DAVID MACEY

The Lives of
Michel Foucault

David Macey lives in England. He is the author
of *Lacan in Contexts*.

The Lives of
MICHEL FOUCAULT

ACKNOWLEDGEMENTS

My gratitude is due to those who shared their memories of Foucault with me, provided information and supplied contacts, to a number of institutions, and to one who listened and read:

Maurice Agulhon, Michel Almaric, Jacques Almira, Claire Ambroselli, Didier Anzieu, Sylvie-Claire d'Arvisenet, Association pour le Centre Michel Foucault, Margaret Atack, Robert Badinter, Etienne Balibar, Jean-Pierre Barou, Zygmunt Bauman, Neil Belton, Bibliothèque du Saulchoir, Pierre Bourdieu, Roy Boyne, Brotherton Library (University of Leeds), Catherine von Bülow, Georges Canguilhem, Robert Castel, Hélène Cixous, Jeannette Colombel, Jurandir Freire Costa, Régis Debray, Daniel Defert, Frédéric Deneuville, Laurent Dispot, Jean-Marie Domenach, Bernard Doray, Jean Duvignaud, Gregory Elliott, Didier Eribon, François Ewald, Arlette Farge, Serge Fauchereau, Alain Finkielkraut, John Forrester, Denys Foucault, Gérard Fromanger, Francine Fruchaud, Henri Fruchaud, Mike Gane, Carl Gardner, Philippe Gavi, Célio Garcia, Colin Gordon, André Green, Félix Guattari, Malcolm Imrie, Douglas Johnson, Chaim Katz, Georges Kiejman, Denise Klossowski, Pierre Klossowski, Bernard Kouchner, Jean Laplanche, Annette Lavers, Antoine Lazarus, Jacques Lebas, Dominique Lecourt, Serge Livrozet, Jean-François Lyotard, Roberto Machado, Pierre Macherey, Edmond Maire, Claude Mauriac, Philippe Meyer, Jean-François Miguel, Françoise-Edmonde Morin, Jean-Pierre Mignard, Modern Languages Library (University of Leeds), Liane Mozère, Toni Negri, Michelle Perrot, Jean-Pierre Peter, Jean Piel, Danièle Rancière, Jacques Rancière, Jonathan Rée, Christian Revon, François Roustang, Yves Roussel, René Schérer, Dominique Seglard, Lucien Sève, Anne Thalamy, Georges Verdeaux, Jacqueline Verdeaux, Marie-Thérèse Vernet, Paul Veyne, Pierre Vidal-Naquet, Simon Watney, Jeffrey Weeks.

TEXTUAL NOTE

Unless otherwise stated, all translations are mine. All quotations from the works of Michel Foucault have been retranslated; existing English-language translations are listed in the bibliography.

Introduction:

'I, MICHEL FOUCAULT...'

In his masterly life of Bernard Shaw, Michael Holroyd remarks: 'Biographies of writers are written in collaboration with the posthumous subject of the biography.'[1] Some posthumous subjects are less cooperative than others and Foucault, who shared Nietzsche's scorn for 'all the learned dust of biography',[2] is rather more recalcitrant than Shaw. Alive, he would have rejected the advances of any biographer; in death, he still struggles to escape them.

On 25 June 1984, Michel Foucault died at the age of fifty-seven from the complications attendant upon his infection with the human immuno-deficiency virus. His last two books had just been published and were being widely discussed in the press. When he died, he was without doubt France's most prominent philosopher, and had achieved the unusual distinction of entering the best-seller lists with *Les Mots et les choses*, a dense and difficult book written, according to its author, for a small audience of specialists. He had successfully crossed the great divide that separates the purely academic world from the broader cultural sphere. For almost fourteen years, he had taught at the Collège de France, the most prestigious institution in the French academic world. He had been fêted in the United States, and translations of his works had given him an international reputation from Brazil to Japan. Indeed, his international reputation has almost eclipsed his reputation in France. Many if not most of the studies of Foucault to be found in Parisian bookshops are translations from the English.[3]

Foucault lived many lives – as an academic, as a political activist, as a child, and as a lover of men. He lived a very public life, and also a very private one. To a large extent, Foucault's life was also the intellectual life of France. There are few changes that are not reflected in his work, and there are few developments that he did not influence. His biography is also of necessity an intellectual history of his times. In an unexpectedly generous tribute, the German philosopher Jürgen Habermas, who could be very critical of Foucault, wrote: 'Within the circle of the philosophers of my generation who diagnose our times, Foucault has most lastingly influenced the *Zeitgeist*.'[4] As a student,

Foucault had witnessed and reacted against the dominance of Sartrean existentialism, and had been part of the generation that discovered or rediscovered Hegel, Nietzsche and Heidegger. He was taught by Louis Althusser and Maurice Merleau-Ponty. In the 1960s, he was popularly perceived as being one of the structuralist Gang of Four, its other members being Jacques Lacan, Roland Barthes and Claude Lévi-Strauss. A decade later, he was associated with the so-called new philosophers in their precipitate retreat from Marxism and Maoism. In his final years, another change of direction led him to the quiet contemplation of Stoic philosophy and to the exploration of a possible new ethics.

The multiplicity of Foucault's lives makes it difficult to arrive at any satisfactory periodisation of his work. In their very influential study, Dreyfus and Rabinow propose a four-stage schema: a Heideggerean stage, an archaeological or quasi-structuralist stage, a genealogical stage and, finally, an ethical stage.[5] The schema is not entirely unsatisfactory, but it has the disadvantage of reducing a complex life and body of work to a uniquely philosophical dimension. It makes no allowance for the trajectory that took Foucault from membership of the Parti Communiste Français, through a period of political quietism to a period of full-blooded leftist militancy and then to a concern for human rights. Nor does it take account of the important literary phase in Foucault's career.

In November 1971, Foucault took part in a debate with the American linguist Noam Chomsky on Dutch television. The debate was to have been preceded by a short film on Foucault; he flatly refused to provide any biographical information and the film was never made.[6] Yet in May 1981, he stated quite clearly: 'In a sense, I have always wanted my books to be fragments from an autobiography. My books have always been my personal problems with madness, with prisons, with sexuality.'[7] The same view was expressed with even greater force in Vermont a year later: 'Each of my works is a part of my own biography.'[8] To say that the history of his books is to a large extent the biography of Michel Foucault is, at one level, almost a truism. His biography is, that is, the story of a thought, a work in progress. In such statements, Foucault appears to be hinting at some deeper relationship between author and text. In a discussion of a favourite author, he was slightly more explicit, and can even be seen as supplying a formula for his own biography. Referring to the novelist and poet Raymond Roussel, he argued:

Someone who is a writer is not simply doing his work in his books, in what he publishes . . . his major work is, in the end, himself in the process of writing his books. The private life of an individual, his sexual preference, and his work are interrelated not because his work translates his sexual life, but because the work includes the whole life as well as the text. The work is more than the work; the subject who is writing is part of the work.[9]

Foucault rarely spoke of his life – particularly of his early life – in any detail. He ended an unusually personal interview in 1983 by saying:

Anyway, my personal life is not at all interesting. If someone thinks that my work cannot be understood without reference to such and such a part of my life, I accept to consider the question. [*Laughter*] I am ready to answer it if I agree. As far as my personal life is uninteresting, it is not worthwhile making a secret of it. [*Laughter*] By the same token, it may not be worthwhile publicising it.[10]

The teasing tone, in which it does not require a psychoanalytic training to detect a strong element of narcissism, is not typical. More characteristic is the defensive aggression to be seen in a celebrated passage from *L'Archéologie du savoir*. To the imaginary interlocutor who complains: 'Are you saying yet again that you have never been what you have been reproached with being? You are already preparing the get-out that will enable you in your next book to spring up somewhere else and to mock at us as you are doing now: "No, no, I'm not where you are lying in wait for me, but over there, laughing at you" ', Foucault replies: 'I am no doubt not the only one who writes in order to have no face. Do not ask who I am and do not ask me to remain the same: that is an ethics for the *état civil*; it governs our identity papers. It might leave us free when it's a matter of writing.'[11] The *état civil* is France's equivalent to the Office of the Registrar General. Elsewhere, Foucault called it 'that strange body that turns individual existences into an institution' and described its civil servants as 'the primal form of the law' because they 'transform every birth into an archive'.[12]

Real dialogues of the kind parodied in *L'Archéologie du savoir* occurred quite regularly in seminars and lectures given by Foucault, who habitually declined to say just who or what he was. Questioned about his intellectual identity in the Brazilian city of Belo Horizonte in 1973, Foucault finally defined himself simply as 'a reader'.[13] In 1981, an audience in Louvain was warned not to press him too closely on whether he was a philosopher or a historian.[14]

Foucault's refusals to state his identity or to trace his history could be witty. Paolo Caruso was told: 'It would be a little difficult for me to describe the itinerary that has brought me to my present positions, for the very good reason that I hope I have not yet reached the point of arrival.' Another interviewer, who had reproached him for saying nothing about his background or childhood, was told: 'my dear friend, philosophers are not born . . . They exist, and that's all there is to it.'[15] The witticisms were an expression not of flippancy, but of a deeply seated conviction. As Foucault told a free-lance writer in Vermont in October 1982:

> I don't feel that it is necessary to know exactly who I am. The main interest in life and work is to become someone else that you were not in the beginning. If you knew when you began a book what you would say at the end, do you think you would have the courage to write it? What is true for writing and for a love relationship is true also for life. The game is worthwhile insofar as we don't know what will be the end.[16]

On occasion, the famous reticence extended to the work itself. On a rare visit to London's Institut Français in the mid-1970s, Foucault refused to give the expected lecture, and announced that he would answer questions put to him by the audience on any subject . . . except his work. He then sat on the steps that led from the stage to the auditorium, thus ensuring that the microphone on the table captured nothing of what he said. Many in the audience were not amused. Nor were the invited guests greatly amused by Foucault's very early departure from the reception that had been organised for him in order to catch the next flight back to Paris.[17]

'Writing in order to have no face' was the stated ambition of a man who had many faces, who led many different and very compartmentalised lives. Few, if any, people knew all the many Foucaults who coexisted. After Foucault's death, Daniel Defert, who shared his life for over twenty years, was astonished to find that his partner had been giving large sums of money to the Dominicans of the rue de la Glacière in gratitude for the hospitality they accorded him in the Bibliothèque du Saulchoir.[18] Family and friends were kept separate. The compartmentalisation of his life was such that a number of male acquaintances were sincerely but wrongly convinced that they were, at a given moment, Foucault's 'only heterosexual friend'. Many people, most of them men, speak of Foucault's profound misogyny; the charge is denied by women like Catherine von Bülow, Hélène Cixous and Arlette Farge, all of whom worked closely with him at different times.

The Lives of
MICHEL FOUCAULT

A BIOGRAPHY

David Macey

VINTAGE BOOKS

A DIVISION OF RANDOM HOUSE, INC.

NEW YORK

To Aaron, John and Chantelle,
for all you have given us in such a short time,
and in affectionate memory of Antoine Roquentin

The Library of Congress has cataloged the Pantheon edition as follows:
Macey, David, 1949–
The lives of Michel Foucault / David Macey.
p. cm.
Includes bibliographical references and index.
ISBN 0-679-43074-1
1. Foucault, Michel. 2. Philosophers—France—Biography.
I. Title.
B2430.F724M327 1994
194—dc20
[B] 93-28220
CIP
Vintage ISBN: 0-679-75792-9

Author photograph courtesy of David Macey

Manufactured in the United States of America
LSI 001

CONTENTS

Subjective impressions of Foucault are confusingly varied. He could be seductive, and, like Jacques Lacan, had the ability to make his interlocutor of the moment believe that he or she enjoyed a privileged relationship with him. He could also be cruel and brutally dismissive of those who approached him with innocent questions about his work. He could be a generous host who had a free hand with the whisky bottle, though he rarely drank himself.[19] He could combine generosity with offhandedness. When, in the late 1970s, a group of young German 'autonomists' found their way to his apartment, Foucault greeted them warmly, listened to them and joked with them, stroking his cat all the while. He prepared food for them and then disappeared, saying that he would not eat with them and had some important work to do on EEC milk quotas. To his discomfort, Laurent Dispot, who had been invited to join the company by Foucault, suddenly realised that his function was to be that of proxy host.[20] Many met a charming Foucault with a very warm personality; at a dinner party in the early 1960s, the psychoanalyst André Green encountered someone who made almost sadistic use of irony to undermine the arguments of a fellow guest.[21] Jean Laplanche, another analyst who first met Foucault in his student days, arrives at an almost perfect compromise-formation by speaking of his 'distant warmth'.[22] There are those who knew only the professor at the Collège de France; others knew, or claim to have known, a Foucault who, clad in black leather and hung with chains, would slip out of his apartment in the rue de Vaugirard in search of anonymous sexual adventure. The immigrant population of the Goutte d'Or district in Paris knew a white intellectual who was willing to face arrest – and beatings – in the fight against racism, though certain of them thought he was Sartre.

An ambiguous desire for anonymity characterised both Foucault's intellectual and personal identities. The Foucault who took part in a Gay Pride march in Toronto in 1982 was also the Foucault who hated being recognised as he entered a bar or club – and this despite the shaven head, the startlingly blue eyes and the habitual white rollneck sweater which combined to make him instantly recognisable. He relished the anonymity afforded by saunas and bath-houses where 'you stop being imprisoned inside your own face, your own past, your own identity', where 'it's not the assertion of identity that's important; it's the assertion of non-identity'.[23] The writer and artist Pierre Klossowski, for one, is convinced that Foucault's goal was, like that of their mutual friend Gilles Deleuze, 'the liquidation of the principle of identity'.[24]

In 1980, Foucault gave an interview to *Le Monde* on condition that he remained anonymous:

> Why did I suggest to you that we should use anonymity? Out of nostalgia for the time when, being quite unknown, what I said stood some chance of being heard . . . Choosing anonymity . . . is a way of addressing the potential reader, the only person who interests me here, more directly: 'Since you don't know who I am, you will not be tempted to look for the reasons why I am saying what you are reading: just let yourself go and say quite simply: "That's right; that's wrong. I like this; I don't like that." '[25]

Anonymity was something to be fought for in a number of domains: 'We have to win anonymity . . . For anyone who writes, the problem was once tearing oneself away from the anonymity of all; in our day the problem is finally erasing one's own name and succeeding in lodging one's voice in the great, anonymous murmur of discourses.'[26] One of the ways in which Foucault did, on occasion, achieve anonymity was to speak in the third person, or to remove himself from his own discourse by adopting an objectively neutral tone. Discussing a film about psychiatric hospitals, he mentioned a carnival that took place each year in the Swiss village of Musterlingen. He described how the patients from a clinic there would process through the streets, all wearing masks, before burning a giant figure representing Carnival.[27] From Foucault's description alone, it would be impossible to tell that he had seen the procession and had even attempted, unsuccessfully, to film it. In the 1980s, Foucault gave a number of interviews about gay culture and sexuality which would have given an intimate self-portrait, were it not that he never said: 'I, Michel Foucault . . .' Here, the anonymity is reduplicated in a distinctly impersonal account of sexual encounters with anonymous partners.

Maurice Blanchot, a man even more anonymous than Foucault aspired to be and whose books bear the biographical note 'Maurice Blanchot, novelist and critic. His life is entirely devoted to literature and to the silence that befits it', captures something of his elusiveness thus:

> Let me say first of all that I had no personal relations with Michel Foucault. I never met him, except one time, in the courtyard of the Sorbonne, during the events of May '68, perhaps in June or July (but they tell me he wasn't there), when I addressed a few words to him, he himself unaware of who was speaking to him . . . It's

true that during those extraordinary events I often said: 'But why isn't Foucault here?' thus restoring to him his power of attraction and respecting the empty place he should have been occupying. But I received replies that didn't satisfy me: 'He's somewhat reserved', or 'He's abroad.'[28]

Foucault was indeed abroad, in Tunisia, though he was briefly in Paris at the end of May. He lived abroad for relatively long periods, and often thought – or fantasised – of leaving Paris and settling elsewhere. Yet Foucault remained profoundly French, or rather Parisian. Many visitors remarked that he was on the whole reluctant to discuss Anglo-American cultural life, and that his intellectual references were predominantly French. Ambivalent he may have been, but Foucault in some senses needed Parisian intellectual life.

Lecture tours took Foucault all over the world; holidays were spent mainly in North Africa and sometimes in Spain. Britain was not a frequent destination and Foucault 'had no great love of England, which he tended to think of as already half-dead'.[29] On one visit, he insisted that the only thing he wanted to see was Petticoat Lane's market in east London, and it was only with great difficulty that Defert once persuaded him to travel to Skye.[30]

The lectures he delivered abroad made few concessions to his geographical displacement. It was rare for him to preface them with the usual polite banalities about being glad to be in, say, Rio de Janeiro, and his normal approach was to plunge directly into his subject matter. Despite his theoretical interest in 'heterotopias', and otherness in general, Foucault remained largely unchanged by his extensive travels. In Tunisia, he expressed an interest in Arabic languages, but his main intellectual project was a study of Manet, and not his own initiation into Islamic art. Virtually all the lecture tours left time for discussions with political activists, academics, mental-health professionals and even Zen Buddhist monks, but the content of those discussions rarely entered Foucault's actual discourse. In interviews, he very occasionally made anecdotal reference to his travels, but that was usually all. Foucault was also an ascetic traveller. His rather impersonal apartment in the rue de Vaugirard was not cluttered with souvenirs, and no Japanese mask adorned its walls after either of his two trips to Japan, though its owner did occasionally wear a kimono and was photographed in it by Hervé Guibert in 1982.[31] The stetson hat presented to Foucault by his students at Berkeley in October 1983 pleased him greatly, but there is no record of it having been worn in Paris. Faceless but conspicuous, well travelled but apparently little influenced by his experience of otherness, Foucault remained enigmatic, unclassifiable.

Les Mots et les choses opens with the gust of laughter provoked by reading Jorge Luis Borges's account of the classificatory system to be found in a Chinese encyclopedia in which animals are divided into the following categories:

> (a) belonging to the Emperor, (b) embalmed, (c) tame, (d) sucking pigs, (e) sirens, (f) fabulous, (g) stray dogs, (h) included in the present classification, (i) frenzied, (j) innumerable, (k) drawn with a very fine camelhair brush, (l) *et cetera*, (m) having just broken the water pitcher, (n) that from a long way off look like flies.[32]

Characteristically, Foucault gives no reference for his quotation; the allusion is to 'El Idioma de John Wilkins', in which Borges describes a 'Celestial Emporium of Benevolent Knowledge'.[33]

Foucault's work poses classificatory problems of its own as it migrates through disciplines as diverse as history, philosophy, sociology, medical history and literary criticism. The story of the hapless librarian who catalogued *L'Archéologie du savoir* as 'Ancient History and Archaeology' is probably as apocryphal as that of his or her colleague who reputedly shelved Augustine's *City of God* under 'Town-Planning'. It does, however, encapsulate something of the problems that arise from any attempt to locate Foucault within a genre classification. Both the man and his work, to use a conventional dichotomy which would have exasperated him, were enigmatic, elusive and protean.

When Foucault died, the lawyer Georges Kiejman remarked in *Le Monde* that France had lost not only a philosopher, but also a street fighter. Although it is not always apparent from his major works, Foucault was, among other things, an occasional political activist and militant. For a very short time in the 1950s, he was a member of the Parti Communiste Français but never again joined a political party. His activities took a variety of forms, ranging from the foundation of the Groupe d'Information sur les Prisons at the beginning of the 1970s to organising support for Soviet dissidents and the boat people, and from a brief involvement with the campaign to legalise abortion to actions in solidarity with immigrant workers in France.

It has often been reproachfully noted that no truly coherent politics emerges from all this activity, and the Parisian press at times took malicious pleasure in mocking *les foucades de Foucault* ('Foucault's whims'). His political activities were not the application of a theory, and it is not always easy to find any consistent attitude behind them. Accusations that he was inconsistent or acted on the basis of mere whims amused Foucault:

> I think I have in fact been situated in most of the squares on the political checkerboard, one after another and sometimes simultaneously: as anarchist, leftist, ostentatious or disguised Marxist, explicit or secret anti-Marxist, technocrat in the service of Gaullism, new liberal etc. . . . It's true that I prefer not to identify myself and that I'm amused by the diversity of the ways I've been judged and classified.[34]

Malraux and Sartre both remarked that death turns a life into a destiny, contingency into necessity. We do know how the game ended. A life which becomes the subject of a narrative looks even more like a destiny, but Foucault's life was as untidy as anyone else's. It is only in a narrative that there can appear to be a connection between a taste for Nietzsche and for the cheeses of Poitou. Nothing predestined Paul-Michel Foucault of Poitiers to end his career at the Collège de France and, in his own view, the recognition he achieved there was not the outcome of some existential project or even of a planned career: 'I don't think I ever had the project of becoming a philosopher.'[35] Foucault's career was to a surprising degree the result of chance encounters and sudden decisions. As he told Jean-Pierre Barou, it could all have been very different. He could have fought in the Resistance, but did not.[36] He could have been a cultural attaché in Rome, head of the French broadcasting service, the director of the Bibliothèque Nationale in Paris, or a clinical psychologist. No destiny or necessity was at work in his life.

The 'autobiography' contained in Foucault's writings is fragmentary in the extreme, not least because the extant written corpus itself is so lacunary. In 1977, he told a friend: 'When I die, I will leave no manuscripts.'[37] He came close to fulfilling that promise. Hervé Guibert, a close friend and, according to some, Foucault's last lover, was ordered to destroy the drafts of the final volumes of *Histoire de la sexualité* and all the preparatory materials. Foucault had little sympathy for Max Brod and his decision to publish Kafka's manuscripts despite the express wishes of his late friend, and was determined to prevent anyone following that famous example.[38] He died without leaving a proper will but a letter found in his apartment made his intentions perfectly clear: 'I leave my apartment and all it contains to Daniel Defert. No posthumous publications.'[39]

His desire has been respected by his family and friends and if any manuscripts did survive, they remain beyond the reach of scholars and biographers. A great deal of unpublished material does survive in the Bibliothèque du Saulchoir, where it may be consulted but not reproduced. There will be no 'Complete Works of Michel Foucault'. For similar reasons, it is improbable that there will ever be an edition of what must be a voluminous correspondence whose addressees ranged from friends and lovers to Japanese publishers. Controversy surrounds the fourth volume of *Histoire de la sexualité*, virtually completed in June 1984, but unlikely to appear in print.[40] The situation created by Foucault is a frustrating one, but it has preempted the emergence of the almost embarrassingly productive postmortem industry that has grown up around Sartre and Simone de Beauvoir as more and more 'unknown' manuscripts are disinterred from various cupboards. Foucault was ready to argue that the 'complete works' of Nietzsche should perhaps contain the notebooks in which laundry lists are jumbled up with outlines for aphorisms.[41] He took the view that the same argument did not apply to his own laundry lists.

In death, the writer who proclaimed the death of the author continues to exercise authorial rights and privileges. In life, the man who often argued that an author did not have the right to lay down the law as to the meaning of his work, was also the author who, together with his assistant at the Collège de France, penned the article on 'Foucault' in a 'Dictionary of Philosophers', signed it 'Maurice Florence' and thus provided an authorised version in more than one sense: 'If Foucault is indeed inscribed within the philosophical tradition, he is inscribed within the *critical* tradition which is that of Kant, and his undertaking might be called a *Critical history of thought* . . .'[42] The paradox of Foucault's posthumous authorship is compounded by his own wish for there to be no posthumous publication; if it continues to be respected, he will always have been the author of completed books and not the industrious producer of draft texts which would allow him to become someone else yet again.

Foucault strongly resisted the notion that he was producing an *oeuvre* or a 'complete works': 'I do not speak of my *oeuvre* for the very good reason that I do not feel myself to be the bearer of a potential *oeuvre*.' [43] According to François Ewald, who was Foucault's *assistant* at the Collège de France and who worked closely with him from 1975 onwards, he insisted that his texts were a toolkit to be used or discarded by anyone and not a catalogue of theoretical ideas implying some conceptual unity.[44] His attitude towards his published writings was, however, strangely proprietorial, as he effectively disowned his first works, refused to have them reprinted and thus removed them from the toolkit. The many occasional pieces were never collected into a volume during his lifetime and he disliked the idea of their being brought together. For Foucault, occasional writings were specific interventions, with little or no utility or interest after the event, and he could say of them: 'Writing interests me only to the extent that it is incorporated into the reality of a combat as an instrument, a tactic, a means of shedding light . . . I certainly do not see what I do as a body of work [oeuvre], and I am shocked to see anyone can call me a writer . . . I sell tools.'[45] No 'selected essays' were ever published in French, but Foucault had no objections to being anthologised in other languages and was quite happy to approve, for instance, the useful collection edited by Colin Gordon.[46] Until very recently, the valuable series of interviews conducted by Duccio Trombadori in 1978 existed only in Italian; there is now an English translation, but no French version.[47] The controversial articles on the Iranian revolution written for *Corriere della sera* have appeared in French. Other texts exist only in Portuguese, English or German. Shortly before his death, Foucault did come around to thinking that publishing a volume of interviews 'might not be a bad idea' but did not live to see its realisation.[48] An edition of all the occasional pieces published by Foucault during his lifetime is now being prepared by Defert and Ewald and will be published by Gallimard.

One effect of this stance on the part of Foucault is that the compilation of a bibliography is a nightmarish task. The best bibliographies are those compiled by James W. Bernauer and Jacques Lagrange, and they supersede Clark's annotated bibliography (still an essential work of reference on the secondary literature), but neither is exhaustive.[49] Not all Foucault's contributions to the left press in his activist days were signed, and it is far from certain that all have been identified. One important and fascinating book appeared without anything to identify Foucault as a contributor. *Vingt Ans et après* consists of transcripts of taped dialogues between Foucault and Thierry Voeltzel, a young hitch-hiker picked up by Foucault in 1975. The dialogues centre on Voeltzel, providing a remarkable account of the life of a young gay man involved in the youth culture of the day, but they also afford some glimpses into the life of a now truly anonymous Foucault. This was 'Thierry's book' and was published under his name alone. It therefore does not appear in Bernauer's otherwise compendious bibliography. What is more, not all the tapes were transcribed, and the unpublished material remains in the possession of Claude Mauriac, the editor of the '*Enjeux*' collection in which the book appeared.[50] Its fate too is determined by the ban on posthumous publication.

Foucault's lectures at the Collège de France were a major part of his work and provided the starting point for the books written after 1970. Most of the lectures themselves remain unpublished and they too are unlikely to appear in print. Unauthorised transcripts of tape recordings do circulate, though many owners are jealously possessive of their totemic tapes, and pirate versions appear from time to time, at risk of legal action by the Foucault Estate. This has led to some absurd situations. An extract from the 1976 lecture course was published in Italian in 1990, and then appeared in French in *Les Temps Modernes*.[51] There is a definite irony here in that Foucault never forgave the journal for its neglect of his *Histoire de la folie* or for its harsh treatment of *Les Mots et les choses*, and made only one contribution to it.[52] The absurdity arose when the Estate and Gallimard took legal action against *Les Temps Modernes*, and were awarded symbolic damages against a journal published by Gallimard.[53] In Italy, the Florentine publisher Ponte alle grazie was prevented by legal action from publishing any more of the lectures. Such incidents are part of a legal controversy, also affecting the work of Barthes and Lacan, over whether or not a public lecture or seminar is by definition within the public domain. Current interpretations of the law pertaining to intellectual property suggest that it is not.

Some transcripts of the lectures can be consulted and others can be heard on tape in the Bibliothèque du Saulchoir, which holds the archives of the Centre Michel Foucault, but, like the other unpublished material, they cannot be reproduced. The tapes are of very variable quality, and many of them are incomplete recordings. In 1989, Seuil published cassette recordings of two lectures: the introductions to the 1978 and 1979 courses on 'Security, Territory, Population' and 'The Birth of Biopolitics'.[54] The best overall account of the lectures remains the course summaries Foucault produced each year for the *Annuaire* of the Collège de France, now available in book form.[55]

Foucault's reticence and the lacunary nature of the 'autobiography' contained in his works pose a major problem for a biographer. There are no journals available for consultation, and the diary Foucault is said by some to have kept appears to have contained little more than notes on the books he read. No American university houses a cache of correspondence and manuscripts. There are rumours of the existence of mysterious unpublished texts, and the persistent legend that a pornographic novel by Foucault still languishes in a filing cabinet or drawer somewhere in Paris. The available documentation is very uneven, and some periods of his life remain obscure while, in other areas, it is the sheer abundance of material that creates problems. Little is known, for instance, of the year Foucault spent in Hamburg; the early 1970s, a period of intense political activity, are exhaustively documented both in the press and by the various volumes of Claude Mauriac's diaries. Foucault's childhood years in particular remain little known.

The written record has been supplemented here by interviews and conversations with many friends and colleagues of Foucault. *The Lives of Michel Foucault* whatever its shortcomings, owes a great deal to the kindness of many strangers. I owe a lot to Foucault's first biographer, Didier Eribon.[56]My particular thanks go to Denys Foucault and to Francine Fruchaud (née Foucault). And above all to Daniel Defert, who will almost certainly disagree with much of what I have written.

1

PAUL-MICHEL

HER family was solidly respectable, well-established and well-connected.[1] Anne Malapert was the daughter of Dr Prosper Malapert of Poitiers, a provincial city 300 kilometres to the southwest of Paris. He was a surgeon with a profitable private practice and taught anatomy in the university's school of medicine. Prosper Malapert was a wealthy man, rich enough by the turn of the century to build a large white house near the railway station and within easy walking distance of the town centre. The house gave on to both the rue Arthur Ranc and the boulevard de Verdun and had a small garden to the rear, though, when Michel Foucault was a child, it contained rather more cement than greenery.

Prosper Malapert had two brothers: Roger and Paulin. Roger opted for a military career, rose to the rank of colonel and fought with distinction in the First World War at the head of a regiment which he had reputedly personally recruited among the *apaches* of Montmartre. Paulin studied philosophy, but never held a university post. In his own view, his chosen speciality was a further obstacle to his career; he was a characterologist, and suffered from the prestige attaching to the then dominant philosophy of Bergsonism, with its emphasis on the fluidity of 'becoming' rather than on the stability of character. Paulin Malapert's career was spent in a Parisian *lycée*, but he published quite widely, producing a treatise on the theory of character, textbooks on psychology and philosophy and a study of Spinoza.[2] He founded no school and achieved no great academic distinction. The academic honours went to his son-in-law, Jean Plattard, editor of standard editions of Rabelais and Montaigne and sometime lecturer at the University of Poitiers and then the Sorbonne.[3]

Anne Malapert married a young doctor, Paul Foucault, originally of Fontainebleau, but later resident in Poitiers. Born in 1893, he was the son and grandson of doctors, both called Paul. His grandfather was the dynasty's deviant. Rather than treat the provincial middle classes, this Paul Foucault chose to work with the poor of Nanterre in the days when it was still a country village a few miles outside Paris. Little is known about him, other than that he died, as befits a *médecin des pauvres* who treated his patients at no charge, with only five francs in his pocket and, presumably, the world. His only bequest was a silver pen given to him by grateful patients, and that vanished in a burglary at the home of his great-grandson Denys. He did, however, achieve a degree of municipal recognition: Nanterre boasts a rue du Dr Foucault.

Like his father-in-law, Dr Paul Foucault taught at the medical school in Poitiers and eventually took over the Malapert practice in addition to his own. As a surgeon, Paul Foucault was at the top of the medical hierarchy and enjoyed much greater prestige than a mere doctor of medicine. He was a *notable*, with a social standing equal to that of a banker or a notary. He was one of a handful of surgeons in the city and an obstetrician whose patients were drawn mainly from the urban middle classes. His practice extended into rural areas and he was also consulted by the Benedictines at Ligugé, the famous abbey eight kilometres to the south of Poitiers, as well as by farmers and landowners. For a surgeon, the accumulation of income from a variety of sources and jealously guarded positions was the key to success, and Paul Foucault was successful. He worked long hours and, given the surgical and medical technology of the day, his professional activities involved a lot of physical effort, especially on rural calls. They also called for a certain talent for improvisation. A folding operating table was carried in the boot of one of the two cars he ran, and Dr Foucault's driver could, if the need arose, act as an assistant anaesthetist. The surgeon was accustomed to the exercise of authority, both professionally and at home, and was not always an easy man to live with.

Anne Foucault was in many respects his match. A woman who knew her own mind and who was accustomed to having her own way, she ran with great efficiency a household of servants and was, with the help of a secretary, largely responsible for the management of her husband's practice. Anne Foucault was no *femme d'intérieur*. Unusually for a woman in the provinces at this time, she could drive, and did so very competently. She was wealthy in her own right, and owned land. The Malapert home was Le Piroir, a large house built in the middle of the last century and standing in its own grounds at Vendeuvre-du-Poitou, some fifteen kilometres outside Poitiers. Le Piroir was approached down a drive flanked by two huge wellingtonias and an avenue of pollarded limes, but it was not of great architectural beauty and, being built of local limestone, had an unfortunate tendency to suffer from damp. Although large, Le Piroir was not, as has sometimes been claimed, known to local people as 'the château'.[4] Vendeuvre does have its château – the sixteenth-century château des Roches with its machicolated towers – but that was never in the possession of the Malaperts. It is revelatory of the values of the times, and of the provincial bourgeoisie, that, though no architect's plans for Le Piroir survive – it was probably built by local masons – there do survive records of the purchase and sale of land and of boundaries.

The Foucaults were members of a prosperous bourgeoisie and enjoyed considerable prestige in Poitiers, a small town with a population of under 40,000 at the outbreak of the Second World War. They had little or no contact with the surviving aristocracy but retained rural connections through Le Piroir and the land attached to it. Land-ownership and agriculture provided the basis for Poitiers's wealth. There was little industry, but this relatively rich stock-rearing region produced wine, asparagus and garlic. The town itself was quiet, and best known for its churches, especially Notre Dame La Grande which, with its splendid façade, is one of the best examples of romanesque sculpture in France. The glories of the university, a Renaissance foundation, were a thing of the past and it was now best known for its law faculty. The medical school was small and taught only the first three years of the degree course; further studies had to be pursued elsewhere. In political terms, the city was radical, meaning that it was dominated by the Parti Radical et Socialiste, which was neither radical nor socialist but moderately conservative. A countervailing political force was provided by fairly strong clerical influence. Outsiders found the town rather dull, and its inhabitants complacent, introverted and not particularly welcoming.

It was into this family and this milieu that Paul-Michel Foucault was born on 15 October 1926. Paul was the second of three children. His sister Francine was his elder by fifteen months, and his brother Denys was born five years after him. The three children bore a striking likeness to one another, and all had the same fair hair, the rather prominent nose and the bright-blue eyes that were to stare from the rimless glasses Foucault wore in so many photographs.

The tradition of the Foucault family was that an eldest son was always called 'Paul', and it was at his mother's insistence that the child was called Paul-Michel. He referred to himself as Michel. For administrative purposes, and at school, he was Paul; for his adoring mother, he was always Paul-Michel. Other members used the same appellation, which could lead to some confusion, even in later years. His niece Anne Thalamy, for example, knew him as 'Paul-Michel' and addressed him as *vous*; to her husband, he was 'Michel', to be addressed with the informal *tu*.

Paul-Michel had a traditional middle-class upbringing. His family was nominally Catholic, but its Catholicism extended little beyond the celebration of rites of passage like baptism, first communion, marriage and burial. The children attended mass in the church of Saint-Porchair, but as often as not it was their grandmother and not their mother who took them. Such nominal Catholicism, combined with a measure of anti-clericalism, was not atypical of *la France bourgeoise*, with its contradictory heritage of Voltairean agnosticism and *bien-pensant* Catholicism. At least occasional attendance at mass was a social obligation, but the doctors and surgeons of the Third Republic were not, as a social group, noted for their piety. Even so, Paul-Michel took his first communion and was, for a while, a choirboy, despite his lack of musical ability. There is no record of any traumatic loss of faith on Paul-Michel's part and it appears that he simply drifted away from his childhood religion. On the other hand, he retained a certain affection for the more camp aspects of organised religion, and once described the Catholic Church as 'a superb instrument of power . . . completely woven from imaginary, erotic, carnal and sensual elements. It's superb.'[5]

The family was never poor, and was becoming more prosperous during Paul-Michel's early years. At the beginning of the 1930s, Paul and Anne Foucault bought, at low cost, land at La Baule and built a villa there. La Baule, which stands on a glorious sweep of sand seventeen kilometres from the port of Saint-Nazaire, was just beginning to develop as a holiday resort and had none of the aristocratic chic of, say, Normandy's Deauville and Cabourg, which was the original for Proust's Balbec. La Baule was primarily a resort for the middle classes of the industrial towns of Nantes and Saint-Nazaire. The Foucault villa, large enough to accommodate a family of five and servants, was to the south of the town in the area known as La-Baule-des-Pins, pines being one of the region's great beauties, and not in the more fashionable streets near the casino. La Baule became the traditional site for family holidays in the summer, whereas the Easter holidays were normally spent at Le Piroir.

Foucault very rarely spoke of his childhood, and when he did so it was usually in very negative terms. He spoke, for instance, of coming from an 'incredibly narrow-minded' provincial background,[6] but the class element in such comments was probably influenced by the disdain which so many Parisians, and especially Parisians by adoption, like Foucault, traditionally display for the so-called 'French desert'. He was later to recall how the narrow-mindedness of his background imposed on him 'the obligation of speaking, of making conversation with strangers ... I often wondered why people had to speak.'[7] The strangers in question were guests at his parents' dinner parties. Entertaining was an important part of the life of Dr Foucault, whose social and professional interests merged imperceptibly, and the dinners he gave for colleagues and local *notables* were effectively business meetings. Although the children were expected to make polite conversation with visitors, they were also required to remain silent at dinner. The contradictory demands for polite intercourse and for silence were, naturally enough, a source of tension and irritation. In the considered view of Paul-Michel and his siblings, very formal dinners were preferable; on such occasions, they ate separately and in much more relaxed circumstances, safe from the demands and conventions of adult society.

Foucault's family background may well have been narrow-minded in many ways, but it was also an immensely privileged background. The house in Poitiers, where cats and dogs were in permanent residence, was large enough to give each of the children a bedroom of their own. Paul-Michel, his sister and his brother naturally took everything for granted, but relatively few children in pre-war France were able to spend their summer holidays in a family villa by the sea. La Baule provided the traditional pleasures of long days on the beach, games of tennis and cycling excursions. Cycling and tennis were the only sports Paul-Michel enjoyed, and his enjoyment of the latter was somewhat spoiled by his short-sightedness. He was, on the other hand, a good cyclist and, as a teenager, regularly rode out to Le Piroir to visit his grandmother.

One holiday stands out in his sister's memory. Shortly before the war, the family went on a skiing holiday in the Pyrenees with their cousins the Plattards. The children were not terribly enthusiastic, and Paul-Michel in particular complained about the cold. His mother, on the other hand, greatly enjoyed the week's stay in a hotel; even on holiday at La Baule, she was the mistress of a house and responsible for all domestic arrangements. The stay in the hotel was a further index of prosperity. Even among the professional middle classes, it was more usual to spend holidays with relations or in private rented accommodation than in a hotel.

Family life in Poitiers was usually quiet. The Plattard children were slightly too old to be suitable company, and the Foucault family unit tended to be self-contained. The children had little contact with the older generation, their grandmother being the main exception. Great-uncles who were soldiers and who taught in Paris were distant figures and not real presences. Entertainment was largely home-made and long evenings at 10 rue Arthur Ranc were spent playing cards and word games, and listening to the radio. Commercial entertainment for children was a rarity. Poitiers did have cinemas but, although the 1930s was a golden age for the French cinema, few films were made specifically for children. Visits to the cinema were therefore not frequent and a trip to see *Snow White and the Seven Dwarfs* (1937), just before the outbreak of war, was something to be remembered for years. Trips to the theatre, on the other hand, were a regular occurrence. They did not introduce Paul-Michel to the heights of dramatic experience, as most of the performances he saw were by travelling companies playing a standard repertoire of Molière, Corneille and Racine to an unappreciative and often rowdy audience of school children.

Poitiers was not, of course, self-contained and was affected by events taking place on the world stage. Some of the rare childhood memories Foucault evoked in interviews are surprisingly political. He remembered the assassination of Austria's Chancellor Engelbert Dollfuss in 1934, and the arrival of Spanish and Basque refugees fleeing the Civil War in 1936. He remembered playground fights and arguments with schoolfriends over the war in Ethiopia. Even as a boy, Foucault sensed that there was a threat to his personal and private existence. When he was ten or eleven, he was unsure whether he would remain French or grow up as a young German. School and home offered a sometimes stultifying safety, but the world outside was becoming increasingly dangerous as Paul-Michel entered adolescence. He was quite aware of the possibility that he might die in an air raid.[8]

On 1 September 1939, the Foucault family drove back to Poitiers from La Baule for the last time. There would be no more summer holidays on the coast for five or six years. France and Britain had declared war on Germany. In May 1940, the Maginot Line was outflanked. As France fell, her troops retreated southwards in disorder. Emergency medical units were set up in Poitiers to care for the wounded. Dr Paul Foucault was actively involved in their preparation and his wife's organisational and managerial skills were a major factor in their successful operation.

Among the thousands fleeing Paris in panic was a young woman who was just completing her medical training. Jacqueline Verdeaux's parents were friends of the Malapert family and, as a very young girl, she had been dandled on the knee of the scar-faced Colonel Malapert.

In the spring of 1940, she found herself working as his nephew's anaesthetist in the military hospital that had been rapidly improvised in a Jesuit school. She did not find Dr Foucault easy to work with. He had all the authority of a surgeon accustomed to heading a team of subordinates, and his behaviour in the operating theatre was that of a tyrant. Verdeaux was not in Poitiers for long, and moved south as the German armies advanced. She did, however, have time to renew a passing acquaintance with Paul-Michel, whom she had first glimpsed at his sister's birthday party: a strangely quizzical presence, already in glasses, still in short trousers, and looking oddly out of place at a children's party.[9]

By May–June, the British were evacuating their expeditionary forces from the beaches of Dunkirk. The French government had left Paris for the safety of Bordeaux. On 17 June, Marshal Pétain requested an armistice and informed France's battered army that the time had come to cease fighting. Under the terms of the armistice, Poitiers was some thirty kilometres inside the occupied zone, and German soldiers patrolled the streets. Even the small village of Vendeuvre-du-Poitou had its German military presence. The house in La Baule was requisitioned as an officers' billet. Official portraits of Pétain appeared in public buildings and schools and Paul-Michel, like every other boy and girl of his age, now began his school day by singing 'Maréchal, nous voilà'. For the next four years, his childhood was lulled by official talk of 'Fatherland, Labour, Family' and of the new world of solidarity and sacrifice which was going to replace the 'egotistical, individualist, bourgeois cultural world'.[10] Much more sinister was the presence of the armed troops on the streets of Poitiers. In a rare allusion to these years, Foucault recalled the arrests, and the silent crowds watching as people were taken away.[11]

The Foucault family remained in Poitiers throughout the Occupation years. Like the vast majority of French families, they expressed no political sympathies in public and conformed to the requirements of the Vichy regime. Dr Foucault became a member of the medical guild established by Pétain in his attempt to inculcate 'corporatist' values into the nation. None of the family was pro-Vichy, but none had any direct involvement in the Resistance either. Anne Foucault, in particular, was something of an anglophile, so the family listened to the BBC's broadcasts to occupied France, though being caught listening to the BBC could have serious consequences, including death or deportation. The family's main concern was with food. Increasingly, providing adequate food for two adolescents and one pre-adolescent was a difficult task. The population of Poitiers did not suffer the same privations as that of Paris, but the shortages were real and gradually became more acute. Relatively easy access to a rich agricultural hinterland ensured that few Poitevins actually went hungry, and the Foucault family had the resources of Le Piroir to fall back on. Even so, clandestine expeditions into the countryside to buy food on the black market were necessary. The main forager was Anne Foucault, who rode a bicycle, now that rationing made it impossible to use a car.

The outbreak of war and the Occupation coincided with a more personal crisis for the young Paul-Michel, and it took the form of difficulties at school. He had begun school at the age of four, but, unlike most French children, he did not begin his academic career in a nursery school. In 1930, he was enrolled in the elementary class at the Lycée Henri-IV. The normal age for enrolment was six, but an exception was made for the boy, who simply refused to be separated from his sister when she began school. Together, Paul-Michel and Francine entered the elementary classroom in the right-hand corner of the *lycée*'s rectangular courtyard. Paul-Michel was left largely to his own devices at first, but did succeed in learning to read and write at an early age. Originally a Jesuit foundation established during the reign of Henri IV, whose portrait, together with that of Louis XIV, adorns the entrance, the school was built in the classical style, with some baroquely Jesuit flourishes in the adjoining chapel. With its internal corridor watched over by 'plaster statues of great men',[12] it must have been an intimidating place for two small children.

They had entered a serious, disciplined world. They came from a background in which education was a cardinal virtue and in which children were expected to work. Homework, in the form of reading and spelling exercises, was set from a very early age. The Foucault family was supportive, shared the values of the education system and actively reinforced them. To adopt the sociological terminology of Pierre Bourdieu and Jean-Claude Passeron, Paul-Michel and his siblings were 'inheritors' whose social privileges were translated into – or legitimised as – personal gifts and talents. The creation of inheritor is the joint task of family and school.[13] Wealth could be inherited, but a successful career was based upon the acquisition of professional skill and qualifications. Paul-Michel learned the lesson well: for the adult Foucault, disciplined devotion to intellectual work was almost an ethic.

When they began school at Henri-IV, Paul-Michel and his sister also entered an elite world. Although legislation adopted in the earliest years of the Third Republic guaranteed compulsory, free and non-denominational education for all,[14] the education system was in fact segregated. 'Primary' and 'secondary' referred to parallel systems rather than to chronological divisions within a single system. The vast majority of children began their studies in free elementary schools, and completed them at the age of thirteen. Most attained only a *certificat d'études*, but a talented minority went on to train as primary teachers in an *école normale*, and thus reproduced the sector that had produced them. The *lycées* of the secondary system, which charged fees until the 1930s, were very largely the preserve of the children of the middle classes and the liberal professions. At the age of four, Paul-Michel was already on the path that led to a *baccalauréat* and possible entry to higher education. As he told a radio interviewer over thirty years later, he had entered

a whole environment in which the rule of existence, the rule of promotion, lay in knowledge, in knowing a bit more than the others, being a bit better in the classroom, even, I should imagine, in having sucked one's bottle better than the rest, having taken your first steps before the rest, etc. Competitive exams, competition, doing a bit more than the rest, being first . . . someone like me has always lived in that environment.[15]

Paul-Michel spent two years in the elementary class, moving into the primary class of the *lycée* proper in 1932 and remaining there until 1936, the year in which he saw refugees arriving from Spain. He received the first four years of his secondary education in the same establishment. Until now, he had always been a good pupil. He was not particularly brilliant at mathematics, but his prowess in French, history, Latin and Greek more than compensated for that. He did not appear to make any great effort, but was regularly either at or very near the top of his class. In the early summer of 1940, something went wrong: he performed very badly in his end-of-year examinations, and was told that he would have to take them again in the autumn.

Two possible explanations have been put forward for this sudden crisis. The education system itself was in chaos. Fearing that Paris would be attacked, many schools had evacuated their staff and pupils to the provinces, and Henri-IV now shared its facilities with the evacuees from the Lycée Janson-de-Sailly, a prestigious Parisian school. It is possible that the influx of pupils from a much more sophisticated background led to a severe crisis of confidence; the boy who had always excelled in competition with his provincial schoolmates now had to compete with the products of a superior system. A second possible explanation, put forward by some of Paul-Michel's contemporaries and by his brother, is that the French master took a sudden dislike to him. M. Guyot was very much a radical teacher who had little sympathy for the provincial notability from which Foucault came, and it is conceivable that the boy lost confidence when faced with such obvious hostility.

Whatever the reasons for the poor results of 1940, Paul-Michel's mother took immediate action. In the autumn, her son transferred to a new school. This was the Collège Saint-Stanislas, an establishment run by the teaching order of the Frères des Ecoles Chrétiennes. It was not the only religious school in Poitiers, and it was not the best. The Jesuit-run Collège Saint-Joseph had a much better reputation, but it also imposed a much more rigorous discipline on its pupils, and made greater religious demands of them. Saint-Stanislas was a compromise between the godless *lycée* and the devout Jesuit college. The brothers who ran Saint-Stanislas were not priests, and Paul-Michel was thus spared the need to make a daily confession to his teachers. According to another former pupil of the Frères des Ecoles Chrétiennes, also known as the Ignorantines, the staff of their schools were excellent at bringing up children, but had no particular talent for actually educating them in any broader sense.[16]

The change of school had the desired effect. Paul-Michel's scholastic performance recovered quickly and he once more gained excellent marks over the next three years, regularly taking class prizes in French, history, Greek and English. By now he was beginning to explore areas outside the school curriculum, not least because he and a friend had access to the library of the Abbé Aigrain, a teacher at the Catholic University of Angers and a well-known figure in Poitiers, who lent them books on philosophy and history.[17] Saint-Stanislas itself did not appeal to him, and he would later describe the years he spent there as having been an 'ordeal'.[18]

In 1942, Paul-Michel went into *terminale* (equivalent to an English sixth form), the class in which he would begin the formal study of philosophy. His teacher was to have been a Canon Duret, a man greatly respected by his colleagues. Duret was, however, actively involved in a Resistance network which had been detected by the Gestapo. On the first day of term, he was arrested and disappeared, never to be seen again. The temporary replacement proposed by the school was a literary specialist. The suggestion outraged Mme Foucault, in whose view the teaching of philosophy was a task for a philosopher and not a

literary man. It was she, and not the school, who found an apparently
acceptable substitute for Duret in the form of a Dom Pierrot from
Ligugé. Dom Pierrot proved to be no more than adequate; his lessons in
the classroom were restricted to a fairly banal commentary on the
syllabus, but he did make time for wider-ranging discussions with
favoured pupils, including Paul-Michel, outside school hours.

As it was obvious that the teaching at Saint-Stanislas was dis-
organised in the extreme, Paul-Michel's mother again intervened by
employing a young student to give her eldest son extra tuition at home.
This was the classic solution to the problem: what was not readily
available could be bought. Louis Girard was only in his twenties and
had no extensive knowledge of the philosophy he was supposedly
teaching. On the whole, he simply recycled the Kantianism he had
recently studied at university. He was to remember the young Foucault
as a demanding pupil, not perhaps the most gifted boy he had ever
taught, but certainly one of the quickest to grasp an idea, and one of the
most talented at organising his thoughts into a coherent whole.[19] The
combination of school and private tuition was a successful one. In June
1943, Foucault passed his *baccalauréat* with better than average results.

Having completed his secondary education, Paul-Michel was now
faced with important choices. He was qualified to go to university and
could have begun to study for a degree in the autumn. He chose not to
do so. At this stage, he appears to have had no particular ambition, and
certainly did not plan to become a professional philosopher. Insofar as
he did talk about the future, he spoke vaguely of a career in politics or
journalism. Dr Foucault, on the other hand, had definite plans for him:
his eldest son would, of course, study medicine in Poitiers and then
Paris, and would eventually take over his practice.

The plan had more to do with the doctor's expectations than with
any discussions with his son. Dr Foucault had relatively few dealings
with his children; domestic life was very much his wife's domain. He
seems simply not to have noticed that Paul-Michel had never shown
any great interest in the natural sciences, and that his talents leaned
towards the humanities. Paul-Michel simply refused to contemplate
studying medicine, and had different plans for his future studies, if not
his future career. The discussions between father and son were difficult,
even violent, but Mme Foucault eventually persuaded her husband
that the boy should not be forced into anything he did not want. A
reluctant and disappointed father finally agreed. It was left to Denys to
become the next doctor and surgeon in the family.

Accounts of the bad relations between Foucault and his father have no doubt been inflated. In later life, Foucault reputedly often spoke to friends of having hated his father and of having quarrelled bitterly with him. Surviving members of the family speak of a relationship which was at times difficult and which cooled over the career issue, but regard talk of bitter hatred as exaggerated. It may, on the other hand, be significant that it was remarkably difficult for anyone to persuade Foucault to consult a doctor. In an unusual reference to this period of his youth, Foucault speaks enigmatically of 'relationships in which there were conflicts over specific points, but they represented a focus of common interest from which it was difficult to detach oneself'.[20] One factor that might lend credence to the rumoured loathing of his father was Foucault's refusal to use the name Paul-Michel and his insistence on referring to himself as 'Michel'. It is possible to see this as evidence of a refusal to identify with his father, but the temptation to indulge in psychological speculation should be tempered by two other possible explanations. Foucault often jokingly claimed that he did not like the name 'Paul-Michel Foucault' because it gave him the same initials as Pierre Mendès-France, the veteran politician. His sister has another explanation: in the schoolyard, 'Paul-Michel' was all too easily corrupted into 'Polichinelle'. Her brother disliked being known as the equivalent of Punchinello or Punch, and loathed the implication that he was a misshapen figure of fun.

Paul-Michel's own vision of the future was one in which he became a student at the Ecole Normale Supérieure in Paris. Entrance to ENS, at the time the most prestigious educational establishment in France, was by competitive examination. The annual intake of arts and humanities students was less than forty. Like the other *grandes écoles*, ENS bypassed the normal university system and provided a fast track to the highest academic qualifications. A twenty-year-old who was admitted could reasonably expect to leave three years later after having passed the *agrégation*, the highest competitive examination in the French system. He would have taken a degree in his first year and a Diplôme d'Etudes Supérieures (roughly equivalent to a British Master's degree and awarded on the basis of a *mémoire*, or dissertation) in his second. The new *agrégé* would then be on course for either advanced academic research leading to a doctorate, or a period teaching in a *lycée* and then a university. Candidates for the ENS *concours* already had their *baccalauréat* and spent a further two years of intensive studies in preparatory classes. The syllabus itself was less important than broad coverage of the subjects that might come up in the all-important oral.

Saint-Stanislas could not provide tuition at the required level, and

Paul-Michel accordingly went back to the Lycée Henri-IV for the next two years. In normal circumstances, he would have spent a year in *hypokhâgne* followed by a year in *khâgne*, but wartime conditions meant that the two classes had been merged into a single group of thirty or so pupils.[21] To prepare the ENS *concours*, or entrance examination, in a provincial *lycée* was to attempt the near-impossible. The vast majority of *normaliens* were graduates of the *khâgnes* of great Parisian *lycées* like Louis-Le-Grand and Henri-IV, though a few did come from exceptional provincial schools like Lyon's Lycée du Parc. Pupils in these schools were inevitably taught by young *profs* who had themselves recently studied at ENS, and the system was as self-perpetuating and self-reproductive as the *école normale* sector. A candidate from Poitiers stood little real chance of success. In 1943, however, it was quite impossible to send a seventeen-year-old to study in Paris on his own, and Paul-Michel returned to his old *lycée*.

His main interests were history and philosophy. Jean Moreau-Reibel, a graduate of ENS and formerly a teacher in Clermont-Ferrand, was not, it seems, noted for giving particularly well-planned classes in philosophy, but his almost conversational mode of teaching succeeded in interesting Paul-Michel in Bergson, Plato, Descartes, Kant and Spinoza. The boy was also fond of his history teacher, Gaston Dez, whose chosen pedagogical method was to dictate his lessons. As a result, his classes proceeded very slowly, and there was a brisk trade in handwritten copies of the previous years' classes. Paul-Michel was a hard-working, somewhat solitary pupil, and most of his waking hours appear to have been devoted to his studies. He was, however, a popular student, not least because of the jokes with which he interrupted the classical plays to which the *classe de philo* were taken en masse.[22]

Although his studies took up most of his time, Foucault was also reading quite widely. He speaks of enjoying Stendhal, Balzac and Gide, authors who were, in his view, on the borderline between the approved curriculum and 'what one calls literature'.[23] If the testimony of Hervé Guibert is to be believed, one book by Gide must have had a special significance for Foucault, namely *La Séquestrée de Poitiers*. According to Guibert, a very young Paul-Michel used to walk with mingled pleasure and fear past a courtyard off the rue de la Visitation.[24] It was a courtyard that was associated with one of Poitiers's hidden scandals. At the turn of the century, a young woman had been imprisoned in a locked room here by her mother and brother because she had had an illegitimate child. For twenty-five years Blanche Monnier, Gide's *séquestrée de Poitiers*, lived in the locked room, half starved and lying in her own excrement, until she was finally rescued by chance.[25]

Paul-Michel's very dreams were dominated by reading. Ever since his childhood, he told an interviewer in 1967, he had been haunted by a recurrent nightmare: 'I have before my eyes a text I cannot read, or of which I can decipher only a tiny part; I pretend to read it, but I know that I am making it up. Then the text clouds over completely, and I can no longer read or even make it up. My throat goes tight, and I wake up.'[26] This is one of the very few insights into his early subjective life given by Foucault.

The picture that emerges from these few comments on his childhood is that of a very serious boy, almost exclusively concerned with work. There are indications that this is not the complete picture. He was, for instance, fond of practical jokes, many of them directed against his father's secretary. At a relatively early age, he developed an acute sense of the absurd, and a talent, encouraged no doubt by his observation of his father's dinner parties, for seeing through the pretensions of those around him. Hence, perhaps, the quizzical look Jacqueline Verdeaux noticed on his face at his sister's party. He was in some ways precocious, and given to lecturing Denys on the issues involved in the Munich Agreement of 1938 in terms sufficiently sophisticated to impress a younger brother. He could be brave, and at times recklessly brave. During a cold wartime winter, a group of boarders from Henri-IV stole some firewood from the headquarters of the collaborationist militia. Foucault and a girl called Lucette Rabatté signed a paper stating that they had supplied the wood from their own resources. The school authorities chose to believe them and no more was heard of an affair that could have had very unpleasant consequences.[27]

As an adolescent, Paul-Michel wrote poetry, but his mother could find no surviving trace of his early literary ventures after his death,[28] and it can only be assumed that he destroyed them. At her son's funeral, his mother spoke in tears to his friends and to the priest who buried him of a little boy who wanted to be a goldfish. When she pointed out that he loathed cold water, he still insisted that he wanted to be a fish . . . just for a moment, just to see what it was like.[29]

There are even fewer insights into Foucault's early sexual life. Ever since he could remember, he said in 1981, he had been attracted to members of his sex, and had always wanted to have sexual relations with other boys or men. The question 'How is it possible for men to live together, to share time, meals, a room, loves, grief, knowledge, trust?' was one that haunted him from an early age. It was, he added, a widespread 'desire, a worry or a worry-desire'.[30] Whether or not he acted upon his 'worry-desire' as an adolescent is not known, but he is on record as saying that he met his first 'friend' when he was twenty, which implies a first relationship established when he was at ENS in Paris.[31] During Foucault's teens, homosexuality was viewed with horror by the ideologues of Vichy, obsessed as they were with the defence of the values of the patriarchal family. Poitiers was a small town. Paul-Michel's family was quite close-knit, and most of his early life was spent under the kindly but vigilant supervision of his mother. Neither the age, the place nor the family in which he lived was conducive to experiments in the use of pleasures, and it appears unlikely that Foucault had any great sexual experience before he moved to Paris.

Foucault's preparation for the ENS *concours* was inevitably interrupted by the war. Only days after the first Allied landings in Normandy, parts of Poitiers, including the rue Arthur Ranc, had to be evacuated in anticipation of bombing raids directed against the station and its installations: Poitiers was an important staging post for the supply of the German garrisons on the Atlantic wall. The Foucault family retreated to Le Piroir for the summer and then returned to rented accommodation, as their home had suffered some bomb damage. As the fighting came nearer to the town, the normal structures of everyday life disintegrated and all schools were closed.

The confusion continued throughout the next year, but not all of it was the result of military action. Administrative incompetence had its own contribution to make. In the spring of 1945, Foucault and thirteen other candidates from Poitiers presented themselves at the faculty of law to begin the written part of the ENS *concours*; successful candidates would then go forward to the oral. They had to do so on two other occasions, and sat the examination three times. On the first occasion, their scripts had to be ignored because it was rumoured that a teacher in Paris had leaked the examination questions to his pupils; it then transpired that essential official documents had not arrived from Paris. The ritual was finally over, and the results were announced in July. Two candidates from Poitiers had been successful. Paul-Michel Foucault was not one of them. One hundred candidates were admissible to the oral; he was ranked one hundred and first.[32]

In October 1945, Foucault enrolled in a very different Lycée Henri-IV. The monastic-looking building behind the Panthéon in the Latin Quarter of Paris was one of France's most famous schools. This was the school Sartre had attended before transferring to its great rival, the Lycée Louis-le-Grand. This was where Alain (Emile Chartier) and

Henri Bergson had once taught. Precisely how Paul-Michel gained admittance to Henri-IV is not known, but a pupil from Poitiers could not normally transfer to a Parisian *lycée* which, like any other, in theory recruited its pupils from a geographically limited catchment area. The exercise of various forms of influence in order to secure a boy's admission to a good *lycée* was not unknown, and it is probable that Foucault's parents used theirs. It is more probable still that his mother had something to do with this final change of school.

Shortly before his departure for Paris, Foucault made an acquaintance who was to have a significant influence on his subsequent career. When Poitiers was liberated, Jean Piel was sent there as an assistant to the *commissaire de la République*, who was part of the bureaucracy responsible for the establishment of the new republican order. He knew the family slightly and had, by a curious coincidence, studied Paulin Malapert's philosophy textbook as a schoolboy. Piel had recently been injured in a very bad car accident, and was operated on by Foucault's father – not entirely successfully, because the operation left him with a heavy limp. That did not dim his affection for the Foucault family, or his interest in the young Paul-Michel. In 1962, Piel would ask Foucault to join him on the editorial board of *Critique*, the literary-philosophical journal founded by Georges Bataille. He had been impressed by *Histoire de la folie*, but he also recalled the bright young man he had met a decade and a half earlier, whose career he had watched from a distance.[33]

It was, perhaps, through Piel that another patient consulted Dr Foucault immediately after the war. Piel is the brother-in-law of the painter André Masson, and a man at the centre of a complex set of relationships. Masson married one of the four Maklés sisters, Bataille a second and Piel a third. Sylvia Bataille's second husband was Jacques Lacan. Like Piel, Masson was treated by Dr Foucault, who, in a rather macabre gesture of friendship, showed him the corpse of a stillborn child with a rare lesion that exposed parts of the brain membrane. The corpse provided the theme for a strange, swirling drawing which was given to the doctor by the artist. Michel Foucault inherited it after his father's death, and for years it stood on the desk at which he worked. It is now in the possession of his brother.

Paul-Michel was in a somewhat peculiar situation during his first year in Paris. Unlike most of the provincials at Henri-IV, he was not a boarder. Nor, of course, was he a day pupil who could return home each evening. He was living in a rented room in the premises of a private school run by a woman-friend of his mother's on the corner of the boulevard Raspail and the rue de Rennes. This curious arrangement ensured that he escaped the rituals designed to initiate new pupils into the conventions of communal living (something he was always to detest), but it also condemned him to a rather lonely existence. Paul-Michel made few close friends at Henri-IV. And though his accommodation was quiet and secure, it was not luxurious. The room was unheated and Foucault had to huddle under his bedcovers to work. The ruinous state of the transport system made it almost impossible to return to Poitiers for holidays or weekends. Food parcels from home made conditions more bearable than they might otherwise have been, but this was scarcely the best introduction to life in Paris.

Foucault in fact saw little of Paris during his first year in the capital. Studying for the *concours* left little time for leisure activities, and life consisted mainly of a constant round of study and mock examinations. Henri-IV's *khâgne* had a complement of fifty pupils, and intellectual rivalries were intense. The teaching was of an excellent standard. History was taught by André Alba, a man noted both for his erudition and his 'anti-clerical republicanism', who, in the words of a near-contemporary of Foucault's, 'plunged us up to our necks in event-bound [*événementielle*] and sometimes structural history'.[34] More significantly, Foucault was, albeit very briefly, taught philosophy by Jean Hyppolite, the greatest of the post-war French Hegelians. His first encounter with Hyppolite lasted for only two months, because the philosopher took up an appointment at the University of Strasbourg shortly after Foucault's arrival at Henri-IV. They would meet again at the Sorbonne and at ENS, but he would always recall the voice of Jean Hyppolite as he expounded Hegel's *Phenomenology of Mind* to the *khâgne* of Henri-IV.[35] Hyppolite's replacement was the mediocre Dreyfus-Lefoyer, who was despised by his pupils for daring to cite such nonentities as Emile Boutroux and Jules Lachelier,[36] almost forgotten figures from an earlier generation.

Despite the change of teacher, Foucault was making rapid progress in philosophy, as well as in history, Greek and Latin. At the end of his first term, he had come twenty-second in a philosophy test; at the end of the year, he came first and was described as an 'elite pupil'.[37] He was now ready to sit the ENS *concours* for the second time.

On his second attempt, Foucault had no difficulty with the written papers and was admitted to the oral. The latter involved him in a first encounter with Georges Canguilhem. Canguilhem had an unenviable reputation for severity in the eyes of *concours* candidates. He was a medically qualified historian of science, then teaching at the University of Strasbourg. A graduate of ENS, he had a distinguished Resistance record. For aspiring *normaliens*, however, his reputation was one of abrasiveness and even harshness. Jean-Paul Aron would later describe him as a cross between a peasant and Proust's Charlus.[38] Those who had been taught by him at the *lycée* in Toulouse recalled how he would deliberately disconcert them with his 'semantic nihilism' and his 'eternal "I don't know what that means"'. Anyone foolish enough to mention 'common sense' would receive on his essay that eternal comment, while flawed logic always drew a sharp 'I do not see why.'[39] Reputations like this spread rapidly and widely in student subcultures. The appealing southern accent contrasted sharply with the brusque manners; this was a man whose anti-clericalism led him to address, with calculated but polite malice, the nuns who crossed his path as *mademoiselle* rather than *ma soeur*.[40] In later years, Canguilhem would be an inspector of schools who could reduce philosophy teachers to tears with his criticisms. Althusser described him as deliberately spreading terror in the secondary system 'under the illusion that he could correct the philosophical understanding of teachers by bawling them out'.[41]

For the moment, he was one of the two formidable examiners Foucault had to face, the other being Pierre-Maxime Schuhl from the Toulouse faculty of letters. Canguilhem remembers absolutely nothing of his first meeting with Foucault,[42] but it was clearly neither too bruising nor too traumatic for the latter. Only a few days later, Paul-Michel learned that he had been successful and had been ranked fourth in the entrance examination for ENS.

Foucault's departure for Paris did not mark a complete break with Poitiers. As a student at ENS, he returned to Poitiers for summer holidays, and it was there that he learned to drive in either 1946 or 1947. Passing his test did not immediately grant him the mobility he wanted. A planned journey to Italy had to be adjourned when it became obvious that his competence at the wheel left a lot to be desired, and that he needed extra tuition from his mother. Despite this early setback, Foucault became one of the few French philosophers to have any competence at the wheel. Sartre did not drive, and being driven by Deleuze, whose competence with machines is apparently restricted to the 'desiring machines' described in the *Anti-Oedipe* he co-authored with Félix Guattari, is said to be an unnerving experience.[43]

It was mainly because of his mother, with whom he dined whenever she was in Paris, that Foucault maintained his links with Poitiers. Those links became stronger after the death of his father in 1959; from then onwards, Foucault always spent the month of August in

Vendeuvre-du-Poitou. When her husband died, Anne Foucault left Poitiers, where the old family home was eventually converted into offices by the postal service, and retired to Le Piroir, where she installed a central-heating system which finally overcame the damp problems. Foucault's summer visits were not purely for relaxation, and he worked steadily in a study installed in the original servants' wing of the old house. The study was filled with books, and adjoined a bedroom of almost monastic simplicity.

Days spent at Le Piroir followed a ritual pattern. Most of the day was spent working, with interruptions for sunbathing in fine weather. At the end of the day came the ceremonial watering of the gardens. Carrying heavy watering cans and buckets of water was a rudimentary form of weightlifting which Foucault greatly enjoyed. It was only in the summer of 1983 that he failed to water the gardens of Le Piroir. His stays in Vendeuvre coincided with the gherkin harvest, and one of his preferred pastimes was pickling the family's winter supply – a slow, time-consuming task involving the manipulation of tubs of brine and the careful scrubbing of the little vegetables.

In the 1950s and 1960s, the month at Le Piroir was enlivened by the presence of his five nephews and nieces. His nieces Anne and Sylvie-Claire remember him with great affection as the ideal uncle who was always ready to buy the sweets – and, later, the cigarettes – they were not supposed to have, who would reduce them to helpless laughter by asking for three kilometres of black pudding in the village *charcuterie* and who took a malicious pleasure in mocking the *baronne* who owned the château. Sylvie-Claire also recalls a man with whom she enjoyed a delicious complicity, comparing notes on the relative attractions of the men they passed in the street. This was the Foucault who, when asked by a great-nephew why he had no hair, would reply that he had lots of thick curly hair on the inside of his head.

Despite the many changes that took place in his life and despite his stated loathing of his background, Foucault always retained something of his past as well as a liking for some of the local cheeses. He continued to cycle, often travelling from his apartment to the Collège de France by bicycle at considerable risk to life and limb.[44] It was in Poitiers that he learned to cook, and to cook well. Guests were received with the meticulous attention and courtesy that is typical of a certain French bourgeoisie. Even at the height of his political commitment to the far left, dinner guests would find him fussing about the number of place settings and napkins he required. Foucault's attitude towards his considerable wealth was also in some ways that of a member of the provincial middle classes. His successive homes were comfortable and well furnished, but the ostentatious display of wealth and the conspicuous enjoyment of luxury were carefully avoided. Donations to political and other causes were made discreetly, almost secretively. In some ways, the professor at the Collège de France always remained the bourgeois son who left Poitiers in 1945.

2

THE FOX, THE SCHOOL AND THE PARTY

THE Ecole Normale Supérieure stands in the rue d'Ulm, a quiet street just to the south of the place du Panthéon. It is not far from the Lycée Henri-IV, but the short walk between the two is heavy with symbolism. From the *khâgne* of the *lycée* which had coached him for the *concours d'entrée*, Foucault could walk past the Panthéon, the last resting place of the 'great men' of France, to the school that would groom him to be a member of the next generation of the elite. The year 1946 was the one in which ENS celebrated the 150th anniversary of its foundation with solemn ceremonies in the great lecture theatre of the Sorbonne. Two years earlier, a commission on the reform of the educational system had reported to the government and had spoken disapprovingly of the 'caste' spirit which prevailed in the *grandes écoles*. It had even contemplated their abolition, but retreated in the face of the unthinkable. Institutions with such a 'glorious past' can easily outlive government commissions.[1] No *grande école* was more conscious of its past glories than ENS.

An *école normale* trains entrants for the teaching profession; in principle, the Ecole Normale Supérieure trains entrants to university teaching but in practice many of its alumni go on to other professions, many of them in the state sector. The school was residential and all-male, with *normaliennes* attending the sister institution in Sèvres. *Normaliens* received maintenance allowances from the state, whereas students at the Sorbonne were, with few exceptions, obliged to finance their own studies. In 1946, the accommodation provided in the rue d'Ulm was functional rather than luxurious and the ENS was not greatly renowned for its cuisine. Students slept in a dormitory divided into cubicles by curtains; studies or '*thurnes*' were shared. In the autumn of 1946, Foucault and five other alumni of Henri-IV took possession of a *thurne* on the ground floor. They collectively represented one sixth of the year's intake of student on the arts side.[2]

Normaliens are inevitably conscious of being members of a future elite, very conscious of not being at the lowly Sorbonne – though they are free to attend lectures there – and tend to have a heightened sense of hierarchy. As entry is by a competitive examination, the inhabitants of the rue d'Ulm are numerically graded from the outset and the individual who came last in the *concours d'entrée* can be daily reminded of his lowly status. Virtually any *normalien* who is asked about the years he spent at the school will immediately produce a yearbook to check who came first in the entrance examination and in the *agrégation*, unless, of course, he can supply that information from memory. ENS is characterised by a strong *esprit de corps* and both friendships and rivalries formed there can be long-lasting. Graduates tend to form a powerful old boys' network even when, like Foucault, they do not formally belong to the Association des Anciens Elèves. Like all such networks, this can be an exclusive society. The philosopher Jean-François Lyotard, for example, believes that one of the reasons he never knew Foucault well is that he was not himself a *normalien*.[3]

To enter ENS is to enter a lineage as well as an elite. The three 'models and supports' to whom Foucault paid tribute in his 1970 inaugural lecture at the Collège de France – Georges Dumézil, Canguilhem and Hyppolite – were all graduates of the Ecole Normale Supérieure. In the late 1940s and the 1950s, it was still possible for a student to trace his intellectual ancestry back to 1848 through a chain of masters. Although he was not actually taught by Canguilhem, Foucault regarded him as one of his intellectual masters. Canguilhem was the pupil of Alain, the incarnation of a certain radicalism, and Alain was in turn the pupil of Lagneau.[4] Intellectual lineage is not solely a question of the inheritance of the past. The individual is part of a chain which links him or her to past and future alike. At ENS, Foucault became part of a chain which also included Louis Althusser and, through his agency, would subsequently include a younger generation of theorists such as Jacques Derrida, Etienne Balibar, Pierre Macherey and Jacques Rancière.

Although an integral part of the academic system and a crucial element in its continued reproduction, ENS also has a long history of providing a haven for quietly subversive figures whose influence is out of all proportion to their physical presence. When Jean Hyppolite was at the Sorbonne in 1925, Lucien Herr was one such figure. ENS's almost legendary librarian had published a fragmentary study of Hegel – one of the first by a French academic – and was the shadowy figure behind many a conversion to socialism. As Hyppolite puts it, 'from the library of the Ecole Normale, he influenced many minds, not only in the domain of science, but also in that of action'.[5] When Foucault entered ENS, it housed another gentle subversive.

Louis Althusser had passed the *concours d'entrée* in 1939 but his academic career was immediately interrupted by the outbreak of war and by his mobilisation. Captured in the opening campaign of the war, he spent the next five years in a prisoner-of-war camp in Germany and did not return to the rue d'Ulm until 1945. He took his *agrégation* in 1947 and in 1949 was appointed as a philosophy tutor or *répétiteur* (*caïman* in the hermetic slang of ENS; precisely why a philosophy tutor should be known by this crocodilian name is one of the mysteries of Paris), replacing Georges Gusdorf when he moved to Strasbourg. A year later, he was appointed secretary of the arts side of the school, a post that involved ill-defined duties but made him essential to the life of 'his' school. Althusser was to spend thirty-four years in the rue d'Ulm. He asked rhetorically in his autobiography:

> What did the school become? Very rapidly, from the very beginning, I ought to say, it became a real maternal cocoon, the place where I was warm and at home, protected from the outside world, the place I did not need to leave in order to see people because they passed through and came there, especially when I became famous; in short, a substitute for a maternal environment, for the *amniotic* fluid.[6]

A slender man endowed with a fragile, almost melancholy beauty, Althusser soon became an institution within the institution, his aloofness adding greatly to the mystery that surrounded him. His role was to coach students for the *agrégation de philosophie* but, apart from giving first-year courses on Plato, he in fact taught relatively little. This quiet, gentle man was already suffering from the depressive illness which would have such a horrific outcome over thirty years later. Althusser was permanently domiciled in the school's sanatorium, where he was visited daily by his partner, Hélène Ritman, who, as 'Hélène Legotien', had won a very distinguished Resistance record. He occupied the first room in the sanatorium, and this gave him very easy access to the piano at the end of the corridor.[7] He played it well. Diagnosed by Pierre Male as suffering from dementia praecox (an old term for schizophrenia), and by Julian Ajuriguerra as being afflicted with a manic-depressive psychosis, Althusser endured years of intermittent hospitalisation, electro-convulsive treatment and narco-therapy,[8] a form of therapy involving the injection of penthatol to induce a trance-like lethargy which supposedly removed the barrier of censorship. From 1950 onwards, he was also in analysis with Laurent

Stévinin.[9] Few people knew of Althusser's true condition; the regular periods of hospitalisation were passed off as holidays.

The source of his influence on his students was quite simply his availability and the courteous readiness with which he offered advice to anyone who strayed into his tiny office. His technical advice on the conventions to be followed in *agrégation* examination papers was particularly sought after. At the beginning of the year, Althusser would ask his first-year students to write him an essay. This was returned, with his comments and corrections written on a separate sheet of paper. In his view, comments written directly on the essay would have been a source of humiliation. In an interview, he would offer advice on which courses to follow and on suitable topics for the second-year DEA. Unless they made appointments with him or wandered casually into his office, his students would probably not see him again until they began to prepare for their *agrégation* in their third year.[10]

In 1946 Althusser was not a Marxist, was still heavily influenced by the 'social Catholicism' of his youth in Algeria, Marseille and then Lyon, and was active in Catholic politics. It was to be another two years before he joined the Parti Communiste Français and almost two decades before his influence began to be felt outside ENS. It was not until 1952 that he finally abandoned his Catholicism.[11] He had published virtually nothing and a projected doctoral thesis on politics and philosophy in eighteenth-century France (together with a complementary *petite thèse* on Rousseau) had been abandoned, though elements of it survive in the 1959 study of Montesquieu. It was only in 1975 that Althusser was awarded a doctorate for his published work.[12]

Even when he became a member of the Party, Althusser was not politically active in any normal sense of that term. According to one eye-witness, he failed to attend a number of important meetings, notably one at which the school authorities suspended all student political activity for fear of a physical clash between the Gaullists and the Communists, who had respectively invited Jacques Soustelle and André Marty to speak on the same evening.[13] Yann Moulier Boutang's biography reveals an Althusser who was politically rather more active than earlier accounts would suggest, but it is true that his activities were strictly confined to the micro-world of ENS. He had, however, quietly begun to weave the subtle theoretical web that would influence so many in the 1960s and 1970s. A student from a later generation describes the charm of 'the philosophy teacher who guided our work and our reading. He tactfully gave us the chance of working with him, in such a way that we did not realise that it was he who actually did the work, that he was working for us.'[14]

Foucault and Althusser became close friends in the late 1940s, and the former profited greatly from the older man's counsels. It was on Althusser's advice that Foucault rejected hospitalisation as a solution to his depressive problems, and his early career was to be heavily influenced by 'old Alt', as he was affectionately known at ENS. The very real friendship that developed was to be proof against all political differences and disagreements and was to survive bitter personal tragedies too. It was also proof against the sarcasm Althusser often directed against those around him. Not all Althusser's comments on Foucault were charitable. When he learned that Foucault was studying madness and was spending time at the Sainte-Anne psychiatric hospital, he remarked in the presence of the young English historian Douglas Johnson, who spent the years 1947–49 at ENS, that he should be kept there.[15]

Althusser and Foucault had a mutual friend in Jacques Martin, 'a distressed homosexual, but a warm man despite the distance of his latent schizophrenia . . . Michel Foucault loved him as much as I did'.[16] Four years younger than Althusser and four years older than Foucault, Martin was a member of the *promotion* (class) of 1941. He was a brilliant Germanist with a special interest in Kant. In 1943, he interrupted his studies and went to Germany to work. As a student, he could have avoided the Service de Travail Obligatoire (the system whereby French workers were recruited – and conscripted – to work in Germany), but his intellectual curiosity was greater than his need for comfort. On his return to ENS in 1945, he was at a loss to understand how one could study Germany philosophy after Auschwitz. Despite his bewilderment, he was still studying that subject, with Hegel and then Marx replacing Kant as the focus of his interest.

Martin was a brilliant student, and Merleau-Ponty called him 'the prince of the mind'. Althusser later recalled reading his DEA dissertation: 'He talked about questions I only half understood, despite his explanations. Everything was dominated by the concept of problematic.'[17] The concept of 'problematic' is basic to the highly intellectual brand of Marxism Althusser would forge in the 1960s, where it refers to the ideological or theoretical framework without which a concept cannot exist and cannot be studied. In *Pour Marx* Althusser pays tribute to his student: 'These pages are dedicated to the memory of Jacques Martin, the friend who, in the most terrible ordeal, discovered the road to Marx's philosophy – and guided me onto it.'[18]

Like Althusser, Martin suffered from severe depression and, despite his brilliance, wrote nothing, or nothing that has survived. For Foucault and Althusser, he was a *philosophe sans oeuvre*, a philosopher with no works. The phrase occurred again and again in Yann Moulier Boutang's many conversations with Althusser when he was preparing his biography; Boutang believes that the expression was originally Martin's. In 1948 and then again in 1950, Martin failed his *agrégation*. His planned academic career was in ruins, and he drifted into poverty and depression. Occasional work as a translator (of, among other things, Hermann Hesse's novel *Das Glasperlenspiel*) did not provide a living. Martin was given generous financial support by friends, including Althusser and Foucault. He committed suicide in 1963. According to Boutang, the almost mythical *philosophe sans oeuvre* was, for Althusser and Foucault, the 'ghost of failure', the mirror of what they could have become.[19] Foucault never spoke of Jacques Martin in print, but, like Althusser, he may have borrowed something from him. From 1961 onwards, he would define madness as '*l'absence d'oeuvre*'.

Foucault's years at ENS were not always easy for him. Even though he was largely indifferent to his environment and to considerations of physical comfort, he did not find it simple to adjust to communal living. He also had to live in an atmosphere of intense intellectual competition and rivalry exacerbated by the fact that the community in which he lived was so small. In this closed environment, great importance attached to the verb *briller* – 'to shine', 'to be brilliant'. The compulsion to be brilliant was reinforced by the structure of the final goal: the *agrégation*. As the three written papers dealt with questions relating to the history of philosophy in its entirety, the object of a *normalien*'s study was the mastery of a culture rather than familiarity with a syllabus.

If it was hierarchical, ENS was also segregated in other ways. The division between arts and sciences was particularly marked, with students of the former considering themselves vastly superior to the relatively uncivilised scientists. Within the arts community philosophy was seen as the noblest of noble disciplines. Vertical divisions between years were important. Even physical living arrangements tended to promote divisions. Meals were taken communally at tables of eight in the dining room and it was the custom to remain at the same table for the full three years. It was therefore quite possible to spend three years in a relatively small institution without having any real acquaintance with many of one's contemporaries. Lucien Sève, who was in the 1945 *promotion*, spent two years in a *thurne* almost opposite Foucault's room on the dusty third-floor corridor which housed the DEA and *agrégation* students; their paths crossed frequently, yet they never really knew one another.[20] ENS was a strange combination of enforced communality and separation.

Political divisions were also significant. Catholicism was still a force to be reckoned with, though the strength of the anti-clerical republican tradition meant that many students had nothing but scorn for the so-called '*talas*', a slang expression derived from '*ceux qui vonT A LA messe*' ('those who go to mass'). The traditional right was in decline, while the Parti Communiste Français was begining to make inroads and would gradually increase its influence throughout the 1950s; a modern historian estimates that, at this time, some 15 per cent of *normaliens* belonged to the PCF.[21] To its left there soon stood Jean Laplanche and a handful of other members of Socialisme ou barbarie, the neo-Trotskyist group founded by Cornelius Castoriadis in 1948–49. Political divisions could lead to bitter exchanges, but they were also soluble in alcohol, and there were evenings on which the 'Marseillaise', 'Le Chant du partisan' and the Vichyist 'Maréchal nous voilà' were sung one after another in rowdy chorus.[22]

In 1946, Foucault was largely indifferent to politics, even though he did exhibit some sympathy for the PCF. It was not until 1950 that indifference gave way to commitment. In earlier years, Foucault displayed a curious attitude towards organised politics. According to Maurice Agulhon, then secretary of the Party cell, he was willing to join the cell, but refused to be active in the student union on the grounds that student politics were pathetic and far removed from revolutionary communist ideals.[23] Such nice distinctions and mental reservations were not acceptable to the PCF, and Foucault therefore remained on the fringes.

There are no contemporary accounts of Foucault at ENS. Eye-witness accounts from his fellow students are therefore inevitably influenced by hindsight, and no doubt coloured by subsequent impressions of an older and vastly more important Foucault. They are, on the other hand, relatively consistent. Everyone agrees that the young Foucault had a remarkable capacity for work, that he made notes on everything and stored them neatly in boxes. It is also well known that he suffered serious bouts of depression. Depression was by no means an unknown condition at ENS, where it sometimes seemed that everyone was carefully nurturing a neurosis, but in Foucault's case matters were serious. The psychoanalyst Jean Laplanche, who entered ENS in 1945 after spending a year at Harvard on a scholarship, attributes these episodes to the oppressive and competitive atmosphere. Others offer different explanations. Both Didier Anzieu and Jacqueline Verdeaux recall that Foucault would occasionally disappear from ENS for days at a time, returning exhausted and very dejected, the inference being that he had departed on some lonely sexual expedition.[24] It would be dangerous to see his homosexuality as the sole cause of Foucault's depression. Only a few years later, when he was sharing a flat with his brother Denys, the two would joke easily about their respective girl- and boyfriends, which does not suggest any great feeling of guilt or self-oppression.[25] Foucault drank quite heavily, if episodically, during his years at ENS, but it is uncertain whether this was a symptom or the cause of his depression. There are rumours of drug-taking, though that was unlikely to involve anything harder than cannabis or possibly opium. There are stories, persistent but un-confirmed, of a suicide attempt in 1948 and even of the suicide by hanging of a lover. It is difficult to diagnose the precise reasons for Foucault's depression. There is no extant record of any previous depressive episodes; the crisis of 1940 and his initial failure to pass the ENS *concours* resulted in disappointment, but not real depression. In later years, there was a close association between writing and depressive interludes, but they were relatively short-lived. The depression of the years at ENS probably resulted from a combination of factors: a competitive atmosphere, a culture of the neurotic, possible worries about sexuality, a conviction of being ugly,[26] and fear of failure could all have played a part.

Reports of Foucault's depressions filtered back to Poitiers, and in the year of the supposed suicide attempt his father arranged a consultation with Jean Delay, a very distinguished psychiatrist at Sainte-Anne Given that Delay's reputation was based as much upon his adminstrative and literary expertise as his clinical skills, he may not have been the ideal choice but the consultation did have one beneficial result. With the agreement of Pierre Etienne, ENS's doctor, Foucault spent his third year in the relative luxury and privacy of a single room in the school's sanatorium, thus achieving the ambition of many of his contempo-raries. It also resulted in a lasting friendship – and mutual respect – between Delay and Foucault, who always greeted one another warmly when their paths crossed in the Bibliothèque Nationale. The friendship was punctuated by the exchange of the books they published, including a copy of Delay's classic psychobiography of André Gide.[27]

In the meantime, Jacqueline Verdeaux, now fully qualified, was keeping a watchful eye on Foucault at his mother's request. In her view, the depressive episodes would, in later years, have been an indication for the prescription of psychotropics but such remedies were not available in 1948.[28] It was presumably at this time that Foucault went into analysis, and that he rejected the option of hospitalisation on Althusser's advice. The name of the psychoanalyst in question is not known, and the entire episode is somewhat enigmatic. According to his friend Maurice Pinguet, Foucault was in analysis for a few weeks and reported a dream in which he saw a surgeon's lancet floating in liquid; the analyst had no difficulty in interpreting this as a castration dream. The treatment came to a sudden end when the analyst announced that he was going on holiday; Foucault would not tolerate the interruption and broke off the analysis in retaliation.[29] Foucault's own account, given in response to a question from a Brazilian journalist many years later, is less picturesque. He merely notes that he had entered a very traditional Freudian analysis, and broke it off after only a few weeks because he was bored – not an explanation which any psychoanalyst is likely to accept.[30]

Foucault remained discreet about his depressions. Although his parents obviously had some knowledge of his mental state, his sister, now married and resident in Paris, usually encountered a very cheerful younger brother and saw no signs of depression when she attended ENS's annual ball with him and her husband, Henri Fruchaud.[31] Foucault may have wished to conceal his depression from her, but this is also an early sign of his undoubted ability to live several lives, to be different things to different people.

Not everyone who knew Foucault at ENS encountered a depressive. Although Pinguet learned later that the years at ENS had been almost intolerably painful for Foucault, he met someone very different in the summer of 1950. Foucault was dressed in shorts, laughing and addressing friends in a loud, almost aggressive tone. The word *Dasein* figured prominently in the snatches of conversation Pinguet overheard. Foucault was leaving the dining room, and was carrying a fork, a knife and a spoon.[32] At this time, students were issued with cutlery which they had to take into the dining room at every meal. They were also responsible for washing their cutlery, for which purpose they were naturally supplied with tea towels. Foucault was often involved in horseplay, in the theft of towels and napkins and in chases through the corridors which involved their use in mock battles. The boy who had enjoyed playing practical jokes in Poitiers was far from dead. Not everyone appreciated this boisterous side to Foucault, and some were disaffected by his intellectual arrogance and his ruthless use of irony and sarcasm in arguments and disputes.

Foucault may have been a boisterous student, but he appears to have shunned two aspects of *normalien* tradition. No one recall him climbing on to the roof, a dangerous pastime which can and does cause the occasional fatality. And on only one occasion, to his subsequent regret, did he indulge in the traditional sport of stealing books, preferably from Gibert's bookshop in the boulevard Saint-Michel. In the 1970s, he told Claude Mauriac that he had once stolen something, adding: 'I had to force myself, and was shaking with fear.' An undated cassette recording of Foucault in conversation (probably in 1972) reveals that the stolen object was a volume of poetry by Saint-Jean Perse.[33]

All were struck by his physical appearance. With his short hair, already thinning, his intense blue eyes and his rimless spectacles, he was not a figure who was easily missed or overlooked. Just as Verdeaux had been struck by Foucault's incongruous presence and persona at the children's party where she first met him, Didier Anzieu was constantly surprised to see that the body of a fit adolescent was surmounted by the head of a much older-looking *savant*. Foucault's physical vitality and intelligence resulted in his being nicknamed *Fuchs*, the German word for 'fox'. A fox, like Foucault, explains a fellow *normalien*, has a sharp pointed face and is cunning.[34] This was not the last time that animal imagery would be used to describe Foucault. In his diaries, Claude Mauriac, who first met Foucault in 1971, habitually refers to him as having a 'carnivorous' smile. The *Fuchs* was intelligent, but he could also bite.

If Foucault was discreet about his depressions, he was very discreet about his sexuality. Relatively few people knew of his orientation. He had good reason to remain silent. Whereas the wider intellectual-literary world was tolerant, the same could not be said of the academic community. The relationship between Jean Marais and Jean Cocteau was scarcely shrouded in secrecy, but rumours of homosexuality could and did break academic careers. Prejudice was backed up by legislation. A law passed in 1946 stated that only persons of 'good morality' could be employed in the service of the state. That law subsequently became article 16 of the *statut général du fonctionnaire*.[35] In France, teachers, including university teachers, are *fonctionnaires*, or civil servants. The fact that such legislation was rarely, if ever, acted upon was less relevant than its contribution to an atmosphere of fear and self-oppression. The more general climate can be gauged from the fact that a decree issued by the Préfet de Paris in February 1949 made it an offence for men to dance together in any public place or establishment open to the public. The pursuit of homosexual encounters was therefore a somewhat lonely and potentially dangerous activity.

In philosophical terms, the French intellectual landscape of Foucault's youth was of course dominated by phenomenology, the two great monuments of French existentialism being Sartre's *L'Etre et le néant* (1943) and Merleau-Ponty's *Phénoménologie de la perception* (1945). It is not, however, entirely accurate to claim that Sartre's dominance of the cultural field was complete. His polymathic activity in so many fields – philosophy, literature, theatre, journalism – tends to mask the fact that, for many, the post-war years were marked primarily by the new interest in Hegel. In 1930, Alexandre Koyré drafted a conference report on the state of Hegelian studies in France and found to his embarrassment that he had almost nothing to say: there was no Hegelian school in France.[36] In 1946, Merleau-Ponty could write:

> All the great philosophical ideas of the past century – the philosophies of Marx and Nietzsche, phenomenology, German existentialism and psychoanalysis – had their beginnings in Hegel; it was he who started the attempt to explore the irrational and to integrate it into an expanded reason, which remains the task of our century.[37]

His words may seem hyperbolic, and the Hegel-Nietzsche line of descent in particular is far from self-evident, but Merleau-Ponty was expressing a truth universally acknowledged at the time. Georges Canguilhem, for one, concurred: 'Contemporary philosophical thought is dominated by Hegelianism. Compared to this, many doctrines can be regarded as literature.'[38] In 1948, Hegel appeared to be the source and origin of all things modern; the *Phenomenology* had become 'the basic book that is consulted in all French philosophical milieux'.[39]

For pre-war French philosophers, Hegel had been a dubious, if not dangerous, spokesman for Germanism and pan-Germanism. Until 1930, even the word 'dialectic' had pejorative connotations, meaning 'logic of appearance' to a neo-Kantian and 'pure verbiage' to a Bergsonian; after 1930 it was used more positively to indicate the transcendence of 'analytic reason' (again, a Kantian notion).[40] In the mid-1940s, it had acquired its Hegelian-Marxist meaning. The pre-war masters who, like Léon Brunschwicg, had effectively denied Hegel a place in the history of philosophy, were objects of derision for Foucault's generation. Bergson himself was becoming a rather dusty figure, though he was still sufficiently alive to appear in the *agrégation* paper sat by Foucault in 1951.[41]

The Hegel who was so dominant in the years Foucault spent at ENS was largely a French creation, and his first creator was Alexandre Kojève, whose lectures on the *Phenomenology of Mind* at the Ecole Pratique des Hautes Etudes between 1933 and 1939 had a formative influence on everyone from Georges Bataille and André Breton to Klossowski and Lacan. A summary of the lectures based upon notes taken by Raymond Queneau (and approved by Kojève) appeared in 1947 and brought the previously legendary reading of Hegel into the public domain.[42] Kojève's reading produces a violent Hegel, the author of what Vincent Descombes terms a 'terrorist' conception of history. This Hegel is the theorist of the unhappy consciousness, of the master–slave dialectic and of the struggle unto death for recognition, and the anthropologist of desire.

In the interval between the delivery of the lectures and their publication, a second major event contributed to the new interest in Hegel. The first volume of Jean Hyppolite's translation of the *Phenomenology* appeared in 1939, the second in 1941. The ironic historical symmetry has often been noted: the book completed as French cannon thundered at the gates of Jena in 1807 was translated as France fell to German armies.

Foucault first encountered Hyppolite at Henri-IV, where he was immediately struck by the voice of that small, stocky man as he led his pupils through the labyrinth of the *Phenomenology*: 'In that voice which constantly started over again as though it were meditating inside its own movement, we perceived more than the voice of a teacher; we were hearing the voice of Hegel, and perhaps even the voice of philosophy itself.'[43] He would once again hear the voice of Hyppolite – or of Hegel speaking through Hyppolite – at the Sorbonne and at ENS. As he taught at Henri-IV, Hyppolite was in fact rehearsing aloud the themes of the vastly influential thesis he would submit in 1946.[44]

The importance of Hegel for the generation that attended ENS in the immediate aftermath of the war can be gauged by the titles of the DEA dissertations written by three *normaliens* between 1947 and 1949: Louis Althusser, *La Notion de contenu dans la philosophie de G. W. F. Hegel*; Jacques Martin, *La Notion d'individu chez Hegel*; Michel Foucault, *La Constitution d'un transcendental dans 'la Phénoménologie de l'esprit' de Hegel*.[45] Tragically, Foucault's DEA thesis appears not to have survived and nothing is known of its content. In its absence one can only savour the irony: Foucault, so much of whose work is directed against the attempt to totalise or to produce absolute knowledge, actually began his philosophical career by writing on the master of totalisation, so great was his desire to be part of the 'modernity' represented by Hegel. It was after reading Hegel that Foucault moved on to Marx, Heidegger and finally Nietzsche.[46]

The importance of Hegel greatly outweighed that of Sartre for anyone at ENS in the years 1946–50. In 1945, Sartre lectured on the topic 'Existentialism Is a Humanism' at the Club Maintenant in Saint-Germain; the room was so crowded that people fainted and the speaker could not be heard. He would have received a much cooler reception in the rue d'Ulm, where preference was given to Merleau-Ponty, deemed a technically more interesting philosopher than the popularising Sartre: 'It was fashionable to affect scorn for Sartre, who was fashionable.'[47] Foucault made precisely the same point in conversation with Claude Mauriac in 1973: 'When we were young, it was Merleau-Ponty, who counted, not Sartre. We were fascinated by him.'[48] Foucault quite regularly attended Merleau-Ponty's lectures at the Sorbonne, and stated many years later: 'I remember clearly some lectures in which Merleau-Ponty began speaking of Saussure who, even if he had been dead for fifteen years, was quite unknown, not so much to French linguists and philologists, but to the cultured public.'[49] Hegel was, however, only one of the 'three H's' identified by Descombes as dominating this period, the others being Husserl and Heidegger. Preferring Husserl to Sartre was no doubt in part a classic example of *normalien* intellectual snobbery. As Paul Veyne puts it: 'Husserl is difficult. So a *normalien* would read Husserl.'[50] Foucault was no exception.

An affected distaste for Sartre was not purely a matter of snobbery. Looking back at his career, Foucault often spoke of a dichotomy between a philosophy of consciousness and a philosophy of the concept. In his preface to an American translation of Canguilhem, for instance, he spoke of a dividing line that ran between 'a philosophy of experience, of meaning, of the subject, and a philosophy of knowledge, of rationality and of the concept'. On one side of it stood Sartre and Merleau-Ponty, and on the other Jean Cavaillès, Gaston Bachelard, Koyré and Canguilhem.[51] This was of course a retrospective view, but it is one that is shared by the sociologist Pierre Bourdieu, according to whom one of the supports for opposition to existentialism, especially in its vulgarised version, was a philosophy closely related to a history of the sciences and the epistemology of Bachelard, Canguilhem and Koyré, with its concern for 'seriousness and rigour'.[52] While he was fascinated by the philosophy of the concept, Foucault was also fascinated by something quite different, namely the novels of André Malraux, which provided Sartre with many of the most striking formulas of *L'Etre et le néant*. Indeed, he was able, he claimed, to recite by heart whole pages from Malraux.[53] We do not know just which novels he knew so well; like most readers, he was probably most enthusiastic about *La Condition humaine* (1933) and *L'Espoir* (1937).

Of the 'three H's', it was Heidegger who meant most to Foucault at this stage. He accumulated 'tons' of notes on him ('many more than on Hegel or Marx'),[54] and Heidegger was obviously the main reference for his first important piece of work – the introduction to an essay by the existential psychotherapist Ludwig Binswanger published in 1954. Reading Heidegger in the late 1940s and early 1950s was not the easiest of tasks. Despite the impact of Sartre's *L'Etre et le néant*, even basic Heideggerean terminology was unfamiliar. Although fragments of the text known in English as *What Is Metaphysics?* had appeared in translation in *Bifur* as early as 1929, little was available in French. Part of the *Letter on Humanism* appeared in 1947, and the accompanying presentation by Jean Beaufret was one of the few reliable introductions to Heidegger in circulation.[55] Articles by Koyré and others began to appear in *Critique* shortly after its launch in 1946, but Heidegger still remained a relatively unknown quantity. In the absence of translations, Foucault was obliged to tackle Heidegger in the original. He does not specify just which texts he struggled with, but the introduction to Binswanger suggests at least some familiarity with *Sein und Zeit*, which was not to be translated for many years to come.

For most academic philosophers in France, Nietzsche was almost as unknown a quantity as Heidegger. In the immediate post-war years, there was a growing interest in his work on the part of individuals like Bataille and Klossowski, but the associations with Nazism were still an obstacle. To the extent that his work was known, it was known primarily through a literary tradition which can be traced through Paul Valéry, the Gide of *Les Nourritures terrestres* (1897) and *L'Immoraliste* (1902) and, according to some readings, the Camus of *Le Mythe de Sisyphe* (1943).[56] It is also possible to identify a Nietzschean strand in Malraux. Reading both Heidegger and Nietzsche was a lonely task.

In later years, Foucault would describe his intellectual formation as being based upon a pantheon of authors read 'against' Sartre and Hegel: Nietzsche, Maurice Blanchot and Bataille.[57] It seems in fact unlikely that he read Nietzsche in his student days; Maurice Pinguet dates the crucial encounter with *Untimely Meditations* to the summer of 1953 or, in other words, after the *agrégation*,[58] and the absence of any reference to Nietzsche in any of Foucault's first writings strongly suggests that Pinguet's memory is accurate on this point, and Foucault in fact confirmed that this was the case in an interview given in the 1980s.[59] Foucault's own claim to have joined the PCF in 1950 with the ambition of becoming a 'Nietzschean communist' is a retrospective projection rather than an accurate memory.[60]

The young Foucault was also reading texts on the history of science which would greatly mark his subsequent work. He was, for instance, interested in Bachelard's reflections on 'discontinuities in the theory of science' but Bachelard was to remain a general rather than a specific influence.[61] It is clear that by the time he took his *agrégation* in 1951, Foucault was already interested in the terrain that was to become his, a domain demarcated by the history of the sciences, by a Heideggerean (and subsequently Nietzschean) philosophical discourse and by a certain literary vision. His interdisciplinary terrain was further marked by his growing interest in the psychological sciences.

Foucault's unease during his years at ENS did not stem from his sexual isolation alone. It was compounded by his uncertainty as to just where his future lay. He did not feel that he had any particular vocation for teaching in higher education, and no interest at all in working as a *prof de philo* in a *lycée*. His uncertainty can be seen in his elected areas of study. Although the atmosphere at ENS was highly pressured and although the prospect of the *agrégation* loomed, the school allowed its students great intellectual latitude, and to a large extent Foucault was able to pursue his own interests. He was of course studying philosophy, but he also took considerable interest in psychology.

The relationship between the two disciplines was complex. Traditionally, psychology, as opposed to the medical specialism of psychiatry, was a philosophical discipline; the syllabus for the *baccaulauréat*, which has an important role in the institutional definition of disciplines, always included a section on 'general psychology'. There was no *agrégation* in psychology, which was not a school subject in its own right, and would-be psychologists therefore tended to study philosophy. Many of the psychoanalysts who were later to be associated with Lacan came from this philosophy-psychology tradition. Not surprisingly, psychoanalysts originally reared on a diet of Hyppolite's lectures on Hegel tend to be more philosophically oriented than their British or American counterparts.

It was only in 1947 that the first degree in psychology was created by Daniel Lagache, who had recently succeeded Paul Guillaume as professor of social psychology at the Sorbonne after several years in Strasbourg.[62] Lagache, a member of the glittering ENS *promotion* of 1924 which included Canguilhem, Sartre, Paul Nizan and Raymond

Aron, was one of the first to promote the integration of psychoanalysis into the university curriculum, but his grand design was the integration of all forms of psychology (behavioural, clinical and psychoanalytic) into the one unified discipline he sketched in his inaugural lecture at the Sorbonne.[63]

Foucault followed Lagache's lectures with enthusiasm, and took a psychology degree in 1949, the year after he graduated in philosophy. Althusser's predecessor George Gusdorf had asked his friend Georges Daumézon, one of the founders of a distinctively French style of 'institutional psychotherapy', to organise a monthly series of open lectures which would acquaint normaliens with the major tendencies in a discipline which was now in a period of rapid change. Foucault and his contemporaries were therefore able to hear a sequence of distinguished lecturers including Daumézon himself, Henri Ey and Lacan. The last-named enjoyed an excellent reputation as a clinician and diagnostician but was not yet the enfant terrible that he would become after 1953, when both he and Lagache were driven out of the Société Psychanalytique de Paris and the International Psychoanalytic Association.

Didier Anzieu, who attended Lacan's lecture with Foucault, recalls a talk on identification illustrated by the wielding of glass test tubes containing two different species of crickets. One species modified its morphology as a result of identification with the group, whereas the other did not. The fact that the behaviour of locusts and sticklebacks is used by Lacan to illustrate the process of identification in major papers of the 1950s is a reminder of how much his early theories owe to ethology and even psychobiology and how little they owe to linguistics.[64]

Foucault's knowledge of psychology and psychiatry was not derived from lectures alone. Daumézon also encouraged his students to frequent Sainte-Anne, the great psychiatric hospital that serves central Paris. Here, they witnessed the ritual of the présentation des malades, as practised by Delay and Ey. The présentation was (and is) a combined exercise in diagnosis and pedagogy in which a patient undergoes a preliminary assessment in the presence of an audience of students and trainees. The custom of visiting Sainte-Anne was continued by Althusser when he replaced Gusdorf as caïman and Foucault was a regular attender.

Foucault was following a trajectory which led some of his contemporaries to a career in psychiatry or even psychoanalysis. Didier Anzieu, who became a very distinguished analyst after analysis with Lacan that began in 1949, was convinced that Foucault, with whom he was on cordial but not intimate terms, would take that course. He now explains his conviction as a projection of his own ambitions.[65] Jean Laplanche also went into analysis with Lacan, and then took a medical degree (at Lacan's suggestion) before embarking upon a training analysis. He has subsequently pursued a distinguished dual career as an analyst and as the wealthy producer of red burgundies from the family vineyards in Pommard. There are indications that Foucault too was contemplating a career in either psychology or psychiatry. While still a student, he asked Lagache whether a medical training was a necessary prerequisite for a career in psychology, and received the denial Lagache usually supplied to that question. Foucault is also reported to have investigated the possibility of going into therapy with Lagache, and to have met with a negative response.[66] His interest in psychology was before long to take him in a rather different direction.

Foucault approached the final hurdle of the *agrégation* in spring 1950. This was also the year in which he finally joined the PCF. The Parti Communiste Français had emerged from the war as the single most important political grouping in France, and was able to win five million votes in 1945. By the middle of 1947, its membership reached a high point of 900,000. Authoritarian, highly centralised and disciplined, the Party was a classic Stalinist formation, complete with a somewhat absurd personality cult dedicated to its secretary-general, Maurice Thorez. It was also highly patriotic and still enjoyed and exploited the reputation it had won in the wartime Resistance; this was *le parti des fusillés* – the party which had lost more members than any other to German repression. From 1944 to 1947, the PCF was involved directly in government and cooperated in an unstable coalition with the SFIO (Section Française de l'Internationale Ouvrière, the ancestor of the modern Socialist Party) and the social-democratic Mouvement Républicain Populaire. Tripartism lasted until May 1947, when Prime Minister Paul Ramadier dismissed the remaining Communist ministers. In March, the USA had adopted the Truman Doctrine of 'communist containment'. Later the same year, Andrei Zhdanov, Stalinism's principal ideologue proclaimed the symmetrical doctrine which divided the world into imperialist and anti-imperialist camps. The Cold War had begun. The PCF adopted a resolutely pro-Soviet policy and gradually retreated into a siege mentality. Membership began to decline, and continued to do so, with some fluctuations, for the next two decades.

This was the party which Foucault chose to join in 1950. He took out his Party card at the urging of Althusser, who had taken the same decision two years earlier.[67] In subjective terms, Foucault's newfound commitment was largely a reaction to the apocalyptic despair he had felt as an adolescent living through a disastrous war. Politics had little meaning when the only choice available was one between Truman's America and Stalin's Russia. In France, the choice between the old SFIO and social democracy was equally unappealing. Many young intellectuals, including Foucault, found the idea of a 'bourgeois' profession in teaching or journalism intolerable and were looking for a society that would be

> radically different from the one we had been living in: a society which had allowed Nazism to come about, which had prostituted itself to Nazism and which had then gone over *en bloc* to de Gaulle. Faced with all that, the reaction of a large proportion of young people in France was one of total rejection. They wanted more than a different world and society; they wanted to go further, to change themselves, to revolutionise relationships, to be completely 'other'.[68]

An older Foucault once remarked that the widespread interest in Marxism was 'a means of prolonging that adolescent dream of another world'.[69] Like so many adolescent dreams, Foucault's new vision was not shared by his parents. His refusal to study medicine may or may not have led to serious tensions between father and son but, as Foucault's sister recalls with some amusement, his decision to join the PCF certainly did infuriate Dr Foucault.[70]

Foucault was not a particularly active member of the PCF, and his participation in the life of the relatively small cell at ENS was minimal. His commitment to Marxism extended little beyond the general conviction that material or economic conditions were a dominant, if not determinant, influence on social and political life.[71] Rarely, if ever, was he to be found carrying out the basic task of any true militant – selling the Party's daily *L'Humanité* – and no one can recall him taking part in political demonstrations. Maurice Pinguet recalled that though Foucault rarely took part in the weekly meetings, which were held in a small café in the place de la Contrescarpe, just up the hill from ENS, he did on one occasion launch into a violent denunciation of the coal-steel pact.[72] Jean-Claude Passeron also recalls Foucault giving a talk to a group of Communist students on psychiatry. The talk appears to have originated in the themes of what was to become the second part of *Maladie mentale et personnalité,* and the names of both Pavlov and Stalin were favourably mentioned.[73] His appearances at the beery meetings in the place de la Contrescarpe, and later in the rue Gay-Lussac, were, however, relatively rare.[74]

There are no reports of Foucault's less than assiduous attendance at Party meetings resulting in his being subjected to any serious criticism. According to the historian Le Roy Ladurie, also a PCF member at this time, his fellow members showed him a certain indulgence because they knew that he was absorbed by his research into psychiatry, but it has to be said that even partial exemption from Party commitments on academic grounds would have been, to say the least, exceptional. A more likely explanation is that, while he was teaching part-time at ENS, Foucault was associated with a so-called *groupe folklorique* (very roughly, 'the weird bunch') of slightly younger members including Paul Veyne, Gérard Genette, Passeron and Maurice Pinguet. Also known as the 'Saint-Germain-des-Prés Marxists', the group was not noted for its seriousness and its members were, according to Paul Veyne, regarded by the Party hierarchy as 'future heretics'. Perhaps their future heresies – and all did leave the Party – were such that they were deemed incorrigible, and were therefore left to their own devices.

Many of those who joined the PCF at roughly the same time as Foucault left it after only a few years. Mass resignations followed the revelations about Stalin's Russia made in Khrushchev's 'secret report' to the Twentieth Party Congress of the CPSU in 1956, and Soviet intervention in Hungary that same year led to many more departures. In Foucault's case, the disaffection set in earlier. At the beginning of 1953, *Pravda* announced the arrest of nine doctors on very serious charges. They had allegedly murdered Zhdanov, had planned to murder a number of Soviet marshals and had plotted against the life of Stalin himself. Immediately after Stalin's death from natural causes on 3 March, *Pravda* announced that the nine had been released and rehabilitated; they had been the victims of a machination. Seven of the nine were Jewish. In France, the PCF's press covered the 'doctors' plot' in slavishly pro-Soviet terms, commenting that the security services of the USSR had 'picked off the murderers in white coats, the secret agents recruited among the Zionists and Jewish nationalists' and implying that the entire plot had been hatched in Tel Aviv.[75]

Foucault attended a meeting at which André Wurmser attempted to justify the arrest of the nine. Wurmser laid down the Party line, and his audience of *normaliens* did their best to believe the unbelievable. For Foucault, believing the unbelievable was a way of existing within the Party: continued membership was the source of such tension that it became an exercise in 'dissolving the ego'. After the death of Stalin, the

PCF let it be known that there had been no plot, that it had been pure invention. The ENS cell wrote to Wurmser to ask for an explanation, but received no reply. Shortly afterwards, Foucault quietly left the PCF.[76] The incident left a 'bitter taste' in his mouth,[77] and resulted in both a life-long loathing for the PCF and a distinctly jaundiced view of the USSR.

The 'doctors' plot' had revealed the existence of an ugly strand of anti-Semitism in the Soviet Union. The French Party press was not to be outdone in the matter of anti-Semitism. According to Annie Besse, writing in *Cahiers du communisme*, 'Hitler . . . refrained from harming the Jews of the big bourgeoisie . . . Who will ever forget that Léon Blum, his wife at his side, contemplated from the windows of his villa the smoke from the ovens of the crematoria!' Zionism was 'a mask behind which to conceal espionage operations against the Soviet Union'.[78] Whether Foucault ever read these statements is not known, but in 1953 he was already denouncing the 'odious' attitude taken towards Israel by both the superpowers.[79] His pro-Israeli sentiments were as unswerving as his dislike for the PCF, and it is difficult to believe that there was no connection between the two.

While the doctors' plot and the current of anti-Semitism provided the final stimulus to leave the PCF, Foucault's sexual orientation meant that he had always been uncomfortable in the Party: 'I was never really integrated into the Communist Party because I was homosexual, and it was an institution that reinforced all the values of the most traditional bourgeois life.'[80] As Le Roy Ladurie remarks à propos of a schoolteacher who was forced to leave the Party when it was discovered that he had made sexual overtures to a pupil: 'It was assumed that, in the event of revelations by the bourgeois press, one Party member's homosexual pollution would infect the whole of the communist collectivity.' The individual in question was also forced to resign his teaching position. Ultimately, the education authorities proved to be more progressive than the PCF, and he was allowed to take up a post in a school in Paris, the legislation of 1946 notwithstanding.[81] Such attitudes were disastrously slow to change. As late as 1972 the veteran Jacques Duclos responded to a gay militant's query whether the PCF had changed its views on 'so-called sexual perversions' by saying: 'How can you queers have the cheek to ask us questions? Go and see a doctor. French women are healthy, the PCF is healthy; men were made to love women', while a senior Party spokesman told a journalist that 'neither homosexuality nor drugs have ever had anything to do with the labour movement'.[82] Life in the PCF cannot have been much more comfortable for Foucault than life in pre-war Poitiers.

Foucault's cultural interests, too, conflicted badly with Party orthodoxy. In aesthetic terms, Socialist Realism was the order of the day, whereas Foucault was reading the novelist and critic Maurice Blanchot and was a fervent admirer of Beckett's *En attendant Godot*,[83] which opened at the Théâtre Babylone on 5 January 1953; thirty years later, he could still refer to it as 'a breath-taking performance'.[84] April 1953 saw Foucault at what must have been one of the last PCF meetings he ever attended. It was held in a gallery-bookshop in Lille, was addressed by the same André Wurmser who had justified the arrest of the criminals in white coats, and was concerned with Picasso's portrait of Stalin, which had been reproduced in Louis Aragon's *Les Lettres françaises* on 15 March. Although the paper was under Party control, the leadership had unequivocally condemned the portrait. According to Jean-Paul Aron, who also attended the Lille meeting, Foucault was beginning to be 'swayed' by controversies like this.[85] Sexuality, aesthetic preference and intolerance of dishonesty combined to ensure that he was not the stuff of which docile militants are made. A Communist Party can be left in a variety of ways; Foucault made no public statement, and presumably simply failed to renew his Party card. He never again belonged to an organised political party.

The great mystery pertaining to Foucault's membership of the PCF stems from an exchange between him and Jean-Claude Passeron in December 1971. After a brief altercation with a group of young Maoists in the Goutte d'Or area of Paris, Foucault suddenly remarked to Passeron: 'Do you remember when we worked as ghosts on *La Nouvelle Critique* . . .? And that famous article on Merleau-Ponty that was talked about for so long. "We have to settle Merleau-Ponty's hash." That was the formula we used . . . I think that that article never got written. But there are lots of pages in *La Nouvelle Critique* that we did write and that others signed.' Before Passeron could reply, Claude Mauriac, who records the incident in his diaries, burst in: 'They weren't by any chance signed "Jean Kanapa"?'[86] Founded in December 1948, *La Nouvelle Critique* was one of the PCF's theoretical journals and Kanapa, an ambitious young man with a background in philosophy, was its editor in chief. On the basis of the fragmentary exchange recorded by Mauriac, a legend was born: Foucault had been Kanapa's ghost. In 1977, Foucault himself confused the issue by telling Mauriac, who was apparently contemplating including some mention of the Foucault–Passeron exchange in a further montage from his diaries, 'I did not write "the" Kanapa texts. Two or three of those texts, at most. If you want to be truthful, you should therefore say . . .'[87] At this point the dialogue breaks off.

There is no convincing explanation for either of these exchanges. Despite extensive research, Didier Eribon was unable to find anyone who would confirm the story. Passeron denied ever having written for the journal in question. Kanapa's son Jean encountered Foucault in the 1970s, and discussed the meeting with his father; neither Foucault nor Jean Kanapa mentioned the alleged ghosting. None of the major contributors to *La Nouvelle Critique* remembered seeing Foucault in Kanapa's company, and the latter's secretary claimed never to have heard of Foucault at that time. Eribon was also told by Pierre Daix, a member of the journal's editorial committee, that Kanapa always wrote his own articles and never used ghosts, while a regular contributor asserted that pseudonyms were used only by civil servants who risked dismissal or sanctions if they published openly in the Party press.[88] After the publication of his biography of Foucault, Eribon was congratulated by Daix for having exorcised the 'ghost' legend.[89] Yet a shadow of doubt must remain; Maxime Rodinson, a member of the PCF from 1937 to 1958 and a contributor to its press in the early 1950s, clearly states that certain of Kanapa's phrases appeared under his signature as a result of the heavy and tendentious editing of articles submitted for publication.[90] If Kanapa effectively rewrote other people's articles, it is by no means impossible that he also used ghosts.

In the absence of any evidence to prove (or, by the same criteria, to disprove) that Foucault wrote Kanapa's articles or that he wrote anonymous pieces for *La Nouvelle Critique*, the mystery remains intact. Given his lack of any history of militancy and his failure to display any ambition to rise in the Party hierarchy, it seems improbable that he would have been entrusted with such a task. A second mystery relates to the rationale behind the declarations made in the presence of Mauriac, who can provide no explanation for them. Foucault may simply have been joking, though the context of the exchange was not a particularly light-hearted one. He may also have been suggesting that he was, by the sin of omission, in part responsible for the ideological climate which had created Kanapa. Whatever the explanation, he cannot have been unaware that anything said in the presence of Claude Mauriac was likely to appear in his journals, which were written with publication in mind. A desire to mystify therefore cannot be ruled out, particularly as Foucault read *Et comme l'Espérance est violente* in manuscript and apparently made no comments on the reference to Kanapa.[91]

In retrospect, Foucault found that his relatively short experience of life in the PCF had been useful. He had seen at first hand the spirit of asceticism and intellectual self-flagellation with which so many students had attempted to change themselves in order to become and remain communists,[92] and was left with a healthy suspicion of such commitment. He may also have learned a more philosophical lesson. The Cold War division of the world had its theoretical corollary in the doctrine of the 'two sciences': sciences bourgeois and sciences proletarian. With a few exceptions, like the biologist Marcel Prenant, scientists in the PCF rallied to this doctrine and to the related promotion of Lysenkoism and belief in the inheritance of acquired characteristics in the biological kingdom. Lysenkoism became official Soviet doctrine during the 1948 session of the USSR Academy of Agricultural Science, and was heavily promoted in PCF publications throughout the period of Foucault's membership. Mendelian genetics, in the meantime, was denounced as a 'bourgeois science'.[93]

Foucault's early writings are innocent of any mention of Lysenko, but it is inconceivable that he was unaware of the issues. According to Pinguet, in 1953 Foucault was still struggling to conform to Marxist orthodoxy, but was increasingly intolerant of the 'intellectual *dirigisme*' of Zhdanov and Lysenko.[94] In a conversation recorded over twenty years after his departure from the PCF, Foucault alludes to his student years. One of the issues raised in the period 1950–55 was, he argues, that of the political status of science and the ideological functions science could convey. That issue was typified by the Lysenko affair, which could be summed up in two words: power and knowledge. In the same conversation, Foucault notes that the example of a 'dubious' science like psychiatry might provide a very good instance of how power and knowledge become entwined.[95]

The *agrég* is a fiercely competitive national examination and must be one of the most severe forms of intellectual trial by ordeal to have been devised in any country. Being a national examination, it is set by the highest academic authorities in France, and all candidates sit down to the paper at precisely the same moment. The oral examination involves a confrontation with very senior academics; in 1950, Foucault faced a jury which included an *inspecteur général* and Georges Davy, professor of sociology, dean of the Sorbonne and seemingly a permanent fixture on the jury. In Foucault's day, the first part of the *agrég* consisted of three day-long written papers. Those who survived this preliminary round then faced two orals. The first consisted of a *leçon*, or a verbal extemporisation on a theme chosen by lot. Its function, like that of the written papers, was one of elimination. The second oral comprised a further *leçon* on a set theme and three *explications de texte* or commentaries on texts in French, Latin and either Greek or a modern language. It is no accident that the subculture of ENS has always set such great store by verbal brilliance.

Foucault's written papers covered man's position in nature, and the work of Auguste Comte. These were standard academic topics, and of little interest to someone with an overriding interest in Heidegger and the other two 'H's'. He had no difficulty with the topics, and was now one of the seventy-four candidates who were admissible to the oral. The first oral proved to be his downfall when he failed to improvise successfully on the theme of 'hypotheses'. According to Davy, his mistake had been to try to display his erudition without actually discussing the subject itself.[96] Had he been successful, he would have gone on to discuss the 'notion of the person'.[97]

Foucault was astonished and outraged by his failure. Althusser was furious; his first year as *caïman* had ended with one of his favourite students' failure to pass the examination for which he had coached him.[98] Their astonishment was widely shared, and many of his friends, including Laplanche, hinted darkly at political prejudice, claiming that Foucault had been failed because he was a Communist.[99] That explanation probably has more to do with the PCF's siege mentality than with any objective reality. It had taken Foucault two attempts to succeed in the *concours d'entrée*, followed by two attempts at the *agrégation*. This appear to be a classic instance of underachievement or failure to perform resulting from a combination of high expectations and failure of nerve.

Although friends feared that his failure would result in serious depression or worse, Foucault went back to work with determination, covering countless small sheets of paper with notes on all the topics that might come up in the oral. He was now widely regarded as the candidate most likely to come first.[100] His companion in study was Jean-Paul Aron, who was also resitting the *agrégation*. Aron was not a *normalien* but was attending courses at ENS on an informal basis. Aron too was homosexual and the close association established in 1951 provided the basis for a long-standing rivalry in which intellectual and sexual strands were to become inextricably tangled.[101]

The intensive preparations paid off and Foucault successfully wrote examination scripts on 'experience and theory' and on an imaginary dialogue between Bergson and Spinoza.[102] He now had to face a jury composed of Davy, Hyppolite and Canguilhem. The last-named had no recollection of meeting Foucault in 1945, but retains vivid memories of their encounter at the 1951 oral. When the time came to give his *leçon*, Foucault dipped his hand into the waste-paper basket which contained the topics, each written on a single sheet of paper. His topic was 'sexuality', and his fluent discussion of its natural, historical and cultural aspects convinced his examiners of his worth.

Foucault was outraged; in his considered opinion, sexuality was not a suitable theme for the *agrégation*. It had been proposed by Canguilhem, despite protests from Davy, on the grounds that the *agrég* topics had not changed since he took his oral in 1927 and that it was time for something new. Besides, argued Canguilhem, all candidates for the *agrégation* had read Freud, and they all talked about sex. Foucault shared Davy's more conservative view, and formally protested to Canguilhem.[103] Despite his annoyance, Foucault's second encounter with Canguilhem was a happy one, and he was ranked third *ex aequo* in the *agrégation de philosophie*. The 1951 *agrégation* had been a 'Malthusian' process of elimination: fourteen candidates were successful, and five of them were *normaliens*.[104]

The usual destiny of the young *agrégé* was to spend at least some time teaching in a *lycée*, where he would be better paid and would teach fewer hours than a colleague with less prestigious qualifications, before taking up a post in higher education. One of the peculiarities of the French educational system is that both schools and universities are under the direct control of the Ministry of Education. As a result, it is in theory relatively easy to move between the secondary and higher education sectors. Certain of France's most distinguished thinkers never in fact taught in a university, Sartre and Alain being obvious examples. Foucault first encountered Jean Hyppolite at Henri-IV. A historian as distinguished as Maurice Agulhon, a contemporary of Foucault's at ENS and later professor at the Collège de France, served an apprenticeship teaching in a *lycée*. A transfer into the university sector is, however, by no means guaranteed and many *agrégés* view the prospect of being posted to a *lycée* with dismay. To make matters worse, they can be posted anywhere in the country and exile from Paris is always a very real possibility.

Exile in a *lycée* is not the only ordeal awaiting the graduate, or at least the male graduate. Young men can defer their military service for the duration of their studies, but by the autumn of 1951 Foucault had no option but to face a military selection board. He was excused military service on health grounds. Although his record did reveal a history of depression, it is almost certain that this was a case of medical and military strings being pulled by a paternal hand, particularly since his younger brother, whose health was perfectly robust, was also declared unfit for service on similar grounds.[105] A posting to a *lycée* was preceded by an interview with the *inspecteur général* responsible for the discipline concerned. The *inspecteur* for philosophy was, of course, Canguilhem. Foucault explained that he was not enthusiastic about teaching and expressed a desire to obtain admission to the Fondation Thiers in order to prepare a doctoral thesis.

The Fondation Thiers had originally been established by the family of the statesman and historian Louis Adolphe Thiers who died in 1877, but was now under the control of the Centre National de Recherche Scientifique. Beneficiaries were, technically, researchers attached to the CNRS and received a monthly allowance. Admission was not by examination, and candidates recommended by the director of the institution from which they graduated were simply interviewed by the Fondation's director – Paul Mazon, a classicist – and by representatives from the Académie Française and from the five academies (*inscriptions et belles lettres*, sciences, fine arts, moral sciences and political sciences) that together make up the Institut de France. Armed with Canguilhem's recommendation and, presumably, that of Hyppolite, Foucault had little difficulty in obtaining admission to the Fondation, then housed in a large nineteenth-century building in the elegant sixteenth *arrondissement*.

Like ENS, the Fondation was an all-male boarding establishment but it did offer the comparative luxury of single rooms and rather more creature comforts than the rue d'Ulm. Once more, Foucault was obliged to take meals in a communal dining hall and to adjust to living with twenty or so others. The Fondation proved to be less tolerant than ENS, and Foucault's boisterous aggression, sarcasm and sense of superiority soon made him almost universally unpopular. There are also rumours of an affair with a fellow resident which had an unfortunate outcome. The scholarship had been awarded for three years; Foucault stayed at the Fondation Thiers for only one year. The escape route was provided by a vacant assistantship in the northern university of Lille.

3

CARNIVAL IN MUSTERLINGEN

FOUCAULT was well qualified for the post in Lille, since the small philosophy department was looking for someone to teach psychology to philosophy students and not for a clinician. In the summer of 1952, he had successfully completed the diploma course in psychopathology taught by the Institut de psychologie. This was one of the four diploma courses offered (the others being in experimental, educational and applied psychology), and combined theoretical and practical elements. Foucault was taught by Jean Delay, attended clinical sessions and *présentations des malades* at Sainte-Anne and followed the lectures on the theory of psychoanalysis given by Maurice Benassy, then the scientific secretary of the recently founded Institut de Psychanalyse. His opinion of his chosen discipline was not favourable. It was, he argued, well known that a psychology graduate knew nothing and could do nothing because the revision required for all his certificates could easily be done sitting in the garden on a summer's afternoon. Nor did he have a particularly high opinion of the psychology courses taught in provincial universities; in his view, they were remarkable mainly for their soporific properties.[1]

It was the informal network of contacts and patrons he had established at ENS that took Foucault to Lille. Raymond Polin, the head of the philosophy department, was looking for a suitable candidate to fill the vacant post, and Foucault's name had come up in a conversation with Jules Vuillemin, the professor of philosophy at Clermont-Ferrand and a friend of Althusser's. He had briefly met Foucault in the rue d'Ulm. In October 1952, Foucault therefore joined Polin, Olivier Lacombe and Yvon Belaval in the northern city. He was very much the junior member of the department and does not appear to have formed any particularly close attachment to his colleagues. Indeed, the ground was being prepared for some later alliances and rivalries. Belaval, who had recently published a study of Diderot,[2] would later be one of Foucault's rivals for a chair at the Collège de France, while Vuillemin was to be one of his main sponsors.

The teaching was not demanding. Foucault was given a fairly free hand and most of his courses were based upon his own recently acquired knowledge. He was a highly competent teacher, and was commended by the dean of the faculty of letters in April 1954: 'A young *assistant*, very dynamic. Organises the teaching of scientific psychology with talent. Truly merits promotion.'[3] Foucault's existence in Lille was not unpleasant and he was not isolated since a number of acquaintances, including Jean-Paul Aron, were also working in the area.

Now an *agrégé* in philosophy and the holder of degrees in psychology and the natural sciences, Aron was teaching at the Lycée Faideherbe in Tourcoing, where he would remain for some years before returning to Paris to work at the CNRS and then, from 1960 onwards, at the Ecole des Hautes Etudes en Sciences Sociales. His experiences in Tourcoing provided the basis for *La Retenue*, the novel he published in 1962. Aron and Foucault saw quite a lot of one another and often dined together. It can be safely assumed that Foucault, like other friends, was drawn into one of Aron's favourite pastimes: the devising of imaginary menus. The interest in food eventually developed into one of Aron's most attractive books, namely an analysis of the culture of food in nineteenth-century France, but that lay far in the future.[4]

Relations between the two men soon became strained. After a bitter quarrel, one of Aron's young lovers fled and took refuge with Foucault. Thanks to a peculiar coincidence, the young man in question later worked for Plon, where he would play a role in the publication of *Histoire de la folie*. The rage this incident provoked in Aron added sexual jealousy to the intellectual envy that, as he was to admit after Foucault's death, he already felt for the man whose notes he had shared as they prepared for the *agrégation*. The envy in turn goes some way to explaining the bitterness of some of the remarks about Foucault made in *Les Temps Modernes*, though the text also reveals a general and very definite talent for verbal malice.

The prospect of actually living in Lille, 300 kilometres to the north of Paris and almost on the Belgian border, did not appeal to Foucault. Together with Tourcoing and Roubaix, the city made up a sprawling industrial conurbation dominated by cotton and jute mills, and had suffered very badly in the war. Its main disadvantage was quite simply that it was not Paris. Foucault's solution was to stay at a hotel in Lille for two or three nights a week and to pack all his teaching into the short periods of time he spent there. The rest of the week was spent in Paris, and he commuted back and forth for the next three years. Denys Foucault was now studying medicine in Paris, and parental generosity meant that the brothers were able to share a two-bedroomed flat in the rue Monge. Foucault was by no means alone in commuting to an academic post. The French language even has a term for such university teachers; they are *turbo-profs*, so called, presumably, because they jet in and then jet out again.

The existence of the *turbo-prof* was and is the result of a number of factors. Pastoral duties in a French university are traditionally so light as to be almost nonexistent, and staff–student relations tend to be formal, if not distant. There is therefore little imperative to be on university premises outside teaching hours. Despite repeated attempts at decentralisation, the structure of the educational system is still such that most resources are concentrated in Paris. This is particularly true of research facilities. Even the Parisian faculties are not overendowed with libraries, and the situation in the provinces is certainly not conducive to library-based research. Doctoral and post-doctoral research usually requires access to the Bibliothèque Nationale. The situation is self-perpetuating: academics claim that they would be more willing to work in the provinces if they had better research facilities, and the ministry claims that it would provide better facilities if academics were willing to remain in the provinces.

Foucault required access to Paris for a variety of reasons, not least because he was also teaching part-time at ENS. The putative thesis he had begun at the Fondation Thiers – and which he now described to Polin as being on the philosophy of psychology – meant that he had to work at the Bibliothèque Nationale and he had already become one of its habitués. For the next thirty years, Henri Labrouste's great building in the rue de Richelieu, with its elegant pillars and arches of cast iron, would be his primary place of work. His favourite seat was in the *hemicycle*, the small, raised section directly opposite the entrance, sheltered from the main reading room, where a central aisle separates rows of long tables subdivided into individual reading desks. The *hemicycle* affords slighty more quiet and privacy. For thirty years, Foucault pursued his research here almost daily, with occasional forays to the manuscript department and to other libraries, and contended with the Byzantine cataloguing system: two incomplete and dated printed catalogues supplemented by cabinets containing countless index cards, many of them inscribed with copperplate handwriting. Libraries were to become Foucault's natural habitat: 'those greenish institutions where books accumulate and where there grows the dense vegetation of their knowledge'.[5]

Paris was also the centre of intellectual power and provincial universities, with the possible exceptions of Strasbourg and Toulouse, were unlikely to provide the institutional base for a spectacular career. Foucault's teaching at ENS gave him a base in Paris, and the apartment in the rue Monge served as a pied-à-terre. His continued contact with Althusser, Hyppolite, Canguilhem, Delay and others supplied him with essential elements of a support network. His ability to publish was also greatly enhanced by the fact that he was based in Paris, since French publishing has always been even more centralised than the educational system. No doubt there were also more personal reasons for not leaving Paris. Friends and pleasures like music, theatre and galleries all had a significant pull. Most significantly of all, Jean Barraqué was in Paris.

Althusser had adopted the custom of taking small groups of *normaliens* to prepare for the *agrégation* oral in the relaxed atmosphere of Royaumont Abbey, a Cistercian foundation near Paris which had been converted into an international cultural centre. Both Foucault and Aron were there in 1951, and they returned the following year in the company of a group of students. As they entered the lounge, they heard a young man discussing literature in vociferous terms and denouncing the work of André Gide, who had died the previous year. Later in the evening, the same young man sat down at the centre's magnificent Bechstein and began to play a Mozart sonata. His name, it transpired, was Pierre Boulez.[6]

At twenty-seven, Boulez was already a major figure in French music. A pupil of the great organist Olivier Messiaen, he had composed two piano sonatas (1950 and 1952) in which the influences of Webern and Schoenberg were still evident, and a book of *Structures* for two pianos in which every aspect of the composition – pitch, duration, intensity and attack – is governed by a mathematical series. Foucault and Boulez did not become particularly close friends, but moved for a while in the same circles, together with Michel Fano and Gilbert Amy. They did, however, have some things in common, and notably a liking for the poetry of René Char. Foucault never lost his enthusiasm for Char, and Boulez's *Le Marteau sans maître* of 1955 (a suite of nine pieces for contralto and sextet) is based upon a collection of poems which Char had published under that title in 1934.

It was in the circle of young musicians and composers who gravitated around Boulez that Foucault met Barraqué, whom he believed to be 'one of the most brilliant and most underrated composers of the present generation'.[7] Barraqué was also a pupil of Messiaen's at the Conservatoire National Supérieur de Musique, but he did not have the success enjoyed by Boulez. He had recently completed a piano sonata, though it had yet to be performed in its entirety. Fragments from it had been played during a broadcast entitled 'Tribune des jeunes compositeurs' but a recording project had come to nothing, and it was not until 1958 that the sonata became available on record, together with *Séquence*, premiered in March 1956. In 1952, Barraqué was making a living by teaching and writing for the music press, and performing occasionally. He was two years younger than Foucault.[8]

The short-sighted Barraqué was not, according to friends, particularly easy to get along with and could be very jealous.[9] Although he approached his music with great seriousness, he was no ascetic. On the contrary, he was something of a gourmet. At his suggestion, the group of young musicians and composers would often adjourn to sample his favourite white wines when they left Messiaen's analysis class at the Conservatoire. They were often joined by Foucault, whose technical ignorance of music meant that he had relatively little to add to the conversation. Exchanges between the members of the group were characterised by a deliberate lightness of tone; serious issues were always discussed in apparently frivolous terms.

Relatively little is known about relations between Foucault and Barraqué, but it is clear that an initial friendship soon developed into a passionately stormy affair which lasted for two to three years before finally being broken off by Barraqué when Foucault was in Sweden. There is no full biography of Barraqué, and Foucault's characteristic reticence about his personal life ensures that the relationship is shrouded in obscurity. The brief reference made to Barraqué in an interview with Paulo Caruso in 1967 is the only occasion on which Foucault mentions him by name. In a later interview, he simply speaks of a 'friend who was a composer and who is dead now' and refers to the 'influence of living with a musician for several months'; that interview also contains a totally opaque reference to an earlier relationship: 'The first friend I had when I was twenty was a musician.'[10] Foucault's 'first friend' has never been identified.

While the personal aspect of the relationship remains somewhat mysterious, its intellectual aspect can be traced quite clearly. Both men idolised Beethoven and were increasingly fascinated by Heidegger and Nietzsche, who inspired Barraqué's vision of the composer: 'One cannot be a modest composer, for music is *creation* . . . The poem, in the Nietzschean sense, that which means that man is never himself but speaks beyond himself, is that transposition of self, perhaps ecstasy.'[11] Kafka and Dostoievsky were favourite authors, and both Foucault and Barraqué enjoyed Beckett, though the composer's enthusiasm for him was not entirely unalloyed. Both admired Genet, whose play *Haute Surveillance* was first performed in 1949 and whose film *Un Chant d'amour* began to circulate clandestinely in 1950. Barraqué always cherished the hope that Genet would write a libretto for him, but never approached him directly about that project.[12]

Debts were contracted on both sides; very specific debts on Barraqué's side and more general ones on Foucault's. When the two first met, Barraqué was working on a composition for voice, percussion and instrumental ensemble entitled *Séquence*, which centred on themes inspired by the 'Song of Songs', Baudelaire's prose poems and Rimbaud. Over the next three years, he constantly reworked the fragments, and finally replaced the original texts with fragments from Nietzsche's 'Ariadne's Lament', a version of which figures in *Zarathustra*:

> Who still warms me, who still loves me?
> Offer me hot hands!
> Offer me coal-warmers for the heart!
> Spread-eagled, shuddering,
> Like a half-dead man whose feet are warmed—
> Shaken, alas! by unknown fevers,
> Trembling with sharp icy frost-arrows,
> Pursued by you, my thought!
> Unutterable, veiled, terrible one!
> Huntsman behind the clouds!
> Struck down by your lightning bolt,
> You mocking eye that stares at me from the
> darkness – thus I lie,
> Bend myself, twist myself, tortured
> By every eternal torment,
> Smitten
> By you, cruel huntsman,
> You unknown – God!
> . . .
> He is gone!
> He himself has fled,
> . . .
> My great enemy
> . . .
> No, come back!
> . . .
> My last – happiness![13]

The Nietzsche was Foucault's contribution. *Séquence* was premiered and recorded at the Théâtre du Petit-Marigny in Paris in March 1956; to his sorrow, Foucault was not present.

On Saturday 24 March 1956, Barraqué drafted a two-page outline for a composition provisionally entitled 'La Mort de Virgile'. It was based upon Hermann Broch's philosophical novel *Der Tod des Virgil* (1945), which appeared in a French translation in 1954.[14] Barraqué read the novel, in which he discovered the 'poetry of death', at Foucault's suggestion; sadly, Foucault did not record his own impressions in writing. Foucault was no expert on modern Austrian literature, and it was almost certainly thanks to an article in *Critique* that he discovered Broch.[15] A long, dense novel, *Der Tod des Virgil* deals with the last days of the poet, when he was, according to legend, tormented with a compulsion to destroy the manuscript of the *Aeneid*. Obsessed with death, with the impossibility of total knowledge and with the vanity of all human creations, it has a symphonic structure of four movements (water, fire, earth, air) that lent itself well to a musical translation. It was greatly appreciated by Maurice Blanchot who, in the August and October issues of the *Nouvelle Revue Française*, compared it to the work of Proust, James Joyce and Thomas Mann.[16]

Foucault had provided his friend with a fertile obsession. At least three versions of the work were written before the final score of what was now entitled *Le Temps restitué* was completed in 1968, only two months before its premiere at the Royan Festival. Shortly afterwards, Barraqué began work on a lyrical composition provisionally entitled *L'Homme couché*; this too was derived from his reading of Broch, but it remained unfinished when Barraqué died in 1973. *Le Temps restitué* and the 1962 *Concerto* for clarinet are his best-known works.

In 1967, Foucault told Caruso in rather mysterious terms that the serial and twelve-tone music of Boulez and Barraqué offered him his first escape from the dialectical universe in which he was still living, and that its impact on him had been as great as that of Nietzsche. Fifteen years later, he returned to the subject in an article which is nominally about Boulez but is no doubt coloured by memories of Barraqué (who is not mentioned by name): 'Encountering Boulez and music at a time when we were being taught to privilege the importance of meaning, of lived experience, the corporeal, of primal experience, subjective content or social significance, meant seeing the twentieth century from an unfamiliar angle: that of a long battle about form.' Boulez and Barraqué introduced Foucault, that is, to a musical equivalent of the philosophy of the concept, to the current that goes from Russian formalism to structuralism, and taught him a lesson that warned him against 'categories of the universal'.[17]

The encounter with Boulez and Barraqué must have represented the classic shock of the new for someone whose basic musical culture was symphonic. However, Foucault's recollections are not entirely accurate. Barraqué does not seem to have regarded himself as an iconoclast; he adored Beethoven and was influenced by Debussy, to whom he devoted his only book,[18] as well as by Webern. He was no mathematician and one informed observer has described his work as expressing a contradiction between the constraints of the combinatory basis of serial music and the physical *jouissance* of sound.[19]

Passionate affairs and the discovery of contemporary music were the purple passages in a life lived mainly, if somewhat reluctantly, on the academic plane. Foucault's position as a *répétiteur agrégé*, or junior tutor, at ENS gave him the right to an office of his own. It was in fact a room previously used to house a record library and was cluttered with dusty seventy-eights. Here, Foucault both worked and held court. He was now regarded as the 'leader' of the *groupe folklorique*, who visited him regularly in his new quarters.

Another regular visitor was Maurice Pinguet, three years younger than Foucault, homosexual, and a candidate for the 1953 *agrégation*. Pinguet, who died in 1991, was to spend much of his career in Japan, where he became director of the Institut Français, and his major work was to be on suicide in Japanese culture.[20] He later recalled afternoons spent in Foucault's room, chatting about everything and nothing. He also reveals a characteristic trait. When he asked Foucault about how his research was progressing – Foucault was working on his first book, *Maladie mentale et personnalité* – the reply was a smile or at best an anecdote. There was no serious discussion.[21] Foucault rarely talked in public about his ongoing work; those who met him in the Bibliothèque Nationale were greeted with a smiling *Ça va?* but were soon given to understand that detailed enquiries into his work would not be welcomed. No enquiries into their work would be forthcoming either.[22]

Pinguet's impression was that Foucault was as sensitive as he was intelligent, and that his biting humour and bitter laughter were defences. The smile, in contrast, was gentle and full of confidence. Foucault's self-confidence was also noted by Paul Veyne, a member of the *groupe folklorique*, who was then studying history. He was for some time very close to Foucault and was the recipient of certain confidences. Foucault was convinced of his own future greatness, but confessed to a strange ambition. He did not want to be a teacher. He wanted to write like Maurice Blanchot.

Blanchot began to contribute articles or essays entitled 'Recherches' to the *Nouvelle Revue Française* in 1953. These were essays in the *belles lettres* tradition and not reviews, and rapidly established Blanchot's reputation as one of France's most influential critics, while austere novels like *L'Arrêt de mort* and *Le Très-haut* (both published in 1948) won him great literary acclaim. Wanting to write like Blanchot was a curious ambition for someone who appeared to be embarking on a career in psychology, and a further index of Foucault's uncertainty of where he was going. Perhaps aware of Blanchot's deep-seated conviction that a life devoted to literature should also be devoted to silence, Foucault made no attempt to meet him, just as he made no attempt to meet René Char. Ambitions notwithstanding, Foucault did not write anything ressembling Blanchot's dense, classical prose at this time; it was only in the years 1963 and 1964 that he produced literary essays in that style. Significantly, one of them is devoted to Blanchot himself.

The friendship with Veyne was to be relatively short-lived and was effectively destroyed by the very different sexual orientations of the two men. Veyne found Foucault misogynist in the extreme; Foucault, for his part, found Veyne's almost flamboyant heterosexuality at best irritating. After Veyne's *agrégation* and subsequent departure from ENS, the two lost contact and the friendship was not renewed until the 1970s, when both men were at the Collège de France.[23] Foucault's affection for Pinguet, in contrast, remained constant and life-long. In August 1953, they drove together to Rome in a green *quatre chevaux* owned by Foucault and spent a fortnight exploring the city. When they were not sightseeing, Foucault was reading Nietzsche, producing a bilingual edition of the *Unzeitgemässe Betrachtungen* (*Untimely Meditations*) whenever they sat down in a café, and reading it on the beach at Civitavecchia.[24] Serial music was not the only escape route from the dialectical universe. It is in the second of the 'Meditations' that Nietzsche makes the case against Hegel that was to mean so much to Foucault: 'The belief that one is a latecomer of the ages is, in any case, paralysing and depressing: but it must appear dreadful and devastating when such a belief one day by a bold inversion raises this latecomer to godhead as the true meaning and goal of all previous events.'[25] Whether or not he read it at this time is uncertain, but a passage in *Die fröhliche Wissenschaft* seems to adumbrate the whole of Foucault's future career. Here, Nietzsche describes a task for the industrious: 'So far, all that gives colour to existence still lacks a history. Where would you find a history of love, of avarice, of envy, of conscience, of pious respect for tradition, or of cruelty? Even a comparative history of law or at least of punishment is so far lacking competely.'[26]

Foucault's teaching at ENS effectively duplicated his work in Lille. Technically, he was employed to teach psychology, but he also gave classes in general philosophy. Veyne, for example, recalls a dazzling lecture on Descartes but, unfortunately, nothing of its content. Psychology was, however, the staple fare. *Gestalt* theory, Rorschach tests, academic psychology and the theory of psychoanalysis all found their way into lectures which impressed everyone – Veyne, Passeron, Pinguet, Bourdieu and a very young Jacques Derrida – with their flair and technical competence. Pinguet, for example, recalled Passeron emerging from Foucault's lecture on 'Beyond the Pleasure Principle' and exclaiming: 'The Fuchs is brilliant.'[27] Depressive interludes and occasional hangovers did not prevent Foucault from performing very well in the lecture room. Although he could be dismissive about psychoanalysis in conversation, he was also furthering his knowledge of the subject by attending the seminar given at Sainte-Anne from 1953 onwards by Lacan, and was therefore one of the first to bring to the rue d'Ulm news of the 'return to Freud', or in other words of Lacan's reformulation of psychoanalytic principles in the light of modern liguistics, anthropology and philosophy and of his dismissal of the 'ego-psychology' which, he claimed was reducing psychoanalysis to a banal psycho-social engineering.

Foucault's experience of psychology and psychiatry was not confined to the lecture room and the library. His own accounts of this period are, however, fairly vague, if not actually misleading, and are the products of either a hazy memory or a reluctance to supply the information that would allow his identity at any given moment to be established with too great a precision. In 1983, he described himself as having worked for 'two or three years' at Sainte-Anne and defined his status, or lack thereof, thus:

> There was no clear professional status for psychologists in a mental hospital. So as a student in psychology . . . I had a very strange status there. The *'chef de service'* [Delay] was very kind to me and let me do anything I wanted. But nobody worried about what I should be doing; I was free to do anything. I was actually in a position between the staff and the patients.[28]

A year earlier, he had described the motives for his work at Sainte-

Anne: 'After having studied philosophy, I wanted to see what madness was: I had been mad enough to study reason; I was reasonable enough to study madness.'[29]

An earlier interview, published in Italian, clearly indicates that in the early 1950s he was in fact contemplating a career as a psychiatrist. An encounter with a patient named 'Roger' seems to have had a negative influence on that project, and left Foucault with an indelible image of suffering. Roger had been hospitalised because his family and friends feared that he would injure or even kill himself during one of his bouts of depression. Foucault and Roger became friends, but the latter was convinced that he would never be allowed to leave hospital, and that belief provoked serious anxiety states. Drugs having failed to have any effect, he was eventually given a prefrontal lobotomy, a form of intervention which Foucault regarded as a way of bypassing both the patient and the illness itself. Although lobotomy might well remove the 'affective overload', it signally failed to penetrate the 'internal mechanism of the illness'.[30]

The encounter which, given Foucault's own depressive tendencies, must have had a considerable impact, left the would-be psychiatrist wondering whether death might not be preferable to Roger's non-existence. Ultimately, he concluded that 'even the worst pain is preferable to a vegetable existence because the mind really does have the capacity to create and beautify, even if the starting point is the most disastrous of existences'.[31]

Foucault was at once more and less closely involved in the life of the hospital than he suggests. It is true that he was not a salaried employee, but nor was he merely an outside observer. He was of course there on sufferance; had he not enjoyed the patronage of Jean Delay it is improbable that he would have been allowed into the hospital. On the other hand, he was directly – if unofficially – involved in clinical work. Again, it was a personal connection that made this possible. Georges and Jacqueline Verdeaux had recently established a small electro-encelography unit at the request of Delay, and Foucault occasionally took part in its work.

In 1944, Georges Verdeaux had completed a thesis under the direction of Lacan and was now working, together with his wife, on neurophysiology and emotivity. The work of the unit at Sainte-Anne was in part an extension of their interests. Measurements of brain waves, respiration and other physiological indicators were taken and collated, with Foucault occasionally acting either as an experimental subject or as an experimenter. Polygraph tests were used, and experiments were carried out on responses to music. The unit was not purely experimental, but was integrated into the hospital's clinical work and was responsible for drawing up psycho-neurological profiles of patients. It was also here that Foucault learned to carry out the Rorschach projective tests that he was to inflict on so many of his friends and acquaintances. He did not find Sainte-Anne unpleasant; it was better than many of the provincial hospitals he was to visit later, and did not give a particularly negative impression of psychiatry.[32] His impression was in keeping with the times. The immediate post-war years were a reformist period for both the penal system and the psychiatric sector. Many of the men who had taught Foucault – Daumézon and Ey in particular – were associated with Evolution Psychiatrique, a group that represented a liberal tendency within the profession. His subsequent doubts about the very notion of progress in the mental-health sector notwithstanding, Foucault first came into contact with it at a time when reforming efforts were being made.

Foucault's clinical involvement was not confined to Sainte-Anne. In 1950, the Administration Pénitentiare had established a Centre National d'Orientation at Fresnes, the prison that houses the penal system's main medical facilities.[33] The centre was founded in order to meet the legal requirement for the medico-psychological examination of all inmates. Prisoners arrived at Fresnes with files comprising their criminal records, social reports and medical and psychiatric reports. At the Centre National d'Orientation, the files were completed by the addition of data on their subjects' past and present mental states and on any relevant personal or hereditary factors. The information gathered was used to determine suicide risks and to ascertain whether individual prisoners would benefit from being sent to specific prison workshops or specialist units. Fresnes was also equipped with an ECG unit, which was used mainly to try to distinguish between real and simulated psychopathological, and particularly epileptic, disorders.

The unit was run by the Verdeaux, with some assistance from Foucault. Twice a week, Jacqueline Verdeaux would collect him from ENS and drive him to the unit at Fresnes, where he occasionally donned the white coat of the professional. As at Sainte-Anne, Foucault had no official status and permission had to be obtained for him to gain admittance to the prison. It was not difficult to obtain; Verdeaux recalls, with considerable amusement, that the fact that her son and the prison governor both played rugby greatly reduced the need for formalities. The regime at Fresnes was relatively liberal, and Verdeaux and Foucault were given access to all prisoners. They were thus able to work with all categories of inmates, from killers to juvenile delinquents.

Two conclusions emerge from Foucault's experiences at Sainte-Anne and Fresnes. Although he rarely mentioned them, it is clear that they provided an early insight into the interface between psychiatry and criminology and that his later interest in that topic was rooted in experience and not in purely historical or philosophical theorisation. It is also clear that Foucault, by now in his late twenties, was still unsure about his future career. In a sense, Foucault was trapped by the dilemma he describes in an early article: 'One of the sharp-witted white-coated men of psychology . . . asked a beginner if he wanted to do "psychology" like M. Pradines and M. Merleau-Ponty, or "scientific" psychology like Binet.'[34]

As well as being a doctor and psychiatrist, Jacqueline Verdeaux was a translator specialising in psychiatric texts. Her first translation was of a treatise by Bochner and Halpern on the clinical interpretation of Rorschach tests – a subject close to her professional heart – followed by Wyrsch's study of schizophrenia.[35] In the early 1950s, professional contacts introduced her to the work of Roland Kuhn, whose *Phénoménologie du masque* she translated in 1957. When she visited Kuhn at the clinic he ran in Musterlingen, he suggested that she might also find the work of his colleague Ludwig Binswanger of interest.

Verdeaux accordingly went on to Kreuzlingen on the Swiss-German border, where Binswanger had been running the Bellevue sanatorium – founded by his grandfather – since 1911. He was to go on doing so until 1956. Binswanger, an associate of Jung and Freud – with whom he corresponded – was the founder and principal promoter of '*Dasein-Analyse*', a version of existential psychotherapy heavily influenced by Heidegger's phenomenology. After some discussion, Binswanger himself suggested that Verdeaux should translate his paper 'Traum und Existenz'; this was the text which, in his opinion, should be his first publication in French.[36] She immediately agreed and set to work, even though a publisher had yet to be found for the proposed translation. The clinical vocabulary posed no problems, but Verdeaux found that she required some assistance with Binswanger's dense philosophical terminology. Her chosen consultant was Foucault, whose intensive study of Heidegger now found a very practical application. In terms of translation practice, the most interesting feature of the text is the joint decision, reached after lengthy discussion, to render *Dasein* as 'presence in the world'. The term is problematic, and had been translated both as 'human reality' and as 'being there'; later translations, both French and English, tend to retain *Dasein* in the original.

The two worked together in Foucault's office at ENS, usually in the

late afternoon or evening when Verdeaux had finished her day at
Sainte-Anne. Or rather, they worked side by side. The office was
divided by a flimsy partition which did not even reach the ceiling, and
Foucault insisted that Verdeaux should work on the other side of it, her
explanation being that he was reluctant to be seen with a woman in the
all-male precincts of Normale. Foucault was not particularly easy to
work with, and was given to making somewhat dogmatically negative
comments about psychiatry, just as he was given to passing dismissive
judgement on psychoanalysis in discussions with friends like Maurice
Pinguet. He was capable of telling Verdeaux, in terms which were not
purely humorous, that he and his friends had been saying 'nasty things'
about her and her work. His negative comments could also spill over
into print. When, in an article on research in psychology published in
1957, he refers scathingly to 'research on the cutaneous resistance,
blood pressure and breathing rhythms of people listening to the
"Symphony of Psalms" ', he is describing Verdeaux's research at
Sainte-Anne.[37]

Foucault could also be disagreeable in other ways. After a visit to
Binswanger, he and Verdeaux spent a short holiday in Italy, where
Foucault displayed a sophisticated appreciation of Renaissance painting. Vehement declarations of his loathing of 'nature' and the
ostentation with which he turned his back on sunsets proved to be less
endearing. Such gestures may have reflected nothing more than the
legendary arrogance of the normalien, but they were not attractive.

Despite his ambivalence towards psychiatry, Foucault was fascinated by Binswanger's paper. He stated some thirty years later: 'I was
looking for something different from the traditional grids of the medical
gaze, a counterweight.'[38] His enthusiasm was such that Verdeaux
suggested that he should write a preface for the translation. Some
months later, while she was on holiday in Provence with her husband,
she received a note saying: 'You'll get your Easter egg.' The 'Easter
egg' was a voluminous manuscript; at 128 pages (roughly 25,000
words), the printed text is twice the length of the essay it purports to
introduce. Despite its unwieldy bulk, Verdeaux liked the preface; so too
did Binswanger, who was particularly gratified at being read by a
philosopher with at least some clinical knowledge. Publishers were less
enthusiastic. The disproportion between text and introduction was
blatant. Foucault was completely unknown, and Binswanger himself
was something of an unknown quantity in Paris. With some difficulty,
Verdeaux persuaded Desclée de Brouwer, who would also publish her
translation of Kuhn, to accept the book, and it appeared in 1954. It was

not a success. The print run was 3,000 copies; three years later, only three to four hundred had been sold, and the remaining copies were pulped.[39]

Jacqueline Verdeaux was to have a considerable influence on Foucault's career in one other way. She was convinced that work and, more specifically, writing would have a quasi-therapeutic effect and would help to counteract his recurrent depression. To that end, she introduced Foucault to Colette Duhamel, an old schoolfriend of hers and now an editor at La Table Ronde, the small, independent publishing house run by Roland Laudenbach. Two projects emerged from their discussions. One was for a 'History of Death', which appears to have been a joint project. The other was for a 'History of Psychiatry'. Neither book was ever written, even though contracts were drawn up and signed, but, by Foucault's own account, the latter was the germ that developed into *Histoire de la folie*. He was not entirely happy with the idea of writing a history of psychiatry, and proposed a study of relations between doctor and madman, of the 'eternal debate' between reason and unreason'.[40] It is significant that the original suggestion came from someone else. Prior to writing *Histoire de la folie*, Foucault published only five texts, and all were commissioned.[41] Although ambitious and confident of his own future greatness, he obviously felt no great compulsion to write.

One other incident from this period is of considerable significance. In 1952, Foucault went with Georges and Jacqueline Verdeaux to visit Roland Kuhn at the psychiatric hospital he ran at Musterlingen on the shores of Lake Constance. They arrived on Shrove Tuesday and witnessed one of the stranger survivals of the ancient rite of Carnival. It was the custom for the inmates to spend much of the spring making large, ornate masks to be worn in a procession. Doctors, nurses and inmates all wore masks and were indistinguishable from one another. Having left the hospital grounds, the procession wound through the village, led by the giant figure of Carnival himself. When it finally returned to the hospital, Carnival was burned with great ceremony and the masks were discarded. The evening ended with a ball. A very short film privately made by Georges Verdeaux shows the procession and the ritual burning of Carnival; the figures have the slightly sinister air that so often characterises manifestations of Carnival. Foucault also attempted to film the event, but failed to operate his borrowed camera correctly.[42]

Foucault was greatly impressed by the spectacle, but only once spoke of it in print. He did so in impersonal terms and never hinted that he had been present:

On carnival day, the mad dressed up and went out into the town –
not those whose condition was serious, obviously. They acted out
a carnival, and the population watched, from a distance, but
frightened, and, ultimately, it was quite ghastly, as the only day
they were allowed out *en masse* was the day when they had to dress
up and literally pretend to be mad.[43]

Histoire de la folie opens with a well-known – and now controversial –
passage decribing the Ship of Fools as it drifts slowly along the canals
and rivers of northern Europe. It is difficult to believe that it was
written without some recollection of a real carnival in a peaceful Swiss
village.

The fact that Foucault was given commissions is an indication of his
perceived intellectual status. The first was a contribution to the
revision and updating of a venerable history of philosophy which had
reached its fourth edition in 1886, and its eighth in 1914.

Commissioned by Denis Huisman in 1952, written the following
year, but not published until 1957,[44] 'La Psychologie de 1850 à 1950' is
in many ways simply an academic survey of trends within psychology
from John Stuart Mill onwards, supplemented by bibliographical
notes. It also reflects the content of Foucault's teaching in both Lille
and Paris. Much of the text gives the impression that it is a display of
knowledge already acquired and digested rather than the product of
highly original research. Foucault displays an impressive command of
the relevant literature in French, English and German, but it is the
short introduction that is of most interest. He rapidly identifies the
history of psychology as being the history of a contradiction between a
desire, inherited from the Enlightenment, to bring the discipline into
line with the natural sciences and the growing realisation that 'human
reality' is not simply a sector of 'natural objectivity', that it must be
studied with the aid of methodologies other than those supplied by the
natural sciences. The problem facing contemporary psychology is its
ability, or otherwise, to master that contradiction by abandoning its
'naturalistic objectivity'. It is the history of psychology that will
pronounce upon that ability.[45] The essay ends with an aphoristic
manifesto: psychology will be possible only if it marks a return to man's
conditions of existence and to what is most human in man, namely his
history.[46]

Foucault's choice of vocabulary is as revelatory of his concerns as his
subject matter. The reference to 'human reality' indicates his growing
interest in Heideggerean phenomenology and in the *Dasein-Analyse* of

Kuhn and Binswanger, for whom psychology is 'an empirical analysis of the way in which human existence is given in the world' based upon an 'existential analysis of the way in which that human reality is temporalised, is spatialised and finally projects a world'.[47] The notion of the history of a discourse pronouncing upon its validity, on the other hand, locates Foucault's history of psychology firmly within an epistemological tradition within the history of science.

One of that tradition's best representatives is, of course, Georges Canguilhem. In a relatively late essay based on a lecture delivered in 1966, Canguilhem uses the metaphor of a court of law to illustrate how the history of the sciences strives to understand and demonstrate how outdated notions and methods were in themselves a supersession of previous methods, and how 'the outdated past [*le passé dépassé*] is still the past of an activity for which we have to retain the name scientific'.[48] The formulation dates from 1966, but it derives from Bachelard and something of its content can already be seen in Canguilhem's *Essai sur quelques problèmes concernant le normal et le pathologique*, originally a doctoral thesis in medicine published in 1943.[49] Foucault's familiarity with the essay is clear from the argument that, whereas psychology was 'an analysis of the abnormal, of the pathological', it has become 'a psychology of the normal'.[50] The unspoken irony is that, having argued, on phenomenological grounds, that psychology cannot employ the methods of the natural sciences, he now invokes an epistemological model constructed with reference to biological and medical science.

To the extent that it announces the project of going beyond existing academic psychology, or even of founding a psychology, 'La Psychologie' can be read as a prologue to Foucault's essay on Binswanger and to his first book, *Maladie mentale et personalité*. Both were published in 1954, but it is not entirely clear which was written first. Conventional bibliographical wisdom has it that *Maladie mentale* was the earlier of the two, but internal evidence suggests that this may not be the case. Although *Maladie mentale* makes reference to Binswanger, Foucault does not use Verdeaux's translation and does not refer to his own introduction to 'Rêve et existence'. It is an immoderately modest young author who does not refer to his own publications, and it therefore seems likely that the essay on Binswanger was either unwritten or still being written when Foucault was working on his first book. In the absence of direct documentary or manuscript evidence, it is impossible to resolve the question with any certainty, but it is clear that both texts provide answers to the problem raised at the end of 'La Psychologie'.

Maladie mentale was commissioned by Jean Lacroix, the editor of PUF's 'Initiation philosophique' collection. Foucault was known to Lacroix, a Catholic philosopher, through Althusser, who had been taught by Lacroix in Lyon before the war. Foucault's first book was the twelfth in a series which, at the time of its publication, included Lacroix's own *Les Sentiments et la vie morale*, Gaston Berger's *Caractère et personnalité*, Georges Gusdorf's *La Parole* and André Bidoux's *Le Souvenir*. At twenty-eight, Foucault was being accepted into distinguished company; the series's *comité de patronage* included eminent philosophers such as Ferdinand Alquié, Gaston Bachelard and Paul Ricoeur. He was being published in the same series as one of his teachers. As the generic title indicates, the 'Initiation philosophique' series consisted of short introductions to philosophical topics, and was aimed primarily at a student audience. But just as Foucault had used a contribution to a history of philosophy to launch what was in effect a manifesto, he was to use his introduction to the question of mental illness to further a polemic and to promote his own concerns.

The history of *Maladie mentale et personnalité* is a curious one. Foucault revised it for the second edition, which appeared in 1962, and completely rewrote the final section, which became a summary of *Histoire de la folie*. There is nothing in the 1962 edition to indicate to the reader that this was a revised version.[51] A further reprint of the second edition appeared in 1966, but Foucault would not allow any further editions. He also attempted, unsuccessfully, to prevent the publication of the English translation.[52] The first (1963) edition of *Naissance de la clinique* still lists *Maladie mentale* as 'by the same author' but the earlier text then disappears from that category; *Histoire de la folie* had become Foucault's first book and was to remain so.

Maladie mentale opens with an introductory section on mental and organic illness, and the main text consists of two parts discussing, respectively, the psychological dimensions of illness and its real conditions of existence. Arguing that organic pathology cannot be employed as a model because its use would lead to the conclusion that mental illness is a natural illness manifested by specific symptoms,[53] Foucault propounds the view that mental illness must be analysed by looking at the concrete forms it can take in the psychological life of an individual, at both its psychological dimensions and its actual conditions of existence: 'I would like to show that the root of mental pathology must not be sought in speculations about some "meta-pathology", but simply in man's reflection upon man.'[54] Throughout, he argues against purely negative or privative definitions of mental illness; the apparent chaos of schizophrenia, for instance, finds its point of coherence in the personal structure of the patient who guarantees the lived unity of his consciousness and its horizon. No matter how ill [*malade*] a patient [*un malade*] may be, that point of coherence inevitably exists. The science of mental pathology can only be the science of the ill personality.'[55]

Only a phenomenological psychology can afford an entry into the experience of mental illness: 'It is only by understanding it from within that it is possible to establish within the morbid universe the natural structures constituted by evolution and the mechanisms individualised by psychological history.[56] The second section of the text represents an excursion into the territory staked out by Marx's *1844 Manuscripts* (available to Foucault in Volume 6 of the Costès edition of the *Oeuvres philosophiques*) and by the associated theory of alienation. Foucault is able to play on the multiple meanings of the term, signalling both the legal alienation of a property or essence, the alienation or estrangement of the human essence, and mental alienation, a sense which is stronger in French than English. Arguing on socio-anthropological grounds and invoking Emile Durkheim and Margaret Mead to demonstrate that the notion of illness is culturally relative, Foucault concludes: 'The contemporary world makes schizophrenia possible, not because its technologies make it inhuman and abstract, but because the use man makes of his technologies is such that he can no longer recognise himself in them. Only the real conflict of conditions of existence can explain the paradoxical structure of the schizophrenic world.'[57] More generally: 'The ill man cannot recognise himself as man in the conditions of existence which man himself has constituted. With this new content, alienation is no longer a psychological aberration; it is defined by a historical moment.'[58]

Maladie mentale is an extraordinarily hybrid text in which Foucault explores, but ultimately cannot reconcile, a number of different ways in psychology. The most surprising section is Chapter Six, 'The Psychology of Conflict', in which he suddenly turns to Pavlov and claims that his physiology comprises an experimental study of conflict. References to I.P. Razenkov, the vice-president of the Soviet Academy of Medical Sciences, are perhaps even more surprising. By 1954, Foucault's brief sojourn in the PCF was already over, but his first book is something of a monument to his Party membership. Although Pavlov did not consider himself to be either a materialist or a Marxist, his physiology and the psychology predicated upon it became part of Soviet orthodoxy. Ironically, Pavlovianism was first promoted by

Trotsky but it became incorporated into a Stalinist version of materialism at the 1930 Soviet Congress for the Study of Human Behaviour. In the Cold War period, Pavlov's work, together with that of Lysenko, became part of the 'bourgeois science/proletarian science' debate and was held to supply the basis for a materialist psychology. It was this model that was heavily promoted by the PCF, largely as a stick with which to beat psychoanalysis, the interest of Pavlovianism being that it provided arguments against both the existence of the unconscious and the importance of sexuality.[59]

If Foucault's incorporation of Pavlov into his text is a reminder of his Party membership, his references to phenomenology signal his distance from anything approaching ideological orthodoxy; Heidegger and Binswanger were not exactly part of the PCF's canon. In conversation with Duccio Trombadori in 1978, Foucault remarked that in the 1950s 'many psychiatrists' took an interest in Pavlov and reflexology in an attempt to elaborate a materialist psychology, but their researches did not lead them very far.[60] His own modest contribution to that unrealisable project goes unmentioned.

The references to Pavlov are not the only monument to Foucault's membership of the PCF. As a perceptive critic notes, when Foucault refers to the need to rid mental pathology of 'metapathological abstractions' and argues that it is the 'real man' who is the support for the actual unity of 'various forms of illness', he is arguing a case very similar to tnat put forward by Georges Politzer in his search for a concrete psychology.[61] Politzer (1903–42) was the author of a violent attack on Bergson and the artisan of a concrete psychology based in part upon a critique of psychoanalysis. Like classical psychology, psychoanalysis promotes, according to Politzer, the roles of agencies like the superego in such a way as to obscure the concrete social reality of the individual.[62] Foucault argues, in his 'La Psychologie', that, while psychoanalysis has facilitated a transition from 'evolution' to 'history', its negative features are its continued reliance on the 'metaphysical or moral prejudices' generated by its naturalistic origins'.[63] It is not surprising that Foucault should have read and been influenced by Politzer, who is one of the PCF's great heroes; he was executed by the Gestapo and died shouting: 'Long live the German Communist Party.' He was one of the very few PCF theorists to make a contribution to psychological theory in the interwar period. Anyone in or close to the PCF in the late 1940s and early 1950s would inevitably have come into contact with his work.

Although its commissioning editor thought it 'excellent',[64]

Foucault's first book attracted almost no critical interest. In the only review published at the time, Roland Caillois found it 'well written', but thought the references to 'materialism' superfluous and his excursions into metaphysical considerations simply unnecessary.[65]

For a long time, Foucault's introduction to Binswanger was a very neglected part of his *oeuvre*, at least because it was impossible to find it outside a very few libraries. Like the other early writings, it tends to be overshadowed by *Histoire de la folie*, but the appearance of an English-language version stimulated more discussion of it in more recent studies of Foucault.[66] The introduction is, however, the best indication of where Foucault's intellectual interests lay in the early to mid-1950s. It also represents the starting point for a project which was either abandoned or never begun: 'A later work will attempt to situate existentialist analysis within developments in contemporary thinking about man; by following phenomenology's drift towards anthropology, we will attempt to demonstrate the foundations that have been proposed for concrete thinking about man.'[67]

'Traum und Existenz' centres upon a discussion of dreams of falling and of expressions such as *'aus allen Himmeln fallen'* ['to fall from the clouds'; that is, 'to be bitterly disappointed']. The link between the sensation or dream of falling and the metaphor is provided by the Heideggerean proposition that 'it is language that "envisions and thinks" for all of us before any one individual brings it into the service of his own creative and intellectual powers'.[68] Metaphors of falling are to be taken literally:

> When, in bitter disappointment, 'we fall from the clouds', then we fall – we *actually* fall . . . Our harmonious relationship with the world and the men about us suddenly suffers a staggering blow, stemming from the nature of bitter disappointment and the shock that goes with it. In such a moment our existence actually suffers, is torn from its position in the world and thrown upon its own resources.[69]

Rather than representing the fulfilment of a wish, a dream of falling reveals a basic ontological structure. For Binswanger, a dream is 'nothing other than a particular mode of human existence in general'. Soaring and falling are fundamental, 'the systole and diastole of human existence'.[70]

From the outset, Foucault makes it clear that he does not intend to 'introduce' Binswanger's text in any real sense: he will not follow the path traced by the author in accordance with the 'paradox commonly found in prefaces'.[71] He uses the text as a springboard for his own phenomenological reflections and for his critique of other psychological and psychiatric discourses. Foucault also makes it clear that his alliegance to Binswanger is provisional:

> Let us say, in provisional fashion, and subject to possible review, that man's being [*Menschsein*] is, after all, no more than the effective and concrete content of what ontology analyses as the transcendental structure of *Dasein*, of presence in the world . . . It seemed to me worth following, *for a moment*, the track of this reflection and using it to see whether the reality of man is only accessible outside the distinction between the psychological and the philosophical, whether man, in his forms of existence, is the only means of reaching man.[72]

For Foucault, the interest of 'Traum und Existenz' is twofold. On the one hand, the privileging of the dream

> defines the analysis's concrete move towards the basic forms of existence; the analysis of the dream is not restricted to the level of a hermeneutics of symbols; on the basis of an external interpretation, it will, without having to take refuge in a philosophy, be able to arrive at an understanding of existential structures.[73]

More generally, it offers the possibility of 'an anthropology of the imagination'.[74]

Binswanger also provides Foucault with the basis of a critique of Freud, and the introduction therefore marks the beginning of a long and fraught relationship with psychoanalysis.[75] Although Foucault acknowledges that *The Interpretation of Dreams* marks the entry of the dream into the 'field of human significations', his main criticism is that it grasps dream language 'only in its semantic function' and overlooks its morphological and syntactic structures. It explores only one version of the oneiric world, and has an inadequate understanding of symbolism. Binswanger, in contrast, is attempting to deal with concrete individuals (a phrase which echoes Politzer) and to reveal the articulation between forms and conditions of existence.[76]

The critique of psychoanalysis is based largely upon readings of *The Interpretation of Dreams* and of Freud's major case histories, particularly the 'Dora' case. Foucault's knowledge of his subject was not, however, confined to those texts or to Freud. He detected two main tendencies within the more recent history of psychoanalysis: the Kleinian and the Lacanian. In his view Melanie Klein attempts to trace the genesis of meaning in fantasy alone, whereas Jacques Lacan has done his best to find in the imago, 'the point where the signifying dialectic of language becomes frozen, and where it becomes fascinated by the interlocutor it has constituted for itself'.[77]

The sources for Foucault's knowledge of Lacan and Klein are not clear, particularly as he fails to supply references to specific texts. He had heard Lacan lecture at ENS and had attended some of the seminars he gave at Sainte-Anne from 1953 onwards, and it is probable that most of his knowledge derived from these oral presentations rather than from the published work. According to Jacqueline Verdeaux, he had little sympathy for Lacan's overall project and poured scorn on his philosophical pretensions. The psychoanalyst's pilgrimage to see Heidegger in Fribourg in 1950 provoked great mirth on Foucault's part, as well as some very disparaging comments on Lacan's philosophical competence in unpublished letters to Verdeaux.[78] It is not possible to identify the source of Foucault's knowledge of Klein with any certainty. Little of her work had been translated into French, but her ideas had been given a certain currency by Merleau-Ponty's lectures on psychology at the Sorbonne.[79]

The introduction to Binswanger also contains some critical comments on Sartre and it is one of the few texts in which Foucault engages with Sartre, rather than side-stepping or dismissing him. Sartre's theory that the image negates its object by positing it as unreal is refuted by the argument that the 'imaginary' is not a mode of unreality, but an oblique approach to presence or being, which reveals its 'primitive dimensions'. Foucault refers here to the 1940 essay on the 'imaginaire', a text which he admired, despite his general dislike of Sartre's phenomenology; he also spoke with respect of the earlier outline for a theory of the emotions.[80] In his criticisms of Sartre, Foucault cites with qualified approval the work of Gaston Bachelard on the 'dynamics' of the imagination. For Foucault, Bachelard goes some way towards capturing the lived reality of the imagination (and therefore the dream), but does so in purely subjective terms and fails to grasp its social or historical dimensions.[81] There were two Gaston Bachelards. The Bachelard who theorised epistemological breaks and whose work, like that of Canguilhem, had such an impact on Foucault's vision of the history of the sciences, was also the author of quasi-psychoanalytic studies of the imagination. Foucault admired this Bachelard too, and saw him as an author who had unleashed a surprising dimension of epistemology. As he was to write twenty years later:

For Bachelard, studying the concept of fluidity does not, for example, imply studying the equations of fluid mechanics. Any epistemologist who has passed his epistemological A-levels [*son bachot d'épistémologue*] can do that! It means something very different. It also means showing all that fluid can be, all it represents in people's imagination, in the imagination of the masses.[82]

Foucault's introduction to Binswanger is a virtuoso display of the erudition of the *agrégé de philosophie*. Plato, Aristotle, Heraclitus, Leibniz and Spinoza are all pressed into service. This is the traditional repertoire of the academic philosopher. Foucault's command of Husserl and Heidegger, on the other hand, indicates his membership of the rising generation. There is also a more personal side to his erudition. Sections of the text abound in literary references and allusions, most of them designed to demonstrate that Binswanger is working within a 'classical' tradition. The most striking thing about them is that they are, for the most part, to the literature of what Foucault would, in *Histoire de la folie*, dub the classical age. They are also remarkable for their relative obscurity. The fact that Foucault should be able to cite *Macbeth* or Racine's *Athalie* is not surprising; that he was familiar with seventeenth-century court poets like Benserade (1613–91) or Tristan l'Hermite (1601–55) and with Théophile de Viau's *Pyrame et Thisbé* is, to say the least, intriguing. None of these authors is likely to have figured on any of the programmes of study followed by the young Foucault; their works are normally read only by those concerned with the dustier corners of the seventeenth century. One can only assume that Foucault read them of his own accord, and speculate that his interest in the classical era predated even the beginnings of *Histoire de la folie*. The Binswanger introduction also contains two quotations from René Char's *Partage formel*, first published in 1945 as part of *Seuls demeurent*.[83] The second quotation reveals what was to be a regular failing on Foucault's part; fragment XVII of Char's prose sequence is wrongly identified as fragment LV. This is a very early instance of the author's notoriously cavalier attitude to the use of quotations and references.

Within a year of the publication of the Binswanger translation, Foucault had left France for Sweden. His first publications were followed by a period of silence which was to last until 1961. The fact that he did not publish articles or follow up any of the proposals contained in his first essays indicates, perhaps, that he realised that they were not leading anywhere in particular. The decision to leave France for Sweden and to take up a position as a cultural diplomat was also a farewell to any practical involvement in psychiatry.

Two final features of these early works deserve mention. They are all very content-oriented and have none of the stylistic flamboyance that was to become one of Foucault's hallmarks. He had yet to discover the rhetorical device of using a particularly seductive passage to open his books: the image of the Ship of Fools at the beginning of *Histoire de la folie*; the analysis of Velázquez's *Las Meninas* in *Les Mots et les choses*; the description of the execution of Damiens in *Surveiller et punir*. One of the results of the years of silence was the discovery of a style. In terms of their content, the early writings are characterised by an absence: that of Nietzsche. In many ways, Foucault was still becoming Foucault.

4

NORTH

LIKE so many events in Foucault's career, his departure for Sweden in August 1955 was the result of a chance encounter or, rather, of an encounter which did not actually take place. Georges Dumézil, the great specialist in Indo-European religions and mythologies, had spent some time at the University of Uppsala in the 1930s and was in the habit of returning to work there for a month or two every summer. In 1954, friends at the university asked him if he knew of a suitable candidate for the post of 'French assistant' in the Department of Romance Studies. Dumézil was at something of a loss for an answer, since he had few contacts with the younger generation, but mentioned the problem to his archaeologist friend Raoul Curiel, who had just returned from Afghanistan. By chance, Curiel had just met a young *normalien* and *agrégé de philosophie* called Foucault who was uncertain where his career was taking him. Curiel described him as the most intelligent person he had ever met. Suitably impressed, Dumézil wrote unannounced to Foucault to describe the attractions of life in Uppsala and to ask if he would be interested in the vacant post. Foucault applied.[1]

He was not the only candidate. His rival was Algirdas Julien Greimas, a Lithuanian who had studied in Grenoble before the war and who was to become an outstanding semiologist.[2] He was currently teaching in Alexandria and was anxious to return to Europe, but his plan was frustrated by Foucault's successful application for the Uppsala post.[3] Foucault had yet to meet Dumézil; the latter spent the summer of 1955 in Wales and did not return to Sweden until the following spring. It is, however, more than probable that it was thanks to his influence in Sweden that Foucault was appointed in preference to Greimas.

Although well qualified and already the author of published works, Foucault had not achieved any great academic success. Neither his post in Lille nor his part-time teaching at ENS looked like a promising start to a brilliant career, and there was no sign that his thesis was nearing completion. His involvement in psychiatry had led him to take an ambivalent view of that specialism, and further progress in that direction would probably have meant taking medical qualifications. Uppsala offered at least a temporary solution to the uncertainty. It also meant a change of direction. Foucault was appointed as a reader in French, meaning that he was responsible for taking *ab initio* language classes open to all and for teaching courses on French literature. Language-teaching was not a very professionalised occupation at this time, and the fact that Foucault's nationality was his only real qualification posed no obstacle to an appointment which placed him, however, on the lowest rung of the academic hierarchy. He was simultaneously appointed director of the Maison de France, the Swedish outpost of the Quai d'Orsay's department of '*Relations culturelles*'. At least the possibility of a career in the cultural-diplomatic field was opening up. Foucault was already a long way from the psychiatric unit at Fresnes which had fascinated him so much.

Career considerations were not the only thing on Foucault's mind. In a late interview, Foucault stated that he left France because 'I have suffered and I still suffer from a lot of things in French social and cultural life . . . Well, I think that, at the moment when I left France, freedom for personal life was very sharply restricted there. At this time Sweden was supposed to be a much freer country.'[4] His comments sound very much like a veiled allusion to the difficult social situation of French homosexuals in the mid-1950s. Sweden enjoyed a reputation for liberalism in sexual matters; for anyone living in post-war France, it must also have seemed the prosperous homeland of a fashionable modernism. Elsewhere, Foucault explained his departure for Sweden by stating that he had 'had enough of French university culture'.[5] Yet if Foucault was expecting to find a sexual utopia, he was to be sadly disappointed. The University of Uppsala proved to be rigidly hierarchical and very puritanical in its collective outlook. The town, an hour to the north of Stockholm, was pleasant but very quiet.

Many of Foucault's later comments on life in Sweden are bitterly sardonic. He found, he said, that 'a certain kind of freedom' could have 'as many restrictive effects as a directly repressive society',[6] that Sweden showed him 'what we will be in fifty or a hundred years' time, when we are all rich, happy and aseptisised'.[7] Elsewhere, he remarked that Swedish society was 'overmedicalised' and that all 'social dangers were in some way muffled by subtle, sophisticated mechanisms'.[8] Foucault also discovered that life in Sweden posed other difficulties. He frequently referred to 'the Swedish night', and found the long dark winters oppressive. Nor was the cold to his liking, and, influenced by chilly memories of a pre-war holiday in the Pyrenees, he was reluctant to indulge in the popular recreation of cross-country skiing. Friends and relations in France were given a lugubrious picture of Nordic gloom. His brother recalls Foucault describing the time he asked how many students he could expect. He was told that there would not be many, and that their numbers would fall when the winter set in and the inevitable wave of suicides began.[9]

Such anecdotes obviously contained a degree of gallows humour, and the above comments were made with hindsight. The bitterness was not, however, simply a reflection of a frustrated search for a utopia, but of a very real academic and intellectual disappointment. Foucault was prone to making pronouncements which conformed to a desired self-image rather than to the realities of his daily life. As in Italy with Jacqueline Verdeaux, he insisted that he loathed nature, that his natural habitat was a library. Yet, though he spent long hours in the library in Uppsala, he also enjoyed long walks through the woods and even, despite his dislike of the cold, on the frozen lakes of the winter countryside.[10]

Foucault arrived in Uppsala at the end of August to take up his teaching post and moved into the two rooms reserved for the director in the Maison de France, which was itself no more than a large flat on the fourth floor of a building in Sankt Johannes Street. A few days later, he was joined at the university by Jean-François Miquel, a young biochemist who was taking up a post-doctoral research post. They immediately took to one another and decided to eat together regularly at the Maison de France. Before long, the French duo became a trio with the arrival of Jacques Papet-Lépine, a physicist working on thunder and lightning and preparing a thesis entitled, with some wit, 'A Mathematical Contribution to the Theory of Thunderclaps' [*coup de foudre*, also meaning love at first sight].[11] The three quickly became a closely knit group, taking it in turn to cook for one another (with Foucault specialising in pasta dishes, about which he elaborated an entire culinary theory) and spending most of their free time together.[12] They were often joined by Costanza Pasquali, the Italian reader, and by her English counterpart, Peter Fyson. The latter was a poetry specialist capable of reciting long passages from Dante and other European poets, and an opera enthusiast. He was related to the Guinness family and his social contacts allowed the group at least some access to higher reaches of Swedish society than those normally frequented by such junior academic figures.

With the exception of Fyson and Pasquali, Foucault's closest professional associates in Uppsala were scientists. Although he had by now seemingly lost interest in clinical psychiatry, as opposed to the history of psychiatry, Foucault took an interest in other sciences and frequently visited the biochemistry and biology laboratories with Miquel. He had no background in the natural or life sciences but soon acquired sufficient competence to be able to discuss his friends' research in at least general terms, and was sometimes heard to regret his schoolboy decision not to study science. Biology was not the only domain in which he took an amateur interest. Uppsala boasted a particle accelerator which soon came to fascinate the young philosopher, who was instructed in the general principles of its workings and purpose by the chemist Theodor Svedberg, the winner of the 1926 Nobel Prize.

The French group quickly acquired a somewhat dubious reputation in both town and university, not least because of their noisy drinking parties. Foucault, in particular, was drinking quite heavily at this time. His notoriety increased when he purchased a powerful beige Jaguar sports car – not the type of vehicle normally owned by a junior member of faculty. The car was second-hand, but still expensive; Foucault was still receiving an allowance from his family and was not reliant on his salary alone. The Jaguar was his pride and joy, even though its mechanical condition left something to be desired and gave him a lot of trouble, and the driver's overindulgence in alcohol meant that it ended up in the ditch on more than one occasion.[13]

Despite his subsequent comments about Sweden, Foucault was in fact leading a much more active and relaxed social life than in Paris. Jean-François Miquel recalls that while he himself had more than one girlfriend in Uppsala, Foucault had rather more than one boyfriend at any given moment, and at least implies that some of their partners were interchangeable. If Foucault ever did have heterosexual encounters, it was at this time. One woman in particular was the special focus of his affections, though in her case the attachment was platonic. Dani was a young French secretary who came to work in Sweden at the suggestion of Jean-Christophe Öberg, the son of a diplomat based in Paris. He returned to Sweden to study law and subsequently became a major figure in the diplomatic world. Dani became Foucault's secretary at the Maison de France, and also undertook secretarial work for Miquel. She became a member of the small French community, watched over with rather more than paternal affection by Foucault. Dani and Foucault remained very close; when Foucault first met Daniel Defert, the latter was vetted for suitability by his lover's former secretary.[14]

Forays into Stockholm, either for pleasure or for professional reasons, were not infrequent and one of them resulted in an unexpected encounter. Miquel and Foucault went on impulse to a performance given in the city by the singer Maurice Chevalier. After the show, Foucault suggested that they should invite Chevalier for a drink and made for the stage door. Chevalier readily accepted the invitation and then agreed to return with them to Uppsala, driven by Foucault. The singer spent an unofficial and unscheduled weekend in the Maison de France, entertaining the company with anecdotes culled from his long career. Foucault proved to have a talent for persuading people to tell stories, and Chevalier performed well in response. It is a little surprising that Foucault should have taken any interest in Chevalier. His usual taste in music tended to the classical, and he constantly listened to Bach or Mozart as he worked in his rooms, though he also professed an interest in the serial music to which he had been introduced by Barraqué. The fact that he had accumulated a large collection of different recordings of the same pieces – especially Bach – was an indication that he had developed a very good ear for music.

Although Foucault's life in Sweden was in some ways quite frivolous, he took his teaching responsibilities very seriously and succeeded in the difficult task of capturing and retaining the attention and interest of his predominantly female *ab initio* students, one of whom subsequently became Miquel's wife. His literary classes began in the spring of 1956 with a fairly conventional course on contemporary French theatre, but the next semester found him lecturing on 'The Conception of Love in French Literature, from the Marquis de Sade to Jean Genet'. These were public lectures open to all, given on the main university campus, and were apparently not universally appreciated. De Sade and Genet represented an aspect of French culture which was not normally promoted by missionaries from the Quai d'Orsay. As Foucault was not teaching to a syllabus, his choice of subjects is a clear indication of his personal preferences; de Sade and Genet were to prove lasting interests. Foucault also gave seminars on standard subjects such as classical French theatre. None of the lectures or seminars given in Sweden has survived, but it is possible that the discussion of the image of madness in Racine's *Andromaque* to be found in *Histoire de la folie* originated in a seminar for students taking French as an optional subject.[15]

At the Maison de France, Foucault was responsible for a variety of cultural activities, organising play readings and performances and leading discussions of surrealist poetry and of the work of René Char, as well as of Edouard Manet and the impressionists. He displayed a considerable talent for organisation and improvisation. On one occasion, he was sent a print of Fernand Rivers's 1951 film adaptation of Sartre's *Les Mains sales* at very short notice. Without having seen the film, he prepared a very successful introduction to it in two hours or so. His other responsibilities included inviting guest speakers: Marguerite Duras, Roland Barthes, the novelist Claude Simon and Jean Hyppolite were all Foucault's guests in Uppsala.[16] In order to ensure a lively discussion, Foucault had his friends read the work of the guest of the moment and rehearsed the introduction he would make with them. They were then planted in the audience to ask prepared questions.[17]

Foucault was a capable and efficient organiser. In January 1956, *inspecteur général* Santelli wrote to the ministry in Paris to report that Foucault was conscientiously carrying out 'his heavy task with a devotion to which the dreadful way he looks bears testimony, for I have the impression that M. Foucault is working too hard and not taking the rest he needs'.[18]

In the spring of 1956, Dumézil returned to Uppsala for his habitual two months' stay in the small flat lent to him by the university. His first meeting with Foucault was marked by a curious ritual; the two recited their respective academic titles and it was duly noted that Dumézil had taken his *baccalauréat* long before Foucault. That point having been established, Dumézil suggested that they should address one another as *tu*. Foucault thanked him in his halting Swedish: '*Tack ska' du ha*', and the encounter was toasted in schnapps.[19]

Dumézil was born in 1898, and his *baccalauréat* dated from just before the First World War. His publishing career began two years before Foucault was born with the appearance of the first of his many studies in comparative mythology.[20] After having spent a lot of time in Poland, Turkey and Sweden, he was appointed to a lectureship at the Ecole des Hautes Etudes in 1933 and then made a *directeur d'études* two years later. In 1948 he was elected a member of the Collège de France and, after his retirement, became a member of the Académie Française in 1978. To the extent that his innovative work concentrates on comparisons between the various Indo-European pantheons and on sets of relations rather than discrete elements, it can legitimately be considered one of the formative stages in the development of structuralism. It is also a significant influence on historians like Georges Duby.[21] For the young Foucault, Dumézil was simply '*le professeur*'.

In the original preface to *Histoire de la folie*, Foucault thanks Dumézil, 'without whom this work would not have been begun – would neither have been begun in the course of the Swedish night nor completed in the great stubborn sun of Polish freedom'.[22] When interviewed by *Le Monde*'s Jean-Paul Weber about the influences that had marked his book, Foucault immediately cited '*le professeur*'. A surprised Weber asked how a historian of religion could have inspired a work on the history of madness, and received the reply: 'Because of his idea of structure. I attempted to discover structured forms of experience whose schema can be found, with modifications, at different levels, just as Dumézil did with myths.'[23] There is no textual evidence to suggest that Foucault had read anything by Dumézil before his departure for Sweden.

Dumézil was to be rather more than an intellectual mentor. He was influential, widely respected for his scholarship and erudition, and a man whose name could open doors. Like Hyppolite, he was to become an important part of the support network which Foucault, not having worked for any length of time in a French university, would eventually need in place of the more direct networks of patronage on which so many academic careers are based.

In Dumézil's view, one of the great attractions of Uppsala was the great library known as the *Carolina rediviva*, which he described in his initial letter to Foucault. One of its great treasures is the 'Bibliotheca Walleriana', a collection that includes a vast library on the history of medicine and related subjects. The collection had recently been completely catalogued and Foucault was therefore able to utilise it fully. If *Histoire de la folie* has a single place of birth, it is the library at Uppsala, even though it is obvious that a great deal of the research was carried out in libraries in Paris. It was in the Bibliotheca Walleriana, for instance, that he encountered Sebastian Brandt's *Das Narrenschiff* of 1494; this is the collection of allegorical poems and woodcuts illustrating the varieties of human folly to which he refers in the opening chapter of his first major book.

Teaching and administrative commitments permitting, Foucault worked in the library every day from morning to night, except when it was his turn to cook, in which case he would leave rather earlier than usual. The manuscript notes gradually accumulated, fed into Foucault's writing and eventually travelled with him to Poland and Germany. In 1968, Foucault told a Swedish journalist that, when he left France, he had no intention of writing anything. 'It was in Sweden, during the long Swedish nights, that I contracted this mania, this filthy habit of writing for five or six hours a day.'[24] There is a degree of exaggeration in this claim, Foucault was in fact under contract to write a history of psychiatry for La Table Ronde, and he was already no stranger to hard intellectual work. His plans were, however, somewhat vague and the history of psychiatry was never written. What was written was *Histoire de la folie*.

In December 1957, Foucault seems to have still been thinking of publishing in Paris. In a letter to Jacqueline Verdeaux, he thanked her for 'books from Sainte-Anne' and then went on:

> I will probably have to ask you for two or three things, but there is a magnificent library there. I've written about 175 pages. I'll stop when I get to 300 . . . Why not approach the question this way: madness and the experience of unreason within the space opened up by Greek thought . . . do you think the publisher would accept a book like that, with twenty-five to thirty pages of Latino-erudite notes at the end? I'd like to send you what I've done, but it's such scribble. It will have to be rewritten by the typist. Or perhaps a tape-recorder? If it's ready by next June or September, could it be published in December or January 58?[25]

The plan to publish in Paris was abandoned, probably before this letter was written. Disregarding the Table Ronde project, and ignoring his contractual obligations, Foucault had decided that his work in progress would be submitted as a Swedish doctoral thesis. The research facilities available to him in Uppsala were excellent and they tempted him to stay there – this was the first fantasised attempt to leave France for good – despite his unwillingness to spend even the university vacations in Uppsala. A Swedish doctorate would not necessarily have been acceptable to the French academic system, which must have cast doubts upon the outcome of an eventual return to France. There was also a language problem, as Foucault spoke only very basic conversational Swedish and would certainly have been unable to teach in anything but French. Nor, obviously, could he have written a thesis in Swedish.

Whether or not he took any of these problems into serious consideration is not on record, but Foucault did approach Professor Stirn Lindroth with his doctoral proposal. Lindroth was a specialist in the history of science and the history of ideas, and a figure of major importance in the university. He spoke French, had worked on Renaissance philosophy and medicine and was not at all ill-disposed towards Foucault, whom he had invited to dinner on several occasions. He was not, however, very impressed by the manuscript he was shown in 1957. He objected, in particular, to its speculative generalisations, which, in his view, offended against Uppsala's traditions of empiricism and positivism. Although Foucault revised his manuscript at least four times, Lindroth was still unwilling to consider its acceptance. He would certainly have been interested in a thesis on the history of medicine based on the Walleriana's holdings, but had no sympathy for this project. In vain, Foucault apologised for his failings and tried to win over the professor:

> I was wrong not to define my project, which is not to write a history of developments in psychiatric *science*. But rather a history of the *imaginary moral and social* context within which it developed. For it seems to me that until the nineteenth century, not to say until the present, there was no objective knowledge about madness, but merely the formulation, in terms of scientific analogy, of a certain experience (moral, social, etc.) of Unreason. Hence the very unobjective, unscientific and ahistorical way in which I approach the question. But perhaps the undertaking is absurd and doomed in advance.[26]

Lindroth proved deaf to Foucault's pleas and made it clear that Foucault's doctoral project had no future in Uppsala. According to Jean-François Miquel, it was Lindroth's hostility to the project that precipitated Foucault's abrupt departure from Sweden. The published teaching programme for the autumn of 1958 announced a lecture by Foucault on 'Religious Experience in French Literature from Chateaubriand to Bernanos'. It was never delivered, and by October 1958 Foucault was in Warsaw.

Hurt pride goes a long way to explaining the bitterness of his later comments on Sweden. Loneliness may also have been a real problem. By the end of the 1957 university year, Miquel, Dani and Papet-Lépine had all left Uppsala. Although Foucault had good Swedish friends – including Eric-Michel Nilsson, the young friend and future filmmaker to whom *Histoire de la folie* was dedicated – the nucleus of his social world had largely disintegrated.

Foucault had rapidly established what was to become the pattern for the years he spent abroad. Despite the 'sufferings' inflicted upon him by life in France, he frequently returned to Paris during vacation periods and never spent a full summer in Sweden, leaving for France in the famous Jaguar as soon as his teaching commitments were fulfilled. This may in part explain the references to the dark Swedish nights; Foucault had no real experience of the white nights, when the sun does not set and when the population of Stockholm leaves the city for the archipelago of small islands to its east. In December 1955, only four months after his arrival in Uppsala, Foucault returned to Paris for the Christmas vacation. The visit had two significant results: a break and a meeting.

The relationship with Barraqué was now going very badly. Foucault spent part of the vacation with him, and the rest of the time at Le Piroir. Shortly after the premiere of *Séquence*, Foucault received a letter: 'I want no more "Decembers"; I no longer want to act out or watch that "degradation". I have escaped that mad vertigo.' A friend then advised Barraqué to have no more to do with Foucault: 'This man will destroy you when he has destroyed himself.' In May 1956, Foucault attempted a reconciliation but was rebuffed.[27] The relationship with Barraqué was over. Barraqué's reference to 'degradation' is enigmatic, but, with hindsight, it is very tempting to see it as an allusion to some sado-masochistic strand in the relationship.

It was through the intermediary of Robert Mausi, a fellow student at ENS, that Foucault first met Roland Barthes in December 1955.[28] At forty, Barthes was not a well-known figure. He had spent much of his youth in a tuberculosis sanatorium and had therefore not been able to take the *agrégation*, the essential rite of passage for anyone looking for a regular academic career. In 1955, he was largely reliant on freelance work but was also working as an editor on *Théâtre populaire*, a review that had done much to popularise Brecht in France. He had published his *Le Degré zéro de l'écriture* to some acclaim in 1953 and his *Michelet par lui-même*, on which he had been working sporadically for years, appeared in 1954. The essays which were to be anthologised as *Mythologies* in 1957 were appearing regularly in *Les Lettres nouvelles*, *Esprit* and *France-Observateur* and Barthes was beginning to establish a reputation as a cultural critic, but he was not yet the major literary figure he was to become.

Barthes and Foucault had interests in common but they were also very different. There were, for instance, political differences which would, ironically, be inverted in the 1970s. At this stage, Barthes was still working within a quasi-Marxist framework, while Foucault was indifferent to politics. Their attitudes to their shared homosexuality was also strikingly different. Although it would be anachronistic to speak of Foucault 'coming out' in the 1950s, his sexual orientation was no secret to his friends, or to his brother. His mother was probably aware of it, too. Barthes, in contrast, was anxious to conceal his sexuality from his mother, with whom he lived, and succeeded in doing so until her death in 1977. Even so, the two became close friends and occasional lovers. They ate together whenever Foucault was in Paris, and spent their nights in the cafés and clubs of Saint-Germain-des-Près. Barthes was one of the guest lecturers invited to Uppsala by Foucault and they holidayed together in North Africa on a number of occasions. The relationship was to last until 1960.

In the summer of 1957, Paris was the scene for a significant encounter of a rather different kind. In search of 'I can't recall what book', Foucault strayed into 'that huge bookshop across from the Luxembourg gardens', or, in other words, into the premises of the formidable José Corti, bookseller and publisher, in the rue de Medicis. Corti himself was deep in conversation with a friend and, as he waited, Foucault began to glance at an old series of yellow-covered books published by the Librairie Lemelle, best known for its editions of the Parnassian poets. He started to browse through one of them out of idle curiosity. The book was Raymond Roussel's *La Vue*, a 2,000-line poem describing a seaside view engraved on a penholder. Foucault was immediately struck by the similarity between *La Vue* and Robbe-Grillet's *Le Voyeur* (1955). Roussel was quite unknown to him. When Corti had finished his conversation, Foucault timidly asked him who Roussel was. 'Corti looked at me with a generous sort of pity and said: "But, after all, Roussel . . ." I immediately understood that I should have known about Raymond Roussel, and with equal timidity I asked if I could buy the book, since he was selling it. I was surprised or rather disappointed to find that it was expensive.'[29] Corti then advised Foucault to read *Comment j'ai écrit certains de mes livres*. Over the next few years, Foucault gradually acquired the complete works of Roussel; he had found a new enthusiasm, almost an obsession, but kept this secret love to himself: 'You know, he was my love for several summers . . . and no one knew it.'[30]

Corti's rather patronising smile notwithstanding, Foucault had no reason to be particularly ashamed of his ignorance of Roussel. Born in 1877, Roussel died in dubious circumstances in Palermo in 1933 and his work had been largely forgotten, despite the interest taken in it by the surrealists and by Leiris. At this point, only one book had been devoted to Roussel.[31] The second, which coincided with a revival of interest in an unduly neglected author, appeared in 1963 and was by Michel Foucault.

While Foucault was in Sweden, France had begun to change rapidly as the Algerian war continued and as the Fourth Republic crumbled. Foucault took little interest in these developments. The bitter taste of the PCF was still in his mouth, and for the moment he was thoroughly disenchanted with politics. He and his friends read *Le Monde* and *Le Figaro* regularly but took the detached and cynical stance of the uncommitted expatriate towards events in France. There were a small number of Algerian students at the University of Uppsala and meetings were organised in support of the independence movement led by the National Liberation Front (FLN). Foucault had some contact with these students, and invited some of them to dinner in his rooms. He had vague sympathy for the Algerian cause, but was not a militant supporter.[32]

Despite that sympathy, he was also very impressed by Albert Camus's speech when he accepted the Nobel Prize in December 1957. In his role as director of the Maison de France, Foucault had a hand in the preparations for Camus's visit and was present when he delivered his speech of acceptance on 10 December. Two days after the Nobel ceremony, Camus took part in a debate at the University of Stockholm and was asked by an Algerian student why he had not taken a pro-independence stance. As the discussion became more and more heated, an angry Camus made the notorious statement: 'I have always condemned terror, and I must also condemn a terrorism which is being used blindly, in the streets of Algiers, for example, and which might one day strike my mother or my family. I believe in justice, but I will defend my mother before I defend justice.'[33]

Camus's subsequent lecture in Uppsala on 14 December, organised in part by Foucault and devoted to the topic of 'The Artist and His Time', went ahead without incident, and no political issues were raised. Foucault is not on record as having expressed any doubts or reservations about Camus's Stockholm declarations. The director of the Maison de France was not, of course, in a position to make public statements in favour of the FLN; what is surprising is that even a close friend like Miquel does not recall Foucault making any private statements either. Years later, Foucault did claim that he had been opposed to the war, but added, almost with regret, that, being abroad at the time, he had not himself participated in one of modern France's decisive experiences. He also noted that the war put an end to 'a long period in which it was widely believed on the left that PCF, correct struggle and "just cause" were synonymous'.[34]

Despite his professed indifference to politics, Foucault found it impossible to ignore the events of May 1958, when de Gaulle returned to power in a climate that seemed dangerously close to outright military rebellion in Algeria. Foucault drove from Uppsala to Paris with Oberg at the end of the month, and the two mingled with the excited crowds who thronged the Champs-Elysées and waved red, white and blue flags.[35] Foucault spent at least a month in Paris, staying with his brother in the rue Monge and only returning to Uppsala to pack his bags. His views on the May events are not on record, but many of his acquaintances recall that Foucault was not unsympathetic to de Gaulle and believe that he had Gaullist leanings at this time. What is certain is that he did not support the view – not uncommon on the left and a matter of dogma in the PCF – that de Gaulle's return was a coup d'état which heralded the emergence of 'a presidential regime oriented towards personal dictatorship and opening the way to fascism', and that he took a broadly positive view of the general's handling of the Algerian situation and of the subsequent process of decolonisation.[36]

October 1958 found Foucault in Warsaw, and in charge of the university's Centre Français. The appointment had been arranged at very short notice, and Dumézil once again had a hand in it. The head of the Quai d'Orsay's 'French-language-teaching section' was Philippe Rebeyrol, a contemporary of Dumézil's at ENS. Diplomatic negotiations with Poland had resulted in the establishment of a French centre, and Rebeyrol was looking for someone to run it. Dumézil put forward Foucault's name. Dumézil's judgement was, in Rebeyrol's view, sound and Foucault had established a solid reputation for efficiency in Uppsala. His references were good. In May 1958, a report on the director of the Maison de France had been sent to the Quai d'Orsay: 'M. Foucault is a brilliant foreign representative of French culture. He is succeeding magnificently in Uppsala, where he has won the trust of teachers and students alike. In this post, he is indispensable and one wonders who could replace him if, as is, alas, predictable, he finally tires of the Nordic climate.'[37] Whether or not – and, if so, when – Foucault actually approached Dumézil to express unease about remaining in Sweden remains an obscure question. Even when negotiated by friends, it takes time to arrange diplomatic-cultural appointments and the Quai d'Orsay has never been noted for its rapidity of action. If, as seems at least possible, Poland was being proposed as an option in May 1958, the seriousness with which Foucault viewed his plan to submit a doctoral thesis in Uppsala must be called into question.

To move from Sweden to Poland was, in Foucault's words, to move from a 'social-democratic country which functioned "well" ' to 'a people's democracy that functioned "badly" '.[38] Warsaw was still partly in ruins and material shortages were common; immediately after his arrival, Foucault stayed in the decrepit Bristol Hotel near the university, and was forced to work on the manuscript of *Histoire de la folie* by candlelight. In political terms, too, it was a gloomy city. Memories of the 'Polish October', when Gomulka defied the threat of Soviet intervention and when a 'permanent festival of exultant avant-gardism'[39] was celebrated in the university, still flickered but only fitfully. As Gomulka began to reassert his authority, the alliance between the party and the intellectuals began to break down. In late 1957, students had rioted against the suppression of the 'revisionist' press and Party membership declined precipitously.[40]

Foucault was struck by two things. On the one hand, the Polish people saw their regime as something that had been forced upon them by the outcome of the Second World War and the occupation. Party and government were a foreign bloc that they were forced to live with. On the other, the disastrous economic situation was regarded as a painful sequel to the war. Everything had a provisional or temporary feel to it.[41] For most of his students, Marxism was an object of disgust, an irrelevant theory which they had to study as a French schoolboy might have to study the catechism.[42] Catholicism, on the other hand, represented a form of passive resistance: 'A lot of people went to mass, and they went to mass only in order to show their opposition to the regime.'[43] The university itself was a fairly liberal enclave; it was, reports one of its former lecturers, quite possible to walk across the campus without realising that there was a tight ideological lid on Polish society as a whole.[44]

Foucault's responsibilities in Warsaw were initially similar to those he had had in Uppsala, the differences being that he answered in part to the university authorities and that he had to create his 'Centre' by procuring chairs and tables as well as books and newspapers. As well as teaching French-language classes, he lectured on topics similar to those he had already covered, with particular reference to the contemporary theatre. He succeeded in making himself popular in the university, and quickly won the friendship of Professor Kotarbinski, the distinguished president of the Academy of Sciences and something of a major power in academic circles. In short, the Centre Français quickly became a success.

Foucault's activities were not restricted to his embryonic Centre Français. De Gaulle attached considerable importance to France's Warsaw embassy, which he saw as providing a window on to the East, and that view was shared by his ambassador, Etienne Burin des Roziers. Burin des Roziers knew nothing of Foucault when he appeared in the embassy in the autumn of 1958, but was soon impressed by his energy and efficiency. The French cultural attaché had recently been granted leave to allow him to complete a doctoral thesis, and Foucault became his unofficial replacement. He was now effectively a member of the embassy staff.

His new position gave him some insights into the rituals of diplomatic life, which he viewed with amusement; it also provided him with an opportunity to travel and to give lectures in other cities. In 1986, Burin des Roziers could still recall the 'dazzling' lecture on Apollinaire given by Foucault in Gdansk. So impressed with Foucault was the ambassador that he offered him a permanent position as cultural attaché. Foucault was amenable to the proposal, but was prepared to accept the post only if his own conditions were met. He took the view that the Quai d'Orsay was wrong to believe that cultural attachés could simply be transferred at will from, say, South Africa to Poland as though they were men for all seasons and all places. He wanted to recruit a team of young Polish specialists who could establish a network of French centres throughout the country. Burin des Roziers did not disagree, but unexpected circumstances put paid to the project before it could even be finalised.[45]

The director of the Centre Français was less successful than his creation in that he became embroiled in an unfortunate sexual débâcle. Although the prevailing Catholic atmosphere means that many people take a dim view of homosexuality, it has never actually been made illegal in Poland, which has never known an equivalent to the Oscar Wilde trial.[46] In the artistic and intellectual circles in which Foucault moved, it was quite possible to be openly gay. This was, however, a dangerous option for a foreigner and especially for one who was working as a cultural attaché at an embassy. One of the young men with whom Foucault had become involved proved to be working for the police. He was the son of an officer murdered at Katyn and therefore, given the ideology of the day, under suspicion of having a bourgeois-nationalist background. Agreeing to work for the police was the price he had paid for his university education. Political indoctrination also ensured that he believed that the French Communist Party was working in clandestinity and that his activities as *provocateur* would eventually further the cause of the French proletariat. Foucault had been caught up in a classic entrapment ploy – the 'honey trap' of so many espionage thrillers – designed to cause embarrassment and, possibly, to permit blackmail. When the affair broke, he was advised by his ambassador that he would do well to leave Warsaw as quickly as possible.[47] This was not the first occasion on which Foucault's sexuality had intruded upon his career in Poland. Its previous intrusion may also have had an impact on his career in France.

On a visit to Cracow, Foucault was accompanied by an inspector from the Ministry of Education in Paris who was preparing a report on French cultural work in Poland. Already something of a power in the land, she was later to become the director of the women's Ecole Normale Supérieure. One morning, she was unable to locate the acting cultural attaché and, in frustration, finally burst into his hotel room, where, to her horror, she found Foucault in the arms of a young man he had met the night before. In later years, Foucault told the story with great relish, claiming that the farcical incident had prevented him from presenting to de Gaulle a plan for the reform of higher education that would have forestalled the explosion of May 1968.[48] Whether or not the Cracow incident did in fact affect his career is unclear; it is, however, known that in 1962, Foucault did, with some help from Burin des Roziers, gain an interview with the civil servant responsible for the universities, and did present him with an outline plan for the reform of that sector.

It was to be over twenty years before Foucault returned to Poland. He retained a lasting impression of the 'restrictive and oppressive power of the Communist Party',[49] but also a lasting affection for the Polish people. He later derived considerable satisfaction from the knowledge that, while Poland was still ruled by the puppets of Moscow, the Catholic Church was ruled by a Pole.[50]

The incident in Warsaw left Foucault without employment, but that was soon remedied by a visit to Rebeyrol at the Quai d'Orsay. Despite the incident, his credit was good and he was given excellent references by Jean Bourilly, whom he had temporarily replaced as cultural attaché. A number of positions were vacant in French cultural institutes in Germany, and Foucault opted for Hamburg, another city which still bore the scars of the Second World War.

He resided in the director's quarters at the Institut Français in Heidmer Strasse, taught small groups of language students and gave lectures on the topics already covered in Uppsala and Warsaw. He invited guest lecturers to the Institut, including Alain Robbe-Grillet, whose work he had read but whom he had not previously met. Not all their conversations were strictly literary; it appears to have been Foucault who introduced the novelist to the strip-tease clubs of Hamburg, as well as to the fairground and the 'fun-house maze of mirrors' which, according to Foucault, provided the starting point for Robbe-Grillet's novel *Dans le labyrinthe* (1959).[51]

Foucault was not unacquainted with the seedier side of life in Hamburg. He was involved in a relationship with a transvestite and was familiar with the Sankt Pauli red-light district.[52] One of the official guests Foucault had to welcome was the novelist Pierre Gascar, who provides a rare account of the year spent in Hamburg.[53] Gascar arrived by train from Hanover, knowing only that he would be met by someone carrying a placard bearing the legend 'Institut Français'. As he stepped on to the platform, he saw a motionless figure holding at chin level a piece of cardboard with the expected words. Looking rather like a condemned man tied to the stake, Foucault introduced himself and gave a smile in which his surprised guest – who had assumed he would be met by a minor official or even a driver – read both irony and provocation:

> It was the perfect attitude of the exhibitionist offering to the other, with perfect serenity, that part of himself which has the value of an invitation. That image of his character was to remain imprinted on my memory. It defined him for ever, imprisoning him, here in the midst of the moving crowd, in the smiling 'against-the-current' impassiveness which he would subsequently never cease to demonstrate in the midst of the philosophical or political movements of his times.[54]

Gascar had never previously visited Hamburg, even though, as a prisoner of war, he had seen it burning on the horizon. Foucault proved to be a good guide to the city, well versed in its history and familiar with its streets. The two visited the Kunsthalle, where Foucault commented unfavourably on the collection of German romantic paintings, and eventually strayed into the Sankt Pauli quarter, with its female mud-wrestlers, prostitutes and other varied attractions. For Gascard, the area was a somewhat sordid tourist attraction of which he had heard scandalised and scandalous stories. Foucault was more familiar with it, and was known as 'Herr Doktor' in some of the bars and strip clubs.

Sankt Pauli was only part of Foucault's life in Hamburg. It was here that *Histoire de la folie*, which was discussed at some length with Gascard, was finally completed. By now Foucault had resolved to submit it as a doctoral thesis in France, and had made his intentions known to Hyppolite in Paris. *Histoire de la folie* was to be his principal thesis; the Sorbonne's regulations meant that it had to be supported by a 'complementary thesis', also on a philosophical topic. Foucault elected to translate and introduce Kant's *Anthropologie in pragmatischer Hinsicht* (*Anthropology from a Pragmatic Point of View*) of 1798,[55] and much of the year in Hamburg was devoted to a fastidious task which reactivated the German he had originally learned in order to read Heidegger and Nietzsche. He had finally resolved on an academic career, and a post was available in Clermont-Ferrand.

The introduction to the *Anthropologie* which formed the first volume of the 'complementary thesis', the other being the translation itself, is in many ways a classically academic piece of work which Foucault never attempted to publish. A lot of the 127-page typescript is taken up with discussions of the issue of textual dating and with editorial points, but it does mark an important stage in Foucault's intellectual development. It was here that references to an 'archaeology of the text' begin to appear, and that Foucault begins to refer to the emergence of the 'human sciences' (a generic term, current in French since the nineteenth century, designating such disciplines as sociology, psychology and linguistics) and to ask: 'If it were possible, would not the archaeology of the text allow us to see the birth of a "*homo criticus*", whose structure would be essentially different to the man who preceded him?'[56] More generally, Kant's description of man as world citizen is read against a background of contemporary medical and legal texts, or the 'whole network of empirical knowledges' that constituted the domain of anthropology.[57]

It is the end of the thesis that is most startling. Suddenly breaking off his discussion of Kant, Foucault evokes Nietzsche in prophetic terms:

> Nietzsche's undertaking might be understood as finally putting an end to questions about man. Is not the death of God in effect manifest in a doubly murderous gesture which, by putting an end to the absolute, is at the same time the murder of man himself? For man, in his finitude, is not separable from the infinity of which he is both the negation and the herald. Is it not possible to conceive of a critique of finitude which would be liberating with respect to both man and the infinite, and which would show that finitude is not an end, but that curve and knot of time in which the end is beginning?
>
> The trajectory of the question *Was ist der Mensch?* through the field of philosophy ends in the answer which challenges and disarms it: *der Übermensch.*[58]

The similarity with the famous passage towards the end of *Les Mots et les choses* is astonishing: 'What Nietzsche's thought announces is not so much the death of God . . . as the end of his murderer; it is the shattering of man's face in laughter, and the return of masks.'[59] More astonishing still is the similarity with an unpublished manuscript drafted by Louis Althusser in December 1946: 'We have all taken to heart these words from A. Malraux: "At the end of the century, old Nietzsche proclaimed the death of God. It is now up to us to ask ourselves about ourselves, and to ask ourselves whether man might not be dead henceforth." I quote from memory and these might not be his exact words.'[60] Althusser refers here to the speech given by Malraux to the inaugural meeting of UNESCO on 4 November 1946.[61] He identified a persistent theme in Malraux, whose work was well known to Foucault. In a very early novel written in 1921–25, which takes the form of an exchange of Spenglerian letters between 'A.D.', a European living in China, and 'Ling', a Chinese traveller in Europe, Malraux wrote: 'In order to destroy God, and after having destroyed him, the European mind destroyed everything that could oppose man; having accomplished its attempt, it finds only death.'[62]

Whether or not Foucault had read Althusser's manuscript will probably never be known. It should be recalled, however, that Alexandre Kojève had ensured that the notion of the death of man, and the expression itself, was in the public domain in the late 1940s.[63] It is perhaps not surprising that Althusser should invoke the notion, as mediated by Malraux, given the importance of Kojève's Hegel at this time. The fact that it appears in Foucault's thesis on Kant and then reappears in Les Mots et les choses, is more curious but it is a reminder that the philosophical territory he was to claim for his own was marked out by Kant and Nietzsche, and that the death of man was no structuralist discovery. Malraux, Kojève and Foucault obviously do not use the 'death of man' trope in precisely the same way. For Malraux, the death of man is part of a tragic vision in which the absence of God and the encounter with the absurd negate the idea of humanity, and may signal the appearance of a nihilistic barbarism. For Kojève, Hegel's anthropological philosophy speaks of the death of man to the extent that man is a being who is conscious of death, who freely accepts its inevitability. For Foucault, writing in 1966, the death of man indicates the impossibility of continuing to think with an abstract notion of Man; the noble notion of an autonomous human subject has been rendered untenable by the discoveries of psychoanalysis, linguistics and Marxism. In his doctoral thesis of 1961, he is appropriating a bleakly Nietzschean vision of a post-theological world in which a divinely guaranteed notion of man is being called into question. The famous formula of Les Mots et les choses proves to have a complete history or pre-history.

5

A HISTORY OF MADNESS

THE France to which Foucault returned in the autumn of 1960 was changing. The Fourth Republic had given way to the Fifth, and de Gaulle had been in power for two years. France was beginning to modernise. In February, the country had exploded its first atom bomb, and in the summer legislation was introduced to allow the construction of the first toll motorways. The new franc was in circulation. Godard's *A Bout de souffle* was on release in the cinemas and had been seen by a quarter of a million people by the end of the year. January had seen the death of Camus in a car crash; March, the launch of a new literary journal entitled *Tel Quel*. In May, Sartre published his monumental *Critique de la raison dialectique*, which proclaimed that the late twentieth century was the moment of Marx, just as earlier centuries had once been the moment of Descartes, Kant or Hegel, and that Marxism was the only humus out of which individual thought could grow, the horizon that bounded all culture.[1] In September, 121 intellectuals and artists signed a declaration in support of the increasing number of young men who were refusing to fight in Algeria or deserting from the French army. No national newspaper dared to publish it. The war in Algeria was all but over, but within a year vicious fighting would break out in Paris itself as the Organisation Armée Secrète tried desperately to resist the inevitability of Algerian independence.

The developing trend towards modernisation did not extend to all areas of French culture. On 18 July 1960, the Assemblée Nationale met to debate a bill authorising the government to take measures against social scourges such as prostitution and alcoholism, and diseases such as tuberculosis. An amendment was then proposed by one Mirguet, the elected representative for the Moselle constituency, who urged the adoption of measures against homosexuality, which he described as a scourge from which children must be protected at all cost. The bill and the amendment were voted through and as of 30 July 1960, the French government was officially committed to reducing the incidence of alcoholism, cutting the price of soft drinks ... and combating homosexuality.[2] The Mirguet amendment, which remained on the statute book until 1981, did little to affect anyone's day-to-day life, but it was of immense symbolic importance, particularly as the 1946 legislation was still in force.

There had been changes in Foucault's life, too. His father had died the previous year. His reactions are not on record, but it is symptomatic that he now began to stay with his mother, who had retired to Le Piroir, on a much more regular basis. With the money he inherited on his father's death, Foucault was able to purchase his first apartment in the rue du Dr Finlay, off the quai de Grenelle. The high-rise block of flats was functional and modern; this was one of the most modern *quartiers* in Paris, almost directly across the river from the Maison de la Radio. The flat was well lit and airy, with views across the Seine. Foucault was fairly indifferent to where he lived, but the furnishings reflected a definite taste influenced to a degree by Swedish modernism. Dark, modern furniture in teak predominated, with some relief provided by attractive wooden bookshelves housing a collection of surrealist texts. Here, Foucault worked with the drawing by André Masson left him by his father propped up on his desk. Daniel Defert describes Foucault's new home as having been an apartment for a scientist, or a protestant pastor from Sweden.[3]

In September 1960, Daniel Defert was about to begin his studies at the Ecole Normale de Saint-Cloud, having failed the oral part of the *concours* for the rue d'Ulm. Defert, born in Vézelay in Burgundy, was in his twenties and had been cheerfully and openly – with the connivance of his mother – gay since his teens. In Lyon, he had been taught by Robert Mausi, who had known Foucault at ENS. Disappointed by his pupil's unexpected failure in the oral, Mausi offered to introduce him to the 'best philosopher of his generation', adding that he would be sitting on the ENS jury next year and that Defert should resit the *concours*. Defert did not follow Mausi's suggestion about the *concours* since he had already been accepted by Saint-Cloud, but he did meet Foucault.

The young Burgundian was soon accepted into Foucault's circle and mingled easily with Barthes and other friends. There ensued a close friendship, eventually maturing into a sexual relationship. It was not an exclusive relationship; Defert was avidly discovering the pleasures of Paris, and had the impression that Foucault was rediscovering them just as avidly. Foucault acted as friend and mentor, advising Defert on his philosophy studies and counselling him as he in his turn went through the rites of degree, DEA and *agrégation*.

There was one area in which Defert did not require advice. Unlike most of Foucault's friends, he was a political activist and was very much involved in the campaign against the continuing Algerian war. At Easter, the powerful Union National des Etudiants Français had resolved to establish links with the Union Général des Etudiants Musulmans Algériens, which was effectively the student branch of the FLN, and threw its weight behind the independence struggle. For many young people, this was the beginning of a progressive disenchantment with the PCF, whose support for Algerian independence was widely perceived as being less than lukewarm. Defert was active in the anti-war movement, and it was here that he began to acquire the political skills and the taste for semi-clandestine activity that would be so useful a decade later. He was also acquiring some familiarity with the Arab ghettoes of the suburb of Nanterre and in doing so came, to his great amusement, across the rue du Dr Foucault. Foucault had no real experience of political militancy; Defert was a new species.[4]

Despite the presence of Defert, Foucault did not become involved in political life at all, and continued to pursue a classically literary and intellectual existence. The association with Barthes continued, and the two dined together, with a group of friends (mainly but not exlusively gay), as often as three times a week. Barthes's fortunes and intellectual visibility were now improving. In 1960, he was appointed *chef de travaux* at the Ecole Pratique des Hautes Etudes, which was to be the institutional fortress of structuralism, and displayed an unexpected talent and relish for administrative work. His collected *Mythologies* had appeared in 1957, and he was now working on the essays which would eventually go to make up *Système de la mode* (1967).

Foucault, for his part, was primarily concerned with the publication of his first major work, which would give him a doctorate and a tenured position in a French university. He had returned from Hamburg with his translation of Kant and with a bulky manuscript of 943 pages (plus a further forty pages of notes and bibliography), the product of some five years' research and writing. What had begun life as a planned history of psychiatry for La Table Ronde, and had then metamorphosed into a projected Swedish doctoral thesis, had finally become Foucault's first major work: *Folie et déraison: Histoire de la folie à l'âge classique.*

In the original preface, dated 'Hamburg, 5 February 1960', Foucault wrote that the book was begun 'in the Swedish night' and completed in the 'great, stubborn sunlight of Polish freedom', and he often claimed that most of the work was done in Uppsala, but his footnotes tell a slightly different story. The text was actually written in exile, but much of the research was obviously carried out in Paris, partly in the manuscript and printed-books departments of the Bibliothèque Nationale, partly in the Archives Nationales and partly in the Bibliothèque de l'Arsenal in the rue de Sully. Foucault also relied to some extent on Sainte-Anne's library facilities, as he confirms in the privately printed brochure written to support his candidature to the Collège de France:

> In *Histoire de la folie à l'âge classique*, I wished to determine what could be known about mental illness in a given epoch ... An object took shape for me: the knowledge invested in complex systems of institutions. And a method became imperative: rather than perusing ... only the library of scientific books, it was necessary to consult a body of archives comprising decrees, rules, hospital and prison registers, and acts of jurisprudence. It was in the Arsenal or the Archives Nationales that I undertook the analysis of a knowledge whose visible body is neither scientific nor theoretical discourse, nor literature, but a daily and regulated practice.[5]

A long love affair with the archive had commenced, and it began with a lengthy sojourn in the 'somewhat dusty archives of pain'.[6]

It is, perhaps, the preface to the first edition of *Histoire de la folie*, sadly truncated in the abridged version of 1964 and replaced by a new preface in later editions, that provides the clearest insight into what Foucault is about in his 'first book'.[7] It opens abruptly with a quotation from Pascal: 'Men are so inevitably mad that not to be mad would be to give a mad twist to madness.'[8] Foucault's history is a history of that further 'mad twist', 'whereby men, in an act of sovereign reason, confine their neighbours, and communicate and recognise one another in the pitiless language of non-folly', an attempt to 'rediscover the moment of that exorcism, before it was definitively established in the realm of truth, before it was revived by the lyricism of protest'. The concepts of psychopathology will be of no help in the search for 'the degree zero of the history of madness', a phrase in which it is tempting to see a playful allusion to the title of Barthes's *Degré zéro de l'écriture*, in which the term 'writing degree zero' refers to the flatly natural style of Camus's *L'Étranger*. It is not the categories of nosography that will guide Foucault. On the contrary, it is necessary to grasp something much more primal: 'Constitutive, the gesture that divides madness, and not the science established once the gesture has been made, once calm has returned. Primal, the caesura that establishes the distance between reason and non-reason.'[9]

The preface goes on:

> In the midst of the serene world of mental illness, modern man no longer communicates with the madman; on the one hand, there is the man of reason, who delegates madness to the doctor, thus authorising a relationship through the abstract universality of illness alone; on the other, there is the man of madness who communicates with the other only through the intermediary of an equally abstract reason, namely order, physical and moral constraint, the anonymous pressure of the group, the demand for conformity. There is no such thing as a common language. Or rather, there is no longer such a thing; the constitution of madness as mental illness, at the end of the eighteenth century, takes formal note that a dialogue has been broken off, assumes that the separation has already been made, and plunges into oblivion all those imperfect words, somewhat stammered and with no fixed syntax, in which the exchange between madness and reason once took place. The language of psychiatry, which is reason's monologue *on* madness, could only be established on the basis of such a silence.[10]

Foucault's ambition is to write, not the history of a language, but the archaeology of a silence. His history will be one of limits, 'of the obscure gestures, necessarily forgotten as soon as they have been made, with which a culture rejects something which will become its Outside'.[11] It is also an attempt to capture something else:

> The space, at once empty and populated, of all those words without a language which allow the person who lends an ear to hear a muffled noise from below history, the stubborn murmuring of a language which seems to speak quite by itself, without a speaking subject and without an interlocutor, huddled in on itself, a lump in its throat, breaking down before it has achieved any formulation and lapsing back without any fuss into the silence from which it was never separated.[12]

Beneath the Heideggerean accent, it is possible, perhaps, to hear another muffled noise and to recall a boy dreaming of 'a text I cannot read, or of which I can decipher only a tiny part, but I know that I am making it up; then the text clouds over completely, and I can no longer read, or even make it up'.[13] As in his childhood dream, Foucault is trying to listen to something almost inaudible, to capture something that remains frustratingly elusive: the experience of madness itself.

Histoire de la folie is not an easy text to read, and it defies attempts rapidly to summarise its content. Foucault refers to a bewildering variety of sources, ranging from well-known authors such as Erasmus and Molière to archival documents and forgotten figures in the history of medicine and psychiatry. His erudition derives from years pondering, to cite Poe, 'over many a quaint and curious volume of forgotten lore', and his learning is not always worn lightly. The chronology of his history is not always respected as he employs contrasts to illustrate the salient features of the classical age's experience of unreason. Vignettes culled from the archives interrupt discursive flights of philosophy; empirical arguments mingle with theoretical claims. The taste for paradox can result in intimidatingly dense formulations. Thus, the threat posed to the classical order by the threatened triumph of folly or madness is said to 'reveal the irreparable fragility of relations of belonging, the immediate collapse of reason into the having wherein it seeks its being: *reason is alienated in the very movement whereby it takes possession of unreason*'.[14] The reader is rarely allowed to forget that this is a book by a *normalien*. The display of erudition is one of its best defences. Foucault's exploitation of archival material and forgotten lore helps to put him beyond criticism. Few of his potential readers are likely to be able to challenge his references to, say, Paracelsus. And fewer still are in a position to query both the references to Paracelsus and Foucault's reading of de Sade and Artaud.

Yet the text affords even its most casual reader a great deal of pleasure. Its overall arguments and structures are seductively persuasive, and do win over the reader, just as they were to win over and convince the members of the jury which examined Foucault for his doctorate. As one wanders through the botanical garden of 'species' like dementia, mania, hysteria and melancholia, or encounters strange references to 'a madman who became an imbecile' and to 'a man who was once mad, but is now feeble-minded and imbecilic',[15] one experiences a pleasing bewilderment akin to that provoked by Borges's Chinese encyclopedia. And beneath the bewilderment, one senses that a relativism is increasingly at work as any intellectual conviction about the validity of judgements about madness is undermined.

The history is basically a triptych or a tragic drama in three acts, and a similar periodisation will be used in *Les Mots et les choses*. The first panel or act depicts the experience of madness in the late Middle Ages and the Renaissance; the second, the classical era which stretches, according to Foucault, from 1657, when the Hôpital Général was founded and when the poor of Paris became the victims of the 'great confinement', to 1794, when the inmates of Bicêtre were set free from their chains by Philippe Pinel, an act which inaugurates the age of the asylum. The final act is concerned with the modern experience of madness. The history has a further underlying theme: 'During the reconstruction of this experience of madness, a history of the conditions of possibility of psychology virtually wrote itself.'[16] The preface ends with the second of two unacknowledged quotations from René Char's 'Partage formel' (1948): 'Pathetic companions who can barely murmur, go, with your extinguished lamps, and give back the jewels. A new mystery sings in your bones. Develop your legitimate strangeness.'[17]

On the one hand, *Histoire de la folie* is a positive history of the transition from '*folie*' to 'mental illness'. '*Folie*' is a difficult term to translate, since it encompasses both 'folly' and 'madness'; in French, Erasmus praises 'folly'; and both Lady Macbeth and King Lear fall prey to it. On the other, it is an attempt to listen sympathetically to 'the great lyrical protest which one finds in poetry since Nerval and Artaud ... an attempt to restore to the experience of madness a depth and a power to reveal which were reduced to nothing by confinement'.[18] In the years that followed the publication of *Histoire de la folie*, Foucault was to devote a great deal of effort to tracing and deciphering that experience and its literary expression, rather as though he detected some primal relationship between writing and madness.

The text itself opens in dramatic fashion, and reveals the way in which Foucault has now acquired a style marked by the use of arresting initial images or declarations: 'At the end of the Middle Ages, leprosy disappeared from the western world.'[19] In a dense and rapid survey replete with references to an extraordinary and sometimes forbidding variety of sources, Foucault decribes the disappearance of leprosy from Europe and the transference of all the fears and fantasies once inspired by the leper on to a new object. As the lazar houses empty, a new object appears in the imaginary landscape of the Renaissance: the Ship of Fools, the *Narrenschiff* that drifted slowly along the rivers of the Rhineland and the canals of Flanders with its symbolic cargo of madmen. Whereas the Middle Ages had been haunted by the fear of death from plague or war, the Renaissance attempted to exorcise a new fear: fear of madness, no longer seen as an external threat, but as a possibility inherent in human experience. Folly haunts the work of men, turning thought to derision, reducing all human endeavour to vanity. The overall structure of fear remained the same; men still feared 'the nothingness of existence, but that nothingness is no longer recognised as an external and final term, at once a threat and a conclusion; it is experienced from within, as the continuous and constant form of existence'.[20] Folly outdoes wisdom in Erasmus, denying the existence of any dividing line between reason and unreason, and mocks at reason in many a painting. Folly can even be a higher form of wisdom: Lear understands more in his madness than in his regal sanity, and the Fool is always wiser than Lear. Folly has not yet been totally excluded from the world; it speaks – and often speaks the truth – in Shakespeare and in Cervantes. The muffled sound of its voice had yet to be silenced. The individual madman, present in the everyday life of the Middle Ages, is isolated from the world, but his status has yet to be medically defined; he is the object of a particular solicitude and even hospitality.

Folly was silenced and exiled by the 'great confinement' of the seventeenth century. It was confinement that now provided the most visible structure of the experience of madness. A decree of 1656 allowed for the foundation of Paris's Hôpital Général, which had a mission to house the poor, the indigent, the sick, curable and incurable, the mad and the sane, vagrants, mendicants and 'libertines' in a bedlam familiar to any reader of Prévost's *Manon Lescaut*. The great confinement was not primarily concerned with the insane as such. The Hôpital Général, and the workhouses, Bridewells and houses of correction of England were all part of a police system, and Foucault uses 'police' in what he claims to be its original sense of all those measures which make work both necessary and possible for all those who cannot live without working'.[21] Established at the same time as the great manufactures, with their barrack-room discipline,[22] they were in part a response to the economic crisis of the seventeenth century, a way of regimenting labour. They were also the product of an epistemological shift exemplified by Descartes's *Méditations métaphysiques*, published in Latin in 1641 and in French in 1647: 'While *man* can still be mad, *thought*, being the exercise of the sovereignty of a subject who makes it his duty to perceive the truth, cannot be insensate. A dividing line is traced, and will soon render impossible the experience – so familiar to the Renaissance – of an unreasonable Reason and a reasonable Unreason.'[23] The combination of epistemology and police ensures that 'madness is perceived in terms of an ethical condemnation of idleness'.[24]

It was within institutions like the Hôpital Général that western reason encountered, or even created, those it deemed mad, within institutions that housed a varied population of debauchees, syphilitics, sodomites, alchemists, blasphemers and others who represented unreason, who offended against the canons of classical rationality. From the classical age onwards, the insane would be distinguished by their 'halo of guilt'.[25] Confinement was not initially a first, crude attempt to hospitalise madness but, rather, the likening of the mad to all those who came within the remit of a reason which confined all that it deemed to be unreason.[26] The decision to confine a given individual may have been taken on medical grounds; the practical definition of unreason was constructed by legal, social or even theological discourses. Folly or madness is not a natural phenomenon defined once and for all. It is a shifting constellation which can be displaced. It is, however, always the object of a consciousness which denounces it in the name of an assumed rationality.

Foucault identifies four modalities of this consciousness: critical, practical, enunciative and analytic.[27] A critical awareness or consciousness of madness is essentially a denunciation which is confident of its own rationality, sure of not itself being mad, whereas practical consciousness is primarily a perception of a deviation from the norms of a group or society. The latter involves the tracing of dividing lines, and the denunciation of those who transgress them. The enunciative consciousness relies for its existence upon the statement 'He is mad', but it neither qualifies nor disqualifies madness as such. It is therefore reversible into its opposite and can give rise to the endless ironies of a text like Denis Diderot's Le Neveu de Rameau, later analysed by Foucault at some length and seen by him as exemplifying 'the necessary instability and ironic reversal of any form of judgement which denounces unreason as being external to it and inessential'[28] because it introduces the motif of de te fabula narratur. The analytic consciousness looks at the forms, phenomena and modes of appearance of its object. For this modality, madness is not mysterious; it is simply the totality of its phenomena. It provides the basis for an objective knowledge of madness, and will dominate the age of the asylum, just as practical consciousness dominated the classical period.

During the eighteenth century, madness is forced to enter what Foucault terms 'the garden of species'. In an analysis which foreshadows major sections of Les Mots et les choses, he characterises the Enlightenment as a period of taxonomy, a period in which the phenomena of madness enter the logical and natural domain of medicine, a field of rationality typified by the attempt to apply the principles of Linnaean classification to what once defied categorisation.

Disorder is now subject to an ordering that seeks to invoke the parameters of natural history and the ideals of the herbarium. A discursive knowledge now becomes possible. The garden that was originally planted with such species as frenzy, delirium, mania, melancholia and stupidity by Thomas Willis (1621–73) gradually becomes the more recognisable garden tended by Pinel (1745–1826) and his disciple Esquirol (1772–1840), where species such as dementia, mania and melancholy mutate into hysteria, hypochondria and nervous illnesses.

The emergence of a positive or discursive knowledge of madness does not, however, signal a linear progress towards any final clarity, nor does it necessarily signal a liberalisation. It emerges against the background of the great fear that suddenly developed in the mid-eighteenth century: that some mysterious contagion might spread from institutions like the Hôpital Général or Bicêtre.[29] It was as though the ancient fear of leprosy had returned in a new form. The reforms initiated in the revolutionary period had their origins in a response to this irrational fear: 'reducing contamination, by destroying the impurities and vapours . . . preventing ills [les maux] and evil [le mal] from vitiating the air and spreading their contagion through the atmosphere of the towns. The hospital, the maison de force and all places of internment must be better isolated, surrounded by a purer air.'[30]

The birth of the asylum was marked by the founding of an institution and by an act of apparent liberation: the York Retreat first opened its doors in 1796, and Pinel struck off the chains that bound the insane inmates of Bicêtre in 1794. The Retreat was a Quaker foundation established by Samuel Tuke to provide a more enlightened regime for the insane. Its foundation was made possible by changes in the Poor Law and it was a charitable institution, initially housing only Quakers but soon able to take patients from all sectors of society, regardless of creed. Set in pleasant rural surroundings outside York, it provided an environment in which it was hoped that exercise, regular walks, work in the gardens and a quiet family-like atmosphere would facilitate the return of its inmates' reason. Pinel, in the meantime, had discovered in the course of a visit to Bicêtre that the bestiality he saw there lay, not in the mad but innocent inmates, but in the unthinking cruelty of those who had incarcerated them alongside criminals.

To Foucault, the birth of the asylum represents a new form of confinement, and also signals the new importance of the doctor of medicine. Confinement is now a medicalisation of madness, but the authority of the doctor is not purely medical: the role of the medical profession is to supply a moral and legal guarantee that confinement is justified. The Retreat sought to reproduce the structure of a Quaker community: sober, and much given to self-examination, to a dialogue with one's own conscience, and to a constant awareness of the presence of both Law and Sin. In this climate, madness, being curable, will no longer inspire fear. On the contrary, fear and guilt will be instilled into the mad, entrusted as they are to a pedagogy of good sense, truth, morality and the internalisation of constraints, and living as they do under the constant gaze of the staff who were, quite literally, their brothers' keepers.[31]

Pinel's liberation of the inmates of Bicêtre began, at least in part, as a political manoeuvre. It was rumoured that the old prison harboured criminals, the insane, political prisoners incarcerated by the Ancien Régime and, most sinister of all, enemies of the Revolution masquerading as lunatics. Before they could be treated more humanely, the mad had first to be identified as such. The mad were, thanks to the logic of confinement, silent: they now had to speak their madness in order to be seen as mad. Convincing the individual that he was in fact mad became an essential precondition for treatment. Pinel established a regime in which confession was essential: the madman had to recognise himself in the judgement of madness that had been passed on him and that organised the enveloping structures of surveillance, judgement and condemnation. The conclusion is chillingly pessimistic:

> The madman 'freed' by Pinel and the madman of modern confinement who came after him, are characters who are on trial; while they have the privilege of no longer being mixed up with or assimilated to the condemned, they are, at every moment, condemned to face an accusation, the text of which is never given, as it is the whole of their life in the asylum that formulates it. The asylum of the positivist age ... is not a free domain for observation, diagnosis and therapy; it is a judicial space in which one is accused, judged and condemned, and from which one is freed only by the version of this trial in psychological depth, in other words by repentance. Madness will be punished in the asylum, even if it is found innocent outside. For a long time to come, and until our own day at least, it is imprisoned in a moral world.[32]

Throughout *Histoire de la folie*, Foucault hints at the existence of a muffled noise that resists confinement's attempts to silence it. The voice is heard in the work of poets like Gérard de Nerval and Antonin Artaud, in Goya's *Disparates* and *Caprichos* and the last paintings of van Gogh, in the madness of Nietzsche as he proclaims himself to be both Christ and Dionysus, and in the writings of de Sade, which outline a theory of *libertinage* or of the 'use of alienated reason in the unreason of the heart'.[33] The almost inaudible words of unreason murmur through these texts and paintings, amplified into cries of madness, into the final disintegration of speech that overtook Artaud on the stage of the Vieux Colombier theatre in 1947. Although Foucault's thought is certainly influenced here by his perception of Jacques Martin as a *philosophe sans oeuvre*, it is probably Artaud who provides him with his definition of madness: madness is the absence of an *oeuvre*, meaning a work in the literary sense. Thus, 'Artaud's madness does not lie in the interstices of the work; it is precisely the *absence of an oeuvre*, the reiterated presence of that absence, its central void, experienced and measured in all its endless dimensions'.[34] Foucault gives no hint as to just which text by Artaud he is referring to here, but he may have in mind a passage from 'Le Pèse-nerfs', a fragmentary and almost hallucinatory piece first published in 1925: 'I've told you: no works [*oeuvres*], no language, no speech, no mind [*esprit*], nothing. Nothing, except a fine Nerve-Scale. A sort of incomprehensible and totally upright stance in the middle of everything in the mind.'[35]

The publication, in 1964, of an article entitled 'La Folie, l'absence d'oeuvre' does little to clarify matters. Here, Foucault speculates that, one day, we will no longer know what madness once was, and dreams of a utopia in which 'Artaud will belong to the ground of our language, and not to its rupture; in which neuroses will belong to the constituent forms of our society (and not to deviations).'[36] Arguing that *folie* and mental illness – 'two different configurations which fused and merged from the seventeenth century onwards'– are now beginning to be separated out,[37] Foucault again speaks in very enigmatic terms of the relationship between madness and literature. *Folie* and *oeuvre* exist in a relationship of 'geminous incompatibility': '*Folie* neither manifests nor recounts the birth of an *oeuvre* . . . it designates the empty form from which it never ceases to be absent, where we will never find it, because it was never to be found there. There, in that pale region, beneath that essential mask [*cache*], the geminous incompatibility of *oeuvre* and *folie* is unveiled.'[38]

A rather clearer exposition of what is meant by the *absence d'oeuvre* comes in a discussion of Nerval published in 1964:

For us, Nerval is not an *oeuvre*, not even an attempt to translate into a vanishing *oeuvre*, an experience that seems obscure to it, alien or reticent. For modern eyes, Nerval means a certain relationship, continuous and jagged, with language. From the outset, he was dragged forward by an empty obligation to write. Nerval's texts do not leave us fragments of an *oeuvre*, but the repeated observation [*constat*] that we must write, that we live and die only through writing.[39]

The relationship between Foucault's *absence d'oeuvre* and Artaud is far from clear, but there is a marked parallel between the pantheons of writers celebrated by the two. Artaud certainly saw himself as belonging to the same line as Nerval, Nietzsche and Hölderlin. In 1946, Artaud saw the major van Gogh exhibition held at the Orangerie and was inspired to write 'Van Gogh le suicidé de la société' ('Van Gogh or Society's Suicide'), in which he draws upon Van Gogh's paintings and his own experience of nine years' confinement in various asylums to arrive at his own definition of the 'authentically insane man': 'A man who would rather go mad, in the sense in which that word is socially understood, than forfeit a certain higher idea of human honour . . . a man to whom society did not want to listen, and whom it wanted to prevent from stating unbearable truths.'[40]

At this stage, Foucault does not actually explore the tradition of writing and painting to which he alludes throughout his history of madness. Few references are given, and names such as Nerval, Nietzsche and Artaud function as emblems or tutelary deities which are simply evoked in counterpoint to the saga of the medicalisation of madness. It will, however, be explored in some detail in a sequence of essays and articles produced in the years that separate the publication of *Histoire de la folie* and that of *Les Mots et les choses*.

In order to submit *Histoire de la folie* and his translation of Kant for a doctorate, Foucault was obliged to find an academic patron willing to provide a report on his work and to sit on the thesis jury. There was no question of supervision in any normal sense of the word; both texts were written in isolation during the years spent in Sweden, Poland and Germany. At this time, a thesis had to be published in order to be accepted as a doctorate, and Foucault therefore required the *imprimatur* of the Sorbonne. He initially approached Hyppolite, who had become the ENS's director in 1954; being a Germanist, Hyppolite was quite prepared to act as a director of studies for the *petite thèse* on Kant, but opined that *Histoire de la folie*, which he had read with admiration, was not within his area of competence. He suggested that Foucault should approach Canguilhem, who had succeeded Gaston Bachelard at the Sorbonne in 1955.[41]

The role played by Canguilhem is somewhat obscured by Foucault's comments in the original preface to *Histoire de la folie*. Here, Foucault thanks Dumézil, Hyppolite and 'above all, M. Georges Canguilhem, who read this work when it was still shapeless, advised me when not everything was simple, helped me to avoid many errors and showed me how much it can cost to be heard'.[42] Canguilhem strenuously denies that he gave Foucault any advice. He was, he recalls, presented with a complete piece of work, and had never been consulted about it. His advice amounted to a few recommendations about rhetoric, and he is not sure that they were followed. In his view, the tribute paid him by Foucault was simply a matter of academic politeness.[43] An alternative explanation might be that Foucault was placing his work under the symbolic authority of a 'master' he admired rather than acknowledging any specific debt.

If Canguilhem's role in the genesis of *Histoire de la folie* is far from clear, nor is it entirely clear why Hyppolite suggested him as a *rapporteur*. Most of Canguilhem's work had been on the history of medicine and the life sciences, and he was no expert on the history of many of the varied topics covered by Foucault. His own explanation is that Hyppolite recommended him on the strength of a recent article he had written on psychology. 'Qu'est-ce que la psychologie?' was a lecture delivered to the Collège Philosophique in December 1956 and published in the *Revue de Métaphysique et de morale* in 1958.[44] It is in fact a violent attack on the very notion of psychology on the grounds that psychologists are quite incapable of coherently defining the object of their studies, the definition of a theoretical object being a key part of Canguilhem's criterion for scientificity.[45] As it is, psychology is little more than a 'composite empiricism' which has been codified in literary fashion for teaching purposes. What is more, psychology easily becomes a police discipline. Canguilhem ends with a fable. The philosopher gives the psychologist the following directions: If you leave the Sorbonne by the rue Saint-Jacques, you can either go uphill or downhill. If you go uphill, you may reach the Panthéon, a shrine to a few great men; the downhill road leads inescapably to the Préfecture de police.[46]

On 19 April 1960, Canguilhem submitted his typewritten report on Foucault's thesis to the dean of the Sorbonne, and recommended its publication and submission to a jury drawn from the faculty of letters and human sciences for examination.[47] It was elogious: 'We are truly in the presence of a *thesis* which represents something new, not only in the domain of ideas, but in the techniques of grasping and presenting facts in the history of psychiatry.' Canguilhem later compared Foucault's submission to Raymond Aron's *Introduction à la philosophie de l'histoire* (1938), one of the most memorable theses of the inter-war period.[48] Much of his report is taken up with an objective summary of Foucault's text, but its tenor and tone are also instantly recognisable as representative of Canguilhem's own concerns:

> M. Foucault uses the term 'classical era' to designate the seventeenth and eighteenth centuries of the history of Europe or, more accurately, the period which stretches from the end of the sixteenth century to the constitution, in the first third of the nineteenth century, of a mental medicine and a psychiatric practice with pretentions to, respectively, the dignity of science and the efficacy of an application of theory . . . M. Foucault attempts essentially to show that madness is an object of perception within a 'social space' which is structured in diverse ways throughout history, an object of perception produced by social practices rather than being grasped by a collective sensibility, and, more importantly, rather than being analytically broken down by speculative understanding.

Canguilhem read the thesis as a confirmation of his own views on the dubious scientificity of psychiatry and psychology:

> It is . . . the meaning of the beginnings of positivist psychiatry – before the Freudian revolution – that is in question in M. Foucault's work. And, going beyond psychiatry, it is the meaning of the appearance of positivist psychology that is being re-examined. Not the least of the surprises occasioned by this study is the calling into question of the origins of psychology's 'scientific' status . . . As to documentation, M. Foucault has on the one hand reread and re-examined and, on the other, read and exploited for the first time, a considerable amount of archival material. A professional historian cannot fail to be sympathetic to the effort a young philosopher has made to gain access to first-hand material. On the other hand, no philosopher can criticise M. Foucault for having alienated the autonomy of philosophical judgement by submitting to the sources of his historical information. In its use of considerable documentation, M. Foucault's thought has throughout retained a dialectical vigour which in part derives from his

sympathy for the Hegelian vision of history and from his familiarity with the *Phenomenology of Mind*.

The last comment is deeply ironic, given that Foucault himself believed that Nietzsche and serial music had at last freed him from the prison of Hegelianism, but it is a reminder of just how much Hegel still meant in 1960. As a recent critic has pointed out, Canguilhem is correct to mention Hegel, as *Histoire de la folie* does demonstrate how Foucault 'learned from phenomenology – the phenomenology of the early Hegel mediated through Hyppolite – to freeze historical moments within constellations consisting of both abstract categories and concrete examples which are presented without interpretation, without reference to any tradition of scholarship and dispute'.[49]

Canguilhem's report was approved by the academic authorities and Foucault was given permission to publish his thesis. Finding a publisher was to prove surprisingly difficult. Foucault's first choice was Gallimard. Gallimard, which grew out of the *Nouvelle Revue Française* and which began to publish under its own Librairie Gallimard imprint in 1919, was by far France's most prestigious publisher. To be published in its plain white covers was the ambition of all young writers; Gide, Proust, Sartre, Camus, Malraux and Blanchot were all Gallimard authors. Acceptance or rejection by Gallimard was not a matter for an individual, but for the fabled *comité de lecture*, or readers' committee, which met weekly in conditions of secrecy and wielded immense literary and intellectual power.

In 1961, one of its most prestigious members was Brice Parain. A philosopher by training, Parain was the author of essays on the philosophy of language and on the Platonic *logos*.[50] He was also the legendary editor who, together with Gaston Gallimard, had helped Sartre to transform a manuscript entitled 'Melancholia' into the best-selling *La Nausée* in the 1930s.[51] He had belonged to the committee since 1927 and was a friend of Dumézil, whom he had first met at ENS just after the First World War. In the 1940s, he had published some of Dumézil's work, including the *Jupiter, Mars, Quirinus* series, in an academic collection entitled La Montagne Sainte-Geneviève.[52] The collection had not been a particular success, and he may have been reluctant to publish more academic works. Whatever the final explanation, he rejected *Folie et déraison*.

The book did, however, find some admirers on the *comité de lecture*. Daniel Defert believes that Raymond Queneau was in favour of publishing it, and Roger Caillois was definitely in favour. Caillois, a member of the committee since 1945 and the editor of 'La Croix du sud', an imprint of Latin-American literature (the first title was a French translation of Borges's *Ficciones*), had in pre-war years been a member of the Collège de Sociologie and an associate of Bataille's.[53] He worked for UNESCO, a factor which was to prove relevant to the fate of *Les Mots et les choses* in 1966. He too knew Dumézil, and had once studied under him. Caillois was impressed by Foucault's book, but puzzled by its style, finding the combination of splendour and precision disconcerting.[54] He was, however, unable to overcome Parain's objections. He passed on the text to Maurice Blanchot, who read at least part of it in manuscript. Both Blanchot and Caillois were members of the jury that awarded the annual Prix des Critiques, and wondered whether Foucault might not be a worthy laureate. Their plotting came to nothing.[55]

Being rejected by Gallimard is something of an honourable tradition. The first volume of Proust's *A La Recherche du temps perdu* was rejected and was privately published at the author's expense; legend has it that André Gide turned it down because there were 'too many duchesses' in its pages. Rather more recently, Parain had made the mistake of rejecting Claude Lévi-Strauss's *Anthropologie structurale*. The knowledge that he had distinguished antecedents was no consolation to Foucault, who was bitterly disappointed. He desperately wanted to be published by Gallimard and even rejected Jean Delay's offer to publish it in a collection he edited for Presses Universitaires de France, presumably because of a desire to escape the academic ghetto.[56]

Anthropologie structurale was eventually published by Plon and, following the advice of a friend, Foucault submitted his manuscript to the same publisher. (The friend, Jacques Bellefroid, was the young man who had been involved with Jean-Paul Aron in Lille.) The receipt of the script was greeted with silence. Foucault himself describes the course of events thus:

> I . . . took my manuscript to Plon. No answer. After a few months, I went to get it back. I was given to understand that they would first have to find it before they could return it. And then one day, they found it in a drawer, and even noticed that it was a book on history. They gave it to Ariès to read.[57]

Rumours were currently circulating in Paris to the effect that a banana importer had just written a revolutionary study of the history of childhood and the family: the study was *L'Enfant et la vie familiale sous l'ancien régime*, and its author was Philippe Ariès.[58] Ariès was not in fact an importer of bananas, but an information officer who worked for an institute dealing with tropical agriculture. He described himself as a 'Sunday historian', and never held any academic post. He and Foucault had never met, but Foucault did know *L'Enfant*, which figures in the bibliography appended to *Histoire de la Folie*.

Ariès was a bundle of contradictions. A supporter of the monarchist Action Française in his youth, he became a friend of Foucault's at a time when the latter was moving far to the left of the political scene. Described by the broadcaster Philippe Meyer, who came to know him well in the 1970s, as having the utmost respect for all symbolic authorities and none whatsoever for any real authority,[59] Ariès was a devout Catholic who, in his later years, regularly attended mass wearing earplugs so as not to be disturbed by all the 'nonsense' that had emerged from the Second Vatican Council.[60] The historian Arlette Farge saw Ariès's relationship with his wife as a rare example of conjugal *amour fou*. Yet his wife walked behind him, carrying his umbrella.[61] This was the man who was to publish *Histoire de la Folie*: 'One fine day, a fat manuscript reached me: a philosophy thesis on relations between madness and unreason during the classical epoch, by an author who was unknown to me. When I read it, I was dazzled.'[62] According to Ariès it was 'the devil's own job' to persuade Plon to publish Foucault. The company had recently been taken over by, in his words, a 'banker assisted by a playboy' and was not actually interested in publishing books, and especially not academically prestigious titles with little market potential. He persevered and *Folie et déraison* appeared in his *Civilisations d'aujourd'hui et d'hier* collection alongside *L'Enfant et la vie familiale* and Louis Chevalier's *Classes laborieuses, classes dangereuses*.

Canguilhem's report was a passport to more than publication. While Foucault was still in Hamburg, Jules Vuillemin had written to ask him if he would be willing to accept a position at the University of Clermont-Ferrand. Foucault indicated his willingness, but a number of academic formalities had first to be fulfilled. In order to be appointed, Foucault had to be included on the *liste d'aptitude*, his inclusion being equivalent to official recognition as a qualified and competent lecturer. Georges Bastide was commissioned to write the requisite report in June 1960: 'Michel Foucault has already written a few minor works and translated some German works, mainly on history and method in psychology, works of vulgarisation. All that is respectable. But it is certain that it is the candidate's theses that are his best qualifications.'[63] Bastide was uncertain as to how to categorise Foucault in disciplinary terms: was he a psychologist or a historian of science?

Foucault was eventually categorised by the authorities as a philosopher.

Bastide's comments, Canguilhem's report on the thesis and a letter of recommendation from Hyppolite were more than sufficient to guarantee Foucault's appointment to Clermont-Ferrand as of October 1960. He was at first appointed to replace Professor Cesari who was absent on sick leave; when Cesari died in 1962, Foucault succeeded him as full professor. Officially he was a philosopher; in practice he was required to teach psychology.

Foucault never lived in Clermont-Ferrand. He refused to leave Paris, crammed his teaching into the minimal time possible and stayed at the Hôtel Elisabeth when it was necessary to remain in the capital of the Auvergne. Between 1960 and 1966, he made the six-hour train journey in both directions once a week throughout the academic year.

Clermont-Ferrand was Foucault's first real academic appointment within the French system. It provided him with a base and offered the possibility of moving into the educational establishment. As in any educational system, the acquisition of power required participation in a number of fields, while the centralisation of the system meant moving between its various levels. Over the next few years, Foucault duly sat on the jury for the ENS *concours*, for the final examinations at ENA and, at a more lowly level, on a *baccalauréat* jury in Lille. Although he was a relative latecomer to the university system – he was thirty-five in 1961 – Foucault had already established a network of powerful institutional contacts. From now on, his power base would be within the university. Unlike Bataille, who was by profession a librarian and not a university teacher, or Sartre, Foucault was in many ways a product of the system and was never to be a freelance intellectual.

Life in Clermont, or such time as Foucault deigned to spend there, was not at first unpleasant. The company of Vuillemin was agreeable, and so was that of colleagues like Michel Serres. In 1962, however, Vuillemin was elected to the Collège de France, where he took up the chair left vacant by the sudden death of Merleau-Ponty. His proposed replacement was Gilles Deleuze. Foucault and Deleuze had met, but were not yet close friends. Deleuze had published relatively little, but his *Nietzsche et la philosophie* had greatly impressed Foucault.[64] Both the department and the faculty found Deleuze a more than acceptable candidate, but his appointment was never ratified.

The appointed candidate was Roger Garaudy, the PCF's official philosopher in residence and an important member of the Political Bureau. The reasons for his appointment in preference to Deleuze are mysterious, but there are rumours of undue political influence. More specifically, it is often claimed that he was appointed at the insistence of Georges Pompidou, who became prime minister in 1962. Legend has it that the friendship the two had established at ENS had outlasted their party-political differences and that Pompidou was anxious to promote the career of his old friend. Daniel Defert, for one, still insists that Garaudy was forced upon an unwilling department at ministerial insistence.[65]

Garaudy was, in the words of an English commentator, 'formerly witch-finder general, now dispenser of extreme unction, in quick succession champion of Stalin and defender of the Khrushchevite faith'.[66] Until recently, Garaudy had been the classic Stalinist; he was now the promoter of dialogues with Christians and a champion of Marxist humanism.[67] Indeed, he seems to have had a genius for being converted to various causes; after his expulsion from the PCF for 'factionalism' in 1970, he turned to Christianity, and finally to Islam.

Foucault detested him, partly because of his Stalinist past, partly because of his 'soft' humanism. He also had a very poor opinion of his philosophical competence. There was an underlying reason for his hostility to the new appointee. Garaudy was the arch-enemy of Althusser, for whom Foucault had immense affection and admiration. Garaudy was one of those who, in 1965, blocked the publication of *Pour Marx* and *Lire le Capital* by Editions Sociales, the PCF's publishing outlet, and forced Althusser to turn to Maspero. The animosity between Foucault and Garaudy was open and violently expressed. Foucault constantly found fault with him, and seized every opportunity to criticise and humiliate him, preferably in public. On one occasion, Garaudy apparently asked a woman student to translate from Marcus Aurelius's Latin; the text was in Greek, and Foucault was not slow to point out the error.[68] The sociologist Jean Duvignaud claims to have overheard the following exchange: 'Garaudy: "What do you have against me?" Foucault: "I've nothing against you. Just against stupidity." '[69] Some speak of physical violence between the two.[70] Eventually, Garaudy conceded defeat in this campaign of attrition and thankfully accepted a transfer which took him, ironically, to Poitiers. The departure of Garaudy did not put an end to the scandals at Clermont-Ferrand; Foucault himself unleashed a storm of protest from the establishment by appointing Daniel Defert to an assistantship in preference to an older and better-qualified woman candidate. When it came to the brutal wielding of power, Foucault was a match for Pompidou.

Foucault defended his thesis on the afternoon of Saturday 20 May 1961 in the Sorbonne's Louis Liard lecture theatre. A French *soutenance de thèse* is a complex ritual and a difficult rite of passage for the candidate. It is a public event, open to all and announced in the press. For the jury of examiners, it can be a blood sport and the candidate is often the excuse for the settling of old scores. On this occasion, the wood-panelled lecture theatre was crowded. The usual public, some of whom went to every *soutenance* as others go to the theatre, had been joined by a cohort from ENS. Other students, including a young Pierre Macherey, had been urged to attend by Canguilhem. Daniel Defert, who had recently seen the proofs of *Histoire de la folie* arrive at the flat in the rue du Dr Finlay, was sitting next to Jean-Paul Aron.

Given the hybrid nature of Foucault's work, the jury was of necessity interdisciplinary in its composition. Henri Gouhier, who had once agreed to supervise the thesis Foucault planned to write at the Fondation Thiers, presided over it by virtue of academic seniority. The complementary thesis on Kant was examined by Hyppolite and by Maurice de Gandillac, a specialist in medieval and renaissance studies; *Histoire de la folie* by Gouhier, Daniel Lagache, now professor of pathological psychology, and Canguilhem. This was a very prestigious jury indeed.

The *soutenance* began with Foucault's defence of his translation of Kant and of his introduction to the *Anthropology*. Gandillac found that the translation was in need of some revision, and suggested that the introduction should be expanded for publication so as to produce a full critical edition of a neglected text. Hyppolite saw it as an outline for a book on anthropology, and commented that, despite its ostensible subject matter, it owed much more to Nietzsche than to Kant. In the event, the translation was published by Vrin in 1964 with a brief historical introduction; Foucault never attempted to publish his 130-page thesis.

After a short break, it was time for the examination of *Histoire de la folie*. Foucault expounded his theories about reason and unreason, making delicate gestures with his hands that reminded Defert of the gestures of an orchestral conductor and that were striking enough to provoke audible comment from Aron.[71] As he ended his exposition, the candidate ruefully complained that, in order to make audible the voice of the confined, one needed the talent of a poet. Ruffled by this display of false modesty, Canguilhem snapped: 'You have it, *monsieur*.'[72]

Again, there were objections from the jury. Lagache, in particular, challenged many of Foucault's assumptions about the history of medicine and psychiatry, while Gouhier wondered whether Foucault might not be attaching too much value to the experience of madness described by Artaud, Nietzsche and van Gogh. As Foucault would later tell *Le Monde*'s Jean-Paul Weber with an indulgent smile, 'One of the jury's objections was that I had tried to rewrite *In Praise of Folly*.'[73] More seriously, Gouhier challenged the interpretation of Descartes that saw in the words '*Mais quoi, ce sont des fous*' the tracing of a dividing line between reason and unreason, and concluded by admitting that he quite failed to understand what Foucault meant when he defined madness as the 'absence of *oeuvre*'.[74]

Although criticisms were made of both theses, they were not made in an aggressive manner. Gouhier was, he subsequently explained, simply doing what was expected of a historian of philosophy who had been asked to sit on a jury, and Lagache's doubts were voiced with such urbanity as to be quite inoffensive. Macherey, for one, was surprised at the reception given to Foucault: someone who was effectively unknown in France was being treated with respect, even as an equal, by men with the reputation of Hyppolite, and with the famed temper of Canguilhem.[75] Aron was impressed, and later spoke of Canguilhem receiving Foucault into the Sorbonne as Virgil welcomed Dante to Parnassus, 'with the melancholic rapture of an old baron knighting an intrepid gentleman.'[76] At the end of the afternoon, Gouhier officially announced that Foucault had been awarded the degree of *doctorat ès lettres* with an honourable distinction. He was also awarded one of the twenty-four bronze medals given by the Centre Nationale de la Recherche Scientifique to the authors of the most distinguished theses submitted over a three-year period. The ceremony ended with a glass of wine – the traditional *pot de soutenance* (pot being a slang term for a drink).

Five days later, Henri Gouhier submitted his official report on Foucault's *soutenance*. Praising Foucault for his breadth of culture, strength of personality and rich intellect, he wrote:

M. Foucault is more of a philosopher than an exegete or a historian . . . The main thing one recalls of this *soutenance* is the curious contrast between the undeniable talent which everyone recognises in the candidate and the many reservations that were expressed throughout. M. Foucault is certainly a writer, but M. Canguilhem speaks of rhetoric in relation to some passages and the chairman finds him overanxious to create an 'impression'. The erudition is not in doubt, but the chairman cites cases which stem from a spontaneous tendency to go beyond the facts themselves; one has the feeling that there would have been more criticisms of this type, had the jury included an art-historian, a literary historian or an institutional historian. M. Foucault has a real competence in psychology; M. Lagache finds, however, that his information on psychiatry is a little limited and that the pages on Freud are a little cursory. The more one thinks about it, the more one realises that both theses gave rise to many serious criticisms. The fact remains, however, that we are in the presence of a truly original thesis, of a man whose personality, intellectual dynamism and talent for exposition qualify him to teach in higher education. This is why, reservations notwithstanding, the distinction was awarded unanimously.[77]

From the moment that Canguilhem gave *Histoire de la folie* the imprimatur of the Sorbonne, it was a foregone conclusion that Foucault would be awarded his doctorate. It is not, however, surprising that the *soutenance* should have given rise to numerous criticisms of his work. A *soutenance* is, by definition, an agonistic or adversarial process and the raising of objections is part of its *raison d'être*. The fact that the doctorate was awarded despite the jury's criticisms and reservations is indicative of the very nature of Foucault's thesis. It is the overall brilliance that convinces, and not the detail of the demonstration. Had Gouhier's hypothetical historian of literature been present, he might, for instance, have raised the minor objection that when he cites Molière in Part I, Chapter Three, Foucault gives faulty references for his quotations, or that the account of de Sade owes rather more to Blanchot's 'La Raison de Sade' than Foucault's text suggests (and that the given page references are incorrect)[78]. The art historian might have noted that in the Dürer woodcuts illustrating the Apocalypse, the four horsemen do not represent the triumph of folly; they represent the scourging of the world prior to the establishment of the new celestial order.[79] Other specialists would no doubt have raised similar points of detail. Foucault's thesis was not judged on points of detail, but on its overall quality as a startlingly new approach to his topic.

Foucault was proud of his *Histoire de la folie* and was to remain very 'attached to it', though he did admit in 1972, when it was reprinted for the second time, that, if he had to write it again, it would contain 'less rhetoric'.[80] He was also disappointed by its critical reception. Interviewed by an Italian journalist in 1978, he stated that, while people like Blanchot, Klossowski and Barthes welcomed it, on the whole it was greeted with indifference and silence. 'I thought that there was something in my book that ought to have interested those intellectuals who devoted themselves to analyses of social and political systems . . . I was convinced that [it] ought to have been of interest to Marxists, if no one else. But there was simply silence.'[81] The same complaint was voiced in other interviews: 'It has to be said that neither the philosophical community nor even the political community took the slightest interest. None of the journals that are institutionally responsible for registering the slightest upheavals in the world of philosophy paid any attention.'[82]

More generally, Foucault claimed that his early attempts to explore the relationship between power and knowledge were greeted with silence from the intellectual left, perhaps because of a refusal on the part of Marxists to look too closely at the problem of confinement, at the political use of psychiatry.[83] In terms of the institutionalised left, Foucault was right; no PCF journal discussed *Histoire de la folie*, probably for the reasons he outlines. He was, however, using retrospective arguments; there was no particular reason why his book should be seen as a political text in 1961, and he himself said nothing at the time to suggest that it should be read as such. Part of Foucault's disappointment at the reception given to his first major work stemmed from the fact that it had been ignored by mental-health professionals, something which he often complained about in private.[84] It was to be a decade before Foucault's theses had any impact in that milieu.

It is not in fact the case that *Histoire de la folie* was greeted with critical silence. It was quite widely reviewed in relatively favourable terms. It also led to an interview published in *Le Monde*, an unusual accolade for the author of what was, after all, an academic thesis. According to Weber, the interviewer, *Histoire de la folie* had made Foucault a 'known, even famous, philosopher' and he was the archetypal young intellectual, absolute and timeless: 'He has a dialectical smile; he speaks with intonations which seem intended to teach, that is to disturb, and to reassure. A rather absent-minded, misty look in his eyes, absorbed in something else.' The interview, which was to be the first of many, allowed Foucault to restate his thesis in relatively simple terms. Asked about 'influences', he referred briefly to Blanchot, Roussel and Dumézil and then went on:

> Madness cannot be found in a wild state. Madness exists only within a society, it does not exist outside the forms of sensibility which isolate it and the forms of repulsion which exclude it or

capture it. We can therefore say that in the Middle Ages, and then in the Renaissance, madness is present within the social horizon as an aesthetic or day-to-day fact; then, in the eighteenth century – as a result of confinement – madness goes through a period of silence, of exclusion. It has lost the function of manifestation, of revelation, that it had in the epoch of Shakespeare and Cervantes (Lady Macbeth, for instance, begins to speak the truth when she goes mad), and becomes mendacious, derisory. Finally, the twentieth century collars madness, and reduces it to a natural phenomenon bound up with the truth of the world. This positivist appropriation gave rise to, on the one hand, the scornful philanthropy which all psychiatry displays towards the madman and, on the other, the great lyrical protest we find in poetry from Nerval to Artaud, an effort to restore to the experience of madness a depth and a power of revelation which had been destroyed by confinement.[85]

Histoire de la folie appeared in May 1961, but most reviews did not appear until the autumn. August did, however, bring something of a surprise in the form of a remarkably generous letter from Gaston Bachelard. On 1 August, Bachelard finished reading Foucault's 'great book' on the 'sociology of unreason' with great attention and great pleasure: 'Sociologists go great distances to study strange peoples. You have proved to them that we are crossed with savages. You are a real explorer.' Bachelard then explained that he would have liked to send Foucault a study he had written long ago, but could not find it in the 'chaos of notes in which I spend my life'. Finally, he invited Foucault to visit him at home after the summer holidays.[86] There was no time for Foucault to visit Bachelard in the rue de la Montagne Sainte-Geneviève, where he did indeed live in a chaos of mythical proportions; Gaston Bachelard died in October at the age of eighty-six.

The first review appeared in the *Nouvelle Revue Française* in September and was decidedly mixed. The author, Henri Amer, refers favourably to 'a remarkable and fascinating essay', but goes on to refer to Foucault's 'lack of historical qualities' and to his willingness to distort chronology in order to preserve his 'system'. He is also highly critical of the haste with which Foucault 'canonises' Artaud and of what he sees as a failure to admit that not all madness is of artistic interest. The claim that madness exists only within a society is, finally, interpreted as a surrender to a dream of anarchy propped up by an implicit metaphysics.[87]

In the next issue, Maurice Blanchot took up Foucault's defence. It is obviously highly unusual for any journal to review the same book twice, and shows just how much power the reclusive Blanchot could wield. His piece did not appear in the review pages; he incorporates his 'review' into a more general article entitled 'L'Oubli, la déraison'. For Blanchot, the book was rich, insistent and 'almost unreasonable', and the clash brought about between the university and unreason by a doctoral thesis was an added source of pleasure. He agrees with Foucault that the language of madness is to be heard in the literature and art of Goya, de Sade, Artaud and van Gogh and suggests that the enigmatic relationship between thought, impossibility and speech is the basis on which we can begin to understand works simultaneously rejected, accepted and objectified. One author of such works is Bataille,[88] not mentioned in *Histoire de la folie*, but soon to be of considerable interest to Foucault.

For Barthes, writing in *Critique*, Foucault had shaken France's 'intellectual habits': 'This book . . . is something other than a history book, even if this history is conceived audaciously, even if, as is the case, this book is written by a philosopher. So what is it? Something like a cathartic question asked of knowledge.'[89] At the beginning of December, *Le Monde* also published a highly favourable review by Jean Lacroix, who referred to 'an astonishing book, a real masterpiece of a new kind which brings disquiet to the innermost realms of modern culture and which, with its seven hundred pages, has the merit of being accessible to all'.[90] A week later, a piece by the psychoanalyst Octave Mannoni was printed in *Les Temps Modernes*, though Foucault tended in later statements to insist that Sartre's journal ignored his work completely. Mannoni found the book somewhat confused and difficult to read, and referred to the ambiguity of its methodology, which at times views history as the field in which the concepts used by abstract thought are constituted, and at times as the privileged arena for a universal misrecognition.[91]

It was not until the summer of the next year that the final reviews of *Histoire de la folie* appeared. Barthes had suggested that 'Lucien Febvre would have liked this audacious book'. Lucien Febvre was, with Marc Bloch, the founding editor of *Annales* and the patron saint of a distinctively French school of historiography. Two of his heirs certainly did like the audacious book. Robert Mandrou found Foucault's thesis 'impassioned and decisive' and praised this 'orchestra of a writer' for his ability to write simultaneously as a philosopher, a psychologist and a historian.[92] Foucault's reflections on history were a challenge to 'the whole of Western culture' and his book put him in the forefront of contemporary research.[93] In a brief note appended to Mandrou's article, Braudel refers to the pioneering character of 'this magnificent book'. Further praise was forthcoming from Michel Serres in *Mercure de France*. According to Serres, the book was a milestone because of its methodology, its technique and its erudition, because of Foucault's 'miraculous' writing and the 'sumptuous severity' of his descriptions.[94] He draws a parallel with the work of Bachelard:

> M. Bachelard shows that the alchemist does not consider a natural phenomenon so much as the psychological subject himself. The object of that archaic knowledge is nothing more than a projection of the cultural universe itself on to the unconscious subjects of emotions and passions. *Mutatis mutandis*, it is the same with Foucault: in the classical age, the object of archaic psychiatric knowledge is not so much the madman . . . as a projection of the classical cultural universe on to the space of confinement.[95]

Only seven reviews (plus Braudel's 'note') appeared in the first year of the book's life and not all of them were particularly positive. The sales reflected the critical reception; it was not until February 1964 that the initial print run of 3,000 copies was sold out.[96] Foucault's disappointment is understandable, but theses are rarely widely reviewed. Of the favourable critics, most were known to Foucault. Serres was his colleague at Clermont-Ferrand; Barthes was, of course, a personal friend, and rather more than a friend. Lacroix had published *Maladie mentale et personnalité* in his 'Initiation philosophique' series and knew Foucault through Althusser. There may have been an element of personal loyalty in these favourable reviews, though it would be absurd to suggest that loyalty outweighed intellectual conviction. It is more a question of the respective authors' mutual recognition of themselves as belonging to an emerging trend within the human sciences. Blanchot, on the other hand, did not know Foucault personally, though he had read at least part of the text before its publication. Mandrou and Braudel were both strangers.

The fact that Foucault was favourably reviewed in *Critique*, the *NRF* and *Annales* is significant. Of the three, only *Annales* is associated with an academic institution, whereas *Critique* and the *NRF* are independent. They are points at which the academic world intersects with a wider literary and intellectual world. Foucault's escape from the academic ghetto was further facilitated by the *Monde* interview; the daily is a journal of record and a barometer of French intellectual life, but is far from being an academic publication. The *NRF* still represented a tradition of fine writing, though it no longer enjoyed the authority it had in the 1920s and 1930s. In the 1940s *Critique* had been influential in introducing authors like Heidegger to a French audience. In the 1960s, it would become one of the leading journals of the new 'structuralist' criticism. On the strength of *Histoire de la folie*, Foucault was invited to join its editorial board by Jean Piel, who became editor when Bataille died in 1962, and thus became part of the journal that had consecrated his work. The review in *Annales* is the most intriguing of all. It signals a rare moment of agreement between Mandrou and Braudel, and seems to promise acceptance by professional historians. This was not to be. The promise was a false dawn: between 1963 and 1969, not one article in *Annales* so much as mentions Foucault.[97] The review did not spell wholehearted approval, but signalled the beginning of a fraught and complicated relationship with the historians. Foucault's sole contribution to *Annales* was a review-article on Jean-Pierre Richard's *L'Univers imaginaire de Mallarmé*.[98]

Histoire de la folie also attracted some attention outside France. Two academic journals specialising in French studies reviewed it in quite favourable terms, with Yale's John K. Simon finding in it a 'disorientating iconoclasm' which reminded him of the work of Huizinga, and Jacques Ehrmann describing it as an essential work of reference for any future discussions of the cultural heritage of western civilisation.[99] Of rather more significance was the long review which appeared in the *Times Literary Supplement* in October 1961. Foucault was given the accolade of a front-page review, an unusually generous tribute to an unknown French author from Britain's leading literary periodical. After this welcome, a translation must have seemed a distinct possibility, but it did not materialise until 1965.[100] Richard Howard found the book 'difficult and obscure but subtly argued', and devoted most of his review to an exposition of the author's 'highly individual conception of . . . the dialogue which went on century after century as Western societies tried to fix the limits which separated reason from unreason'. Describing Foucault as 'a philosopher-historian with some animus against doctors', he concluded: 'His brilliant book, erudite, but overloaded with antithesis and abstruse generalisations, is the most original contribution that has been made to the wretched story of unreason in the Age of Reason. Carried to a later period, his studies might illuminate problems that have contemporary urgency.'[101]

Howard's prescient allusion to 'contemporary' problems hints at what was to become an important element in the history of Foucault's history of madness. As Robert Castel notes, *Histoire de la folie* can be – and has been – read in two different ways. Initially, it was read as an academic study which belonged to the French tradition of the epistemology of the sciences; after the upheavals of May 1968, it became part of 'an anti-repressive sensibility'.[102] For the moment, it remained an academic work.

6

DEATH AND THE LABYRINTH

FOUCAULT now quickly established himself as a major intellectual figure in France. He was associated with Barthes, acquainted with Robbe-Grillet and, for a while, close to the *Tel Quel* group of avant-garde novelists and critics. Through Barthes, he became acquainted with Pierre Klossowski, writer, artist and translator of, *inter alia*, Hölderlin, Nietzsche and Wittgenstein.[1] He was, in other words, at the centre of an exciting world, one which was much more exciting and open-minded than an academic department in even a good provincial university. It was also a relatively small world in which personal, social and intellectual interests easily merged, and in which it was not difficult to dine with the psychoanalyst André Green, or to meet the actors Simone Signoret and Yves Montand at a private screening of *Mourir à Madrid*.

Foucault was very busy and was publishing widely. The appearance of *Histoire de la folie* marked the beginning of a very productive period for him and he was now active in a number of different areas. *Maladie mentale et personnalité* was reprinted in a revised edition as *Maladie mentale et psychologie* in 1962. While working simultaneously on *Naissance de la clinique* and *Raymond Roussel*, both of which were published in 1963, he began to contribute reviews and articles, mainly on literary topics, to journals like *Critique* and the *Nouvelle Revue Française*. He also published his second – and last – translation, of an essay by Leo Spitzer.[2] He was in demand as a speaker at conferences and colloquia, and took part, for instance, in the May 1962 Royaumont conference on 'Heresy and Society in Pre-Industrial Europe', when he spoke to an enthusiastic audience on 'Religious Deviations and Medical Knowledge'.[3] He was an active member of *Critique*'s editorial board, which usually met over a meal *chez* Piel.[4] One young critic has affectionate memories of Foucault's mode of operation. Serge Fauchereau, now a successful art critic and historian, had submitted an unsolicited manuscript on the American poet e. e. cummings. He received no reply and no comment until the proofs unexpectedly arrived through the post. His first article had been accepted by *Critique*.[5]

Foucault was also becoming, at first in a fairly minor way, an international figure, being invited by the French cultural attaché to lecture on 'Madness and Unreason' in Copenhagen in 1962,[6] and speaking at Saint-Louis in Belgium in 1964.[7] He was also invited to contribute to journals published outside France, his initial contributions to the international scene being an essay which expands the discussion of the water–madness association noted in the first chapter of *Histoire de la folie* in a Swiss medical journal, an afterword to a German version of Flaubert's *La Tentation de Saint Antoine* ('La Bibliothèque fantastique') and a contribution to an exhibition catalogue published in Hamburg.[8]

Just as there had been a Foucault who seemed likely to become a psychologist or psychiatrist, there was now a Foucault who seemed likely to become a major literary critic, to write like Blanchot or even to become Blanchot. His interest in literature was at its most intense in the early 1960s, when he produced a series of literary reviews and articles, as well as a lengthy preface to Rousseau's *Dialogues* which was deemed 'not always clear' by its one academic reviewer.[9] Some of the articles are, inevitably, of little import and of only circumstantial interest. Foucault reviewed, for instance, Jean-Edern Hallier's first novel, *Les Aventures d'une jeune fille* (1963). Hallier was one of the founders of *Tel Quel* and, for a time, a friend of Foucault's; the review was a gesture of friendship rather than a major statement.[10]

Taken together, the articles from this period represent a considerable body of work, but until very recently they had received relatively little attention from Foucault's critics.[11] If they were to be anthologised and read in isolation from the rest of Foucault's work, there would be little or no indication that their author was a professional teacher of psychology and philosophy in Clermont-Ferrand. Only one short review reveals Foucault's interest in the history of science, namely a short piece on Alexandre Koyré's *La Révolution astronomique, Copernic, Kepler, Borelli*.[12] Only one review-article deals with a psychological topic: it discusses Jean Laplanche's psychobiographical study of Hölderlin, and in it Foucault displays considerably more knowledge of the poet and his work than in *Histoire de la folie*, where the name 'Hölderlin' is little more than an emblematic cipher. Foucault expresses little sympathy for most traditional writing on 'relations between art and madness'; Laplanche's text is one of the few that should be saved from a dynasty 'without glory'.[13] Clinical psychology, for its part, is dismissed with a contempt worthy of Canguilhem as 'an eclecticism without concepts',[14] while the vast majority of the 'psychological race' are said to gravitate in accordance with 'the law of the greatest platitude possible' and are scornfully dismissed for their lingering belief that 'the involuntary fasting of rats' provides 'an infinitely fertile epistemological model'.[15]

In terms of their subject matter, the articles range from a review essay devoted to Crébillon *fils*'s *Les Egarements du coeur et de l'esprit* (1736–38) and a remarkably obscure novel by one Reveroni de Saint-Cyr (1767–1829), to a piece on works by members of the *Tel Quel* group, and from a review of Roger Laporte's novel *La Veille* to a discussion of Jean-Pierre Richard's *L'Univers imaginaire de Mallarmé*.[16] In many ways, they reveal an aesthetic similar to that hinted at in *Histoire de la folie* and further explore both the relationship between *folie* and *oeuvre* and the contention that 'every literary work belongs to the indefinite, undefined [*indéfini*] murmuring of the written'.[17] Similar formulations occur throughout the articles of this period. Thus, in the one article he published in *Tel Quel*, Foucault insists:

> In our day, writing has come infinitely closer to its source. That is, to that disturbing noise which, from the depths of language, announces, as soon as one lends it an ear for a moment, that against which we seek shelter and that to which we simultaneously address ourselves . . . an *oeuvre* whose meaning is to close in on itself so that its glory alone speaks, is no longer possible.[18]

Whereas literature had once been a matter of rhetoric, a discourse in which every figure referred ultimately to some primal Word, it has now entered Borges's Library of Babel where

> everything that can be said has already been said . . . And yet, above all these words and covering them, a rigorous, sovereign language, speaking them and, truth to tell, giving birth to them; and this language itself is supported by death as it is at the moment when he falls into the pit of the infinite Hexagon that the most lucid (and therefore the last) of the librarians reveals that even the infinity of language is multiplied to infinity, repeating itself endlessly in the reduplicated figures of the Same.[19]

Foucault's aesthetic is resolutely modernist, and defines Flaubert as the first modern. Flaubert is the literary equivalent to Manet; the one paints with constant reference to the museum, the other writes with constant reference to the library.[20] Modernism is, in other words, reflexive and self-referential. It is also anti-realist and anti-humanist.

The articles also reveal, however, some rather unexpected aspects to Foucault's literary erudition. The article on Crébillon and Reveroni is one example. *Les Egarements du coeur et de l'esprit*, a 'libertine' novel with a delicately erotic tone, had been reprinted in 1961 in an elegant edition prefaced by Etiemble, and was an obvious subject for review. Foucault cites *Pauliska* in its first edition, and could have discovered this novel of terror only in a library, probably the Bibliothèque Nationale. References to novels of terror are frequent in his writings of this period, and his taste for them is no doubt explicable in terms of their generic similarity to de Sade. Foucault's article begins: 'The scene takes place in Poland, that is to say, everywhere.'[21] This is a parody of Alfred Jarry's speech introducing the first riotous performance of *Ubu Roi* in 1896 ('The action takes place . . . in Poland, that is Nowhere') and the article also contains references to Jarry's *Le Surmâle* (1902), a novel dedicated to the proposition that 'the act of love is of no importance, since it can be performed indefinitely'.[22] Ultimately, the proposition is demonstrated both by a pair of human lovers and by a love-making machine. It is the machine that supports the Jarry–Reveroni association: in *Pauliska*, the heroine's lover is captured by a band of Amazons who construct a strange mechanical statue of the young man, and in a reworking of the Pygmalion myth one of the women falls in love with it.[23] Even so, the presence of Jarry is somewhat unexpected here. Many of the works discussed by Foucault are austere in their self-conscious modernity, yet Jarry introduces a note of outrageous comedy. One of the ancestors of surrealism, he is also a reminder that Foucault's literary concerns were not totally alien to those of André Breton and his allies, and that the seriousness with which he elaborates a modernist aesthetic had not destroyed his sense of humour.

A further gust of laughter is provided by a very short piece contributed by Foucault to the *NRF*, not a journal one usually associates with frivolity. Its subject is Jean-Pierre Brisset, author of a number of works published in Agen at his own expense in the late nineteenth century, and artisan of two main theses: Latin does not exist (it was merely an artificial code used by bandits to confuse common mortals), and Man is descended from the frog. The latter thesis is demonstrated philologically.[24] Foucault does not say how or when he came to discover Brisset, but the most likely explanation is that he read Breton's *Anthologie de l'humour noir* of 1939, where Brisset is described as an important link between Jarry's 'pataphysics' (the science of imaginary solutions), Dali's critical paranoia, and the work of Raymond Roussel and Marcel Duchamp.[25] Foucault presents brief extracts from Brisset's writings, and prefaces them with some remarks of his own:

> Brisset belongs to . . . that family of shades who inherited what linguistics left in escheat during its formation. In their pious, avid hands, speculations about the origins of language that had been denounced as rubbish became a thesaurus of literary speech . . . Brisset is perched at an extreme point of linguistic delirium, where the arbitrary is accepted as the cheerful and unbreakable law of the world; each word is broken down into phonetic elements, each of which is equivalent to a word; in its turn that word is no more than a contracted sentence; word by word, the waves of discourse spread out into a primal swamp, into the great, simple elements of language and the world: water, sea, mother [*mer, mère*], sex.[26]

Foucault's short presentation of Brisset led to a gradual revival of interest in this mad philologist or etymologist. In 1970, he prefaced a new edition of *La Grammaire logique* and it is largely thanks to him that it is possible to read Brisset at all.[27] The comic appeal aside, Brisset has proved to be of considerable interest to Lacanian psychoanalysts, who find in his work an equivalent to Schreber's *Ursprächer*. Foucault too finds an *Ur*-element at work in Brisset: a language which exists before man.

> Words are fragments of discourses . . . modalities of statements which have been frozen and reduced to being neutral. Before there were words, there were sentences; before there was a vocabulary, there were statements; before there were syllables and the elementary arrangement of sounds, there was the indefinite murmur of all that was being said. Long before there was language, someone was speaking [*on parlait*]. But what about? What, if not about man, who did not yet exist, because he had no language; if not about his formation, of the slow process that wrenched him out of his animality, about the swamp from which his tadpole existence was emerging with difficulty? And so, beneath the words of our language, we can hear sentences . . . spoken by men who did not yet exist and who spoke of their future birth.[28]

This is the language of unreason *par excellence*, the constant murmuring in a dream of something that is perpetually out of reach, but also perpetually present.

The major literary text of this period is of course *Raymond Roussel*.

This is the only book by Foucault to be devoted to a literary topic. It is therefore somewhat apart from the rest of his work, and its very apartness means that it has received relatively little critical attention.[29] Its neglect was a strange source of satisfaction to Foucault, who told his American translator Charles Ruas: 'No one has paid much attention to this book, and I'm glad; it's my secret affair.'[30]

Raymond Roussel (1877–1933) was one of French literature's great eccentrics. Enormously rich, he travelled the world but rarely left his hotel room or his cabin. He financed the publication of his own writings and the staging of his own plays, which were invariably expensive failures accompanied by riots among the audience. His writings excited little interest in his lifetime, though some of the surrealists – notably Breton in his *Anthologie de l'humour noir* – appreciated them. For much of his life Roussel suffered from serious neurotic illnesses provoked (or at least triggered), it is thought, by the spectacular failure of *La Doublure* (1897), a long verse-novel, written in alexandrines, about a stand-in actor. He was treated by Pierre Janet, who failed to see any literary talent in him and described him as *un pauvre petit malade*; Roussel is the 'Martial' whose case is discussed in the first volume of *De l'Angoisse à l'extase* (1926). Roussel was homosexual, though little is known about his sexual tastes or activities, and became totally dependent on barbiturates in his later years. He died in Palermo, where his body was found in his hotel room, lying on a mattress which he had – presumably with great difficulty, given his physical state – pushed up against the door connecting his room to that of his travelling companion. The door, habitually left unlocked, was locked. Whether Roussel was murdered or committed suicide has never been determined. At the time of his death, he had been planning to go to Kreuzlingen, where he had hoped to consult Ludwig Binswanger.

Foucault's fascination with Roussel grew out of the chance encounter in Corti's bookshop in 1957. Roussel's works had long been out of print, but Foucault gradually succeeded in acquiring first editions. Not having sold well in the first place, these were not great rarities and could still be found without too much effort at the beginning of the 1960s.[31] There had for some years been a growing interest in Roussel. The first book appeared in 1953, but it was Michel Leiris's 1954 article in *Critique* that really marked the revival of interest.[32] Leiris's father had been a financial adviser to Roussel's father; the two men knew each other slightly, and Leiris was the main source for biographical information on Roussel. Like many others before him Foucault consulted Leiris, whom he had met through Jean Duvignaud, for information, but was disappointed to find that 'everything he had to say about Roussel was contained in his articles';[33] Leiris was not, however, impressed by Foucault's study and claimed that it ascribed philosophical ideas to someone who had none.[34] Comments from Robbe-Grillet, in the meantime, had added a contemporary interest. Foucault himself first refers to Roussel in *Histoire de la folie*, where, like Diderot's 'Neveu de Rameau' and Artaud, he is one of the emblems of 'the experience of unreason'.[35]

Foucault has described the circumstances of *Raymond Roussel*'s publication. He had originally planned to publish a short article on Roussel, in *Critique*, but he was so in love with his subject that he shut himself away for two months and, to his own surprise, produced a book.

> One day I received a telephone call from an editor asking what I was working on. 'Oh, I'm working on a book on Raymond Roussel.' 'Would you let me read it when you've completed it? Will it take you a long time?' For once in my life I, who take such a long time with my books, could answer proudly: 'I'll be finished with it very soon.' 'When?' he asked. I answered: 'In eleven or twelve minutes', an answer that was completely justified by the fact that I had started typing the last page. That's the story of this book.[36]

Foucault's account is not entirely accurate; an early version of the first chapter of *Raymond Roussel* had already appeared in a literary journal in the summer of 1962, and it was therefore no secret that he was working on Roussel.[37]

Foucault does not identify the editor who telephoned him, but it was almost certainly Georges Lambrichs, responsible for the 'Le Chemin' collection. Foucault thus became a Gallimard author almost by accident. Jean Piel would have been only too happy to publish *Raymond Roussel* in the 'Critique' series he edited for Minuit, but could not make an offer in time.[38] Gallimard's eagerness to publish Foucault's study was not entirely disinterested. Its appearance coincided with that of a new edition of Roussel's *Locus Solus*, which was intended to be the first volume in a comprehensive series of reprints. Foucault immediately became involved in the campaign to promote Roussel: the fifth chapter of *Raymond Roussel* was published in the *NRF*, and the short piece he contributed to *Le Monde* in August 1964 was clearly intended to promote both *Locus Solus* and his own study.[39] Gallimard's project was unexpectedly frustrated. Acting on somewhat uncertain legal grounds, Roussel's nephew Michel Ney, Duke of Enchingen, sold the rights to

Pauvert and had the Gallimard edition impounded.[40] The complete works of Raymond Roussel were therefore issued in scarlet covers by Pauvert, a small publishing house known at this time mainly for its editions of de Sade and assorted erotica.

Raymond Roussel is in many ways a very personal book, and the product of a love affair. Foucault told Ruas that this 'is by far the book I wrote most easily, with the greatest pleasure, and most rapidly; because I usually write very slowly, I have to rewrite endlessly, and finally there are countless corrections'.[41] The speed with which it was written shows; although Foucault had read the available literature on Roussel and cites Ferry, Janet and Leiris, the text makes no concessions to the reader in that no bibliographical information is provided. One has the impression of reading a sequence of personal explorations which were written for subjective purposes rather than in order to convince a reader. Foucault was well aware of this: 'I imagine it must be a complex work to read, because I belong to that category of people who, when they write spontaneously, write in a slightly convoluted manner.'[42]

And, as Gilles Deleuze suggests, the book probably has a great deal to do with Foucault's own sense of identity or non-identity.[43] Foucault suggests that Roussel's fiction has something in common with Leiris's *La Règle du jeu*, which is an extraordinarily intimate exploration of how personal mythologies combine to create the unity of an individual ego.[44] Leiris slowly gathers together his own identity from 'so many insignificant things, so many fantastic *états civils . . .* as though absolute memory slept in the folds of words, with chimeras that never quite died'. Roussel opens out those folds 'so as to find in them an unbreathable void, a rigorous absence of being which he can have at his sovereign disposal, with which he can fashion figures with no kin, no species'.[45] Given Foucault's constant refusal to have an identity thrust upon him and his scorn for the bureaucrats of the *état civil*, Roussel's 'absence of being' must have had a considerable appeal.

At a less speculative level, it is clear that the fascination that Roussel exercised over everyone from the surrealists to Foucault stems mainly from his method of composition, which is described in the posthumously published *Comment j'ai écrit certains de mes livres* (1935). His novels, and the plays adapted from them, are structured around a complex wordplay. The best-known example is as follows. The sentence '*les lettres du blanc sur les bandes du vieux billard*' ('the letters in white around the edges of the old billiard table') can very easily be transformed into '*les lettres du blanc sur les bandes du vieux pillard*' ('the white man's letters about the old plunderer's gangs'). If the shift from /b/ to /p/ is ignored, we have 'a series of identical words saying two different things'.[46] The first sequence of words was constructed from random letters by the characters of a story about a group of friends amusing themselves on a wet afternoon. The difference between it and the second generates a narrative about a white man who is shipwrecked and captured by a black robber-king, and who describes his experiences in letters written to his wife.

The original short story, *Parmi les noirs*, then generated *Impressions d'Afrique* (1910), the best known of all Roussel's works. Here, a further formal game commences. The novel contains twenty-four chapters, and begins *in medias res* with the grandiose ceremonies held to mark the coronation of the Emperor of Ejur. In the fourth edition of the novel, printed in 1932, a pasted slip advises any reader unfamiliar with Roussel to begin at Chapter X, which starts '*Le 15 mars précedent . . .*' ('On 15 March the previous year . . .'). Anyone who follows that advice will read a novel which is chronologically coherent and concerns the adventures of a shipwrecked company of musicians, artists, circus performers and bankers who have been held to ransom. While they wait for the return of the envoy who will bring the ransom, they spend their time organising the gala performance with which the novel opens. The reader who takes Roussel's advice will, on the other hand, deprive himself of the pleasure of seeing the puzzle finally make sense. Foucault concisely describes Roussel's *procédure* as follows: 'Take a sentence at random – from a song, a poster, a visiting card – break it down into its phonetic elements and use them to reconstruct other words which have to be used as a set theme.'[47]

Roussel's books abound in language games and wonderfully inventive machines. In *Impressions d'Afrique*, for example, an engineer carefully constructs a loom [*métier*] which functions on the principle of the water-wheel by scooping up water in its vanes [*aubes*]. He wanted to find, it is explained in *Comment j'ai écrit certains de mes livres*, a profession [*métier*] which required him to rise at dawn [*aube*].[48] The construction of the loom illustrates Roussel's 'procedure' in miniature: the difference and similarity between two words (*métier*: loom/profession; *aubes*: dawns/vanes) generates part of a narrative.

For Foucault, the *metier à aubes* is a figurative representation of the workings of the entire text, illustrating the self-referentiality of the modern. The river generates movement, just as the flow of language generates the *procédure*. The vanes dip into the water and drive the mechanisms that weave a complex pattern of threads. Shuttles move spontaneously, functioning as inductor words which spring from the dense fabric of language, and the woven thread acts as a connecting thread linking the river of language to the stretched canvas of the text. Gradually, the loom weaves an image: that of the Flood and then that of the Ark, of the threat of death and of rebirth.[49] Significantly, the loom is supported by a locked box which resembles a coffin: death is at the heart of the entire process.

What is at work here is 'a reduplication of language, which, beginning with a simple nucleus, moves away from itself and constantly gives birth to other figures (proliferation of distance, a void opening up under the feet of the double, a labyrinthine growth of corridors which are both similar and different)'.[50] The text becomes a labyrinth of words and, as Foucault points out, at the centre of a labyrinth there lurks a minotaur.[51]

Roussel's machines are always described with extraordinary precision. The description of the *métier à aubes*, for instance, is in part based upon technical illustrations from encyclopedias. Its almost clinical accuracy recalls the manner in which Jules Verne, an author greatly admired by Roussel and referred to by Foucault as having written about 'knowledge's negentropy',[52] depicts his inventions. And it is Roussel's precision of description that provides the link with the objectivism of Robbe-Grillet: In both Roussel and Robbe-Grillet, description is not language's fidelity to its object, but the perpetually renewed birth of an infinite relationship between words and things.'[53] The wordplay and the fantastic humour mask something universal. 'Like any literary language', Roussel's language is 'the violent destruction of everyday hackneyed clichés, but it remains indefinitely in the hieratic gesture of that murder'.[54] It is also a language that exists within the space 'between *folie* and *oeuvre*, a place at once full and empty, invisible and inevitable, the place of their mutual exclusion'.[55]

Raymond Roussel appeared in May 1963. Foucault also published another book that month: *Naissance de la clinique*. It was at Foucault's insistence that they appeared simultaneously. To achieve simultaneity involved negotiations with Gallimard and PUF: the cover of *Naissance de la clinique* describes *Ramond Roussel* as 'forthcoming', and its publication was slightly delayed to acccommodate Foucault's wishes. The insistence that the two books should appear together was not merely a self-conscious display of polymathy; it was a strong hint that *Raymond Roussel* and *Naissance de la clinique*, apparently so dissimilar, had something in common, and contradicts Foucault's later claim that *Raymond Roussel* 'doesn't have a place in the sequence of my books'.[56]

It is sometimes claimed that *Naissance de la clinique* was commissioned by Georges Canguilhem,[57] but this was not the case. Canguilhem was indeed delighted to be able to publish it in the short-lived 'Galien' collection ('History and Philosophy of Biology and Medicine') he edited for Presses Universitaires de France, which also included his own *Formation du concept de réflexe* and a reprint of Claude Bernard's classic *Principes de médecine expérimentale*. He strenuously denies, however, having had anything to do with its genesis. Like the editor at Gallimard, he was presented by Foucault with a finished manuscript, and had been involved in no prior discussions of its content.[58]

Precisely where and when the research that went into *Naissance de la clinique* was carried out is not known, but it is probable that it overlapped with that undertaken for *Histoire de la folie*. It would be difficult, if not impossible, either to verify or invalidate Foucault's claim to have read every book 'with any methodological importance' produced between 1790 and 1820, but a bibliography listing almost two hundred items, many of them running to several volumes, is an eloquent testimony to the researcher's industry. It is also a testimony to the extent of his ambitions: 'One should read everything, study everything. In other words, one should have at one's disposal the general archive of an epoch at a given moment.'[59] *Naissance de la clinique* is in many ways Foucault's most technically specialist book, and is probably unlikely to appeal to the general reader, not the least of its difficulties being its use of medical vocabulary and Foucault's uncompromising decision to cite works like Sydenham's *Observationes medicae* and Morgagni's *De Sedibus et causis morborum* in the original Latin. Yet, despite its subject matter, it has a surprising amount in common with Foucault's more literary texts.

The preface opens with a beautifully austere sentence whose quasi-legalistic tone tends to be lost in any English version: 'This book is about space, language and death; it is about the gaze' ['*Il est question dans ce livre de l'espace, du langage et de la mort: il est question du regard*]. Two vignettes follow. In the mid-eighteenth century, a doctor named Pomme treated a hysteric by making her take 'baths for ten to twelve hours a day, for ten whole months'. After this period of treatment against the desiccation of the nervous system and the heat that sustained it, he saw 'membranous portions similar to pieces of wet parchment . . . peel off with some pain, and be passed daily with the urine, and the right ureter peel away and be passed in the same way'. The same happened with the intestines, as their internal tunics were lost and passed through the rectum. The oesophagus, the arterial trachea and the tongue then peeled, 'and the patient rejected the various pieces either by vomiting or by expectoration'. Less than a century later, Bayle observed a lesion of the brain and the 'false membranes' often noted in patients suffering from chronic meningitis: 'Their outer surface, which is next to the arachnoidian layer of the dura mater, adheres to this layer, sometimes very loosely, in which case they can be easily separated, sometimes very firmly and tightly, in which case it is sometimes very difficult to detach them. Their internal surface is merely contiguous with the arachnoid, and is not attached to it . . .'[60]

The difference between the two vignettes is total. Pomme is working with the old myths of nervous pathology; Bayle with a precision of observation that is not completely unfamiliar to the modern reader. 'What has changed is the silent configuration in which language finds support, the situational or postural relationship between what is speaking and what is being spoken about.'[61] More succinctly, the old question 'What is wrong with you?', which once inaugurated the dialogue between doctor and patient, gives way to a different question in which we recognise the principles of clinical medicine: 'Where does it hurt?'[62] The transition from one to the other is Foucault's subject matter:

> In order to grasp the mutation in discourse at the moment when it took place, we must no doubt investigate something other than thematic contents or logical modalities, and address ourselves to that region where 'words' and 'things' have not yet been separated, where ways of saying and ways of seeing still cleave together at the level of language. We must question the primal distribution of the visible and the invisible insofar as it is linked to the division between what is stated and what remains unsaid: the articulation of medical language and its object will then appear in a single figure. But there is no priority for the person who asks no retrospective questions; only the spoken structure of the perceived – that full space from whose hollow language takes its volume and size – deserves to be brought into the deliberately indifferent light of day. We must position ourselves, and remain, once and for all, at the level of the basic *spatialisation* and *verbalisation* of the pathological, where the loquacious gaze that the doctor lets fall on the venomous heart of things is born, and communes with itself.[63]

A great deal could be said about this passage. The notion of grasping a division as it is taking place in the moment of its institution is reminiscent of *Histoire de la folie*'s attempt to grasp the primal caesura that 'establishes the distance between reason and non-reason',[64] whereas the reference to 'words' and 'things' obviously looks forward to the title of *Les Mots et les choses*. The version of the first chapter of *Raymond Roussel* published in *Lettre ouverte* was entitled 'Saying and seeing in Raymond Roussel', and the 'full space in whose hollow language . . .' is a variant on Foucault's discussion of the 'solar hollow' that is 'the space of Roussel's language, the void from which he speaks'.[65] In the context of a book on the history of medicine, references to 'the pathological' inevitably recall Canguilhem, whereas those to a primal distribution of visible and invisible are reminiscent of Merleau-Ponty; the relationship between visibility and invisibility is one of the themes of *La Phénoménologie de la perception*.

The subtitle – 'The Archaeology of the Medical Gaze' – introduces a further dimension to this textual labyrinth. Foucault had little philosophical sympathy indeed for Sartre, but it is impossible for any French writer to employ the expression 'the gaze' [*le regard*] without making tacit reference to a central chapter of *L'Etre et le néant*'s discussion of the question of being-for-others: '*Le Regard*'. This is clearly no straightforward essay in the history of medicine.

Naissance de la clinique was described by its author as being 'an attempt at method in the domain, so confused, so little structured and so badly structured, of the history of ideas',[66] but he was subsequently to dismiss completely the very notion of a history of ideas. What Foucault actually understands at this point by a 'history of ideas' becomes slightly clearer when he refers to 'the concept of fever' in the eighteenth century.[67] The use of 'concept' here signals the proximity of Canguilhem and, at a slightly further remove, of Jean Cavaillès, logician, Resistance fighter and victim of the Gestapo, for whom 'it is not a philosophy of consciousness, but a philosophy of the concept that can give a doctrine of science', and according to whom 'the theory of science is an *a priori*, not anterior to science, but the soul of science'.[68] It would be an error to identify Foucault too closely with Cavaillès, as the latter's work is grounded in the pure phenomenology of Husserl, but Foucault too is looking for the 'historical and concrete *a priori* of the medical gaze'.[69] Unlike Cavaillès or Canguilhem, Foucault does not define his *a priori* in purely logical or conceptual terms, and his history is at least in part an institutional and sociological history, but his very vocabulary signals his definite awareness of working within the tradition of Bachelard, Canguilhem and Cavaillès. Foucault is concerned with the conditions

in which medicine emerged as a clinical science, 'conditions which
defined, together with its historical possibility, the domain of its
experience and the structure of its rationality. They form its concrete *a
priori*.'[70] Such statements inevitably have a Kantian ring to them, and
are a reminder of Foucault's self-inscription within a 'critical' tradition.

The archaeology of the medical gaze is not, then, an empirical
history. Nor is it a history that is likely to give any comfort to believers
in the inevitability of linear progress from Aristotle to Marie François
Xavier Bichat (1771–1802) and in the gradual process of enlightenment. The transition from the observations of Pomme to those of Bayle
is not necessarily one centred upon a conflict between 'young
knowledge and old beliefs'. The conflict is one between 'two figures of
knowledge'.[71] Similarly, Foucault stoutly asserts that he is not writing
against one form of medicine and in favour of another: this is 'a
structural study which attempts to decipher, within the density of the
historical, the conditions of history itself'.[72] *Naissance de la clinique* does
not provide, and does not set out to provide, the basis for relative
judgements of value.

Like *Maladie mentale*, *Naissance de la clinique* was revised for republication, though not so drastically as its predecessor. Most of the revisions
can be more conveniently discussed in the context of Foucault's
relationship with structuralism, as exemplified by *Les Mots et les choses*.
In the 1972 edition, the sentence cited is altered to read: 'a study which
attempts to disentangle, from within the density of discourse, the
conditions of its history'. One of Foucault's most perceptive readers
convincingly suggests that the change indicates the destruction of
evidence that, in 1963, the Hegelian theme of grounding history and
reason within the development of history, as interpreted by
Hyppolite, still exercised a 'lingering attraction'.[73] If Bernauer is
correct, the alteration of the text is further evidence of Foucault's
marked tendency to obliterate elements of his past in order to redefine
himself in terms of his concerns of the moment, and thereby to frustrate
attempts to situate him in absolute terms through the exploitation of an
interplay between identity and non-identity.

To return to the 1963 text. The *clinique* of the title is a complex entity,
and one which poses a translation problem: it designates both 'clinical
medicine' and the teaching institution that replaced the faculties of the
Renaissance and still earlier periods. In both senses it is distinct from the
hôpital which, like its English cognate, was originally a charitable
institution caring for the indigent as well as the sick. Its birth signals a
major shift in the understanding of illness, in the very concept of disease.

Foucault begins by remarking that our perception of the body as the natural 'space of the origin and distribution of disease', as a space determined by the 'anatomical atlas', is merely one of the various ways in which medicine has spatialised illness.[74] It owes a great deal to the *clinique* of the nineteenth century and to the emergence of pathological anatomy, and the birth of the *clinique* can best be understood by looking at what went before it. Before it was localised in the body, disease was organised hierarchically into families, genera and species. Hence the relevance of the advice proffered to physicians by Gilibert in 1772: 'Never treat a disease without being sure of its species.'[75] From Sauvage's *Nosologie* of 1761 to Pinel's *Nosographie* of 1798, medical perception was dominated by a theory of species inscribed in a table which recorded neither a sequence of cause and effect nor a chronological series of events nor yet its visible trajectory through the body. That perception was defined by a space with what Foucault terms a horizontal and a vertical axis. The vertical axis is that of a temporal sequence, which may or may not actually be observable in an individual case: a fever may occur in a single episode or in several episodes. The horizontal axis is that of analogy and resemblance: catarrh is to the throat what dysentery is to the intestine. It is within this space and along these axes of perception that 'disease, emerging before the gaze, inserts its own characteristics into a living organism'.[76] Analysis and diagnosis are so abstractly structured that the individual patient actually becomes a potential obstacle to the perception of the formal class or species.

Foucault has identified or defined two levels of spatialisation: a primary spatialisation which locates disease within a conceptual configuration, and a secondary configuration relating disease to the body. The latter is an attempt to answer the question: 'How can the flat, homogeneous space of classes become visible within a geographical system of masses differentiated by their volume and distance? How can a disease defined by its *place* in a family be characterised by its *seat* in an organism?'[77] Foucault then completes his triangulation of the space of medical perception by introducing 'tertiary spatialisation', a term designating 'the body of gestures by which disease is, in a given society, medically invested, isolated, divided up into closed and privileged regions, or distributed across curative *milieux*'.[78]

Such, basically, is the classificatory perception of disease. The emergence of the *clinique* requires the construction of a new *a priori*, the formation of a 'completely structured nosographic field'.[79] It is no longer enough to 'situate a symptom in a disease, an illness in a specific set [*ensemble*], and to orient the latter within the general map of the pathological world'.[80] The emergence of the new space implies the recognition that

the place where knowledge is formed is no longer the pathological garden in which God distributed species; it is a generalised medical consciousness, diffused in space and time, open and mobile, bound up with each individual existence, but also with the collective life of the nation, always alert to the infinite domain in which illness betrays, in its various aspects, its great, massive form.[81]

It is within this space that the body of disease and the body of the sick man coincide exactly, that the configuration of disease is superimposed upon the body. This is a space in which the medical gaze is paramount: visible lesions and coherent pathological forms coincide and can be read by the experienced eye.

The birth of the clinic was not a purely epistemological event; Foucault's tertiary spatialisation plays a crucial role in its appearance. During the Revolutionary period in particular, socio-political factors combined with the epistemological demands of developments in medicine. The old classificatory medicine, centred upon a faculty of doctors intent upon discovering pathological essences in the garden, is challenged by teaching institutions demanding a free field of enquiry; the abolition of the privileges of the Ancien Régime was essential to the establishment of a more open society. The needs of the revolutionary armies, and the regular decimation of the physicians in their ranks, made the improved and accelerated training of doctors a military and political necessity.

Nor is the emergence of the *clinique* purely a matter of perception. It is also a matter of language. No pathological essence lies beyond the symptom; the symptom becomes a signifier of illness, and illness is no more than a collection of symptoms. Here, it is Condillac who is the important figure: the signifying structure of the symptom transposes into clinical practice a conceptual configuration elaborated in discursive form by the *Essai sur l'origine des connaissances humaines* of 1746.[82] Within clinical thought, the symptom plays a role analogous to that of the 'language of action' that is, according to Condillac, the original form of linguistic communication. The language of action is a direct manifestation of instinct, the symptom is illness in its manifest form. There is now an isomorphism or formal homology between the structure of disease and that of the language which identifies it:

In the medicine of species, the nature of the disease and its description could not coincide without an intermediary moment, namely the 'table', with its two dimensions; in the *clinique* being *spoken* and *being seen* communicate from the outset in the manifest truth of the disease of which it is, precisely, the whole *being*. Disease exists only within the element of the visible and, therefore of the stateable [*énonçable*].[83]

This configuration is governed by the myth of a pure gaze which is also pure language, of a speaking eye.

The clinical case is, however, a surface gaze. Hence the importance of Bichat's terse advice to the medical profession: 'Open up a few corpses.' The gradual separating-out of pathological anatomy as a discipline made it possible to follow that advice. The medical gaze now begins to focus on death. Death is now asked to account for illness and, by extension, life itself. Life is no longer the form of an organism; the organism is the visible form of life insofar as it resists all that is not life and all that opposes life:

Bichat did more than free medicine from the fear of death. He integrated death into a technical and conceptual *ensemble* in which it acquires its specific characteristics and its value as an experience. So much so that the great break in the history of western medicine dates precisely from the moment when clinical experience became the anatomo-clinical gaze.[84]

The break marks the beginning of a new transition. Now that the space of disease can, thanks to anatomy and dissection, be seen to be the space of the organism itself, the medicine of illnesses has had its day and begins to give way to the medicine of pathological reactions. The concrete *a priori* for a modern medical gaze has emerged.

Despite its austerity, *Naissance de la clinique* is shot through with some surprisingly erotic themes relating to language and death. Discussing the perceptual and epistemological structures of clinical anatomy, Foucault notes that the hidden element takes on the form and rhythm of the hidden content, which means that it is in the very nature of the *veil* to be transparent and then adds in a footnote: 'This structure does not date from the beginning of the nineteenth century; far from it: in its general outline [*silhouette*], it dominates forms of knowledge and eroticism in Europe from the mid-eighteenth century onwards, and it prevails until the end of the nineteenth. I will attempt to study it later.'[85] No such attempt was made, but Foucault does briefly explore this

theme in his essay on Crébillon and Reveroni: 'The veil is that thin
surface that chance, haste or modesty have placed and try to keep in
place, but its line of force is irremediably dictated by the verticality of
falling. The veil unveils thanks to fatality; that of its light fabric and its
supple form.'[86] The structure of the veil is also that of transvestism:
'Like the veil, tranvestism conceals and betrays; like the mirror, it
presents reality in an illusion which masks reality while proffering it . . .
it is an anti-nature which is mimicked and therefore warded off.'[87] A
footnote to a discussion of anatomy leads back to the world of Roussel's
labyrinths.

The title of the Crébillon article – 'Such a cruel knowledge' – is
actually used by Foucault in his description of the innovations made by
Bichat (1771–1802) who was, he notes, a near-contemporary of de Sade
(1740–1814), the man who 'suddenly introduced, in the most discursive language, eroticism and death, its inevitable point'. In the space
opened up by Bichat, 'knowing life is granted only to a cruel, reductive
and infernal knowledge which desires it only when it is dead. The gaze
which envelops, caresses, examines and anatomises the most individual flesh and lists its secret bites is that fixed, attentive, slightly
dilated gaze which, from the heights of death, has already condemned
life.'[88] This is not the gaze of a living eye, but 'the gaze of an eye which
has seen death. A great white eye that unravels life.'[89]

Foucault's archaeology of the medical gaze is also the history of an eye,
and it relates to a different story about an eye. In the autumn of 1963,
Foucault contributed a major essay to a special issue of *Critique*
published in homage to Georges Bataille, who died in July 1962.
Hommage à Georges Bataille was an important stage in the modern
canonisation of Bataille. Leiris, Blanchot and Klossowski all contributed, as did Barthes, with his vitally important 'La Métaphore de
l'oeil'.[90] Foucault's contribution was 'Préface à la transgression'.[91]

'Préface à la trangression' is a densely written exploration of certain
of Bataille's major themes and a continuation of Foucault's own
explorations. Although Foucault provides no detailed references to
specific texts, it is obvious that he was familiar with much of Bataille's
work; the major points of reference are the short novels *Eponine* (1949),
Madame Edwarda (1937), *Le Bleu du ciel* (1957) and the essays
L'Expérience intérieure (1943) and *Les Larmes d'Eros* (1961). The most
important text is, however, the notorious *Histoire de l'oeil*.[92] Despite his
obvious interest in Bataille, Foucault had never made any attempt to
meet him; like Blanchot and Char, he was someone admired from afar.

Foucault's 'Préface' was his first act of homage to Bataille; the second was made seven years later when he prefaced the first volume of the *Oeuvres complètes* with the words: 'Now we know it: Bataille is one of the most important writers of this century . . . We owe to Bataille a great part of the moment in which we exist; but no doubt we also owe to him, and will do so for a long time, what remains to be done, thought and said. His work will become greater.'[93]

Without any preliminaries or hesitation, Foucault plunges into a discussion of the question of limits. Modern sexuality – and by 'modern', Foucault means sexuality since de Sade and Freud – has not been liberated. It has, rather, been taken to the limit, or established as a limit: 'the limit of our consciousness as it dictates, ultimately, the only reading possible, for our consciousness, of our unconscious; the limit of the law, as it appears to be the sole absolutely universal content of the forbidden; the limit of our language: it traces the line of foam of what can just be reached on the sand of silence'.[94] Perhaps, Foucault speculates, the importance of sexuality relates to the death of God, as proclaimed by Zarathustra: the death of God abolishes the limit of the Unlimited, and then transfers the limit into an experience in which there can be nothing outside being: this is an inner experience, the discovery of 'the unlimited realm of the limit' and of the void.[95] Eroticism, for instance, is 'an experience of sexuality which in itself links the crossing of the limit to the death of God'.[96] The existence of limits necessarily opens up the possibility of transgression, but transgression is not negative; it is the self-assertion of the limited being. The experience of limits, defined in this sense, offers the hope of a 'possible philosophy of non-positive assertion'.[97] Foucault looks forward now to 'the collapse of philosophical subjectivity, its dispersal within a language that dispossesses it, but also multiplies it in the space of its lacuna', 'the end of philosophy as the sovereign, primary form of philosophical language'.[98] The labyrinth of dispersal is the language of the literary modernism explored by Foucault in his articles and in *Raymond Roussel*, and it holds out the promise of a release from the 'sleep' of dialectics and anthropology, both of which are defined primarily by reference to Kant. An investigation of limits will replace the philosophical quest for a totality; transgression will replace the movement of contradiction. In authors like Bataille, Foucault finds something which he also glimpsed in Laporte's novel *La Veille*, something he associates with Nietzsche: thought which cannot be reduced to philosophy.

The attempted description of the language of dispersal is strangely poetic:

This language of rocks, this unavoidable language to which rupture, escarpment and a torn profile are essential, is a circular language which refers to itself and turns in upon a questioning of its limits – as though it were nothing other than a little globe of darkness from which there flashed out a strange light, designating the void from whence it comes and inevitably addressing to it everything it lights up and touches. It is perhaps this strange configuration which gives the Eye the obstinate prestige Bataille grants it.[99]

The eye is of course the object that circulates through the darkly erotic *Histoire de l'oeil*, sometimes as an eye torn from its socket, sometimes in the form of an 'equivalent' such as an egg (and here the phonetic play between *oeil* and *oeuf* comes close to Roussel), a saucer of milk used in an erotic game, or the testicle (also an *oeil* in popular usage, according to Barthes[100]) of a bull.

For Foucault, the tearing out of the eye is equivalent to eviction of the philosopher from his position of sovereignty. Novels such as *Histoire de l'oeil* end with scenes of extraordinarily sexualised violence:

What are the great scenes with which Bataille's stories end, if not the spectacle of these erotic deaths in which eyes roll upwards, reveal their white limits and roll towards gigantic and empty orbits? . . . The eye, rolled upwards or enucleated, is Bataille's philosophical space, the void where he holds forth and becomes lost but never stops speaking . . . the space of belonging to language and death, there where language discovers its being in the crossing of its limits: the form of a non-dialectical language of philosophy.[101]

Bataille is not mentioned in *Naissance de la clinique*, and Bichat does not appear in 'Préface à la transgression'. Yet the same imagery is applied to both. Bataille's 'limit' traces a line of foam on the sand of silence. Pathological anatomy does something oddly similar:

Discovering no longer means finally *reading* an essential coherence beneath a disorder, but pushing a little bit further the foam-line of language, making it cut into that region of sand that is still open to the clarity of perception, but already no longer open to familiar speech. Introducing language into that penumbra where the gaze has no more words.[102]

The explanation for the parallel is that Foucault likens Bichat's perception of life in death to the persistent theme of death in Goya, Géricault, Delacroix, Lamartine and Baudelaire, and to the cruel knowledge that it implies. For both Bichat and this artistic tradition, 'death has left its tragic heaven; it has now become the lyrical kernel of man: his invisible truth, his visible secret'.[103]

Naissance de la clinique ends on an unexpectedly philosophical and poetic note. The possibility of the individual's being both subject and object of his own knowledge inverts the play of finitude:

> It is this reversal that acted as a philosophical condition for the organisation of a positive medicine; conversely, positive medicine has been, at the empirical level, the first breakthrough towards the relationship that binds modern man to a primal finitude . . . This medical experience is . . . related to a lyrical experience which sought its language from Hölderlin to Rilke. That experience, inaugurated by the nineteenth century and from which we have not yet escaped, is bound up with the revelation of forms of finitude, death being no doubt the most threatening, but also the fullest.[104]

In terms of their immediate critical reception, neither *Raymond Roussel* nor *Naissance de la clinique* was a particular success. Interestingly, no one critic reviewed the two books together or attempted to establish a connection between the two. The former, in particular, received very strange treatment at the hand of Alain Robbe-Grillet in *Critique*. In theory, he was reviewing the Pauvert edition of Roussel's *Oeuvres complètes* as well as Foucault's study. He exploited the freedom *Critique* has always afforded its contributors by writing a short essay on Roussel, and by saying not a word about *Raymond Roussel*.[105] Writing in *Esprit* on Foucault's book and Michel Butor's *Essais sur les modernes*, Yves Bertherat remarked that the critical essay was developing into a genre which existed independently of the works to which it supposedly referred, and commented that it was quite possible to develop a passionate interest in Barthes's *Sur Racine* without ever having seen or read a play by Racine. Insofar as it actually touches upon *Raymond Roussel*, his review is a fine example of the development he notes. Only the last two sentences are devoted to Foucault:

> We are familiar with the passion the author of *Histoire de la folie* and *Naissance de la clinique* has for what lies beyond human actions and works, and the art with which he hunts down meaning where we do not normally expect to find it. Here, he pursues, through

Roussel, a personal meditation whose most striking contribution is, perhaps his attempt to locate where, in the language, history and works of men, the boundary between reason and unreason lies . . . if there is one.[106]

There were a few other reviews of rather less interest and importance,[107] but it was Philippe Sollers who really sang the praises of Foucault's 'admirable study' in a five-page article in *Tel Quel*. Much of the article is expository, and it is a final footnote that contains the real eulogy. For Sollers, *Raymond Roussel* was part of the fascinating series of investigations that had begun with *Histoire de la folie*. The profundity of Foucault's investigations, the subtlety and depth of his thought, and the beauty of his writing, all promised him a very important position as a writer. What Foucault thought of this rather patronising comment from a man ten years his junior is not, unfortunately, on record, but it is difficult to believe that he would have been displeased by Sollers's conclusion: 'His *Roussel* . . . is, together with Maurice Blanchot's *Lautréamont* [*Lautréamont et Sade*], the most dazzling critical (poetic) book to have appeared in recent years. One is almost tempted to call it, with reference to *Naissance de la clinique*, *Naissance de la critique*.'[108]

Naissance de la clinique received even less critical attention on publication. Strangely enough, the first review appeared in a British journal. F. N. L. Poynter of the Wellcome Historical Medical Library devoted most of his review to expounding Foucault's theses, but began and ended it with highly positive comments. Whereas the pictorial splendour of most French books on the history of medicine was, in his view, matched only by the superficiality and anecdotal character of their text', Foucault's study provided 'evidence of a new spirit . . . which probably springs from contact with the modern school of French historians of science who have already produced much distinguished and scholarly work'. Although he expressed some reservations about the advisability of establishing a link between Rilke and Hölderlin and the *idéologues* of the nineteenth century, Poynter accepted that the book was 'so packed with ideas and fertile seeds for arguments as to be positively exciting'. 'The next English historian to write about our own great school of early nineteenth-century clinicians or the organisation of our own profession from 1858 onwards, and even the medical politician who is agitating for changes in our own health service today, will find a great deal that is relevant to his theme in these pages.'[109]

The only member of the 'modern school of French historians of science' to review *Naissance de la clinique* was not entirely enthusiastic about the author he described as a 'prodigious archivist, a subtle archaeologist'. Stressing that the book was very much a sequel to *Histoire de la folie*, François Dagognet detected the Kantian strand in Foucault who, he claimed, was less interested in the reality of psychiatry or medicine than in the assumptions and conditions that make them possible. The noumenal reality of unreason is, for instance, condemned to exist in negativity, either in the despair of the unformulated or the tragedy of violent protest. Dagognet also had doubts about some of the detail of Foucault's argument, but his main regret was that he had not painted a full enough picture. He ended by expressing the hope that, when history took over from achaeology in Foucault's 'dazzling dialectic', the reader's remaining uncertainties would be dispelled.[110]

Naissance de la clinique may not have been a resounding critical success, but it soon became a cult book. In 1963, Bernard Kouchner was a young doctor, a member of the Centre National des Jeunes Médicins, and an influential figure in the Union des Etudiants Communistes. He became fascinated by Foucault's study of the genealogy of his chosen profession; it provided him with the intellectual tools which allowed him to see that medicine was not simply a mechanical practice, but also a language which had evolved over time. The CNJM read and discussed the book chapter by chapter in a series of impassioned meetings, many of them held in Kouchner's home. It provided a vital antidote to the dull, academic history of medicine which had been their staple diet at medical school. Kouchner made no attempt to meet or even contact Foucault at this time, but the interest he and his group took in *Naissance de la clinique* was one of the factors that would eventually turn Foucault into an icon for the new left.[111]

Although Foucault had gained considerable prestige and had won the respect of his peers, he was also open to attack: Parisian intellectual society was not a demilitarised zone. One of the first and, in personal terms, most wounding came from close to home. Jacques Derrida, born in Algeria in 1930, began his studies at ENS in 1950 and took his *agrégation* in 1956. At ENS, he had been close to both Althusser and Foucault, whose lectures he attended with enthusiasm; he was later to describe himself as Foucault's 'admiring and grateful disciple'.[112] In 1963, Derrida's philosophical reputation was already considerable as his first major publication – a translation of and introduction to Husserl's *Origin of Geometry* – had won him the Prix Jean Cavaillès, awarded for an outstanding contribution to modern epistemology. On 4 March 1963, Derrida, who was then teaching at the Sorbonne, gave his first lecture to the Collège Philosophique. His topic was 'The Cogito and the History of Madness'.

Derrida's lecture began with a eulogy of Foucault which was in fact the prologue to a savagely critical reading of *Histoire de la folie*. The book was 'admirable in so many respects, powerful in its inspiration and its style', and it had been Derrida's good fortune to have had Foucault as a teacher. He was, however, a disciple and when the disciple begins a dialogue with the master, his consciousness is an unhappy consciousness: 'The interminable unhappiness of the disciple may perhaps have to do with what he does not yet know or still conceals from himself: that the master, like real life, is, perhaps, always absent. We therefore have to break the glass [*glace*], or rather the mirror, the reflection, the disciple's infinite speculation on the master. And begin to speak.'[113]

Derrida then began to speak at length to an audience which included Foucault himself. He attacked on two fronts. Firstly, he challenged Foucault's interpretation of the passage in the first of the *Méditations philosophiques* in which Descartes speculates about the possibility of denying that his hands and body are in fact his. To do so would, he concludes, be to behave like poor men who believe they are rich, who believe that they are dressed in purple and gold when they are in fact naked. He dismisses the speculation: such men are mad, and to model his behaviour on theirs would make him as mad as they. In *Histoire de la folie*, Foucault had used this passage to exemplify the self-confident certainties of classical reason.[114] Henri Gouhier had taken mild exception to this interpretation during the *soutenance de thèse*, but Foucault does not seem to have attached great importance to his reading of Descartes. When the abridged edition of *Histoire de la folie* appeared in 1964, this was one of the passages to be excised. It was presumably not thought to be vital to what Foucault, in his very brief prefatory note, called 'the general economy of the book'. Derrida, in contrast, claimed: 'The meaning of Foucault's whole project can be concentrated in these few allusive and slightly enigmatic pages.'[115] The re-examination of Foucault's reading – or alleged misreading – is an exercise in the art of close reading which was to become one of Derrida's hallmarks. His relentlessly, and at times laboriously, critical exegesis of both Foucault and Descartes will not be examined in detail here, but will be touched upon later in relation to Foucault's eventual reply.[116]

Derrida commences by unpicking the implications of Foucault's quotation from Pascal: 'Men are so inevitably mad that not to be mad would be to give a mad twist to madness.' Foucault had attempted to write a history of madness itself, to elaborate the archaeology of a silence. According to Derrida, this is strictly impossible: 'Will not the archaeology of the silence be the most effective, the most subtle recommencement, the *repetition* of the act perpetrated against madness?'[117] The only way to escape the totality of the language of exiled madness would be to remain silent, or to follow the madman into exile. In other words, Foucault is still speaking the language of reason. Derrida is tempted 'to consider Foucault's book a powerful gesture of protection and confinement. A Cartesian gesture for the twentieth century. A recuperation of negativity.'[118]

Secondly, Foucault is held by Derrida to be operating with a structuralist method, 'according to which everything in the structural totality is bound up together and circular . . . Structuralist totalitarianism may be effecting [*opérait*] an act that confines the cogito, an act which may be [*serait*] of the same type as that of the violences of the classical age. I am not saying that Foucault's book is totalitarian . . . I am saying that it sometimes runs the risk of being totalitarian.'[119] Derrida is careful to use the conditional here. This is the tense of insinuation which allows a newspaper to suggest that a minister may be [*serait*] an adulterous murderer without risking a libel case by asserting that he is [*est*] one. One does not have to be a psychoanalyst to doubt the validity of the disavowal of 'I am not saying', while the play on 'totality' and 'totalitarian' has all the ideological crudity of the criticisms the PCF would direct against *Les Mots et les choses* in 1966 and 1967.

Critiques of this nature usually serve two related purposes. On the one hand, they are by definition negative; on the other, they allow a new position to be staked out in an intellectual version of positional warfare. Derrida's 'Cogito' is no exception. As he brought his lecture to a conclusion, he asserted: 'The relationship between reason, madness and death is an economy, a structure of *différence* whose irreducible originality must be respected.'[120] The implication, insinuated rather than demonstrated, is that Derrida's conceptual analysis must replace Foucault's.

'Cogito et Histoire de la folie' was an important moment in Derrida's career, and helped to consolidate his growing reputation as a master and not a disciple. Emergence from discipleship often implies the symbolic murder of the master. Foucault's relationship with psychiatry and the masters who taught him that discipline has been described as murderous, and this type of murder is not unusual in hierarchically organised academic communities. In the case of Foucault and Derrida, the real murder victim was their friendship. Foucault sat through the lecture in silence, and remained silent when 'Cogito et Histoire de la folie' was published in the *Revue de métaphysique et de morale* in 1964. Nor did he respond to its republication in *L'Écriture et la différence* three years later. Foucault's continued silence is puzzling, as he was notoriously intolerant of criticism. A partial explanation may be that the presence of both men on the editorial board of *Critique*, which Derrida joined in 1967, may have resulted in an armed truce. When the response did come in 1970, it was a brutal attack not only on the 1963 lecture, but also on Derrida's deconstructionism as a whole. There are few references indeed to Derrida in Foucault's writings, and they are not complimentary.

Foucault and Defert were now living together in the rue du Dr Finlay, and had resolved to spend the rest of their lives together. Their decision did not imply fidelity on either part, but it did establish a relationship that was to endure until Foucault's death in 1984. It was on the whole a fairly relaxed partnership, and Defert describes Foucault as having been remarkably easy to live with on a day-to-day basis. They did, however, experience certain social difficulties and a degree of prejudice. The fact that they were living together was no secret in their milieu but, in 1963, French society -- and French academic society in particular -- did not take an especially positive view of gay partnerships.[121]

His relationship with Daniel Defert resulted in significant changes in Foucault's life in that it brought about an estrangement from Barthes. At least three versions of what happened are in circulation. Sollers speaks of jealousy between Barthes and Foucault, whereas others talk of an incident that supposedly occurred when Barthes, Foucault and Jean-Paul Aron were on holiday together in Tangier. Foucault complained constantly about not having had any news from Defert and, when he finally did receive a letter, reacted very badly to a sarcastic comment from Barthes.[122] According to Defert, it was a combination of his presence in Foucault's life and pressure of work that brought about the estrangement, and he denies that there was any real quarrel between Foucault and Barthes. By 1963–64, Defert was studying for his *agrégation* and Foucault was already working on *Les Mots et les choses*. Both were regularly working until the early hours of the morning, and Foucault simply had to abandon his old habit of dining with Barthes three times a week. The old friendship therefore cooled considerably, but was not ended by some sudden break. In the early 1970s, political differences finally put an end to it.

The appearance of Defert also had a minor textual effect. When the abridged version of *Histoire de la folie* appeared in 1964, the original dedication to Eric-Michael Nilsson vanished, and it does not reappear in any subsequent edition. The new relationship had erased even the mark of the earlier platonic friendship. Defert was now the most important figure in Foucault's life, and he was to remain so. Both men had numerous more or less casual sexual encounters, and Foucault was often surrounded by a court of admiring younger men. Foucault never referred openly to Defert in any of his published writings, but he did describe the importance of their relationship in conversation with the German filmmaker Werner Schroeter in 1982:

> For eighteen years, I have been living in a state of passion for someone. Perhaps that passion took the form of love at some given moment. In truth, it is a state of passion between us, a permanent state ... in which I am completely involved ... I believe that there is not a single thing in the world, nothing, nothing at all, that would stop me when I have to go back to him, to talk to him.[123]

His love for Defert may not have led immediately to a total break with Barthes, but it did prevent Foucault from realising an old ambition. Ever since he had left Hamburg, he had been fascinated by the idea of going to Japan, and even had the notion of settling there. The fascination was, at least in part, an expression of the conviction that the Orient was one of the limits of western reason. As he wrote in the original preface to *Histoire de la folie*:

> The Orient, thought of as the origin, dreamed of as the vertiginous point that gives birth to nostalgias and promises of return ... the night of beginnings, in which the West was formed, but in which it traced a dividing line, the Orient is for the West all that the West is not, even though it is there that it must seek its primitive truth. A history of this division throughout its long western evolution should be written, followed in its continuity and its exchanges, but it must also be allowed to appear in its tragic hieratism.[124]

The impetus to go to Japan came from a suggestion made by Maurice Pinguet. In 1963, the post of director of the Institut Culturel Français in Tokyo fell vacant. Given his experience in Sweden, Poland and Germany, Foucault was a well-qualified candidate, and he was enthusiastic about the idea, not least because he was becoming increasingly dissatisfied with working in Clermont-Ferrand. The quarrels with Roger Garaudy had always been an irritant, and Foucault was bored with the administrative load he had to carry with little or no secretarial backup. He was, moreover, still unconvinced that teaching in a university was his true vocation. Japan looked like an attractive alternative.

There were two obstacles. One was that Foucault's dean of faculty was unwilling to lose him, particularly because he was the only person qualified to reorganise the university's Institut de Psychologie Appliquée. In an official letter to the Minister for Education, dated 2 September 1963, the dean wrote:

> M. Foucault's departure would, in the present circumstances, seriously prejudice our Faculty. Not only would it be impossible to replace him for the coming academic year; the very critical situation of the philosophy section in Clermont . . . requires that the Director should remain in post next year . . . Given these conditions, I took it upon myself urgently to press M. Foucault to decline the offer he has received. He has accepted the validity of the argument I put to him with a selflessness for which I am very grateful.[125]

Foucault's selflessness may have been more apparent than real. He was not one to be swayed unduly by the academic authorities, and may well have asked his dean to write to the minister while he played for time. The second obstacle to his departure was, of course, the relationship with Daniel Defert. Foucault was unwilling to abandon his new partner, and even suggested that Defert should go with him and retrain as a specialist in Japanese studies. Having little or no idea of how modern Japanese society was developing, the latter had visions of himself studying fans and ceramics, and those visions had no great appeal. There was also the issue of his *agrégation*; going to Tokyo would mean abandoning his studies and, therefore, any real hope of an academic career. Eventually, he made the difficult decision to sacrifice his *agrégation*. Foucault, in the meantime, was being pressed for an immediate decision by the Quai d'Orsay; Prime Minister Pompidou was due to make an official visit to Japan, and it would not do for the Institut to have no director. Having prevaricated by claiming that the university was creating difficulties, Foucault finally said that his answer was no; he had decided to sacrifice the pleasure of living in Japan for the sake of Daniel's *agrégation*. The entire comedy of errors had been played out without any open discussion between the two. Defert now made the silent resolve that he would make reparation for Foucault's sacrifice by producing a major piece of intellectual work. It was never realised, and Foucault never knew of his partner's unfulfilled and unspoken ambition.[126]

Defert successfully completed his *agrégation* in the summer of 1964, and immediately became liable for military service for a period of eighteen months. His experiences in the anti-war movement and as a delegate to UNEF's anti-colonial committee had left him with a totally negative view of the forces, and he was reluctant to serve as a soldier. Unlike Foucault, he did not have a father who could influence an army medical panel, but there was an alternative and it is a reminder of the advantages conferred by education in an openly elitist system. The provisions for the recently established *Service civil de coopération* allowed suitably qualified young men to spend their period of military service in developing countries (usually, but not exclusively, former French colonies). Defert's original plan was to go to Vietnam, but the Tonkin Gulf Incident of 2 August 1964 and the subsequent American strike against North Vietnam made that seem an unpleasantly dangerous prospect and he therefore accepted a teaching post in Tunisia. He spent the duration of his military service teaching philosophy in Sfax, a southern city on the Gulf of Gabès. Foucault was a regular visitor, and the two spent the Christmas holidays of 1964–65 travelling in Tunisia.

September 1963 did not find Foucault in the exotic setting of Tokyo or Kyoto, but in the more familar environment of a colloquium organised by *Tel Quel*. The journal had been founded by Sollers, Hallier and others in 1960 as a platform for the theory and practice of the literary avant-garde. According to its founding declaration: 'What has to be said today is that writing is no longer conceivable without a clear definition of its powers, a sang-froid equal to the chaos from which it is awaking, a determination which will give poetry the highest place in the mind. All the rest is not literature.'[127] Throughout its existence, until it ceased publication in 1983 and was immediately resurrected as *L'Infini*, the journal was much given to the issuing of manifestoes and declarations as it made the transition, marked by sudden shifts rather than gradual developments, from political quietism to critical support for the PCF (until about 1970), and then from extreme Maoism to high Atlanticism in the mid-to late 1970s. Despite the many changes of direction, an underlying continuity was guaranteed by the conviction that the literary avant-garde was the harbinger, or even the agent, of social and political revolution. The conviction finds its supreme expression in Julia Kristeva's monumental attempt to prove that the poetic revolution of Lautréamont and Mallarmé represented a crisis for the bourgeois state.[128] As the founding declaration makes clear, *Tel Quel* was also given to a certain pedantry; the final sentence cited above is a knowing allusion to Paul Verlaine's *Et tout le reste est littérature*, a dictum which makes 'literature' synonymous with frivolity.

In 1960, Maoism was not even on the horizon and 'literature' effectively meant the *nouveau roman*, 'the only form that offers a way of handling literature, both from a formal point of view and from the point of view of a possible ideological reconversion'.[129] The initial pantheon of writers celebrated by *Tel Quel* included Borges, Artaud, Hölderlin, Ponge and Heidegger, and overlapped to a large extent with the tradition Foucault had begun to explore in *Histoire de la folie*. He was an obvious person to be invited to the colloquium held in Cérisy-la-Salle in September 1963, at which he chaired a major debate on the novel. The colloquium was an important one; from this date onwards, according to Sollers,

> the accent was no longer placed merely on formal research in fiction, but on the elaboration of a critical terrain which allowed us no longer to make a distinction between levels of texts, no matter whether they were said to be critical, poetic or fictional. At the same time it clarified our research into the way in which the literary series was inserted into politics itself.[130]

At this stage, Foucault was not terribly interested in the 'insertion' of the literary into politics, and his contribution to the debate is of interest mainly for what it reveals of his own thinking.

Admitting, with some false modesty, that he was not really qualified to speak on the novel and describing himself as a 'naive man whose philosophical intentions were obvious',[131] Foucault opened the debate by pointing to the parallel between the interests of *Tel Quel* and those of the surrealists: a 'constellation' of topics such as dreams, madness, unreason, repetition and doubles. By introducing the notions of 'limit' and 'transgression', Bataille had helped to remove this constellation from the purely psychological dimension, while *Tel Quel* had elevated it to a more intellectual level. Literature itself was now asking the question: 'What does thinking mean? What is this extraordinary experience known as thinking?'[132] Parrying an objection couched in Marxist terminology from Eduardo Sanguinetti, Foucault went on to argue that accusations of spiritualism or mysticism were not admissible: 'At the moment, we are trying, but with great difficulty, even and especially in philosophy, to see what thought might be without applying the old categories, by trying, above all, to escape the dialectic of mind that Hegel once defined.'[133] Ten years after he had first begun to read Nietzsche, Foucault was still trying to escape from the ghost of Hegel.

The debate did not, to judge by the published transcript, get off to the best of starts. As Sollers hesitantly claimed to work intuitively and added that his work might therefore seem confused to a philosopher, Foucault felt forced to retreat from his 'abstractions', and invited Jean-Pierre Faye to speak. Faye was not slow to accept, and dominated the long discussion by tracing the retreat from realism in the work of everyone from Henry James and James Joyce to Kafka, Sartre and Roussel.

For most of the debate, Foucault's role was that of a rather diffident chairman who prefaced virtually all his contributions with a polite 'Perhaps . . .'. His attempts to introduce a more philosophical note were frustrated. When he noted that from 1945 to 1955, France had had a 'literature of signification' corresponding to the philosophy of signification represented by Merleau-Ponty, and then suggested that the discussion might perhaps turn to the problem of the relationship between what has – since the day of a certain phenomenology – been called significations, and what we are now beginning to discover to be the field of the signifier and the signified, the domain of the sign', Faye rejected the opportunity to explore the differences between Husserl and post-Saussurean theories of language, and immediately plunged back into a critical discussion of Robbe-Grillet.[134] A later attempt by Foucault to broaden the debate to include contemporary music with the suggestion that there might be an analogy between musical language and the problems facing novelists was also frustrated; Gilbert Amy, who had known Foucault since the 1950s, refused to be drawn and contributed only some very general comments.

Although his attempts to steer the debate away from purely literary questions were not successful, Foucault was in complete agreement with the *Tel Quel* group's rejection of Sanguinetti's appeals to realism. When the latter argued that not all events occur within language, Foucault retorted: 'Reality does not exist . . . language is all there is, and what we are talking about is language, we speak within language.'[135]

Foucault also took part in a second debate at Cérisy. The discussion of poetry was not terribly well focused, but it did provide him with an opportunity to explain the isomorphism he detected between his own work and that of *Tel Quel*. He claimed to be working at a discursive level – which he defined in somewhat curious terms as meaning 'without talent' – and admitted that there was no direct connection between the historical analysis of *Histoire de la folie* and the poetic experiments of Pleynet. The common ground lay in their use of the notion of *contestation*: 'one of the most problematical, most difficult and most obscure notions in a minuscule philosophical current . . . whose source, at least, might be found in people like Blanchot and Bataille'.[136]

Foucault never became a close associate of *Tel Quel*. There may have been personal reasons for this. *Tel Quel* was very much the private preserve of Philippe Sollers, not a man given to the sharing of intellectual power, and Foucault may have kept his distance for purely subjective reasons. It is also quite obvious that he did not at this stage share the group's more political concerns; though he was anxious to find a form of thought that was not reducible to philosophy, his hostility to dialectical thinking extended to Marx as well as Hegel. When Foucault did emerge as a political activist, his politics were far removed from *Tel Quel*'s dogmatic but literary Maoism, and there was little or no common ground between him and Sollers.

7

WORDS AND THINGS

At *Tel Quel*'s Cérisy conference, Foucault had been a slightly uncomfortable philosopher in an almost purely literary milieu. At the following year's Royaumont colloquium on Nietzsche, he found himself in more comfortably philosophical surroundings. The colloquium, held between 4 and 8 July 1964 and chaired by Martial Guéroult, brought together distinguished specialists including Pierre Klossowski, Gilles Deleuze, Jean Beaufret and Jean Wahl, with Giorgio Colli and Mazzino Montinari from Italy reporting on their progress towards a full edition of Nietzsche's collected works.

Foucault's paper was dedicated to the three 'masters of suspicion' – Nietzsche, Freud and Marx – and was basically a discussion of techniques of interpretation. Indeed, he began by referring to his 'dream' of constructing a general corpus or encyclopedia of all the techniques of interpretation that have ever been used in western cultures. His illustration of what such an encyclopedia might contain was a discussion of the category of resemblance in Renaissance thought. It is a succinct version of the opening pages of Chapter 2 of *Les Mots et les choses*, and an indication that the book was already well advanced. Taking as his main texts *The Birth of Tragedy*, the first volume of *Capital* and *The Interpretation of Dreams*, Foucault then argued that Nietzsche, Marx and Freud did not give a new meaning to things that previously had no meaning: 'In reality, they changed the nature of the sign, and modified the way in which the sign could be interpreted.'[1] For Renaissance thought, signs existed within a homogeneous space in which earth referred to heaven and vice versa. From the nineteenth century onwards, signs tend to be a matter of depth and superficiality. Nietzsche, for example, refers to 'thorough thinkers, who thoroughly explore the grounds of a thing' and describes himself as having 'descended into the depths . . . tunnelled into the foundations'.[2] Zarathustra's ascent of the mountain, however, leads to the discovery that the depths are no more than a surface fold. Marx discovers that there simply is no depth to bourgeois conceptions of value; and Freud's intepretation of dreams exposes a spoken chain which lies flat beneath the downcast gaze of the analyst.[3]

The spatiality of signs and their interpretation is not, however, Foucault's main theme: it is the infinite nature of interpretation that really concerns him. Marx does not interpret the history of relations of production, but rather relations which present themselves as natural, as, that is, an interpretation. Freud does not interpret signs but fantasies, or the patient's already elaborated interpretations of a bodily experience. For Nietzsche, philosophy is an endless exercise in philology; words do not indicate a signified – they impose an interpretation. Interpretation is endless because the *interpretandum* is already an *interpretans*.

All these formulations relate to the exploration of labyrinths in Foucault's literary articles and in his *Raymond Roussel*, but they also relate to his perceived connection between language and death. Although potentially endless, interpretations inevitably break off. For Freud, it is transference that signals both the inexhaustibility of analysis and the approach of a dangerous area which makes further analysis impossible. For Nietzsche, 'it could pertain to the fundamental nature of existence that a complete knowledge of it would destroy one'.[4] And for Foucault himself, 'what is in question at the point where interpretation breaks down, in interpretation's convergence towards a point which makes it impossible, may well be something like the experience of madness'.[5]

It is obvious throughout the paper that Foucault's real sympathies lie with Nietzsche rather than with Marx or Freud and a brief comment in the ensuing discussion reveals why this should be the case. Nietzsche's theory of interpretation is radically different, and therefore cannot be inscribed within any 'constituted body', whereas Marx can be inscribed within the 'body' constituted by communists, and Freud in that constituted by psychoanalysts.[6] It is the unclassifiable nature of Nietzsche's work that appeals to Foucault, as well as the promise of liberation from dialectical thinking.

Deleuze is always very reticent about just when and how he met Foucault, telling *Libération*'s Robert Maggiori, for instance; 'One remembers a gesture or a laugh rather than dates. I met him in about 1962.'[7] The two had met in Clermont-Ferrand, but the Royaumont colloquium undoubtedly marks a significant moment in their friendship. Foucault referred favourably to Deleuze's *Nietzsche* in his paper,[8] and Deleuze returned the compliment in his closing address on the will to power and the eternal return.[9] Deleuze also mentions a project which was to bring them closer together: the production of a French version of the Colli-Montinari edition of Nietzsche. Based on original research in the Weimar archive, this was a joint French-Italian-Dutch project and there was, strangely, no German involvement. The French side of the project was overseen jointly by Foucault and Deleuze, and publication began in 1967 with Volume 5, which contains Klossowski's translation of *Die fröhliche Wissenschaft*, a variety of posthumous material and a short general introduction by the two supervising editors.[10] The fourteen-volume edition was finally completed in 1990 with the publication of a new translation of the *Unzeitgemässe Betrachtungen*.

In an interview, Foucault explained the need for a new edition, the need to 'demolish the false architecture, the creation of an overzealous third party, and to reconstruct, as far as possible, the texts in accordance with Nietzsche's own perspectives'.[11] The 'third party' was of course Nietzsche's sister, Elizabeth Förster, who was largely responsible for the version of *Der Wille zur Macht* which proved so popular with the ideologues of Nazism: 'Did not the arbitrary interpretations of Nietzsche's sister – whose racist feelings were well known, whereas the philosopher vigorously denounced anti-Semitism in the last years of his life – favour the ideological annexation attempted by the Nazis? A serious edition of the works of Nietzsche is therefore essential, particularly now that the philosopher is once more finding a new audience.'[12]

Foucault knew most of those present at Royaumont, and the company included one person who was particularly close to him at this time. Klossowski, who spoke on the theme of Nietzsche's 'eternal return',[13] had been introduced to Foucault by Barthes, probably in 1963. Born in Paris in 1905 into a family of aristocratic and artistic Polish émigrés, Pierre Klossowski is the elder brother of the painter Balthus, or Balthasar Klossowski de Rola, to give him his full name. Barthes had known him since the late 1940s, when he would go to his apartment in the rue Canivet to play four-handed piano duets with Klossowski's wife Denise.[14] Brought up in France and Germany and therefore bilingual from a very early age, the young Klossowski knew Rilke, and his long career has brought him into contact with an extraordinary range of people. He was at various times an associate of Gertrude Stein, Bataille, Masson and Walter Benjamin, and is one of the very few people to have been close to both Gide and Foucault (one of the others being Claude Mauriac).

Klossowski's career has been a curious one. Immediately before the Second World War, his quest for a religious life led him to begin a noviciate with the Benedictines and then the Dominicans, but he left the community after only three months. The experience provided the basis for his first novel, *La Vocation suspendue* (1949), which takes the form of a discussion of a rare book of the same title which may or may not give an accurate account of a loss of faith. In 1947, having abandoned his religious quest, he married Denise Marie Roberte Morin Sinclaire, a war widow who had been deported to Ravensbrück as a result of her Resistance activities. Henceforth, all his work would be dominated by and dedicated to her haunting beauty. She is the 'Roberte' who figures in his novels and so many of his delicate drawings. Originally a writer and translator, Klossowski began to experiment with drawing shortly after meeting Denise, and has since alternated between the two media. His drawings, influenced by artists as diverse as Ingres and Fuseli, are all on a large scale, made on paper and (with the exception of the very early graphite works) executed with coloured pencils, a medium which requires long hours of painstaking labour.

Klossowski's novels and drawings make up an imaginary world in which erotic, religious and philosophical themes merge, and, being a self-confessed monomaniac, he has little interest in anything outside that world. Although his work – and especially the trilogy known as *Les Lois de l'hospitalité* –[15] is sometimes dismissed as misogynist and even pornographic,[16] he insists that it has a mystical content and belongs to a gnostic tradition. Maurice Blanchot endorsed Klossowski's claims when he described his writings as 'a mixture of erotic austerity and theological debauchery'.[17] Both the novels and the drawings are sequences of scenes, understood in the theatrical sense of that term, and of humiliating encounters between Roberte and characters from a threatening *commedia dell'arte*. Roberte becomes an object of exchange, circulating endlessly in an erotic economy. She is raped and assaulted, is seduced and seduces, and takes on many different identities but remains unpossessed, inviolable, it being the author's conviction that the deepest level of individuality is a core which is both non-communicable and non-exchangeable. Like the *tableaux vivants* imagined and staged by de Sade's libertines, Klossowski's words and images betray an obsession with representation itself: representations of plays, of drawings, of drawings of scenes from plays, books about books. They are a theatre of simulacra in which everything is represented, and nothing is real. The theatrical scenes that make up the trilogy, in particular, originated in planned drawings that were not actually executed.

The notion of the simulacrum is not easy to grasp, Klossowski not being the most conceptual of thinkers. He himself claims that it derives from the aesthetics of the Rome of the decadence, where simulacra or effigies of the gods lined the streets, both manifesting their presence and calling citizens to worship. For Klossowski, their main interest was that they 'sexually determined the divinities they represented. The indeterminacy of their essence was replaced by a materialisation, which was that of a sexuality.' Gradually, the classical reference became combined with a meditation upon the nature of icons, and the simulacrum is finally defined as constituting

> the sign of an instantaneous state and cannot establish an exchange between one mind and another, nor permit the transmission of one thought to another . . . The simulacrum has the advantage of not purporting to fix what it represents or says of an experience; far from precluding it, it implies contradiction.[18]

On the basis of a passage in one of Klossowski's essays on Nietzsche, Foucault related the simulacrum to the 'demon' of Nietzsche's *Gay Science*.[19] This is the demon who says that 'everything in your life . . . will return to you, all in the same succession and sequence'. Nietzsche then asks: 'Would you not throw yourself down and curse the demon who spoke thus? Or have you experienced a tremendous moment when you would have answered him: "You are a god and never have I heard anything more divine"?'[20] The ambiguity of the demon-god is also that of the sign-simulacrum known as Roberte.

For Klossowski, language is an unstable medium in which startling transformations can occur. It is also closely related to the body: Roberte is a word made flesh and her body is of a flesh made of words. The body–language relationship generates texts which must have appealed greatly to Foucault's own enjoyment of wordplay. In *Roberte ce soir*, for example, erotic encounters can be couched in the language of Thomist theology, as when Roberte is penetrated by the *sed contra* of a colossus while she stimulates her own *quid est* to orgasm.[21]

Foucault and Klossowski had a lot in common, notably a fascination with Nietzsche and de Sade. Klossowski's *Sade, mon voisin* was, together with Blanchot's *Sade et Lautréamont*, one of the first serious studies of the Divine Marquis, though there is no indication in *Histoire de la folie* that Foucault had read it at that time. Klossowski, on the other hand, had read *Histoire de la folie* with great interest and enthusiasm. A comment from Deleuze, also a friend of Klossowski's, suggests that Klossowski's work may have had a definite subjective appeal for a man who refused to be defined: in his view, all Klossowski's work 'strives towards a single goal: ensuring the loss of personal identity, dissolving the ego; that is the splendid trophy that Klossowski's characters bring back from a journey to the edge of madness'.[22] There were, on the other hand, limits to their common interests and Klossowski never really succeeded in interesting Foucault in the gnostics who mean so much to him. Yet they enjoyed one another's company and Foucault's visits to the rue Canivet were enlivened by his conversational style, which Denise Klossowski describes as *sautillant*, hopping or skipping from topic to topic.[23]

Inevitably, the private and public sides to the friendship overlapped, as Foucault both defended and celebrated Klossowski in print. In 1964, Klossowski published a translation of the *Aeneid* which begins: '*Les armes je célèbre et l'homme*' ['The arms I sing and the man']. It followed, that is, the original Latin word order and syntax, and made no attempt to transpose Virgil's words into French. Klossowski could almost claim to be a native speaker of Latin: his first grammar book as a child was neither French nor German, but Latin,[24] and his prose often has a Latinate feel to it. The translation of Virgil was not universally appreciated, but Foucault admired it greatly and called it a 'vertical translation': 'Each word, like Aeneas, carries with it its native gods and its sacred birthplace. It falls from the Latin verse to the French line as though its signification could not be separated from its place, as though it could say what it has to say from the precise point where fate and the dice of the poem threw it.' (The half hidden reference is to Mallarmé's '*Un coup de dés jamais n'abolira le hasard*'.) In order to translate, 'Klossowski does not settle himself into the resemblance between French and Latin; he finds lodgings in the hollow of their greatest differences'.[25]

Foucault was also an admirer of *Le Bain de Diane* (1956), in which Klossowski explores the myth of Diana and Actaeon and weaves elegant variations on it. The myth is a recurrent theme in the drawings, and Diane is very similar to Roberte in that her nature remains unchanged despite her physical metamorphoses. Actaeon never succeeds in glimpsing the nudity of the real goddess, but merely a simulacrum; the 'true' Diana is always elsewhere. For Foucault, *Le Bain de Diane* ranked alongside the work of Blanchot and Bataille, which was high praise indeed. It was a 'text dedicated to the interpretation of a far-away legend and a myth of distance (a man punished for having attempted to approach the naked divinity) . . . Diana reduplicated by her own desire, Actaeon metamorphosed both by his desire and by that of Diana.'[26] As he put it elsewhere, Klossowski captured 'the experience of the double, of the exteriority of simulacra, of the theatrical and demented multiplication of the ego.'[27]

Perhaps the greatest gesture of friendship Klossowski made towards Foucault – his greatest reader, as he puts it – was to allow, or ask, him to read his novel *Le Baphomet* (1965) in manuscript. The novel is a strange exercise in medievalism and an exploration of the theme of androgyny, and its very title is a cipher derived from *BAsileus philosoPHOrum METallicarum* ('The King of the Metallurgist-Philosophers').[28] Foucault read it, chapter by chapter, with enthusiasm and spent long hours discussing it with its author, and the novel is dedicated to him. Regrettably, he did not record his impressions in any permanent form.

The friendship endured until the early 1970s, when Foucault found himself increasingly alienated from Klossowski – and other friends from this literary period – by his political interests. The friendship finally died, but it has its monuments. In the late 1980s, Klossowski found a mouldering piece of canvas in Balthus's château and interpreted the patches of damp on it to create two versions of a drawing entitled *The Great Confinement II* (1988). Both include a portrait of Foucault; in the second version he is surrounded by portraits of Strindberg, Nietzsche, Bataille and an anonymous pope, while Freud, to Foucault's right, contemplates a sketch of Leonardo's *Madonna and Child with St Anne*.[29]

Histoire de la folie had won Foucault the respect and admiration of his peers, but he had yet to gain any great public recognition. He appeared on two educational television programmes in February and March 1965. The first was a discussion on philosophy and psychology, with Alain Badiou as interlocutor. Badiou was at the time teaching in a *lycée* in Reims, and had recently published a first novel;[30] within a few years he would be a prominent figure in Maoist circles.

Foucault's response to the questions put to him by Badiou is largely a reprise of the theses of the recently published *Maladie mentale et psychologie* (as it was now called) and his first television appearance is remarkable mainly for the flight of fantasy with which it ends. Asked what he would teach a philosophy class in a *lycée* about psychology, he said that his first step would be to buy a mask. He would adopt a different voice, 'like Anthony Perkins in *Psycho*', so that 'nothing of the unity of my discourse would be apparent'. He would then give a lucid account of current developments in psychology and psychoanalysis, before abandoning his mask, adopting his usual voice and giving a class on philosophy which would demonstrate that psychology was 'a sort of absolutely inevitable and absolutely fatal impasse in which western thought found itself in the nineteenth century'.[31]

The second broadcast involved Foucault in a brief and rather barbed exchange with Paul Ricoeur about polysemy and ontology, and then in a very short discussion with Ricoeur (a specialist in hermeneutics), Hyppolite, Canguilhem and a Mme Dreyfus. It centred on the propositions, advanced by Canguilhem and Hyppolite respectively, that 'There is no philosophical truth' and that 'There are no errors in philosophy'. Arguments about such propositions were the staple diet of the apprentice philosophers at whom the broadcast was directed. Significantly, Foucault and Canguilhem were in agreement that there were no criteria by which a philosophical system could be judged true or false; in other words, that there was no truth as such in philosophical discourse. Foucault, however, argued that there was such a thing as a 'will to truth'.[32]

It was neither educational broadcasts nor colloquia that finally brought Foucault into the limelight, but the appearance of *Les Mots et les choses* in 1966. Foucault gives no indication of how long the research and writing took him. It is, however, obvious from 'Nietzsche, Freud, Marx' that large sections of it were already written by mid-1964, and it is reported that its main themes were outlined in a series of relatively unsuccessful lectures given in Brazil in 1965.[33] Occasional comments made in interviews and elsewhere make it clear that he found it a difficult task. Yet if *Les Mots et les choses* was difficult to write, it was easy to publish.

The submission of the long manuscript to Gallimard brought renewed contact with Roger Caillois, who had been one of the original readers of *Histoire de la folie* in 1961. There was an exchange of letters between Foucault and Caillois, but only the former's contribution to it has survived. From the remaining and fragmentary evidence, it can be surmised that Caillois read the manuscript in his capacity as a member of Gallimard's *comité de lecture*, and that he wrote to Foucault about it in very positive terms. Foucault thanked him effusively in terms that reveal his total mastery of that elegantly polite rhetoric that comes so naturally to the educated French bourgeois: 'When one sends a publisher a long, heavy, dense text with a sediment of notes, one becomes frightened in advance about the reader's fear. But as luck had it that mine fell into your hand, and that it did not displease you too much, I have the impression of having had the benefit of *the* ideal reader.'[34] Caillois suggested that an extract from Foucault's second chapter could be published in *Diogène/Diogenes*, the journal published in both English and French by UNESCO. Foucault readily agreed to the suggestion but hesitated about producing a further 'short, general text', explaining that the book had cost him so much difficulty that he was not yet sufficiently distanced from it. The extract, but no 'general text', duly appeared in English and French, and marked a minor but significant stage in the author's international career.[35] Foucault's English-language career was gradually taking shape. His name had first been made known to the American public in 1963 by an essay by Susan Sontag on Marguerite Duras.[36] *Madness and Civilization* appeared two years later. 'The Prose of the World' was therefore a significant addition to the slowly growing *oeuvre* available in English.

Les Mots et les choses appeared in April and immediately became a best-seller. Foucault believed that he had written a book that would be read by at most 2,000 specialists in the history of ideas, and described it as the most difficult of all the books he had written, 'the biggest pain in the arse'.[37] Yet the original print run of 3,000 copies sold out within a week with virtually no advertising; 800 copies of the second printing were sold in the last week of July alone.[38] The second impression of 5,000 copies sold out within six weeks. In August, La Hune, a well-stocked bookshop on the boulevard Saint-Germain and a reliable barometer of a certain Parisian taste, reported that the book was selling 'like hot cakes'.[39] In the first fortnight of August, *Les Mots et les choses* entered *L'Express*'s non-fiction best-seller list, which was headed by *The Crippled Tree*, the first volume of Han Suyin's autobiography.[40] To his bewilderment, Foucault had published one of the best-selling titles of the year.

Les Mots et les choses was one of the first books to be published in Gallimard's new series, 'La Bibliothèque des sciences humaines', the other lead title being a translation of Elias Canetti's *Masse und Macht*. The series was well received and rapidly became something of an intellectual institution. Its general editor was Pierre Nora, a recent refugee from Julliard and a professional historian. He was to become Foucault's main editor and, for a long time, a close associate and friend. Foucault obviously profited from the publicity surrounding the launch of the series, and in turn lent it his prestige. An unsigned piece in *Le Nouvel Observateur* in May described *Les Mots et les choses* as 'one of the most fascinating books published in a long time'.[41] A week earlier, the same magazine had referred to its author, along with Deleuze and Michel Tort, as one of 'the philosophers people are talking about' when it reported his presence at the lecture on 'Sign and perversion in de Sade' given by Klossowski to an enormous audience at a forum organised by *Tel Quel* in Saint-Germain-des-Prés.[42]

The apparently simple title of *Les Mots et les choses* has a curious history. References to 'words and things' appear in many of Foucault's earlier writings and seem to anticipate the book's title. Yet, according to Pierre Nora, as reported by Eribon, this was not the original title. Foucault originally intended to call his book *La Prose du monde*. That, however, was the intended title of an article found in Merleau-Ponty's desk after his death in 1961 and eventually became that of the volume of unpublished material edited by Claude Lefort in 1969. Reluctant to be closely identified with Merleau-Ponty, Foucault therefore opted for either *L'Ordre des choses* or *Les Mots et les choses*, and used the title 'La Prose du monde' for his second chapter. After some persuasion from Nora, he adopted the definitive title.[43] According to Angèle Kremer Marietti, however, 'L'Ordre des choses' had to be abandoned because there was already a book in print with that title.[44] The English translation, which appeared in 1970, was entitled *The Order of Things*, a literal translation of '*l'ordre des choses*'. A 'Publisher's Note' explains: 'A literal translation of the title of the French edition of this work . . . would have given rise to confusion with two other books that have already appeared under the title *Words and Things*. The publisher therefore agreed with the author on the alternative title *The Order of Things*, which was, in fact, M. Foucault's original preference.'[45] Some years later, Foucault confused matters still further by telling two Brazilian interviewers: 'The title itself is a translation of "Words and Things", which was the great moral, political, scientific and religious slogan in early eighteenth-century England.'[46] It would be idle to speculate on which version of the story is the true one, and we are therefore left with a rather pleasing instance of undecidability.

The subtitle – '*une archéologie des sciences humaines*' – poses no translation problems, but it too has a history which is not without its ambiguities. Dreyfus and Rabinow were told by Foucault that the original subtitle was 'An Archaeology of Structuralism'.[47] *Histoire de la folie* was 'the archaeology of a silence' and *Naissance de la clinique* an 'archaeology of the medical gaze'. Discussing Freud in *Maladie mentale et personnalité*, Foucault remarked that a neurosis is 'a spontaneous archaeology of the libido',[48] an phrase which may have been suggested to him by the frequent archaeological metaphors used by Freud himself. It is, however, in his thesis on Kant that Foucault first uses the expression: 'Would not the archaeology of the text, if it were possible, allow us to see the birth of a *homo criticus*, whose structure would be essentially different to that of the man who preceded him?'[49]

Foucault provides various explanations for his use of the term. In conversation with Raymond Bellour, he defines 'archaeology' as 'the science of the archive' of a given period,[50] and he would in later interviews hint at a possible etymological connection between the two. There is no such connection: 'archive' derives from '*archia*', meaning 'magisterial office' or 'public office', 'archaeology' from the root '*archaeo-*' ('ancient', 'primitive'). The pseudo-etymology is no more than playfulness on the part of a man with a great affection for the etymological wonders to be found in the works of Brisset. Foucault was of course well aware that there is no etymological link between 'archive' and 'archaeology', but argued that 'the law of words – which does not coincide with the law of philologists' authorised his usage.[51] The element of playfulness is much more apparent in the slightly different explanation given elsewhere, when Foucault simply refers to the 'ludic rights of etymology'.[52]

Foucault also provided a much more solid and convincing explanation in the course of an exchange with the critic and academic George Steiner, when he signalled that the term 'archaeology' derives from Kant's work on progress in metaphysics, and dismissed the suggestion that it has anything to do with Freud.[53] Bernauer has identified the reference in question as being to Kant's use of the term '*philosophische Archäologie*', which might be defined as 'the investigation of that which renders necessary a certain form of thought'.[54]

A passage in the foreword written for the English translation of *Les Mots et les choses* provides one of the clearest definitions of just what Foucault now understands by archaeology:

What I would like to do . . . is to reveal a *positive unconscious* of knowledge: a level that eludes the consciousness of the scientist and yet is part of scientific discourse, instead of disputing its validity and seeking to diminish its scientific nature. What was common to the natural history, the economics and the grammar of the Classical period was certainly not present to the consciousness of the scientist; or that part of it that was conscious was superficial, limited and almost fanciful; . . . but, unknown to themselves, the naturalists, economists and grammarians employed the same rules to define the objects proper to their own study, to form their concepts, to build their theories. It is these rules of formation, which were never formulated in their own right, but are to be found only in widely differing theories, concepts, and objects of study, that I have tried to reveal, by isolating, as their specific locus, a level that I have called, somewhat arbitrarily perhaps, archaeological. Taking as an example the period covered in this book, I have tried to determine the basis or archaeological system common to a whole series of scientific 'representations' or 'products' dispersed throughout the natural history, economics, and philosophy of the Classical period.[55]

An archaeology is not a history of ideas, a genre which Foucault now dismisses as teleological. He is anxious to avoid retrospective readings which see in the classical analysis of wealth only 'the later unity of a political economy which is tentatively constituting itself',[56] just as he was anxious in *Histoire de la folie* to eschew analyses which might allow the psychiatrist to relax in the belief that he understood the true phenomenon behind the obscure myths contemplated by the mad-doctor. Foucault's concern is with the thesis that 'in culture and at a given moment, there is never any more than one *épistémè* which defines the conditions of possibility of all knowledge'.[57]

Archaeology is further contrasted with what Foucault terms 'doxology'. The terms refer to different levels and forms of analysis. Doxology would, for instance, study eighteenth-century economic thought by looking at who was a physiocrat and who was not, by analysing the interests that were at stake, and by looking at how the struggle for power was waged. Archaeology, in contrast, ignores individuals and their histories, and defines how it was possible to think in terms of either physiocratic or anti-physiocratic knowledge.[58] The *épistémè* is equivalent to the 'historical *a priori*' of *Naissance de la clinique*. In the preface to *Les Mots et les choses*, Foucault uses Borges's Chinese encyclopedia and its bizarre classificatory system to illustrate 'the stark impossibility of thinking *that*'.[59] It is, that is, apparently quite impossible to conceive of a system of thought which operates with categories such as '*et cetera*' and 'innumerable', and ignores the classical categories of Western philosophy. The role of archaeology is, in part, to demonstrate that it is not only possible but necessary for such modes of thought to exist and operate.

Whereas *Naissance de la clinique* had focused on a relatively short period of history, *Les Mots et les choses* marked Foucault's return to the broad panoramic sweep of *Histoire de la folie* and to a similar division into Renaissance, classical age, modern age. In some ways, the book is a continuation of the earlier works and large sections are expanded from themes that had already been explored. The Royaumont paper on Nietzsche, Freud and Marx outlined in succinct terms the discussion of Renaissance theories of the sign in Chapter 2 ('The Prose of the World'), and a lot of the analysis of the quasi-botanical taxonomy of the classical age is anticipated by sections of both *Histoire de la folie* and *Naissance de la clinique*. Perhaps the most novel and striking feature of *Les Mots et les choses* is the enormous scope of an archaeology that ranges across disciplines as apparently diverse as philology, economics and natural history. It provides an even more sumptuous display of erudition than the thesis of 1961, and Foucault did not employ research assistants.

The first chapter of *Les Mots et les choses* is the celebrated consideration of Velázquez's *Las Meninas*, known in French as *Les Suivantes*, which hangs in Madrid's Museo del Prado. It is a seductively attractive piece of writing, beginning with a flat descriptive neutrality – 'The painter is standing slightly back from the canvas'[60] – and becoming more impassioned as Foucault's gaze moves across every detail of the complex painting. By the end of the chapter, the painting of Philip IV, his wife, members of their court and family, and of Velázquez himself, has become 'the representation of classical representation and the definition of the space it opens up'.[61] The opening pages on Velázquez have lured many a reader into the depths of a complex and difficult book, and they are a *tour de force*. They were not, however, part of Foucault's original schema for the book. A slightly shorter version of 'Les Suivantes' first appeared as an essay published by the *Mercure de France* in its July–August issue of 1965 and was Foucault's first sustained discussion of the visual arts. It was only at Pierre Nora's insistence that Foucault included a revised version of his essay in *Les Mots et les choses*; in the author's own view it was 'too literary' for inclusion.[62]

Had it not been for the editorial intervention of Nora, the reader's first encounter with the text would have been with a rather less immediately seductive discussion of the forms of 'similitude' which governed Renaissance thinking. For the *épistémè* of the sixteenth century, the world was a vast syntactic system in which animals communicated with plants, the earth with the sea and men with their environment thanks to a series of similitudes and correspondences.[63] Hence the title of the chapter: 'The Prose of the World'. Things bore names which signalled their role in this prose: aconite had an affinity with the eyes, but that affinity would remain unknown, were it not for the signature contained in its seeds. The seeds are dark globes embedded in white coverings, and they are what the pupil is to the eye.[64]

This system of thought is, it would seem, as 'starkly impossible' as the Chinese encyclopedia, yet it is made possible and necessary by a structure of knowledge exemplified by 'the great metaphor of the book which one opens, spells out and reads in order to understand nature'.[65] The book metaphor is the obverse of the system which forces language to reside in such natural objects as aconite seeds. Language itself is part of the great distribution of similitudes and signatures, and must therefore be studied in the same way. Hence the etymological search for the secret properties of words, letters or syllables. Hence the accumulation of knowledge in the form of word lists and the compendia which astonished the great naturalist Georges Buffon (1707–88) by listing under the same heading accurate descriptions of snakes, mythological accounts of their supposed properties, and tales of the uses made of them in magic. Foucault cites Buffon's dismissal of Aldrovandi's *Historia serpentum et draconum* – 'All that is legend, not description' – and then comments: 'Indeed, for Aldrovandi and his contemporaries, all that was *legenda* – things to be read.'[66] Aldrovandi was no more credulous than Buffon, nor was he any less concerned with the accuracy of his observations: 'His gaze was simply not bound to things by the same system, not by the same disposition of the *épistémè*.'[67]

As in *Histoire de la folie*, the account given here of the Renaissance is little more than a prologue to the main topic. In his preface, Foucault speaks of the two great discontinuities which punctuate western culture: that which inaugurates the classical age, and that which inaugurates our modernity at the beginning of the nineteenth century,[68] but he is concerned primarily with the classical and modern ages. The Renaissance is the contrasting backdrop against which the classical age stands out. Yet, if it is familiar to readers of his earlier books, not everyone found Foucault's Renaissance familiar. Reviewing *L'Archéologie du savoir* in 1969, Brice Parain, who had reputedly rejected *Histoire de la folie* in his role as a Gallimard reader, recalled that his first reaction to *Les Mots et les choses* had been: 'God, it's beautiful.' His enthusiasm soon gave way to disquiet. This was not a Renaissance he recognised: 'There were people I didn't know: Grégoire, Porlu, Aldrovandi, Campanella, Crollius, Cardan, even Paracelsus, but no Bodin, no Galileo, no Gutenberg, no Rabelais, no Agrippa d'Aubigné, a bit of Montaigne . . . but mainly to tell us to distrust him, and no mention of technological discoveries or architecture.' Parain probably spoke for many.[69]

The collapse of the Renaissance *épistémè* is signalled by the appearance of Don Quixote, already an important minor figure in *Histoire de la folie*: 'A long graphism, as thin as a letter, he has just escaped from the open pages of a book. His whole existence is nothing more than language, text, printed sheets, a history already transcribed.'[70] Don Quixote's life is a quest for similitude in which everything becomes a sign from the books he had devoured, but all signs and similitudes disappoint and deceive him: '*Don Quixote* sketches the negative of the Renaissance world; writing has ceased to be the prose of the world; resemblances and signs have broken off their old alliance; similitudes disappoint, tend towards the visionary and delusion; things stubbornly remain within their ironic identity: they are no longer anything but what they are.'[71] The old relationship between words and things has broken down, and belief in resemblance is now a form of unreason. The classical age inaugurated by the wanderings of the Knight of the Doleful Countenance will be structured by new modes of representation, speech, classification and exchange.

The *épistémè* of the classical age can be schematically described as being governed by an articulated system of *mathesis* (a general, mathematical science of order), *taxinomia* (a classification which operates at a more empirical level) and genetic analysis.[72] Its figures of thought are traced through analyses of the four modes identified by Foucault in chapters on 'representing', 'thinking', 'speaking' and 'exchanging'. It would not be practical to undertake a reading of the entire text here, and comprehensive accounts can readily be found elsewhere.[73] A brief examination of the chapter on 'speaking' will therefore be made in order to outline Foucault's primary concerns and methods.

Whereas the Renaissance was struck by the brute fact of the existence of language in a physical sense, in the knowledge of the classical age, language exists at the level of a different kind of representation: in the form of verbal signs and discourse. Analysis or criticism therefore becomes the examination of *figures*, or types of discourse and their expressive value, and of *tropes*, or the different relations existing between words and the same representative content.[74] Ultimately, analysis is based upon the founding conviction that 'insofar as language can represent all representations, it is quite legitimately the element of the universal. There must be at least one possible language which gathers the totality of the world into its words, and, conversely, the world being the totality of what can be represented, must be able to become, in its totality, an Encyclopedia.'[75]

This encyclopedia is not Borges's 'Celestial Emporium', but the great undertaking of Diderot and his colleagues. And one of its homologues is the *Grammaire générale et raisonnée* published by the logicians and teachers of Port-Royal in 1660, which Foucault prefaced in 1969.[76] General grammar does not mean comparative grammar; its central concern is with the basic representative function of language, the mode in which it articulates thought. 'General grammar will define the system of identities and differences . . . establish the *taxonomy* of every language, that is, that which in every language founds the possibility of discourse.'[77] Given that language is not a simple system of representation, but one which is always reduplicated, grammar must also study 'the way in which words designate what they say, initially in their primitive value (theory of origins and roots), then in their permanent capacity for sliding, extension and reorganisation (theory of rhetorical space and of derivation).'[78]

The classical experience of language from Thomas Hobbes to the *Idéologues*, or for Nicolas de Malebranche, Etienne Condillac and David Hume, centres on a grammar which is both 'science and prescription, the study of words and a rule for building them, using them and reshaping them in their representative function'. And like the medicine of the pathological anatomist, it is haunted by a myth: 'the great utopia of a perfectly transparent language in which things themselves can be named without any confusion, either by a totally arbitrary, but perfectly reflected system (an artificial language) or by such a natural language that it can translate thought as a face expresses a passion'.[79] The fundamental task of language is to ascribe names to things and, in doing so, to name their very being.

It is the taxonomic aspect of general grammar that provides the most obvious link with the other faces of the classical *épistémè*. For the natural historians of the seventeenth century, their discipline is 'the space opened up in representation by an analysis which anticipates the possibility of naming; the possibility of seeing what one will say . . . In classical knowledge, knowledge of empirical individuals can be acquired only on the ordered and universal table of all possible differences.'[80] The analysis of wealth also obeys the same general configuration: 'The role of money, like that of words, is to designate [value], but it constantly oscillates around this vertical axis: price variations are to the initial establishment of the relationship between metal and wealth what rhetorical displacements are to the primitive value of verbal signs.'[81]

If the classical *épistémè* can be described positively with reference to its internal logic, it can also be described in negative terms: 'There is no life in the classical epoch, no science of life; nor is there any philology. A natural history, a general grammar. Similarly, there is no political

economy because production does not exist in the order of knowledge.'[82] This negative picture of the classical age outlines, like a bas
relief, the configuration of the modern era and the emergence of the
major disciplines which will provide the foundations for the human
sciences: economics, biology and philology. All imply the fracturing of
representation and the appearance of a historical dimension which
contrasts greatly with the timeless ideal space of the table.

Very schematically, the classical view of wealth as representation
gives way, with Adam Smith, David Ricardo and Marx, to the concept
of value as product, as the result of a productive process which implies a
temporal dimension. Ricardo, in particular, is credited with having
dissociated the formation and representation of value, and therefore
with allowing the articulation of economics and history.[83] Significantly, Foucault makes no great distinction between the political
economists and Marx: the controversies between them are no more
than ripples in a children's paddling pool.[84]

Georges Cuvier brings about a similar epistemic shift in the proto-
biological sciences. The structure of organs is no longer to be
understood in terms of taxonomic tabulation, but in terms of their
function. Life itself is no longer an uncertain distinction between
animate and inanimate, but the element in which 'all possible
differences between living creatures have their foundations'.[85] The
appearance of the vitalism of Cuvier marks a transition from a
taxonomic to a synthetic notion of life, and is one of the conditions of
possibility for a biology.

Language, in the meantime, loses its transparence and the sovereign
role it had in classical thought. Thanks to the work of Jakob Grimm and
Franz Bopp on philology and on linguistic families, language becomes
an object like any other, to be analysed or studied in the same way as
living creatures, wealth and value or the history of events and of men.
The foundations for the human sciences – psychology, sociology,
economics, literary analysis – have been laid. And so too have the
foundations for their destruction and transcendence.

Les Mots et les choses contains an apocalyptic vision: the modern
épistémè which emerged towards the end of the eighteenth century was
bound up with the dissolution of the reign of discourse and with the
constitution of man as subject and object of knowledge. Its possible
demise is now signalled by shifts to be observed primarily in the domain
of language, and in some ways it will mark a return to the Renaissance.
The difference is that there is no longer any primal word to found and
limit the movement of discourse, merely a language which 'spreads

without any point of departure, without any terminal point, without any promise'.[86] The modern literature Foucault had been analysing over the last years is language's revenge on the German philologist Bopp: 'It takes language away from grammar and returns it to the naked power of speech, and there it encounters the savage and imperious being of words.'[87] And corresponding to it is modern thought's questioning of 'the relationship between meaning, the form of truth and the form of being: in the heaven of our reflection there reigns a discourse – perhaps an inaccessible discourse – which may be a combined ontology and semantics. Structuralism is not a new method; it is the awakened and worried consciousness of modern knowledge'[88] the realisation that, far from being a transparent medium of communication, language is a material force with a being of its own.

Les Mots et les choses closes with an image that stays in the mind of most readers and inevitably coloured all debates about the book: 'Man is an invention easily shown by the archaeology of our thought to be of recent date. And whose end is, perhaps, nigh . . . We can readily wager that man will be effaced, like a face traced in the sand at the edge [*limite*] of the sea.'[89] The image is poetic, bleak and emotive, but it is not new. The image of a line of foam on a beach occurs again and again in Foucault's writings on literature and the experience of limits. Nor is this the first time he had spoken of the imminent death of man. In 1964, he wrote:

> What will not be long in dying, what is already dying within us (and whose very death supports our current language) is *homo dialecticus* – the being of departure, return and time, the animal who loses its truth and finds it anew and illuminated, the stranger to himself who becomes once more familiar to himself. This man was the sovereign subject of all the discourses that were pronounced on man, and particularly on alienated man, for a very long time. And, fortunately, he is dying beneath their chatter.[90]

The man who will soon be found dying is the Hegelian subject;[91] Foucault is celebrating the twilight of a particular idol. The irony is that the first philosopher to proclaim the death of man in France was, of course, the Hegelian Alexandre Kojève.

Foucault gave three major interviews to the literary press around the time of publication.[92] These allowed him to explain his book to a fairly general public, and to answer in advance some of the inevitable criticisms. They also added to the gathering groundswell of publicity. His interlocutors were all distinguished. Raymond Bellour saw the interview or conversation as a literary form in its own right, and had written extensively on the cinema and on Henri Michaux. The interviews with Lévi-Strauss, Barthes, Christian Metz, Jean Laplanche and J.B Pontalis that are, together with his Foucault interview, collected in his *Le Livre des autres* provide an invaluable picture of the public face of French intellectual life from 1966 to 1971. Madeleine Chapsal was an intelligent and sensitive critic as well as a capable journalist, as was Claude Bonnefoy.

Foucault describes *Histoire de la folie* as having been the history of difference, and his new book as being a history of resemblance, of identity.[93] His study of the transition from the classical age to the nineteenth century had led him to a surprising discovery: 'Man did not exist in classical knowledge. What did exist in the place where we discover man, was the power of discourse, of the verbal order, to represent the order of things.'[94] In May, a month after publication, Foucault described his own intellectual formation to Chapsal, who was to review his book for *L'Express*, in terms which made it seem like a revolt against the dominance of Sartre and his generation. Whereas Sartre's generation had been concerned above all with 'meaning', his was concerned primarily with the notion of 'system'; the break between the two generations was signalled by the work of Lévi-Strauss and Lacan. It was declarations like this that led to Foucault's being perceived as a structuralist. That perception of him is enshrined in a famous cartoon by Maurice Henri portraying a structuralist *déjeuner sur l'herbe*.[95] Foucault, Lacan, Lévi-Strauss and Barthes are seated on a lawn, all wearing grass skirts – and, in the case of Lacan, a bow tie – and Foucault is holding forth to the others. Legend has it that the only reason why Althusser did not feature is that no one outside ENS knew just what he looked like.

Foucault's relationship with structuralism was much more tenuous than this popular iconography suggests, and the unity of the supposed structuralist school now looks more fragile than it must have done in 1966. To take the obvious points of reference, Foucault was not, like Lévi-Strauss, in search of 'elementary structures' of kinship whose principles are so innate that their operations provide the equivalent of a philosophy of mind, and was not, like Lacan (whose own loyalty to structuralism was far from unalloyed), exploring the workings and formations of a universal unconscious 'structured like a language'. The model supplied by Saussurean or post-Saussurean linguistics, with its massive emphasis on the systematicity of *langue* (the social phenomenon of a differential system of verbal signs, as opposed to *parole* or speech; that individual phenomenon of language-use), was never paramount for Foucault. The revision of *Naissance de la clinique* for the second edition of 1972 did involve the shedding of a lot of structuralist terminology, as in the replacement of the phrase 'a structural analysis of the signified' with 'an analysis of discourses',[96] but that did little to alter the book's overall conceptual content, and it also involved the shedding of a residual Hegelianism inherited from Hyppolite. The iconography of 1966 is misleading in some senses, but it does capture the negative unity of an alliance of theorists in revolt against the banality of contemporary forms of humanism and the fading charms of existentialist phenomenology.

In the interview with Chapsal, Foucault began to suggest for the first time that there might be an explicitly political dimension to his work:

> Our task at the moment is to completely free ourselves from humanism and in that sense our work is political work. Saving man, rediscovering the human element in man, and so on . . . that is the aim of all these verbose undertakings, both theoretical and practical, to reconcile, for example, Marx and Teilhard de Chardin . . . Our task is to completely free ourselves from humanism and it is in that sense that our task is a political task, in that all regimes, East and West, smuggle shoddy goods under the banner of humanism . . . We must denounce all these mystifications just as, inside the PCF, Althusser and his brave comrades are struggling against 'Chardino-Marxism'.

The reference to 'Chardino-Marxism' is to the attempts by Garaudy and particularly by Jacques Monod to synthesise humanist Marxism and Christianity, science and faith, thanks to a theory of cosmogenesis. In 1967, the struggle against Chardino-Marxism was to be one of the major themes of Althusser's lecture course on the 'spontaneous philosophy' of scientists.[97]

When Chapsal suggested that the logic and mathematics to which he seemed to be appealing might seem abstract to many, Foucault exploded with anger: 'Abstract? I will give this answer: it is humanism that is abstract! All these cries from the heart, all these demands on behalf of the human person, existence, are abstract; I mean they are divorced from the scientific and technical world, and that is our real world.'[98]

Similar points are made in the interview with Bonnefoy, albeit in slightly less violent terms. Foucault also made some ill-tempered comments about Sartre, whose *Critique* had put a full stop to an episode in our history that began with Hegel: 'The *Critique de la raison dialectique* is a nineteenth-century man's magnificent and pathetic attempt to think the twentieth century. In that sense, Sartre is the last Hegelian and, I would even say, the last Marxist.'[99] The ground had been prepared, deliberately or otherwise, for a violent polemic. Foucault had effectively defined himself as being in opposition to Sartre, hostile to the Marxism of the PCF and favourable to Althusser.

Foucault's best-seller was to become a source of controversy. Seven reviews appeared in the dailies and weeklies in the last week of May and the first ten days of June. For the period, this was virtually maximum media exposure and the results were impressive; every review which mentioned the phenomenal sales figures resulted in yet more sales. Unexpectedly, *Les Mots et les choses* became popular summer reading. It was not, however, the most improbable best-seller of the season; the glossy magazines were also recommending Lacan's *Ecrits* as holiday reading. One can only speculate on the likely discrepancy between the number of both titles that were sold and the number of copies that were actually read. A sardonic Michel de Certeau well captures the mood of the moment: 'The work, though long and difficult, numbers among those outward signs of culture the trained eye should find on display in every private library, alongside the art books. Have *you* read it? One's social and intellectual standing depends on the response.'[100]

Thanks to *Histoire de la folie*, Foucault had long escaped the academic ghetto, but the reception given to *Les Mots et les choses* was something new. His previous books had been reviewed by intellectual monthlies like *Esprit* and *Critique*; *Les Mots et les choses* was widely discussed in mass-circulation magazines such as *Le Nouvel Observateur* and *L'Express*. Of the two, *Le Nouvel Observateur* was the more intellectual. Throughout the next decade and beyond, many academics and intellectuals – including Foucault – would write for it and it would become an important conduit for the dissemination of a certain culture. *L'Express* was a rather different publication. Once a major organ for opposition to the war in Algeria, it was increasingly modelled on the American *Newsweek*. Its target readership was mainly the increasingly affluent professional middle class, or the legendary *jeune cadre dynamique*. The average reader of *Le Nouvel Observateur* was likely to be a graduate student, an academic or a member of liberal professions, who was on the left but critical of the PCF. Many of Foucault's hypothetical 'two thousand specialists' would have read *Le Nouvel Observateur*; few of them were likely to read *L'Express* on any regular basis. Foucault was now reaching a very different audience and had unwittingly become a cultural commodity. From 1966 onwards, his life was very much a public one. When André Breton died at the end of September, it seemed quite natural for a journalist to approach Foucault for comment.[101] That would not have happened in 1961.

The main characters in Simone de Beauvoir's novel *Les belles images* (1966), an architect and a woman working in advertising, are probably not atypical of Foucault's new public, obsessed as they are with the acquisition of commodities and concerned with 'image' to the exclusion of almost everything else. They and their friends read the same periodicals, which easily convince them that 'the idea of man has to be revised and will probably disappear; it was an invention of the nineteenth century, and is now out of date'.[102] De Beauvoir herself is on record as saying that the satire is directed not only against the intellectual snobs among Foucault's readership, but also against Foucault himself. In her view the *nouveau roman*, *Tel Quel* and especially Foucault 'provide bourgeois consciousness with its best alibis. They suppress history, praxis, that is to say commitment, and suppress man.'[103] Foucault read *Le Monde* regularly, and can scarcely have avoided seeing this vituperative assessment of his work.

Not all the initial responses were so hostile. At the beginning of June, Foucault received a letter from the Belgian surrealist René Magritte, much of whose *oeuvre* can be interpreted as a profound meditation on the relationship between words and things. Magritte was impressed by Foucault's book, and his letter consisted of a short and rather enigmatic disquisition upon 'resemblance' and 'similitude'. According to Magritte, similitude was a property of things, and resemblance a property of thought, which 'resembles by being what it sees, understands or knows'. Thought was as invisible as pleasure or pain, but painting introduced a difficulty: 'There is such a thing as thought which sees and which can be described visually. *Las Meninas* is the visible image of Velázquez's invisible thought. Can the invisible therefore sometimes be visible? Provided that the thought consists exclusively of visible figures.' Magritte attached to his letter reproductions of 'paintings I painted without preoccupying myself with original research into painting'. They included 'This is not a pipe', with a legend inscribed on the verso: 'The title does not contradict the drawing; it states it differently.'

Foucault promptly replied, asking for some information about *Perspective – The Balcony of Manet* (1950). The painting is a variant on the canvas in the Louvre which shows the painters Berthe Morisot and Antoine Guillement, the violinist Fanny Klauss standing on a balcony, with Léon Koëlla in the background. In Magritte's version, the figures are replaced by coffins. Foucault thought he detected a parallel with Roussel, but wanted to know why the coffins had been introduced.[104] The painter liked the suggestion that his work had something in common with Roussel, but his answer to Foucault's question was less than illuminating: 'Your question . . asks what it already contains: what made me see coffins where Manet saw white figures is the image shown by my painting, where the décor of "The Balcony" provided a suitable place for coffins.' He ended by expressing the hope that he could meet Foucault when he was in Paris at the end of the year for his exhibition at the Iolas gallery. Foucault was not in Paris at the end of the year, and the exchange was not pursued any further: René Magritte died in September 1967. The correspondence with the artist did, on the other hand, lead Foucault to write an essay entitled 'Ceci n'est pas une pipe', which, in a slightly revised and expanded version, was republished as an elegant little illustrated book in 1973.[105]

Although it was the monthlies published in the spring of the following year that created the real controversy over Les Mots et les choses, the initial reviews provided a glimpse of what was to come. The book was very favourably reviewed in Le Monde by Jean Lacroix, who was one of the few to stress the Kantian strand in Foucault's exploration of 'the internal conditions of possibility' that allowed the history of thought to be articulated by thought.[106] For François Châtelet, there was no doubt: this was 'the theoretical analysis which will give the human sciences the reflexion which they so notoriously lack. Foucault's rigour, originality and inspiration are such that a reading of his book inevitably gives one a radically new insight into the past of western culture and a more lucid conception of its present confusion.'[107] Deleuze was similarly enthusiastic; Foucault's analyses were so masterly and his tone so new that the reader was immediately aware that the book represented a 'new way of thinking'. Foucault was indeed 'founding the human sciences', but the foundation he provided was 'poisonous', and had been destroyed by his archaeology.[108] In the more popular L'Express, Madeleine Chapsal hailed, in rather brash terms, the advent of 'the greatest revolution since existentialism'.[109] In Le Figaro littéraire, Robert Kanters was somewhat more sceptical about a book he found 'curious . . . rich and difficult'. For Foucault, he wrote, the 'classical order' was the enemy and 'man' was a useless hypothesis. The book was a call to 'burn Descartes'.[110] The veteran Catholic novelist François Mauriac complained, not without some justification, that all this talk of the death of consciousness would soon make his old enemy Sartre look like a brother.[111] Jacques Brosse, in the meantime, firmly situated *Les Mots et les choses* in the context of the structuralism inspired by linguistics,[112] whilst a sardonic Jean-Marie Domenach wondered how the 'devotees of systems' could possibly appeal against the present system in the name of a 'liberating society'.[113]

Domenach did, however, take the book very seriously. When, in December, *Esprit* organised a conference on structuralism, *Les Mots et les choses* was high on the agenda. The major themes of the coming controversy had been outlined by the summer. Foucault represented something new and revolutionary, and was part of the structuralist camp. He was Sartre's rival heir apparent.

The first of the influential monthly journals to discuss *Les Mots et les choses* was *Les Temps Modernes*. Unusually, two articles and a total of forty-eight pages were devoted to Foucault in the January 1967 issue. Both articles were negative, and strongly influenced by the comments made by Sartre in an interview with Bernard Pingaud in October 1966. The interview was concerned mainly with Sartre's views on structuralism, but his immediate response on being asked if he saw a common inspiration in the younger generation's attitude towards him was to identify

> At least a dominant tendency, as the phenomenon is not general: the rejection of history. The way Michel Foucault's latest book has become a best-seller is typical . . . The success of his book is proof enough that it was something that people were waiting for. Now, truly original thought is never something that people are waiting for. Foucault gives people what they needed: an eclectic synthesis in which Robbe-Grillet, structuralism, linguistics and *Tel Quel* are used one after another to demonstrate the impossibility of historical reflection.

Foucault's perspective was historical only insofar as it distinguished between a 'before' and an 'after': 'He replaces cinema with a magic lantern, movement with a succession of immobilities.' In a footnote to *L'Archéologie du savoir*, Foucault replied sardonically to this point, and pointed out that a *tableau* is a 'series of series' and 'not a small fixed image placed in front of a lantern, all the better to disappoint children, who, given their age, naturally prefer the vivacity of the cinema'.[114] Sartre went on to claim that Foucault's main target was not history as such, but Marxism: the point was 'to construct a new ideology, the last rampart the bourgeoisie can erect against Marx'.[115] The interview was widely publicised and was given even further exposure when extracts were published in *La Quinzaine littéraire*'s issue of 15–31 October.

Pingaud's interview with Sartre is obviously one of the main sources for de Beauvoir's comments in *Le Monde*. It is also the source of many of the points made by Sylvie Le Bon, the adopted daughter of de Beauvoir, in her article on Foucault's 'despairing positivism'.[116] She begins:

How can one suppress history? Michel Foucault proposes a despairing solution to this impossible problem: don't think about it. Exclude it from knowledge, if not from the real. That is the aim of his book *Les Mots et les choses*, and in order to pursue it, the author is ready to sacrifice anything. Sacrificing his predecessors, honesty and even his object of study is easy. Foucault goes further than that, and would rather expose his book to death by unintelligibility than abandon his positivist postulate.[117]

For Le Bon, Foucault is a 'positivist' because his archaeology is not concerned with explaining 'a progression, an evolution or, in short, a history'; it simply provides a description of three stages, with 'the analysis of three historical *a priori*s, which adequately account for the apparently anarchic profusion of knowledges'.[118] Foucault's historical *a priori* is no more than a 'retrospective artifice' designed to 'transform the historical evolution of ideas and knowledge into a juxtaposition of atemporal necessities'. His attempt to uncover *a priori*s is comparable to the attempts of a 'tyrannical ethnographer' to apply his own social categories to an alien society.[119] Like Sartre himself, Le Bon contends that Foucault's book is a sustained attack on Marxism, and that its author has failed to learn the lesson taught by the opening pages of *Critique de la raison dialectique*: ' "schools of thought" which claim to have transcended Marxism are in reality pre-Marxist.' The second *Temps Modernes* article, by Michel Amiot, was rather more measured but reached equally negative conclusions. Although he was elogious of Foucault's erudition, he saw in it 'an unstable mixture of Spengler and Heidegger' and concluded that Foucault's philosophy was no more than 'a variety of historicist scepticism'.[120]

The chorus of disapproval from the Sartre clan was soon amplified by representatives of the PCF, who also introduced some curious variations of their own. For Jacques Milhau, writing in *Cahiers du communisme*, Foucault's 'anti-historical prejudice' stood up only because it was supported by 'a neo-Nieztschean ideology which, whether he knows it or not, serves only too well the aims of a class whose interests lie in masking the objective paths of the future'.[121] Jeannette Colombel, a philosophy teacher from Lyon and a long-standing Party member, found that, while Foucault's relativism was in some respects healthy, his 'catastrophism' could be a consolation to both the

> '*intellectuel de gauche*' who is disappointed, impatient, and anxious without in some cases having ever been committed, and the technocrat who believes only in the virtues'of the system . . . The human sciences . . . are used by Foucault to demonstrate the illusory nature of all undertakings: all we can do is accept the system: lucidity of despair, lucidity of laughter. Made in USA [English in the original].[122]

Noting, quite accurately, that Foucault's analysis made no mention of contradictions between forces and relations of production or of the class struggle, she concluded that his work embodies an 'ideology of despair'. The real task was to analyse contradictions as a preliminary to changing the world and to 'smashing the system'.[123]

Both PCF reviewers were using a coded language. Milhau's 'objective paths' lead, obviously enough, to the eventual victory of the PCF. Colombel is writing from a perspective which associates structuralism with technocracy and either Americanism or Gaullism, and disingenuously transforms Foucault's professed interest in systems of thought into support for the economic system of capitalism. Ultimately, their criticisms are a truism: Foucault was not a supporter of the PCF and his cardinal sin had been to declare, in a phrase that was to become famous: 'Marxism exists in nineteenth-century thought as a fish exists in water; that is, it ceases to breathe anywhere else.'[124]

The 'technocracy' argument reappeared elsewhere in an even more curious form when Foucault was accused of trying to emulate de Gaulle by plotting 'a sort of intellectual 13 May or apocalypse after which the old human sciences will be replaced by the ethnography of Lévi-Strauss's subcontractors, the puns of the Lacanian squad and the "concept" of "wrenching" [*déchirure*; *reissen*] as defined by Monsieur Martin Heidegger', and of having elaborated a theory which was technocratic in that it both 'applied the methods of technocracy and supplied it with the explicit ideology it lacked'.[125] Indeed, Foucault's book represented a threat to reason and to reason's twin sister: democracy.[126]

The same argument appears in a more moderate form in *Esprit*, where Pierre Burgelin explains Foucault's success as follows:

> We no longer know what it means to speak the truth. Hence the anonymous power that it is used by those who claim to know in

order to lead us where an unavoidable destiny is leading us: the scientific and technical civilisation which manufacture conditions of existence, the men who have to adapt to them . . . For if man, carried off by the death of God, disappears, destiny is all that remains.[127]

Jean-Marie Domenach, writing in the same issue, took a slightly more charitable view, arguing that 'structuralism' might help in a 'great clean-up of conceptualisations' and sensing that *Les Mots et les choses* contained a genuinely tragic vision.[128]

Foucault had succeeded in provoking the hostility of a grand coalition of Sartreans, Marxists and Catholic humanists. He had accomplished, or almost accomplished, the feat of reconciling Sartre and the man he had once cruelly dismissed with the words: 'God is not an artist. Nor is Monsieur Mauriac.'[129] It would be some time before it emerged that he did have allies on the left, and even within the PCF. For the moment, his main champion was Canguilhem. Canguilhem's defence of Foucault was the work of an angry man, and one whose anger produced an ironically modest proposal: Foucault's critics should establish 'A League of the Rights of Man to be the subject and object of philosophy with the motto: "Humanists of all parties, unite".'[130] Foucault had caused a scandal:

> Because history today is a sort of magic field in which, for many philosophers, existence is identified with discourse and the actor of history with the authors of histories, even if they are stuffed with ideological *a priori*s. And that is why a programme for the overthrow of historical discourse is denounced as a manifesto for the subversion of the course of history. The subversion of a progressivism can only be a conservative project. And that is why your structure is neo-capitalist.[131]

Here, Canguilhem is parodying a line from Molière's *Le Médecin malgré lui* (1666) so famous as to have become proverbial: '*Et voilà pourquoi votre fille est muette*' ('And that is why your daughter is mute'). Molière's thesis is that a girl brought up in silence will have nothing to say; Canguilhem's that Foucault's critics are so blinded by their belief in the progressive nature of history that they inevitably perceive criticisms as an apologia for neo-capitalism. Canguilhem ends his case for the defence with an argument in which epistemological and *ad hominem* arguments combine to brutal effect. Over twenty years ago, Cavaillès had outlined a critique of phenomenology and had stressed the need for a philosophy of the concept. The self-proclaimed Spinozist who was shot by the Germans for acts of resistance had refuted in advance existentialist theories of history and 'the argument of those who try to discredit what they call structuralism by condemning it for, among other misdemeanours, generating passivity in the face of a *fait accompli*'.[132]

Canguilhem has never been noted for his moderation of tone and it is clear that some old scores are being settled here, the suggestion being that while Cavaillès fought and died, Sartre and the theorists of commitment did not. Canguilhem's comments also revive the distinction between philosophies of consciousness and philosophies of the concept, and firmly situate Foucault's work among the latter. He was, probably without realising it, preparing the ground for an alliance between Foucault and representatives of a new generation. For the moment, Foucault himself did not reply to his critics.

One of the stranger by-products of the media success of *Les Mots et les choses* was an invitation to lecture in Hungary, presumably on the strength of the coverage in *Les Lettres françaises*. Foucault states that this was in 1967, whereas Daniel Defert believes that it was in 1966. The only documentary evidence is inconclusive: a card with a postmark so blurred as to be illegible.[133] Foucault's tour took him to university lecture theatres, but when he made it known to the authorities that he intended to speak on structuralism, he was informed that he would have to speak to a small team of specialists meeting in the rector's office. When he raised the issue in private with his student interpreter, he was told that there were three topics that could not be discussed in the university: Nazism, the Horthy regime, and structuralism.[134] In retrospect, he began to realise that there was a connection between the ban on discussing structuralism in Budapest and the hostile reception given to structuralist works and to *Les Mots et les choses* by *Les Temps Modernes* and the PCF. Although matters were obviously much more serious in the Eastern-bloc countries, the aim was the same: the suppression of an emerging non-Marxist culture on the left.[135]

The only other source of information about Foucault's experiences in Hungary is Daniel Defert. Foucault apparently rejected the opportunity to meet Georg Lukács (a privilege accorded to all visiting philosophers), in whose work he had no interest, and that rejection greatly enhanced his interpreter's opinion of him. There may also have been a more private reason for accepting the Hungarian invitation, and Defert suggests that Foucault was eager to see the Manets in Budapest's Museum of Fine Arts. If Defert is correct, these would have been a wash drawing made in preparation for the lithograph version of

The Barricade and a line drawing of *The Execution of the Emperor Maximilian.*[136] Foucault could have traced their whereabouts from standard works of reference, and may also have been aware of the international conference devoted to the *Execution* paintings in Budapest in 1965.

Foucault's comments on Hungary point to some uneasy contradictions. In his interview with Chapsal, he complained bitterly about what he called the 'monoglot narcissism of the French' and their wilful ignorance of developments such as Russian formalism and the Anglo-American new criticism. This was, he claimed, fostered by a secondary education system which did not teach 'the basic disciplines which would allow us to understand what is happening in our country – and especially what is happening elsewhere. . . . Our education system dates from the nineteenth century and in it we still see the reign of the blandest psychology, the most outdated humanism, and categories of taste, of the human heart.'[137]

The comments reflect Foucault's involvement in the work of the Fouchet Commission in 1965–66. The commission, established by Fouchet in his capacity as minister for education, first met in January 1965 and dealt with the situation in secondary and higher education. Foucault's presence is explained by the appointment of Jean Knapp as an adviser to the minister; Knapp had been at ENS with Foucault and, during his time as a cultural adviser to the French Embassy in Copenhagen, had invited Foucault to lecture there. He now suggested that he should sit on the commission. Foucault argued strongly that secondary education should concentrate on basic disciplines rather than on topics which were simply a prefiguration of the university syllabus, and also cast serious doubts on the role of the *agrégation*, which he described as a test of 'intellectual vivacity' rather than a preparation for research. The doctoral system also needed revision; in the present circumstances, the 'principal thesis' required such effort that it often left its author exhausted for the rest of his or her life.[138]

Educational reforms were certainly essential. The traditional policy of no selection, which meant that anyone with a *bac* had the right to enter university, had led to both escalating student numbers and to a cruel process of de facto selection by elimination during first- and second-year examinations. The opening of a new faculty at Nanterre in October 1965 had done little to ease the situation. Christian Fouchet was unpopular with students and lecturers like, and had been declared *persona non grata* by militants at the Sorbonne in 1963. For the majority of students, the finer points of the regulations covering the *agrégation* and the doctorate were of no significance; they were concerned with having more lecture theatres and fewer formal lectures delivered to an audience of hundreds. Foucault's comments said more about his own elite background than about student concerns of the moment.

In March 1966, Fouchet's plans for reforms were greeted with a call for a three-day strike from SNESup, the main lecturers' union. In September, an obscure group calling themselves 'Situationists' published a pamphlet in Strasbourg. It was entitled *On Student Poverty, Considered in Its Economic, Political, Psychological, Sexual and Especially Intellectual Aspects, and on Some Ways of Remedying It*, and was one of the omens of what was to come in 1968.[139]

Although there is a considerable literary element in the final pages of *Les Mots et les choses*, Foucault was by now writing much less on literary issues and concentrating more and more on historical and philosophical topics. One of the finest expressions of his interest in the literary was also, paradoxically, one of the last. Foucault obviously continued to read widely and to write occasional pieces on literary topics, but his passion for modernist literature never again reached the peak it had between 1962 and 1966.

Fittingly, his last major article from this period was devoted to Maurice Blanchot. It appeared in the June 1966 issue of *Critique*, which was a homage to Blanchot.[140] Many of the themes of Foucault's earlier articles reappear in a very concentrated manner, but there are also some shifts of accent. While he is again pursuing forms of thought which are irreducible to philosophy, Foucault's perception of the modern is now somewhat different. Self-referentiality and reflexivity define the modern in only the most superficial terms. What is at stake in literature is now seen as a transition to an 'outside':

> Language escapes discourse's mode of being – that is, the dynasty of representation – and the literary word develops from itself, forming a network in which each point, distinct from the others and distanced even from its closest neighbours, is situated in relation to every other point in a space which at once holds and separates them . . . The 'subject' of literature (that which speaks in it and that which it speaks about) is less language in its positivity, than the void in which it finds its space when it enunciates itself in the nudity of the 'I speak'.[141]

The 'I speak' is naked because of its isolation, because it is not a communication addressed to others, but rather an utterance in which speaker ('I') and speech ('I speak') are inseparable and self-sufficient. Within this space, de Sade allows the 'nudity of desire', as non-communicative as Blanchot's 'I speak,' to speak, and Hölderlin announces the 'shimmering absence of the gods'.[142] Mallarmé, Artaud, Bataille and Klossowski all inhabit it. And one of the finest representatives of this 'thought of the outside' is Blanchot, 'not hidden by his texts, but absent from their existence and absent through the marvellous force of their existence, he is . . . that thought itself – the real, absolutely distant, scintillating invisible presence, the necessary fate, the inevitable law, the calm, infinite and measured vigour of that thought'.[143]

Blanchot's fiction and criticism are haunted by two myths: that of the sirens and that of Eurydice. The sirens sing their deadly song of enchantment from a place which can never be reached: 'only the promise of a future song runs through their melody'.[144] Eurydice is effectively invisible, offering only the promise of a glimpsed face. Both are, of course, figures of death. Language and the thought of the outside imply an encounter with death; writing is a transgression against the limit imposed by death.

Foucault never offered any explanation for his failure to pursue his literary-critical interests. Or rather, he offered an explanation which does not explain everything. In an interview first published in 1977 as a foreword to the Italian anthology *Microfisica del potere*, he spoke scathingly of 'all that relentless theorisation of writing we saw in the 1960s' and described it as 'a swan song':

> The writer was struggling to retain his political privileges; but the very fact that it was precisely a theory, that it needed scientific guarantees supported by linguistics, semiology and psycho-analysis, that the theory took its references from Saussure or Chomsky, etc., that it gave rise to mediocre literary works, all goes to show that the writer's activity was no longer at the centre of things.[145]

Had Foucault mentioned his own direct involvement in that relentless theorisation, this would read like a lucid piece of self-criticism. He did not, and his comments therefore become another illustration of how one Foucault can hide another. Before the newly politicised Foucault could emerge, the literary Foucault had to undergo a metamorphosis.

8

SOUTH

BY 1965, Foucault's frustration with Clermont-Ferrand had been such that he was actively seeking an alternative, and he made no secret of that fact. The ideal solution appeared to present itself when the sociologist Georges Gurvitch let it be known that he was willing to support his candidature for a post that had fallen vacant at the Sorbonne. Foucault was very tempted, but did not apply. He had been warned by Canguilhem, whose talents include a complete mastery of university politics, that any candidate backed by Gurvitch would probably be rejected by a grand alliance of sociologists, philosophers and psychologists. Canguilhem was also unsure that Foucault, even if not associated with Gurvitch, would be welcomed with open arms by the Sorbonne's somewhat conservative philosophy department.[1]

Foucault did, however, briefly escape from France in the late summer and early autumn. He went to Brazil, partly to visit Gérard Lebrun, a friend and sometime student at ENS who was now teaching there, and partly to lecture at the University of São Paulo. While the two-month trip was enjoyable, the lectures – whose themes were based on the forthcoming *Les Mots et les choses* – were not particularly successful and did not draw large audiences. Foucault was quite unknown in Brazil, and it was only in 1969 that *Maladie mentale* appeared in Portuguese, as *Dença mentale psicologia*.[2] Despite his lack of success, Foucault liked the country and the relaxed, sensual lifestyle it offered, and sometimes thought of settling there. He would make four other visits in the 1970s.

In the meantime, Foucault continued to look for an escape from Clermont-Ferrand and, according to Eribon, even briefly contemplated applying for a lectureship in the Congo (now Zaïre) but was strongly advised against it by Jean Sirinelli, the head of the Quai d'Orsay's language service.[3] Precisely what he imagined himself doing in Kinshasa remains a mystery. A rather less exotic alternative came to his notice when he learned either from Barthes (according to Eribon[4]) or from Jean Wahl (according to Defert) that a post was available in

Tunis. The post had originally been created for Wahl, who had been invited to Tunis by Gérard Deladelle, a specialist in Anglo-American philosophy and director of the university's philosophy department. Wahl, however, was unhappy away from his family and soon left Tunis. Administratively, Foucault would be accountable to the University of Tunis but his salary would be paid by the French government under a cooperation agreement and would be twice the salary he was receiving at home.[5] The appointment was for three years. The contacts that Foucault had maintained in the cultural-diplomatic service since his return to France ensured that he had no difficulty in arranging his secondment from Clermont-Ferrand; there were no objections from the dean who had wanted to prevent him going to Japan.

As Daniel Defert still says, there was something enigmatic about Foucault's departure for Tunis in September 1966. Their relationship was stable and happy and it is possible, according to his partner, that Foucault thought his temporary absence would give Defert more space for his own work. This was, perhaps, an indication of Foucault's awareness of the danger that he might overshadow his young partner, or a tacit realisation that it is not always easy to live with someone who has suddenly acquired star status in the intellectual world. The decision to leave Paris for three years may also have been motivated by a desire to avoid media attention. Although Foucault enjoyed the publicity he was now receiving, he also found it irritating. In a diary entry for April 1968, for instance, the journalist Jean Daniel records Foucault's 'exasperation' with the fact that 'archaeology' was now a fashionable word on everyone's lips.[6] Its reduction to a cultural cliché was an affront to his very real sense of intellectual seriousness.

Foucault was already familiar with the pleasures that North Africa could afford. He had spent holidays in Morocco and knew Tunisia from the visits he had made to see Defert when he was teaching in Sfax. The climate appealed to him, as did the opportunity to swim regularly in the sea. The cuisine was good and cannabis, which he occasionally used, was quite readily available. So too were sexual partners; gay men from France had long known that North Africa was an agreeable holiday destination. The only explanation given by Foucault himself for his departure from Clermont-Ferrand came in an interview with the daily *Presse de Tunis*, which described him as wearing a well-cut beige suit, carrying a small black briefcase and looking like 'a young civil servant with a brilliant future ahead of him'. Foucault briefly sketched his autobiography: 'After having stayed in the French University long enough to do what had to be done and to be what one has to be, I wandered about abroad, and that gave my myopic gaze a sense of distance, and may have allowed me to re-establish a better perspective on things.' He had been drawn to Tunisia, he went on with some self-mockery, by all the myths that Europeans project on to the country: 'the sun, the sea, the great warmth of Africa. In short, I came to look for a Thebaid without the asceticism.'[7]

Tunisia proved not to be a latterday equivalent to the legendary land of Thebes, where hermits led a solitary and contemplative life. Foucault's life certainly involved contemplation, but it was also a very social life. It taught him, for instance, a great deal about Arab men and the homoeroticism of their society. When, years later, a woman friend complained in his presence about their chauvinist attitude towards women, he responded in lyrically angry terms:

> They live among men. They are men and are made for men, with the fleeting bedazzlement, the brief reward of women. People have succeeded in denying, in breaking that fundamental bond which was, for a long time, the basis of the Spanish army: groups of ten men who never left one another. Those cells of brothers were, obviously, based on a subtle blend of friendship and sensuality. And sexuality (subsequently denied and rejected so constantly) also had its part to play.[8]

Foucault did not live in Tunis itself, but in Sidi Bou Saïd, a village some kilometres outside the city. Sidi Bou Saïd was built by the beys who ruled Tunisia on behalf of the Ottoman Empire from 1547 to 1881, when the country became a French protectorate. Standing on the hills above the city and overlooking the sea, it was a beautiful spot with narrow cobbled alleys winding between the dazzling white buildings with their blue, studded doors. Now something of a tourist attraction, the village had since the 1950s been the centre of an artistic-intellectual colony made up largely of French expatriates. Taking up an appointment in Tunis did therefore not mean intellectual or social exile for Foucault, though he did have to tolerate some of the inconveniences of living in a developing country: at times, for instance, the local bank simply did not have enough money on hand to pay him his accumulated salary. Defert was a frequent visitor, and Foucault remained in contact with friends like the Klossowskis, who occasionally – and much to their amusement – received packets of dried figs and dates from him through the post.[9]

Foucault's editorial involvement with *Critique* continued while he was abroad, and he continued to work on the Nietzsche project with

Deleuze. He went on reading *Le Monde* every day. He also returned to France quite frequently. In March 1967, for instance, he went to Paris to deliver one of his most interesting lectures of this period to a group of architects. His topic was space. Foucault was reluctant to publish his lecture at the time, but later relented and agreed, shortly before his death, to its publication to coincide with an exhibition on 'Idea, Process and Result' in Berlin.[10] Its intrinsic interest aside, it provides some indications of what Foucault was reading early in 1967. He began by arguing that, whereas the nineteenth century had been haunted by the concept of cyclical crisis and drew its mythologies from the second principle of thermodynamics, the twentieth was concerned primarily with notions of spatial organisation. Structuralism could thus be seen as an attempt to localise within a spatial configuration elements which appeared to be distributed across time. It was not a denial of history, but a way of handling time and history. Foucault then traced what he called the 'history of spatiality' in the Western experience, beginning with Galileo's substitution of an infinitely open universe for the closed cosmologies of the Middle Ages. The argument is very close to that propounded by Alexandre Koyré's *From the Closed World to the Infinite Universe*,[11] a French translation of which appeared in 1962.

After a very brief discussion of utopias, Foucault went on to discuss 'heterotopias', defined as the 'other spaces' which are essential to the workings of any society. Critical heterotopias are privileged or sacred spaces reserved for individuals in a state of crisis or transition (adolescents, women in childbirth). They may also be the locus for rites of passage such as the defloration of a newly married woman in a honeymoon hotel which, in terms of normal life, is situated 'nowhere'.

A second type of heterotopia is symbolised by the changing role and location of the cemetery, placed next to the church until the eighteenth century, but gradually displaced to spaces outside the town, where they became the 'other city' in which every family has its dark abode. Although no source is given, Foucault's history of the cemetery is recognisably derived from Philippe Ariès's 1966 'Contribution à l'étude du culte des morts à l'époque contemporaine'. Either Foucault was in direct contact with Ariès at this point and the two were exchanging publications or, which seems rather less likely, Foucault was an assiduous reader of the *Revue des travaux de l'Académie des sciences morales et politiques*.[12]

Foucault's other heterotopias ranged from gardens to travelling fairs, from the Jesuit colonies of Latin America to Scandinavian saunas and the Club-Méditerranée-style huts which were beginning to appear on the Tunisian island of Djerba, and which he could have seen when travelling in the south with Defert.

It is estimated that, in 1968, half of the lecturers at the University of Tunis were French nationals,[13] and many of them resided in Sidi Bou Saïd. The village was characterised by a cosmopolitanism which has been likened to that of Lawrence Durrell's Alexandria, and was home to a bohemian society of 'diplomats, bogus spies and real tramps, artists and adventurers' living among its Turkish-style minarets and Arab cafés.[14] It was a society ruled by the twin cults of sensuality and friendship, and had a tantalising hint of decadence about it. The one cardinal rule was a taboo on touching anyone else's *kif*.

Mingling in this relaxed society, Foucault made a very important contact. Jean Duvignaud, a sociologist who had just left the university but who was still a frequent visitor to Tunisia, introduced him to Jean Daniel, the editor of *Le Nouvel Observateur*.[15] In his turn Daniel introduced Foucault to residents like Jacques Berque, the great French Arabist, and the Tunisian painter Jellal Ben Abdallah.[16]

Daniel is a man with a great personal affection for Tunisia and its people, but that affection is rooted in pain. When Tunisia gained its independence 1956, France retained an important naval base at Bizerta. The Bourguiba government periodically brought pressure to bear in an attempt to regain control of Bizerta and matters came to a head in July 1961, when lightly armed groups of patriots made an assault on the installations. French paratroops responded by opening fire, killing hundreds. Jean Daniel was covering the crisis for *L'Express* and was badly wounded in the upper leg. It was the medical care he received in Tunis and the generosity of his doctors and nurses that led him to love the country; his first doctor displayed, he wrote, 'the skill that only true generosity can procure'.[17]

Daniel was introduced by Duvignaud to 'a sort of frail, gnarled samurai who was dry and hieratic, who had the eyebrows of an albino and a somewhat sulphurous charm, and whose avid and affable curiosity intrigued everyone'. His attitude of 'ceremonious humility and Asiatic politeness' was, thought Daniel, an effective device for keeping unwanted strangers at a distance.[18] The samurai lived in a converted block of stables which had reputedly once belonged to the bey, or provincial governor. The full-length windows overlooked the sea and gave directly on to the street. The main room was kept cool and dark, and at the far end there was a raised platform where Foucault slept on a mat which could be rolled up and put away during the day. Daniel, like most people, was immediately struck by the smile which split the samurai's face in two. His first impression was that this was a man who was torn between the temptations of pleasure and a wish to resist temptation by transforming it into an ascetic conceptual exercise.[19] The room was not only a cool refuge; it was also a place of study where Foucault worked early in the morning. It was here that Duvignaud once found him at Easter 1968 – surrounded by a horde of children and calmly reading Feuerbach in their midst.[20] The news that the man who started work so early in the morning was a philosopher gave rise to a rumour, spread by the old ladies of the village for whom 'philosopher' was no doubt synonymous with 'necromancer', that he kept a human skull on his table.[21]

Jean Daniel was not the only person to be dazzled by Foucault's smile. Catherine von Bülow, once a dancer with the Metropolitan Opera in New York, but now working for Gallimard, was in Tunisia on business with two colleagues. As they walked along the beach below Sidi Bou Saïd, they suddenly saw above them the startling figure of a European dressed entirely in white. Von Bülow's colleagues immediately recognised the figure as Foucault, and introduced her. He invited them for tea in his cool rooms, and it seemed to her that the dark house was illuminated by a smile full of beauty and generosity, by an inner light emanating from Foucault as he sat on the floor sipping his tea. For the moment, this was the only encounter between von Bülow and Foucault; in the 1970s, they would become close political allies.[22]

One of the pleasures afforded by the coastal area, and one which was certainly not resisted by Foucault, was walking along the beach at Porto Farina, where the dunes protect a long peninsula of sand. It reminded Foucault of the lagoons of the Sirte coast in Julien Gracq's haunting novel Le Rivage des Syrtes, which won the 1951 Prix Goncourt and which describes a long and desultory war between two imaginary kingdoms on the shores of the Sirtean sea. Foucault considered it 'one of the most beautiful novels I have ever read'.[23] The ruins of Carthage, unrestored and romantically beautiful, but incongruously overlooked by a middle-class suburb, were also within easy reach. The original Carthage having been destroyed in 146 BC at the urgings of Cato ('delenda est'), this was the later city which rose to be the capital of the Roman province of Africa. As Foucault was fond of reminding visitors, it had once been the home of Augustine of Hippo.

Access to Tunis from Sidi Bou Saïd was provided by the 'TGM', which is one of the world's more charming light railways, its uncomfortable wooden seats notwithstanding. It runs from Tunis to La Goulette, the capital's port, and then on to La Marsa, where the French ambassador has his official residence. Tunis is separated from La Goulette by a brackish and malodorous lagoon, and the TGM crosses it on a dyke which it shares with the main highway. Initially, Foucault used the railway, but later acquired a white convertible and made the journey by car. The TGM would deposit him at the station on the place d'Afrique at the top of the tree-lined avenue Bourguiba. From here, it was a pleasant walk through the medina, with its souks and mosque, and past the National Library, where Foucault often worked in the afternoon, to the university overlooking the salt lake at Sejoumi.

Foucault taught on a recently established philosophy degree course, but he also gave public lectures on Friday afternoons and they soon drew large audiences from *le tout Tunis*. His lecturing style was, as always, dramatic: 'Cocky, self-assured and articulate, he did not stand behind the lectern but stalked up and down the dais like a young naval lieutenant pacing the bridge of his command.'[24] He was impressed by his students, telling *La Presse* that only in Brazil and Tunisia had he encountered such serious intellectual passion in students, such an absolute greed for knowledge. The degree lectures were mainly on Nietzsche, Descartes and psychology, but Foucault also taught a course on aesthetics, focusing primarily on *quattrocentro* painting and Manet. The latter was to have been the subject of a book provisionally entitled *Le Noir et la surface* and a contract had been signed with Minuit before Foucault's departure from France, but the book was never completed. He was also a regular speaker at the Club Tahar Hadad, a centre for Arab-European cultural exchanges run by a young woman called Jellila Hafsia, who later confessed to having been forlornly in love with him.[25]

Manet was a long-standing interest, and Foucault regarded his work as being to painting what Flaubert's novels were to literature, namely the place of the birth of the modern. *Le Déjeuner sur l'herbe* and *Olympia* were not simply precursors of impressionism, but paintings which, 'for the first time in European art', explored painting's relationship with itself and with the mode of existence it acquired in the museum. From Manet onwards, every canvas belonged to 'the great squared surface of painting'.[26] These slightly cryptic comments are from the 1964 afterword to Flaubert's *Tentation de Saint Antoine*, and would presumably have become one of the main themes of the unwritten study. The identification of self-referential elements in Manet is, of course, consonant with Foucault's views on literary modernism.

Foucault's lectures at the University of Tunis were obviously not intended for publication and there is no official record of their content.

Two of the public lectures have been published, one in fragmentary form and one in its entirely. The first was a lecture on structuralism and literary analysis, delivered to the Club Tahar Hadad on 4 February 1967.[27] Foucault in fact had little to say about literary analysis in any specific sense, and his remarks about structuralism were very broad in their application. Structuralism was not, he argued in terms that anticipate *L'Archéologie du savoir*, a 'philosophy', but the sum of attempts being made to analyse the 'documentary mass' constituted by all the signs, traces and marks which humanity had left behind it and with which it continued to surround itself. He outlined two approaches to this mass: research into the laws of its production, and the study of documents insofar – and only insofar – as they are documents. In order to describe the latter approach, he coined the neologism '*deixologie*'. In linguistics, 'deixis' usually refers to a theory of enunciation; deictic categories or forms include the pronouns involved in speech acts. Foucault uses a standard definition of these forms in *L'Archéologie du savoir*, where he refers to them as 'elements which designate the speaking subject and his interlocutor ... pronoun elements or connecting particles which refer to earlier or later sentences'.[28] He argued in his lecture to the Club Tahar Hadad that structuralism had now reached the point where it must disappear as a method in order to recognise that it has done no more than discover an object. The transition from structuralism to *deixologie* would be akin to the movement from pathological anatomy to physiology.

The second lecture was read to a March 1968 conference on linguistics and the social sciences organised at the university by the Centre d'Etudes et de Recherches Economiques et Sociales. Casting doubts on structuralism's claims to have achieved a new threshold of scientificity, Foucault discussed the role of eighteenth-century tabulations of knowledge and later philological models in terms similar to those employed in *Les Mots et les choses*, and argued that modern linguistics did offer new epistemological possibilities relevant to the analysis of discursive productions.

It is obvious from these lectures that Foucault was reading widely in the area of analytic and linguistic philosophy, and his study of those topics would have a marked impact on *L'Archéologie*. It appears that most of his knowledge of the subject was acquired in Tunisia and derived from books lent him by Gérard Deledalle. In something of a new departure, Foucault was also reading Trotsky, Luxemburg and the 'black power' literature that was beginning to appear in the United States.[29] The content of his contribution to the March conference shows that he was also reading Althusser, whose *Pour Marx* and *Lire Le Capital* had both appeared in 1965, with considerable interest, and that he saw in Althusser's work an attempt to discover in Marx neither a 'direct assignation of causality' nor a Hegelian-type logic, but 'a logical analysis of the real'.[30]

In Tunisia, Foucault's pursuit of his intellectual and scholarly interests was for the first time brutally interrupted by politics. Tunisia was ruled by Habib Bourguiba's Destour party, which promoted a 'statist' ideology that eventually resulted in the classic fusion of party and state apparatuses and in the emergence of a distinctly undemocratic system dominated by the technical executives of the large civil service. The university became a focus for opposition to government policies as the National Union of Students began to try – unsuccessfully – to assert its independence from the Destour.[31] Shortly after Foucault's arrival in Tunis, a student strike broke out, in December 1966. The initial issue was trivial – a student's refusal to pay his fare on the bus – but it soon led to widespread agitation and to arrests as the police moved on to the university campus. It also led certain of the French academic community to breach the terms of their contracts, the second clause of which ruled out any political activity or interference in internal Tunisian affairs.

Accounts of Foucault's degree of involvement vary considerably. According to Defert, he expressed solidarity with the students from the beginning and became rapidly politicised as a result. Georges Lapassade, a flamboyant gay ethno-psychologist who had replaced Duvignaud as lecturer in sociology in 1965, and who also lived in Sidi Bou Saïd, tells a very different story, but may not be the most reliable of narrators.[32] According to Lapassade, Foucault agreed not to teach, but broke his promise and was seen lecturing to his usual *mondain* audience; no students were present. Lapassade was, he claims, then accused of having disrupted Foucault's lecture and was informed that he would be deported for having breached his contract of employment.[33] Two things are certain. Foucault and Lapassade quarrelled bitterly, with the latter accusing the former of not having protested loudly enough when he was deported. And Foucault's political involvement became much more serious.

The sequel to the quarrel came in 1975. The two men met by chance outside Lapassade's home on the Ile de la Cité. Without warning, Foucault slapped Lapassade in the face. The astonished ethno-psychologist returned the blow and demanded an explanation. The stimulus to Foucault's anger was a character called 'Machin-chose'

('What's his name') in a novel by Lapassade.[34] Machin-chose (readily identifiable as a fictionalised Foucault) had denounced a character recognisable as the author to 'Bourbigras' (Bourguiba), and had caused him to be deported.[35] The accuracy of Lapassade's account is difficult to determine, and it is obviously coloured by envy.

In Paris, in the meantime, what François Châtelet described as 'the small-scale theoretical war' against Foucault was continuing.[36] Foucault had by now found a new champion. Maurice Clavel, graduate of ENS, man of the theatre and novelist, was Le Nouvel Observateur's television critic. His career had been stormy. In 1952, he had been suspended without pay from his teaching post by none other than Canguilhem, who was appalled by the chaos he found reigning in Clavel's classroom, and horrified to learn that a philosophy teacher could see fit to absent himself from work to pursue his theatrical interests.[37] A monarchist in his youth, Clavel had played a vital role in the liberation of Chartres in 1944 and had become a fervent Gaullist, only to break with de Gaulle over the assassination of the Moroccan leader Ben Barka with French connivance in 1965. Clavel had recently rediscovered a headily mystical Catholicism, and May 1968 would convert him to a religious gauchisme like no other. In late 1967, he discovered Foucault. On 8 November, he informed the readers of Le Nouvel Observateur that Foucault was a new Kant and the greatest philosopher of the day. His work was to the last two hundred years of philosophy what Kant's critical work had been to two hundred years of rationalism. Foucault had confirmed Clavel in his religious faith; the man whose death was proclaimed in Les Mots et les choses was 'man without God.'[38] In the mid-1970s, Clavel could, to the astonishment of Claude Mauriac, be found lecturing on Foucault before the altar in a transept at Notre Dame; 'Bent over his text beneath his mop of thick white hair – combed, for once – and looking medieval, almost monkish: "I am speaking of Michel Foucault who, in one hundred decisive, and in my view immortal, pages of Les Mots et les choses . . ." '[39]

For the moment, Clavel was busily defending Foucault against his 'humanist' critics, and he sent the articles he wrote to Tunis. In April 1968, Foucault replied:

> Everything you say about the attempt to bypass not only the 'humanist' figure, but also the whole structuralist field; that is what I was trying to do. But the task seemed so huge and demanded such an uprooting that I did not pursue it to the end, did not formulate it properly and, at the last moment, closed my

eyes. By articulating thing so forcefully, you have forced me to and freed me. In other words, you understand me better than I do myself.[40]

This was of course a perfect instance of Foucault's ability to flatter, but being compared to Kant was to become as irritating as it was gratifying and amusing. Yet Foucault developed a very real affection for the turbulent Clavel who would, a decade later, be the godfather of the *nouveaux philosophes*.

It was only in March 1968 that Foucault became involved in the theoretical war. He replied to Sartre's claim that he was helping the bourgeoisie to build its last barricades against Marxism in fairly restrained terms in an interview with Jean-Pierre El Kabbach, then at the beginning of a very successful career in radio broadcasting. Part of the interview was broadcast on France-Inter, and the full text was then printed in *La Quinzaine littéraire*. The *Quinzaine* made the most of its story; the cover carried a large photograph of Foucault and the legend 'Foucault replies to Sartre'. Much of the interview was taken up with Foucault's account of his own philosophical positions, and his comments on Sartre were politely dismissive: 'Sartre is a man who has too great a body of work – of literary, philosophical and political work – to complete, to have had the time to read my book. He hasn't read it. What he says about it therefore cannot seem very pertinent to me.'[41] Foucault was probably right here, as there are no real indications that Sartre's knowledge of *Les Mots et les choses* extended beyond what could be read about it in the press.

Foucault then adopted a confessional tone, and admitted that he had, briefly, been a member of the PCF at a time when it was Sartre who was being denounced as the bourgeoisie's last ally in the struggle against Marx. The admission was humorous, but the joke soon turned very sour. In its next issue, the *Quinzaine* was obliged to print a very sharply worded letter dated 'Sidi Bou Saïd, 3 March 1968'. The interview had, Foucault objected, been published without his consent, and it represented an unedited version of the conversation. Certain of his comments on Sartre and the reference to his own 'past life' had been made on the express condition that they were not to be included in the final version, and they had not in fact been broadcast. El Kabbach apologised in print for his error of judgement.[42]

Foucault was no doubt reluctant to become embroiled in a journalistically inspired 'Sartre versus Foucault' confrontation, but it was the leaked 'confession' that he had been a member of the PCF that really provoked him to anger. Former membership of the PCF was no great crime, and Foucault's old political loyalties were no secret to his entourage. Knowledge of that part of his history was not, however, in the public domain, and he did not wish it to be. He was enraged at having momentarily lost control of his image and of his self-definition. The published text of this interview is unique in that Foucault habitually exercised a high degree of authorial control and insisted on seeing – and, if necessary, revising – interviews before publication.[43]

If the *Quinzaine* issue indicates Foucault's concern with controlling his public persona, a brief exchange in the pages of *La Pensée* indicates the way in which he was ready to defend his work against criticism. In February and March 1967, a research seminar at the University of Montpellier organised three debates on *Les Mots et les choses*. The proceedings were then published in the PCF's journal *La Pensée*, the 'review of modern rationalism' founded by Georges Politzer just before the outbreak of the Second World War. One of Foucault's critics was J. Stefanini, who taught at Aix-en-Provence. He claimed that Foucault's discussion of grammar and linguistics contained a number of errors and inaccuracies. Foucault replied by simply going through the list of supposed omissions and supplying page references to prove that he had covered the points in question. He did not enter into any methodological or theoretical discussion. In a covering letter to Jacques Proust, who had organised the debate, he suggested that his remarks scarcely deserved publication, as *La Pensée*'s readers 'could themselves have done the little piece of work on which I have just spent the afternoon' [of 11 March 1968].[44]

The theoretical war did not always take the form of criticism and counter-criticism. It also took the form of more positive dialogues. After its 1967 conference on 'Structuralisms, Ideology and Method',[45] the *Esprit* editorial group submitted eleven written questions to Foucault with a view to obtaining a clarification of his aims and positions. On the whole, *Esprit*, still strongly influenced by the personalism of its founder, Emmanuel Mounier, had little sympathy for either structuralism or Foucault. Unlike the PCF, *Les Temps Modernes* or *Raison présente*, it was, however, prepared to pursue a dialogue rather than indulge in denunciations. Arguing that if he were to reply to all eleven questions, he would have to write another book, Foucault chose to respond to the eleventh. Regrettably, the other ten questions have either been lost or still languish undiscovered in *Esprit*'s archives.[46]

The question that Foucault chose to answer suggested that a mode of thought which introduced the 'constraints of the system' and 'discontinuity' into intellectual history might remove the basis for progressive political interventions, and asked whether it did not result in a dilemma: either acceptance of the system, or an appeal to external violence as the only means of overthrowing the system. Foucault appeared, it was being suggested, to offer an uninviting choice between passivity and nihilistic violence.

Foucault was glad to have the opportunity to discuss his work with *Esprit* and submitted a long written reply.[47] It left Domenach, by his own admission, none the wiser about the basis for political action supplied by *Les Mots et les choses*. Foucault began with some remarks about the notion of 'system', but did not clarify what was obviously a serious confusion between 'the capitalist system' and 'systems of thought or discourse'. He denied having introduced the idea of *system*; he was a pluralist and spoke of *systems* in the plural.[48] Turning to the notion of discontinuity, and no doubt thinking of the common complaint that he had 'frozen' history into a timeless structure, he argued that 'discontinuity . . . is an interplay of specified transformations which are different to one another . . . and bound up together by schemata of dependence. History is the descriptive analysis and theory of those transformations.'[49]

Much of the reply to *Esprit* is a reprise of the arguments of *Les Mots et les choses* and an anticipation of the much more formalised theses of *L'Archéologie du savoir*. The conclusion, in which Foucault outlines a number of hypotheses about 'progressive politics', introduces something that is found in neither of those texts. The first two hypotheses are, perhaps, the most significant:

> A progressive politics is a politics which recognises the historical and specified conditions of a practice, whereas other politics recognise only ideal necessities, univocal determinations and the free interplay of individual initiatives. A progressive politics is a politics which defines, within a practice, possibilities for transformation and the play of dependencies between those transformations, whereas other politics rely upon the uniform abstraction of change or the thaumaturgic presence of genius.[50]

The very notion of a progressive politics signals the emergence of something new in Foucault's work, even though its actual content remains regrettably vague. The dismissal of 'univocal determinations' is recognisable as an attack on the facile certainties of some forms of Marxism with their ritual appeals to objective roads to the radiant future, but the repeated insistence on 'practice' demonstrates that Foucault was now moving closer to Althusser.

Althusser's work of this period, as represented by the essays collected in *Pour Marx* and by *Lire Le Capital*, which was the end product of a seminar held at ENS in 1964, can be read in a variety of ways.[51] At one level, it is an attempt to ride out the storms generated by the Sino-Soviet split. It is also an attempt to renew French Marxism by insisting on the need to read Marx himself rather than the banal work of his commentators. For Althusser, there is a profound difference between Marx and Hegel and his work can, like Foucault's, be read as an attempt to escape the shadow of Hegel (but not dialectical thinking). Above all, Althusser's writings are an attack on humanism, deemed to be an ideological form with which Marxism has broken in its transition to historical materialism or the science of social formations, and dialectical materialism, or the theory of scientific practice. There is an overlap between his anti-humanism and his anti-Hegelianism in that both the various humanisms and Hegel operate with a notion of causality in which everything is a simple expression of a single principle, be it Rome in Hegel's *Philosophy of History*, 'man', consciousness or human freedom.[52]

To the extent that both men were engaged in a battle against the dominance of philosophies of consciousness and were proponents of a philosophy of the concept, Foucault and Althusser had a lot in common, even though Foucault never claimed to be a Marxist. The 'practice' to which Foucault alludes in his reply to *Esprit* is of central importance to Althusser's Marxism, and refers to the economic, political and ideological processes of transformation or production that together make up the social formation, while 'theoretical practice' refers to the transformation of ideology – or the immediate, lived relation to the world – into knowledge.

Foucault and Althusser also had ancestors in common, notably Canguilhem, to whom Althusser admitted owing 'an incalculable debt'. Althusser's sole written comment on Foucault was made in a letter to Ben Brewster, who translated the two books published in 1965 and who added a useful glossary to *For Marx*. It is, however, scarcely a model of clarity:

He was a pupil of mine, and 'something' from my writings has passed into his, including certain of my formulations. But (and it must be said, concerning as it does his own philosophical personality) under his pen and in his thought, even the meanings

he gives to formulations he has borrowed from me are transformed into another, quite different meaning than my own.[53]

In the same letter, Althusser speaks, briefly but with obvious admiration, of 'that *great* work', *Histoire de la folie*. Althusser may have had little
to say in print about Foucault, but he certainly read his work with
enthusiasm and discussed it in upublished correspondence with
Etienne Balibar, one of the young *normaliens* who had collaborated with
him on *Lire Le Capital*.[54] In 1966–67, Balibar was doing his military
service as a cooperant in Tunisia. Both he and Althusser believed that
Les Mots et les choses would help to provide a general theory of ideology.[55]
It was increasingly possible to see Foucault and Althusser as being part
of the same theoretical project, or at least as working on very similar
projects.

The perceived Althusser–Foucault link was an important element in
the reception of the latter's work in leftist circles. The students and
normaliens on the fringes of the PCF had long been split into 'Italian' and
'Chinese' factions,[56] and it was the 'Chinese' or proto-Maoist groups
that really took on board Althusser's theories. In 1966, a schism within
the group that published *Cahiers marxistes-léninistes* resulted in one of the
more exquisitely theoretical projects of the period.

Cahiers pour l'analyse (Notebooks for analysis) began publication in
January 1966, and was the organ of ENS's Cercle d'Epistémologie, a
group of young and fiercely conceptual philosophers.[57] Theirs was a
milieu in which Jacques-Alain Miller could, in June 1964, accuse
Jacques Rancière of stealing his concept of 'metonymic causality'. A
violent quarrel ensued, with Rancière defending himself strenuously
until Althusser restored a semblance of peace by admitting that he was
the culprit.[58] The *pour* of the journal's title alludes to that of Althusser's
Pour Marx, while the *analyse* makes a double allusion to Condillac and to
psychoanalysis.[59] Under the editorship of Miller, the *Cahiers* published
an extraordinary and brilliant range of material. Derrida, Lacan, Luce
Irigaray and Canguilhem all appeared in its pages, as did major pieces
of work by members of the Cercle itself. This was one of the sites were
Althusserian Marxism and Lacanian psychoanalysis met in their joint
search for scientificity. Each issue of the *Cahiers* carried as its theoretical
masthead a quotation from Canguilhem, with whom many of the
contributors had studied: 'Working on a concept means varying its
extension and comprehension, generalising it through the incorporation of external features, exporting it outside its region of origin, taking
it as a model or, conversely, finding a model for it, and in short

gradually conferring upon it, through calculated transformations, the function of a norm.' No source was given for the quotation; in this milieu one was simply expected to be familiar with Canguilhem. His 1956 essay on 'Qu'est-ce que la psychologie?' was reprinted in the second issue, and the critique of psychology became an implicit illustration of the scientificity of Lacanian psychoanalysis.

It was in this milieu, highly intellectualised, increasingly politicised and inevitably centred on ENS, that Foucault found an audience for his *Archéologie du savoir*. The philosophy of the concept once associated with Cavaillès and Canguilhem was beginning to find a new incarnation. Indeed, some spoke disparagingly of a 'party of the concept'. The concept's new incarnation was not simply a reincarnation of the old. In the eyes of Miller in particular, it was to be understood in a strictly logical-mathematical sense rather than in any historical sense. Significantly, *Cahiers pour l'analyse* regularly spoke of 'science' in the singular; Canguilhem habitually speaks of 'sciences' in the plural.

The ninth issue of *Cahiers pour l'analyse* (summer 1968) took as its theme 'the genealogy of the sciences'. It included a set of questions addressed by the Cercle to Foucault requesting him, in somewhat tortured syntax, to 'state, with regard to his theory and the implications of its method, critical propositions which will found its possibility'. He was further requested to 'define his responses in relation to the status of science, its history and its concept'.[60] Foucault responded with a lengthy essay which was in fact a preliminary version of *L'Archéologie du savoir*.[61] It generated a further set of questions and critical comments, including the reproach that Foucault's notion of 'discourse' remained woefully ill-defined and that its value had not really been established. The Cercle ended its comments by asking Foucault to define himself in relation to Freud and Marx, and announced that his reply would appear in a forthcoming issue.[62] The reply never materialised; after a final issue on 'formalisation', *Cahiers pour l'analyse* suddenly ceased publication.

The greater part of Foucault's two years in Tunisia was not devoted to politics but to the writing of *L'Archéologie du savoir*, which was written in Sidi Bou Saïd and published in Paris in 1969. It was in part an expanded version of the replies Foucault had given to the questions put to him by *Esprit* and *Cahiers pour l'analyse*, but it had obviously been planned before those dialogues took place. This was the study of the methodological problems inherent in his archaeological project that he had announced in a footnote to *Les Mots et les choses*,[63] and to which he again referred in the April 1967 interview given to *La Presse de Tunis*, where he described himself as working on 'a methodological work concerning forms of existence and language in a culture like ours'. *Esprit*'s readers had been told that it was one of two similar essays, the other being a study of the problems of historical discourse which Foucault was thinking of calling 'Past and Present: An Other Archaeology of the Human Science'.[64] When the *Archéologie* was published, Foucault again referred to a second volume. The book he had just published was 'at once a reprise of what I have already attempted to do prompted by a desire to rectify certain careless inaccuracies in the earlier books, and an attempt to trace in advance the path for a later work which I truly hope never to write, owing to unexpected circumstances'.[65] For reasons which have never been elucidated, that second volume was never written. Foucault's reply to queries about its fate would, no doubt, have been the remark he made in Vermont in 1982: 'I like to write first volumes, and I hate to write second ones.'[66]

Gérard Fellous's introduction to the *La Presse* interview described Foucault's ongoing project as 'the Bible of structuralism'. That description proved to be not entirely accurate. This time, Foucault had succeeded in writing something that would be read only by a small audience of specialists. In *L'Archéologie*, he assumes that his reader is very familiar with his earlier work and makes few concessions to the uninitiated. Outside that specialist audience, the book is probably best known for the last lines of the introduction, where Foucault defiantly describes himself as writing in order to have no face and defies the bureaucratic morality of the *état civil*. Throughout the book, Foucault dwells at length on the need to abolish or overcome the notion of a sovereign subject or author but, paradoxically, no other text by him is so marked by the persistent use of the first person pronoun, by the massive presence of an 'I' which defines, reformulates and refutes. It is as though Foucault were torn between a desire to escape into the anonymity of pure textuality and a need to express that desire in the first person.

In many ways, *L'Archéologie du savoir* is distinctly less attractive than its predecessors. The reader is neither carried along by the broad sweep of *Histoire de la folie* or *Les Mots et les choses*, nor seduced by the dark poetics of *Naissance de la clinique*. There is something relentless about the way in which Foucault defines concept after concept, and his style has a certain aridity that is far removed from the almost baroque splendour of his earlier books. When Frank Kermode complained in a review of the English translation about Foucault's 'wanton neologisms and gratuitous syntactical inventions', he was no doubt voicing the complaints of many a frustrated reader.[67]

This is Foucault's only purely methodological work, but it is also more than that. It is a work of self-criticism. *Histoire de la folie*, in particular, is criticised for giving too great and too enigmatic a role to 'experience' and for thereby coming dangerously close to accepting that history had an 'anonymous and general subject'.[68] It now transpired that it was not possible to describe 'what madness itself could be, as initially given to some primitive, basic and muffled experience that was scarcely articulated'. As the footnote makes clear, the criticism is directed against one of the explicit themes of *Histoire de la folie*, and notably of the original preface.[69] Yet, as late as 1964, Foucault had been arguing that it was possible to speak of an experience of madness in connection with Nietzsche, and made the point repeatedly to an uncomprehending interlocutor at Royaumont.[70]

Naissance de la clinique is now criticised by Foucault for its 'infelicitous' use of the expression 'the clinical gaze'; that expression suggested the synthetic or unifying function of *a* subject.[71] Although Foucault does not actually make the point, this self-criticism can be read as indicating the fading of the literary-modernist vision: it was the insistence on the gaze and the eye that allowed the connection to be made between the medical and the literary, as exemplified by *Histoire de l'oeil*. The thematic link provided by the eye-gaze connection is being broken, or at best made most tenuous, as the emphasis on the literary fades and as Foucault begins to move away from the Blanchot-like contention that 'language is all' to a broader notion of discourse.

It is clear from the introduction that Foucault now regards his archaeology as deriving from – or as annexing for its own purposes – two existing schools of historiographical thought. On the one hand, there was the *Annales* school of historians, with their focus on 'long periods as though, beneath political events and episodes, they were attempting to reveal stable equilibria which culminate and are reversed after centuries of continuity'.[72] On the other, there was the history of the sciences, as practised by Bachelard and Canguilhem, with its concentration on epistemological breaks and thresholds, and on the displacement and transformation of concepts. Here, a distinctly Althusserian note creeps in as Foucault cites *Pour Marx* on the work of theoretical transformation which 'founds a science by detaching it from the ideology of its past and by revealing that past to be ideological'.[73] Although there may appear to be a contradiction between the focus on the stable structures of the *longue durée*, and the search for the discontinuities that punctuate the history of a science, Foucault argues that they have a common core. Both schools are in effect dethroning the supposed subject of history and opposing the philosophy of consciousness that views the history of thought as the site of an uninterrupted continuity or as a smoothly evolutionary process, one by depersonalising history, the other by breaking down its apparent simplicity. And both are operating with a notion of structure.

The archaeological project begins with 'a negative work' or a conceptual clear-out of notions such as tradition (which attempts to give a conceptual structure to a set of phenomena which are both successive and identical), influence (a vague and untheorised idea of causal transmission), 'mentality' or 'spirit' and so on. Even such apparently innocent notions as 'book' and *'oeuvre'* are called into question. In what sense, asks Foucault, does a volume of Michelet have the same status as a treatise on mathematics? Should posthumous publications, rough drafts, abandoned works and scraps of conversation noted by third parties all be included in the 'complete works' of, say, Nietzsche, and given the same status as *Zarathustra* and *Ecce Homo*? The unity of an *oeuvre* is, that is, by no means self-evident. In the face of all these uncertainties, Foucault proposes an alternative. Rather than continuing to rely upon these untheorised notions, we must elaborate the theory they demand, 'and that theory cannot be elaborated unless the field of the facts of discourse from which they were constructed appears in its non-synthetic purity'.[74]

Take the example of madness. The psychiatric discourse of the nineteenth century is characterised not by the existence of pre-shaped objects to which it addresses its attention, but by the way in which it forms its own objects. Their formation is governed by a set of relations between 'surfaces of emergence' (family, social group, working environment, all of which are in different ways thresholds for the exclusion of the mad), 'instances of delimitation' (medicine, justice, religious authority) and 'grids of specification' (systems which identify forms of madness, and either relate them to one another or differentiate between them). The conceptual clear-out and subsequent theorisation will lead to the identification of 'discursive formations' and 'rules of formation'. The discursive formations of the classical era included, for example, general grammar, natural history and the analysis of wealth. They are anonymous constructs without a creative subject:

Whatever their generality, the rules for the formation of concepts are not the result of operations effected by individuals, deposited in history and sedimented in the density of collective habits; they do not constitute the fleshless schema of a whole abstract labour, in the course of which concepts emerge out of illusions, prejudices, errors or traditions. The preconceptual field reveals discursive constraints and regularities which make possible the hetero-geneous multiplicity of concepts.[75]

The object of Foucault's analysis exists at the level of discourse and not at the level of empirical phenomena. Discourse is not to be interpreted in such a way as to reveal a history of the referent[76] – of, that is, an object existing outside or prior to discourse. Archaeology is not concerned with physical objects, but with the discursive process which makes it possible to speak about objects such as madness or clinical medicine.

The basic unit of analysis is the statement [*énoncé*]. A discursive formation is essentially a body of statements, and a statement can be defined as

a function of existence which belongs specifically to signs and on the basis of which one can decide, through analysis or intuition, if they 'make sense' or not, according to the order in which they follow one another or are juxtaposed, of what they are the sign and what kind of act is effected by their formulation (oral or written).[77]

Foucault explores and then rejects a possible parallel between his 'statements' and the 'speech acts' of Austin and Searle,[78] but the precise relevance of speech acts and performatives to his discourse analysis remains rather obscure, particularly as concrete examples are rarely presented. Foucault is on much more familiar ground, and a ground that brings him closer to Althusser's work on ideology, when he argues: 'To describe a formulation as a statement does not consist in analysing relations between the author and what he says . . . but of determining the position any individual can and must occupy in order to be its subject.'[79] At this stage, Foucault appears to be combining elements of 'speech-act' theory with a theory of the production of individual subjects that owes at least something to Althusser's description of ideology as an imaginary relation to the real world that enables or obliges the individual to emerge as a subject positioned within an ideological or discursive formation. The similarity between Althusser and Foucault was to become more marked with the publication of Althusser's essay on 'Ideology and Ideological State Apparatuses' in 1970.

Foucault ends his *Archéologie* by outlining three possible objects for future study: sexuality, painting and political knowledge.[80] In the case of sexuality, a study oriented towards the *épistémè* (defined here as 'a set of relations capable, in a given period, of uniting discursive practices giving rise to epistemological figures, to sciences'[81]) would look at how 'epistemological figures' such as the biology and physiology of sexuality took shape in the nineteenth century, and at how Freud broke with them and established a scientific discourse; a strictly archaeological study would look at 'ways of speaking about sexuality', and would thus demonstrate that sexuality is invested in a system of prohibitions and values. In that sense, it would tend towards an ethics. Neither approach would look at actual sexual behaviour. An archaeology of painting, for its part, would demonstrate that painting is not purely a matter of vision, and that it is always traversed by scientific knowledges [*connaissances*] and philosophical themes which are inscribed not only in theories, but in the very gestures of the painter. A study of political knowledge would concern itself neither with the moment of the emergence of a revolutionary consciousness nor with the biography of revolutionaries; it would examine the emergence of a discursive practice and a revolutionary knowledge which together generate strategies and give rise to a theory of society and of its transformation.

While he was writing his methodological treatise, Foucault became caught up in a conflict that was far from theoretical. The years 1967 and 1968 were tumultuous in Tunis. Pro-Palestinian demonstrations during the Arab-Israeli war of June 1967 led to renewed anti-government protests, but also degenerated into anti-Semitic riots in which Jewish-owned shops in central Tunis were burned and looted. Foucault was horrified by what he saw and tried to remonstrate with some of the student demonstrators. They attempted to justify their actions in the name of solidarity with the Palestinian cause, but the supposed distinction between anti-Zionism and anti-Semitism had ceased to operate, even for the politically sophisticated, and racial perceptions were becoming dominant.[82] In their support for their Palestinian brothers, groups of students and youths attacked and burned Jewish property. Foucault described what he had seen in a letter written to Canguilhem on 7 June:

A good fifty fires. 150 or 200 shops looted – the poorest ones, obviously; the timeless spectacle of the synagogue gutted, carpets dragged into the street, trampled on and burned; people running through the streets, taking refuge in a block that the mob wanted to set on fire. Since then, silence, the shutters down, no one or almost no one in the area, children playing with broken knick-knacks . . . Nationalism plus racism adds up to something very nasty. And if you add that, because of their *gauchisme*, the students lent a hand (and a bit more than a hand) to it all, you feel quite profoundly sad. And one wonders by what strange ruse or (stupidity) of history, Marxism could give rise to that (and supply a vocabulary for it).[83]

If he was horrified by the unexpectedly savage anti-Semitism of his students, Foucault was astonished by the fierceness of their Marxism: 'For those young people, Marxism did not merely represent a mode of analysing reality; it was at the same time a kind of moral energy, an existential act . . . For me Tunisia in a sense represented an opportunity to reinsert myself into the political debate.'[84] The bitter taste left in his mouth by his experiences in the PCF was being replaced by a real sense of excitement. The Marxism of the students, grouped mainly around a journal entitled *Perspectives*, was not particularly sophisticated, and veered somewhat unsteadily from Trotskyism to Maoism (the Communist Party itself had long been effectively marginalised, and had been completely banned in 1966). It was, however, passionate, very concrete, and far removed from the mumbled political discourses and quarrels over the ownership of concepts that Foucault had heard in Paris.[85]

Agitation continued throughout 1968 and reached new heights between March and June, when tensions were further exacerbated by an official visit from US Vice-President Hubert Humphrey. The British and US embassies were attacked, and Bourguiba responded by levying a tax on every household in the city to pay for the damage caused in the riots, which were restricted to the capital.[86] In 1978, Foucault described the events to Duccio Trombadori: 'Strikes, lecture-boycotts and arrests continued throughout the year. The police entered the university, attacking the students, throwing them into jail. I was to some extent respected by the local authorities, and that allowed me easily to accomplish a series of actions.'[87]

Foucault overestimated the degree to which the 'respect' of the authorities would protect him, and the situation was rapidly becoming dangerous. At one point, he allowed a Roneo machine used for printing

anti-government leaflets to be concealed in his garden, despite the fact
that he realised he was under police surveillance. Daniel Defert, in the
meantime, was taking major risks by smuggling messages to Tunisians
in Paris after his regular visits to Foucault, sometimes concealing them
in his socks to avoid discovery.

Foucault was convinced that his telephone was being tapped;
whenever he took a taxi, his driver seemed to have an uncanny
foreknowledge of his destination. Unconvincing beggars loitered on his
doorstep. As he drove through the area near his home one evening, he
realised that he was being followed by police motorcyclists, who
signalled him to stop. Fearing the consequences, Foucault drove on,
but quickly decided that the distinct possibility of being shot was the
greater of two evils, and pulled over. He was politely informed that one
of his brake lights was not working, and was advised to have it repaired.
The leftist student cowering in the back of the car somehow escaped
detection.

Then came a definite warning. The tactic was a familiar one. A boy
with whom Foucault had spent the night asked to be driven home. In a
narrow lane, Foucault's car was forced to a halt, and he received a
savage beating – Defert describes him as having been tortured – at the
hands of men who may or may not have been police officers. It was
increasingly clear that the philosophy lecturer who looked like a civil
servant was rapidly becoming an undesirable alien.[88]

In September, the trials of the arrested students began, with some of
Foucault's surplus salary going to swell the defence fund. A futile
approach asking the French ambassador to intervene met with a rebuff.
Foucault's attempts to speak at the trial of a student called Ahmed Ben
Othman were frustrated, and the case was heard *in camera*. By October,
it was obvious that it was not possible to stay in Tunis any longer.
Foucault returned to France, and abandoned his plans to buy a house
overlooking the bay at Sidi Bou Saïd. It was not until 1971 that
Foucault returned to Tunisia, to lecture on 'Madness and Civilisation'
to the Club Tahar Hadad.[89]

Like a number of individuals with some experience of the Third
World, notably Régis Debray and Pierre Goldman,[90] Foucault often
tended to take a slightly jaundiced view of May 1968. Although he did
not deny the importance of the May events, he was only too aware that,
whereas a student demonstrator caught by the police in Paris was
unlikely to suffer more than a beating, the students arrested in Tunis
had risked a great deal more: 'There is no comparison between the
barricades of the Latin Quarter and the real risk of doing fifteen years in

prison, as in Tunisia.'[91] At the time, Foucault did not publicly comment on or write about what he had seen and experienced in Tunis. His support for the students had been practical, public and courageous, but it was never expressed in print and it was only in the 1970s that he began to speak of it. The Foucault of the 1970s, always prompt to denounce what he saw as 'the intolerable', would not have remained silent in this way. One can only speculate that it was precisely his Tunisian experience that allowed a much more vocally militant Foucault to emerge.

It was only weeks after the first riots in Tunis that Paris erupted into the chaos of the May events.[92] They were the culminating expression of a growing discontent, but took most of France by surprise. The Situationist pamphlet of September 1966 had been a warning that something was seriously amiss in the French education system. Signs that a flashpoint had been reached became obvious in January 1968, when a dispute over the right to visit the rooms of students of the opposite sex led to the occupation by women students of a male residential block at Nanterre. When riot police were called in to clear the building, violence broke out. In March, the arrest of the leaders of the Comité National Vietnam led directly to the occupation of a lecture theatre and then the administration block. A month later, a series of debates at Nanterre on the future of the universities ended in uproar. On 2 May, the campus was closed indefinitely, and students were violently attacked by the police as they evacuated the courtyard. The Sorbonne and the science faculty were then closed on ministerial orders.

Demonstration followed demonstration in a climate of escalating violence, and on 6 May the first barricades to have been seen in Paris since 1944 were thrown up in the streets of the Latin Quarter. The night of 10–11 May was 'the night of the barricades', when pitched battles were fought in central Paris. Two days later, the Sorbonne was occupied; within days the transport system was paralysed, and most of France was on strike.

Foucault was fascinated by these developments in Paris and, although he was kept informed of what was going on by Defert and others, frustrated at not being there. Jean Daniel records a conversation with him on 25 April in Tunis. Daniel was passionately interested in what was happening, and was surprised to learn that the author who had announced the death of man and who seemed to take a sceptical view of slogans about 'freedom', was equally interested. Foucault insisted that nothing interested him more than 'politics, the present, today' and argued that the agitation at Nanterre just might be announcing a revolution in everyday life. He also suspected that the events in Paris might lead to the departure from power of de Gaulle.[93]

Foucault saw nothing of the night of the barricades or of the endless meetings in the occupied Sorbonne. He was, however, in Paris for a few days and was present at the 50,000-strong meeting in the Cherléty stadium on 17 May, which demanded workers' power in the factories and student power in the universities. Seeing a student demonstration in the street, he remarked to the *Nouvel Observateur*'s editor that the students were not making revolution: they *were* the revolution.[94]

Foucault's later comments on May, such as those made to Trombadori in 1978, are somewhat at odds with Jean Daniel's description of a Foucault who was only too anxious to see what was happening in Paris. It was undoubtedly true that the Tunisian students risked considerably more than their French counterparts, but there was also an element of self-justification in Foucault's subsequent comments; in the milieu in which he moved after 1970, not having taken part in the May events was a serious sin of political omission, and he was often tempted to explain his non-participation by finessing potential critics with accounts of direct involvement in a struggle with much higher stakes.

Foucault left Tunis in October 1968. His future was not entirely certain, but there was no hint of a return to Clermont-Ferrand. One possible change of direction had already been rejected. Burin des Roziers was now France's ambassador in Rome and was looking for a new cultural attaché. A telephone call to Tunis resulted in Foucault's provisional acceptance of the post, but nothing came of the plan; according to the ambassador, the minister for education had something else in mind for Foucault.[95]

Mysterious ministerial plans aside, it is clear that Foucault's intention was to return to Paris. A second opportunity now presented itself. Didier Anzieu was now head of a new department of psychology at the University of Nanterre. He had had little direct contact with Foucault since ENS, but he had followed his career from a distance and had been impressed by it. His aim at Nanterre was to bring together a young and dynamic team, and Foucault was, he thought, an obvious appointment. The author of *Histoire de la folie* was eminently acceptable to Anzieu's colleagues.

Yet it was only on paper and only for a couple of weeks that Foucault was a member of the Nanterre faculty. To Anzieu's great disappointment, his recruit announced that he was not interested in teaching psychology again and that he was accepting the offer of a post in philosophy at the newly created University of Vincennes[96]. Nanterre had been the original storm centre of May 1968; by going to Vincennes, Foucault was to find himself at the centre of some rather different but equally violent storms.

9

VINCENNES

THE Foucault who returned to Paris in the autumn of 1968 was a changed man. He had undergone his political baptism of fire, and had had the first of many direct encounters with violence at the hands of the police. He had also changed physically. It was in Tunisia that he had first shaved his head and thus inaugurated a morning ritual which he was to perform for the rest of his life. As he told Pinguet some years later, it stopped him having to worry about losing his hair;[1] others were told that he had shaved his head in order to reveal his true face. Foucault had created his self-image and had become the familiar figure that stares from so many photographs, almost always wearing the white rollneck sweater which spared him the chore of ironing shirt collars.

The society in which he was to move for the next few years was somewhat different from the artistic-literary circles in which he had lived in the early 1960s, and was increasingly politicised. The transition was not, however, total and therefore resulted in some odd combinations of events. Four days after he delivered a solemn eulogy in memory of Jean Hyppolite at ENS on 19 January 1969, Foucault was arrested during the violent occupation of the new University of Vincennes. A month later, the street fighter reverted to being the philosopher who, in front of an extremely distinguished audience from the Société Française de Philosophie, expanded his comments on authorship in *L'Archéologie du savoir* into one of his most celebrated lectures: *'Qu'est-ce qu'un auteur?'*[2]

Foucault had hoped that May would be the beginning of a revolution in everyday life, and in some ways that revolution was indeed under way. Foucault's world was now one in which the PCF was perceived as representing the far right of the political spectrum. The events of May had politicised many young people and had left a heritage that was to become more and more violent. On 1 June 1968, as France began to return to normal, a 50,000-strong demonstration marched across Paris from the Gare Montparnasse to the Gare d'Austerlitz chanting: *'Ce n'est qu'un début, continuons le combat'* ('This is only a beginning, we fight on').

The following February, a book by three young leftists was openly calling for the fight begun in May to be transformed into a civil war.[3]

The next few years were to be stormy ones. Even those who participated in the clashes of the early 1970s now find it difficult to explain – or even imagine – the violence in which they were so frequently implicated.[4] At times, it seemed to some that civil war was a real possibility, and not merely an extremist scenario. The drift into violent confrontation reflected a widely held view that political change would not be brought about by normal means. Despite the upheavals and hopes of May, the same politicians were still in power. De Gaulle resigned in April 1969 after losing a referendum on senate and regional reforms, only to be replaced as president of the Republic by Georges Pompidou, the prime minister he had sacked almost a year earlier. Matters were not helped by the violent tactics of the police under the command of Raymond Marcellin, a notoriously heavy-handed minister of the interior. Talk of 'anti-youth racism' on the part of the police was commonplace.

As Foucault moved to the left, his books became part of the cultural infrastructure of the hoped-for revolution in everyday life. *Histoire de la folie*, in particular, had by now become a different book. In 1961, it had been read primarily as an academic work; after 1968, it was read in the context of 'a social movement characterised by political activism and a generalised anti-repressive sensibility'.[5] The theme of the great confinement now seemed to provide the archetype for the confinement of workers in factories, students in universities and of desires in repressive structures. As Foucault himself would put it in 1975, there was nothing surprising about this when 'prisons resemble factories, schools, barracks and hospitals, which resemble prisons'.[6]

The parallel also had an obvious and immediate relevance for discontented radicals working in the mental-health sector. March 1969 saw the publication of a special issue of *Partisans*, a periodical published by Maspero, entitled *Garde-fous arrêtez de vous serrer les coudes*. The title was a clever pun: a *garde-fou* is literally a railing on an exposed parapet or balcony designed to hold back anyone mad enough to go too close to the edge, but here it also means 'those who guard the mad'. The warders were being told to stop 'sticking together'. The opening lines of the introduction by François Gantheret and Jean-Marie Brohm indicate the extent to which Foucault's book had become part of a leftist culture:

Not so long ago, the mad were still locked up any old how together with prostitutes, the unemployed, thieves and underworld characters, in a word with all those who were not 'normal' in terms of the sacred values of class society; with those who upset the norms of private property and the institutions of moral conformity.[7]

Histoire de la folie was becoming a key text for the so-called anti-psychiatry movement.[8] Its changing status owed a lot to developments in England. In the English-speaking world, the first academic reading described by Castel was conspicuous mainly by its absence and when *Histoire de la folie* appeared in translation it almost immediately became an icon of the 'counterculture' of the late 1960s. Richard Howard's translation was not of the complete text. In 1964, Foucault himself abridged his book for publication in the 10/18 pocket-book library, and reduced its length by more than half. The abridged edition, now long out of print, provided many readers with their first introduction to Foucault. It gave English readers their only introduction to him, as it was this edition which, presumably for commercial reasons, was translated, with the addition of some material from the original.[9] The translation, *Madness and Civilization: A History of Insanity in the Age of Reason* was published by Pantheon in New York in 1965, and by Tavistock in London two years later. Significantly, the English edition was prefaced by David Cooper, one of the major figures in the anti-psychiatry movement, who noted:

> Madness, as Foucault makes so impressively clear in this remarkable book, is a way of seizing *in extremis* the racinating groundwork of the truth that underlies our more specific realisation of what we are about. The truth of madness is what madness is. What madness is is a form of vision that destroys itself by its own choice of oblivion in the face of existing forms of social tactics and strategy.[10]

He also claimed, with more partisanship than accuracy, that Foucault 'hints at' the social pressures which, according to 'recent research', allow or force certain people to drive others mad.[11]

The identification of Foucault with anti-psychiatry was further reinforced when R. D. Laing reviewed *Madness and Civilization* in the *New Statesman*, and the association was strengthened by the appearance on the facing page of an article by Cooper entitled 'Who's Mad Anyway?'[12] The two pieces were bracketed together with the generic title 'Sanity and Madness'. Although Laing viewed Foucault's verbal 'pirouettes' with some suspicion, he was in no doubt of the book's value or its relevance to his own concerns:

> The history of madness documented here is the history of the projection onto the few who were destroyed or forgotten, of the lunacy of the majority who won the day. . . . Until a few years ago, the collective definition of European man as sane by his own consent imposed such an iron vice on consciousness that hardly anyone was able to break out without breaking down. I do not know any other book which *sees through* (that is, *dia-gnoses*) what has been going on, in such a scholarly and systematic way. It remains itself fully within the idiom of sanity, while undermining the presuppositions of its own foundations. To define true madness – is to be nothing else but mad.[13]

British reviewers tended to agree that Foucault was at least an ally of the anti-psychiatrists. Edmund Leach remarked: 'After reading this book even the most bigoted rationalist must reflect with anxiety upon the unreasonableness of reason.' *New Society*'s reviewer noted: 'All this fits in with the current anti-psychiatry movement.'[14] A more clinical and professional journal commented that Foucault's 'thesis raises much that is disturbing and disputable, but its relevance today is unquestionable. This is stressed by Cooper, whose own work may be seen as a contemporary study of the process which Foucault saw developing during the Classical Age.'[15]

Foucault was somewhat bemused at being retrospectively seen as part of a 'movement', remarking in 1974: 'When I wrote *Histoire de la folie*, I was so ignorant that I did not know that anti-psychiatry already existed in England.'[16] He could have been forgiven for his ignorance; Laing's *The Divided Self* dates from 1959, although the research on which it is based was completed by 1956. The term 'anti-psychiatry' itself appears to derive from Cooper's *Psychiatry and Anti-Psychiatry* (1967), a French translation of which appeared in 1970. There was no real reason why a French academic working in Hamburg should have been in contact in 1960 with currents within English psychiatry which, at the end of the 1950s, had yet to find an audience outside the professional milieu. Popularisation came about thanks to events like the Dialectics of Liberation congress held at London's Roundhouse in July 1967.[17]

In France, the association with anti-psychiatry was strengthened by Maud Mannoni's *Le Psychiatre, son 'fou' et la psychanalyse* (1970), which employed a broadly Foucauldian framework to describe 'psychiatric segregation' and its alienating effects. Significantly, Mannoni was one of the few psychoanalysts to attempt a rapprochement with the British anti-psychiatrists, whom she invited to a congress on psychosis in 1967,[18] and her book is a brave attempt to combine Lacanian psychoanalysis and Laing's theories into a viable way of approaching the problems of institutional psychotherapy.

There were obvious differences between the positions of Foucault, and Cooper and Laing. Foucault was not a practising psychiatrist, nor was he proposing alternative forms of therapy. Unlike Cooper and Laing, he had no overriding interest in schizophrenia. And, ironically, their work was, as is apparent from their study of Sartre, deeply rooted in the phenomenological tradition Foucault disliked so much.[19] In 1969, the niceties of such differences counted for less than the perceived similarity.

Foucault was further identified with anti-psychiatry, defined in a rather different sense, when *Histoire de la folie* was discussed at length at a congress organised by Evolution Psychiatrique, France's oldest professional grouping of psychiatrists and psychoanalysts.[20] Foucault was invited to attend the congress in Toulouse in December 1969, but politely declined the invitation. In subsequent interviews, he described Evolution Psychiatrique's discussion of his work as an 'excommunication', as a 'psychiatric court' set up to denounce him as 'an ideologue, a bourgeois ideologue'.[21]

Those who took part in the debates in Toulouse were not tender towards *Histoire de la folie* and Foucault was indeed accused of having elaborated 'an ideological conception' of madness, but he was not in fact accused of being a '*bourgeois* ideologue'. In his opening remarks, Henri Ey praised Foucault for his 'extraordinary erudition, courage, style and lucidity' but went on to accuse him of 'psychiatricide'.[22] In the paper he later read to the congress, he expanded that comment to define 'psychiatricide' as 'genocide with respect to humanity's system of values'. In Foucault's 'perspective – let us call it "ideological" – being mad, seeming mad or being treated as mad has nothing to do with any natural phenomenon: in both history and in the practice of the concept of mental illness, it is as though its "pathology" were purely artificial and its therapy purely social'.[23] Ey was not using 'ideological' in any Marxist sense, and effectively makes it synonymous with 'idealist'.

Other contributors to the debate were, if anything, harsher. Henri Sztulman, who drew a parallel with the work of the American Thomas Szazs on the manufacture of madness, accused Foucault of having no real interest in the mad: 'Not one human cry is heard in these thousands of pages, in the closed and aseptic world of disembodied thought in which M. Foucault moves.'[24] Georges Daumézon, highly critical of Foucault's historical accuracy, accused him of constantly confusing madness as a 'category of day-to-day language' with the 'mental disturbances we are responsible for treating'. Perhaps more significantly, he was worried about the effect the book was having on young psychiatrists whose 'daily practice was being influenced by the torments inflicted on them by this distorted view', whose 'behaviour when faced with a patient was being dictated by their fear of being the medical jailer described by Foucault'.[25] Speaking from the floor, H. Aubin stated baldly: 'Foucault is an anti-psychiatrist because the whole of his philosophy is inscribed within the revolutionary current, in the wake of Marcuse.'[26]

Eight years after its publication, *Histoire de la folie* was still sending shudders through the psychiatric world. Certain of the speakers were not unknown to Foucault, and there is a personal note to some of their remarks. Daumézon had taught Foucault in the late 1940s, and Ey had at least some acquaintance with him, having prefaced the translation of Weizsaecker's *Der Gestaltkreis* on which Foucault collaborated with Daniel Rocher in the 1950s. At the age of eighty-three, Eugène Minkowski was more than old enough – and enough of a bibliographer – to recall Foucault's introduction to Binswanger, which had rarely been mentioned in print since its appearance in 1954. He was generous enough to speak of it in generally positive terms in his contribution to the debate, even though he had little sympathy for Foucault's attempt to see madness as a complete 'manifestation of human life' or for his neglect of clinical data.[27] If this was a court, the judges were quite familiar with the accused. In the 1950s, Foucault had rejected his mentors in psychiatry and psychology. It was now their turn to reject and disown him. Wildly inaccurate accusations that he was part of the same current as Herbert Marcuse, author of *One Dimensional Man*, can only have enhanced the increasingly widespread view that *Histoire de la folie* was part of the radical counterculture.

Despite the hostility of Evolution Psychiatrique and his own growing reputation as a leftist, Foucault continued in many ways to pursue a conventional and distinguished career. He addressed the Société Française de Philosophie, and spoke at the 'Journées Cuvier' conference held at the Institut d'Histoire des Sciences in May 1969.[28] Although this was not a particularly productive period in terms of his writing, Foucault also wrote occasional reviews, including a very favourable piece on Deleuze's *Différence et répétition*.[29] He was also willing, and able, to use his growing prestige on behalf of others. When, for instance, Daniel Defert's brother Maxime showed his paintings at the Galerie Daniel Templon, the short catalogue was prefaced by Michel Foucault, and extracts appeared in the press.[30]

L'Archéologie du savoir appeared in the spring of 1969, to a somewhat muted reception, and with none of the extensive publicity that had surrounded *Les Mots et les choses*. Foucault gave two interviews about the book, patiently explaining yet again why he used the term 'archaeology' and reiterating his opposition to humanism and teleological visions of history. He was also anxious to distance himself from structuralism and to challenge those who subsumed him under that most vague of generic labels, pointing out to *Le Monde*'s Jean-Michel Palmier that *langue* or the linguistic system was of less interest to him than the 'operations' that gave rise to the said system. When pressed on whether there was any real similarity between his work and that of Lévi-Strauss and Lacan, he teasingly replied with a riddle: 'It is up to those who used the same label "structuralists" to refer to diverse works to say to what extent we are structuralists. You know the riddle: what is the difference between Bernard Shaw and Charlie Chaplin? There's no difference, because they both have beards, except for Chaplin, of course!'[31]

The main reviews were not by journalists like Madeleine Chapsal, but by colleagues like Châtelet and Duvignaud. The former saw *L'Archéologie* primarily as a welcome assault on the tired discipline known as the history of ideas, as a work of demolition which was intended to liberate spaces and forces, 'to break the annoying surge of the humanist, subjectivist and empiricist schools of thought which clutter up, with all their immense good will, the road that leads to the destruction of speculative ideology'.[32] In the *Nouvel Observateur*, Jean Duvignaud referred to Foucault as a *flâneur*, 'a traveller who is unwilling to be shut up in the academic "ghetto"'. The description is an attractive and not inaccurate one, as is that of Foucault's work as being less 'reassuring' than it might seem to those who insisted on seeing him either as a structuralist or as a disciple of Wilhelm Dilthey and Ernst Cassirer (as, that is, a historian of ideas). Yet, though he admired the book, and particularly its style, Duvignaud had doubts. His doubts focused upon the suggestion that 'the totality of experience' was reducible to language and that the analysis of discourse was the sole means to discover existence, and he saw in that suggestion an assumption common to Foucault, *Cahiers pour l'analyse* and *Tel Quel*. 'What', he asked, 'if language were no more than one of the possible and necessarily relative modes of representing an experience which was anonymous and infinite?'[33]

The real celebrant of the man he called 'a new archivist' was Deleuze, writing in *Critique*.[34] Much of Deleuze's review-article is a rhapsodic improvisation inspired by Foucault rather than a critical account of the book itself, but a number of points emerge clearly from the plethora of spatial metaphors. For Deleuze, the final pages of this 'poem-archaeology' are a 'call for a general theory of productions which must merge with a revolutionary practice in which the active "discourse" takes shape in the element of an "outside" which is indifferent to my life and my death'.[35] Deleuze concludes by citing Boulez on Webern, and by suggesting that this judgement might well apply to Foucault and his style: 'He [Webern] created a new dimension, which we might call a diagonal dimension, a sort of distribution of points, blocks or figures which exist in space, not on a plane.'[36] The suggestion is not luminously clear, but it is an effective reminder that, according to Foucault himself, the music of Boulez and Barraqué was one of the things that liberated him from the academic philosophy on which he was raised as a student.

Discussion of *L'Archéologie* was not widespread in the press, but Foucault did not really need media publicity at this stage. The reception of his book by *Cahiers pour l'analyse* and the association with Althusser and Canguilhem were more than enough to consolidate his reputation in the intellectual circles that mattered much more to him than the readership of, say, *L'Express*. Foucault was, for instance, particularly pleased with the favourable review-article by Dominique Lecourt that appeared in *La Pensée* in April 1970. Although Lecourt was not a Party member, *La Pensée* is a PCF journal; this was the first non-hostile review of Foucault to appear in the Party press, and signalled a consolidation of the Foucault–Althusser–Canguilhem alliance. Lecourt had, significantly, studied with Canguilhem.[37] Lecourt was critical of Foucault's failure to adopt a 'class position' in politics; he was convinced that Foucault's 'discursive formation' was in fact 'a materialist and historical theory of ideological relationships and of the formation of ideological objects'.[38]

Canguilhem, in the meantime, was elaborating a notion of 'scientific ideology' which was, he acknowledged, influenced both by Althusser and by Foucault's thresholds of positivity, scientificity and formalisation.[39] The enthusiasm for theories of scientific ideologies was not long-lived, but it did seem to cement an important alliance in its time.

Although he never became a member of any established political organisation and restricted his activities to ad hoc bodies like the Groupe d'Information sur les Prisons, Foucault shared many of the assumptions of the younger generation of *gauchistes*. Their loathing of the PCF matched his, but stemmed from rather different sources, being based upon the argument that the PCF, or the ex-PCF as it was often described in these circles, had abandoned basic principles of Marxism and had become 'revisionist'. Foucault's distrust and dislike of the PCF reflected his own disillusionment of the 1950s, his experiences in Poland, his clashes with Roger Garaudy and the representatives of Marxist humanism, as well as a revulsion from the totalising ambitions of Marxism, revisionist or not.

Originally a pejorative term applied by the PCF to those it judged irresponsibly 'leftist' and derived from Lenin's comments on the 'infantile disorder' of 'left-wing communism', *gauchiste* came increasingly to refer to the myriad groups spawned in the aftermath of the May events, and primarily to the Maoist and anarchist tendencies, though it was sometimes to cover Trotskyist groups too. Organised Trotskyism was of no interest to Foucault, but *gauchisme* certainly had its attractions. He had been politicised by what he had seen and experienced in Tunisia, and Daniel Defert was already moving in *gauchiste* circles. More generally, May had led to an extension of the notion of the political: madness, sexuality, prisons could now all be seen as political issues in a way which had not really been possible in the 1950s or the early 1960s. As Foucault put it:

> The boundary of politics has changed, and subjects like psychiatry, confinement and the medicalisation of a population, have become political problems. With what has been happening over the last few years, political groups have been obliged to integrate these domains into their action, and they and I have come together, not because I've changed – I'm not boasting; I'd like to change – but because I think I can say with some pride in this case that it is politics that has come to me.[40]

In general ideological terms, he now found himself close to the Gauche Prolétarienne, the most notorious and most dynamic of the self-styled Maoist groups.

The Gauche Prolétarienne, which took its name from that applied to the 'rebels' who opposed the 'capitalist roaders' in China's Cultural Revolution, grew out of the fusion of elements of two *gauchiste* groups in the spring of 1969. It was formally established in September 1968, mainly by members of the UJC(ml) [Union des Jeunesses Communistes (marxiste-léniniste)], but really came to life when it merged with elements from the Mouvement du 22 mars. The UJC(ml), based mainly at ENS, had been strongly influenced by Althusser's reading of Marx, and in particular by his success in placing Mao on the philosophical map in his 'Contradiction and Overdetermination'.[41] From Althusser, it inherited an obsession with rigour and correctness which, once it shed its philosophical guise, easily translated into sectarian fanaticism. The '22 mars' group, originally based at Nanterre and led by Daniel Cohn-Bendit, had always been characterised by its stress on spontaneity. The combination of Maoism and spontaneism resulted in a volatile and potentially violent ideology. In some quarters, it also meant that the young Maoists were dismissively known as '*Maos-spontex*', Spontex being a brand of cleaning sponge.

Although nominally Maoist, the GP displayed some peculiar ideological features. Most Maoist parties and groups, including the dogmatically dull Parti Communiste Marxiste-Léniniste Français, traced their ancestry from Marx and Engels through Lenin and, with varying degrees of embarrassment, Stalin, to Mao. The GP wrote Lenin and Stalin out of its pedigree, not out of any concession to liberalism but because of its rejection of Lenin's endorsement in *What is to be done?* of Karl Kautsky's claim that 'the vehicle of science is not the proletariat, but the *bourgeois intelligentsia*',[42] and his insistence that a revolutionary movement could not be founded upon the spontaneous instincts of the proletariat alone. As a GP member known only as 'Jean' put it in an interview: 'A Maoist has nothing to teach the masses. What a Maoist does have to do is try to free the initiatives of the masses, by which we mean: helping the masses to fight the old bourgeois ideas. How? By starting out from the correct, but perhaps confused, ideas which are to be found among the masses.'[43]

Although its leadership and much of its membership were 'intellectuals' by any definition, the GP was resolutely anti-intellectual. Insofar as the intellectual had a role, it was one of self-abnegation. The role model was that of the *établi*, the young intellectual who succeeded in gaining factory employment and 'establishing' himself inside the proletariat. According to 'Jean', 'Maoists act a bit like catalysts: they melt into the people and try to help it to organise. But it is the people itself, the people alone which is marching towards the Revolution.'[44] Even those who formulated the notion tended at times to think in terms of literary images, like Jean, whose own theories reminded him of

Zola's *Germinal*: 'The guy who lands up in the mines in the Nord, ends up by winning the confidence of the masses, by unleashing their enthusiasm.'[45]

At the time, GP members would have been horrified by any suggestion that their position had profoundly religious overtones, but it is almost impossible not to be reminded of Simone Weil's pre-war search for latter-day sainthood in the factory,[46] or of the worker-priest experiments of the early 1950s. The practice was not the invention of the GP, had already been adopted by the UJC(ml), and became more common as the militants resolved to move out of the Latin Quarter and into the factories in the summer of 1968. For the individuals concerned, the attempt to become an *établi* was often brutally destructive. Possibly the best account is Robert Linhart's autobiographical novel about the years he spent on the shopfloor in Citroën's Porte de Choissy plant, a saga of brutalisation and exhaustion which led to a mental breakdown and years of chronic depression for its author.[47]

Foucault did not subscribe to the mythology of the *établi*, and spoke disapprovingly to Defert about the move into the factories, arguing that May would have had much farther-reaching effects in the sphere of knowledge if the struggle had been concentrated on the universities. He had no interest in arcane interpretations of Lenin. Nor did he share the contemporary enthusiasm for 'studying Mao Tse-Tung thought', an activity which he regarded as quite meaningless. Yet he was to make many friends in the *gauchiste* milieu, and to drift away from older friends like Klossowski as he became more politically active. He occasionally wrote for the GP's paper *La Cause du peuple* and was involved in at least some GP activities. The attractions were considerable. *Gauchisme* and the GP in particular offered an appealing image of naked revolt against authority which was not without its Nietzschean overtones. So too did the physical hardness of the young street-fighting man, and the GP was nothing if not a man's organisation. Had the GP ever designed an icon, it would have featured a young man in a tight leather jacket, boots and a crash helmet defying police lines. Some of those police lines were to be drawn up at Vincennes.

The University of Vincennes, officially known as the Vincennes Experimental University Centre, was the offspring of May 1968 and Edgar Faure, the minister for education. It seemed to respond to many of the demands put forward in May: it was resolutely interdisciplinary, introduced novel courses on cinema, semiotics and psychoanalysis, and was the first French university to open its doors to candidates who did not have the *baccalauréat*. It therefore succeeded in attracting considerable numbers of wage-earners and people outside the normal recruitment pool.

Vincennes was immediately affected by Faure's other innovation: the *loi d'orientation* of 12 November 1968. The law introduced major changes into university administration and did away with the previous system under which universities were governed by a dean, a secretary general and a council of tenured professors. The existing faculties and departments were replaced, in the first instance, by Unités d'Enseignement et de Recherche [Teaching and Research Units], which were expected to group themselves into universities at a later date, and which did evolve into institutions designated as Paris VIII (Vincennes) and so on. The UERs were to be run by elected councils representing the student body, the teaching corps and the administration.

The underlying principle was that of 'participation', and it was this that was to cause Vincennes so many problems in its early years. Participation had become the slogan of Gaullism in its later phases, and was duly adopted by Pompidou. The slogan of participation was launched by de Gaulle in a speech made on 24 May 1968, and referred to both profit-sharing schemes and a vague notion of co-management. 'Participation' in the management of industry was immediately denounced as trap: a poster produced at the Ecole des Beaux Arts bore the declension: 'I participate, you participate, we participate, he profits.' The extension of 'participation' to the higher education sector was clearly not to be unproblematic. Broadly speaking, the PCF supported the idea of participation on the grounds that it would make higher education more democratic. It was also well aware that it could exploit it to its own ends. As Foucault was wont to argue at the time, the PCF might not be interested in seizing power but it was certainly interested in obtaining positions of power.[48] Emmanuel Terray, who taught anthropology at Vincennes, put the case against Faure's law in *Le Monde*, arguing that the ideology of participation was 'a resurrection of the old liberal ideology: it consists of a denial of the reality of class antagonisms and of the assertion that the citizens of a nation – or all members of a company – have an equal interest in its prosperity'.[49]

In administrative terms, the new university existed as of October 1968 but it was not until the following January that teaching actually got under way. Raymond Las Vergnas, the dean of the Sorbonne, was given responsibility for its organisation and for chairing the Commission d'Orientation, or steering committee. The commission's membership was prestigious and included Barthes, Derrida, Le Roy Ladurie and Canguilhem. It appointed the university's first professors, who in turn formed the *noyau cooptant* ('coopting nucleus') which recruited the teaching staff. Foucault was appointed to the *noyau* on 25 October on the recommendation of Canguilhem. His colleagues included Robert Castel and Jean-Claude Passeron in sociology, Jacques Droz in history, and Hélène Cixous in English. The last-named, better known at this time as a Joyce specialist than as a feminist novelist, was to become a particularly close friend.[50]

Foucault was a fairly obvious choice for the chair in philosophy and his nomination had been recommended to Las Vergnas by Canguilhem. At this point a bureaucratic muddle developed. As a member of the coopting group, Foucault could not, technically, coopt himself to a chair and therefore had to resign from the *noyau* in order to be coopted by his colleagues. Ten of the eleven members voted for his appointment; the eleventh member was absent. As of the beginning of December, Foucault was officially Vincennes's professor of philosophy.[51]

There was nothing surprising about Foucault's appointment. *Les Mots et les choses* had brought him immense prestige, and he was now probably the most distinguished, and certainly the best-known, philosopher of his generation. In ministerial eyes, he was politically uncontroversial and had played no part in the May events. Nor had he spoken publicly about his experiences in Tunisia. It is also possible that his continued friendship with Burin des Roziers gave him a certain reputation in government circles. In the eyes of the *gauchistes* who were to play such an active role at Vincennes, however, Foucault's absence in Tunisia had seriously compromised him. In the autumn of 1968, not to have been involved in May was almost as damning as admitting in 1945 that one had not been active in the Resistance. It was common for young lecturers to begin courses by describing what they had done during the 'events'; the display of battle honours did not always imply any great change at the level of pedagogical practice. Foucault was convinced that he had risked more in Tunisia than anyone on the Paris barricades, but cautiously resisted the temptation to say so in public.

If Foucault did enjoy ministerial confidence, the appointments he made to the philosophy department must have shaken it somewhat. The opportunity to create *ex nihilo* a new department in a new university gave him a lot of power, and he used it with a skill that impressed those around him. As he had done when he appointed Defert as his assistant at Clermont-Ferrand, he in a sense exploited his power: all his appointees were personally known to him, and there was no sign of an open recruitment policy. Daniel Defert, in the meantime, was drifting away from philosophy and secured an appointment in Castel's sociology department, where he soon acquired a reputation as a highly competent and popular teacher. This change of academic direction was not particularly unusual; there is no *agrégation* in sociology, and many of France's best sociologists are, like Bourdieu, *agrégés de philosophie*. Like Anzieu at Nanterre, Foucault was determined to recruit the best members of the rising generation. He also approached some of his own contemporaries. Deleuze declined the invitation to come to Vincennes on health grounds: his recurrent respiratory problems made it impossible, and he did not arrive until two years later. Michel Serres, René Schérer and François Châtelet accepted with enthusiasm. So too did Jeannette Colombel, a teacher from a Lyon *lycée* who met Foucault at Deleuze's *soutenance de thèse*; he had obviously decided to ignore the criticisms she had levelled at *Les Mots et les choses* in 1967. The rest of the staff were from a younger and more militant generation. Etienne Balibar, one of the young co-authors of Althusser's *Lire Le Capital*, was appointed on secondment from a suburban *lycée* and was joined by Alain Badiou, who advised Foucault on possible appointees, and Jacques Rancière, also a co-author of *Lire Le Capital*.

It was in fact psychoanalysis rather than philosophy that became the real source of controversy. At Vincennes, psychoanalysis and philosophy were to exist in a curious symbiosis. In July 1968, Serge Leclaire, a close associate of Lacan's and one of the most respected figures in the entire analytic community, entered into discussion with Las Vergnas over the possible creation of a department of psycho-analysis at Vincennes.

Psychoanalysis had begun to make inroads into the universities after 1945, mainly thanks to the efforts of Lagache, but was usually still taught under the rubric of general or clinical psychology. At Nanterre, Didier Anzieu had some freedom to pursue and develop his psycho-analytic interests, but the Sorbonne was still under the influence of a psychological tradition which owed rather more to Janet than to Freud. At Censier, Jean Laplanche finally succeeded in establishing a Laboratory of Psychoanalysis and Psychopathology; his own teaching centred on the conceptual reading and exegesis of Freud in a manner reminiscent of the *Language of Psychoanalysis*.[52] The importation of psychoanalysis to Vincennes was to take a rather different course. Leclaire's discussions with Las Vergnas were extended to a consul-tative group including Cixous, Derrida, Canguilhem and Foucault, acting in his capacity as the professor-designate of philosophy. Leclaire's aim was to create a space for psychoanalysis rather than a department as such, and Vincennes became the first university in France to teach psychoanalysis without being subsumed under either medicine or psychology.

Foucault's role was crucial. He supported Leclaire and the department of psychoanalysis was initially established as a constituent part of the philosophy department.[53] Foucault's relationship with psychoanalysis had always been ambivalent, and he was certainly not committed to the hard-line Lacanianism which became dominant at Vincennes. According to Robert Castel, his real motive was a desire to prevent the establishment of a department of psychology which would, he feared, be experimental and behavioural. He also suspected that it would provide a bridgehead for the PCF.[54]

The department of psychoanalysis was headed by Serge Leclaire. One of his and Foucault's appointments was to prove both significant and controversial. Jacques-Alain Miller was teaching in Besançon, and had become a member of the GP in the spring of 1969. He was not, apparently, Leclaire's first choice, and was appointed when more senior figures declined Leclaire's invitation to join him in the woods at Vincennes. Knowing of his membership of a group whose stated goals included the destruction of the university, Leclaire suggested that Miller should move to philosophy. Miller opted to remain in psychoanalysis, where he was joined by his wife Judith and his brother Gérard. Although he was a member of Lacan's school, Miller was not a psychoanalyst and had not at this time been in analysis, a fact which would have ruled out his participation in the teaching offered by any conventional institute of psychoanalysis. His real qualifications were at once theoretical, political and personal. As editor of *Cahiers pour l'analyse*, he had been influential in promoting a brand of psychoanalysis which owed as much to formal logic as to Lacan, and he was now a member of the GP. His wife Judith was Lacan's daughter.

Lacan's own attitude to the Vincennes experiment was not unambiguous. On the one hand, the new department obviously provided him with a platform for the diffusion of his theories; on the other, it represented a potential threat to the central authority of his own seminar and of the crisis-ridden Ecole Freudienne de Paris. He had little direct involvement with the department, and his one encounter with the students of Vincennes ended in a spectacular display of chaos. In December 1969 he made the first of four planned visits to the new university. He was challenged over a number of issues, notably the futility of following courses on psychoanalysis which did not confer any psychoanalytic qualifications. There was an incident in which a male student began to undress and was promptly told by Lacan, who had recently seen the Living Theatre's rather more daring exploitation of on-stage nudity, to have the courage to strip completely. The psychoanalyst then accused the *Vincennois* of being slaves to the Pompidou regime: 'You don't understand that either? The regime is putting you on display. It's saying – *Watch them come*. Goodbye for today. *Bye* [English in the original]. It's over.'[55]

If Foucault still enjoyed ministerial confidence, it must have been somewhat shaken by his appointments. And they did have their repercussions in the spring of 1969. Foucault was due to speak at the French Institute in London and at two British universities, but when he went to the Quai d'Orsay to make the final arrangements for his journey, he was informed that it had been cancelled on ministerial instructions. The story was leaked to the *Nouvel Observateur*, whose Patrick Loriot assumed that Faure was behind the cancellation and that Foucault was being prevented from speaking against the *loi d'orientation*.[56] Foucault then wrote to the magazine, stating that it was Michel Debré who had cancelled the visit in order to prevent 'questions and discussions that might embarrass the French embassy. The English public has therefore been no less censored than I.'[57] The source of the leak was undoubtedly Foucault himself, and his subsequent letter appears to have been an act of deliberate provocation.

The politics of Foucault's appointments are intriguing. They represented a broad political spectrum, ranging from the PCF (Balibar) to an extreme variety of Maoism (the Millers) and completed, surprisingly, by Trotskyism (Henri Weber). Although on the left, Serres and Châtelet had no particular sectarian loyalties. Didier Eribon argues that Foucault's aim was to secure a built-in political balance, and to use the moderation of some to cancel out the extremism of others.[58] His interpretation is not implausible, but Defert suggests a rather different one. Most of Foucault's recruits were having difficulties of one kind or another with the educational establishment. The Millers had encountered political problems at Besançon and had effectively been marginalised. The career of René Schérer, a Fourier specialist who had first met Foucault when they sat together on a *baccalauréat* jury in the early 1960s, was in jeopardy because of his alleged involvement in a paedophile scandal. Châtelet's work was scarcely appreciated by the Sorbonne establishment. For Balibar, Vincennes provided a welcome escape from the secondary sector (because of administrative delays, Balibar's secondment was never officially ratified; he taught a seminar at Vincennes, but was officially still a *lycée* teacher). According to this view, Foucault was trying to create a space in which individuals who had been marginalised by the system would be able to work without the constraints found elsewhere. Etienne Balibar, on the other hand, recalls a discussion in the rue de Vaugirard in which Foucault spoke of bringing together representatives of the new French philosophy, and of recruiting both 'specialists in power' and 'specialists in knowledge'. Whatever his precise motives, Foucault had succeeded in creating a political hornets' nest.[59]

The university was built in the Bois de Vincennes on land leased from the army for a ten-year period. In the summer and autumn of 1968, prefabricated buildings sprouted with remarkable speed. They were modern and well equipped. For the first time, a French university was fitted with television sets and with public telephones in the corridors. The rooms were carpeted, and the university restaurant rapidly came to enjoy a good reputation. Vincennes was, however, very isolated. The experimental centre was a long way from the nearest metro station at the Château de Vincennes, and was served by an inadequate bus service. Many students were reduced to hitch-hiking – and it soon became obvious that this was a somewhat dangerous practice, particularly for women – in order to get to lectures. The problem was obviously most acute for the part-time students who attended lectures in the evening, when the bus service did not operate. The physical location of the university gave it something of the appearance of a luxury ghetto. As a cynically realistic student put it: 'The administration talks about an experimental university, but the only experiment going on there is to see whether the government can take a group of leftist students and keep them out of trouble by giving them a playground to fight over.'[60] Student recruitment was not, initially, easy. By Christmas, only 2,000 students had enrolled, and it was feared that Vincennes would recruit too few students to make it a viable concern. The fears were to prove groundless. By January 1969, over 5,000 students had enrolled, and the new university was already overcrowded when it opened.

It was not the issue of participation that provided the initial spark for the inevitable explosion. It was the memory of May 1968. On 23 January 1969, a group of school students at the Lycée Saint-Louis on the boulevard Saint-Michel were forbidden by the school administration to show a number of films about the May events, and the electricity was cut off. Power sources were illegally tapped, and the film show went ahead. An almost ritualistic clash with the police followed, and the school students crossed the boulevard into the courtyard of the

Sorbonne. Here, a meeting to protest about inadequate grants was in progress. A proposal to occupy the rectorate, which adjoined the Sorbonne, was overwhelmingly voted through in protest at developments in the *lycée*. The rectorate was duly occupied by about 150 students, and the police moved in, cordoning off the area around the Sorbonne and evicting the protesters. There were thirty-six arrests, and sporadic violent clashes continued until late in the evening.

News of developments in the Latin Quarter soon reached Vincennes, where a crowded general meeting immediately voted to occupy. Building D was taken over, and the entrances and staircases were barricaded, with a number of the famous television sets finding their way into the fortifications. One of those involved in building the barricades was Foucault, dressed in a black corduroy suit and ably abetted by Defert. Before long, the building was surrounded by 2,000 police in full riot gear. An ultimatum was given: the protesters could either leave freely or face the consequences. Most chose the latter alternative.

At 1.30 in the morning, the attack came. Salvoes of tear-gas grenades were fired through the windows and a full-scale battle broke out. Defert and Foucault retreated up the stairway, blocking their path behind them and then joining those who were flinging assorted missiles from the roof. Foucault was, in Defert's phrase, having a whale of a time [*il s'amusait comme un petit fou*] and was no doubt experiencing a definitely Nietzschean 'joy in destruction'.[61]

The result of the first battle of Vincennes was a foregone conclusion, and some 220 people were soon being herded into the main lecture theatre. Two of the last to be bought in were Defert and Foucault, coughing and spluttering with the effects of the gas. All were transferred to the police holding centre in the rue Beaujon and held for a few hours before being released, mostly without being charged. Foucault had been arrested for the first time, and his status in the eyes of his *gauchiste* colleagues and comrades was enhanced accordingly.

As a result of the Sorbonne occupation, thirty-four students were expelled from the university for a year and the possibility that they might be called up early for military service was being openly discussed. Students enjoyed the privilege of deferred military service, and it was an axiomatic part of *gauchiste* folklore that militants who were drafted in these circumstances would have a hard and dangerous time of it. On 11 February, 3,000 people packed into the Mutualité for a protest meeting that ended at midnight to the strains of the *Internationale*. The speakers included Sartre and Foucault, who now really entered the political scene for the first time. It was on this occasion that the first indication was given that Sartre's standing with the *gauchistes* might not be beyond challenge; when he reached the platform, he found a note telling him to 'keep it short'. To the backdrop of a banner reading *'Non à l'Université policière'*, Sartre summarily denounced 'participation' as a mug's game, but later admitted that his attempt to analyse Faure's law had disappointed his audience; for them, the problem was how to meet violence with violence, not how to analyse laws.[62]

There is no accurate record of just what Foucault said. According to contemporary press accounts, he claimed, somewhat disingenuously, that the students had caused no damage, that everything that had occurred was the result of police provocation and that the students found themselves faced with a policy of calculated repression.[63] Defert recalls a rather different speech, in which Foucault advised on the correct handling of television sets in the construction of barricades. Given the climate of the meeting, those present probably failed to realise that it was the scene of a significant encounter. Not only were Foucault and Sartre sharing a public platform for the first time; it was the first time they had met.

The Mutualité meeting was not Foucault's only protest. On the same day, a letter was sent to the rector of the Academy of Paris:

> We are a few of the teachers who occupied the premises with the students, and for the same reasons as they. We are in complete solidarity with the action they undertook, we behaved in the same way as they on this occasion, and we do not accept that any distinction should be made between their case and ours.
>
> We are therefore asking you to face up to your responsibilities, just as we have done, and to take the disciplinary measures provided for by the law, to the extent that they exist.

The letter, which was released to the press,[64] was signed by Alain Badiou, Daniel Defert, Michel Foucault, Sylvain Lazarus, Judith Miller, Viviane Regnot and Emmanuel Terray. The rector did not respond to the challenge.

After the first occupation, Vincennes rapidly became notorious. Las Vergnas resigned and was replaced by Inspector General Seïté, who proved as incapable of calming the situation as his predecessor. Physically, conditions deteriorated rapidly: vandalism, most of it politically inspired, was rampant and aggressively militant graffiti covered every available surface. The university's most famous feature was the 'souk', an improvised and unofficial market which flourished on the premises. *Merguez* sandwiches (*merguez* are spicy mutton sausages, originally from North Africa) and records were sold along-side a jumble of political and hippy commodities. A brisk trade in 'second-hand' books developed, many of them stolen from Maspero's 'Joie de lire' bookshop in the Latin Quarter, which had a deliberate policy of not prosecuting shoplifters. Books from the Vincennes library were beginning to disappear at an alarming rate, and it is probable that they helped to increase the 'souk's' turnover. Drugs were quite easily available. The university that was to have shown the way for the late twentieth century was rapidly becoming chaotic. There was a regular police presence on campus, and Foucault, to his amusement, was often shadowed by officers who mistakenly believed him to be a Maoist 'leader'.

The 'participation' issue was of course central to life at Vincennes, but it overlapped with broader ideological differences. For the Trotskyist minority led by Weber, Vincennes offered the chance to turn a leftist ghetto into a 'red base', and to transform the avant-garde of the bourgeois university into the weakest link of the system.[65] The most extreme current found expression in the grandiosely entitled '*Comité de base pour l'abolition du salariat et la destruction de l'Université*' organised by Jean-Marc Salmon, Jean-Paul Dollé and André Glucksmann.

Born in 1937, Glucksmann was significantly older then his comrades, and was officially a researcher at the CNRS. A former student of Raymond Aron's, he was the vocal advocate of an extreme *gauchisme*. As its name indicates, the Comité's goal was the destruction of the university and the abolition of the wage system. The latter aim was unlikely to be achieved at Vincennes, but the former was not entirely unrealistic. For the Comité de Base, the destruction of the university was a long process which required an understanding, on the part of the 'student masses', of the futility of the university and its examination system and of the uselessness of its 'perverted teaching.'[66] Many members of the Gauche Prolétarienne held similar views, notably Judith Miller, who unwisely told two women researching a book on the crisis in education:

> I will do the best to make sure it [the university] functions worse and worse. The university is a state apparatus, a fragment of capitalist society, and what appears to be a haven of liberalism is not one at all. I don't think that it can be shattered without the whole system. All one can say is that one will make it function as little as possible.

Her comments subsequently appeared in a magazine article which was apparently read by Pompidou himself. At his insistence, Edgar Faure's successor Oliver Guichard promptly dismissed Miller, who returned to the secondary sector.[67]

Behind Miller's wild pronouncements, there lay the very real issue of modular course units, dubbed *unités de valeur* ('units of value') in the terminology introduced by the *loi d'orientation*. In order to obtain a degree, students had to accumulate thirty *unités*, twenty from a major discipline such as philosophy, and ten from a sub-major such as psychoanalysis. The examining and awarding of credits soon became almost farcical, particularly on Judith Miller's course; credits were effectively awarded on request to all those who had enrolled for courses, even if they had never attended a single lecture. For the GP, this was all part of destroying the university; elsewhere it led to the increasing conviction that a Vincennes degree was quite worthless.

Hostility to the PCF could take the form of physical violence on the part of those who were convinced that they were involved in a Cultural Revolution of their own. It was not unknown for PCF members to have to descend staircases while being spat upon by their political opponents.[68] In the summer of 1970, when the 'participation' issue was at its height, a meeting of Rancière's students voted to exclude PCF members from his classes. He was spared the embarrassment of having to defend a political party for which he had no sympathy by the communist group's decision to depart of its own accord.[69] One of the main victims of the Maoist faction was Balibar. According to the Comité and associates, the PCF was the bulwark of the bourgeoisie, and Althusser was the PCF's ideological bulwark. Attacks on Althusser and his followers would lead to the destruction of the PCF, and hence to the final collapse of the bourgeoisie. Balibar was in the front line. His lectures were regularly interrupted, and pickets and demonstrations eventually made it quite impossible for him to teach. One of the side effects of this was the formation of an unlikely alliance between Balibar and Weber; for once, the PCF and Trotskyism were on the same side. Balibar has no recollection of Foucault doing or saying anything to remedy the situation, though it is probably true that neither party would have appreciated his intervention. Balibar was eventually forced to admit defeat, wrote to the Ministry of Education requesting not to be seconded to Vincennes, and retreated to his *lycée*.[70]

It being axiomatic to the Maoism of the day that moderates were the worst of all enemies, Foucault also came under attack. He had not participated in the May events, and was still seen in some quarters as a

Gaullist technocrat. His lectures were interrupted and he was finally forced to abandon the format of the formal lecture and to take part, much to his annoyance, in rambling forums and open debates. On occasion, he was locked out of his own lecture room and passed the time in rather desultory conversation with Colombel and others.[71] For someone with his commitment to intellectual work, the climate was rapidly becoming intolerably frustrating. Balibar recalls one occasion on which Foucault became so irritated with an endless general meeting that he fled, with Balibar and Serres, to seek refuge in a cinema showing Straub's recently released *Chronicle of Anna Magdalena Bach*.

In terms of course content, the new department of philosophy had been given a free hand. Foucault himself taught lecture courses on Nietzsche, which were immensely popular but not always appreciated by the *gauchistes*, and on 'sexuality and individuality'. The lectures of Nietzsche owed a great deal to Klossowski's recently published study, which Foucault described as 'the greatest book on philosophy I have read'.[72] It is mainly a commentary on posthumously published fragments dating from the period 1880–88. The courses taught by his colleagues were much more openly political and dealt, *inter alia*, with Marxism and revisionism, Marxist dialectics and cultural revolution. It is true that Serres and Châtelet taught more traditional courses on the history of science and Greek political thought respectively, but it was the more politicised topics that gave Vincennes its notoriety. The same courses soon attracted ministerial attention. In January 1970, Guichard announced that the content of the philosophy course was 'too specialised' and that any degrees awarded would not be nationally recognised. The direct implication of his pronouncement was that Vincennes graduates would be denied teaching posts in both the secondary and higher education sectors.

Foucault replied to Guichard in an interview published in *Le Nouvel Observateur*. He began by making the obvious point that it was virtually impossible to provide 'developed and diversified courses' with eight members of staff and 950 students, and defended his choice to experiment with

freedom, which I would not say is total, but as complete as possible in a university like Vincennes.

We have defined two broad areas of teaching: one that is basically devoted to the political analysis of society and one that is devoted to the analysis of the scientific fact and to the analysis of a certain number of scientific domains. These two regions, politics

and science, seemed to all of us, students and teachers alike, to be
the most active and the most fruitful.[73]

He insisted that the struggle would go on until the Vincennes degree
was fully recognised. Neither Foucault's pleas nor the promised
struggle had any effect, and it was to be years before the degree – by
then very different – was recognised.

Even as he defended his department and its work in print, Foucault
was well aware that his future lay elsewhere. Despite his obvious
commitment to Vincennes, his stay there had always been intended to
be a temporary one. Three days before his arrest at Vincennes,
Foucault had addressed a solemn gathering at ENS. The occasion was
the memorial meeting held to honour Jean Hyppolite, who died in late
October 1968 at the age of only sixty-one. Foucault was one of the main
orators and spoke with moving affection of a man he had greatly
respected, admired and loved.[74] His tribute was to the man whose voice
had introduced the presence of Hegel into a classroom at Henri-IV in
1945, and to the master who had supervised his thesis on Kant.
Foucault's eulogy was a skilful piece of rhetoric, bringing in quiet
allusions to virtually every stage in Hyppolite's career, from the early
thesis on mathematical method and Descartes to the final interest in
information theory and genetics, without ever becoming a dry résumé.

Hyppolite's chair at the Collège de France had been in the history of
philosophical thought, a description which Foucault understood to
mean the history 'of that torsion and that turning back upon itself . . .
by means of which philosophical discourse says what it is, pronounces
its own justification and, by stepping back from its immediate form,
manifests what can found it and establish its own limits'. Introducing a
more subjective note, he then went on:

> Conceived in this way, philosophical thought maintains the
> discourse of the philosopher within the instance of an indefinite
> vibration, and makes it resonate beyond any death; it guarantees
> that philosophy will be in excess of any philosophy: a light which
> was awake even before there was any discourse, a blade which still
> shines once it has entered into sleep.[75]

Hyppolite's definition of his specialism as being the history of
philosophical thought, rather than the history of philosophy, is relevant
to Foucault's own project. This is, perhaps, made clear by a passage in
Hyppolite's outline project for his courses at the Collège de France,
where he argues that the history of philosophical thought 'allows us to

explore the interpretations of being that underlie both our everyday life and the positive sciences . . . Contemporary philosophical research . . . answers a double demand: that for rigour in analysis, and that for direct contact with lived experience.'[76] Philosophy, that is, would progress if, and only if, it was constantly in contact with the non-philosophical and if it was a self-questioning rather than a complacently self-sufficient discipline.

Foucault's second and final tribute to his 'master' took the rather different form of a contribution to a collective volume of essays published to honour Hyppolite in 1971.[77] The name of Hyppolite is not mentioned, and the essay is in fact both the clearest statement to date of Foucault's interest in Nietzsche and an indication of a move away from archaeology. It is Nietzsche the 'genealogist' that is of interest to Foucault: 'Genealogy is grey; it is meticulous and patiently documentary. It works on muddled, scratched parchments that have been rewritten several times . . . Genealogy therefore demands minute knowledge, a great number of piled up materials, patience. . . A certain determination in erudition.'[78]

Supporting his argument with detailed references to *Daybreak*, *The Genealogy of Morals*, *The Gay Science* and other texts, Foucault inveighs against teleological histories and puts the case for the effective [*wirkliche*] history of the *Untimely Meditations*, a text he first read on the beach at Cittavecchia in 1953, and for 'history as a concerted carnival': 'The point is to make such use of history as to free it for ever from the model, which is both metaphysical and anthropological, of memory. The point is to turn history into a counter-memory.'[79] Such a history or genealogy would systematically break down identities, revealing them to be so many masks, so many intersecting systems which dominate one another and not some single idea struggling for its self-realisation: when genealogy asks where we were born, what language we speak, or what laws govern us, it does so 'in order to reveal the heterogeneous systems which, beneath the mask of our ego, deny us any identity'.[80] It will sacrifice the subject of knowledge:

> The end of a genealogically directed history is not to rediscover the roots of our identity but, on the contrary, to strive to dissipate them; it does not attempt to locate the unique home from whence we come, that first homeland to which, the metaphysicians promise us, we will return; it attempts to reveal all the discontinuities that traverse us.[81]

A collection of essays written in tribute to Hyppolite, best known for his work on Hegel, may seem an odd place for this celebration of Nietzsche. As Bernauer suggests, it is not in fact totally inappropriate in that Hyppolite's Hegel is always under interrogation by his successors,[82] including Nietzsche and Foucault. As Foucault put it elsewhere, in Hyppolite's vision, philosophy was no longer a totality capable of grasping itself, but an endless task carried out against the backdrop of an infinite horizon; the Hegelian system was not a reassuring universe, but a philosophy which was taking extreme risks.[83] Hyppolite's project for his course at the Collège de France outlined an encounter between philosophical thought and the non-philosophical, and 'thought irreducible to philosophy' was precisely what Foucault was seeking in Bataille and Nietzsche. It is strangely fitting that his final homage to Hyppolite should take the form of a eulogy of Nietzsche.

The death of Hyppolite meant that a chair at the Collège de France was vacant. As early as 1966, Hyppolite had argued, on the basis of the success of *Les Mots et les choses*, that Foucault was a suitable candidate for election to France's most prestigious institution, and had begun to cast around for support. He found supporters in Jules Vuillemin, Georges Dumézil and Fernand Braudel.[84] It seems that the possibility of election to the Collège de France was first mooted in 1967 when, after he had read a paper to Raymond Aron's seminar at the Sorbonne, it was intimated to Foucault that he was unlikely to find a position at the Sorbonne. A post at the Ecole Pratique des Hautes Etudes was a possibility, but it was hinted by Aron and Braudel that that might compromise any later possibility of election to the Collège. Foucault himself thought that the Collège was beyond him, and told Canguilhem that he thought he might as well stay where he was in Tunis.

The election of a candidate to the Collège de France is a complex process, but Foucault's election is well described by Didier Eribon. The election was in two stages: the vote for the creation of a chair, with no candidate's name appearing, and then the election of the candidate. Obviously, a great deal of lobbying and plotting went on; Jean-François Miquel, for instance, was responsible for mobilising support for Foucault among his scientific colleagues. Dumézil was also active behind the scenes, but was modest in his description of his role: 'I simply nudged a few colleagues whom I suspected of not understanding him, or even of ruling him out *a priori*. I was in the United States at the time. So I wrote about six copies of the same letter: "Careful, don't let genius slip through your fingers." '[85]

The candidate had to submit an account of his work in the form of a privately printed brochure to be circulated among the members of the

Collège. It is in part a *curriculum vitae*, listing qualifications, posts held and publications, but also contains a six-page outline of his work to date and of his proposed courses.[86] Foucault's description of his work begins with *Histoire de la folie*, as though everything written before was of no relevance. It was, he explained, an attempt to determine what could be known about mental illness in a given period and had eventually led him to discover his real object of study: 'knowledge invested in complex systems of institutions'. Madness proved, however, to be an insufficiently topical example, since the psychopathology of the seventeenth and eighteenth centuries was so rudimentary as to be indistinguishable from an 'interplay of traditional opinions', and he therefore turned to a much more rigorous object: the origins of clinical medicine. *Naissance de la clinique* had demonstrated that 'the exercise of medicine is not restricted to combining, in an unstable blend, a rigorous science and an uncertain tradition; it has as its scaffolding a system of knowledge which has its own equilibrium and coherence'.[87] *Les Mots et les choses* had, in its turn, revealed that the internal archaeology of areas of knowledge could be defined, and that the identities and analogies between domains revealed an overall configuration of organised regions of empirical knowledge. At this point, Foucault had two sets of findings: on the one hand, he had noted the specific existence of 'invested knowledges'; on the other, he had noted systematic relations in the architecture characteristic of each knowledge. *L'Archéologie du savoir* provided the synthesis: knowledge (*savoir*) was an area intermediate between opinion and scientific knowledge (*connaissance*), and it was embodied not only in theoretical texts or experimental instruments, but in a whole body of practices and institutions.[88]

The *projet d'enseignement*, or proposed course of lectures, was governed by two imperatives: 'never lose sight of a reference to a concrete example which can serve as a testing ground for the analysis; elaborate the theoretical problems I have happened to meet with or which I may encounter'. The sector proposed for analysis was, somewhat surprisingly, 'knowledge about heredity'. Foucault saw the analysis he wanted to make as exploring attempts to improve livestock through breeding and to control epidemics, looking at specific economic and historical constraints such as land-ownership and productivity, the input of knowledge from chemistry and physiology. Ultimately, it would explore theories of heredity and would lead into an analysis of Darwin's understanding of the natural evolution of species.

Having sketched his overall project, Foucault then identified three sets of problems. The first concerns the establishment of a corpus that can encompass an anonymous knowledge which does not take as a model or a foundation individual and conscious knowledge. Precisely how that knowledge is elaborated into a scientific discourse represents a second problem, whose solution requires the examination of its modes of transmission and diffusion. Foucault's third set of theoretical problems concerns causality in knowledge. How, that is, does an understanding of diseases affecting plants combine with a perception of economic constraints to the study and introduction of new plant varieties? Analysis of all three sets of problems will reveal *savoir* to be the organisation of sets of practices and institutions, the anonymous and ever-moving locus of the constitution of the sciences, and the element in which the history of the sciences exists. The history of systems of thought will be located midway between the history of constituted sciences and the history of opinion.[89]

On 30 November 1969, the professors of the Collège de France assembled to vote on a proposal to establish a chair in the History of Systems of Thought, a title which obviously echoes that of Hyppolite's chair. The other proposed chairs were in the Philosophy of Action (Paul Ricoeur) and in the History of Rational Thought (Yvon Belaval). Foucault's main sponsor was Vuillemin, while Ricoeur was backed by Pierre Courcelle, and Belaval by Martial Guéroult. Despite his support for Foucault, Vuillemin had serious doubts about the theory of 'statements' elaborated in *L'Archéologie du savoir* and the two apparently quarrelled seriously over Foucault's defence of his theory. A reconciliation was effected, and Vuillemin read a sympathetic report on Foucault's work to the assembled Collège. He concluded:

> The history of systems of thought is neither the history of men nor that of the men who think them. Ultimately, it is because it remains trapped in the terms of that alternative that the conflict between materialism and spiritualism is one between fraternal enemies . . . one takes as the subject of thought either individuals or groups, but they are still subjects . . . The abandonment of dualism and the constitution of a non-Cartesian subject demands more: eliminating the subject, but keeping thoughts; and attempting to construct a history with no human nature.[90]

When the sponsors of all three candidates had spoken in turn, voting began. Foucault received 21 votes, Belaval 10 and Ricoeur 10. Four voting slips were marked with a cross, indicating disapproval of all three candidates. A majority plus one vote being required by the Collège's statutes, a second round was necessary. Foucault received 25 votes, and Belaval 9. Two slips were marked with a cross. Foucault's election had yet to be ratified by a new vote taken at the Collège on 12 April 1970 (24 votes in favour, 15 marked with the cross signifying hostility to his election) and by one of the Academies that make up the Institut de France. The appointment was also subject to the approval of the minister for education. For reasons that remain obscure, Foucault's candidature was rejected by a large majority of the members of the Académie des Sciences Morales et Politiques: 22 of the 27 votes cast. Twenty-two were marked with a cross and four left blank. The Académie therefore formally refused to endorse his candidature. Foucault was appointed by the minister, who ignored that Academy and followed the convention of not going against the wishes of the members of the Collège de France.[91] Six months before his forty-third birthday, Foucault had been elected to life membership of the most prestigious institution in France.

10

'A PLACE WHERE THOUGHT IS FREE'

BEFORE taking up his appointment at the Collège de France, Foucault finally had the opportunity to realise his cherished dream of visiting Japan. If he had long been interested in Japan, Japan was now beginning to take an interest in Foucault, and particularly in *Histoire de la folie*. His first real contact with the Japanese was a meeting in Paris in 1963 or 1964 with a Professor Maeda, with whom he remained in contact over the years. In 1970, a definite invitation to visit Tokyo came from the newspaper *Asahi janaru* and from Moriaki Watanabe, professor of French literature and translator of Claudel and Genet. Foucault immediately accepted – not least because it offered an opportunity to see his friend Maurice Pinguet again – and went to Tokyo in September 1970.[1]

Although Foucault enjoyed the country, he had had little time to prepare for the journey, did not speak a word of the language, and therefore found Japan bewildering, being particularly puzzled by the architectural and aesthetic conventions to be observed in the imperial palace in Kyoto. It was not the modernisation of Japan that intrigued him but the survivals of the past and especially the culture of Zen, on which subject he accumulated a considerable amount of documentation. He also began to take an interest in contemporary Japanese literature and developed a taste for the novels of Junichiró Tanizaki, which he found vaguely reminiscent of Bataille and Klossowski.

The journey was not, however, a pleasure trip and Foucault's tasks included giving public lectures at the University of Tokyo. As Japanese interest still centred mainly on *Histoire de la folie*, they focused on the themes of 'Madness and Society' and 'Madness, Literature and Society'.[2] Foucault had often spoken on these topics, and the lectures added little of substance to his published *oeuvre*.

The visit also provided an opportunity to reply to Derrida's criticisms of his 'first' book. The journal *Padedia* was planning to publish a special issue devoted to Foucault in 1972, and Foucault was invited to make a contribution of his own. The result was the harsh critique of Derrida contained in 'Mon Coeur, ce papier, ce feu'.[3]

Foucault was, according to Defert, motivated to reply to Derrida at this point by his feeling or perception that a Foucault–Derrida rivalry was being actively promoted in American universities, and that interest in his own work was being eclipsed by the rise of deconstructionism. Although their original disagreement centred on the interpretation of a passage in Descartes, it is therefore interesting to note that Foucault ends by foregrounding the issue of pedagogy. Derrida was, asserted Foucault, the principal exponent of a systematic 'reduction of discursive practices to textual traces':

> A historically well-determined little pedagogy manifests itself very visibly here. A pedagogy which teaches the pupil that there is nothing outside the text, but that in it, in its interstices, its blanks and its silences [non-dits], there reigns the reserve of the origin; that it is therefore unnecessary to search elsewhere, but that there, not in the words, of course, but in the words under erasure, in their *grid*, the 'sense of being' is said. A pedagogy which, conversely gives to the voice of the master the limitless sovereignty which allows it to restate the text indefinitely.[4]

Most of the text is taken up with a meticulously detailed reading of 'Cogito et histoire de la folie', and it is dedicated to demonstrating that Derrida has misread Descartes, largely as a result of his failure to look at the 'discursive differences' that generate the categories used by Descartes's comments on madness and, at a much more banal level, by his failure to compare the French and Latin versions of the *Méditations métaphysiques*. The appearance of 'Mon corps . . .', written, according to Defert, at the suggestion of Japanese colleagues, ensured that the rupture with Derrida would last for almost a decade. On his return to France, Foucault had, however, more pressing matters on his mind than disagreements with Derrida: he was due to give his inaugural lecture to the Collège de France on 2 December.

While Foucault was in Japan, Daniel Defert was negotiating the purchase of a new apartment on his behalf, and they would move into it together in the new year. After Tunis, Paris had seemed a dark, lightless city and even the flat in the rue du Dr Finlay looked gloomy in comparison with Sidi Bou Saïd. Foucault had found his new home in the rue de Vaugirard, reputedly the longest street in Paris. Number 285 rue de Vaugirard was a modern block of no particular architectural beauty directly opposite the Vaugirard metro station. It had one major advantage over the traditional *immeuble* in that it afforded off-street parking – a rare luxury in central Paris. The apartment block, which fronted on to the street, was L-shaped and built overlooking a courtyard with lawns at right angles to the white-painted frontage. The seventh of eight entries gave access, via either a claustrophobic lift or a precipitous spiral staircase, to the flat on the eighth floor. Its greatest attraction was immediately obvious to anyone who entered it. A large room running the full length of the apartment had been created by knocking two rooms into one. Full-length French windows gave access to a terrace. The building faced southwest, was not overlooked and had a spectacular view across the Paris basin to the woods at Saint-Cloud and Sèvres. For Foucault, the view was much less important than the light which flooded into the room; he told Charles Ruas that it was 'the clarity of light for thought that he appreciated'.[5]

The main room was used by Foucault as a study combined with a lounge or reception room. It was predominantly white, quite austerely furnished with anonymously modern pieces and was not cluttered with the ornaments that invade so many homes. A few photographs and pictures hung on the walls, pride of place being given to the Masson Foucault had inherited from his father and to a fine Francis Picabia (*La Femme aux deux visages*) dating from 1932.[6] Inevitably, the dominant feature was the collection of books and of runs of periodicals that lined the walls. Until the end of Foucault's life, this was to be a workplace, a place for relaxation and occasionally a political meeting place. It was also a place for receiving guests; they included Jean Genet, who would sit writing on the suitcase balanced on his knees and who succeeded in interesting Foucault and Defert in Cocteau; Paul Veyne; and, most surprising of all, the English actress Julie Christie, a friend of Defert's, for whom Foucault carefully prepared vegetarian meals.[7] The sheltered terrace, where more than one visitor noticed the cannabis plants nestling among the petunias, provided a convenient spot for sunbathing and was large enough for dining on warm evenings. It also supplied a vantage point for the gentle art of voyeurism, the pleasures of which Foucault described in a letter dated 28 July 1983 to the young novelist Hervé Guibert:

I wanted to tell you about the pleasure I take in watching, without moving from my table, a boy who leans out of a window on the rue d'Alleray at the same time every morning. At nine o'clock, he opens his window; he wears a small blue towel, or blue underpants; he leans his head on his arm, buries his face in his elbow; he does not move, apart from making occasional, rare, slow movements when he takes a puff at the cigarette he is holding in his other hand. . . . . And I wonder what dreams his eyes found in the fold of his arms, what words or drawings are being born, but I tell myself that I am the only one to have seen from the outside the gracious chrysalis in which they were born, take shape and lose shape. The window is closed this morning; instead, I am writing to you.[8]

Foucault was ambivalent about giving his inaugural lecture, not because he shrank from the honour or from the attendant publicity, nor because he was reluctant to perform in public, but because the very idea of the 'inaugural' went against his deep conviction that absolute origins and beginnings are a myth. When asked what he would be speaking about, he mused:

An inaugural lecture. A surprising expression, indeed. Making an absolute beginning is something we can do if we put ourselves in the position of the student, and that position is, to say the least, mythical. But an inaugural, in the strict sense of the term, takes place against a background of ignorance, of innocence, of absolutely primal disingenuousness; we can speak of inauguration if we are faced with something of which we know nothing, or of which we have never spoken, thought or known. And yet this inaugural is a lecture. Now, a lecture implies that you are surrounded by a whole collection of already constituted knowledges and discourses. I think I will give my lecture on that paradox.[9]

'Undistracted by the gravity of the moment from an irrepressible irony, a shaven-headed figure with an ivory complexion came forward, something of the Buddhist in his style and a Mephistophelean look in his eye. He submitted to the initiatory ceremony with the ease of a deacon in an age of heresies', and looked like 'a courteous iconoclast'.[10] Foucault was being solemnly welcomed by Etienne Wolff, the *administrateur* of the Collège de France, into what the latter termed the 'land of freedom'. Wolff's phrase provoked dissenting grumbles from the crowded lecture theatre presided over by a bronze statue of Henri Bergson. Although luminaries like Dumézil and Lévi-Strauss were present, many of the audience were young and had made their way to the Collège through streets lined by vans and coaches with the hated CRS riot police caged inside them. Nothing was happening on the streets on 2 December 1970 but the Latin Quarter was, as usual, under a virtual police siege. Although Wolff's reference to 'freedom' may have sounded incongruous in the circumstances, it had a history of which many of the audience were probably unaware. During the Occupation, Paul Valéry, professor of poetry at the Collège from 1937 to 1945, was asked by a German officer: 'What is taught in this school?' Valéry replied: 'This is a place where thought is free.'[11] The fact that it was not occupied in May 1968 also seems to say something about the Collège's unique position and reputation as a place apart. The Latin Quarter at times looked like a war zone in the early 1970s; the Collège de France remained a demilitarised enclave.

Originally founded during the reign of François I at the suggestion of the great humanist scholar Guillaume Budé, the Collège de France is unique among French educational institutions. It is not, and never has been, part of the university system and, unlike the universities, is quite autonomous. The Collège de France has no student body and awards no degrees or other qualifications. All lectures and seminars are open to the public. Professors are elected by their future peers, and appointments are for life. They do not teach to any syllabus and are required to base their teaching on completely original research. As one of Foucault's predecessors, the historian Ernest Renan (1823–92), put it, the Collège is an institution where the public can see 'science in the making'. The research is presented in the form of twelve two-hour public lectures a year and at related seminars.

In many ways, the Collège de France was the ideal place for Foucault. He was now free from all administrative responsibilities, which he loathed, and from all political or bureaucratic interference. Whereas his situation at Clermont-Ferrand had frequently led him to complain about a lack of secretarial backup, he now had a loyal and devoted secretary in Françoise-Edmonde Morin. Indeed, her loyalty and discretion were such that she now declines, gently but firmly, to discuss Foucault because of her conviction that his privacy must be safeguarded even beyond the grave.[12]

Foucault was free to choose to direct doctoral research projects, or to refuse to do so. Those who did persuade him to supervise their projects found to their dismay – like Danièle Rancière, who began a thesis on nineteenth-century philanthropy with him – that he was not a particularly directive director of research.[13] His election honoured him with complete recognition by the intellectual elite and was a form of public consecration. Unlike the Académie Française, which Foucault regarded as fossilised, the Collège was at the very centre of intellectual life. It also offered some concrete advantages. The Collège's year is short, running from late November to May, and Foucault's lectures often did not actually begin until January. He was thus free to travel and to take up visiting professorships, and was often to spend at least part of the autumn term in the United States.

Yet, as Foucault was to discover, life at the Collège is not always easy. Like Bergson, he attracted huge numbers of people to his lectures, only to find himself isolated in the midst of an anonymous crowd. And, like Valéry, he found the isolation wearisome and could no doubt have echoed his predecessor's lament: 'Oh, if only I had an audience of only five, like Renan! It would go like clockwork. But a room full of anonymous people is tiring. One wonders who to aim it at, what degree of culture, desire and tension one should be trying to satisfy.'[14] One historian of the Collège divides its teachers into three broad categories: hermits, leaders of sects, and prophets. The prophets can be subdivided into high priests and messiahs.[15] Like Barthes, elected to the Collège in 1978, Foucault was somewhat reluctantly cast in the role of high priest. Many casual observers who strayed out of curiosity into Foucault's lectures had the distinct impression that they were attending some secular high mass.

The newly elected professor of the history of systems of thought began to read the text of his inaugural lecture by referring to his wish that he could slip unnoticed into the speech (*discours*) he had to give, to be enveloped in it and to be carried to a point that existed before any possible beginning. Rather than being the source of a discourse, he wanted to be situated at random within its unfolding, to be the point of its possible disappearance. He wished that he could hear a voice saying:

> I must go on, I cannot go on, I must go on, I must speak words so long as there are words to speak, must speak them until they find me, until they speak me, perhaps it's already happened, perhaps they have already brought me to the threshold of my history, to the door that opens on to my history, it would surprise me if it opened.

Foucault gave no source, but his words were adapted from the last lines of Samuel Beckett's *L'Innommable*.[16] The expressed desire to be anonymous, to be swallowed up into some pre-existing discourse, was obviously in part a rhetorical device whose function was to become apparent later and it typified Foucault's more general longing to win anonymity, but it was also a sign of something else: Foucault was nervous, and remained nervous every time he had to give his lecture at the Collège.

He ended his inaugural by paying tribute to his 'models', paying a triple homage to Dumézil, Canguilhem and Hyppolite. Dumézil, whom he had first met in Sweden, had encouraged him to work 'at an age when I still thought that writing was a pleasure' and had taught him to analyse 'the internal economy of a discourse in ways very different to the methods of traditional exegesis or those of linguistic formalism', whereas it was the work of Canguilhem that had first suggested that the history of science could be 'a coherent and transformable set of theoretical models and conceptual instruments'.[17] His highest praise was, however, reserved for Jean Hyppolite. 'Our whole age' was an attempt to escape Hegel via either logic or epistemology;

> But any real escape from Hegel presupposes that we have an accurate understanding of what it will cost us to detach ourselves from him; it presupposes that we know the extent to which Hegel, perhaps insidiously, has approached us; it presupposes that we know what is still Hegelian in that which allows us to think against Hegel; and that we can assess the extent to which our appeal against him is perhaps one more of the ruses he uses against us and at the end of which he is waiting for us, immobile and elsewhere.[18]

Hyppolite was the essential guide in the escape from Hegel in that it was his pioneering work that had made it possible to read him. The tribute to Hyppolite brought Foucault back to his starting point:

> I now have a better understanding of why I had such difficulty in beginning just now. I am now well aware by which voice I would have liked to be preceded, borne along, invited to speak, and which voice I would have liked to lodge itself in my own discourse. I know why beginning to speak [*prendre la parole*] was so fearful, because I was speaking [*je la prenais*] in this place where I listened to him, and where he is no longer there to hear me.[19]

In paying tribute to Hyppolite in this way, Foucault was of course inscribing himself within the history of the Collège de France by taking up a legitimate position within a succession of thinkers. He had already inscribed himself within its present by briefly invoking the work of François Jacob, professor of cell genetics and joint winner, with Jacques Monod and André Lwoff, of the 1965 Nobel Prize.[20] The allusion is discreet – Foucault makes no mention of Jacob's *La Logique du vivant*, which he had very recently reviewed in *Le Monde*[21] – but enough to signal Foucault's self-integration into a scholarly community.

Within the circular structure of his inaugural, Foucault elegantly deals with the themes that had already appeared in the later sections of *L'Archéologie* and in the February 1969 lecture to the Société Française de Philosophie on the notion of the author, now described as 'that which gives the disturbing language of fiction its units, its knots of coherence and its insertion into the real' and as 'a principle for grouping together discourses . . . the unity and origin of their significations . . . the focus of their coherence'.[22]

He also outlined a programme for 'the work I would like to do here in the coming years'. Four parameters were set in the form of principles of reversal, discontinuity, specificity and exteriority. By introducing a principle of reversal, Foucault signalled the need to reject the idea of continuity and authorship in favour of the negative play of cutting out and rarefying discourses. Discontinuity indicated that no analysis would ever succeed in uncovering some primally unspoken or unthought element which would at last become perceptible or amenable to analysis: 'Discourses must be treated as discontinuous practices which intersect and are sometimes juxtaposed, but which also know nothing of one another or exclude one another.'[23] Specificity meant that discourse was not an interplay of prior significations; 'Discourse has to be seen as the violence we do to things, or in any case as a practice which we impose upon them; and it is within that practice that events in discourse find the principle of their regularity.'[24] The principle of exteriority indicated, finally, that analysis should not be directed towards some hidden nucleus, but should begin with discourse itself and then look for its external conditions of possibility.

In his *Titres et travaux*, Foucault had outlined a definite programme of research on heredity; in his inaugural he sketched a more general programme in which heredity was only one possible object of study. Two overlapping *ensembles* were mentioned, one 'critical' and the other 'genealogical'. An initial body of critical studies could be carried out on various 'functions of exclusion', like the classical age's distinction between reason and madness. The prohibition on speaking about sexuality was another. By this, Foucault did not mean the gradual elimination of a prohibition, but its displacement from the practice of confession (in which prohibitions were named and hierarchically classified) to nineteenth-century medicine and psychiatry. The 'will to knowledge' could provide a further theme: this analysis would explore how effective discourse came, with the sophists, to be organised around a division between true and false discourse, and a later examination of the same theme would look at that same 'will' in the natural philosophy of the seventeenth century. A third dimension would be added by the founding acts of modern science, the formation of industrial society and the positivist ideology that went with it: 'Three sections through the morphology of our will to knowledge; three stages in our philistinism.'[25] Medicine, the origins of the penal system, and literary criticism's construction of the author and the figure of the *oeuvre* were also possible topics. All the critical examples represented an analysis of 'agencies of discursive control'; genealogy would look at the effective formation of discourses, both inside, outside and astride the agencies or instances of control.

Foucault was outlining a vast research project, or rather a vast range of possible projects. By no means all of them were followed through. Foucault in fact had little more to say about literary criticism and the construction of authors, for instance. The inaugural lecture does, however, adumbrate many of the topics that would be dealt with in the future books and lectures, and notably the themes of criminality, psychiatry and sexuality.

Foucault's weekly lectures frequently attracted many more people than the lecture theatre could hold and closed-circuit television monitors had to be installed in the next room. Like the movable feast of Lacan's seminar, which Foucault occasionally attended,[26] it was an attraction for *le tout Paris*, but it also drew a lot of foreign visitors. James Bernauer, for one, was struck by the 'cacophony of foreign tongues heard before each of his classes'.[27] The audience included the inevitable eccentrics, like the old lady who told Daniel Defert that she had attended every lecture to have been given on philosophy at the Collège for the last sixty years. She was perhaps the only living person to have heard both Bergson, who died in 1941, and Foucault.[28]

For Foucault himself, the lecture theatre was a lonely place, and he often complained to friends and to his niece Anne Thalamy about his isolation, the lack of dialogue and the failure of his audience to ask him questions.[29] In 1975, he made the same point to a journalist:

> Sometimes, when the lecture was not good, something, a question, was needed to bring it all together. But the question never comes . . . And as there is no feedback, the lecture becomes a piece of theatre. My relationship with the people who are there is that of an actor or an acrobat. And when I have finished speaking, a feeling of total solitude.

For years, he was to see the same people sitting in the same seats, but was unable to speak to them: 'When I leave the room, they have already gone. Sometimes I would like to interrupt my lecture, to ask them why they are there, what they are looking for.'[30] Those who rushed towards Foucault at the end of the lecture were not trying to ask him questions, but hurrying to retrieve the tape-recorders and microphones they had placed on his desk. Later the same year, Foucault told the radio journalist Jacques Chancel that he was terribly nervous before every lecture, that he felt the way he had as a student facing an important exam. It was as though his anonymous public were perpetually judging him, putting him on trial.[31]

His isolation did, on the other hand, have advantages. While lecturing at the Collège, Foucault told Chancel, he did not have the impression that he was teaching, that he stood in a relationship of power to his audience. When he complained about his loneliness, Foucault seems to have been oblivious to the fact that asking questions in front of an audience of up to 2,000 is something that would intimidate most people. He also overlooked the question of his own daunting public persona. Even those who dared approach him found his entourage intimidating. When Arlette Farge began to collaborate with him on what was to become *Le Désordre des familles*, she agreed to meet Foucault after a lecture. As she climbed the staircase leading to his room, she felt that she was running a gauntlet of hostile stares, all of them silently asking 'Who does she think she is?'[32]

Few people saw any signs of Foucault's nervousness as he pushed through the people crowding his dais, cleared the clutter of microphones to make room for his papers, and plunged into a lecture that would last without a break for two hours. He spoke quickly in a 'regular, almost monotonous voice',[33] reading from a prepared text and rarely improvising. Another listener describes the scene:

> People were scrambling at the doors two hours in advance, as though it was a first night. Inside, emissaries kept places; people tore each other to pieces to get half a buttock on a quarter of a foldaway seat, and the old ladies from the *beaux quartiers* showed off their best *haute couture*. And on the platform, standing midway along an endless desk of polished wood, his bumpy skull lit *mezzo giorno*, surrounded by a thousand mikes linked up to a thousand tape recorders, with a troop of trendy young men curled round his feet, Foucault would speak.[34]

Both Claude Mauriac and the cartoonist Wiaz (Pierre Wiazemski) thought that the theatrical lighting made Foucault look like an alchemist as he huddled over his pile of notes.[35] As he spoke, silence reigned in the theatre where Bergson had once given equally memorable performances.

The lectures followed the model outlined in the inaugural rather than that of *Titres et travaux*. In his first year at the Collège de France, Foucault began to outline what he called a 'morphology of the will to knowledge' and to look at the very different models offered by Aristotle's *Nichomachaean Ethics* and Nietzsche's *Gay Science*, which provided a 'model of a basically self-seeking knowledge, produced as an event of the will and determining the truth-effect through falsification'.[36] For Aristotle, there was a direct relationship between pleasure and sensation, and therefore between the intensity of pleasure and the quantity of knowledge supplied by sense-perception. The desire for knowledge was a variant on the natural search for happiness and 'the good'. For Nietzsche, knowledge is a product of a play of conflicting instincts or desires, and of a will to appropriate and dominate. Always provisional and unstable, it is always a slave to primal and violent instincts. Nietzsche's model was then applied to a series of examples taken from the history and institutions of archaic Greece, namely the use of oaths in legal conflicts, the search for a golden mean in commercial exchanges and social relations within the *polis*, the search for a just law which would both ensure order within the *polis* and reflect the order of the universe, and ritual purification after acts of murder.

Foucault's second obligation as a member of the Collège de France was to conduct a weekly seminar. Towards the end of the year he therefore announced that the seminar would begin early in 1971 and asked those who wished to take part to write to him outlining their interests and stating what they were willing to contribute. His request for written statements was an attempt to limit numbers. In his view, the seminar was to be a 'place of work' and he wished it to be restricted to those who were willing to undertake serious research and to write as a collective enterprise. It was also a forum for invited speakers who could broaden its scope or make specialist contributions.

In stating that access to the seminar was to be restricted, Foucault was consciously going against the spirit and the letter of the laws governing the Collège. To the surprise of those who did write to him, it was a small group that met in the Collège at the beginning of 1971. Working with a small, committed group was a welcome relief. Foucault found the presence of casual observers a source of profound irritation, and occasionally tried to close his seminar, only to be called back to order by the Collège authorities. The issue would not go away in the years to come.

The first year of the Monday seminar was devoted to the development of penal psychiatry during the Restoration period, but gave rise to no publications in the short term. The research material was provided by contemporary journals like the *Gazette des tribunaux* and the *Annales d'hygiène publique et de médicine légale*. Most of the cases described were lurid accounts of murders: stories of servant girls who suddenly murdered children entrusted to them, of a woman who killed and ate her child, of a former wine grower who lived in the woods and who, having failed in his attempt to rape a little girl, mutilated her and drank her blood. Although they no doubt provided something of a *frisson*, the main interest of such cases was that they were reported by the medical press and that they exemplified the intersection of medical and legal discourses about insanity and criminality.[37] In short, they anticipated some of the major themes of *Surveiller et punir* and of such papers as the lecture on the concept of the 'dangerous individual' delivered to a symposium on 'Law and Psychiatry' at York University (Toronto) in 1978.[38]

It was in the pages of the *Annales* that Foucault first encountered the case of Pierre Rivière, which provided the subject matter for the next two years. In the meantime, the weekly lecture was taking as its theme penal theories and institutions, and Foucault was beginning to elaborate his theory of 'power-knowledge': 'No power is exercised without the extraction, appropriation, distribution or retention of knowledge. At this level, we do not have knowledge on the one hand and society on the other, or science and state; we have the basic forms of "power-knowledge".'[39]

In his résumé of the second year of the seminar, Foucault lists the participants as Jean-Pierre Peter, Robert Castel, Gilles Deleuze, Alessandro Fontana, Philippe Riot and Maryvonne Saison. Deleuze was not, however, a regular attender. The published text of *Moi, Pierre Rivière* also includes the names of Blandine Barret-Kriegel, Jeanne Favret, Georgette Legée, Gilbert Barlet-Torvic and Patricia Moulin. Barret-Kriegel was a latecomer who joined the seminar group some time after its constitution, and Favret's participation was apparently minimal. Numbers fluctuated somewhat, but there were no more than fifteen regular participants.

For Jean-Pierre Peter, the discovery of the Rivière case was a bittersweet surprise. A historian who had studied with Braudel, he had become interested in the history of scandal. To the displeasure of Braudel, he then began to move away from economic and social history and was asked by Le Roy Ladurie to assist him with his research on nineteenth-century medical archives. His work in that area meant that he found *Naissance de la clinique* somewhat abstract and far removed from the day-to-day practice of medicine, but he was still eager to work with Foucault. At this point, the breach with Braudel became complete, and resulted in a bitter quarrel that led to a rather blighted career. Peter is half convinced that if he had continued his research for only another three months, the discovery of the Rivière case would have been his. As it was, he was to become a major figure in the tightly knit seminar group.

A systematic exploration of the history of Pierre Rivière was proposed. The account published in the *Annales* was not complete, but hinted that Rivière's own handwritten account could be found in Normandy. Not entirely optimistic, Peter went to Caen to consult the archives of the *département* of Calvados. Like many towns in Normandy, Caen was virtually razed to the ground by the Allied invasion of 1944 and many of the city's archives were destroyed. Peter had heard sinister stories of charred fragments of documents blowing around the streets near the archives. By chance, the 'memoir' written by Pierre Rivière had survived the bombing and the fire, and a highly emotional Peter was able to return to Paris with a photocopy of the complete manuscript. Miraculously, the departmental archives in Caen also still held the files containing all the legal documents and press coverage relating to the case. At Foucault's request, the whole dossier was transferred to the Archives Nationales in Paris, though the transfer was delayed by a civil servants' strike. It was now possible to transcribe the entire dossier; the transcription was largely the work of Peter. The group now had its real working document.[40]

Foucault's description of the case in his *Résumé des cours* is flat and gives no indication of the real passion it inspired in the group: 'Pierre Rivière: a little-known nineteenth-century murderer; at the age of twenty, he slit the throats of his mother, brother and sister; after his arrest, he wrote an explanatory *mémoire* which was handed to his judges and to the doctors responsible for writing a psychiatric report.'[41]

In 1835, the young Pierre Rivière brutally slaughtered his mother, sister and brother with a sickle and then fled to live rough in the countryside of Normandy. He was soon arrested and committed for trial. Parricide was not a particularly unusual crime in rural France, but Rivière's case attracted a lot of attention, largely because of the astonishing memoir he submitted to the court. Although he was reputedly illiterate and was regarded by many as little more than a village idiot, he proved capable of writing a long and sophisticated document, and to be able to quote the books of Deuteronomy and Numbers in his defence. There was no doubt as to Rivière's guilt: his memoir began: 'I, Pierre Rivière, having slaughtered my mother, my sister and my brother . . .' He had, he explained at length, killed his mother to avenge his father for the persecutions she had inflicted on him, and his brother and sister because they loved their mother. He had been acting on the orders given him by God and his angels. What was in doubt was his sanity; the law of 1832 had introduced the notion of a defence based upon 'extenuating circumstances', a category which included insanity. Hence the importance of Rivière's own account of his actions to both his judge and Foucault's seminar:

> The story of the murder . . . was an element which was an integral part of his rationality or his unreason. Some said: the same signs of madness can be seen in the fact of the murder and in the details of what is recounted; others said: the same proofs of lucidity can be seen in the preparation and the circumstances of the murder and in the fact of having written it down. In short, the act of killing and the act of writing, the deeds performed and the things recounted were interwoven, like elements of the same nature.[42]

Rivière's text was asked a triple question about truth: factual truth, the truth about public opinion and scientific truth.[43] The young peasant was trapped in a discourse from elsewhere, one that asked questions about his past, about his alleged acts of cruelty towards animals and children, about the solitary walks on which he talked to himself in order to establish whether or not he was a 'dangerous individual'.

Eventually, Rivière was found guilty and sentenced to death. Here, other circumstances came into play. Parricide was viewed as a variant on regicide, and there had recently been an attempt on the king's life; the death sentence was probably predictable. Rather less predictably, the sentence was commuted on appeal to life imprisonment on the grounds that Rivière had killed as a result of his religious hallucinations. In 1840, he committed suicide in prison.

The Rivière case had an obvious historical and theoretical fascination in that it so clearly exemplified the play between the legal and the psychiatric. It also had a more subjective appeal. As Foucault put it, the seminar group was quite simply seduced by the beauty of Rivière's text: 'We were captivated by the parricide with the auburn eyes' ('*le parricide aux yeux roux*'; an odd expression in that *roux* usually applies to hair colour).[44] It would be easy to interpret this statement as evidence of a homoerotic infatuation on Foucault's part, were it not that Rivière had precisely the same appeal for everyone in the seminar group, regardless of their sexual orientation. Rivière invaded all their lives and dominated all their conversations for months. So strong was their imaginary affective bond with their killer that the group members were even reluctant to take royalties from their published account of the case, and thought of using them to finance a foundation named after him. The plan came to nothing, but indicates the captivation they felt.

In the published text, Pierre Rivière's memoir and contemporary accounts and documents are given pride of place, and the accompanying essays – described simply as 'notes' – are not intended to be interpretations, and least of all are they intended to provide a psychoanalytic interpretation.[45] Rivière is allowed to speak for himself, and his words are framed rather than explained by the contributions of the seminar group. Ultimately, the only explanation for the triple murder is that given by its perpetrator. As Foucault put it in a discussion of René Allio's film adaptation of *Pierre Rivière*, the publication of the book was 'a way of saying to psychiatric gentlemen: "Right, you've been in existence for one hundred and fifty years; here is a case that is contemporary with your birth. What do you have to say about it? Are you any better placed to talk about it than your nineteenth-century colleagues?" '[46]

A decision to publish the Rivière dossier was soon reached. It was in part a panic decision. At the insistence of the Collège authorities, Foucault had opened the seminar to the public, or, as an angry Peter saw it, to 'vampire-like hordes of consumers of knowledge'. The seminar became a second lecture course, complete with intrusive microphones and tape recorders. A rumour began to spread that someone was going to publish an abbreviated version of the memoir, together with a commentary based on tape recordings of the seminar. Whether or not there was any truth behind the rumour has never been demonstrated.[47]

The decision to publish was to occasion controversy within the otherwise harmonious seminar group. The argument that broke out was not really over the contents of the proposed volume, though it is said that a contribution by a young woman no one is willing to name was brutally rejected by Foucault. It was, rather, the format of publication that was the source of conflict. Foucault had obviously spoken of his ongoing work to Pierre Nora, his editor at Gallimard and the co-*directeur* of the 'Archives' series. Nora immediately assumed that *Moi, Pierre Rivière* would appear in that series. The 'Archives' series began publication in 1964, and was originally published by Julliard.

Later a joint Julliard-Gallimard imprint, it is a paperback format, designed to make original documents – edited and selected by eminent specialists – available to the general public at an affordable price (*Pierre Rivière* was priced at 12.5 francs; seven years earlier, *Les Mots et les choses* sold for 26 francs). Early titles ranged from a documentary history of the Popular Front to contemporary accounts of the foundation of the PCF.[48]

The seminar members did not take kindly to Nora's assumption that the book was for him: the 'Archives' format was too small, the typography was poor, the collection was not sufficiently prestigious . . . They suggested that another Gallimard series would be preferable. Foucault was, for once, adamant. Although he had been open-minded, tolerant and eminently democratic throughout the working life of the seminar, he now exercised his full professorial authority. He was unwilling to do or say anything that might compromise his relations with Gallimard or Nora's 'Bibliothèque des histoires', and the text duly appeared as a volume in the 'Archives' series, with some concessions won over the layout and typography.

Reviews were quite favourable but rather muted. As with the later *Désordre des familles*, the fact that the volume was not by Foucault alone may have detracted from its interest. One review in particular provoked Foucault to fury. Although he did have some favourable comments to make, Le Roy Ladurie criticised *Moi, Pierre Rivière* for its neglect of social and economic history and concluded that the book suffered from 'an insufficient dose of provincialism. The only person that the brilliant team assembled by Michel Foucault lacked was a Norman. A Norman social anthropologist.'[49] The comment is barbed in two ways. Le Roy Ladurie is himself a Norman, and the clear implication is that he could have written a better book. Although no Norman, Jeanne Favret is an anthropologist and was at this time undertaking research on witchcraft in Normandy. The research, based on participant observation, provides an almost unique insight into the popular culture of rural France.[50] For weeks, Foucault would tell anyone who cared to listen that the eminent historian of Montaillou was a crass fool.[51]

Neither the two years he spent at Vincennes nor the first year at the Collège de France was particularly productive in terms of Foucault's written output. He was still involved in a literary world to some extent but that aspect of his life was becoming less important than it had once been. As of the autumn of 1970, he ceased to be an active member of the editorial board of *Critique*, though he continued to sit on the advisory *conseil de rédaction.* His departure from the board resulted from lack of time rather than lack of interest in a journal to which he owed a great deal.

Foucault's final contribution to *Critique* was a lengthy essay on two books by Deleuze: *Différence et répétition* and *Logique de sens*, both of which appeared in 1969 [52] He had already reviewed *Différence et répétition*, which he described as 'something very different from the *Nth* account of the beginning and the end of metaphysics. It is the theatre, the stage, the rehearsal for a new philosophy on the bare platform of every page.'[53] 'Theatricum philosophicum' is a celebration rather than a critical review, and, no doubt a direct response to Deleuze's celebration of *L'Archéologie du savoir* in his 'Un nouvel Archiviste'.

Both Deleuze's publications of 1969 are further stages in the anti-Platonic onslaught that began with his *Nietzsche et la philosophie* in 1961.[54] They are at once very serious and very playful, mingling literary, philosophical and artistic themes and references in the characteristic style that reaches its apotheosis with the *Anti-Oedipus* of 1972.[55] Foucault does not expound or explain Deleuze's texts; he celebrates them by joining a dance in which his partners include Leiris, de Sade, Bataille, Klossowski and Lewis Caroll's Alice. Deleuze's language is described as being 'a perpetual phono-decentring', meaning that it captures something of the formation of language and the 'lightning flash' of thought, and is compared to the work of Brisset, the 'fantastic grammarian, the sombre predecessor who well identified the remarkable points of this decentring'.[56] In rather more conventionally philosophical terms, Deleuze is credited with having discovered the preconditions for conceptualising fantasies and events alike: 'the suppression of categories, the assertion of the universality of being, the repetitive revolution of being around difference'.[57] Repetition and the resultant encounter with 'stupidity' recall both Andy Warhol's soup cans and Flaubert's *Bouvard et Pécuchet*.

The most surprising feature of Foucault's article is, however, its lyrical account of the virtues of LSD:

One can easily see how LSD inverts relations between ill humour, stupidity and thought; no sooner has it short-circuited the suzerainty of categories than it tears away the ground from its indifference and reduces to nothing the glum mimicry of stupidity; not only does it reveal this whole univocal and a-categorical mass to be rainbow-coloured, mobile, asymmetrical, decentred, spiraloid and resonating; it makes it swarm constantly with event-fantasies; sliding across this surface, which is at once punctiform and immensely vibratory, thought, freed from its catatonic chrysalis, has always contemplated the infinite equivalence which has become an acute event and a sumptuously adorned repetition.[58]

Foucault then goes on to discuss the very different properties of opium and its inducement of 'a weightless immobility' before speculating that drugs may produce a 'half-thought' by displacing the thought–stupidity relationship and replacing the brief lightning flash of thought with a continuous phosphorescence. At which point Deleuze asks in a footnote: 'What will people think of us?'[59]

The real mystery is not what 'people' thought about this phantasmagoria, but why and on what basis it was written. Foucault was no stranger to the pleasures afforded by cannabis or, probably, opium, but he had yet to take LSD; his first encounter with the hallucinogen was to be a Californian experience, and it did not take place until 1975. LSD was not a commodity in short supply in Paris in 1970, and an abundant literature was devoted to its celebration. In the absence of any real documentation, it can only be assumed that the professor at the Collège de France had an unusual, but probably second-hand, familiarity with the acid culture of the 'underground'.

Reverting to a more recognisable philosophical discourse, Foucault ends by singing the praises of Deleuze's 'genital thought, affirmative thought, a-categorical thought' and of his construction of philosophy as theatre rather than thought, as a theatre in which Plato, Duns Scotus, Spinoza, Leibniz and Kant enter a masked ball. Reaching the pinnacle of the pyramid, Leibniz discovers that the music of the spheres is in fact Schoenberg's *Pierrot Lunaire*. Finally, a strange figure appears: 'In the cabin in the Luxembourg, Duns Scotus pokes his head through the circular lunette; he has an imposing moustache; that of Nietzsche, disguised as Klossowski.'[60]

Although much of 'Theatrum philosophicum' is a puzzling and mysterious game being played out between Deleuze and Foucault, its final image is easily explained. Foucault was still in contact with Klossowski, though the association would not last much longer, and had recently read and reread his latest production.[61] *La Monnaie vivante* is one of the stranger products of Klossowski's imagination, and describes a utopian stage in economic development in which the medium of exchange will not be currency, but living beings. The gold standard will give way to a pleasure standard, and producers will be paid in girls and boys. A graphite drawing dating from 1969 illustrates the process by depicting 'The Recuperation of Surplus Value' as an act of sodomy.[62] The notion had considerable appeal for the philosophers of desire.[63] And it took Foucault's breath away. As he told Klossowski, *La Monnaie vivante* was a distillation of Blanchot and Bataille: 'That is what had to be thought: desire, value, simulacrum – the triangle that has no doubt dominated and constituted us in our history for centuries. Those who struggled to do so in their mole-runs used to say, and still say: "Freud-Marx." Now we can laugh at them, and we know why.'[64]

Thought may have been free inside the Collège de France, but it was not always at total liberty outside its walls. As Foucault was to learn from personal experience, censorship, on both political and sexual grounds, was a very real issue in Pompidou's France. Daniel Defert recalls that, when Foucault was asked to preface the first volume of Bataille's *Oeuvres complètes*, it was in the hope that his growing prestige and status would protect the text from the censor. Whether or not it was the association with Foucault that preserved Bataille's work from censorship is open to debate, but it is a matter of record that no action was taken against the notorious author of *Histoire de l'oeil* and *Mme Edwarda*. The lesser-known Pierre Guyotat was less fortunate in his encounters with the agencies of control.

In September 1970, after a year of hesitation, Gallimard finally published Guyotat's *Eden, Eden, Eden*, protected by a triple carapace of prefaces by Barthes, Leiris and Sollers. The author's first novel, *Tombeau pour cinq cent mille soldats* (1967), was a violently lyrical portrayal of war, set in Algeria and full of sexual and physical brutality. It had done moderately well, selling 1,500 copies, and was translated into a number of foreign languages. *Eden, Eden, Eden* was even more shocking: it was what a sympathetic journalist called 'an eternity of fornication', involving men, women, children, Arabs, blacks and soldiers in endless permutations of copulation.[65]

In an open letter to Guyotat, Foucault warned that his book would cause a scandal, but praised his vision of sexuality. Guyotat was saying something which had been known for a long time, but which was carefully concealed so as to protect the primacy of the subject and the unity of the individual. In other words, sexuality

is not something like 'sex' at the limit of the body, nor is it a means of communication; it is not even the individual's fundamental or primitive desire; the very texture of its processes exists prior to the individuals. The individual is no more than its precarious prolongation, provisional and quickly effaced; ultimately, the individual is no more than a pale form which arises for a moment from a great stock that is both stubborn and repetitive. Individuals – the pseudopodia of sexuality, quickly retracted. If we wish to know what we know, we must abandon up what we imagine about our individuality, our ego, our position as subject. In your text, relations between the individual and sexuality are openly and completely reversed, perhaps for the first time; they are no longer characters which are effaced for the benefit of elements, structures or personal pronouns; sexuality moves to the other side of the individual and ceases to be 'subjectified'.[66]

Sensing that the publication of Guyotat's novel would pose problems, Foucault, Leiris, Barthes, Sollers, Derrida and others offered themselves as 'guarantors of its existence' in an attempt to prevent censorship. Their gesture of support was not entirely futile. The novel was not banned outright. On the other hand, it could neither be advertised, displayed in bookshops nor sold to minors under the age of twenty-one. The bans continued to apply until 1981, when *Eden, Eden, Eden* finally went on open sale.

11

'INTOLERABLE'

JUST over two months after giving his inaugural lecture at the Collège de France, Foucault inaugurated something very different. For the next two years, his life was to be primarily that of the political militant, caught up in a flurry of confused events and reacting to them quickly and not always wisely. The political platform and even the street corner replaced the lecturer's dais. Elegant and erudite essays on Bataille and Blanchot gave way to hastily drafted statements to the press. His academic life continued at the Collège, but he simultaneously led an exhausting political existence which involved him in meeting after meeting, demonstration after demonstration and confrontation after confrontation. Nothing in his previous life – neither the stormy days in Tunis nor the chaos of Vincennes – had prepared him for the coming years. His involvement in Tunis and at Vincennes had been that of someone who was drawn into events. With the foundation of the Groupe d'Information sur les Prisons' (Prison Information Group), he became an instigator. The goal of Foucault's political activity was the empowering of others by giving, for instance, prisoners the voice they were denied. His own voice tended therefore to fade, or to be merged into a collective discourse. For the period 1971–73, Foucault's biography was part of a collective biography, and part of the sequence of events in which he was involved. Although it embroiled him in a number of dramatic episodes, Foucault's new existence also meant that he spent a lot of time performing the mundane tasks essential to the existence of any political group: addressing envelopes, drafting press releases and handing out leaflets were all part of his daily life.

On 2 December 1970, Foucault had spoken in a crowded lecture theatre once used by Bergson; on 8 February 1971, he found himself speaking in the Chapelle Saint-Bernard, a gloomily cavernous structure beneath the Montparnasse railway station. A press conference was in progress and as it ended, a microphone was handed to Foucault. The professor began to speak:

None of us can be sure of avoiding prison. Less so than ever, today. Police control over our day-to-day lives is becoming tighter: in the streets and on the roads; over foreigners and young people; it is once more an offence to express an opinion; anti-drug measures are leading to increasingly arbitrary arrests. We are living under the sign of *la garde à vue*.[1] They tell us that the courts are swamped. We can see that. But what if it were the police who had swamped them? They tell us that the prisons are over-populated. But what if it were the population that were being overimprisoned?

Little information is published about prisons; this is one of the hidden regions of our social system, one of the dark areas in our lives. This is why, together with a number of *magistrats*,[2] lawyers, journalists, doctors and psychologists, we have founded a *Groupe d'information sur les prisons*.[3]

The aim of the group was not to promote reforms, but to gather and disseminate information about the prison system. Convinced that the information it wanted would not be found in official publications, the GIP decided to distribute questionnaires to anyone with any know-ledge of the system: prisoners, ex-prisoners, social workers, *magistrats* and so on.

Foucault himself was not directly involved in the prelude to the foundation of the GIP, which was played out over a period of six or seven months. On 27 May 1970, the Gauche Prolétarienne was proscribed by Raymond Marcellin. Le Dantec and Le Bris, the editors of its newspaper *La Cause du peuple*, were in prison awaiting trial. On the night of the GP's proscription, a 5,000-strong meeting in the Mutualité called for their release and at its height, Alain Geismar, one of the most prominent figures in the events of May 1968, appealed to everyone present to take to the streets in protest. He was arrested after the meeting and later sentenced to two years' imprisonment for inciting violence. On 28 May, Le Dantec and Le Bris were sentenced to eight months and one year respectively. A night of violent rioting in the Latin Quarter followed, and both the faculty of science and the Censier faculty were briefly occupied.[4] The next day, the so-called *loi anti-casseurs* ('anti-wreckers' law) was adopted; the organisers of demonstra-tions were now collectively responsible for any violence or destruction of property that might occur on the streets.

The GP, or the 'ex-GP' as the press habitually described it, did not in fact disappear and continued to flourish in semi-clandestinity. *La Cause du peuple* had not been banned and it continued to appear under the nominal editorship of Sartre, though its street-sellers faced constant police harassment and a number of issues were illegally confiscated. Widespread protests followed, many of them organised by Secours Rouge, the broad front founded in June by Sartre and others to support the 'victims of oppression'.[5] In the autumn, hunger strikes began in the prisons as some thirty militants, the youngest aged eighteen, the eldest twenty-six, claimed political status.

There was a precedent for this. A decree passed in August 1960 had introduced a *régime spécial* for FLN prisoners in France, the last thing de Gaulle's government wanted being an epidemic of suicides by hunger strike at the height of the Algerian war. OAS prisoners also enjoyed the more relaxed regime, which gave them access to books and news media and greater freedom of association. In an unexpected ruling, the Appeal Court accepted in September 1970 that a common-law offence – defacing the walls of a public building with slogans calling for solidarity with the jailed leaders of the Gauche Prolétarienne – could be of an 'objectively political nature'.[6]

On 1 September 1970, a statement 'written in the prisons of France' appeared in the press:

> We demand full recognition of our status as political prisoners. We are not, however, demanding privileges denied to so-called 'common law' prisoners; in our view, they are the victims of a social system which, having produced them, refuses to re-educate them and is content to degrade and reject them. Indeed, we want our struggle, which denounces the present scandalous regime in the prisons, to help all prisoners.[7]

Although René Pleven, the minister for justice, rejected the demand for political status, the strikers' conditions of detention were relaxed and the strike was called off after three weeks, by which time the prisoners were in a dangerously weak state.

A new wave of strikes involving another thirteen 'political prisoners' broke out towards the end of the year. This time, the demands were slightly different. The *régime spécial* should be automatically extended to anyone imprisoned as a result of their political actions. All political prisoners should be held together in a small number of prisons, preferably in or near Paris, as opposed to being dispersed across France. They should be able to meet on a daily basis, visiting arrangements should be improved, and all books and newspapers should be available on request. The list of demands ended with a reference to the need to speed up deliveries of mail.[8]

Protests were now spreading, and even parliamentary voices were being raised in mild protest. In a written question to Pleven, François Mitterrand, then *député* for Nièvre, argued that men and women whose actions, although open to criticism, were the result of 'an ideological choice' were being subjected to 'an unacceptably repressive regime'.[9] Demonstrations continued in Paris and by February 1971 the violence was escalating to dangerous levels. On 5 February, the police station in the place du Panthéon was fire-bombed and police vehicles outside came under attack. The most notorious incident came four days later, when a Secours Rouge demonstration was violently broken up in the place Clichy. In the confusion, Richard Deshayes, a young Vive la Révolution militant,[10] tried to help a girl who had been knocked to the ground. He was struck in the face by a grenade of an unidentified type, lost one eye, suffered serious facial injuries and was then kicked by riot police as he lay on the ground in a pool of blood. Deshayes became the most celebrated victim of the illegal tactic of firing grenades at head height, and his picture, which appeared on the front page of the 18 February issue of VLR's newspaper *Tout*, was soon pasted on walls all over Paris, together with the slogan 'They mean to kill'. A *lycéen* called Gilles Guiot was arrested in the vicinity of the same demonstration; he had been positively identified as having struck a policeman and was sentenced to six months. Guiot had not been part of the demonstration and had no history of political involvement. Within days, the *lycées* of Paris were on strike and 10,000 students took to the streets in peaceful protest. Guiot was released on appeal for lack of evidence.

Street demonstrations were not the only form of solidarity action to be undertaken. An initial hunger strike at the Sorbonne was followed by the occupation of the Chapelle Saint-Bernard by eleven militants from Secours Rouge. Father Bernard Feillet, the priest in charge, insisted that the chapel had been occupied against his will but also acknowledged the hunger strikers' right to sanctuary.[11] The chapel became the site of a permanent political meeting and the strikers received a stream of celebrity visitors, including Maurice Clavel, Simone Signoret, Yves Montand and Foucault, who begged them to end the strike before it was too late.[12] On 29 January, some of the strikers, accompanied by Sartre, made their way to the Ministry of Justice, where they asked to see Pleven. With a sensitivity worthy of Marie-Antoinette, his *chef de cabinet* announced that the minister could not receive them as he was attending an official lunch. Before long,

Pleven did, however, begin to retreat and on Monday 8 February Georges Kiejman and Henri Leclerc, the lawyers acting for the imprisoned militants, held a press conference in the chapel to announce that most of their clients' demands had been met. It was at this point that the microphone was handed to Foucault.

Foucault's knowledge of recent events had not been culled from the newspapers. Geismar was an acquaintance he had met through Defert. He had come to know many of those involved with the GP at Vincennes and had previously known some of them in their earlier incarnation as Althusserian philosophers. More significantly, Daniel Defert had himself joined the GP after its proscription by Pleven. He immediately immersed himself in the work of its 'political prisoners' group, which brought together the families and friends of those in prison. He suggested that a commission should be set up in order to pass judgement on the prison system and to investigate conditions of detention. What he was thinking of was something similar to the 'people's court' set up in the northern town of Lens to investigate the circumstances leading to the methane explosion which killed sixteen men in the Number 6 Pit at Hénin-Liétard in late 1970.[13] The Maoist leaders had, as Defert put it later, assumed that 'Foucault should go to the jails and say: "I am from the GIP; I want to visit the jails", and of course they will refuse, and we will make a big protest against the jails in the press'.[14] This was not quite what Defert and Foucault had in mind. Defert initially proposed that his commission should be chaired by Casamayor, a lawyer of legendary status for those on the left and a permanent irritant to his legal establishment, who is known only by his enigmatic pseudonym. Casamayor declined the invitation and then suggested that Jean-Marie Domenach might be interested. A phone call was made by Foucault. The result was the GIP.

The statement read out in the Chapelle Saint-Bernard was made in the joint names of Jean-Marie Domenach, Michel Foucault and Pierre Vidal-Naquet, and the address given was Foucault's. Its author was Foucault, who also wrote the undated leaflet that accompanied the questionnaire distributed to those present on 8 February:

> The situation in the prisons is intolerable. Prisoners are being treated like dogs. The few rights they do have are not being respected. We want to bring this scandal to light.
>
> Recent events have alerted public opinion and the press to the way in which people are being sent to prison nowadays, and to the

life that awaits them once they are inside; but we do not want the movement to decline or pass into oblivion.

We must see to it that real changes take place, and in order to do that we intend to wage a long campaign.

We need your help in order to gain concrete knowledge about prisoners' real situation (and not simply what the administration tells us about it).

To begin with we would like to know more about and publicise prison living conditions: the state of the prisons, hygiene, food, the nature of the victimisation and the punishments; visits, visiting rooms, relations between families and prisoners, the rights that the administration does not respect, relations between prisoners and the legal system. In order to help us gather this information, the attached questionnaire should be filled in with the help of prisoners or former prisoners.

If you cannot hand it to us, please send it to the GIP, 285 rue de Vaugirard, Paris XVe.[15]

A second questionnaire, concentrating on relations between prisoners and the legal apparatus, was sent out to a number of *magistrats*. Its findings were not published, but it was probably instrumental in fostering and cementing links between the GIP and radical members of the legal profession. The links established with the Syndicat de la Magistrature, formed in June 1968, were to be important and Foucault thought highly of the organisation. One of his nieces was now studying law, and he recommended the Syndicat to her as 'an observatory' for the study of the legal machine.[16]

In an interview published in July 1971, Foucault explicitly relates the foundation of the GIP to the hunger strikes of the previous winter: 'Last December, a number of political prisoners, *gauchistes* and Maoists went on hunger strike in order to struggle against conditions of detention, political and common law, in general. This movement began in the prisons and developed outside them. It was from that moment on that I began to take an interest.'[17] In the same interview, he comments that his previous work had been on somewhat abstract subjects like the history of the sciences and that he now wanted to move away from that abstraction. Particular circumstances and events had displaced his attention on to the prison problem. They also offered an escape from his boredom with 'literary matters' ('*la chose littéraire*').

Foucault's new concern with prisons was obviously an extension of his long-standing interest in madness and confinement. As a very young man, he had gained some personal – and indeed professional – insight into the mechanisms of the prison system through his work with the Verdeaux at Fresnes. At the Collège de France, Foucault's seminar was currently looking at nineteenth-century penal psychiatry. A number of different strands were beginning to combine as the GIP was founded. Its foundation was not the application of some abstract theory. In Tunisia, Foucault had spontaneously supported his students without ever claiming to share their Marxist ideology. He was now acting in support of Maoists – though the focus of the GIP was soon to shift considerably – without sharing their belief in cultural revolution and without subscribing to their scenario of imminent civil war. On the contrary, in the summer of 1972 he was predicting a Socialist-Communist electoral victory, followed quickly by the return to power of the right.[18] He saw himself as working *alongside* the Maoists and was 'unable to conceive of any other form of political commitment'.[19] The one constant in his behaviour was a willingness to commit himself both politically and physically, together with a revulsion from what he saw as the intolerable.

The names of Foucault's co-signatories are highly significant. Domenach was the editor of *Esprit*. As a young man he had fought in the Resistance and he was to rediscover in the GIP the spirit of spontaneous self-organisation and of continual improvisation he had found in the mountains of the Vercors in 1944. In the early 1960s *Esprit* was one of the platforms for opposition to the war in Algeria and he saw the work of the GIP as a continuation of that work of denunciation. Although Foucault and Domenach had their political differences, *Esprit* became an important platform for the GIP, which was virtually ignored by *Les Temps Modernes*. Pierre Vidal-Naquet, a distinguished classical historian, had been one of the first to denounce the French army's widespread use of torture in Algeria. The experience of Vichy and then Algeria had bred in both men a deep distrust of – and even contempt for – a legal system which had compromised itself both during the Occupation, when magistrates and judges condoned the deportation of Jews, and during the Algerian war, characterised as it was by flagrant breaches of both human rights and French law.[20]

Resistance to the intolerable proved to outweigh the earlier disagreements between the three signatories. Domenach and *Esprit* had been dubious about *Les Mots et les choses*; Vidal-Naquet was a founding editor of *Raison présente*, which had been openly hostile to Foucault's 'archaeology of the human sciences'.

Although the founding statement was signed by three men, the GIP was very much Foucault's creation – and that of Daniel Defert. Indeed, when Bernard Kouchner wanted information on the GIP for an article for *Actuel*, he initially approached Defert and not Foucault.[21] Vidal-Naquet freely admits that his presence was largely symbolic and that he took little part in the GIP's day-to-day activities. Domenach took a much more active part, but agrees that it was Foucault's tireless energy and commitment that made the GIP an effective force. It was Foucault who made the phone calls, addressed meetings across France and held open house for GIP activists and supporters in the rue de Vaugirard.

The GIP was not characterised by any particular ideological unity or by any one political line. Christians, Maoists and nonaligned individuals succeeded in coexisting, if not always entirely peacefully. Indeed, it was at times characterised by an almost deliberate lack of organisation. There was no formal constitution. There were no membership cards and no subscriptions. It is impossible to state how many people were involved: estimates vary from a few hundred to thousands, but it was certainly possible for the group to mobilise impressive numbers for demonstrations. No permanent premises were ever acquired and most non-public meetings took place in Foucault's apartment.

While the emphasis on spontaneity may have evoked memories of the wartime resistance for Domenach, it was also very much in keeping with the ethos of the Gauche Prolétarienne. The GP was not, however, always united in its support for Foucault's group. When Robert Linhart, with support from Foucault, proposed devoting a special issue of *La Cause du peuple* to the prison mutiny that broke out at Toul in December 1971, more workerist comrades like Christian Jambet and Pierre Victor argued that not all forms of revolt were 'politically correct' and that the workers at Renault – the Maoists' political touchstone – would not understand support for such causes. Linhart and Foucault won the argument.[22] The possibility of manipulation by the Gauche Prolétarienne was, however, always present, and Danièle Rancière recalls Foucault having to insist again and again: 'This is the GIP, not Secours Rouge, and not the Gauche Prolétarienne.'[23]

Individuals rallied to the GIP for a wide variety of reasons. Many, like Deleuze, were drawn into it simply out of loyalty to and affection for Foucault. Given his past history of criminality and repeated imprisonment, it was perhaps inevitable that Jean Genet would have some involvement, but he in fact remained on the fringes of the group and never become a central figure in its work. For members of the GP, the primary motivation was solidarity with their imprisoned leaders and a search for revolutionary change. Since some members of the GP had strong anarchist leanings and a somewhat romantic view of banditry, there was a tendency to see the prison population as an ersatz proletariat. Foucault himself was at times prepared to describe criminality as a form of political revolt and to quote from Victor Hugo's *Les Misérables*: 'Crime is "a coup d'état from below"'.[24] He was also ready to justify shoplifting from supermarkets on political grounds, though it was not an art he practised himself.[25] This was not a theoretical issue; three weeks before its proscription, the GP had organised a successful commando raid on a luxury delicatessen. The spoils were distributed to the immigrants in the shanty towns of the suburbs.

Philippe Meyer, then a young sociologist and now a popular radio broadcaster, sensed echoes of his parents' Resistance activities, but also speaks of the mythological power of the image of the prisoner conveyed by the songs of Georges Brassens and notes that the Christian connotations of the prisoner as icon of suffering must have had a definite appeal to those of a religious persuasion. He describes his own position as being that of the classic liberal democrat, happy to work with Maoists, but convinced that he would be shot, 'come the Revolution'. The ideological fluidity of the GIP, on the other hand, was such that he felt perfectly able to say '*merde*' to the Maoists, and he was not slow to do so on occasion.[26]

Friends and associates of Foucault's, like Danièle Rancière (who initially met him because she studied for her *agrégation* alongside Defert at Saint-Cloud) and Hélène Cixous, found involvement with the GIP so natural that it was only *in medias res* that they thought to ask themselves *why* they were involved.[27] Cixous eventually realised that there was a link between her commitment to the GIP and the themes of her first novel,[28] but acted first and came to that conclusion later. The memory of May 1968 was still powerful and inspired in some young supporters an enthusiasm which could take an almost comically naive form: both Domenach and Meyer recall with great amusement the telegram of support received from a group of *lycéens* in a provincial town. Their support for the GIP was total, their only regret being that they could do little . . . because there was, unfortunately, no prison in their town.[29]

Although the GIP proved to be an effective instrument, it did have its political limitations. It was able to alert sections of public opinion to conditions in prison. Its position on the political spectrum ensured that it was not able to work with trade unions or political parties. For the

PCF, any *gauchiste* action was of course a provocation which 'objectively' served the interests of the ruling class. In a polemical exchange with Aimé Paistre, the secretary of the prison officers' union affiliated to the pro-Communist Confédération Générale du Travail, Foucault quotes, no doubt with a certain satisfaction, a local communist paper which had described the GIP as a 'hooligans' union'.[30] Paistre himself was on the right of the Gaullist Union des Démocrates pour la République and, like many of his members, in favour of the death penalty for murderers. He was also reported to be the only CGT secretary to have called upon his members to vote for Pompidou in the 1969 presidential election.[31] Although Domenach had some success in using his church contacts to publicise the work of the GIP, his attempt to persuade his friend Edmond Maire, the secretary of the Confédération Française du Travail, that prisoners should be unionised was a total failure. Like the CGT, the CFDT had a prison officers' section and was unwilling to offend its membership by appearing to support mutinous prisoners. Maire does, on the other hand, think that the GIP may have subsequently had an influence on the more liberal members of the union.[32]

The nature of the 'investigation' is described in an undated leaflet headed '*ENQUETE – Intolérance*'. The author – or authors – remains anonymous, but it can be safely assumed that Foucault had at least a hand in its drafting.

Insofar as it is possible, this investigation

– must give those held in various prisons the opportunity to say for themselves what their conditions of detention are, what they find particularly intolerable, and what outside actions they wish to see developing. The only way to avoid '*reformism*'.

– must reveal what is happening in the prisons without delay and as it happens (ill-treatment, suicides, hunger strikes, agitation, revolts). The only way for the investigation to be an *effective weapon* against the prison administration.

– must publicise what is uncovered as quickly as possible and as widely as possible. They only way to unite inside and outside in *one struggle*.[33]

The immediate task was to distribute the questionnaires and make contact with the prison population. GIP groups were assigned to different prisons, with Foucault concentrating on La Santé in the fourteenth *arrondissement*, and Domenach on Fresnes in the southern suburbs. A third group concerned itself with the 'model prison' of

Fleury-Mérogis, some twenty-five kilometres north of the capital. As it was obviously impossible to enter the prisons themselves, the groups gathered outside at visiting time in an attempt to make contact with prisoners' families. Despite some initial setbacks, the results were surprisingly encouraging. Foucault and Vidal-Naquet described the process in an interview:

> To give an example: every Saturday, we go to the gates of La Santé, where prisoners' families are queuing up for their hour's visit. We distribute our questionnaires. The first week, the welcome was very cold. The second week, people were still very suspicious. The third week, someone said to us: 'All that's just a load of talk. It should have been done long ago.' And suddenly, this woman told all. Exploding with anger, she talked about visits, the money she gives to a prisoner, the rich who are not in prison, the filth. And everyone noticed the plain-clothes cops pricking up their ears.
>
> The fourth week was even more extraordinary. The people in the queue were talking about our questionnaire and about the scandal of the prisons even before we arrived. That day, instead of making people wait in the street until 1.30 as usual, they opened the gates of La Santé three-quarters of an hour early.[34]

There is some evidence to suggest that the questionnaires and perhaps other GIP publications did circulate inside the prison walls. Defert claims that copies were smuggled in, and speaks with considerable relish of this clandestine work. The original questionnaire was published in *Esprit*, whose target audience has always included social workers, and in February 1971 Domenach received a curious reply when he protested to the authorities that inmates in Clairvaux had been refused permission to subscribe to his journal. Pleven wrote: 'For local administrative reasons, prisoners in the Maison Centrale de Clairvaux have been asked not to take out new subscriptions. But they can buy single issues of periodicals.'[35] The implication is that 'subversive material' was circulating. And, as Serge Livrozet points out – having been involved in the protests organised in the Melun 'Centrale' in 1971–72, he is certainly in a position to know – the fact that it is illegal has never prevented anything from circulating inside a prison.[36]

The questionnaires were sorted and the findings collated at a series of informal gatherings in Foucault's apartment. The open-house policy that was adopted, with large numbers of prisoners' wives and ex-inmates coming and going, may have occasioned some surprise to Foucault's concierge and to the eminently bourgeois inhabitants of 285 rue de Vaugirard, but there is no record of it resulting in conflict or disputes with neighbours. Most participants recall the meetings as being effective, if at times chaotic, with Foucault sprawled on the floor – a characteristic pose – surrounded by papers and talking for hours with his informants. He enjoyed the work and the company, and took a malicious pleasure in attempting to shock more liberal comrades by whispering that so and so was a 'lifer' who had been amnestied.[37] Deleuze recalls

> moments of great fun, particularly during the first encounters with former prisoners. There was a kind of rivalry among them, and it was hard to have two or three together as each badly wanted to be more of a prisoner than the others. If one had served five years, the other would say, 'I did seven', always outdoing the first. 'And where were you? Oh, that's an easy prison.'[38]

The questionnaires formed the basis for the GIP's first pamphlet, *Enquête dans vingt prisons*, which appeared at the beginning of June 1971.[39] A forty-eight-page document printed in green on white and adopting the odd format of 29 by 10 centimetres, it was published by Champ Libre, the anarchist house run by Gérard Lebovici, and sold for three francs, roughly equivalent to the price of a paperback book. The back cover gives an insight into the group's general stance. The following are tersely described as 'intolerable': 'the courts, the cops, the hospitals, the asylums, school, military service, the press, the TV, the State'.

Enquête reproduces two completed questionnaires in full, then gives two first-hand accounts of prison life, one by an inmate in La Santé, the other from Nevers. A selection of the 'most characteristic' answers completes the pamphlet, though the absence of any statistical break-down of the responses makes the very notion of 'characteristic' rather dubious. The three-page introduction, unsigned but written by Foucault, is worth citing at some length:

> 1. These investigations are not designed to improve or soften an oppressive power, or to make it tolerable. They are designed to attack it at those points where it is exercised under a different name – that of justice, technology, knowledge or objectivity. Each investigation must therefore be *a political act*.

2. They are aimed at specific targets, at institutions which have names and places, people in charge and governors – and which claim victims and inspire revolts, even among those in charge of them. Each investigation must therefore be the *first episode in a struggle.*

3. They bring together, around these specific targets, different social strata which the ruling class has kept apart thanks to the interplay of social hierarchies and divergent economic interests. They must bring down barriers which are indispensable to power by uniting prisoners, lawyers and *magistrats*, or even doctors, patients and hospital personnel. Each investigation must constitute a *front* – an *offensive front* – at each important strategic point.

4. These investigations are not being made by a group of technicians working from the outside; the investigators are those who are being investigated. It is up to them to begin to speak [*prendre la parole*], to bring down the barriers, to express what is intolerable, and to tolerate it no longer. *It is up to them to take responsibility for the struggle which will prevent oppression being exercised.*[40]

It is further argued that the 'exploited class' has always been able to recognise its oppression and has always resisted it. What was new was that oppression now proved intolerable to those who were not its direct victims: social workers, lawyers, journalists and other professionals were now protesting about the power structures in which they were implicated.

That the 'investigators-investigated' should begin to speak for themselves was axiomatic to the work of the GIP, which had no intention of speaking on their behalf. Deleuze once told Foucault: 'In my view, you were the first to teach us a basic lesson: speaking for others is shameful.'[41] Foucault's 'new social strata' were not being asked to speak in the name of supposedly universal values such as justice, but from the position within which their own specific practices bring them into conflict with the demands of power. In later writings, Foucault outlines the notion of the 'specific intellectual' who speaks out against the intolerable on the basis of his or her sectoral knowledge, his usual example being Robert Oppenheimer, who spoke out against nuclear power *as* a nuclear physicist.[42] In December 1971, a spectacular example was to be provided by Dr Edith Rose, the prison psychiatrist at Toul, whose accounts of what she had seen there were to have a devastating political effect.

Foucault's introduction ends with a series of four demands, all concerning the abolition of the *casier judiciaire*. Originally introduced in 1850, the *casier judiciaire* is a system of keeping criminal records. All convictions are recorded, but become 'spent' after varying lengths of time. By checking against the registers of the *état civil*, it is possible to trace the record of any individual; this is often the object of the identity checks carried out during a *garde à vue*. The difference between this and the British system is that everyone has a *casier judiciaire*, which may or may not be 'clean' (*vierge*) in the sense that a British driving licence may be said to be clean. Extracts from the *casier* are available on request to employers or potential employers.[43] The GIP's point was that the system made the rehabilitation of offenders almost impossible and therefore made recidivism virtually inevitable by confining them to low-paid work and to the greyer areas of the labour market.[44] The publication of a pamphlet dealing with the issue was announced, but never materialised. In arguing for the abolition of the *casier judiciaire*, the GIP was not demanding a reform but challenging the whole system. As Foucault put it in an interview with *Actuel*, the point was to blur the distinction between innocence and guilt, between good and evil.[45]

On 1 May 1971, small groups of GIP activists and supporters gathered outside La Santé and Fresnes. May Day is the *fête du travail* and a bank holiday; as well as handing out leaflets and questionnaires, the groups distributed sprigs of lily of the valley in accordance with the long-established tradition of the left. Although initially peaceful, the demonstrations were short-lived as the police immediately moved in and arrested all those present. At Fresnes, Domenach and three comrades were taken into custody and held for four and a half hours for 'identity checks'. He had no complaints about his treatment, but later reported the following exchange: '*Brigadier*: "The fact that most jailbirds go back to jail proves that the situation in the prisons is fine." Domenach: "It proves just the opposite. Prisons are supposedly designed to make prisoners better people. They make them rot." ' He concluded: 'We have a long way to go.'[46]

Outside La Santé, Foucault and others were arrested on the grounds that their leaflets had not been duly registered for copyright. Foucault later commented: 'The streets are starting to become the private preserve of the police; arbitrary police decisions have the force of law: move along, keep moving, don't talk; don't give anyone what you've written; no gatherings. Prison begins far away from the prison gates. Just outside the door of your house.'[47] The incident seemed minor and no one was unduly concerned at being arrested. Danièle Rancière recalls that everyone sang cheerfully as they were driven away – much to the annoyance of the arresting officers. At the *commissariat* of the fourteenth *arrondissement* in the avenue de Maine, events took an uglier turn. When the detainees were asked to identify themselves, they were asked how many of them had 'proper French names'. A young woman agreed that her name was 'not really French', and that during the Occupation talk about 'proper French names' had resulted in the death of some of her family in the gas chambers. A quarter of an hour later, a policeman pretended to aim and fire an imaginary revolver at her, shouting 'Heil Hitler'. A senior officer had the grace to look embarrassed.[48] Someone was heard to say 'Dirty Jewish bitch' and 'dirty queer', and Foucault was struck in the back and publicly insulted by a policeman who followed him for some distance.[49]

On this occasion, Foucault decided to press charges in an attempt to demonstrate in court that the police were using their powers in an increasingly arbitrary manner. The charges included false arrest, illegal imprisonment, premeditated violence and use of abusive language. The charge of false arrest was a response to the charge that the GIP leaflets breached copyright law. Under French law, every publication must carry the name, not necessarily of the publisher, but of the printer. The leaflets bore Foucault's address and he was effectively claiming to be the printer. The assault and false arrest charges were brought before examining magistrate Sablayrolles, and Foucault was represented by Georges Kiejman. All those involved were called before the magistrate, and Foucault identified the police officer who had struck him. Even so, Sablayrolles ruled that there was no case to answer and overruled all Kiejman's objections.

The copyright issue later came up before an examining magistrate for whom Kiejman had a high regard. The lawyer's case was that the leaflets had been duplicated by Foucault and carried his address; he had in fact brought the printing equipment – a crude duplicator known as a *vietnamienne* – to court with him and had it under his arm. The magistrate did not accept the argument, ruling that 285 rue de Vaugirard was not the address of a printer. Foucault was ordered to pay a nominal fine.[50] Despite his defeat, Foucault congratulated Kiejman on his conduct of the case, telling him that he had behaved 'regally, if the word could be applied to a revolutionary defence plea'. Indeed, he later sent the lawyer a signed copy of *Moi, Pierre Rivière*; the inscription states that, with Kiejman as his defence lawyer, Rivière would have been acquitted.[51]

As the year progressed, Foucault was struck by the changing

contents of the letters the GIP was receiving from inside the prisons of France:

> In June, the letters were talking about the cold and the screws; in September, they were talking about Attica, and about Bengal. Between those two dates, the outside world began to exist for prisoners. The warders are in fact complaining about this newfound freedom. When the Clairvaux business blew up, they immediately blamed the newspapers. Wrongly, in the case of that suicide-operation, which is typical of a closed world.[52]

The 'Clairvaux business' was the most serious incident of a hot summer. On 22 September, a nurse and warder were taken hostage by Claude Buffet and Roger Bontems in Clairvaux, originally a monastic building with a venerable place in the history of mysticism, but often said to be France's most sinister and dangerous prison. The two barricaded themselves inside the prison hospital, demanding weapons and cars for their escape. When the hospital was stormed, both hostages were killed. In February 1971, a nurse and a social worker had been taken hostage by two prisoners in Aix-en-Provence; both men died in the police assault. In July, a warder was shot dead in Saint-Paul's prison in Lyon and in October, a prisoner was fatally wounded in Les Baumettes (Marseille) during another hostage-taking incident.

Pleven's response was both heavy-handed and disastrous. In a circular issued on 2 November 1971, he announced that prisoners could no longer receive Christmas parcels from their families. What they had assumed to be a right was in fact no more than a privilege. At the end of the Second World War, when it was generally recognised that conditions in French prisons were deplorable, inmates were accorded the right to receive food parcels from their families, but that right was withdrawn in 1958. An exception was made for the Christmas period. The November circular referred to 'recent events' which had demonstrated that, even with strict security precautions, the custom of sending in parcels represented an unacceptable risk. What was more, thorough searches almost inevitably resulted in damage to the contents of the parcels. Finally, the prison service did not have time to search parcels.

Pleven's circular helped to publicise the GIP. On 11 November, it was able to organise a large public meeting in the Mutualité. It was devoted to the situation in French and American prisons and featured a film on Attica (the site in New York State of a violent mutiny and siege in September 1971) and San Quentin, California, the main focus of attention being the death of George Jackson, a young prisoner associated with the 'black power' movement. The domestic situation also figured prominently; for the first time, ex-prisoners and their families were able – and ready – to describe in public their experiences of the prison system. For the GIP, this was a historic event, but some of the political purists in the audience found it embarrassing that the speakers were 'so insufficiently proletarian'.[53]

The abolition of the 'right' to receive parcels provoked an immediate outcry. On 5 December, a group of fifty protesters, including Foucault and Claude Mauriac, gathered outside the Ministry of Justice in the place Vendôme. They were carrying a large package symbolising the banned parcels and handed it over to an official, watched by five or six vanloads of police.[54] A small delegation of women was allowed inside the ministry for what proved to be a pointless discussion with officials. For Foucault, it had been a long day. Having spent the morning in the Bibliothèque Nationale, he had earlier made a brief appearance in the Goutte d'Or, where a protest about racism was going on; Mauriac found him frugally lunching in the street on a bar of chocolate and a *pain au lait*.[55] The next two months were to be even busier.

Genet objected that Pleven's circular represented an abuse of power; parcels were one of the few things that allowed inmates to participate in normal life, and the minister had no right to interfere.[56] A press release from the GIP referred to the deliberate creation of a 'climate of psychosis' inside the prisons, and claimed that an attempt was being made to convince prison staff that their lives were in constant danger.[57] Representatives of the CGT trade-union federation apparently agreed that this was indeed the case, and applauded the ministerial circular.[58] Aimé Paistre claimed that the dominant feeling was one of acute anxiety; prison officers were terrified that the events at Clairvaux would be repeated.[59] Charles Dayant, a former prison doctor, warned in an open letter to the authorities that an outbreak of suicides could be expected on Christmas night and that the level of tension was dangerously high.[60] Jean Lacombe, an inmate of La Santé, wrote to the minister himself: 'The last symbol has collapsed. The one thing that made us men like other men no longer exists. Yes, it's serious, more serious than it seems. Isn't being deprived of freedom enough?' Lacombe was immediately transferred to Fresnes, where he was thrown into solitary confinement in *le mitard* (an unheated punishment cell) and placed on a bread and water diet. He then announced his intention of remaining on hunger strike until Christmas.[61] Commenting on the Lacombe case, the GIP noted that a further step had been taken towards the dehumanisation of French prisons.[62] For his part, Domenach argued that all prisoners were being punished for the actions of Bontems and Buffet, and were being held hostage to guarantee the good behaviour of their fellow inmates.[63]

Faced with this reaction, Pleven did make concessions and announced on television on 8 December that women prisoners and minors could receive parcels from their families. Parcels could be sent to other inmates through the Red Cross or church agencies; their value was not to exceed thirty francs and, in order to avoid petty jealousies and tension, they must contain nothing that could not be bought from prison canteens.[64] The inmates of France's prisons had effectively been given prisoner-of-war status.

Hunger strikes started in Draguignan and Poissy in November, but the real explosion was to take place in Toul, a small town with a population of only 15,000, politically dominated by the UDR, and noted for its Gothic church, which rates two stars ('worth a detour') in the Michelin guide. Toul lies 283 kilometres from Paris and 23 from Nancy. The prison, the Centrale Ney, stands on the outskirts of the little town. Originally an army barracks built in 1917, it was turned into a prison in 1947. In December 1971, it held 540 prisoners in two wings.

On 5 December, 200 adult prisoners refused to go back to their cells after exercise in protest at the conditions in which they were being held. They were eventually persuaded back into their cells by the chaplain, Abbé Velten. Over the next two days disturbances broke out in the youth wing and 200 inmates were transferred to other prisons. On 9 December, full-scale riots broke out: the carpentry shop was ransacked and the library set on fire. Prisoners took to the roof, chanting slogans calling for 'more potatoes and less work'. The talk was now of revolution and the men were demanding the dismissal of the governor and three warders with a reputation for violence. Calm was restored after negotiations with Abbé Velten and his Protestant colleague. The prisoners were assured that they would not be victimised and that their complaints had been noted. They also believed that they had received assurances that Governor Galiana would be transferred elsewhere.

Overnight, hundreds of CRS and *gardes-mobiles* moved into the town and surrounded the prison. On 13 December, the rest of the prison was sacked before three squadrons of riot police put a brutal end to the riot. One warder gloatingly told a journalist that rifle butts had been broken on the heads of prisoners.[65] Until then, the only violence had been that directed against the prison itself. No hostages were taken and when the rioters took over the armoury, they escorted the remaining warders to safety. The one part of the prison not to be damaged was the chapel; its door was daubed with the legend: 'We respect those who treat us like men.'

As the riots continued, a '*Comité pour la vérité sur les événements de la centrale Ney*' was set up and began to organise leafleting and meetings. '*Comités-vérité*' ('truth committees') were loose coalitions, usually organised by Secours Rouge and the Gauche Prolétarienne, designed to publicise situations judged to be intolerable. In the case of Toul, the truth was devastating. In a leaflet distributed by the Comité-vérité before the storming of the prison, a former inmate described how he had been punished for a series of trivial breaches of discipline. Breadcrumbs had been found in a toilet, and a supply of bread in his cupboard. He had asked to see a doctor without good reason. His work output was unsatisfactory, and he had turned up in the workshop wearing espadrilles. He had indulged in whispered conversations at work. His punishment was a series of weekends in the *mitard*, the final turn of the screw being that Sunday was visiting day. Postal orders sent to him from outside had been withheld for months.[66] Over the next few days, many more damaging truths were to emerge from behind the walls of the Centrale Ney.

The most damning statement came, not from a prisoner, but from Dr Edith Rose, the prison psychiatrist, in an open letter sent to the inspector general of the prison administration, the president of the Republic, the minister of justice and to the president of the Ordre des Médecins. Extensively quoted in the press, the letter was published in *La Cause du peuple-j'accuse* and then printed as a paid advertisement in *Le Monde* on 26–27 December. Dr Rose begain by citing concrete examples of the climate in Galiana's prison. Inmates did not have the right to play sports until they had won a 'merit stripe' for a year's good conduct. Prisoners had the right to have only a certain number of photographs in their cells; she had recently treated a young man for 'mental problems' after warders had taken away a photograph of his younger brother sent to him by his mother. A severely depressed inmate refused to take the anti-depressants she had prescribed; he feared that they would slow down his work rate and that he would be punished as a result. A mentally ill prisoner was placed in the *mitard* because he had refused to work; she swore that he was incapable of working. Frequent use was made of straitjackets, and she had heard of prisoners being 'restrained' for up to a week at a time, supposedly in an attempt to prevent suicide bids. Some had reportedly been left to lie in their own excrement.

Suicide attempts, sometimes by hanging, were common; other suicidal inmates had swallowed spoons, forks or sections of neon tubing. When the disturbances began, she was refused access to the prison. She had been told that the riot had been fomented by the two chaplains in a bid for 'fame'.

Perhaps the most vital part of Edith Rose's statement concerns the nature of the prison population: 'We have no "hard men" in the Centrale Ney.' She then gives an identikit picture of the typical young inmate: the product of a broken marriage or the son of an alcoholic, who had first been taken into custody as a child.

> Many of them first went to prison at the age of fourteen. When they leave, with 100 francs in their pockets, and with every door closed to them, there is only one thing on their minds: making the beautiful dream they have cherished for years come true – speeding along in a beautiful car. They steal a car and go back to prison. Then they become 'dangerous recidivists.'

Dr Rose ended by stating that she had no religious beliefs and belonged to no political party. Needless to say, she was forced to leave the prison service. Within the service, her statement was greeted with total silence.[67]

A reporter on *L'Express* added more graphic details. A prisoner had been refused permission to write to the mother of his four children because they were not married. A social worker explained with irrefutable logic: 'Either she is a respectable girl, and should have nothing to do with the guy, or she is not a respectable girl, and he has no business writing to her.' He attempted to commit suicide. Suicides or incidents of self-mutilation were occurring at a rate of one a week. The prison's one nurse commented: 'I don't call it a suicide attempt if a prisoner cuts his wrists when a warder goes by.' According to the authorities, the use of straitjackets was a medical practice; straitjackets were never used unless a medical certificate had been signed. Rose commented that the violently insane were her concern; she had never signed a certificate allowing anyone to be restrained. *L'Express*'s reporter laconically referred to the Centrale Ney as 'Attica-on-Moselle'.[68]

For Foucault, Dr Rose's statement was 'the discourse of Toul':

> Toul's psychiatrist has spoken. She has given the game away and broken the great taboo. She was part of a system of power, but instead of *criticising* its workings, she *denounced* what was

happening, what had happened on such and such a day, in such and such a place, in specific circumstances. . . . This woman who, after all, and if only because of her knowledge, was 'part of power', 'involved in' power, has had the singular courage to say 'I swear it' . . . The 'discourse of Toul' may be an important event in the history of the penal and psychiatric institution.[69]

Foucault also drew a parallel between the situation in Toul and that in Algeria a decade earlier: it was one thing to say that the army was using torture, but quite another to say that Captain X had tortured Y or that so many corpses had been brought out of a particular police station. Dr Edith Rose was one of those brave enough to take the latter course.

On Christmas Eve 1971, Foucault got home after midnight after the long drive from Toul, where he had been chairing the meeting addressed by Dr Rose, and heard on the radio that a small GIP demonstration had taken place outside La Santé. About forty people had gathered in the boulevard Arago. Bengal lights flickered in the darkness and firecrackers were let off. The night was mild and those inside La Santé shouted their enthusiasm from their cell windows.[70] On New Year's Eve, Foucault took part in a similar peaceful demonstration outside Fresnes.

The meetings in Toul and Nancy – where one drew an audience of over a thousand – could be stormy. Deleuze describes a meeting in Toul at which a group of warders tried to shout down the speakers. They were silenced by ex-inmates who were prepared both to say why they had gone to prison and to identify publicly warders who had brutalised them. The phrase 'I know who you are' had once been used by warders to intimidate prisoners; it now became a weapon used to silence warders.[71] Not all warders were silenced. In early January, forty of them held a meeting to denounce the 'slanders' being put about by the Comité-vérité,[72] and a joint statement put out by the CGT, CFCT and FO unions expressed surprise that people 'outside the prison administration' had done more to turn the prison population against 'those who were responsible for guarding them' than to calm the situation.[73] The possibility of violence was always present, and sometimes it became a reality: as Domenach left a meeting in Metz, he narrowly escaped being run over by a car that was deliberately driven at him.

One meeting is of particular significance, not because of what it disclosed about Toul, but because of what it reveals about Foucault's politics and those of the GIP. On 5 January 1972 Foucault addressed a

Comité-vérité meeting in Toul and challenged Pleven to tell the truth. His speech was not reported by the national press. What was reported at some length by *Le Monde* was the message from Sartre read to the meeting:

Two hundred young men have been taken away from the Centrale Ney. Two hundred young men who took part in the revolt and who have therefore moved from an individualistic rebellion to a common action undertaken for common interests. It is possible that they will carry into the prisons where they have been placed this new aspect of their condition and their behaviour: a collective revolt . . . If this generalised revolt breaks out, will we watch it from the outside with mixed feelings, will we see in it another infamy on the part of this hellish race – prisoners – and will we let a rotten administration settle it alone by claiming that it is to protect us that it has unleashed the CRS, or will we see it as the beginning of our struggle against the repressive regime which keeps all of us . . . in a concentration-camp world?[74]

Foucault's one comment at the time was that it was sad to see *Le Monde* devoting so much space to Sartre and failing to mention the prisoners' demands.[75] He could have said more. Sartre appears to have thought that he had found a 'group in fusion', or even an agent for revolutionary change, and was accordingly criticised in print by Domenach, who argued that, in the unlikely event of a general revolt breaking out, it would not be the beginning of anything, and would be put down with severe repression.[76] Perhaps more significantly, Sartre referred to 'a concentration-camp world' (*un univers concentrationnaire*). As he knew, having worked with its author in the 1940s, *L'Univers concentrationnaire* is the title of David Rousset's classic study of the camps,[77] and the term is therefore both very emotive and ideologically loaded. It was not uncommon in the early 1970s for French Maoists to assert that France had been occupied by the bourgeoisie and that their struggle was a new Resistance, but as Domenach remarked, it was improbable that the 'masses' shared Sartre's view. The difference between Foucault's claim that 'No one can be sure of avoiding prison' – forceful, but not untrue to the experience of many young people – and Sartre's claim that we are all living in a concentration-camp world says a lot about the respective political judgement of the two men.

The first weeks of January were punctuated by sporadic hunger strikes and disturbances in the prisons: Nîmes, Amiens, Loos-lès-Lille, Rouen, Ecrouves and Fleury-Mérogis were all affected in turn. In all cases, demands for improved conditions were put forward. On 15 January, prisoners in the Charles III prison in Nancy mutinied at 7.30 in the morning. At 1.30, the police assault began with volleys of teargas grenades from both police on the ground and a gendarmerie helicopter hovering over the prison. Within an hour, the police were in control; damage was estimated at two million francs. In the meantime, the mutineers had succeeded in communicating a leaflet outlining their demands to the 3,000 spectators who had gathered in the streets outside the prison walls, where a dozen or so young people were arrested for demonstrating their overenthusiastic support for the mutiny. The demands concerned the need for justice inside the prison, and echoed the GIP's claim that prisons were, paradoxically, outside the law. Demands for better food, an end to the censoring of newspapers, decent hygiene and heating in all dormitories also figured on the list. According to the GIP, development at Nancy had followed the same pattern as at Toul: after a peaceful demonstration, the inmates had been promised that their demands would be noted and that no reprisals would be taken. They were then persuaded in from the exercise yard and thrown into the punishment block.[78]

Shortly after the mutiny was put down, Pleven issued a statement to the press:

> The mutiny which broke out this morning was not the result of any serious cause for discontent. It is clear that certain subversive elements are currently trying to use prisoners, who are likely to suffer the consequences, to provoke or rekindle dangerous agitation in various penal establishments . . . The real purpose of those who are instigating the current troubles is to hamper the announced reforms so as to foment reasons for agitation.[79]

The 'subversive elements' argument was to be used again when disturbances occurred at Fresnes in February. GIP militants were actively organising meetings for prisoners' families and the local prefect claimed that the protest, in which a head warder was overpowered without any use of weapons, was the direct result of propaganda which was being 'remote-controlled' from outside the prison, a nice variant on the 'outside agitator' theme. Foucault merely replied that the inmates were big enough to organise their own protests without any need for remote control.[80]

Shortly after the Nancy events, Foucault received a statement from within Melun prison, where the situation was tense but still calm. He proposed that it should be made public at a press conference at the

Ministry of Justice. On 18 January, Mauriac, Deleuze and Sartre, jokingly referred to by Deleuze as 'our mascot' and accompanied by his close friend and sometime lover Michelle Vian, met in the rue de Castiglione, which leads into the place Vendôme from the south. They were joined by Foucault and a large group of supporters, moved into the place Vendôme and then into the entrance to the ministry. A second group moved down the rue de la Paix to join them. A barrier was pushed aside, and the demonstrators announced to the bewildered porters that they had come for the press conference.

As Foucault began to read his statement, a few CRS arrived and began to push the press conference into the street. Foucault, red-faced and his muscles swollen with the effort, led the resistance. Outside the ministry, scuffles broke out and the journalist Alain Jaubert was seized by a policeman. Sartre – who, given his age and state of health, cannot have been of much real help – Foucault and others promptly grabbed his arm and tried to pull him away. The situation now bordered on the farcical: those involved in the tug of war were surrounded by a circle of CRS who took no action and merely watched.

Jaubert, together with Marianne Merleau-Ponty and another journalist, was finally bundled into a police van. Mauriac tried to intervene, showed his press card, and was allowed to speak to the *commissaire* in charge. He agreed that the demonstrators would disperse if their comrades were freed. It was with a definite embarrassment that the police learned just whom they had arrested, and the three were released: Jaubert was in the process of bringing charges of false arrest and assault against the police. Although the atmosphere was tense and potentially dangerous, the arrest of Merleau-Ponty, a lawyer and the daughter of the philosopher, also occasioned somewhat hysterical laughter and cries of 'We must not lose Marianne' – 'Marianne' being the icon of the Republic whose statue sits in every *mairie*.

As Foucault moved closer to the CRS lined up in front of the van, the butt of a gun was banged down on his foot. With fury in his face, he pushed it aside. The riot police remained as impassive as robots. Finally, a civil servant arrived and announced that he would see to it that the minister received the petition. Foucault's cutting reply was that it was a report, not a petition, and that the minister would, like every other citizen, be able to read it tomorrow, adding that he did not deserve special treatment.

The incident was over, and an impromptu press conference on the Nancy events and the situation in Melun was held in the premises of Agence de Presse Libération in the rue Dussoubs.[81] The statement from Melun began by noting that prisoners had two means of alerting public opinion: rooftop protests and violence, or the present statement, the implication being that violence would ensue if it was ignored. The main demand concerned the establishment of democratically elected prisoners' committees empowered to negotiate with the prison authorities without being regarded as 'ringleaders' or 'troublemakers'. The other demands were the release of prisoners being held on bail conditions, the commutation of life sentences to fixed-term sentences after seven years, the abolition of the *casier judiciaire*, social-security rights, the right to work and enough money to live for three months on release, and the repeal of laws preventing prisoners from communicating freely with the outside world.[82]

The GIP and Secours Rouge called a demonstration in Paris for 21 January, mobilising around calls for the establishment of prisoners' commissions and for guarantee of no reprisals. Some 800 people took to the *grands boulevards*, and the demonstration ended with the almost ritual exchange of Molotov cocktails and gas grenades.[83] In an attempt to preempt police intervention, the initial leaflets had given no specific meeting place and simply told potential demonstrators to contact Secours Rouge militants for further information. That 800 people could be mobilised in semi-secrecy and in only a couple of days is no small testimony to the organisational skills of the groups concerned.

The government's response to the Toul mutiny was the appointment of a commission of inquiry headed by Robert Schmelck, *avocat général* to the Court of Appeal and president of the European Committee for Criminal Problems. The commission reported in January 1972 and concluded that the disciplinary regime in Toul had been excessively strict: in October and November alone, disciplinary sanctions had been taken against inmates on 191 occasions. This was considered excessive for a prison population of 540. The main problem in the young offenders' wing, where the disturbances had begun, was identified as boredom, combined with inadequate training facilities. The commission admitted that it could neither confirm nor deny Dr Rose's claims. Schmelck also referred to the existence within the prison of organised gangs, speculating that an attempted *réglement de comptes* may have been at the origin of the riot.[84]

Shortly after the appearance of the report, Galiana was transferred to another post. A GIP press release described the work of Schmelck's team as 'inadequate' and commented unfavourably on the decision to hold a press conference – which lasted for five minutes – in conditions of virtual secrecy. More specifically, it criticised Schmelck's failure to point out that Galiana's use of disciplinary procedures meant that release dates had been put back for many prisoners, and called for an independent inquiry.

One of the GIP's primary weapons was the press release, and it soon proved adept at using the media. Favourable coverage was usually provided by *Le Nouvel Observateur* and *Témoignage chrétien*, a Christian newspaper whose origins lie in the Resistance. Throughout 1972, *Le Monde*'s regular reports on the wave of prison suicides habitually juxtaposed the official statistics and those provided by the GIP.

Television, on the other hand, was almost out of reach, being under tight state control. In February 1972, the weekly *Dossiers de l'écran* was devoted to the prison issue. The normal format was adopted: a feature film followed by a debate lasting for one and a half hours. The film in question was Maurice Cloche's 1956 *Prison de femmes* which, to judge by the synopsis given in *La Semaine Radio-Télévision*, is a typical prison melodrama.[85] The two-page article by one J. Parrot which introduces the programme consists entirely of stories of notorious murderesses. Parrot does, however, point out that women's prisons were in need of reform, and expresses the hope that viewers' questions would help to open up the debate.

The debate was to remain closed. The personalities invited to give their accounts of prison life included the CGT's Paistre, Le Cornu, a prison psychiatrist, a lawyer, the chairman of a prison visitors' organisation and a nun. No representative of the GIP was invited to take part, and no ex-inmate was seen on screen. Claude Mauriac describes the debate's non-content: 'Not only was there no allusion to any of our interventions . . . there was no mention of the serious events that have recently taken place in the prisons or even, to cap it all, of the Schmelck report.'[86] *Les Dossiers de l'écran* normally accepted questions phoned in by viewers for on-air discussion. Well aware that their questions would be ignored, a number of GIP members and supporters called the programme: Sartre, de Beauvoir, Domenach, Cixous, Deleuze, Faye, Foucault and Clavel. Not one of their questions was broadcast. The questions, duly published in *Le Nouvel Observateur*, asked, among other things, why Dr Rose had not been invited to take part, and why there had been no discussion of living conditions in La Roquette – the women's prison in Paris.[87]

Although politics and the GIP were taking up much of Foucault's time, his academic life continued too. In April, he went, somewhat reluctantly, according to Deleuze,[88] to the United States, where he lectured on 'the history of truth' at the State University of New York at Buffalo and on 'political ceremony' in seventeenth-century France at the University of Minnesota.[89] This was not his first visit; he had already been to Buffalo the previous winter, and had been less than enamoured of the climate. The one consolation had been the presence of Cixous, also on a lecture tour and equally depressed by the cold.[90]

Foucault's reputation in the United States had yet to become firmly established, and it was probably not enhanced by the fact that he could only lecture in French. The fascination of America had not yet really begun to work on him. For the moment, 'America such as it is viewed by a European like me who is a little bit lost and not very resourceful [is] gigantic, technological, a little terrifying, that Piranesi aspect which permeates the view that many Europeans have of New York'.[91] Nor was he pleased by his American students' complacent assumption that he was available for discussion at all hours – something which is certainly outside the experience of most teachers in French universities.[92]

The trip to Buffalo was not purely academic. John K. Simon, the chairman of the department of French at Buffalo, was able to arrange for Foucault to visit Attica. Disingenuously, Foucault told him that he had never before set foot inside a prison and chose not to mention his work at Fresnes in the 1950s. He found the sight of Attica prison 'overwhelming':

> At Attica what struck me perhaps first of all was the entrance, that kind of phony fortress à la Disneyland, those observation posts disguised as medieval towers with their *machicoulis*. And behind this rather ridiculous scenery which dwarfs everything else, you discover that it's an immense machine . . . Attica is a machine for elimination, a form of prodigious stomach, a kidney which consumes, destroys, breaks up and then rejects, and which consumes in order to eliminate what it has already eliminated.[93]

Shortly after Foucault's return to France, six of the Nancy mutineers were brought before the town's *tribunal correctionnel*, where they were defended by Albert Naud and Henri Leclerc. The GIP organised demonstrations in Nancy, and was again met with violence by the police. In one incident, Hélène Cixous was clubbed to the ground and left unconscious.[94] The six mutineers, the youngest of whom was nineteen, received additional sentences of between five and eight months and were ordered to pay fines of 250 francs. The court recognised that there had been 'mitigating circumstances' and the prosecutor's plea for 'long terms of imprisonment' to preserve society from chaos was ignored. In his summing-up, he referred to the GIP as the '*Groupe d'intoxication du public*' ('Public Brainwashing Group'). In Foucault's view, the six 'ringleaders' had been scapegoated, and it was no accident that two of them had particularly long records of previous offences.[95]

The GIP regarded the relatively lenient sentences handed down in Nancy as a partial victory. On the other hand, the tactics adopted by the judge had frustrated all attempts by Naud and Leclerc to politicise the proceedings by raising the issue of just who went to prison and of how inmates were treated. Some grim details did, however, emerge from exchanges between Leclerc and the head warder. No films were ever shown in Charles III. There was no television. There were no sports facilities. The prison was not heated, even though winters can be extremely cold in Nancy. It was not possible to read, write or smoke in the dormitories, which were wire 'pens' housing four to six men. When the part-time chaplain remarked that the age and state of the buildings, the lack of privacy and the lack of heating seemed to him to provide adequate grounds for mutiny and that it seemed unfair to bring only six of the prisoners involved before the court, he was silenced by the judge.

The trial was attended by a number of GIP activists, including Defert. They carefully transcribed the court proceedings.[96] The transcripts were to become the basis for the script of a short play performed by members of the Théâtre du Soleil after the scheduled performances of *1792* at the Cartoucherie de Vincennes in July. The theatre's director Ariane Mnouchkine, who had been drawn into the orbit of the GIP by her friend Cixous, played the role of Leclerc, and Foucault that of the second assessor. Defert and Meyer appeared as police officers. At Vincennes, the performance was followed by open discussions; given Mnouchkine's reputation and the nature of the Théâtre du Soleil's usual audience, it was almost guaranteed a good reception. Other performances seem to have been less successful, but not because of the police intervention which put a rapid end to many of the GIP's attempts to put on playlets on the streets. *Le Procès de Nancy* was played in the open air outside a housing estate in Créteil, but no record of its reception appears to exist.

A performance was also planned for the rue de la Butte aux Cailles, where an eviction was due to take place the day before the Vincennes performance. A thunderstorm scattered the actors. The only people present were a group of political militants, who were trying to prevent the eviction from going ahead. The inhabitants of the *quartier* failed to turn out, and it seemed pointless to go ahead, particularly since most of the militants present planned to go to Vincennes the next night. As a result, Claude Mauriac found a rather bewildered Foucault sitting alone in a local café.[97] Unfortunately, no photographs were taken, either, of *Le Procès de Nancy*. Mnouchkine, in particular, insisted that this was a purely political action and not a vehicle for personalities.[98]

Not all the GIP's productions were as sophisticated as this. More typical were the agitprop sketches in which Foucault sometimes participated. A typical example was the playlet based on a clever perversion of the proverb '*Qui vole un oeuf vole un bouef*' ('He that will steal a pin will steal a pound'), which became '*Qui vole un oeuf va en prison, qui vole un boef va au Palais-Bourbon*' ('He who steals a pin goes to prison; he who steals a pound gets into Parliament').[99] Theatre was not the only weapon; the GIP also made a documentary film about prisons. It was professionally directed, technically quite sophisticated and was distributed with some success through the thriving 'alternative' network.

The spate of prison mutinies abated after Nancy, and the GIP now turned its attention to the alarming increase in suicides in France's prisons. Until 1971, the suicide rate had been falling; in 1972 and 1973, it reached an exceptionally high level, with thirty-seven and forty-two suicides respectively. In statistical terms, the rate was 131 per 100,000 between 1972 and 1975, and most of the victims were under twenty years old. One study showed that a twenty-year-old in prison was twenty times more likely to kill himself than a twenty-year-old in the outside world. The official attitude to suicides was harsh. *Le Monde* cited Le Cornu as saying that most suicide attempts were made in an attempt to obtain a transfer to the hospital block, the belief being that escapes could be planned more easily there. Suicide bids – officially described as self-mutilation – were therefore severely punished. The Ministry of Justice was quick to issue a complete denial of this claim.[100] Yet the GIP's fourth and last pamphlet reproduces a document smuggled out of La Santé: it is a summons ordering a prisoner to appear before a disciplinary hearing because he had slashed his left arm.[101]

Prison suicides soon became a matter for widespread concern, and were the subject of a public meeting organised by the Mouvement d'Action Judiciaire in November. The meeting, attended by GIP members, *magistrats*, lawyers and former prisoners, was a good example of how Foucault and the GIP were able to work with professional groups involved with the penal-legal system. Chaired by Jean-Jacques de Félice, a lawyer who had resigned from Pleven's commission of inquiry into the demand for political status, the meeting drew an audience of between two and three hundred. Foucault and Mauriac were both present, together with Gilles and Fanny Deleuze.

Although serious, the meeting did have its moments of hilarity, most of them provoked by a transvestite from FHAR (Front Homosexuel d'Action Révolutionnaire, a gay liberation group founded in 1971) who interrupted an exchange about the role of judges by commenting in camp tones that they too wore *robes*, meaning both 'robes' and 'dresses'. The gay issue was also raised in rather different terms by references to the case of Gérard Grandmontagne, a twenty-five-year-old drug-user jailed for dealing as a result of police entrapment. Although he had been diagnosed as a suicide risk, he was put into the *mitard* for having committed 'homosexual acts' in Fresnes. The result was predictable, and he hanged himself with a length of flex torn from a light fitting.[102] Understandably, he became something of a martyr for FHAR, and discussion of the case threatened to dominate the whole meeting.

Asked to speak on behalf of the GIP, Foucault refused to be drawn, and simply said that while they knew about Grandmontagne, they knew little about the other twenty-seven suicides that had taken place in the course of the year, and appealed for more information about them. At the beginning of the meeting, Foucault had been laughing and joking with Deleuze. He was now very serious, and patiently answering questions from unknown participants.[103]

At five in the morning of 29 November, Bontems and Buffet were guillotined for the murder of the nurse and warder in Clairvaux. Their case had been heard in June and had been surrounded by controversy, not least because the court's deliberations had been broadcast to the crowds in the Palais de Justice's waiting room through loudspeakers. Bontems had been armed only with an Opinel, a cheap pocket knife with a three-inch blade, on which no blood was found, and the jury found that he had not killed either of the hostages. He was, however, found guilty of 'complicity' with Buffet and was sentenced to death. Many observers concluded that the court had been swayed by the argument of Buffet, who claimed that his accomplice must take his share of responsibility and who seemed determined that Bontems should go to the guillotine with him.[104]

Like many people, Foucault was convinced that Bontems would be pardoned by Pompidou, who was on record as being opposed to the death penalty.[105] He was wrong, and the pardon never came. In a virulent article in *Le Nouvel Observateur*, Foucault argued that Pompidou had taken a calculated political decision. If only Buffet had been executed, the death machine would probably have jammed and

Pompidou would have had the unenviable honour of being the last president to have put it in motion. At least part of the responsibility for Bontems's death would be attributed to Buffet, which reduced the presidential responsibility. The execution of Bontems for 'complicity' served as a warning to all prisoners by introducing the principle of collective responsibility and guilt. More generally, Foucault argued that the guillotine was merely the visible symbol of a system governed by death. The possibility of death, especially by suicide, was inherent in any prison sentence. Life sentences and the death sentence meant the same thing: 'When you are certain of never getting out, what is there left to do? Except risk death in order to save your life, risk your life even though you may die. That is what Buffet and Bontems did.' Foucault ended by accusing the prison system of murder.[106]

Although its front cover gives the date '1972', *Suicides de prison* in fact appeared at the beginning of January 1973. The opening section lists the thirty-two suicides that occurred in 1972, adding that, given that they were based on death certificates signed by prison doctors, they might not be entirely accurate; this may explain the discrepancy between the GIP's figures and those given by Chesnais. One quarter of the suicide victims were immigrants, and the majority were in their twenties. A series of 'case-histories' follows. They are almost clinically bleak:

> Fleury-Mérogis, 27 March 1972. Saïd Bleid, aged 19. Algerian, family resident in France. Placed by a judge in the Foyer des Epinettes [a halfway house for young workers facing criminal charges]. Arrested; the warden of the foyer refuses to take him back on his release from prison. Deemed to be without any fixed abode, he is deported. Having no family ties in Algeria, he comes back to France. Arrested and threatened with deportation. Hangs himself.[107]

The title makes telling use of the conjunction *de*: these are not suicides which simply happen to occur in prison. They are caused by the prison system: the prison's suicides.

The most moving section of the pamphlet reproduces the prison letters of 'H.M.', a petty criminal with a record going back to his teens, when he was sentenced to youth custody for stealing sweets. Remanded in prison on drug charges (he had sold opium to a plain-clothes officer posing as an addict) in the summer of 1972, H.M. was, like Grandmontagne, put in the *mitard* for committing 'homosexual acts'. He too hanged himself. The letters, written under the influence of tranquillisers, range from requests for a copy of Sartre's *Saint Genet* to a discussion of the anti-psychiatry of Laing and Cooper. H.M. talks of taking up yoga, of his old fantasy of going to India, discusses the psychotherapy he is undergoing, and describes making a picture frame decorated with slogans about love borrowed from John Lennon. There is no mention of physical escape, but the desire to flee to some other realm is obvious throughout. The letters are accompanied by an unsigned commentary which is almost certainly by Foucault. It ends thus:

> What is on trial is not only a social system in general, with its exclusions and condemnations, but all the provocations – deliberate and personified – thanks to which the system functions and ensures its order, thanks to which it manufactures those it excludes and condemns in accordance with a policy, the policy of Power, the police and the administration. A certain number of people are directly and personally responsible for the death of this prisoner.[108]

Suicides de prison was published jointly by the GIP, the Comité d'Action des Prisonniers and the Association pour la Défense des Droits des Détenus, and by the time it appeared, the GIP had effectively ceased to exist. The CAP, founded in November 1972, was largely the creation of the charismatic Serge Livrozet, who had been one of those involved in the Melun protest movement. Like the GIP, the CAP had no formal membership and was held together primarily by the forceful personality of its founder, a former burglar who turned to writing and political activism after his release. In Livrozet's view, the GIP had shown the way, and it was now up to the recently released prisoners in the GIP to organise themselves and to continue the revolts that had begun behind the walls and on the rooftops.[109] The stated objective of the CAP, which was to survive until 1980, was the constant improvement of the lot of prisoners both during and after their incarceration.

Given that the GIP had always claimed to be providing prisoners with a means of expression and not to be speaking on their behalf or in their place, its self-effacement was now a logical development. Its disappearance may also have been the result of political and personal exhaustion. Danièle Rancière, at least, admits to having breathed a sigh of relief when the GIP was dissolved, and cannot have been alone in finding two years of close involvement with prisoners and their families a tiring, and ultimately stifling, experience. The break-up of Secours Rouge in the summer of 1972 must also have robbed the GIP of at least some of its natural constituency. French Maoism, and the Gauche Prolétarienne in particular, was entering a period of crisis that was soon to lead to its demise. Foucault's involvement with the prison question was not over, but the moment of the GIP itself had passed by the end of 1972.

The ADDD was established at Foucault's suggestion, though he took little part in its activities. Unlike the GIP, which had no formal status in law, it was a legally constituted and registered association founded to act on behalf of prisoners and to ensure that loss of liberty was the only sanction they suffered. Its creation was also in part a response to the wishes of prisoners' families, who understandably feared that their legitimate concerns might be exploited by too close an alliance with the *gauchiste* tendencies within the GIP.[110] Its committee was eminently respectable and very prestigious, including, as it did, Dominique Eluard, the widow of the poet, Claude Mauriac and Gilles Deleuze. Its honorary president was Vercors, the author of *Le Silence de la mer*, perhaps the most famous of all literary expressions of the wartime Resistance. ('Vercors' was the pseudonym of Jean Bruller; it was taken from the mountainous region which saw some of the most tragic and heroic episodes in the history of the Resistance.)

Largely as a result of the work of the GIP, the prison issue had been placed on the public and political agenda, much more so than in either Britain or the USA, where no comparable group ever succeeded in organising large-scale actions outside the walls of prisons.[111] In their different ways, the ADDD and the CAP continued its work, but, as *Le Monde* was to note, Foucault's leadership was sorely missed.[112]

12

THE PROFESSOR MILITANT

THE GIP was Foucault's primary political preoccupation from 1971 to the beginning of 1973. It was not his sole preoccupation. At times, he seemed to be active everywhere at once, taking part in demonstrations against the continuing war in Vietnam and, at a more local level, against racism in France and threats to immigrants.[1] He could be found in strange places and was occasionally seen wielding a broom in houses squatted by immigrant families. He could be seen distributing CAP leaflets on the *grands boulevards* with Livrozet and others.[2] Yet Foucault was not always where he might have been expected to be.

When an attempt was made to establish a group which would do for psychiatric hospitals what the GIP had done for prisons, Foucault was an obvious person to be contacted. He went with Robert Castel to an initial meeting which drew some two hundred people – ex-patients, anti-psychiatry enthusiasts and a variety of leftists – to a church hall in the fourteenth *arrondissement* in late 1971. The meeting was stormy and devoted to violent and often very personal attacks on named individuals and institutions. Foucault and Castel, who describes the atmosphere as *bordelique* ('shambolic'), listened in silence and soon reached the conclusion that nothing positive could be done in cooperation with these 'ultra-*gauchistes*'.[3] A GIA (Groupe d'Information sur les Asiles) was indeed founded, and led a shadowy existence for years, but it was founded and functioned without any help from Foucault.

He was rather more actively involved in the GIS (Groupe d'Information sur la Santé; 'Health Information Group'), at least in its early days. With six other members, he took part in round-table discussions which led to the production of a manifesto in late 1972: 'Our objective is not to form an interdisciplinary group which could merge with other practitioners of different sciences, but to challenge the division between scientific knowledge and day-to-day practice, between manual and intellectual labour.'[4] The GIS has left few documentary traces of its existence, but was involved in campaigns to investigate and denounce lead poisoning in a Lyon factory, in the denunciation of the profit motive in the drugs industry and in attacks on the oppressive use of forms of knowledge by doctors.[5]

As a result of his involvement with the GIP, Foucault inevitably became involved in one of the classic manifestations of French, or rather Parisian, politics: the signing of political petitions and open letters. In its modern form, the practice is normally seen as dating back to the Dreyfus affair, but as a recent study makes clear, the first recognisable petition signed by massed intellectuals was in fact a protest against the construction of the Eiffel Tower in 1887.[6] Classically, the petition is an open letter with appended signatures published as a paid advertisement in the daily press, Le Monde and, later, Libération being the loci classici. Signing petitions and collecting signatures are delicate operations; no one wishes to be found in the wrong political company. 'Who has already signed?' and 'Who is being asked to sign?' are the questions which are immediately asked. Petitions represent a knowing exploitation of the cultural capital or visibility of the signatories; Foucault's signature was obviously 'worth' much more than that of an unknown novelist. They also have the effect of confirming the status of the signatory; he or she becomes more of an intellectual by the very act of giving a signature. There is, of course, also the danger that signing too many petitions might devalue the individual's signature by making it appear that he or she was an indiscriminate supporter of totally heterogeneous causes. Sartre and Marguerite Duras, both prolific signers of petitions and protests, often ran that risk. A historian of the 'intellectual' in France summarises the three main assumptions behind the classic petition as follows: intellectuals have the right to create a public scandal; they have the right to unite to give their protests more weight; they have the right to use their academic qualifications as a symbolic form of power.[7]

Foucault's view of petitions in general was not particularly sanguine. In most cases, he signed them because pressure had been brought to bear by friends. Asked by a journalist on the weekly Nouvelles littéraires what he thought of petitions, he sighed and replied: 'Signing everything, or signing nothing, it all comes down to the same.' He did, he went on, sign, but 'only when the life or freedom of an individual is at stake'.[8] That statement is not strictly accurate, but it does indicate a certain selectivity. At times, the requests to sign petitions became so regular that evasive action became necessary. Foucault's telephone number was never a particularly closely guarded secret and he refused to buy an answering machine on the grounds that it would have forced him to return calls. Friends had to use a code, letting the phone ring, hanging up and then calling again. Alternatively, Defert would answer, telling callers that this was the number for today's petitions; requests to sign next week's should be addressed elsewhere.[9] In 1979, Foucault expressed the forlorn hope that the publication of his comments in *Les Nouvelles littéraires* would result in his being asked to sign fewer petitions; he claimed, no doubt with some slight exaggeration, that he was asked to sign one almost every day.[10]

The first petitions signed by Foucault concerned the war in Vietnam: a protest against the threat that the dykes of North Vietnam would be bombed (*Le Monde*, 9–10 July 1972) and a collective statement from French scientists and research workers denouncing the aggressive use of modern technology by US forces (*Le Monde*, 23 December 1972). He also endorsed an appeal on behalf of the Palestinian people (*Le Monde*, 14–15 January 1973). Opposition to the war in Vietnam was a *sine qua non* and solidarity with Palestine was also a popular cause in the circles in which Foucault was moving, and his endorsement of such protests shows little more than a general commitment to positions that were very widely held.

His signing of petitions does, however, indicate a certain incoherence in Foucault's views on the role of the intellectual. Although he consciously rejected the notion of a 'universal intellectual' – the prototype being the Zola of *J'Accuse* (1898) – the petitions he signed are inevitably couched in the language of that very universal intellectual. Many of Foucault's criticisms of the universal intellectual are directed against Sartre, but Zola remained the classic example. As Foucault told a Japanese journalist in 1978, it was not because he was a miner that Zola wrote *Germinal*.[11]

In practice, Foucault often went against his own stated principles. Early in 1973, for instance, he lent his name to a Third Worldist journal which dealt mainly with North Africa and the struggles of Polisario in Western Sahara, and agreed to act as its nominal editor. *Nouvelles Afrique-Asie*, which rapidly changed its name to *Zone des tempêtes*, published only three issues in the spring and summer of 1973 and then folded.[12] Foucault's nominal editorship, like Sartre's editorship of *La Cause du peuple*, was a classic example of the use of intellectual power to protect the right to political protest, but Foucault was no more a North African guerrilla than Zola was a miner. He was a professor at the Collège de France, and was consciously exploiting the prestige that conferred upon him. Foucault's visibility and his constant solicitation by various left-wing groups meant that there was a danger of overcommitment and dissipation of his considerable energy. On the whole he resisted the temptation to be drawn into too many issues and was selective about his commitments. A number of those issues were dramatic and implied a very physical involvement.

The case of Alain Jaubert added weight to Foucault's claim that no one was safe from arrest. On the afternoon of Saturday 29 May 1971, Jaubert, a science correspondent on the *Nouvel Observateur* and a lecturer at Vincennes, left the Pub Poster, a restaurant in the place Clichy, where he had just had a meal with his wife and family. There was a heavy police presence in the area, as a demonstration in solidarity with the people of Martinique had been called by a West Indian student organisation. The demonstration had just dispersed peacefully, but police squads were actively breaking up groups of demonstrators in the streets around the Barbès area. As Jaubert and his family crossed the rue de Clignancourt, they came across a man bleeding from a head wound; he subsequently proved to have been expelled from the demonstration by the stewards because he was carrying weapons. Jaubert and others helped him into a nearby *pharmacie* for first aid. The police emergency services were called, and the injured man was dragged roughly into a van. Jaubert, a slightly built man who wore glasses, approached the police, showed his press card, and said that he had seen the incident and was prepared to accompany the man to hospital. The police made no objection and Jaubert climbed in. The official version of what happened next was given in a press release from the Préfecture de Police:

> As the injured man was about to be taken to hospital, a man appeared and asked to accompany him, claiming that he knew him and wanted to help him. The police officers agreed and allowed the individual who had intervened to get into the van. This was M. Alain Jaubert. After about 200 metres he became very agitated, insulted the officers by calling them 'swine' and 'SS', and then, taking advantage of the momentary inattention of the officers, who were busy with the injured man, he opened the van door, leaped from the moving vehicle and injured himself as he fell. Policemen in a second van which was following the first tried to help M. Jaubert to his feet. He struggled violently, threw punches causing injuries to three police officers.[13]

Jaubert was taken to the Lariborisière hospital, then to the Hôtel-Dieu, placed under arrest and held for forty-eight hours. Charges of resisting arrest and assault were immediately filed against him by an examining magistrate.

Jaubert denied the official version of the story completely and said that as he tried to calm the injured man, one of the policemen suddenly struck him without provocation. The *brigadier* told his subordinates to 'throw him out'. Jaubert was butted in the stomach and propelled out of the moving vehicle. He fell full length in the road, and found himself surrounded by about fifteen policemen. One of them broke his spectacles. He was beaten and dragged into the second van, where the beating continued. His protestations that he had done nothing and that he was a journalist merely provoked more violence. His trousers were removed and his testicles were punched and twisted. Jaubert was convinced that he was going to die, or at best be castrated. When he was finally taken to an emergency ward, a nurse phoned his wife, Marie-José, who immediately began to contact the press.[14]

No one in the world of journalism found it difficult to believe that a colleague had been badly beaten. Relations between the police and the press were at a very low ebb. Only weeks earlier, the *Nouvel Observateur*'s Michèle Manceaux had been arrested at six in the morning by four policemen. Her flat was searched, documents were taken and she was held in a Latin Quarter police station for six hours. No warrant was produced and no charges were brought. The reason for the arrest was apparently that her car had been seen outside the Renault factory in Flins, where Maoist groups were active and where she was researching her *Les Maos en France*. For weeks, Claude Angeli, a reporter on *Politique Hebdo*, had been followed by police officers who refused to identify themselves.[15] It was common knowledge that the police used forged press cards to gather information for their files; earlier in the year, an undercover officer of the Renseignements Généraux section was unmasked at the University of Aix-en-Provence. He was carrying a forged press card. Other forged cards had been found at the universities of Vincennes, Nanterre and Grenoble.[16]

What was now known as the 'Jaubert affair' fuelled the anger of the press corps still further. On 4 June, an unprecedented demonstration took place as journalists marched from *Le Figaro*'s offices on the Champs-Elysées to the Ministry of the Interior in the place Beauvau, calling for Marcellin's resignation. For once, *Le Figaro* and *La Cause du peuple* were united.

On 1 June the lawyers Henri Leclerc and Pascale Legendre filed charges on Jaubert's behalf; he accused the police of assault and false arrest. The regular press conference given by the prime minister's secretary of state was interrupted on 2 June by questions from the hundreds of journalists present, including the formidable and highly influential Jean Daniel. The secretary of state, Léo Hamon, was lost for a response, and tried somewhat unconvincingly to argue that the matter was before the courts and justice should be allowed to take its course.[17] On the same day, a commission of inquiry was set up by a number of intellectuals acting in collaboration with the Comité de Défense de la Presse et des Journalistes: its members were Denis Langlois, lawyer and author of *Les Dossiers noirs de la Police française*, which was at the time the object of a police prosecution for libel;[18] Dr Daniel Timsit, Claude Angeli, Michèle Manceaux, a Protestant pastor called Cazalis, Pierre Vidal-Naquet and Michel Foucault. Its object was to gather eye-witness accounts of what had happened on 29 May and to publish its findings in an attempt to establish the responsibilities of those involved. At the inaugural press conference Foucault declared that police savagery had reached a new threshold. Jaubert had been attacked because he was a journalist; journalists were loathed by the police because they saw things and talked about them. By bringing charges against Jaubert, the examining magistrate was covering up for the police. Foucault ended by quoting article 15 of the 1958 Constitution, which defines society's right to ask any public servant to justify his actions.[19]

The Jaubert Commission was to have one more member. At the initial press conference, Foucault had noticed the presence of Claude Mauriac, who was representing *Le Figaro*. At the suggestion of Maurice Clavel, Foucault telephoned Mauriac to ask him if he would be prepared to help with the inquiry. The phone call was to lead to a long and seemingly unlikely friendship. Mauriac, the son of the novelist François Mauriac and an acclaimed novelist himself, had in his youth been a secretary to de Gaulle and was not known for his leftist sympathies. Claude Mauriac is also a diarist. The relevant volumes of his journals provide the most detailed account of Foucault's activities during these crowded years. Well-connected in both the literary and the political worlds, Mauriac was to become a close friend, and was a frequent guest in the white apartment in the rue de Vaugirard. The invitations were returned, and Foucault and Defert often dined at Mauriac's home on the Ile de la Cité, where he received guests in a flat crowded with books, paintings and photographs and where pride of place was given to a superb white-on-black drawing by Jean Cocteau.

On 12 June, Mauriac went to 285 rue de Vaugirard, where the door was opened by Jaubert.

And there, in that sunlit apartment on the eighth floor, among these unknown people, some of whom are so well known, including our host, a professor at the Collège de France and a philosopher of such importance, sitting near me on the couch and then, when there were too many people, on the floor to my right – young, suntanned, his head naked, shaven, polished (and not far away from him Gilles Deleuze sat silently, another prestigious philosopher – long grey hair, a worn, tired face . . .) . . . I suddenly had the impression that I had gone through the curtain in our society that separates those on whose behalf the state uses its might, and the rest.[20]

The inquiry got under way. A bus driver who had been on the scene was traced and questioned, as was an Algerian who claimed to have seen a bleeding man who might have been Jaubert being taken into the hospital. The search for that witness took Foucault into the Goutte d'Or area for the first time; by the end of the year, it would be a familiar place. It proved to be a futile search. When he was eventually found, the witness was certainly willing to talk to Mauriac and Foucault, but they had the distinct impression that he was saying what they wanted to hear.

The evidence of the bus driver proved to be crucial. He had seen the police van pull away from the rue de Clignancourt at 5.40; the records of the Larib01sière hospital showed that Jaubert had been admitted at 6.15. It took Mauriac and Timsit exactly five minutes to make the same journey. On 18 June, M. Paolini, the *chef de cabinet* of the Prefect of Police, had stated on television that the Police-secours vehicle had reached the hospital within seven minutes. The missing half-hour added to the veracity of Jaubert's accusations. The traffic had not been heavy and there was no plausible explanation of why a police vehicle should have taken so long to make such a short journey.

Regrettably, none of the people interviewed was willing to be identified or appear in court and it was apparent that the police had been busy in the rue de Clignancourt. A number of people had been seen to watch the police beating Jaubert from their windows; those who dared to open their doors to strangers now claimed to have been away from home on 29 May.[21] Foucault was uncomfortably reminded of the Occupation, and of the French population's opinion of the Gestapo; like Mauriac, he was convinced that the police had become a state within the state.[22]

Foucault and his fellow investigators presented their case to the press on 21 June. In his opening statement, Foucault declared that the Jaubert case represented a serious crisis, and that the role of the police was a central element in that crisis. A deliberate campaign of disinformation had been organised by the police and the Ministry of the Interior. The truth about the Jaubert affair had not been difficult to establish, and the evidence had been gathered in the space of two days. The examining magistrate, in contrast, had undertaken no investigations and had simply taken the police at their word.[23] Nine days later, an open letter signed by Deleuze, Foucault, Langlois, Mauriac and Denis Perrier-Daville effectively accused Paolini of having lied on television.[24] The ensuing silence from the ministry was eloquent.

The epilogue came in April 1973, when the police who had assaulted Jaubert were given suspended sentences of thirteen months. Jaubert himself was fined 500 francs for assaulting the police.[25]

In many ways Jaubert's experience was a fairly banal example of police brutality. It replicated the arbitrary exercise of power which Foucault so frequently saw in his work with the GIP. In the eyes of many in the Gauche Prolétarienne, the answer to this abuse of power by the police was 'people's justice'. The notion of 'people's justice' was initially promoted as the result of a mining disaster that occurred early in 1970, when sixteen men died in a methane explosion in the Number 6 Pit at Hénin-Liétard. The accident immediately provoked a violent response from local people and their political supporters, and the colliery offices were fire-bombed. Towards the end of the year, a people's court was organized in the nearby town of Lens, with Sartre as one of its leading figures. Perhaps predictably, it ruled that the nationalised Compagnie des Houllères and the mine engineers responsible for the safety of the Number 6 Pit were jointly guilty of murder because safety had been sacrificed to profit. In its published conclusions the court stated, in a parody of the opening words of the Penal Code, that 'Nul n'est censé ignorer la loi du peuple.[26]

Foucault himself had no involvement whatsoever in the Lens court, but it did provide Defert with the initial inspiration that led to the establishment of the GIP. The issue of people's justice was also to result in a set-piece debate between Foucault and major representatives of the Gauche Prolétarienne at the beginning of 1972. In the meantime there were attempts to organise people's courts to deal with other issues in Paris, Grenoble and Clermont-Ferrand, the most spectacular being the attempt to put the police on trial in Paris in June 1971. None of these planned trials actually took place; the projects were abandoned in the face of government opposition and in view of the high level of violence that would probably have ensued had they gone ahead. Not without a sense of humour, the organisers admitted that there was little point in a people's court sitting *in camera*. The projects did, however, serve to put the notion of popular justice on a certain political agenda. Again, Foucault was not directly involved in the trials, but publicly associated himself with the position taken by the Ligue des Droits de l'Homme and, more surprisingly, the Trotskyist Ligue Communiste Révolutionnaire. A statement attributed to Foucault and the former organisation pointed out that justice and power were inseparable; courts which could reach meaningful decisions could only be established by those who held power, and in the present circumstances the criteria establishing precisely who was on trial and who was the judge were sadly ill-defined. The model of the commission of inquiry used during the Jaubert affair appeared preferable.[27]

The existence of a clandestine armed wing of the Gauche Prolétarienne suggested a possible shift to terrorism and to attacks by the New People's Resistance on the bourgeoisie that was 'occupying' France. The potential for violence could also be channelled in other directions. One particular incident helped to focus Foucault's attention on the issue of people's justice and, according to Defert, to raise serious doubts in his mind about just where the GP was heading.

In the autumn of 1971, the GP reached the conclusion that Moussa Fofana, who had been given responsibilities in the north and who was living underground in Belgium, was a traitor and a police informer. Fofana was given to understand that the armed struggle was about to begin and was lured into a cave which he had been erroneously convinced contained a munitions dump. His companions pulled guns and informed him that he had been condemned to death by the justice of the people. He was then told that the sentence had been suspended, and was advised to disappear. The guns were not loaded.

According to *La Cause du peuple*, only people's justice in the true sense could hand down and carry out such a sentence; the demands of clandestinity conflicted with the need for publicity inherent in people's courts, which remained an empty form, a hope for the future.[28] Nothing was made of the fact that Fofana was one of the GP's very few black cadres.

Foucault discussed the Fofana case again and again with the leaders of the GP, and readily agreed to a more formal exchange of views which could be published. His main interlocutor was 'Pierre Victor'. This was the *nom de guerre* of Benny Lévy who, in December 1972, became Sartre's

last secretary. A *normalien*, Victor was one of the founders of the GP and
its principal ideologue; his emergence as a Maoist warlord was
preceded by a long immersion in the complex world of student politics.
In 1971, his headquarters were in ENS in the rue d'Ulm, which he
rarely left. He was born in Egypt in 1945 into a Jewish family which was
forced into political exile; he was stateless and had yet to gain French
nationality. The leader of the GP was thus forced by his own
circumstances to avoid the violent clashes his group instigated, as his
arrest would have certainly led to his deportation.

The debate was taped and transcribed for a special issue of *Les Temps
Modernes* coordinated by a group from the GP and entitled *Nouveau
Fascisme, nouvelle démocratie*. It was in fact something of a dialogue of the
deaf. Foucault was, in his own words, primarily interested in looking at
the 'history of the juridicial state apparatus',[29] whereas Victor and his
comrade 'Gilles' were intent upon defending their dogmatic version of
Maoism. At times it lapsed into an almost grotesque comedy, as when
Foucault asked what Victor understood by the 'ideology of the
proletariat'. He received the predictable reply 'Mao Tse-Tung
thought', and commented: 'Right. You'll grant me that what the
majority of the French proletariat thinks is not Mao Tse-Tung
thought, and that it is not necessarily a revolutionary ideology.'[30]

Foucault's basic hypothesis was that a court is not a natural
expression of people's justice, and that the historic function of courts
had always been to master and strangle people's justice by reinserting it
into the institutions characteristic of a state apparatus. His primary
example of what he understood by people's justice was supplied by the
September massacres of 1792, when prisoners in the jails of Paris were
killed by the revolutionary troops before they marched off to Valmy,
the justification being that traitors could not be allowed to live and to
threaten the revolution from within at a time of extreme danger. For
Foucault the massacres represented 'at least a first approximation of an
act of popular justice; a response to oppression which was strategically
useful and politically necessary'.[31] The emergence of actual courts, in
contrast, signalled the appearance of an institutionalised division
between 'the ruling bourgeoisie' and the 'Parisian pleb'.

Foucault's insistence on talking about the French Revolution was a
source of some annoyance to his interlocutors, who constantly tried to
bring the discussion back to China, about which Foucault admitted he
knew very little. Nor was Foucault's position on more contemporary
matters greatly appreciated. He argued that effective forms of people's
justice had yet to be invented: 'The act of justice whereby one replies to

the class enemy cannot be entrusted to a sort of instantaneous spontaneity which has not been thought through, which is not integrated into an overall struggle. Forms for the need to reply, which certainly exists among the masses, have to be elaborated through discussion and information.'[32] The danger was that those potential forms would be coopted or recuperated by a state apparatus.

It is only towards the end of the long discussion (the transcript is over thirty pages long) that the question of Lens actually arises, and the Fofana affair is never touched upon. Foucault argues that the people's court had not been a 'counter-justice', but agrees that it had played an important role in supplying information to combat 'the bourgeois court' which had tried those who fire-bombed the colliery offices. Even so, a conversation reported by Mauriac suggests that Foucault may have conceded the point for emotional rather than political reasons: 'Out of weakness. To keep Victor happy. Out of exhaustion.'[33] In more general terms, however, he insisted that: 'I don't think there can be any counter-justice in the strict sense of the term. Because the function of justice, functioning as a state apparatus, is inevitably to divide the masses. The idea of a proletarian counter-justice is therefore contradictory; it cannot exist.' For Victor, Foucault's position was 'totally idealist'.[34]

Foucault's position in this debate was in some ways confused and ambiguous. Although no Maoist, he did use some Maoist terminology, simply because of the need to engage with the discourse of his interlocutors. His use of the notion of a 'state apparatus' reflected a reading of Althusser's 1970 paper on ideology and ideological state apparatuses,[35] but he was soon to reject completely the concept of 'state apparatus' and even that of ideology. The notion of the 'pleb' – a term which was to take on considerable importance, and a rather different resonance, in the writings of the *nouveaux philosophes* and in the work of Glucksmann in particular – clearly owed something to the Marxist concept of the lumpenproletariat, but it also derived from the description of the mechanisms of exclusion and marginalisation provided by *Histoire de la folie* ten years earlier. The 'pleb' included the 'dangerous individuals' who have to be removed from society; the penal system divides them from the proletariat by stigmatising them as deviant or criminal, so as to prevent them from being the 'spearhead of movements of popular resistance'.[36] Foucault repeatedly avoided the question posed by Victor: is the contradiction between prisoners (or the pleb) and the proletariat, the major contradiction within the people? The tension between Victor's Maoism and Foucault's apologia for the pleb was palpable, reflected their differing views of the prisoners' movements, and remained unresolved.

Foucault's views on the possibility or otherwise of 'people's justice' did not evolve in a vacuum, but reflected the way in which he was reacting to specific events. One event in particular had a significant effect. In the spring and summer of 1972, Bruay-en-Artois, a declining mining town 213 kilometres to the north of Paris and some forty kilometres from Lille, became the theatre for a drama which gripped the whole of France, Foucault included.[37] On 6 April, the body of sixteen-year-old Brigitte Dewevre was found on a patch of waste ground. She had been strangled and partly stripped. Her breasts were badly cut and mutilated, but there was no indication of penetration. A post-mortem revealed that her wounds had been inflicted after her death.

The girl was the daughter of a local miner and had grown up virtually in the shadow of the spoil heaps that dominated the skyline. The waste ground where she was found was bordered by a tall hedge beyond which stood the house of Monique Mayeur, the owner of a furniture store and the fiancée of Pierre Leroy, a prominent notary and member of the local Rotary Club. Suspicion immediately fell upon Leroy: his car had been seen in the area, as had a man answering his description, and his mother admitted to the police that she had washed two of his suits in ammonia water rather than sending them to the cleaners. The hedge had recently been cut low opposite the point where the body was found. Acting on the basis of circumstantial evidence, Henri Pascal, the examining magistrate assigned to the case, had Leroy committed to Béthune prison pending investigations.

The murder polarised the small town and quickly took on political overtones. Neither Leroy nor Mayeur was popular; he had been involved in dubious land transactions made on behalf of the Compagnie des Houllères, and she had a reputation for being a hard woman to deal with. What was more important, they represented the local bourgeoisie. In an area where wages where low and unemployment high, they could afford to eat expensively. Leroy owned a boat. Leroy was also apparently well known in the local bars and brothels, and was said to have a taste for sadistic practices. The growing conviction in the community was that Brigitte had been killed in some sadistic orgy and that her lacerations had been caused as her body was dragged through the hedge and across the wall, which was studded with safety glass. In short, the innocent daughter of a miner had been brutally murdered by a bourgeois sadist, presumably with the collusion of his fiancée.

When the Rotary Club closed ranks and began to demand Leroy's release from preventive detention, the class dimension became even more pronounced. Mayeur's house was stoned by a crowd calling for vengeance and howling for Leroy to be castrated or dragged through the streets behind a speeding car. A placard soon appeared on the waste ground. It bore the legend: 'On this spot, Brigitte Dewevre, the daughter of a miner, was murdered by the bourgeoisie of Bruay.'

Bruay had for about two years been a focus for the activities of the Gauche Prolétarienne, which had had some success thanks to the work of an 'Anti-Silicosis Committee', and had made some political inroads in an area traditionally dominated by the PCF. One of the most prominent Maoists was François Ewald, a young and energetic philosophy teacher at the local *lycée*. Initially, the GP took little or no interest in the murder, seeing it simply as a criminal matter with no political significance. That view soon changed. The GP was, as Ewald puts it, convinced of the necessity of 'being where the masses are', and the 'masses' were certainly interested in the case.[38] Its initial hesitations gone, the GP became deeply involved. The appearance of the placard was probably the work of some of its members. A Comité pour la Vérité et la Justice was organised on Ewald's initiative, with support from both the GP and local members of Secours Rouge.

It was not unusual for the GP to attempt to exploit situations it had not created, but the unusual feature here was that it found itself supporting a judge who was well known for his belief in the benefits of preventive detention, a practice which most of the left found abominably repressive. Pascal was coming under pressure either to release Leroy or to bring charges, and his refusal to do so brought him into conflict with his superiors in the prosecutor's department.

On 1 May, *La Cause du peuple* appeared with the banner headline: 'And now they are killing our children'. The murder was seen as an extension of the violent exploitation the miners had suffered for more than a century, as an act of social cannibalism by a man rich enough to eat 800 grammes of meat in a single meal, a man whose woman-friend was affluent enough to eat crayfish. *La Cause du peuple*'s coverage struck a note of moral outrage: 'The main problem is not that the filthy life of some bourgeois has been seen in broad daylight; they can spy it out, they can smell it. Besides, these bourgeois morals, these foul orgies stink too highly; the miners don't like to talk about them; it's shame enough that they exist.'[39] The paper was more than ready to justify the bloodthirsty calls for the death or castration of Leroy.

Bruay was now the centre for intense media attention. Journalists described the brick-built houses of the *corons*[40] in terms which could have come straight from Zola, to the annoyance of many local people, who were extremely proud of their flowers, vegetable plots and spotless interiors. It also drew a number of celebrity visitors, including Clavel and Sartre, who was quick to warn against the danger of lynch mobs. For Sartre, popular justice implied the assumption that Leroy was innocent until proven guilty; the collective reply fom *La Cause du peuple* was that nothing should obstruct the people's spontaneous instinct for justice.[41]

In June, Foucault and Defert also drove to Bruay to see what was happening. Although he had taught in Lille, Foucault had not previously visited the mining regions and was surprised to find that the *coron* was so separate from the 'bourgeois town' that it was a ghetto 'in the grey colours of the north'.[42] He visited the site of the crime, noting with a surprising botanical expertise that the hedge was not of hawthorn, as most reports had it, but of hornbeam, and rapidly reached the conclusion that Leroy was indeed guilty. In conversation with Claude Mauriac later in the month, he defended the 'outside interference' of the GP and others on the grounds that, without it, Pascal would have given in to pressure and Leroy would have been freed. 'This is the first time that the bourgeoisie of the Nord, which has always been protected, has ceased to be protected, and that is why what has happened in Bruay-en-Artois is so important.'[43]

Foucault visited Bruay briefly – he spent only a day there – and he may have been helped to his conclusion by the fact that his host and guide was François Ewald. Ewald insists, however, that Foucault's role should not be overstated, and that he had simply come to see what was happening: 'Basically, Foucault was someone who came to look without saying anything; Sartre spoke without having seen anything.'[44]

Such a dismissive attitude towards Sartre is not unusual on the part of Foucault's associates. In this case, Ewald is probably being over-dismissive. Sartre had in fact visited Bruay in connection with the Lens trial, knew at least something about the area and was already acquainted with Foucault's other main guide.[45] This was André Théret, an old miner and Maoist sympathiser with a long history of political activity and militancy.[46] In a dialogue cited by Gavi, Théret is one of the proponents, identified only by their forenames, of a harsh 'class against class' line, the other being Joseph [Tournel], seen by the GP as a 'model worker'. Ewald, Théret and Tournel were at least in part responsible for the notorious 1 May number of *La Cause du peuple*.

Neither Foucault's own political leanings at this time or his political associates would have been likely to persuade him of the innocence of Leroy. He did not write a single word about the affair, but obviously discussed it with friends.[47] His general view appears to have been that Leroy was the murderer and that the militancy of the mining community and its supporters had succeeded in politicising a sordid crime in an unprecedented way. In later years, he revised that view, admitted to Mauriac in 1976 that he no longer believed in the lawyer's guilt and dismissed with a laugh all the theories he had constructed.[48]

The Bruay murder has never been solved. In July, Pascal was removed from the case and Leroy was freed without any charges being brought. A local teenager confessed to the murder, and then withdrew his confession on the grounds that he had been acting out of bravado. No one has ever been brought to trial for the murder of Brigitte Dewevre.

The affair, or rather *La Cause du peuple*'s coverage of it, came to represent a turning point for the GP. A number of prominent militants – Jean-Pierre Le Dantec, Robert Linhart, Christian Jambet and André Glucksmann – objected violently to the tone and content of the May issue. Le Dantec, in particular, protested about the naivety of coverage which operated with a myth of proletarian moral purity and with crude dichotomies such as 'spotless virginity of miners' children/sexual perversity of members of the Rotary Club'. The protesters were overruled, and dismissed as 'vipers who are poisoning the editorial committee'.[49] Le Dantec immediately realised that he was no longer part of the militant family.

Bruay also revealed some unpleasant truths about proletarian morality, particularly when Théret insisted in the pages of *Les Temps Modernes* that 'all the bourgeois of Béthune are "queers" ', but that 'there are no "queer miners" '.[50]

The next issue of *La Cause* contained what amounted to a call for the lynching of Leroy. According to Pierre Victor, what was happening in Bruay represented 'the beginnings of people's justice, of a justice which, unlike bourgeois justice, does not separate the investigation from the sentence, or the execution of the sentence'.[51] Objections were dismissed with cruel arrogance. When a young woman raised doubts about Leroy's guilt, Serge July, one of the main cadres in the region, replied that she had reservations simply because: 'You are the daughter of a bourgeois, and you're afraid of seeing your father's head on a pike.'[52]

Foucault made no comment on *La Cause du peuple*'s stance at the time, but he was disturbed by the reaction of the local population which, in his view, bordered on the fascistic. Bruay represented an important stage in his retreat from the very notion of people's justice. The retreat was not, however, complete. On the night of 13–14 July, a squatted house in the Paris suburb of Issy-les-Moulineaux was attacked by a mob of some forty men armed with clubs and gas grenades. The squatters were Yugoslav immigrants who were holding a dance with Secours Rouge, their attackers a commando from the nearby Citroën factory organised by the Confédération Française du Travail, a virulently anti-communist 'scab' union whose origins go back to the Vichy period. In the course of the attack, two young women were kidnapped and one was raped several times.

Two of the attackers were captured and badly beaten before being handed over to the police the next day. In a scene reminiscent of the liberation of Paris, they were forced to walk through the streets to the *commissariat* wearing placards reading: 'I am a fascist from the CFT. I belonged to a commando which attacked a dance, wounded five people, kidnapped two girls and raped one of them three times. What should be done with me?'[53]

A statement from 'a certain number of celebrities' was issued to the press, denouncing the aggression, calling for solidarity with its victims and for participation in 'the popular responses that truth and justice demand'. The signatories included Sartre, Pierre Halbwachs representing Secours Rouge, Marguerite Duras, the actress Delphine Seyrig and Foucault, and the reference to 'truth and justice' strongly suggests at least some GP presence behind the scenes. Despite his doubts, Foucault was clearly still prepared to call for and justify acts of people's justice in the summer of 1972.

Searching for the Algerian who had supposedly seen the injured Alain Jaubert being taken into hospital, Foucault had set foot in the Goutte d'Or for the first time. He was now to become quite familiar with it. He was also to renew his acquaintance with Catherine von Bülow, who was active in a local Secours Rouge goup.[54] One of von Bülow's responsibilities at Gallimard was taking care of Jean Genet on his occasional visits to Paris. Given that the writer had no known address and tended to disappear without trace for days on end, this was not the easiest of tasks. Von Bülow was supposed to mother him and take care of his material needs. He was not an easy man to deal with. As von Bülow told Mauriac, she only once succeeded in getting him to talk about his writing. He owned nothing, except the books he was reading, and, once read, they were unceremoniously thrown away.[55] Through von Bülow, Foucault finally met Genet, whose work he greatly admired. There is nothing to suggest that Genet had ever read Foucault, or that he had any intention of doing so. For a short time, there was a certain complicity between the two, but Genet's nomadic tendencies meant that it never developed into a deep friendship.

The area known as the Goutte d'Or is in the eighteenth *arrondissement* and is overlooked by the hills of Montmartre and the Sacré-Coeur. Like Montmartre, the quadrilateral between the boulevard de la Chapelle, the boulevard Barbès, the rue Doudeauville and the rue Max-Dormoy has its place within the urban and literary folklore of Paris. This is where Zola's Nana was born, but by the 1950s it had become an area for immigrants, most of them packed into multi-occupied housing which had not improved, or had even deteriorated, since Nana's day. When Foucault first visited the area with Mauriac, he remarked that it was not the 'medina' he had expected. Nor was it a true ghetto; it was a mixed area remarkable for its poverty rather than for its ethnic homogeneity. By the early seventies, it was estimated that about one fifth of the population was of North African or black African origin. Few of the immigrants owned their property; the majority lived in furnished rooms, small hotels or *immeubles* belonging to the SNCF, a major landlord in the area. Virtually all the local shops and cafés, on the other hand, were immigrant-controlled. Normally quiet during the week, the Goutte d'Or would come to life at weekends, when Algerians and Africans from other parts of Paris, or even from outside the capital, came to shop, gossip and gather in the cafés. The queues that formed outside the brothels on Saturday mornings, calmly ignored by the police, were one of the area's more notorious sights. Foucault had never had any reason to visit that part of town.

The family of fifteen-year-old Djellali Ben Ali was not untypical. He was the eldest of nine children, the son of a labourer who, in 1971, was working for the RER, Paris's new transport system. Overcrowding – the whole family lived in one room in the rue Charbonnière – meant that Djellali had to live with his uncle, M. Djahafi, who had four children himself. Djahafi was a relatively prosperous man who had lived in France since 1948, and the owner of 'Aux tissus et soieries de l'Orient', a draper's at 53 rue de la Goutte d'Or, where the bright colours of the fabrics in the window stood out against the greyness of the street.[56] Djellali had effectively grown up in the street and had a history of involvement in petty crime. He had a reputation for being able to hold his own in a fight, and was typical of the young Algerians who were rapidly becoming the successors to the '*titi parisien*' of legend.

Djellali's uncle's relative prosperity may have made some of his white neighbours jealous. Certainly, relations with Daniel Pigot, who lived in a single room with the building's concierge and their five children, were strained. Djellali became the target of their racist insults, and Pigot soon added threats of violence to his repertoire. At some point at the beginning of October 1972, Pigot – quite legally – acquired a shotgun from a gun shop on the boulevard Barbès. Early in the morning of 27 October, Djellali went out to buy bread and milk for breakfast. Pigot shot him dead on the staircase.[57]

The murder became the area's sole topic of conversation and provoked an influx of white journalists into the Goutte d'Or. Most of their reports expressed horror at the killing, but were tinged with a flavour of exoticism and filled with references to the smell of *merquez*. The murder also attracted the attention of a number of intellectuals, including Foucault, Mauriac, Deleuze, Genet and the filmmaker Michel Drach, who formed an ad hoc Comité Djellali in protest. On 30 October over 2,000 demonstrators marched through the narrow streets with red carnations in their hands. A number of arrests were made, one of those detained being a young woman who was held for thirty hours and eventually sentenced to six weeks' imprisonment, three of them suspended. In her account of her detention, she spoke of having been called an 'Arabs' whore' and of hearing a police officer say that all the 'wogs' – and their white friends – should be machine-gunned.[58] No one found it difficult to believe her claims.

Tension in the area was high, and the police presence heavy. Djellali's uncle was quoted as saying that the Algerian war was starting all over again; and the *quartier* had suffered badly during that war. The cellars of one house in the rue de la Goutte d'Or had been used as a torture chamber by the notoriously vicious *harkis* (members of the French army's 'native auxiliary units'). A committee to clean up the area was currently circulating a leaflet complaining about the 'Harlemisation' of the Goutte d'Or and the excessive concentration of immigrants. On the day of the murder, a petition addressed to the local UDR *député* was circulating, calling for the release of Pigot on bail so as to placate the 'spirit of vengeance'.[59] Another leaflet called for improved street lighting and a strengthened police presence. The comments reported by the woman arrested on 30 October indicate why the last demand was not likely to be appreciated by the nonwhite population. Among the Algerians, grisly rumours were circulating to the effect that corpses had been seen floating in the nearby canal de l'Ourcq. The rumours proved to be unfounded but, only ten years earlier, Algerian corpses had indeed floated in the Seine and it cannot have been difficult to believe such stories.

The Djellali Committee organised two further demonstrations in the Goutte d'Or, on 27 November and 3 December, and began to broaden its concerns. Arguing that the area was under threat from organised racism, it appealed to the white and nonwhite populations to unite. An office was set up and manned in the Salle Saint-Bruno, a hall belonging to the local church (which, confusingly, is in fact dedicated to St Bernard), with the support of Abbé Gallimardet. Sartre let it be known that he was interested in working with the committee, and his offer was somewhat reluctantly accepted by Foucault and Mauriac. His presence was in fact useful. On 27 December, he headed the demonstration, handing out leaflets and occasionally addressing onlookers through a megaphone – which did not prevent him from being virtually inaudible. Orders had clearly been given to the police that Sartre was not to be arrested, and he acted as an efficient 'lightning conductor'.[60] His role was to remain symbolic; Genet successfully persuaded him that he was in no physical state to help man an office.[61] Foucault also spoke, though his need for a megaphone was less than obvious.

His involvement in the Goutte d'Or was intense but sporadic, as his main concern was with the GIP, which obviously took up most of his time. Both demonstrations and the drafting of the appeal were preceded by investigations into the circumstances of Djellali's death and into allegations that a number of young Algerians had been arrested and beaten. The investigations were the work of Mauriac and Foucault, who spent hours in local cafés discussing the situation, often using the services of an Arabic-speaking interpreter. Foucault's one fear was that he would be mistaken for a policeman; he was not, but was – to his amusement – mistaken for Sartre in a restaurant.[62]

As in the GIP, Foucault was happy to work alongside the Maoists of the GP and Secours Rouge, but did not fully share their politics. One meeting in the Goutte d'Or, in particular, gave rise to angry exchanges between the Maoists and a group of local teenagers. According to the latter, the Maoists' slogans were futile: the Maoists had plastered the area with posters bearing Djellali's picture, and had called for vengeance, but had in fact done nothing. Foucault had no sympathy for the subsequent call for the murder of Pigot, but no doubts about the pertinence of their 'radical critique of the contradiction of Maoism, which is always the same: using big words (vengeance in this case) to which there is, and can be, no corresponding reality or action'.[63] In fact, all calls for the punishment of Pigot put Foucault in a difficult position; given that the GIP was 'against prisons', he found he could not even demand his imprisonment'.[64] Nor did his sympathies extend to the representatives of the liberal Mouvement contre le Racisme et pour l'Amitié des Peuples (MRAP), whom he deliberately and even rudely ignored.[65] This was a typical reaction: Mauriac observed that, if Foucault was not interested in what a speaker was saying, he would pointedly read a magazine or talk to whoever was next to him.[66] More generally, his relations with the pro-Palestinian tendency within the GP, which inevitably saw the Goutte d'Or as a potential recruiting ground, were strained by his own pro-Israeli sympathies.

Clearly, not everyone active in the Goutte d'Or was there for the same reasons. Genet, for instance, refused to describe himself as being politically active. His militancy was confined to the black ghettoes of the USA and the refugee camps of Palestine; in France, he was a poet and no more.[67] His presence in the Goutte d'Or must therefore be construed simply as a gesture of pro-Arab solidarity. Mauriac's prime concern was with justice, a notion with little meaning, in the abstract, to Foucault. Foucault himself remained silent on the work in the Goutte d'Or, but the issues raised there certainly intersect with the denunciation of the intolerable that was so basic to all those involved in the GIP.

The intervention in the Goutte d'Or was short-lived and not entirely well considered. Conflicts with the local Palestine committees and the definite possibility that the verbal violence of sections of the local youth would turn to real violence soon persuaded Mauriac and his associates to withdraw. The Djellali Committee was, however, briefly revived in 1977, when Pigot finally came before the courts. He was sentenced to five years in prison, three of them suspended. There were no street demonstrations.[68]

In December 1972, Foucault became involved in events which, though not directly related to the prison issue, did, like the Jaubert and Djellali affairs, raise the question of power and its abuse. They were also to lead to some unpleasant personal encounters with the police. The cause of Mohammed Diab's death was never in doubt: three bullets from a machine gun ended his life in a Versailles police station on Wednesday 29 November 1972. The circumstances surrounding the incident, on the other hand, were a matter for controversy. Earlier in the evening, Diab, a thirty-two-year-old Algerian lorry driver and father of four, had visited his mother, who was seriously ill in a local hospital. He refused to leave the hospital when asked to do so and became more and more agitated. The police were called, assumed that he was drunk and took him to the local *commissariat* for a blood test. Here, his shoes were removed and he was body-searched. Shortly afterwards, three shots were heard and Diab was dead. During a five-hour hearing before an examining magistrate, *sous-brigadier* Marquet insisted that he had acted in self-defence.

According to Marquet, Diab had seized a metal chair, broken windows and knocked out two officers. Their guns fell to the ground and were within Diab's reach. Marquet, for unexplained reasons, was not wearing his regulation handgun, but armed himself with a machine gun from a cupboard. According to Marquet's statement, Diab grabbed the barrel, at which point the gun went off with fatal results.

A very different story was told by Diab's sister, Fatma Sahlioui, and his wife Zara, who had gone of their own accord to the police station and who gave their account to a group of sympathetic academics on 2 and 3 December. They saw Diab being struck and subjected to racist insults by the police. He grabbed a chair in an attempt to defend himself and a scuffle broke out. Marquet picked up the gun and advanced on Diab, who retreated down a corridor before being shot dead at a range of five or six metres.[69]

The case became the subject of wide press coverage, the usual inference being that no white Frenchman would have been treated like this. Diab also became the focus for political action. A statement was prepared by Sartre, and Mauriac and others were asked to sign it. It eventually gathered 136 signatures. Mauriac signed it reluctantly, commenting that the text was too long and that Foucault could say in ten lines what Sartre could scarcely say in ten pages.

The statement finally appeared in *Le Nouvel Observateur* under Sartre's name. Sartre argued at some length that the death of Diab was the inevitable result of the resurgence of racism in the police force since the end of the war in Algeria. A point of no return had been reached; either racism must be crushed, or France must resign itself to living under the 'government of fear' which the terrified bourgeoisie had returned to power in 1968. 'Between 1956 and 1962, we struggled to ensure that victory would remain in Algerian hands. For their sake, but also for our sake: so that the shame of racism would disappear from French thought.'[70] Genet remarked that the fact that the statement had appeared under the name of Sartre alone did nothing to improve it.[71]

Sartre called for 'direct action', and a demonstration was called for 16 December, a Saturday, by the Comité de Défense des Droits et de la Vie des Travailleurs Immigrés, which had grown out of the Djellali Committee. On Friday, Sartre was informed by the police that the proposed route was not acceptable. The plan was for a peaceful march from the Bonne-Nouvelle metro station to the Ministry of Justice in the place Vendôme. This would have taken the demonstrators through a busy shopping area, and the police objected that the streets would be crowded and that inadequate notice had been given by the organisers. A delegation including Mauriac, Geismar and Vidal-Naquet (Sartre was too ill to join them) went to the Préfecture, but was told that the ban still stood. Mauriac's suggestion that the march could perhaps go in the other direction, to the place de la République – a traditional site for demonstrations – was rejected. Those who ignored the ban would be exposing themselves to the rigours of the law, and would, if necessary, be met with force. A press release was prepared, making the point that it was too late to call off the demonstration and that the organisers felt themselves morally obliged to gather at the Bonne-Nouvelle metro station at four in the afternoon of 16 December.

The decision to march from this particular point is far from self-explanatory, but the metro station does have its political significance. As the frustrated delegation left the Préfecture, conversation turned to the Algerians who died there at the hands of the police on 17 October 1961. The FLN had called a peaceful demonstration in protest at the dusk-to-dawn curfew imposed on the Algerian population of Paris in an attempt to halt FLN activity. The unarmed Algerians who attempted to march into central Paris, many of them dressed in their best clothes so as to look 'respectable', were met with extreme force. Eleven thousand arrests were made. The precise number of deaths remains unknown; the usual estimate is 250. The main killing ground was the courtyard of the Préfecture de Police. For weeks, corpses floated in the Seine.

In a different context, Foucault and Vidal-Naquet pointed in an interview to one of the more embarrassing features of modern French history: no one speaks of the Algerians who died in October 1961, but everyone knows about the nine French demonstrators killed by the police at the Charonne metro station during an anti-OAS demonstration the following year; two million people attended the funeral. It was only in 1991 that the massacre of October 1961 was commemorated by a march organised by the MRAP. Twenty years earlier, Foucault and Vidal-Naquet had commented:

> In our view, this means that there is always one human group . . .
> at the mercy of others. In the nineteenth century, that group was
> called the dangerous classes. It's still the same today. There is the

population of the shanty towns, that of the overcrowded suburbs, the immigrants and all the marginals, young and old. It's not surprising that it is usually them one finds before the courts or behind bars.[72]

Early on Saturday afternoon, a planning meeting took place at the Ecole Normale, where a group of Maoists, no strangers to illegal demonstrations, carefully drew a map of the streets around the boulevard Bonne-Nouvelle on a blackboard. Few people were present, much to the annoyance of some militants, who grumbled about lack of discipline. Genet arrived with Foucault, who had not signed Sartre's appeal and claimed, no doubt disingenuously, not to know who had written it.

By three in the afternoon, the police had begun to pick up North Africans for identity checks as they emerged from the metro; most were probably more interested in Christmas shopping than demonstrating. As the demonstrators began to gather, a *commissaire*, resplendent in a tricolour sash, approached Genet, addressed him as '*maître*', a term of almost obsequious respect, and asked him if he could stop the demonstration. Genet replied: 'Call me *monsieur*', and refused to do anything. Small groups of demonstrators now began to move up the side streets, using the queues outside the cinemas as cover. They were repeatedly broken up by police charges. Shortly afterwards, a squad of police charged demonstrators leafleting the queues. As the Rex cinema was showing Walt Disney's *101 Dalmatians* for the holiday period, there were large numbers of children in the area, and panic ensued. A six-year-old boy and his grandmother were knocked over, and the child suffered a nose bleed. The sight of a bleeding child being carried away did little to calm tempers.

Initially, the police concentrated their attentions on Arab demonstrators and, presumably acting on orders, ignored the intellectuals present. As a result, a number of those arrested were snatched back from the hands of the police by Genet, Foucault and others. By six, intellectual immunity had been lifted. As a vanload of prisoners was driven off to applause from the remaining demonstrators, the CRS charged again. Mauriac was struck in the kidneys and a truncheon blow aimed at his groin narrowly missed its target. Foucault was surrounded and dragged into a police van, where he was soon joined by Mauriac. Foucault was pale with anger, but his main concern was that Deleuze might have been arrested too. A young CRS officer warned Foucault that if he tried to be clever, he would make him eat his glasses.

Foucault challenged him to repeat his words, and a potentially ugly incident was only averted by the intervention of an officer. A total of 161 arrests were made. Foucault and Mauriac were taken to the police holding centre in the rue Beaujon, where they encountered Genet and Geismar, also under arrest. The centre, which Foucault had first seen after his arrest during the occupation of the University of Vincennes in 1969, has a sinister reputation; as Geismar pointed out, it was here that student demonstrators had been forced to run the gauntlet between lines of club-wielding CRS in May 1968. On this occasion, no violence occurred, though the calculated insults directed at his captors by Genet raised the temperature to a potentially dangerous level. Unusually, telephone calls were allowed, and Foucault was able to warn his mother that he would not be able to have dinner with her after all. He was separated from Mauriac and Geismar and held with forty-five others in a holding cell designed for twenty. Shortly after ten, he was told that he could go, but refused to leave until his temporary cellmates were freed. All were set free at about midnight. Foucault's first concern was to make certain that no North Africans were still being held.[73]

Although it had a considerable impact in the short term, the Diab case soon disappeared from the press and the loss of media attention effectively put an end to its public discussion. Marquet was charged with manslaughter, but it was not until October 1975 that his case was heard by a Versailles court, which promptly declared that because of the 'disturbing circumstances' surrounding Diab's death, the case was beyond its jurisdiction and should be referred to a higher authority. In April 1976, the case went to a higher court, but Marquet failed to appear, pleading ill health. Both Mauriac and Foucault were called as witnesses by Gisèle Halimi, who was acting for Diab's family and who hoped to establish that Marquet's actions had been racially motivated; both declined to appear on the grounds that their knowledge of the case was not first-hand, and that they were reluctant to testify *against* anyone. In May 1980, almost eight years after the event, the *procureur général* ruled that Marquet had been acting in self-defence and recommended that the charges against him should be dropped.[74]

One of the side effects of the Jaubert affair, the killing of Djellali and Diab and the events in Bruay was the growing realisation of the need for a publication which could cover such events without falling into the ideological dogmatism of *La Cause du peuple*. The eventual result was *Libération*, affectionately known to its journalists and its readers alike as 'Libé'. It was to become synonymous with a disaffected leftism that gradually took on the issues of sexual and lifestyle politics that had been largely ignored by the Maoist groups. Initially a rather chaotic enterprise run on collective lines and paying all its staff equal – and low – salaries, *Libération* gradually evolved, after many splits, crises and near-bankruptcies, into a major left daily, providing many young journalists with their first professional experience. It rapidly became an integral part of the life of many young people, who used its correspondence columns and classified advertisements as a grapevine. The expression *prix libé* ('*Libé* price', meaning 'inexpensive') became a distinctive part of a certain sociolect.

Libération did not begin life as a newspaper but as a press agency called Agence de Presse Libération, founded on 18 June 1971. The agency's name was a clever pun. 'APL' was the French abbreviation of 'People's Liberation Army', and made an obvious reference to China. The 18 June 1940 was the date of de Gaulle's call [*appel*] for continued resistance to the German occupation. 'APL' is phonetically indistinguishable from *appel*; in keeping with the ideology or myth of the New Resistance, this was a new *appel du 18 juin*. Its first manifesto read:

> A collective of journalists belonging to the revolutionary press and to the traditional press is engaged alongside us in a new battle on the news front. We want to create, all of us, a new instrument to defend the truth. That instrument is the Agence de Presse Libération . . . After the Jaubert affair, a great need for freedom was born in the street. It remains the same, despite the government's attempts to smother journalists' anger. APL's ambition is to be a new tribunal which will give a voice to journalists who want to tell all, to people who want to know all. It will give the people a voice.[75]

APL, run by a very small group headed by Jean-Pierre Vernier, who had been one of the hunger strikers in the Chapelle Saint-Bernard, and under the general direction of Maurice Clavel, was an artisanal undertaking whose first releases were stencilled onto poor-quality paper and printed on a second-hand Roneo machine in Vernier's apartment. The initial experiment did not work, because the news produced was of little interest and often unreliable. By September, premises had been found; a ten-page bulletin was being produced on a regular basis, a volunteer team was hard at work in the rue Dussoubs and a nationwide network of correspondents had been established. In December the agency had its first exclusive: the release from prison of Alain Geismar. In March of the following year, it had an even better scoop. An ALP photographer was on hand in the Renault factory at Boulogne-Billancourt when Pierre Overney, a young Maoist, was shot dead by a security guard as he and his comrades tried to hand out leaflets. The evidence was incontrovertible: there had been no fight; Overney was armed only with a stave, and had been shot quite deliberately. The photographs were widely reproduced, and were shown on television. APL now had to be taken seriously.

Overney's funeral brought 200,000 people, including Foucault, on to the streets on 4 March. Althusser was present, and remarked with prescient cynicism that it was *gauchisme* itself and not just Overney that was being buried.[76] Four days later, the New People's Resistance took reprisals for 'Pierrot's' murder by kidnapping a social-relations officer from Renault. The guns were not loaded, and the victim was eventually released unharmed. It seemed that the terrorist option was being rejected.

The APL was soon talking of producing a daily paper. Support for the idea came from the Gauche Prolétarienne which had shown little interest in the APL until it reported the release of Geismar, but the emerging consensus was that the daily, although obviously *gauchiste*, should be free of specific political allegiances. It title was to be *Libération*, taken from a resistance paper and indicative of the ideological climate in which it was born: '*Libération* was born in '41, at a time when arms gave the people a voice . . . Today, France's underbelly [*la France d'en bas*] needs to express itself again. *Libé* is the answer to that need . . . To that extent, we think we are continuing a tradition which was born with the Resistance.'[77]

Finance was a major problem, and was to remain one. Inevitably, an appeal was made to the usual fellow travellers. Clavel donated the royalties from one of his books and a film, and Sartre the 30,000-francs advance he had negotiated with Gallimard for a collection of interviews with Philippe Gavi and Pierre Victor.[78] Foucault donated an unspecified amount of money.

The first full meeting to prepare for the launch of *Libération* took place in December 1972. As Claude Mauriac entered APL's new premises in the rue de Bretagne, he saw fifteen or so people sitting around two tables.[79] Sartre and Foucault were sitting side by side, flanked by Pierre Victor from the GP and Serge Livrozet from the CAP. To his embarrassment, Mauriac realised that he was the only person present wearing a collar and tie. Foucault, in his usual rollneck sweater, alternated between taking copious notes and staring at his fingernails. When Philippe Gavi made the point that 'the people should control every aspect of its life', Foucault intervened with great precision. In his view, 'control' meant four things; information, stopping power from achieving its ends, substitution and innovation. Information or news had to be provided about topics that were usually shrouded in secrecy, such as the workings of estate agents and drug companies. His example of how power should be frustrated was bizarre: women should be prevented from buying cosmetics, 'which are rubbish'. 'Popular control' meant, finally, that groups outside the paper itself should be involved in the project: 'Popular control must be exercised through the agency of the paper, but thanks to the action of outside groups. That way, we will not be talking in a vacuum.' He agreed with Gavi that *Libération* should cover topics usually ignored by the left press, such as horse-racing, adding that it should also provide a voice for 'homosexuals . . . and offenders'.[80] The coverage of Bruay in the Maoist press was obviously on everyone's mind, and Foucault saw it as an editorial problem, asking just who had reported the murder of Brigitte Dewevre for *La Cause du peuple*, and just how the editorial hierarchy had been organised. The issue had been raised but it was not resolved, and for a long time *Libération* devoted much space to correcting the erroneous reports it had published.

Discussion now turned to the contributions that might be expected from the paper's distinguished fellow travellers. Sartre simply said that he would write articles when he was asked to do so. Foucault's proposed contribution was more specific. He was not interested in writing the '*Justice*' column; he quipped that he had already served his two years, and that it was time for the CAP to take over from the GIP. Nor was he particularly taken with July's assumption that he would either spontaneously write on specific topics, or allow himself to be sought out to write as required. He had his own suggestion to make:

> I was thinking about chronicles from working-class and proletarian memory, that is, historical fragments from the nineteenth century . . . Or earlier, and until recent years. For example, the *canuts*, [81] the first great revolt of the carpenters of Paris in 1855 (or 45?). And prison mutinies. The first dates from 1829, the other from 1830. So it would be a historical chronicle related to current event. I think that would interest our readers.[82]

At the beginning of 1973, *Libération*'s manifesto was released to the press. The text was drafted by Pierre Victor, emended by Gavi, revised by Sartre and discussed at length by Foucault. *Libération* was to be a democratic newspaper which would do all it could to combat the power of the press barons. Its main source of news would be the people: news from the people and news for the people. Contributions were invited. The paper would be a daily critique of daily life, and it would reflect the lives of all those who were usually ignored by the media. No paid advertisements would be published; finance would be sought from readers' groups, support committees and subscriptions.[83] According to Foucault, interviewed in July 1978, a '*Libération* committee' was designed to be a collective writer, and, borrowing a phrase from Félix Guattari, he described the whole enterprise as a 'federation of molecular revolutions'[84] meaning that it would be an open enterprise functioning on flows of information rather than a static institution.

On 18 April 1973, after four issues numbered 'oo', the first issue of *Libération* appeared, its front page taken up with an appeal for money and a list of previous donors. It was not until the autumn that it began to come out regularly. The 'oo' issue dated 22 February carried Foucault's first contribution. In a brief piece entitled 'Pour une chronique de la mémoire ouvrière', he answered the questions put to him by 'José', identified as 'a worker from Renault-Billancourt'. A later issue further identified him as an immigrant 'OS' ('*ouvrier spécialisé*', a semi-skilled worker) and a member of the Comité de Lutte who had been sacked for political reasons. Such figures were of crucial importance to the political iconography of both the Maoist left and *Libération*. Renault was the great prize: a nationalised company with a reputation for repression, dominated in political terms by the PCF and the CGT. Winning over the OS was seen as the victory that would break the hegemony of both state and Communist Party. Nothing more is known about 'José', but Foucault was talking to an icon as much as to an individual.

In this first interview, Foucault described the project he had outlined in January. In a second conversation with José, Foucault speaks mainly of his perception of the role of the intellectual. Responding to José's opening suggestion that the intellectual 'who serves the people' is a mirror who reflects back the information he gathers from the exploited, Foucault argues that the role of the intellectual should not be overstated:

The workers don't need intellectuals to tell them what they are doing; they know perfectly well what they are doing. In my view, the intellectual is the guy who is plugged into the information network, not the production network. He can make his voice heard. He can write in the newspapers, give his point of view. He is also plugged into an older information network. He has the knowledge acquired by reading a certain number of books, knowledge which other people do not have at their direct disposal. His role is therefore not to shape a working-class consciousness, as that consciousness already exists, but to allow that consciousness, that working-class knowledge, to enter the information system . . . The intellectual's knowledge is always partial compared to working-class knowledge. What we know about the history of French society is very partial, compared to the massive experience that the working class has.[85]

Foucault's project on the history of working-class struggle never materialised, and these were his only contributions to *Libération* in the first year of its existence. He published a few more pieces in the 1970s,[86] but it was only in the 1980s that his contributions became more regular. It was obvious from his comments at the pre-launch meeting of December 1972 that he intended to play an active role in the life of the paper, and was not prepared to be a mere figurehead. His silence and his failure to produce his planned serial are therefore at first sight somewhat puzzling, but there are a number of probable explanations. Working on *Libération* was a full-time occupation and involved constant participation in the personal and political quarrels, many of them caused by the existence within the collective of a Maoist cell. As Clavel remarked, those working on *Libération* 'quickly ceased to love one another. If they had had a secular arm, they would have exterminated one another within a few months.'[87] Foucault's professional commitments as a teacher, researcher and writer did not permit the almost total involvement demanded by life in *Libération*'s offices. It is also likely that, as Philippe Gavi suggests, the increasing professionalisation – and unionisation – of the team made them less willing to accept regular, as opposed to occasional, contributions from fellow travellers.[88]

When he expressed the hope that *Libération* would be able to give a voice to homosexuals, Foucault touched upon an important issue and signalled a blank in the discourse of *gauchisme*. Although one of the notorious incidents that eventually led to the May 1968 events had had a sexual origin – a ban on visiting the rooms of students of the opposite sex – sexual politics remained relatively undeveloped. A first attempt to raise the gay question was made in May 1968 when eight posters signed 'Comité d'Action Pédérastique Révolutionnaire' appeared on the walls of the Sorbonne, but they were almost immediately torn down and no more was heard of the group.[89]

In its initial stages, French feminism was largely a reaction against the 'machismo' spirit of so many *gauchistes*. The climate at Vincennes was not untypical. There, an attempt to organise a women's meeting was disrupted by a Maoist commando shouting: 'Power comes from the end of the penis.' Conversely, a small demonstration by a group of women eloquently and effectively showed what the emerging feminist movement saw as the problem. On Armistice Day 1971, wreathes were laid on the tomb of the unknown soldier under the Arc de Triomphe and banners were unfurled proclaiming: 'One in two men is a woman' and 'There is someone more unknown than the unknown soldier: his wife.'[90] The police response was immediate and brutal.

For a while the gay and feminist movements coexisted, but in the spring of 1971, the foundation of the Front Homosexuel d'Action Révolutionnaire marked the appearance of an independent gay movement. The first major manifestation of FHAR's presence was the publication of a four-page spread in the April issue of *Tout*. The tone was aggressive and the artwork erotic. FHAR proclaimed that its members would no longer stay in the shadows: 'Yes, we've been buggered by Arabs; we're proud of it and we'll do it again.'[91] FHAR meetings were held mainly at the Ecole de Beaux Arts in a riotous celebration of gay sexuality. Most of the participants were young – the veteran anarchist Daniel Guérin was very much the exception – and in rebellion against the puritan left as well as 'normal' society. Predictably, *Tout* was banned on the grounds that it was pornographic. No less predictably, the major Maoist bookshop, the Librairie Norman Bethune, refused to stock it on the same grounds. FHAR did not last long, having been designed to self-destruct once it had made its point simply by existing.

Although Foucault was generally sympathetic, feminism was not one of his overriding concerns. The gay issue was closer to his heart but he did not become actively involved in FHAR. He attended a few of the gatherings in the Ecole des Beaux Arts, but was oddly suspicious. He welcomed FHAR's existence, but feared that it might result in a new form of ghettoisation, and suspected that 'gay' could be as oppressive a label as any other.[92] In that context he first met the young Guy Hocquenhem, soon to become one of the most visible figures in the gay movement and author of a book which saw gays as the successors to the excluded and confined of *Histoire de la folie*.[93]

Foucault's first public association with the new gay movements took a slightly different form. In March 1973, *Recherches* published an issue entitled *Trois milliards de pervers: La Grande Encyclopédie des homosexualités*

('Three Billion Perverts: The Great Encyclopedia of Homosexualities'). It contained a variety of material written by anonymous gay men and women, ranging from accounts of self-oppression to highly erotic fantasies. The artwork, much of it prepared by Laurent Dispot, a graduate of FHAR, was described thus by a rather squeamish *Le Monde* reporter: photographs, dated engravings . . . drawings in which the phallus plays an eminent and often gigantic role.[94]

In publishing this, Felix Guattari was knowingly running the risk of prosecution, and in an attempt to ward off censorship, Foucault, Deleuze, Sartre, Genet and Guattari himself all claimed authorship of the anonymous material. The strategy did not work; the journal was seized and banned, and Guattari was charged under the obscene publications laws. The trial, at which Guattari was represented by George Kiejman, was farcical, as the accused insisted on reading aloud the most 'pornographic' passages. Foucault was called for the defence, but did not appear, being away on a lecture tour. Guattari was ordered to pay a fine, but boasts that he has never done so, and the main outcome of the trial was a brisk clandestine trade in the surviving copies of *Recherches*.[95]

In the meantime, Foucault had become involved in two other campaigns around sexual politics. In June 1972, Dr Jean Carpentier was suspended and forbidden to practise medicine by the Ordre des Médecins. His offence had been to distribute a leaflet entitled 'Apprenons à faire l'amour' ('Let's learn to make love') outside a school in the suburb of Corbeil. The leaflet, published by a Comité d'Action pour la Libération de la Sexualité, supplied basic sexual information, placing the emphasis on pleasure, and offered some contraceptive information.[96] It referred in favourable terms to masturbation, both individual and mutual. Other versions soon began to circulate widely.

The pamphlet had originated in a pathetically trivial incident, in which a boy and girl were caught kissing on *lycée* premises. The school authorities wrote to their parents to complain, and the couple then informed Carpentier of what had happened in the hope that a more open dialogue could be established.

One of the speakers at the press conference given by Carpentier on 29 June was Foucault. Rather than dwelling on the details of the case itself, he took the opportunity to discuss the thesis that medicine serves as the guardian of morality. In Foucault's view, the Ordre des Médecins felt that it was under attack because Carpentier's leaflets represented a challenge to the 'individualist practice' of medical tradition. He continues:

They criticise you [Carpentier] for having encouraged children in practices which, they say, 'whether normal or not, inevitably lead to psychical disturbances'. Now, ever since the eighteenth century, one of the major functions of medicine, of psychical, psychopathological and neurological medicine, has of course been to take up where religion left off and to reconvert sin into illness . . . I see that at the end of the paragraph in which these practices were defined as 'normal or not', they are suddenly defined as 'debauchery', in other words that medicine also has a juridical function. It is medicine that defines, not only what is normal and not normal, but, ultimately, what is legitimate and what is not legitimate, criminal and not criminal, what is debauchery and what is a harmful practice.[97]

Despite the popularity of the leaflet, and despite the defence put forward by Foucault and by Carpentier himself, the doctor was eventually forbidden to practise for a period of one year.

The text is of interest not only in that it illustrates the political *disponibilité* of Foucault, but also in that it exemplifies the manner in which his theories have a surprisingly immediate applicability. It is also remarkable for its restraint. Carpentier had opined: 'The interest of homosexuality stems mainly from the fact that a hypocritical moral authority usually forbids young people to have heterosexual (girl–boy) relations (and has the cheek to condemn homosexuality). Heterosexual relations do, however, seem to be richer in pleasure.' At a public meeting organised in his support in October, Carpentier was forced by an intervention from FHAR to admit: 'Where homosexuality is concerned, I'm still a bit behind the times.'[98] Foucault did not pick up the gay issue and confined his remarks to general comments about medical power.

A year later, Foucault was embroiled in a rather different, but not unrelated, aspect of sexual politics. In October 1973, he and doctors Alain Landau and Jean-Yves Petit were called in by the Police Judiciaire on the instructions of an examining magistrate. Foucault was amused by the summons to appear, and told Claude Mauriac, 'with one of his most sarcastic smiles, an ironic smile which was both bitter (almost) and triumphant: "You know, I might be charged with performing abortions . . ."'[99] He and the two doctors were assumed to be the authors of a pamphlet issued by the Groupe d'Information sur la Santé and entitled '*Oui, nous avortons*' ('Yes, we carry out abortions').

This was not the first declaration of its kind; in February, 331 doctors, including three Nobel prizewinners, had issued a statement to the effect that they carried out abortions, demanding that abortion was a woman's right and should be reimbursed by the social-security system. Abortion was made illegal in France in 1920 and was to remain so until 1975. It was not one of Foucault's great causes, and even as he discussed his possible arrest he had to be gently reminded by Defert that there *was* a difference between abortion and contraception.[100]

Foucault's actual involvement is impossible to determine, but it is likely that he simply lent his name to a collective publication. In a joint article, the three (who were not charged) described the methods in use in illegal abortion clinics and ended by asserting the right to abortion, their refusal to see the establishment of a medical monopoly and their fear that it would become a source of profiteering. A bill legalising abortion was being discussed, but the attempt to use the law against the GIS indicated an attempt to drive a wedge between 'good doctors' and those who wished to establish abortion and contraception as political rights.[101]

13

THE ARCHIVES OF PAIN

THE period 1971–73 was the most intensely political in Foucault's life and the multiple activities in which he was involved left little time for writing. *L'Archéologie du savoir* appeared in 1969 and he published no more major works until *Surveiller et punir* appeared in 1975; *Moi, Pierre Rivière* was a collective undertaking in which Foucault's role was that of a facilitator rather than an author. Most of his publications from the intervening period were transcripts of lectures, discussions and other verbal exchanges. Foucault was in demand for interviews, mainly concerning the GIP and his views on prisons,[1] and as a visiting lecturer at foreign universities. He wrote prefaces for books like Livrozet's *De la Prison à la révolte* and took part in round-table discussions on social work with a group from *Esprit* in the spring of 1972.[2] Perhaps the most dramatic piece of writing produced in this period was the catalogue essay written for an exhibition by Paul Rebeyrolle in March 1973.

The exhibition, held at the prestigious Maeght gallery, consisted of ten large mixed-media works (oil on canvas, wood, wire mesh) so installed as to give the viewer the impression of being totally confined: 'You have come in. You are now surrounded by ten paintings arranged around a room, all of whose windows have been carefully closed. Is it now your turn to be in prison, like the dogs you see jumping up and hurling themselves against the wire?'[3] The canvases depict the struggles of a dog to escape from a tightly confined space; their titles – 'Condemned', 'Torture', 'The Cell' – all describe a carceral world. Most of the canvases are in shades of grey and white, but something changes in '*Dedans*' ('Inside'), which is the eighth in the sequence. The dominant whites give way to a vibrant blue as escape at last becomes a possibility:

> The wall cracks from top to bottom, as though it had been split by a great blue sword. The vertical, which was once the mark of power thanks to the relief of the stick, now opens up freedom. The vertical sticks which hold the mesh in place cannot prevent the

wall from cracking. A muzzle and paws struggle to open it with an intense, electrical quivering. In the struggles of men, nothing great ever comes through windows; everything always comes through the triumphal collapse of walls.[4]

In the next canvas, the dog crouches, ready to leap from the wall, and stares into a blue immensity from which it is now separated only by the torn mesh. And then:

The last great canvas unfolds and disperses a new space, until now absent from the whole series; it is divided between the dark fortress of the past and the storms of future colour. But all across its length, there are traces of galloping paws – 'a description of an escapee'. It seems that truth comes softly, like a dove. Force leaves the claw marks of its flight on the ground.[5]

Throughout this period, Foucault obviously continued his research activity, mainly in the Bibliothèque Nationale but also in the Archives Nationales, the Arsenal and the archives of the Préfecture de Police. Further collections of archival material were consulted in Vincennes and, further afield, in Nantes. Foucault rarely spoke to anyone of his ongoing research, but it fed into both his lectures and seminars at the Collège de France and into what was to become *Surveiller et punir*. The lecture series for 1972–73 was devoted to 'punitive society' and in it Foucault began to outline the themes for his next book. It was at this point that he first encountered the utilitarian philosopher Jeremy Bentham's astonishing project for a 'panopticon' (an architectural construction that would guarantee a regime of total visibility in a prison), and first spoke of the nineteenth century as having inaugurated 'the age of panopticism'.[6] The seminar for that year was devoted to preparing the Pierre Rivière dossier for publication in 1973. In 1973–74, the lectures dealt with the topic of 'psychiatric power', and the seminar with the history and architecture of hospitals in the nineteenth century, and the role of expert psychiatric reports in forensic medicine.

The seminar group which worked on hospital architecture provided the kind of working environment that Foucault enjoyed most: a small group of individuals willing to collaborate closely on a specific project. The group met at the Collège, but also more informally at Foucault's home and sometimes even in a café. One of the members was Anne Thalamy, Foucault's niece, who recalls the experience of working with him as a pleasant and very rewarding one. Papers were read, eighteenth-century plans for hospitals were unearthed from libraries and discussed in a relaxed and tolerant atmosphere. Foucault was always available for consultation by the small group, and Thalamy found that she could even interrupt him in the Bibliothèque Nationale without incurring his anger; she admits, however, that she may have been unconsciously exploiting the family connection, and that her experience may not have been typical.[7]

The seminar was unusual in that it received finance for research costs from Guattari's CERFI (Centre d'Etude, de Recherche et de Formation Institutionnelles), an alliance of psychiatrists, town planners, economists and political activists. CERFI published the interdisciplinary journal *Recherches* and operated from crowded premises in the boulevard Beaumarchais. Its multiple activities reflected the varied interests and concerns of its libertarian founder originally trained in both pharmacy and philosophy, and then as a Lacanian psychoanalyst. Félix Guattari, who died in September 1992, worked for almost forty years at the clinique de la Borde and was a key figure in the alternative psychiatry movement. Active on many political fronts, he was in many ways an embodiment of the spirit of the late 1960s. CERFI functioned as a collective of organisations carrying out research into a wide range of institutional matters, with Deleuze and Guattari functioning as what one member called a 'bicephalous wise man' in charge of the whole enterprise. After much soul-searching, CERFI concluded that taking money from government sources was not a cardinal sin and began to tender for research projects. In 1973, it was quite a wealthy organisation.[8]

Foucault had already had dealings with CERFI when a group working on the genealogy of the city approached him for comments on its work in progress in the autumn of 1971. One of those who approached Foucault was Marie-Thérèse Vernet, an economist from the University of Vincennes. She found him open-minded and sympathetic, but rather resented the suggestion, which came from within the group itself, that an 'expert' should be approached for advice. On a more anecdotal level, she was amused to see, when she made her way to the rue de Vaugirard, that the famous archivist did not, as she had half expected, live in a clutter of dusty papers, but in a pristine modern apartment.[9] The research, carried out and written up in chaotic conditions, was published as *Les Equipements du pouvoir*.[10] Foucault's contribution was restricted to two brief exchanges with Deleuze and Guattari on the role of the city as productive force.[11] The integration of these exchanges into the wider debate over the history of urbanisation is not entirely happy, and one does have the impression of outside experts being drawn rather unnecessarily into a collective undertaking.

The work of the Collège seminar centred upon the emergence of recognisable health policies and upon the professionalisation of medicine in the eighteenth century. As a result of these twin processes, medicine became integrated into a general policy of economic and political management designed to rationalise society as a whole. In his general introduction Foucault identifies the three main themes that dominated the discussions: the new focus on childhood and a medicalisation of the family; the new importance given to hygiene; and the transformation of medicine into an instrument of social control. Finally, discussion concentrated on the emergence of the hospital as a specifically medical space, with its own planning and architecture.[12] The publication of the group's research went almost completely unnoticed. Only the faithful Canguilhem commented on it in print, and described it as 'an incomparable document relating to the French origins of the modern hospital'.[13]

The clearest indication of Foucault's concerns of the moment comes from a series of lectures given in Brazil in the spring of 1973. His second visit to the country resulted in part from invitations from Brazilian institutions, but Foucault was also travelling under the auspices of the Alliance Française. For the latter, he was '*en mission*', which, to his amusement, meant that he was technically a '*missionaire*', a missionary. His schedule was not a light one. During the five days (21–25 May) he spent in Rio de Janeiro, he gave five major lectures to enthusiastic audiences at the Pontificia Universidade Catolica on the general theme of 'Truth and Juridicial Forms'.[14] The specific topics covered ranged from a general discussion of Nietzsche and genealogy to a reading of the Oedipus myth, described as 'the first eye-witness account we have of Greek juridical practices',[15] and an analysis of the role of 'panopticism' in the emergence of a disciplinary society.

Foucault's mission then took him north for his only visit to Belo Horizonte, the state capital of Minas Gerais and Brazil's third largest city. He spent only three days in the city, but gave informal talks at the Alliance Française and to the philosophy department of the Universidade Federal, and lectured on 'Mental Illness and Psychiatric Institutions' and 'Psychiatric Institutions and Anti-Psychiatry'. In Rio, his audience had been primarily philosophical; in Belo Horizonte, Foucault spoke mainly to psychiatrists and psychoanalysts. The lectures were a denunciation of the power/knowledge exercised by mental-health professionals via their diagnoses, prescriptions and normalisation of behaviour, and an exploration of the alternatives offered by anti-psychiatry.

His hosts were attentive and generous, but not all their attentions were entirely welcome. Considerable publicity had been given to the missionary and a press conference had been called, but Foucault interrupted it to complain about the presence of the many photographers, whose flashguns were so intrusive as to become a form of torture. He was ill at ease, gnawing at his fingernails and displaying a variety of nervous tics.[16] Nor did the social functions he was obliged to attend appeal to him greatly. An evening at the home of Consuelo Albergaria introduced him to many of the city's academics, but was also something of an ordeal in that it meant having to be polite to 'women in long evening gowns'; Foucault was polite enough to conform but privately voiced his irritation to Defert, his unofficial companion on his mission.

Other aspects of the stay in Belo Horizonte were more agreeable. Foucault enjoyed the atmosphere of Brazil and the relaxed life of the streets and bars. Unexpectedly for one who now rarely drank, he also acquired a taste for *caipirinha*, an apéritif based on sugar-cane alcohol and served with lemon, sugar and ice cubes. As Defert in particular found to his cost, too many *caipirinhas* can have an almost lethal effect.

The mission included brief visits to local psychiatric hospitals and discussions with their inmates and staff organised by Célio Garcia, the psychoanalyst and lecturer who acted as Foucault's main guide and interpreter. Foucault's work was known to many of the young professionals he met, and they were happy to discuss the fragile state of Brazil's psychiatric institutions with him. There was also time for more leisurely pursuits, including a day in Ouro Preto, 100 kilometres to the southeast. The small town, famed for its School of Mines, is classified as a historic monument and, with its steep cobbled streets, is one of the best examples of the baroque architecture of eighteenth-century Brazil. From here, Foucault went via Brazilia to Belém, where he lectured at the Universidade Federal do Parà before going on to Amazonia for purely hedonistic reasons.[17]

Back in Paris, Foucault returned to his research on the origins of the prison system. As usual he was solicited on all sides for signatures to petitions and, as usual, tried to avoid signing most of them. Not all solicitations, however, were political. One of the penalties of his fame and media prominence was that Foucault was also frequently approached by aspiring authors who hoped that he would be able to help them publish their books. Such requests plunged him into deep depression, since the manuscripts he was asked to read had usually already been rejected countless times. On Christmas Eve 1973, he was telephoned at midday by an unknown young man who insisted that he must read his manuscript. Foucault prevaricated, claiming that he had no time, that he could do nothing for his caller, and that he knew nobody in literary publishing. The unknown voice insisted that that did not matter, and Foucault capitulated, telling him to bring the manuscript at two in the afternoon. His change of heart was, in part, motivated by boredom; in Foucault's view, Christmas was a season in which nothing had happened for thousands of years. He was also struck by the beauty of the unknown voice, and remarked to Defert that it was impossible to resist its charm. At two, a very nervous young man arrived, clutching a large manuscript. He had walked almost the full length of the rue de Vaugirard to reach the eighth-floor flat, where he found Foucault and some friends finishing lunch. With some hesitation he accepted a cup of coffee, and left his manuscript with Foucault.

The young man was Jacques Almira, then aged twenty-three. His novel had been rejected by Robbe-Grillet at Minuit and by Georges Lambrichs at Gallimard, but he was convinced that Foucault should read it and could help him. Almira had long admired Foucault, having been introduced to *Les Mots et les choses* by an enlightened philosophy teacher in a provincial *lycée*. He shared Foucault's enthusiasm for Raymond Roussel, and had followed the saga of the Groupe d'Information sur les Prisons with interest. When he moved to Paris in 1973, he began to attend Foucault's lectures at the Collège de France and had always intended to approach him afterwards. His courage inevitably failed him, and the decision had been put off week by week.

On New Year's Eve, Almira, who had no telephone, received a telegram: Foucault had read the novel, was wildly enthusiastic about it, and promised to do what he could at Gallimard.

Foucault was both a persuasive advocate and a good judge. *Le Voyage à Naucratis* was published early in 1975, and won the Prix Medicis. The joint interview given by Almira and Foucault to Jean Le Marchand on its publication provides a rare insight into what Foucault was reading in the mid-1970s. He had lost his earlier interest in the very formal experiments of *Tel Quel*, but was still fond of Gracq's *Le Rivage des Syrtes*. He also speaks of enjoying Malcolm Lowry's *Under the Volcano*, which was to remain a favourite text, and the erotic fantasies of Tony Duvert.[18]

In November 1975, Almira dined with Foucault and others in the rue de Vaugirard. The guests included Claude Mauriac and Olga Bernal, a friend of both Foucault and Robbe-Grillet, to whose work she had devoted one of the first serious studies.[19] As Foucault bustled about serving his guests, Almira remarked, with a poor taste that apparently went unnoticed, that in fifty years' time, when Foucault was long dead, he would tell people about the day he brought him the manuscript of *Le Voyage*.

Foucault and Almira were to become good friends who dined together frequently, and the young novelist found something of a spiritual father in the philosopher. The friendship remained nonsexual and, despite its warmth, the two always used the formal *vous* to one another. Almira remembers Foucault as someone who constantly encouraged him with his writing, who was always prepared to assure him in moments of doubt that he did possess a genuine talent. In the spring of 1984, Almira published his third novel, *Terrass Hôtel*, and dedicated it to Foucault. The dedication reads 'This novel is dedicated to Michel Foucault, thanks to whom I published my first novel, whose friendship does me honour, as a token of my affectionate gratitude and of my admiration.' It is almost certain that Foucault did not have time to read it.

Of the many aspiring authors who approached Foucault for help, only Jacques Almira received it in this way. Even Hervé Guibert, who was on very intimate terms with Foucault from the late 1970s onwards, and whose work Foucault both enjoyed and admired greatly, was left to make his own literary way. The one convincing explanation is that Foucault was seduced by a voice.[20] There is one instance of a much more casual generosity on Foucault's part. In 1975, he was approached by a young man called Gérard Dupont who asked him for an interview, explaining that if he got the interview, he would earn 500 francs. Foucault acquiesced. The result was an interesting discussion of sadism in the cinema; Foucault later told Mauriac that he had said the first thing that came into his head in order to make sure that Dupont was paid his money.[21]

'In 1757, Robert-François Damiens was condemned to death for regicide after a pathetically unsuccessful attempt on the life of Louis XV. According to the terms of his sentence, the flesh was to be torn with pincers from his breast, arms, thighs and calves, and his right hand, which had wielded the knife, was to be cut off. His wounds would then be daubed with molten lead, boiling oil, burning pitch and a mixture of molten wax and sulphur. His body would then be quartered and his limbs torn from his torso by four horses. The corpse was to be burned, and the ashes scattered in the wind. In the event, Damiens's sufferings were even more hellish than the sentence. The four horses were unable to perform their task. Even the harnessing of a further two horses to the chains on his legs failed to have the expected result. Damiens's limbs were severed by his human executioners. Only then could the horses do their work.

'In 1838, Léon Faucher published an essay on prison reform and described the rules he had drawn up for the Maison des Jeunes Détenus à Paris. Article 17 read: "The prisoners' day will begin at six in the morning in winter and at five in summer. They will work for nine hours a day in all seasons. Two hours a day will be devoted to instruction. Work and the day will end at nine in winter and at eight in summer." '

So begins *Surveiller et punir*: with a diptych of a public execution and a timetable which, stylistically, recalls the opening pages of *Naissance de la clinique*.[22] The execution and the timetable punish neither the same crimes nor the same category of criminals, 'but they both certainly define a certain penal style. Less than a century separates them. It was an era in which, in both Europe and the United States, the whole economy of punishment was redistributed.'[23] *Surveiller et punir* is the history of that redistribution.

Foucault's objective is to provide 'a correlative history of the modern soul and of a new power to judge; a genealogy of the present-day scientific-judicial complex in which the power to punish finds its supports, receives its justifications and rules, extends its effects and masks its exorbitant singularity'. He outlines four preliminary rules for methodology. Punitive mechanisms are not to be studied merely as repressive measures; they may have positive effects too, and punishment should be regarded as a complex social function. Methods of punishment are not simply an expression of legal rules; they are techniques which find their specificity in a broader field of mechanisms of power. They are therefore to be viewed as tactics of power. The history of penal law and that of the human sciences are not separate series but may well derive from an 'epistemologico-juridical' formation: the technique of power may govern both the humanisation of the penal system and our knowledge of man. Finally, the entry of the soul on to the legal stage and the insertion of scientific knowledge into juridical practice may be the effect of a transformation in the mode of the body's investment by relations of power.[24]

The transition from Damiens's execution to the publication of Faucher's timetable is one which sees the disappearance of the body from public view as the art of inflicting unbearable suffering is replaced by an economy of suspended rights. Symptomatically, the convicts who once marched chained together in a column to the ports from whence they would be deported, were, by the end of this period of transition, transported in closed vehicles with individual cells. The old system, in which crime was an attack on the symbolic body of the sovereign – here, Foucault is heavily influenced by Kantorowicz's study of the king's two bodies[25] – and was punished in public, gives way to a system in which individual crimes and punishments can be calibrated on a sophisticated scale.

The legal disappearance of torture and the emergence of the prison as the standard form of punishment is not, in Foucault's view, necessarily a process of gradual and humanising reform. The object of the reforms of the late eighteenth century was not to 'punish less', but to 'punish better', to insert the power to punish more deeply into the body social: 'to constitute a new economy and a new technology for the power to punish'.[26] The new economy and technology together generate what Foucault calls a 'semio-technique' based upon six rules.[27] His identification of those rules is based upon a reading of a range of works published during the Enlightenment and Revolutionary periods, one of the most significant being Beccaria's *Dei Delitti e delle pene* of 1764 (Foucault cites the French translation and not the original Italian edition). The rules represent, that is, a model rather than a reality, but the model is established by close readings and is the result of the patient and meticulous work of the grey genealogy described in 'Nietzsche, la généalogie, l'histoire'.

The first of the rules is that of 'miminal quantity': the advantage of committing a crime must be slightly outweighed by the disadvantage of being punished. Here, the careful calibration of crime and punishment replaces the conspicuous display of 'surplus power' on the part of an offended sovereign. The 'rule of sufficient ideality' implies that physical pain will give way to the idea of pain, and to the elision of the body from the spectacle of punishment. A rule pertaining to 'side effects' describes the idea of disseminating fear of punishment; ultimately, if it were possible to convince everyone that a criminal would cease his activities, there would be no actual need to punish the individual. The rule of 'perfect certainty' is almost self-explanatory: punishment will follow crime with perfect certainty and inevitability. Hence the notion that the legal apparatus of the courts must be reduplicated by a police apparatus which will be all-seeing. Hence too the need for justice to be seen to be done in a public court or equivalent.

The fifth 'rule' identified by Foucault pertains to truth and to truth-telling, and is thus related to the reading of the Oedipus myth given in the Brazilian lectures of 1974, as well as to his lectures at the Collège de

France from 1971 onwards. Degrees of suspicion and degrees of corresponding punishment are swept away by a concern with a truth – and a standard of proof – which, like mathematical truth, can be accepted only if it is fully proven. Empirical enquiries replace the old inquisitorial model. Judges are no longer answerable to themselves alone as courts rely increasingly upon a proliferation of scientific discourses, including psychiatry. Finally, the rule of optimal specification allows the new semiotics to codify the whole field of illegality and punishment. A link between the individual offender and categories of offences is sought in a model provided by the natural history of the day: the ideal would be a Linnaean classification of crimes, criminals and sanctions. The process is one of individualisation: the criminal is now of greater interest than the crime itself. Hence, for example, the minute investigations into the past and character of Pierre Rivière, who, curiously, is not mentioned in this text. 'A whole individualising knowledge is organised, taking as its domain of reference not so much the crime committed . . . as the virtuality of dangers concealed within an individual, dangers which manifest themselves in his behaviour, which is under daily observation.'[28]

Surveiller et punir is subtitled 'Naissance de la prison' ('Birth of the Prison'), but the institution in question proves to have more than one place of birth. A whole range of institutions and discourses contribute to the emergence of a pervasive notion of discipline. In the military arts, the soldier becomes a manufactured object whose every movement, real and potential, can be measured and recorded. Barracks, classrooms and monastic establishments all provide models for the enclosure or confinement of bodies whose slightest movements can be observed and corrected. The manufacturies of the early industrial period, which resembled prisons in many respects, rely upon the subdivision of the time required to carry out tasks and the synchronisation of the appropriate physical gestures on the part of workers.[29] Hospitals and clinics organise space in such a way that they themselves become operatives or 'curing machines'. From this multiplicity of discourses, practices and institutions, there emerges a 'disciplinary power . . . organised like a multiple, automatic and anonymous power . . . in the hierarchical surveillance of these disciplines, power is not something to be held like a thing, and is not transferred like property: it functions like machinery'.[30] Discipline itself is neither an institution nor an apparatus; it is a type of power, 'a "physics" or an "anatomy" of power, a technology . . . All in all, we can therefore speak of the formation of a disciplinary society in the movement from closed disciplines, a sort of social "quarantine", to the infinitely generalisable mechanism of "panopticism".'[31]

The ultimate expression of the disciplinary society is of course Jeremy Bentham's 'panopticon', described thus by Foucault:

> On the periphery, an annular building; in the centre, a tower. The latter is pierced by broad windows which give on to the inner side of the ring; the peripheral building is divided into cells, each of which runs the full width of the building; they have two windows, one facing inwards and corresponding to the windows in the tower, the other facing outwards to allow light to flood through the whole cell. It then suffices to place a supervisor in the central tower and a madman, a patient, a condemned man, a worker or a schoolboy in each cell. . . . So many cages, so many little theatres in which each actor is alone, perfectly individualised and constantly visible . . . Full light and the gaze of a supervisor capture better than darkness, which was ultimately a protection. Visibility is a trap.[32]

Although it sounds like an architectural fantasy, the panopticon did provide the model for actual prisons. 'Prisons must be seen as a formative place for clinical knowledge about detainees. The theme of the Panopticon – supervision and observation, safety and knowledge, individuation and totalisation, isolation and transparence – found the privileged site of its realisation in the prison.'[33]

Surveiller et punir is obviously a study in history, but the history it studies is that of the present. Although based upon a long study of theories of penology and criminology, of military handbooks on discipline and of the 'archives of pain' material, it is shot through with contemporary allusions and references. Foucault refers in passing to the execution of Bontemps and Buffet in La Santé at dawn on 22 September 1972, an execution which, unlike that of Damiens, took place in semisecrecy, as though the modern state were ashamed of its power.[34] He illustrates the futility of prison reform by juxtaposing the reforms of 1945 with those proposed at a congress held in Brussels in 1847 and showing that they are almost identical.[35] The 'carceral system' has deep roots, as demonstrated by the fact that the model prison of Fleury-Mérogis, opened in 1969, reproduces the panoptic-star shape of the Petite Roquette, opened in 1836.[36] The history of prison reform is coextensive with the history of prisons. It was the present rather than the past which first taught Foucault that 'punishments in general, and prison derive from a political technology of the body'. Recent prison revolts had taken as their target the degrading conditions of crumbling prisons like Clairvaux, but also model prisons with their tranquillisers and psychiatrists:

> It was indeed a revolt, at the bodily level, against the body of the prison. What was at stake was not the prison setting – too crude or too asceptic, too rudimentary or too sophisticated – but its materiality insofar as it is an instrument and vector of power; it was all that technology of the power over the body, which the technology of the 'soul' – that of educationalists, psychologists and psychiatrists – can neither mask nor counterbalance for the very good reason that it is merely one of its tools. That was the prison whose history I wanted to write, with all the political investments of the body that it encloses in its closed architecture.[37]

The publication of *Surveiller et punir* in 1975 was surrounded by considerable publicity. In the week before publication, extracts appeared in *Le Nouvel Observateur* under the title 'Naissance des prisons' and no doubt whetted the appetite of many a potential reader.[38] Four days later, *Le Monde* devoted a two-page spread to 'Michel Foucault and the Birth of Prisons', combining Roger-Pol Droit's interview with Foucault with a review-essay by Christian Jambet, who situates Foucault's work firmly within the tradition of Bloch, Febvre and *Annales*.[39] The June issue of the monthly *Magazine littéraire* appeared with a portrait of Foucault on its cover, and contained a twenty-seven-page dossier devoted to his work. This included a long interview on the new book, a bibliography, an interesting essay by Bernard-Henri Lévy and a discussion between Raymond Bellour and Jacques Revel about Foucault's relations with historians.[40] Foucault was interviewed at some length by both *Les Nouvelles Littéraires* and by the Italian weekly *L'Europeo*, despite the fact that an Italian translation of the book would not appear until 1978.[41]

All the reviews that appeared in the daily and weekly press were favourable, and all sounded as though their authors were somewhat chilled by what they had read. Jean-Paul Enthoven summed up the general view when he suggested in *Le Nouvel Observateur* that all one could do after reading Foucault was listen to the rumble of rebellion from Toul and the other *'écoles normales* of pure discipline', to the voices of the adolescents who hanged themselves in the anonymity of their cells:

Foucault writes on the basis of their rebellion. That is why his book possesses virtues other than those which normally come from his complete erudition, his prodigious sense of the archives or the baroque splendour of his writing. And when an author is, because of his immense talent, far behind the faces of those who haunt these pages, does it still make sense to speak of a masterpiece?[42]

According to Arlette Farge, who once worked as an instructor for prison educators, the book sent 'shock waves' through the prison education and social-work services.[43]

The real celebration of *Surveiller et punir* came at the end of the year, by which time it had already been reprinted. In December, *Critique* published a special 'Foucault' issue, with three major articles devoted to him.[44] Philippe Meyer's article, written at the request of Jean Piel, is not a review but an attempt to follow up a suggestion made in Foucault's book: 'A whole study should be made of the debates that took place during the Revolution about family courts, paternal correction and the right of parents to have their children locked up.'[45] François Ewald's long study of *Surveiller et punir* had an immediate effect on its author's career; it was in part on the strength of this article that the Gauche Prolétarienne's former organiser in Bruay-en-Artois became Foucault's assistant at the Collège de France. It is probably the most sophisticated exercise in tracing the Nietzschean strand that runs through Foucault's study of the birth of the prison. Ewald demonstrates, for instance, that Foucault's history of disciplinary tactics conforms to a model first outlined in his tribute to Jean Hyppolite: 'The forces that are at work in history do not obey a destination or a mechanism, but the hazards of a struggle. They do not manifest themselves as the successive forms of a primordial intention; they do not always take on the appearance of a result. They always appear in the singular randomness of the event.'[46] He also makes the fascinating suggestion that the best way to introduce *Surveiller et punir* might be to tinker with a passage from *The Genealogy of Morals*, and to alter Nietzsche's speculations about the 'problem of pity and the ethics of pity' to read:

At first sight, this problem of prison and the 'ethics of prison' . . . may seem very special, a marginal issue. But whoever sticks with it and learns how to ask questions will have the same experience that I had: a vast new panorama will open up before him; strange and vertiginous possibilities will invade him; every variety of suspicion, distrust, fear will come to the surface; his belief in ethics of any kind will begin to be shaken. Finally he will be forced to listen to a new claim.[47]

Ewald's article also indicates that a major political and philosophical shift was under way among Foucault's public. The former Maoist now asks: 'Who will write the political anatomy of political and trade-union organisations, of those apparatuses for "educating" the masses, for "disciplining" them, for giving them a "consciousness"? . . . What "malevolence" is concealed behind "democratic centralism" '?[48]

In a sense, Ewald has already answered his own question by signalling a link between *Surveiller et punir* and André Glucksmann's study of the Soviet labour camps.[49] He argues that Glucksmann's book is 'an anatomy of Marxist "power-knowledge" ' which confirms the thesis that 'our truths may be built upon police and judicial procedures, that they have been confirmed by the tidal rhythms of the Gulag'.[50] Foucault does indeed refer, in terms which transparently allude to Solzhenitsyn, to the way in which 'the carceral archipelago transports all the technology of the penal institution into the whole body social'.[51] Such themes were to come much more to the fore in the summer of 1976 – the summer of the *nouveaux philosophes*.

For Deleuze, Foucault's book was a 'divine comedy of punishments' and its author 'a new cartographer'.[52] It was as though, at last, something new had appeared since Marx. Like Ewald, Deleuze reads *Surveiller et punir* largely in terms of its contemporary political implications. The GIP, he argues, had, unlike many forms of *gauchisme*, been able to avoid the organisational centralism that still linked the left with Stalinism. The theory of power outlined in the early chapters of *Surveiller et punir* now implied the abandoning of the traditional assumptions of the left. Power was not the 'property' of the class which had supposedly seized it, but a strategy, and Foucault offered a 'new functionalism', a 'functional analysis which certainly does not deny the existence of classes or of their struggles, but which does paint a very different picture, with different characters and different processes, to that to which traditional history, even when it is Marxist, has accustomed us'.[53]

There was originally to have been at least one more essay on Foucault in the December 1975 issue of *Critique*. It was by François Roustang, a Jesuit turned psychoanalyst whom Foucault had known at Vincennes. Roustang both praises and criticises the book, objects to the passing remarks on pyschoanalysis and argues that if visibility is a trap for the prisoner, it is also a trap for power: at the point where everything becomes visible, no one can any longer see anything because the essential contrast between light and shade has been lost, and everyone is dissolved into visibility. The article was rejected by Piel, probably because he was reluctant to publish anything that was openly critical of Foucault. When he learned of its content, Foucault was furious, and let it be known that its publication would cost Roustang dear. Roustang made it clear that he would not be intimidated, and published the offending article in *Les Temps Modernes*, which cannot have done anything to moderate Foucault's anger. Foucault was quite capable of attempting to suppress criticisms of his work and of bearing grudges for a long time, but on this occasion nothing came of his threats and the incident was forgotten.[54]

The publication of *Surveiller et punir* coincided with the opening of Gérard Fromanger's exhibition at the Galerie Jeanne Bucher. The catalogue to 'Le Désir est partout' ('Desire is Everywhere') was prefaced by Foucault's essay on 'La Peinture photogénique', and two of the paintings were of particular significance. The two versions of '*En Révolte à la prison de Toul*' are based on the widely distributed press photographs of prisoners on the roof. They are products of Fromanger's distinctive technique of projecting a photograph on to a surface, and painting directly on that surface before adding splashes of bright colour.

Other paintings in the show were of China and of Paris street scenes, all produced by the same technique. Fromanger's inspiration was not purely technological, and some of his canvases look very much like the 'peasant painters' of China's Shan-Xi province, which enjoyed a considerable vogue on the left at this time.

Foucault's preface to the catalogue was a gesture of friendship to an acquaintance he had known for some years, and Fromanger admits that it did his career a lot of good.[55] Foucault saw the artist's work as a consummation of the long and complicated relationship between painting and photography, which he explores through a brief discussion of Julia Margaret Cameron and the early daguerreotypes of John Jabez Edwin Mayall. Pop art and hyperrealism had introduced a new 'love of images' by allowing artists to 'plug into' the infinite circulation of images. The pop artist does not merely use photographing as an aid to painting; a photographic image is painted and exploited as an image within a painting. Pop art and hyperrealism had plunged painting into an ocean of images. Fromanger, however, introduced something even more novel: 'By covering up photographs, or investing them triumphantly or insidiously, painting is not saying that photos are beautiful. It is doing more than that: it is producing the beautiful hermaphrodite of negative and canvas, the androgyne image.'[56]

In gratitude for the preface, Fromanger painted a portrait of Foucault. *Michel* (oil on canvas, 1976) uses the same technique as the *Le Désir est partout* series. Foucault, in the inevitable white rollneck, seems about to leap from the canvas, laughing and eyes sparkling, while the splashes of colour and the diagonal lines at head height give the portrait a startling vivacity. *Michel* remained in Foucault's possession until his death, and is now in the collection of the Centre Michel Foucault. A second and slightly different version was commissioned by Robert Badinter and hangs outside his office in the Conseil Constitutionnel.

Foucault's reaction to the publicity surrounding *Surveiller et punir* was typical: while he grumbled about the demands made upon him by journalists, he did not refuse to give interviews and generally enjoyed the whole process. As the immediate wave of publicity retreated, he went on with his teaching at the Collège de France, where the year's seminar had been on the legal role of the 'psychiatric report' and where the lecture had dealt with the theme of 'abnormality'. By abnormality, Foucault meant the medical-legal category which defined certain individuals such as hermaphrodites as 'monstrous', which discursively created monstrously incorrigible criminals and which denounced as 'abnormal' the practice of masturbation. The crusade against that abnormal perversion expressed the transformation of the family into a power-knowledge apparatus. The calling into question of infantile sexuality, and of all the anomalies for which it was supposedly responsible, was one of the processes which promoted that new structure: 'the small, incestuous family which characterises our societies, the minuscule and sexually saturated family space in which we were brought up and live'.[57]

In May, the Collège's academic year drew to a close and Foucault left for a brief visit to the United States, having been invited by Leo Bersani to take the post of visiting professor in French at the University of Berkeley. He had already been to America on a number of occasions, but this was his first visit to California. He at once took a great liking to the West Coast, which was always to have an almost utopian appeal for him. He was well received on campus, though it would be a few years before he finally made his triumphant breakthrough and became a major figure in the US. By now he had learned to enjoy the relatively relaxed atmosphere of American universities, and no longer resented the assumptions students made about his availability for informal discussion, as he had done on his first visits. His spoken English had also improved since 1971, and he no longer required an interpreter for all his talks.

Foucault was scheduled to give public lectures and a seminar, but only fragments of what was said have survived. Two fragmentary typescripts, one dated 8 May 1975, the other undated, and entitled, respectively, 'Discourse and Repression' and 'On Infantile Sexuality', indicate that he was working on an early version of *Histoire de la sexualité*.[58]

In both typescripts Foucault speaks of wanting to write a kind of sequel to *Histoire de la folie* and of having attempted to write a history of 'sexual anomalies', which he had recently begun to examine at the Collège de France, and of the repression of sexuality. He had failed to do so because he could not find the necessary documentation. His failure might, he thought, have been related to the role of the 'repressive hypothesis', which he associated with Wilhelm Reich and his 'Sexpol' movement of the 1930s and the belief that sexual liberation would finally dispel the shadows of repression. Against that view, Foucault was now beginning to argue that power does not suppress desire; it produces it, creating the very form of the individual subject. It would therefore be more profitable to study the strategies of power than the prohibitions of the law. Given their fragmentary nature and uncertain status, little more can be said about these typescripts, but it is clear that they represent a stage in the difficult genesis and birth of the planned multivolume *Histoire de la sexualité*.

The pleasures of California were by no means purely academic. Foucault discovered a gay society which was unimaginable in France and a sexual openness which enchanted and enthralled him. On this brief visit, he had little time to explore it, but came to know it well on later trips. It seems that it was now that Foucault began to develop his flirtation with the world of leather and sado-masochism, which were only some of the pleasures available. At this point, he made no mention of them in print and, when he did, it was in a strictly impersonal mode. California, in the shape of two gay academics, also offered LSD, which Foucault now took for the first time. The occasion was almost ceremonial, and had as its setting the desert, and as its background accompaniment a tape of Stockhausen. Rumours abound about the acid trip; this is one of the Foucault stories that everyone seems to know. Reports from those who claim that he told them that it changed his life should probably be treated with some scepticism; the insights granted by LSD tend to be short-lived and illusory rather than real. In

November 1975, Foucault spoke nostalgically to Mauriac of 'an unforgettable evening on LSD, in carefully prepared doses, in the desert night, with delicious music, nice people, and some chartreuse'.[59] Like many users of acid, Foucault claimed that the hallucinogen had had a revelatory effect. Whether or not he was referring specifically to this first trip is unclear, but he reportedly told Defert that 'the terrifying experience had been a sort of psychoanalysis for him'. In conversation with Mauriac in July 1984, Defert confided that Foucault had told him that the drug experience had revealed to him that Daniel had taken the place of his sister Francine in his life.[60] There was now a new addition to the formulary of pleasures, and acid remained an occasional, intense delight.

On his return from California, Foucault was approached by *Le Monde*'s Roger-Pol Droit with a project for a book. Droit suggested that they should collaborate on a series of interviews which would give 'a rather different book'. Droit envisaged a series of conversations that would shed light on the more obscure parts of Foucault's *oeuvre* and explore some of the avenues it had begun to open up. Foucault agreed, and the two met for ten or so working sessions which produced fifteen hours of tape recordings and, eventually, a typescript of some three hundred pages. Increasingly, it became clear that the inevitable concentration on Foucault's past was becoming a source of irritation. The more he was asked to explain things, the more the project began to resemble an intellectual autobiography, which was not a genre to Foucault's liking. It was the future and his new projects that interested him. By common consent, the project was abandoned. One brief extract was published two years after Foucault's death; the remainder languishes in Droit's files.

The surviving extract concentrates on literature and is in some ways a postscript to the writings of Foucault's 'literary period'. He now had little time for the argument, elaborated by *Tel Quel* and other groups, that the act of writing itself was subversive, and that as it became increasingly self-reflexive, it became increasingly revolutionary. Speaking in the past tense, he once more described how Bataille, Blanchot and Klossowski had, like Nietzsche, represented an escape from the constricting discourse of philosophy, an area in which philosophy became permeable to other forms of thought and language. The tone is valedictory, almost rueful. For the moment, Foucault was more interested in the question of how academic and avant-garde discourses effectively collude in defining some texts as 'literary', or promote them to 'literary' status. In the published fragment, he offers no solution.[61]

remarked that his dilemma would be a good subject for Claire Brétecher, the *Observateur*'s devastating cartoonist and chronicler of the comedy of middle-class Parisian life.

The same group met again in the evening, when they were joined by Santiago Carrillo, the secretary general of the Spanish Communist Party (PSOE). Jean Daniel had been in touch with Madrid and had learned that if the delegation arrived on Sunday, they would receive no publicity, as a warm weekend in September was not a time for political debate. Delaying the expedition to Monday – the *Nouvel Observateur*'s publication day – meant that Daniel would not be able to go. Carrillo was now asked for his opinion of the plan, and it was immediately obvious from his expression that he did not approve. In his view, there was no need for haste, since nothing would happen for at least a week. He found the idea of handing out leaflets in the street both dangerous and ridiculous. On the one hand, the leafleters would be exposing themself to immediate arrest under the terms of Spain's draconian anti-terrorist legislation. On the other hand, serious people should undertake serious activities, and leafleting by a group of French 'celebrities' might offend local sensibilities. A press conference, however, would at least allow them to speak, if only briefly.

Foucault replied to the objections. As to possible problems with the police, the whole point of the exercise was, in his view, to be arrested. He did not see himself as 'a serious personage'; on the contrary, his previous political actions, meaning his work with the GIP, had all been intended to break down hierarchies and represented a refusal to be a spokesman for any particular social category. On the other hand, he was now convinced that a press conference was the most appropriate form of action. He proposed that a leaflet should be taken to Madrid; even if they were silenced, the written word would remain.

The text, drafted by Foucault, reads as follows:

Ten men and women have just been condemned to death. They have been condemned by special courts and did not have the right to justice.

Neither the justice that demands proof in order to condemn. Nor the justice that gives the condemned the ability to defend themselves. Nor the justice that ensures them the protection of the law, no matter how serious the accusations. Nor the justice that protects sick men, nor that which forbids the ill-treatment of prisoners.

We have always fought for this justice in Europe. Even today, we must fight for it whenever it is threatened. We do not wish to proclaim innocence; we do not have the means to do so. We are not asking for a late pardon; the Spanish regime's past does not allow us to be that patient. But we are demanding that the basic rules of justice must be respected by the men of Spain, just as they are respected by men elsewhere.

We have come to Madrid to bear this message. Matters are so serious that we had to. Our presence is intended to show that the indignation that shakes us means that we, along with many others, are in solidarity with these threatened lives.[69]

Signatories had now to be found. Sartre and Aragon were obvious choices, and it was rightly assumed that it would not be difficult to persuade them to sign. André Malraux's name was inextricably linked with Spain; he had fought in the Civil War and had later been condemned to death *in absentia* by Franco's courts. His novel *L'Espoir* is still probably the greatest prose work to have been inspired by the Spanish conflict. The problem was that Malraux had said nothing about Spain for years, and very rarely signed petitions of any kind. Obtaining his signature was a task for Claude Mauriac, who had been acquainted with Malraux since the 1940s and who had written on him.[70] He had dined with Malraux in August. In the course of their conversation, the latter began to discuss Foucault, and opined that Maurice Clavel might have been right to suggest that Foucault had had said all he had to say in *Les Mots et les choses*.[71]

Mauriac telephoned Sophie de Vilmorin, who demurred, saying that Malraux would never ask Franco for anything, even a life. She was, however, impressed to learn that the text was to be physically taken to Spain. An hour and a half later, she rang back: Malraux had agreed, with some reluctance, to sign. He did not particularly approve of the plan, and claimed that his signature would bring bad luck, but was willing to allow his name to be used. Malraux's signature had considerable importance for Foucault; as a student, he had admired him so greatly that he had been able to recite whole pages of his works by heart.[72] In the meantime, Foucault had obtained the signature of the Nobel prizewinner François Jacob, his colleague at the Collège de France.

The search for signatures was punctuated by one comic incident. Catherine von Bülow put down the phone and suddenly announced that 'the prince' agreed to sign. Asked which prince she meant, she replied 'Rainier', to the disgust of Foucault, who protested that he would have nothing further to do with the matter. Finally, the misunderstanding was cleared up: the 'prince' in question was Leprince-Ringuet, a member of the Académie Française and not of the Grimaldi family of Monaco. His name did not, for unexplained reasons, figure in the final document. The list of signatories read: André Malraux, Pierre Mendès France, Louis Aragon, Jean-Paul Sartre and François Jacob.

It was decided that the message would be taken to Spain by seven individuals: Costa-Gavras, Debray, Foucault, Father Ladouze, Jean Lacouture, Claude Mauriac and Yves Montand. To his chagrin, Daniel Defert was excluded from the group, as it was thought that his lack of social and media visibility made it likely that he would be harshly treated.[73] Of the seven, Debray, who now dismisses the incident as ridiculous and refuses to discuss it,[74] was probably the most at risk: he had previously been expelled from Spain and his Latin American connections meant that his reputation there was only slightly better than that of the devil himself. Montand and Costa-Gavras were famed for their collaboration on films like Z. In terms of French intellectual politics, Mauriac was the incarnation of his father's opposition to Franco – unusual in that many French Catholics had supported El Caudillo's crusade against the godless Republic.

The delegation, or 'commando' as Jean Daniel called it,[75] was all male. In a token gesture towards feminism, it had been suggested that at least one woman should be in the party. The name of Catherine Deneuve was put forward; she was working with Montand, but was too preoccupied with her part and refused to be distracted. Von Bülow suggested Simone de Beauvoir, who was something of an obvious choice. Unwittingly, she had mentioned one of the names that could not be pronounced in the presence of Foucault, who exploded in rage and completely rejected the suggestion. For a moment, von Bülow thought that he was actually going to strike her. As it was, no woman joined the expedition and 'Les Montand-boys' – the phrase is von Bülow's – left alone.[76]

On the morning of 22 September, Foucault and Mauriac drove together to Charles de Gaulle airport, carrying the text in both French and Spanish (the Spanish translation was by Santiago Carrillo). At the airport they were joined by the other five 'Montand-boys'. The plane was almost empty, and they passed the time by signing copies of their leaflet. It now carried a coda: 'Our physical presence in Madrid must add to the seriousness of our demands, must demonstrate the indignation that moves us and has made us, and many others, demonstrate our solidarity with those whose lives are threatened.'

Customs and immigration posed no problems, and the group emerged into the sunlight. A suite had been booked by Montand and Costa-Gavras on the twentieth floor of the Torre de Madrid hotel. The hotel was also to be the venue for the press conference. After a brief visit to the offices of a clandestine newspaper, they made for the bar. Here, representatives of the foreign press and a few Spanish journalists were beginning to gather. Yves Montand read out the text in French but before Debray could read the Spanish version, plain-clothes members of the Security Police intervened. Everyone was ordered to remain silent and to stay seated. Costa-Gavras slipped Mauriac a scrap of paper with the number of the French embassy scrawled on it. Foucault asked if they were under arrest, and was told that they were not but had to remain seated. He was then asked to hand over the remaining leaflets. He refused, and tension rose immediately. Mauriac was afraid that Foucault would be physically assaulted and a second fear suddenly crossed his mind: perhaps these were not policemen but members of the Guerrillas of Christ the King, a clandestine right-wing paramilitary group. Foucault was pale, trembling with anger, and seemed ready to attack, but finally gave in to Mauriac's whispered entreaties and handed over his leaflets. The arrival of grey-uniformed *policias armadas* reduced the tension somewhat, as it was now obvious that the feared Guerrillas were not in fact present. All the journalists present were arrested, including *The Times*'s William Chislett, and led away in handcuffs. The French were held separately and told that they would immediately be put on a flight for Paris.

Two of the group were allowed to collect their luggage, under police guard, and all were embarked in police vehicles. Mauriac read sympathy and fraternity on the faces of bystanders outside the hotel; the fate of anyone arrested by the *policias armadas* was always in doubt. For a brief moment, Montand was left standing alone on the steps of the hotel and Mauriac had the impression of being in a Costa-Gavras film. So did Foucault:

> Yves Montand read the text signed by André Malraux and the four other French personalities. Plain-clothes inspectors intervened as the reading ended in an impressive silence. There was something fantastic about the look of these policemen and they found the presence of Montand extremely embarrassing: the man who incarnates the image of the 'resistance fighter' in so many

films had suddenly found himself face to face with policemen who recognised him. That gave the scene an extraordinary political intensity . . . [Yves Montand] was the last to leave. He reached the top of the steps of the hotel, with armed policemen on either side; at the bottom of the stairs, the police had cleared the road and their van was much further away. Behind the vans, several hundred people were watching the scene. It was a bit like a rehearsal for the scene in Z where the member of parliament is clubbed. Montand, very dignified, with his head tilted slightly backwards, walked very slowly down the steps. It was then that we felt the presence of fascism. The way people watch without seeing anything, as though they had witnessed the scene hundreds of times before. And at the same time the sadness, and probably the stupefaction, at seeing a very real scene they had lived through hundreds of times, with the imaginary hero they have seen on the screen as an actor in it. They were seeing a film about their own political realities. And that silence . . .[77]

It was not only cinematic memories that were evoked. Foucault could have been back in wartime Poitiers:

It was feeling the presence of fascism that frightened us. We had childhood memories of France under the German occupation, but since then we had lost contact with that presence. But we felt it there . . . We saw once again that sight we had known during the German occupation: the silence of the crowd, watching and saying nothing.[78]

At the airport, it became obvious that the delegation was merely going to be expelled from Spain. They were carefully searched and their passports were examined with unusual care. As they boarded the Air France plane, one of the policeman began to swear at Father Ladouze in Spanish. Costa-Gavras, who was already on the steps, began to shout 'Abajo fascismo! Abajo Franco!' The policeman rushed at him, but found his path blocked by Mauriac and others. Costa-Gavras was now inside the plane, where he found himself surrounded by an impassive group of Japanese travellers. The policeman ordered him to follow him back to the airport. At this point the pilot arrived. After some delicate negotiations in the cabin, the policeman was finally convinced that further action on his part would result in an international incident, since the plane was technically French territory. In the meantime, Montand was handing out the few leaflets he had left to the French passengers on board.

The plane finally took off for Paris. Mauriac later wrote that he had never enjoyed an in-flight meal so much. The seven had been in Madrid for a total of six hours. When they landed in Paris, they were immediately surrounded by a mob of journalists and media people, all of them interested in Montand rather than Foucault. The latter greeted Catherine von Bülow with enthusiastic affection, and generally behaved like a schoolboy who has outwitted the school authorities.[79]

On 27 September, five of the militants – three of them from FRAP – were executed, Franco's only concession being that they were shot and not garrotted. The executions were immediately condemned by the international community. Nine EEC countries recalled their ambassadors and the Vatican expressed its disapproval. Mexico called for Spain to be expelled from the United Nations. The silence of the French government was deafening.

Not all protests were couched in diplomatic language. In Lisbon, still heady with the atmosphere of the previous year's revolution, the Spanish embassy was ransacked and set on fire. There was no police intervention. After an hour of violence, only the smoking walls were left standing. In Paris, demonstrators took to the streets in spontaneous protest and the Champs-Elysées became a battleground. Initially, it seemed that the police had lost control but they regrouped and succeeded in blocking access to the embassy. A bomb exploded outside the Simca-Chrysler showrooms and attempts were made to burn a Spanish-owned bank. It was morning before calm was restored.

At about eight in the evening, Foucault, Mauriac and Defert went to see what was happening. As they reached the avenue Marceau, they encountered a huge procession. The atmosphere was electric, but Defert quickly realised that what they were seeing was in fact the withdrawal of the PCF contingent. Many of the remaining demonstrators were young, and some of them were waving red, yellow and purple flags inscribed with the initials FRAP. According to Mauriac, the majority were Spanish. The young man who approached Foucault on the corner of the avenue Montaigne and the rue du Boccador was not, presumably, Spanish but French. With a remarkably poor sense of timing, he asked Foucault if he would be willing to speak to the group he supported about Marx. The reply was brutal and scornful: 'Don't talk to me about Marx any more. I never want to hear of that gentleman again. Go and talk to the professionals. The ones who are paid to do that. The ones who are his civil servants. For my part, I'm completely through with Marx.'[80]

The night was getting cold, and Foucault and Defert left to look for a taxi to take them to the rue de Vaugirard to pick up sweaters. Mauriac now found himself being asked to link arms with those on either side of him. The demonstrators began to retreat slowly as the massed CRS moved forward. Suddenly, a volley of gas grenades was fired into the crowd, which broke up in panic. Mauriac found refuge in the courtyard of a building, and then watched the scuffles from a safe distance. He later learned that the CRS had been acting on orders when they charged without any provocation; the time for the executions was drawing near and the government wanted the approaches to the embassy cleared at all costs. Mauriac left the scene, uncertain whether or not the two figures he saw in the distance were Foucault and Defert. They had in fact returned to the area at about three in the morning, but could not find Mauriac.

A national demonstration was called by the parties of the left for Sunday 29 September. Tens of thousands of people, many of them carrying or wearing red carnations, marched from the place de la République to the Bastille. A group of FRAP supporters tried to take their place at the head of the demonstration, only to be surrounded by CGT stewards who argued that the CGT had called the demonstration and that the CGT should therefore lead it. CGT stewards are not noted for their gentle handling of political rivals, but on this occasion they were powerless to prevent the inevitable. It was to the chant of 'FRAP', 'FRAP' that the demonstration entered the place de la Bastille over two hours after it had left République. To his lasting surprise, a former secretary to General de Gaulle found himself marching, with clenched fist, in support of a terrorist organisation. Somewhere in the crowd was Michel Foucault.

The September executions were to be the last atrocities of the Franco regime. On 20 November 1975, Franco finally died. Malraux, no doubt to his great satisfaction, outlived him by a year and three days. As his biographer puts it, his last political act had been to make the voices of the fighters of the Sierra de Teruel heard at last.[81] Lecturing at the Collège de France in the following March, Foucault used the 'small and joyous event' of Franco's death to illustrate a new phase in 'bio-power'; people could now be kept living beyond the limits of actual physical life. Franco had been kept alive by medical technology; 'The man who had the power of life and death over hundreds of thousands of people, fell under the blows of a power that organised life so well that he did not even notice that he was already dead, that he was being kept alive after his death.'[82] In 1976, Foucault also commented on the death of Malraux: 'The things that he spoke about were more important to him than the fact that he was saying them.' He then compared Malraux to Bernanos and Céline, asking: 'What are we now to make of men like them, of one who was more than a writer but who was not a saint, one who was more than a writer and who was probably not a swine, and one who was more than a writer, and neither a revolutionary at the age of twenty nor a statesman in old age? Perhaps we are too dedicated to commentary to understand what lives are.'[83]

Foucault's defiance of the police in the bar of the Torre de Madrid is proof of his undoubted physical courage, though, as he remarked to Mauriac at the time, he would have given in a lot more quickly if he had been confronted with a sub-machine-gun. In his own view, it was also the expression of a basic principle: 'I take the view that it is a cop's job to use physical force. Anyone who opposes the cops must therefore not allow them the hypocrisy of masking physical force behind orders which have to be obeyed immediately. The cops must follow through what they represent to the very end.'[84] The individual policeman is the incarnation of power, and power must be constantly resisted. Resistance provides a basis for apparently unlikely alliances:

I do . . . things at the same time with someone (Régis Debray) who probably believes the opposite of what I believe, I don't know, I really don't know any more. What I do know is that we have to be against power, that we always have to hound it into a corner . . . We must not accept, never accept its *raison d'être*, which it cannot, by its very nature, give up: deciding what is permissible and what is not permissible, what it condemns and excludes. We must *never* stop opposing that, so as to force it, *always*, to reach its limits, and try, always, to reduce its domain.[85]

Shortly after his return from Madrid, Foucault left France for a brief lecture tour in Brazil, where he spoke in both Rio de Janeiro and São Paulo. The lectures – for students of social medicine at the Guanabara State University – remain unpublished, but dealt with the themes of criminality, urbanisation and public health.[86] Previous visits to Brazil had been relaxed and pleasant, but on this occasion the political climate was oppressive and Foucault interrupted his brief tour. The specific incident that provoked his disgust was the murder at the hands of the police of a Jewish journalist and member of the clandestine Communist Party:

The Jewish community did not dare give him an official funeral. And it was the Archbishop of São Paulo, Dom Evariste, who organised a ceremony, an interdenominational ceremony, in memory of the journalist in St Paul's cathedral. It attracted thousands and thousands of people into the church and on to the square, and the cardinal, in his red robes, presided over the ceremony, and at the end of the ceremony he advanced towards the faithful and greeted them by shouting '*Shalom, shalom*'. There were armed police all around the square, and plain-clothes police inside the church. The police backed down; they could do nothing against this. I must say that that has a grandeur, a power; there is something of enormous historical weight there.[87]

The spectacle of a Catholic archbishop in the presence of a rabbi confirmed him in his lingering admiration for the church, despite his proclaimed dislike of Christians.[88]

On a cold day a week before Christmas 1975, Foucault, Mauriac, Jean-Pierre Faye, Daniel Guérin and Pierre Halbwachs shivered for over an hour before the demonstration finally moved out. In fact two processions filed out of the place de la Bastille, one consisting of the batallions of the 'united left', and the other made up of miscellaneous leftists, anarchists and celebrities. The two columns were kept apart not by the police but by a *cordon sanitaire* of PCF and CGT stewards. The demonstration was in suport of a number of conscripts who faced trial before the Cour de la Sûreté de l'Etat (State Security Court) on charges of attempting to demoralise the army.[89]

Conscription is not usually a contentious issue in France, and most of those called up view their period of military service as a tedious waste of time to be tolerated as best they can. In the mid-1970s, it did become an issue as a very politicised generation of conscripts objected to being used to break strikes by refuse collectors, and began to demand the right to organise.[90] For many, the primary issue was that of physical living conditions in barracks. The memory of the role plyed by junior officers in the Portuguese revolution of 1974 added a further dimension, and no doubt raised the spectre of insurrection for many military men. Within the soldiers' movement itself, a current of revolutionary anti-militarism coexisted rather uneasily with a more syndicalist current concerned almost exclusively with democratic rights.

Foucault was not a major figure in this movement. He did, however, take part in demonstrations and signed manifestoes.[91] In February 1976, he also put his name to a document which was, potentially, more compromising than any petition. The document was signed by a number of celebrities (de Beauvoir, Sartre, Châtelet, the actor Serge Reggiani, the popular singer Maxime Leforrestier, Mauriac, Foucault . . .), who admitted to such offences as being in possession of leaflets putting forward the demands of the soldiers' commitees, demanding the exercise of democratic rights in army barracks, and supporting the right of association for enlisted men and conscripts alike. Young soldiers were facing charges for these offences, and the signatories demanded to be charged too.[92]

Both Mauriac and Foucault were aware of being in a potentially ridiculous situation. Either they would be charged, in which case they should perhaps have looked more carefully at what they were signing, or they would be ignored and their gesture would be meaningless.[93] Predictably, they were left looking ridiculous. Foucault had no great or lasting concern with the issues at stake, but he was more than willing to express his solidarity with those directly involved in protests against one more form of confinement.

He was more directly involved in one incident. A film shot clandestinely on the 705 Air Base at Tours and entitled *Le Cicogne en rogne* ('The Stork Gets Angry') was being shown at a small cinema in the fourteenth *arrondissement*.[94] Foucault's presence once more brought him into direct conflict with the police. When the cinema was raided, Foucault, to the amazement of many of the young activists present, had to be physically prevented from attacking a police officer. Possible violence then gave way to farce when the *commissaire* who was checking the identity of those arrested referred to Daniel Guérin, who was considerably older than most of those present, as 'Monsieur Foucault.' The real 'Monsieur Foucault' was not amused, and protested loudly.[95]

14

THE USE OF PLEASURES

SIX volumes by Michel Foucault,' announced *Le Monde* on 5 November 1976. The short piece in the lower right-hand corner of the front page, unsigned but probably by Roger-Pol Droit, began:

> Sex repressed? We go on saying it again and again: the West has supposedly smothered, censured and forbidden the healthy exercise of healthy pleasure. And sexual liberation, which has become necessary, would apparently be both felicitous and subversive. Michel Foucault, professor at the Collège de France and one of the 'great gurus' of our young philosophers, now rejects that hypothesis as a received idea.

The six volumes, optimistically planned to appear at the rate of one a year, were to be collectively entitled *Histoire de la sexualité*.

Foucault's thesis had in fact already been in the public domain for several months, thanks to the excitable Maurice Clavel. In a radio debate with Philippe Sollers, he had remarked in July: 'If my information about his [Foucault's] next book, which is devoted to sexuality in the West, is correct, it changes everything, once again! It shows – hold on tight – that for the last three hundred years there have certainly been repressions but that, on the whole, in the dynamism that constitutes our society, *sexuality has not been repressed*! On the contrary: it has been *incited*.' Presenter Jacques Paugam's only response was a spluttered '*Fichtre*' ('Gosh').[1]

The project was an old one. In the original preface to *Histoire de la folie*, Foucault suggested that one of the histories that should be written is that of 'sexual taboos', a history which would speak of 'the continually moving and obstinate forms of repression, not in order to produce a chronicle of morality or repression, but to reveal the tragic division of the happy world of desire to be the limit of the western world and the origin of its ethics'.[2] The same theme reappeared in the opening lines of a major essay on Bataille written in 1963:

We readily believe that, in contemporary experience, sexuality has found once more a natural truth which supposedly waited for a long time in the shadows, under various disguises, before it had the right to come at last into the full light of language, and which only our positive perspicacity now allows us to decipher.[3]

In an interview, Foucault described his planned histories of madness and sexuality as 'twin projects', adding that he had been 'thinking about' the second for twenty years. The project finally crystallised as he was listening to an afternoon radio programme on which a psycho-analyst and a sexologist advised listeners on their sexual problems: 'The only thing they would ask the poor man was "Can you get an erection or not?" Yet there was something very different behind the difficulties he was having with his wife.'[4]

In lectures given in 1970, Foucault sometimes alludes to an abandoned project of writing a history of repression, explaining that he never completed it because he could not find the documentation he required.[5] The same project was at times referred to as being about 'infantile sexuality', and it was probably to this that Foucault referred ('a text on infantile sexuality before Freud') in conversation with Mauriac in August of the same year.[6]

The *Histoire de la sexualité* series opened with *La Volonté de savoir*, which was originally entitled *Sexe et vérité* ('Sex and Truth').[7] The definitive title ('The Will to Knowledge') deliberately makes allusion to Nietzsche's 'will to power', though the point is completely lost in the English translation.[8] 'La Volonté de savoir' had of course been the generic title of the first year's lecture series at the Collège de France, though in that context the term did not apply to sexuality. The back cover of the relatively slim volume announced the completion of Foucault's genealogy by the following volumes: *La Chair et le corps* ('The Body and the Flesh'), *La Croissade des enfants* ('The Children's Crusade'), *La Femme, la mère, l'hystérique* ('Woman, Mother, Hysteric'), *Les Pervers* ('Perverts') and, finally, *Population et races* ('Population and Races'). None of them appeared in the form announced, and the shape of *Histoire de la sexualité* was to change considerably over the next eight years. A footnote announces yet another volume, provisionally entitled *Le Pouvoir de la vérité* ('The Power of Truth'), dealing with torture in Greek and Roman law;[9] this was a topic often touched upon since 1970, and one to which Foucault would often return, but the book itself remained unwritten. Given that it is an introductory and program-matic text, much of *La Volonté de savoir* is given over to outlining future volumes in the planned series. Its programmatic nature also no doubt explains the relative lack of documentary evidence to support its far-reaching hypotheses. Foucault was to regret the tactic of outlining unwritten volumes, claiming that it led to misunderstandings on the part of his critics.[10]

The first volume of the planned history clearly went through a number of different drafts and its argument changed dramatically in the process. Initially, Foucault took 'sex' as a given, and viewed 'sexuality' as a discursive-institutional formation which masked it. Dissatisfied with that thesis, he inverted its terms, arguing that sex is produced by the apparatus (*dispositif*) of sexuality. The discourse of sexuality applies, not to sex, but to the body and the sexual organs, to pleasures and to relations of alliance.[11] The notion of the *dispositif* is the text's major theoretical innovation, and in a sense it replaces the *épistémè* of *Les Mots et les choses*, which was already in eclipse in *L'Archéologie du savoir*.

In a discussion with a group of Lacanians, Foucault defined most clearly what he meant by a *dispositif*. The term refers to a heterogeneous body of discourses, propositions (philosophical, moral, philanthropic and so on), institutions, laws and scientific statements; the *dispositif* itself is the network that binds them together, that governs the play between the heterogeneous strands. It is a formation which, at a given historical moment, corresponds to a dominant strategic function, such as the absorption by a mercantile society of a surplus floating population. The strategic imperative to absorb that population gradually becomes the *dispositif* for the control-subjectification of madness, mental illness and neurosis. In a sense, the *dispositif* represents Foucault's attempt to analyse 'strategies of balances of power supporting types of knowledge'. His attempt to write a history of the *épistémè* in *Les Mots et les choses* had, he now admits, led him into a blind alley. The *épistémè* was no more than a specifically discursive *dispositif*.[12] Dreyfus and Rabinow nicely gloss the notion of *dispositif*: 'The *dispositif* is, of course, a grid of intelligibility constructed by the historian. But it is also the practices themselves, acting as an apparatus, a tool, constituting subjects and organising them.'[13]

The basic thesis of *La Volonté de savoir* quickly gained notoriety. Foucault paraphrased what he called the 'repressive hypothesis' in the following terms, which reveal how much the project had changed since 1961: 'If sex is repressed, that is, condemned to prohibition, non-existence and silence, then the mere fact of speaking about it looks like a deliberate transgression. Anyone who uses this language places himself, to a certain extent, outside power; he upsets the law; he anticipates, ever so slightly, the freedom of the future.'[14]

He then raised three doubts as to its accuracy: that sex has been repressed may not be an actual historical fact; the mechanisms of power may not centre on repression; there is not necessarily any historical break between the age of repression and the analysis of repression.[15] Arguing the case against the repressive hypothesis, he then claims that the last three centuries have seen a 'veritable discursive explosion', a 'discursive fermentation' about sexuality.[16] The nineteenth century, in particular, did not see 'the exclusion of a thousand aberrant sexualities', but rather 'the specification and regional solidification of each of them'.[17] This was the process whereby perversions were incorporated, or literally made flesh, and whereby individuals were specified as perverse. Sodomy, for instance, had once been a category of forbidden acts, whose 'author' was no more than their juridical support or subject; the sexual cosmology of the nineteenth century, in contrast, created 'the homosexual', 'a past, a history and a childhood, a character, a form of life . . .'[18]

The compulsion to talk about sex can be traced back to the Christian pastoral and to the ritual of confession, which finds a strange parallel in the injunctions given in de Sade's *120 Journées de Sodome*: tell all, and in exhaustive detail. Foucault achieves a startling effect by juxtaposing two quotations, one from Liguori's *Préceptes sur le sixième commandement* and one from de Sade. 'Not only consummated acts, but sensual touchings, all impure glances, all obscene remarks . . .' 'Your stories must be graced with the greatest and most searching detail; we cannot judge how the passion you are describing relates to the mores and characteristics of man if you conceal any circumstance.'[19]

One of Foucault's other emblematic sources is the anonymous *My Secret Life*, which he read in the 1964 Grove Press edition and which, like many of its readers, he probably discovered thanks to Steven Marcus's *The Other Victorians*.[20] Marcus's study provides Foucault with the title of his opening chapter: 'Nous autres, victoriens'. *My Secret Life*, probably written between 1890 and 1895 and consisting of eleven small volumes running to over 4,000 pages, chronicles the compulsive sexual exploits of an anonymous Victorian gentleman who is usually identified with the author, 'Walter'. For Walter, the fact that the 'strange practices' he described were indulged in by thousands of people was in itself a justification for publishing his journals; for Foucault, his description of sexual activities was the strangest practice of all, and its principle had been inscribed in the heart of modern man for at least two hundred years. 'Walter' was 'the most direct and in a certain way the most naive representative of a multisecular injunction to talk about sex'.[21]

So taken was Foucault with the book that he was instrumental in the publication of an abridged French translation of the Grove edition in 1978.[22] In his preface to that edition, he speculates that the work is grounded in 'an old spiritual tradition' which had been preserved in Protestant countries: 'keeping a written diary of one's life, examining one's conscience on a blank sheet of paper'.[23] The suggestion is intriguing, but not entirely convincing. A Victorian gentleman such as Walter is unlikely to have been familiar with 'old spiritual traditions', though he would have known of the Anglican Church's Act of General Confession. It may be possible to establish a link between de Sade's narrators and confessors' manuals; that between the detailed chronicles of *My Secret Life* and the remarkably unspecific 'manifold sins and wickedness' alluded to in the communion liturgy is tenuous in the extreme. Whatever the origins of *My Secret Life*, it is improbable that they lie in the practices of a church which has never made individual confession obligatory. Foucault also overlooks the considerable sociological element in the book, and the possibility that Walter may have had more in common with Henry Mayhew and similar chroniclers of the Victorian city than with the confessional tradition.

Any unwary reader who hoped to find a description of sexual practices would be sadly disappointed by *La Volonté de savoir*, which does not offer the vicarious delights of a *Psychopathologica sexualis*. Foucault's aim is not to chronicle sexual practices, but to 'analyse the formation of a certain type of knowledge about sex, not in terms of repression or law, but in terms of power'.[24] Four strategic domains are identified for future research: the hystericalisation of women's bodies; the pedagogisation of the sexuality of children; the socialisation of procreative behaviour; the psychiatrisation of perverse pleasure.[25]

Throughout, Foucault contrasts two primary discourses on sexuality: an *ars erotica* and a *scientia sexualis*. The former, assumed to exist or to have existed in China, Japan, India, Rome or Arab countries, represents an erotic art in which truth is extracted from 'pleasure itself', 'pleasure being understood as a practice and being recorded as an experience'.[26] The West, in contrast, had developed a dismal *scientia sexualis* which, in order to tell the truth about sex, elaborated procedures organised essentially around forms of power-knowledge, as opposed to *ars erotica*'s rites of initiation. Its primary form of power-knowledge is the confessional mode which uses a criterion of truth that gradually migrates from its ecclesiastical origins to domains

as diverse as education and psychiatry and introduces such divisions as
'normal and pathological' (the nod in the direction of Canguilhem is
obvious). All these domains are governed by a will to knowledge.
Sexuality is not some inchoate level of experience existing outside the
discourse or *dispositif* of sexuality, but its product. In that sense, the
only possible liberation is the liberation of pleasures from the regime of
sexuality and sexual identities.

Sexuality is, moreover, the object and target of the power which
speaks of 'health, progeniture, the future of the species, the vitality of
the social body . . .'[27] The exercise of power-knowledge is organised
around two poles: disciplines and regulatory controls that generate,
respectively, an anatomo-politics of the human body and a biopolitics
of population. Foucault would return to these topics, which are merely
outlined in *La Volonté de savoir*, in his lectures rather than in published
works, 'Security, Territory and Population' being the topic for 1977–
78, and 'The Birth of Biopolitics' that for 1978–79. 'Biopolitics' was
schematically defined by Foucault as 'the way in which attempts have,
since the eighteenth century, been made to rationalise the problems
posed for governmental practice by phenomena characteristic of a
group of living beings constituted as a population: health, hygiene,
natality, longevity, races . . .'[28] Gradually, the new topic of 'governmentality' was beginning to emerge.

La Volonté de savoir was given a quiet welcome by the press.[29] Most
reviewers appear to have taken the view that, given that it was an
introduction to a series of works, final judgement should be reserved
until more volumes were available for comment. Droit, in particular,
was somewhat sceptical about Foucault's historical vision of sexuality
and was not convinced by all his arguments. Why, he asks, should the
encouragement of confession not be seen as repressive? And why, in
speaking of *sex*, should Foucault forget so quickly that there are in fact
two sexes?[30] The expectations of the critics, and no doubt those of
Foucault's readers in general, were to be disappointed. *La Volonté de
savoir* inaugurated, not a proliferation of new works, but a silence which
lasted until *L'Usage des plaisirs* and *Le Souci de soi* were published shortly
before Foucault's death in 1984. Those volumes were very different
from what had been promised in 1976, and any manuscript versions for
the original six-volume series that were produced have not survived.

Reviews of *La Volonté de savoir* began to appear in January and
February 1977. In March a major attack on Foucault came in the form
of Jean Baudrillard's *Oublier Foucault* ('Forget Foucault'). The origins of
this polemical pamphlet, which is little more than an extended article,

remain somewhat obscure. The author of an English-language study of Baudrillard gives two accounts, both based on hearsay. One version has it that the polemic originated in a projected study group which was to have included Baudrillard, Foucault, Lyotard, Deleuze and Guattari, and to which Baudrillard presented what was thought to be an overaggressive position paper; the other that it stemmed from an unrealised plan for an exchange of views between Foucault and Baudrillard in the pages of *Les Temps Modernes*.[31] Neither version can be either verified or falsified, but it has to be said that *Les Temps Modernes* was a distinctly improbable venue for any such exchange. Philippe Meyer, on the other hand, claims that the book originated in an article written for the special issue of *Critique* published in December 1975. As noted earlier, it was also planned to carry a critical review by François Roustang, but that was dropped at the insistence of Jean Piel. Foucault reportedly had sight of Baudrillard's article and reacted very badly to it.[32] Baudrillard himself confirms at least some of Meyer's account, and states that *Oublier Foucault* did originate in an article commissioned by Piel. In an interview devoted mainly to his *Cool Memories*, he states that he found Foucault's analysis of power so perfect as to be disturbing. Baudrillard goes on:

> He read my article. We talked about it for three hours. He told me he wanted to reply to it. So I withdrew my article from circulation, so that we could be able to publish our texts together one day. But after a month, Foucault told me: 'I don't want to reply; do what you like with it.' I immediately published it as a pamphlet. And then everything changed. Foucault, who until then had played the game, sudenly became furious. The title which is obviously provocative, much more so than the text itself, was interpreted as an attack on Foucault's intellectual power, which was enormous. I was put into a sort of quarantine, and I am still suffering the consequences.[33]

Baudrillard's criticisms are couched in wounding terms. Foucault's discourse is itself a discourse of power, a mirror of the powers he is describing: 'The only reason why Foucault can paint such an admirable picture is that he is operating at the limits of an epoch (perhaps the "classical era", of which he may be the last great dinosaur) which is collapsing completely.'[34] Most of Baudrillard's pamphlet consists of a reiteration of his own theses about seduction, simulacra and the hyper-real, but it was the attack on Foucault that gave it its notoriety.

The 'great dinosaur' replied to the call to 'forget Foucault' by quipping to friends that he had difficulty in remembering who Baudrillard was, but he also admitted that he was hurt by the criticisms.[35] In public he maintained a dignified silence. It was only in *L'Usage de plaisirs* that he replied to Baudrillard's charge that he had 'said nothing about the simulacrum of power' by alluding to the need to escape the alternative conceptions of 'power seen as domination or denounced as a simulacrum'.[36] To make matters worse, no one came to his defence in print. After Foucault's death, Baudrillard returned to the topic of 'forgetting Foucault' with a comment that combines a certain insight with extraordinary arrogance:

> Paradoxically, Foucault lived his life as though he were ill-loved and persecuted. He was certainly persecuted by the thousands of disciples and industrious sycophants he certainly secretly despised (or at least one hopes he did), who took away from him in caricatural form all sense of what he was doing. To forget him was to do him a service; to adulate him was to do him a disservice.[37]

Baudrillard's last comment on Foucault is the strangest of all: 'Foucault's death. Loss of confidence in his own genius. Leaving the sexual aspects aside, the loss of the immune systems is no more than the biological transcription of the other process.'[38]

Foucault's silence was of course a very relative one. He continued to teach, lectured in various different countries and went on producing numerous occasional pieces. This was also a period of unrealised projects which were begun and then abandoned without explanation. For years, Foucault had planned to write a book based upon the Bastille archives which would look at the history and function of the *lettre de cachet* in the seventeenth and eighteenth centuries. It did not materialise until 1982, but it would seem that he did work sporadically at collecting material for it throughout this period. The Bastille project also spawned another project. In January 1977, Foucault published an essay which purported to be the introduction to a forthcoming book entitled *La Vie des hommes infâmes*.[39] The book was to appear in Gallimard's 'Le Chemin' series.

'Le Chemin', edited by Georges Lambrichs, is primarily devoted to experimental literary texts, but also publishes some critical studies, including Foucault's own *Raymond Roussel*. In his supposed introduction, Foucault stressed that the work was to be 'not a history book', but an 'anthology of existences. Lives consisting of a few lines or a few pages. Countless misfortunes and adventures summed up in a handful of words.' The idea came to him while reading an early eighteenth-century *registre d'internement* in the Bibliothèque Nationale. The texts were to be selected on purely subjective grounds because of the pleasure, surprise or even fear that they provoked on a first, chance reading. The model was obviously the chance encounter with Pierre Rivière in the dusty pages of the *Annales d'hygiène publique et de médecine légale*. Foucault's relationship with archive material was physical:

I would find it difficult to say just what I felt when I found these fragments . . . No doubt one of those impressions we call 'physical', as though there could be any other kind. And I admit that these 'short stories' that suddenly emerge from two and a half centuries of silence struck more chords than what we usually call 'literature'.[40]

The unrealised project also obviously had a lot to do with Foucault's fascination with the institution of the *lettre de cachet*, a fascination evident since *Histoire de la folie*,[41] and which had already inspired the Bastille project:

The *lettre de cachet*-confinement system was no more than a fairly brief episode; scarcely more than a century, and localised in France alone. That does not make it any less important in the history of the mechanism of power. It does not ensure the spontaneous irruption of royal arbitrariness into life at its most quotidian. It ensures, rather, its distribution through complex circuits and in a whole interplay of demands and responses.[42]

A year later, Gallimard launched a new series edited by Foucault and entitled 'Les Vies parallèlles'. The first and only volume to be published was *Herculine Barbin dite Alexina B.*, the tale of a nineteenth-century hermaphrodite discovered in the page of Tardieu's *Question médico-légale de l'identité dans ses rapports avec les vices de conformation des organes sexuels* of 1874. The collection was in part inspired by Plutarch:

The Ancients liked to establish parallels between the lives of illustrious men; one heard those exemplary shades speaking across the centuries. Parallels are, I know, designed to meet in infinity. Let us imagine others which diverge infinitely. No meeting point, and nowhere for them to be recorded: They often had no echo but that of their condemnation. We have to grasp them in the force of the movement that separates them; we have to rediscover the instantaneous and startling wake they left when they plunged into an obscurity where 'the story is no longer told' and where all 'fame' is lost. It would be like an inverted Plutarch; lives that are so parallel that no one can make them meet.[43]

Hermaphroditism was to have been the subject of an unwritten volume in the *History of Sexuality* series, and the topic relates to the content of the 1974–75 lectures at the Collège de France on 'Les Anormaux'.[44] *Herculine Barbin* is a first-person narrative, written in a floridly romantic style, with the charm of a slightly licentious novel, and recounts the life of 'Herculine' or 'Alexina' who is brought up as a girl, only to discover that 'she' is biologically male. A curious romance with a girl friend ensues, before 'Herculine' is finally confronted with the fact of his/her male identity.

Foucault effaces himself from the text, adding only a brief note on its provenance and some documentary material from contemporary sources. In 1980, an English translation appeared. An introduction was added, as was the text of Oscar Panizza's *A Scandal at the Convent*, a story based on the Barbin case. Foucault's introduction is a version of a paper read to the 1979 Congress of Arcadie. Arcadie was France's oldest gay organisation, though there is something uncomfortable about the application of the term 'gay' to a group which always defined itself as 'homophile'. As the inside cover of the published proceedings of an earlier congress put it: 'Arcadie has always been and always will be dispassionate, serene and dignified, and will devote itself to illustrating the homophile problem so that homophiles themselves will live better lives, and so that the heterosexual world will gain a better understanding of what homophiles are and will accept them for what they are, in other words, with their homophile nature.'

In his opening address, Arcadie's founder André Baudry further stated: 'One day we hope to disappear as Arcadie because, on that day, we will, as we wanted in January 1954 when we founded Arcadie, really be side by side with the others, together with the others. There will no longer be any difference between us and the others, and the whole of society will accept us for what we are.'[45]

In May 1979, Foucault accepted an invitation to speak to Arcadie's congress at the Palais des Congrès, a building more accustomed to hosting events like the annual congress of the Association of the Mayors of France than gatherings of 850 homophiles. He had never before been involved with the organisation. Given his sympathies for FHAR, his presence must have seemed somewhat anomalous; to the young militants of FHAR and its successors, Arcadie and its talk of a future 'absence of difference' must have seen a relic from a distant past.[46] As a rather blasé Guy Hocquenhem described it in 1972, Arcadie ran 'a very discreet homosexual institution ... a members-only club, with a weekly dance and public-information lectures, where people go to look for pick-ups. A fairly bourgeois audience, with quite a few young office workers, some rich old homosexuals, and a small minority of lesbians.'[47] The club, which placed great emphasis on the need for respectable discretion, was founded in 1957, three years after its parent organisation, and was known for official purposes as CLESPAL: Club Littéraire et Scientifique des Pays Latins.[48]

By accepting the invitation, Foucault was taking a deliberate stance. He was paying tribute to what Arcadie had represented before the beginnings of gay liberation and expressing his annoyance at the way a younger generation tended to dismiss it. At the end of the congress, Baudry quietly slipped Foucault an envelope containing 2,000 francs. Foucault returned it, saying that a gay man did not have to be paid to speak to other gays. Baudry confided that he was the only speaker to have refused payment in the entire history of Arcadie.[49]

Three years later, Baudry dissolved his organisation, not because homophiles were at last accepted for what they were, but because he found the commercialism of the gay scene totally repellent. French homosexuals, he complained, 'think of nothing but sex. They are wallowing in cowardice, drowning in pornography and vulgarity, or they are being devoured by politics, and Arcadie's members have done nothing to fight against that situation.'[50]

Foucault was one of four guest speakers at the 1979 congress, the others being the novelist and academic Robert Merle, Jean-Paul Aron and Paul Veyne, an old friend from ENS and, since March 1976, professor of the history of Rome at the Collège de France. To their great amusement, the presence of Foucault and Veyne at this congress scandalised the more staid members of the Collège, who would no doubt have been still more scandalised had they heard the speech in which Veyne solemnly explained that in antiquity, the term 'one of them' referred, not to homosexuals, but to adepts of cunnilingus. Most of his address was less provocative and was devoted to the thesis that antiquity did not contrast the love of men with the love of women, but did contrast activity and passivity: 'To be active was to be male, whatever the sex of the so-called passive partner.'[51] Merle, an English-literature specialist, spoke of the Oscar Wilde trial and of the possibility of anti-gay legislation in the Britain of Margaret Thatcher, and Foucault's old associate Aron spoke on the related topic of 'vice trials'.

Foucault's topic was hermaphroditism, and he began by asking how and why western societies had arrived at a male–female opposition, rather than Veyne's 'active-passive' dichotomy, using the figure of the hermaphrodite as a case in point. The notion of homosexuality was, he argued, coloured by old ideas about hermaphroditism, which was traditionally seen as a crime against the law that identified the individual with 'his' or 'her' sex, and which therefore excluded from society 'deviants' such as hermaphrodites and homosexuals. Pleasure had to be freed from the constraints of that law and from the imperative to have a 'true sex': 'Pleasure is something which passes from one individual to another; it is not secreted by identity. Pleasure has no passport, no identity.'[52]

La Volonté de savoir represents a direct challenge to theories of sexual liberation based upon the repressive hypothesis, which suggest, like Wilhelm Reich, that there is some essential sexuality which could be revolutionary if only it could escape the constraints imposed upon it. Yet the text also contains a utopianism, an appeal for a different liberation:

It is from the agency of sex that we have to free ourselves if, through a tactical reversal of the various mechanisms of sexuality, we wish to assert against the hold of power, bodies, pleasures and knowledges in their multiplicity and their possibility of resistance. The basis for the counterattack against the *dispositif* of sexuality must be, not sex-desire, but bodies and pleasures.[53]

The same point is made in rather more graphic terms in two of the interviews given to publicise the book. In one, Foucault told Madeleine Chapsal: 'I am for the decentralisation, the regionalisation of all pleasures.'[54] In a longer and wider-ranging interview with Bernard-Henri Lévy, he spoke of an emerging movement which is not demanding 'more sex' or 'more truth about sex': 'The point is to, I wouldn't say "rediscover", but actually manufacture other forms of pleasures, of relations, of bonds, loves, intensities.'[55] He gives two examples in support of his diagnosis: the fiction of Hervé Guibert and 'the book by Schérer and Hocquenhem'. Guibert had, according to Foucault, attempted to publish some children's stories, only to have them rejected. He then wrote a graphically 'sexual' book, which was successfully published: 'with filthy material, he constructs bodies, mirages, castles, fusions, tenderness, races, intoxication; all the heavy coefficient of sex is volatilised . . . This may be the end of the dreary desert of sexuality, the end of the monarchy of sex.'[56] Foucault's second example, 'the book by Schérer and Hocquenhem' which 'clearly demonstrates that children have a pleasure regime for which the "sex" grid constitutes a veritable prison', was a special issue of *Recherches* – an elegant apologia for paedophilia described as a 'systematic album of childhood' and first published in May 1976.[57]

In counterposing 'sex-desire' and 'pleasures' (and the plural is important), Foucault was distancing himself from the so-called philosophy of desire associated with Deleuze and Lyotard. He explained in an interview given in July 1978:

> I am advancing this term [pleasure] because it seems to me that it escapes the medical and naturalistic connotations inherent in the notion of desire. That notion has been used as a tool . . . a calibration in terms of normality: 'Tell me what your desire is and I will tell you who you are, whether you are normal or not, and then I can qualify or disqualify your desire . . .' The term 'pleasure' on the other hand is virgin territory, almost devoid of meaning. There is no pathology of pleasure, no 'abnormal' pleasure. It is an event 'outside the subject' or on the edge of the subject, within something that is neither body nor soul, which is neither inside nor outside, in short a notion which is neither ascribed nor ascribable.[58]

In the same interview, Foucault referred to the blazons of masculinity and even machismo to be found in gay communities, and suggested that they might not mark a return to phallocracy or machismo, but an attempt to 'invent oneself, to make one's body the place of production of extraordinarily polymorphous pleasures . . . The point is to detach oneself from that virile form of pleasure to order [*commandé*] known as *jouissance*, *jouissance* in the ejaculatory sense, in the masculine sense of the term.'[59] At such points, Foucault comes very close to speaking of his own sexuality.

Desexualisation was part of Foucault's vision of a gay culture. His contribution to it was not purely theoretical. A month before he spoke at Arcadie's congress, he contributed an article to *Gai Pied*, a new monthly magazine. The title itself was Foucault's invention, and was first suggested over a meal with Jean Le Bitoux, the founding editor. ' "*Etre gai et prendre son pied*", those were the two initial intentions.'[60] *Gai pied* defies translation. *Gai* does have the same double meaning in French as in English, but the sexual sense has never become widely used in France, where the majority of gays still refer to themselves as '*homosexuel*'. *Prendre son pied* means, very roughly, 'to be turned on by something', and is often used in a sexual sense. Foucault subsequently extended the wordplay still further and took to referring to the magazine's readers and writers as *les gais piétons* (literally 'gay pedestrians'). The project was to take gay journalism out of the ghetto of the clubs and bars of the rue Sainte-Anne, and to refuse to be confined to the 'role conceded it (the defence and illustration of homosexuality)'.[61] *Gai Pied* was successful enough to go weekly in November 1982.

Foucault's contribution to the first issue was a subdued, almost melancholy meditation on the theme of suicide. Taking his cue from the observation, culled from a treatise on psychiatry, that 'homosexuals often commit suicide', he muses about 'slender boys with pale cheeks' who, being 'incapable of crossing the threshold of the other sex', spend their lives entering the antechamber of death and then leave it, slamming the door on their way out. He argues for the right to commit suicide, the proviso being that it should be a right to die in dignity and comfort, without the horrors (duly catalogued) that so often accompany suicide bids. In a final flight of fancy he suggests that potential suicides should enjoy the benefits of institutions modelled on Japan's 'love hotels' (which he saw in 1978), with 'weird decors . . . in which you could seek out with nameless partners a chance to die without any identity'. To die in that manner would be 'such a simple pleasure'.[62] Suicide is not a constant theme, though it does appear occasionally in Foucault's writings, and there are rumours that he made a suicide bid as a student. Claude Mauriac, for one, was convinced in 1982 that Foucault's future plans included the possibility of suicide.[63]

Foucault did not become a regular contributor to *Gai Pied* and published only two more pieces in it.[64] The first deals with friendship, but clearly got off to an unfriendly start. Asked by an unidentified interviewer for his opinion of the magazine, 'as a man in his fifties', Foucault immediately objected that the identification of 'homosexuality' with 'love between young men' was both problematical and objectionable:

> One of the concessions we make to others is presenting homosexuality purely in the form of immediate pleasure, of two young men meeting in the street, seducing one another with their eyes, putting their hands on each other's bums and having it off in a few minutes. We have there a neat and tidy image of homosexuality, which takes away all its potential to disturb for two reasons: it

corresponds to a reassuring canon of beauty, and it destroys the disturbing element in affection, tenderness, fidelity, comradeship, companionship, for which a fairly controlled society cannot make room, for fear that alliances will be formed, that unexpected lines of force will appear. I think it's that that makes homosexuality 'unsettling': the homosexual way of life, much more so than the sexual act itself. Imagining a sexual act which is against the law or nature doesn't worry people. But when individuals begin to love one another, it does become problematical.[65]

Friendship, which is an important theme in the final volumes of *Histoire de la sexualité*, was not the sole component of a gay culture, as was to become clear from other interviews. In New York in 1982, Foucault was interviewed at some length for the magazine *Christopher Street* by Gilles Barbedette. Shortly afterwards he was interviewed by Bob Gallagher and Alexander Wilson for the *Advocate*. In both cases, Foucault was talking to friends; Barbedette was a young friend from Paris, and Foucault had met Gallagher and Wilson in Toronto, where they were prominent gay activists. A lot of the *Christopher Street* interview is devoted to the issue of gay rights and to the possibility of creating a gay culture. In a sense the two went together: 'The fact of making love with someone of the same sex very naturally involves a whole series of other values. It's not only a matter of integrating this strange little practice of making love with someone of the same sex into pre-existing cultures; it's a matter of constructing cultural forms.'[66] Such cultural forms included 'recognition of relations of provisional coexistence' between men, adoption – including the adoption of one adult by another (here, Foucault may have been thinking of Defert; according to Claude Mauriac, the possibility of Foucault's adoption of Defert was discussed, and a lawyer was consulted shortly before Foucault's death[67]).

More generally, Foucault looked forward to:

a culture which invents ways of relating, types of existence, types of exchanges between individuals that are really new and are neither the same as, nor superimposed on, existing cultural forms. If that's possible, then gay culture will be not only a choice of homosexuals for homosexuals. It would create relations that are, at a certain point, transferable to heterosexuals.[68]

The creation of a culture posed a problem of identity. Gays had to do more than assert an identity; they had to create it, and Foucault was

:stion that its creation was equivalent to the liberation
 ·· was not convinced that the writing of gay novels by
 .he most productive of activities, and the notion of, for
 painting' bordered on the meaningless. Sexual and
ethical cɪɪʋɪ·· provided a starting point for the creation of 'something
that will have a certain relationship to gayness'. The translation of
gayness into other fields, such as painting or music, was not, thought
Foucault, something that was likely to happen. Although he does not
raise the issue, it would seem that the development of a specifically gay
philosophy – or the existence of a 'gay philosopher' called Michel
Foucault – could be ruled out of court, too. Foucault was, on the other
hand, deeply interested in such literary manifestations of a gay culture
as *Masques*, a beautifully produced 'review of homosexualities' published by his friend Jean-Pierre Joecker from 1979 onwards, to which he
contributed a review of Dover's study of Greek homosexuality.[69]

One of the most positive developments in the move towards the
creation of a gay culture was, in Foucault's view, the development of
bars and bath-houses which had 'reduced the guilt involved in making
a very clear separation between the life of men and women, the
"monosexual" relation'.[70] The clubs and bars Foucault was referring
to were those of the gay 'ghettoes' of American cities: Christopher
Street in New York and the Castro Street area of San Francisco.
Spawned in the wake of the gay liberation movement of the 1970s, they
represented a $100-million industry.[71] The Clubs Baths in San
Francisco could hold 800 customers at a time and catered for some
3,000 men a week.[72] In the *Advocate* interview, Foucault was more
graphic in his description of their attractions, and referred to the
subculture of sado-masochism:

The idea that S&M is related to a deep violence, that S&M
practice is a way of liberating this violence, this aggression, is
stupid. We know very well that what all those people are doing is
not aggressive; they are inventing new possibilities of pleasure
with strange parts of their body – through the eroticisation of the
body. I think it's a kind of creation, a creative enterprise, which
has as one of its main features what I call the desexualisation of
pleasure . . . The possibility of using our bodies as a possible
source of very numerous pleasures is something that is
important. For instance, if you look at the traditional constructions of pleasure, you see that bodily pleasure, or pleasures
of the flesh, are always drinking, eating and fucking. And that

seems to be the limit of our understanding of our body, our pleasures.[73]

The extension of pleasure beyond 'drinking, eating and fucking' involved the integration of drugs like amyl nitrate into gay culture, and the creation of new identities. The point was not to liberate desire but to create pleasures. S&M was one such possibility:

One can say that S&M is the eroticisation of power, the eroticisation of strategic relations . . . the S&M game is very interesting because it is a strategic relation, because it is always fluid. Of course there are roles, but everyone knows very well that those roles can be reversed. Sometimes the scene begins with the master and slave, and at the end the slave has become the master. Or, even when the roles are stabilised, you know very well that it is always a game: either the rules are transgressed, or there is an agreement, either explicit or tacit, that makes them aware of certain boundaries. This strategic game as a source of bodily pleasure is very interesting.[74]

In a related interview in which very similar points are made, Foucault referred to 'a whole new art of sexual practice . . . which tries to explore all the internal possibilities of sexual conduct. You find emerging in places like San Francisco and New York what might be called laboratories of sexual experimentation.'[75] They were a by-product of the availability of sex: 'It is because the sexual act has become so easy and available to homosexuals that it runs the risk of quickly becoming boring, so that every effort has to be made to innovate and create variations that will enhance the pleasure of the act.'[76] He agreed with his interviewer that the S&M scene, golden showers, scatological practices and the like' were 'much more openly practised these days'. Elsewhere, he expressed regret that 'such places of erotic experiment do not yet exist for heterosexuals. Wouldn't it be marvellous for them to be able, at any hour of the day or night, to go into a place equipped with every comfort and all imaginable possibilities, and encounter bodies that are at once present and fugitive?'[77] He no doubt thought that their hypothetical opening would be one of the benefits that could be transferred from the gay to the heterosexual community. Foucault was obviously unaware that the Sutro Baths was, as a historian of the AIDS epidemic rather coyly puts it, 'coeducational' and advertised weekly 'Bisexual Boogies'.[78]

Foucault's comments are strangely impersonal. At no point does he say in so many words that 'I, Michel Foucault . . .' His comments are not, however, based on information culled from secondary sources. The exact extent of his involvement in the S&M scene is a matter for rumour rather than objective knowledge. There are no eye-witnesses; this was a culture in which the question 'By the way, what was your name?' came after and not before sexual encounters.[79] Rather archly, a friend of Foucault's refers to 'one French *savant*'s' observation that 'fist-fucking is our century's only brand-new contribution to the sexual armamentarium'.[80] The consensus is that he did indeed frequent the leather bars and establishments like New York's Mineshaft, a leading centre for 'heavy action' located on 'a dark corner in the West Village meatpacking district',[81] and its counterparts in California. The Mineshaft offered a wide variety of sado-masochistic pleasures, including fist-fucking, or the gradual penetration of the rectum by a lubricated and clenched fist. The pleasure-pain involved in such encounters is not necessarily orgasmic in any conventional sense and may not lead to ejaculation. To that extent, Foucault's reference to the 'desexualisation of pleasure' is almost clinically accurate.[82]

The extreme pleasure of a near-death experience was something of which Foucault had a personal understanding. One evening in late July 1978, Foucault was struck by a car or, some say, a taxi as he was crossing the rue de Vaugirard. He was flung into the air and landed on the bonnet of the vehicle, with splinters of glass embedded in his face and head. He was immediately taken to the nearby Hôpital Vaugirard, where he remained for almost a week. The first to be informed of what had happened was Simone Signoret; Daniel Defert was in London, where he was the guest of his friend Julie Christie, and had to be contacted by telephone.[83] There are two possible explanations of why Signoret became involved. One, given by Didier Eribon, is that Foucault asked for her to be contacted;[84] the other is that Foucault was semiconscious, was carrying no identity papers, that her address and number were found in his pocket and that, when telephoned, she recognised Foucault from the description given by the hospital. All are agreed on her reaction; she was startled, and horrified that neither the police nor the hospital staff had recognised Foucault.

On being hit by the car, Foucault immediately thought that he was going to die and experienced a fatalistic sense of acceptance.[85] In 1983, he told a Canadian interviewer:

Once I was struck by a car in the street. I was walking. And for maybe two seconds I had the impression that I was dying and it was really a very, very intense pleasure. The weather was wonderful. It was seven o'clock during the summer. The sun was descending. The sky was very wonderful and blue and so on. It was, it still is now, one of my best memories [laughter].[86]

The experience of near-death may have been an intense pleasure, but its aftermath was not at all pleasant. For over a year, Foucault suffered from headaches and intermittent bouts of nausea and giddiness.[87] In September 1979, he admitted to Claude Mauriac that he had not really recovered from the accident, and that it was still interfering with his concentration as he struggled with his 'second volume of Histoire de la sexualité'[88]

There is a distinct possibility that Foucault was under the influence of drugs on that evening in July. He was certainly using drugs at this period, and had been for some time. Cannabis was not an uncommon digestif in the rue de Vaugirard. Foucault's experience also extended to more exotic products such as opium, cocaine and the LSD he had first discovered in California in 1975. In conversation with Claude Mauriac, he described systematic experiments with drugs and did not rule out the possibility of writing on the subject.[89] He even succeeded in persuading the somewhat reluctant Mauriac to experiment with cannabis, and the experimental subject was disappointed to find that the drug seemed to have no effect on him.[90] Charles Ruas was also told of a projected 'study of the culture of drugs or drugs as culture from the beginnings of the nineteenth century' which 'had to be put aside'.[91] In 1982, Foucault was arguing to Mauriac that drugs were potentially harmless, provided that they were 'culturally integrated', meaning that the young should be taught to use them rather than being left to experiment at random. Not all his own experiments had been entirely uneventful, and he admitted that one LSD experience in New York had been so dreadful that he was on the point of entering a police station to ask for Valium.[92] He had also taken LSD in more controlled circumstances, and had the impression that, far from cutting him off from reality, the whole experience was very much at the level of reality, even truth.[93] Pharmaceutical pleasures also included the use of 'poppers' (amyl nitrate capsules), which Foucault saw as an integral part of gay culture; poppers were, he claimed, the only drug to be so intimately associated with sexuality, and they had the effect of producing 'a prodigious multiplication and intensification' of pleasure which was at once 'unique and unforgettable'.[94]

One of the few projects of the mid-1970s that were actually completed provides further insights into Foucault's views on the use of pleasures. It was the joint project with Thierry Voeltzel, the young hitch-hiker Foucault had picked up in 1975. *Vingt ans et après* is a series of dialogues: 'Thierry, a very young man, is speaking in the presence of an older friend. He is speaking before us and, after many surprises, delays and refusals, we too will become his friends. A tape recorder is recording the conversation. The transcript gives this book, one of the most astonishing books we have read for a long time.'[95] The 'older friend' was, of course, Michel Foucault, who is never named in the book.

In July 1976, Mauriac listened to an initial tape of a conversation between Voeltzel and Foucault, and immediately phoned the latter in Vendeuvre-du-Poitou. Mauriac was astonished by what he had heard, and described it as an 'unprecedented document'. He suggested that, with more direct questioning from Foucault, it could be a sort of modern Socratic dialogue, with the older friend playing Socrates to Thierry's Alcibiades. With the consent of Foucault, he planned to play the tape to an editor at Hachette, but it finally appeared under the Grasset imprint (Grasset is part of the Hachette group). Mauriac also toyed with the idea of giving Thierry other interlocutors, including his daughter Nathalie, a contemporary from a very different background. Foucault was very fond of Nathalie Mauriac, who had pinned the last lines of *Les Mots et les choses* to a wall in her flat, but that part of the project was abandoned.[96]

A series of conversations was taped over the summer, transcribed and then edited by Foucault. Voeltzel describes the life of a young gay man on the fringes of French society, taking casual jobs in the garment district of the Sentier, and in hospitals, mixing with immigrants, with far-left currents, and with the sexual politicians of FHAR and related groups. The talk ranges from rock music to cinema and literature, from sexuality to drugs and even attitudes to religion. Foucault gently prompts Voeltzel, often feigning ignorance in order to produce a response. The result is, as Mauriac rightly claimed, an astonishing document, not least in that it captures Foucault in a relaxed, almost confessional mood.

Safely anonymous, Foucault also speaks more directly of his own pleasures here than in any other text. Speaking of poppers and other drugs, he remarks that they

'deanatomise the sexual localisation of pleasure . . . Kissing on the mouth for two hours with absolutely fantastic pleasure . . . pleasure is displaced in time and space because it is displaced in relation to its sexual localisation, and it's displaced in relation to orgasm, and that makes me wonder whether there isn't something so constrictive in Reichianism, the idea that orgasm ... The apologia for orgasm made by the Reichians still seems to me to be a way of localising possibilities of pleasure in the sexual, whereas things like yellow pills or cocaine allow you to explode and diffuse it throughout the body; the body becomes the overall site of an overall pleasure and, to that extent, we have to get rid of sexuality.[97]

Although he experimented widely, Foucault was not a particularly heavy user of drugs. They were not a utilitarian stimulant. Even when *L'Usage des plaisirs* was proving difficult, Foucault did not use drugs, unlike Sartre, whose consumption of amphetamines during the writing of *Critique de la raison dialectique* was both immoderate and notorious. When Mauriac pointed to the negative example of Sartre, Foucault readily agreed that he would not take stimulants.[98] Drugs afforded an intensity of pleasure which, paradoxically, he sought in disciplined moderation:

Actually, I think I have real difficulty in experiencing pleasure . . . Because I think that the kind of pleasure I would consider as the *real* pleasure would be so deep, so intense, so overwhelming that I couldn't survive it. I would die . . . . some drugs are really important for me because they are the mediation to those incredibly intense joys that I am looking for and that I am not able to experience, to afford by myself . . . A pleasure must be something incredibly intense.[99]

By that criterion, a close encounter with death was also a pleasure.

Almost a year after the publication of *La Volonté de savoir*, Foucault was, to his surprise, contacted by a government commission which was examining the possibility of a reform of the penal code. The invitation was reportedly made at the suggestion of an acquaintance from the Syndicat de la Magistrature who belonged to the commission, and is in itself an index of how *Surveiller et punir*, in particular, had transformed Foucault into a public authority and a potential 'adviser to the Prince'. Foucault was asked by the commission for his views on a number of questions relating to censorship and sexuality. His actual responses to the commission's questions were not made public, but their content and import are obvious from the published text of two discussions. The first was a round-table discussion involving Foucault, the British anti-psychiatrist David Cooper and members of the collective that produced the journal *Change*; the second, a radio debate on France Culture, which took place almost a year later.[100] As Foucault himself remarked, his decision to reply to the commission's questions represented a change of position on his part; he no longer took the view that the role of the intellectual was purely one of denunciation and criticism, and that legislators and reformers should be left to their own unfortunate devices.[101] He would not have taken that stance only a few years earlier; the GIP had not seen the provision of advice on prison reform as part of its remit.

Foucault's general position was that sexuality should not, in principle, be dealt with or controlled by legislation, but he immediately identified two problematic areas: rape and the sexuality of children. His comments on rape were to prove controversial. He floats the idea, also put forward by Hocquenhem in his *Désir homosexuel*, that what should be published in rape cases is the physical violence involved, but concedes that women might not agree with that view. Neither Marine Zecca nor Marie-Odile Faye (respectively one of Cooper's collaborators and *Change*'s editorial assistant) agreed, although the former conceded that rape was a matter of violence rather than sexuality, but was effectively trapped by Foucault's argument that to say that being raped was more serious than being struck in the face was to argue that 'sexuality' had such a role in the constitution of the body that it must be surrounded or invested by a legislation which did not apply to the rest of the body. The Hocquenhem-Foucault argument, as paraphrased by de Weit, was: 'The reasoning on which . . . feminists base their claim for more serious punishment [for rape] is in itself phallocentric, since it implies that some bodily organs are more important than others, i.e. the sexual organs.'[102] Foucault also cited a conversation he had had with an unnamed member of the Syndicat de la Magistrature: he had been told that there was no reason to make rape a penal offence; it could be a matter of civil responsibility, of 'damages and interest'.[103]

Foucault's comments on rape reveal a surprising lack of information about feminist analyses and demands; the possibility that rape may not be a matter of individual violence analogous to a blow in the face is not mentioned. Nor does he appear to have been aware of the fact that most rape complaints made in France at this time eventually came to trial in the form of charges of 'assault' or '*outrage public à la pudeur*' (roughly the equivalent to public indecency).[104] A stinging reply from Monique

Plaza appeared in the May 1978 issue of *Questions féministes*, accusing Foucault of arguing that there is no reason to forbid rape:

Rape is permitted, 'only' the raped woman will go and demand damages and compensation. In other words, she will go and demand payment for a sexual act that a man will have committed 'with' her but without her consent. Therefore: every woman is the sexual prey of men. Either she says nothing and 'consents'; or she exacts retribution before the act (prostitution) or she exacts retribution after the act (rape).[105]

Less polemically, but still critically, one feminist concludes: 'As Plaza argues, Foucault's desexualisation strategy is inappropriate in the realm of rape law since the immediate effects of decriminalisation are focused on women in such a potentially violent way.'[106]

Foucault never replied to Plaza's criticisms, and there is no evidence to suggest that he was even aware of them. He did, however, later shift his position, and argued that 'freedom of sexual *choice*' did not imply 'freedom of sexual *acts*' because 'there are sexual acts like rape which should not be permitted whether they involve a man and a woman or two men'.[107] The abstractly legalistic nature of his initial comments on rape may, in feminist eyes, reflect the fact that he was speaking as a man; it certainly indicates that he had little familiarity with the feminist politics of the day. Susan Brownmiller's *Against Our Will* (1975) was readily available in French translation, but Foucault never addresses her argument that rape 'is nothing more or less than a conscious process of intimidation by which *all* men keep *all* women in a state of fear'.[108] Foucault's arguments may well be in keeping with the 'desexualisation' theme of *La Volonté de savoir*, but they are also a reminder of what one feminist critic calls the 'profoundly androcentric' character of his writings.[109]

Whereas Foucault's remarks on rape reveal a relative lack of familiarity with important debates, his discussion of children's sexuality was very much part of a contemporary controversy. Although he refers to the sexuality of children, the controversy was in fact about sexual relations between adults and children. Foucault had now become involved in a campaign centred on the issue of paedophilia. The immediate issue, to which Foucault referred in passing in the discussion with Cooper[110], concerned three men (a doctor and two teachers) facing charges before the Versailles court for alleged sexual relations with minors. René Schérer had received a letter from one of them, who had been held without trial for almost three years, and had begun to organise a signature campaign calling for charges to be dropped and for the law to be changed.[111] Roland Barthes had already agreed to sign his petition, as had Louis Aragon, who had recently come out as gay, and some forty others. After asking for more details about the case, Foucault also agreed to sign. The signature campaign did not in fact come to anything. The three were found guilty, but were immediately released because of the time they had already spent in custody. It was against this background that Foucault commented on children and sexuality to the Reform Commission. It was also against the background of a growing and violent press campaign about child molestation and child pornography.[112]

In the discussion with *Change*, Foucault raises the question of 'the child who is seduced. Or who begins to seduce you. Is it possible to propose that the legislator should say: with a child who consents, a child who does not say no – one can have any kind of relationship with him; that has nothing at all to do with the law?' Almost immediately, he answers his own question: 'I am tempted to say: once the child does not say no, there is no reason.'[113] Although it is not entirely clear from the discussion itself, Foucault is in fact thinking here of adolescents or pre-adolescents rather than very young children. Elsewhere, he suggests that the age of consent should be lowered to somewhere between thirteen and fifteen, but immediately expressed doubts, 'given the general sexual climate, and what kids can read, or can see on the walls or on their way to school. Legislating about that is therefore a delicate, difficult matter.'[114]

The issues of children's sexuality and paedophilia reappear in the discussion published in *Recherches*. In his introductory remarks, Foucault identifies two trends. On the one hand, the very existence of the commission indicates the emergence of a liberal, reforming trend. That trend seemed to be going against the repressive tendency which had culminated in the adoption of the 'Mirguet amendment' in 1960. As well as defining homosexuality as a 'social scourge', article 331 of the 1960 law increased the penalties facing anyone convicted of committing an indecent or unnatural act with a minor of the same sex (minor being defined as under twenty-one years of age). Yet, if the very existence of the commission represented a possible change of climate, other developments were more worrying. A press campaign against 'child molesters' was in full swing, and in Foucault's view there was a distinct possibility that the climate created in the USA by Anita Bryant's 'Save Our Children' (from homosexuality) campaign would be replicated in France. A campaign had been launched by Hocquenhem and others for the abolition of article 331; it had received support from members of the PCF and even Françoise Dolto, psychoanalytic grandmother to the nation and, as Hocquenhem rightly pointed out, not someone who could easily be described as a paedophile. Foucault strongly supported the call for legal reform and noted that there was no legal definition of the public *pudeur* which could apparently be so easily offended. Much more generally, he used the radio debate as a platform to launch a violent attack on psychological and psychoanalytic theories of 'infantile sexuality' which define it as 'a land which has its own geography, into which adults must not penetrate. A virgin land, a sexual land, of course, but a land which must keep its virginity.'[115] His counter-argument is, again, the objection that children can and do seduce adults. The psychological claim that a child in that position is likely to be traumatised and therefore requires protection against his or her own desires becomes the basis for a dystopian vision of the near future:

We're going to have a society of dangers with, on the one hand, those who are in danger and, on the other, those who bring danger with them. And sexuality will no longer be a type of behaviour with specific prohibitions; sexuality will be a kind of danger at large . . . Thanks to a series of specific interventions, probably made by legal institutions with the support of medical institutions, we will have a whole new *dispositif* [apparatus] for the control of sexuality.[116]

15

DISSIDENT

ON the evening of Friday 17 December 1976, Foucault appeared on *Apostrophes*, the flagship book programme hosted by Bernard Pivot. It was not only the television programme itself that was prestigious; on this occasion, it was recorded in the sumptuous setting of the Louvre. Foucault, the journalist and historian André Fontaine, and the biologist Jean Halburger had been invited to take part in a discussion of 'Man's Future', but the programme also provided Foucault with a platform to publicise the recently published *l'olonté de savoir*. After some teasing comments from Pivot about the irony of asking the theorist of the death of man to speak about man's future, attention turned to Foucault.

To the surprise of his presenter, and presumably his audience, he refused to talk about his book. Instead, he discussed a volume entitled *Un Procès ordinaire en URSS* which had recently been published by Gallimard. Based on tape recordings smuggled out of the USSR, it was the transcript of the trial of Dr Mikhail Stern, who had been accused of accepting bribes and of corruption. The head of an endocrinology unit in Vinnitsa, Ukraine, a doctor with twenty-four years' medical experience and a member of the Communist Party since the late 1940s, Stern had refused the KGB's 'suggestion' that he should bring parental pressure to bear to prevent his two sons emigrating to Israel. At the time of Foucault's broadcast, he was in the third year of his sentence in a labour camp near Kharkov. Partly as a result of Foucault's televised intervention, Stern became something of a celebrity case.

An International Committee for the Liberation of Dr Mikhail Stern brought the case to the attention of the Helsinki Conference and he was released and found his way to Paris.[1] In his review of the *Apostrophes* incident, Clavel spoke with admiration of Foucault's 'abnegation';[2] Foucault himself spoke of the incident in fairly modest terms. He felt he had enjoyed enough media exposure, and was therefore prepared to use his media appearances to bring something 'useful and unknown' to the attention of his viewers. In the circumstances, Stern's book was more interesting than his own.[3] On Sunday, Mauriac telephoned

Foucault to congratulate him on his television appearance. He admired Foucault's gesture, but probably spoke for a lot of people when he said that it was also something of a disappointment.[4] No doubt he too would have liked to hear Foucault talking about his own book. According to Clavel, there was a further twist to the story. Foucault had apparently been approached by the PCF's cultural and theoretical journal, *La Nouvelle Critique*, which was anxious to print something on Pierre Rivière. Foucault responded by offering the journal an article on Stern, which brought the exchange to an abrupt end.

Two days after his appearance on *Apostrophes*, Foucault made another deliberately provocative gesture. Edgar and Lucie Faure were holding a luncheon party for Valéry Giscard d'Estaing. The president was anxious to meet a representative group of writers and intellectuals; the guest list included the feminist lawyer Gisèle Halimi, the cartoonist Claire Brétecher, Jean-Louis Bory, Le Roy Ladurie, Philippe Sollers and Roland Barthes. Foucault was also invited. He was happy to accept, he told the Elysée Palace, provided that he could raise the Ranucci case with the president. Giscard had refused to pardon Christian Ranucci, who had been guillotined in July for the murder of a child near Marseille. The evidence against him was to say the least inconclusive. Foucault was informed that the case was not an acceptable topic of conversation, and he therefore did not lunch with the president.[5]

The Stern issue marked the beginning of an intense interest in Soviet and East European dissidence on Foucault's part. Events soon provided him with an opportunity to give it a concrete expression. In June 1977, Leonid Brezhnev, who had recently added the title of state president to that of secretary general of the CPSU, made a state visit to Paris and was received with all the ceremony France reserves for her official guests. He was also given an unofficial reception. His progress up the Champs-Elysées was watched in silent disapproval by small groups of people, but two hours earlier there had been violent exchanges as right-wing demonstrators mobilised by the Parti des Forces Nouvelles clashed with the police and set fire to the Soviet flags that lined the avenue.[6] On the place de l'Opéra, the police charged a peaceful crowd who had gathered in response to an appeal from representatives of the Soviet Jewish community.[7] Elsewhere on the evening of 21 June, a rather different reception was taking place. The invitation read: 'At the time when Leonid Brezhnev is being received in France, we invite you to a friendly meeting with a number of dissidents from the Eastern-bloc countries at the Théâtre Récamier, 3 rue

Récamier, 75007 Paris at 8.30 pm on 21 June.' It was sent in the joint names of Michel Foucault, Roland Barthes, Pierre Daix, André Glucksmann, François Jacob, Jean-Paul Sartre and Laurent Schwartz.[8]

The idea had emerged from discussions involving Foucault and Pierre Victor. As Foucault put it to Claude Mauriac, it was 'a superb idea. Give a reception for all the Soviet dissidents in Paris on the evening of Brezhnev's reception, so that the journalists will have two receptions. We've found a Russian conservatory of music, a very pretty room . . .' To Foucault's amusement, Mauriac demurred, arguing that it would not be very polite, given that Brezhnev was the guest of France, but eventually agreed to be one of the hosts. The conservatory proved to be unavailable, but the ad hoc organising committee was lent the Récamier, a small, elegant theatre in a side street near the boulevard Raspail, for the evening. Mauriac's wife, Marie-Claude, agreed to take care of the catering, but immediately ran into financial difficulties. Salvation came in the form of donations from the publishers of those involved and the catering was taken care of by the Bon Marché, the long-established department store on the rue de Sèvres.[9]

Foucault was one of the principal organisers and was so preoccupied with the preparations that he took little or no notice of another event that took place on 21 June. A delegation from the CAP, led by Serge Livrozet, was received by Peyrefitte at the Ministry of Justice for discussions about the *quartiers de haute sécurité* ('high-security units') introduced in the wake of the Clairvaux affair. The CAP described the discussions as 'concrete' and Claude Mauriac, who was also present, spoke of a 'historic meeting.' Foucault merely commented that nothing would come of it.[10]

At the Récamier, Foucault, elegant in a white sweater, briefly addressed the assembly from the stage:

> This isn't a meeting – there'll be one at the Mutualité on 29 June – and above all it isn't a reception symmetrical with the one that is taking place at this very moment in the Elysée. We simply thought that, on the evening when M. Brezhnev is being received with pomp by M. Giscard d'Estaing, other French people could receive certain other Russians who are their friends.[11]

He then invited his guests to mingle as they wished, and disappeared behind the curtain. As Foucault had said, this was not a political meeting, but an informal gathering, with people moving from the bar to the buffet and talking in small groups to the accompaniment of music and Russian songs. Foucault was everywhere, acting both as host and head waiter. The Russian guests were distinguished, and it appears that no one refused the invitation. The company included Vladimir Maximov, Artur London, Vladimir Bukovsky, Mikhail Stern, Almarik Sinavsky, Alexander Galitch, and Natalia Gorbanievskaya, who had protested on Red Square against the Soviet invasion of Czechoslovakia in 1968, and who summed up her hopes at the end of the evening thus: 'We can now hope that these people will begin to think about what is happening in the East, using only their conscience and their intelligence. The men of the "independent left" are our hope.'[12]

On the French side, the participants included Glucksmann, de Beauvoir, Deleuze, Jean-Pierre Faye, Jacques Almira, Pierre Victor and Le Monde's Philippe Boucher, but it was the almost incongruous combination of Sartre – walking with great difficulty and leaning on de Beauvoir's arm – and Ionesco that caught the eye of most observers. Political differences did seem to have been transcended in the name of solidarity with the victims of totalitarianism, and Le Nouvel Observateur claimed that 'le Paris des intellectuels' was united, or almost united, for the first time.

The unity was not quite as complete as it may have seemed. Régis Debray, for one, was still denouncing the 'impostors of the Gulag Circus', and preferred to support the Trotskyist Ligue Communiste, 'the only political organisation in France to have commemorated the tenth anniversary of Che's death appropriately'. He had therefore resolved to send the Fémina prize money he had won for his novel La Neige brûle to the Ligue, which had, in his view, for thirty years been denouncing the infamies of socialism without giving up the fight for socialism.[13] Nor was the presence of Sartre, who was later driven home by Foucault,[14] entirely unambiguous. Foucault had recently met Stern, and was astonished to learn that many Soviet dissidents still abominated Sartre because he had refused to meet Solzhenitsyn during his 1966 visit to Moscow.[15] Foucault's argument that all that was in the past and should be forgotten was to no avail. Foucault also claimed, in conversation with Mauriac, that Sartre's greatest wish was now to meet Solzhenitsyn, or to sign a joint statement: Foucault had even been offered a return air ticket to the United States in the hope that he could persuade the Russian writer, who he had never met, to sign a manifesto together with Sartre.[16] Either the air ticket did not materialise, or Foucault did not accept it, but no joint statement ever appeared.

Many of those associated with campaigns to support Soviet dissidents were also associated with the so-called nouveaux philosophes. In the summer of 1977, Foucault's association with the latter was growing more pronounced. The expression *nouveaux philosophes* derives from the dossier published by Bernard-Henri Lévy in *Les Nouvelles littéraires* in June 1976, in which the collective noun referred to Lévy himself, Jean-Marie Benoist, Michel Guérin, Christian Jambet and Guy Lardreau. A month later *Le Nouvel Observateur* published a lengthy article by Gérard Petitjean entitled 'Les Nouveaux Gourous'; this time the cast included – Paul Dollé, Benoist, Jambet, Lardreau, André Glucksmann, Baudrillard, Hocquenhem and, curiously, given that he is normally regarded as a Marxist, Nicos Poulantzas.[17] Although 'new philosopher' was inevitably a somewhat fluid term, the former list dominated public perceptions of the day. For the next year or so it seemed impossible to read a newspaper or to turn on the radio without finding some mention of the new philosophy. Lévy emerged as the central figure in this shifting constellation, not least because most of the 'new philosophers' were published in the 'Figures' and 'Théoriciens' series which he edited for Grasset. His remarkable entrepreneurial and advertising skills helped to launch and promote their work, while his own romantic good looks and photogenic mane of dark hair ensured him maximum exposure in the media.

To the extent that any unity can be found in the work of the somewhat disparate group, it is a negative unity centred upon a violent rejection of Marxism in all its forms. The majority of the new philosophers had a leftist past; Jambet and Lardreau, for instance, were founder members of the GP. It was in that context that they had come to know Foucault. Most were *normaliens* and had, like Lévy, been taught by Althusser. Althusser, Mao and Marx were now rejected *en bloc*; the new theoretical patrons were Lacan, Foucault and Solzhenitsyn. Lacan supplied the figure of the Master (the mythical locus of a discourse which holds that everything and everyone must submit to the law and that total knowledge of the world is possible), Foucault the image of the panopticon, and Solzhenitsyn the overpowering empirical evidence and the messianic zeal. Their Maoist background meant that few of the new philosophers had ever had any great sympathy for the 'revisionist' Soviet Union, but the emerging critique of Marxism went far beyond denunciations of revisionism. What was more, the revelations of Pasqualini's *Prisonnier de Mao* (which disclosed the existence of camps in the People's Republic) and of the Broyelles' account of China destroyed the illusion that 'real socialism' might exist elsewhere.[18]

The Gauche Prolétarienne officially dissolved itself at a final congress held in November 1974, but had been leading a ghostlike existence for at least a year before that. Some had been disillusioned by Bruay and by the implications of the notion of people's justice. Many had been nauseated, or simply terrified, by the flirtation with terrorism. Most commentators agree, however, that the final death knell was sounded in October 1973, when the workers at the Lip watch factory in Besançon refused to accept redundancy notices, occupied their factory and began to produce and distribute watches by themselves – successfully, illegally and without any help from self-appointed and clandestine vanguard militants. A certain *gauchisme* had had its day, and it demise was no doubt hastened by the more liberal presidential regime inaugurated by the election of Giscard in May 1974.

Almost immediately, the new philosophers became an object for both polemic and mockery. Mockery can sometimes be a useful index of social perceptions. In the summer of 1977, *Le Nouvel Observateur* published a *'jeu-test'* which proposed a series of multiple-choice questions to allow readers to decide if they were new philosophers. Anyone who could honestly claim to have rejected Althusser in the last year scored a maximum of three points; rejection of Foucault scored no points. The ideal new philosopher was someone who had at various times been an orthodox communist, a Maoist and a militant catholic.[19] Media exposure was so great as to lead to a new coinage: *pub philosophie* (from *'publicité philosophie'*, which might be translated as 'ad-philosophy'). There was certainly a high level of self-aggrandisement and of mutual congratulation, with virtually every new philosopher taking good care to thank his 'friends' in print and to promote their work. When Lévy, born in 1948, opened his *Barbarie à visage humain* with the words 'I am the bastard child of a diabolical couple: fascism and Stalinism' and continued: 'If I were a poet, I would sing the horror of living and the new Archipelagos that tomorrow is preparing for us',[20] it was immediately obvious that philosophical modesty was not of the order of the day.

Although Glucksmann has always denied being a new philosopher and although his *La Cuisinière et le mangeur d'hommes* predates by two years the publicity orchestrated by Lévy, his work does illustrate the way in which Foucault came to be combined with Solzhenitsyn. The basic thesis of *La Cuisinière* is that 'a camp is a camp, be it Russian or Nazi' and that there would have been 'no Russian camps without Marxism'.[21] Much of the evidence to support the claim derives from *The Gulag Archipelago*. The Russian text became available in Paris at the end of 1973, and Volume 1 appeared in translation in June 1974, followed by Volume 2 in December of the same year. Extracts had appeared in *L'Express* in January 1974, but the crucial event was the appearance of the author himself on *Apostrophes* on 11 April 1975. It was impossible to ignore the power of Solzhenitsyn's testimony, and Lévy captures something of its impact when he describes the author of the *Archipelago* as 'our Dante', as the poet of a new *Divine Comedy*.[22]

Solzhenitsyn was not the easiest of epic poets to come to terms with. One of his interlocutors on *Apostrophes* was a rather apprehensive Jean Daniel, anxious to be 'totally impressed' by Solzhenitsyn but reluctant to agree that, though the colonisation of Vietnam had been wrong, its decolonisation would mean the expansion of an Asiatic communism to which the Vietnamese would soon fall victim. That was not a readily acceptable argument in the spring of 1975. Daniel also failed, by his own account, to convince Solzhenitsyn that Stalinism was only one branch of the tree of communism. *Le Nouvel Observateur*'s editor was not entirely pleased with his own performance, but Foucault was sufficiently impressed to write to say that Daniel, and Daniel alone, had been able to make Solzhenitsyn 'get to the point'.[23] Foucault was greatly impressed by the author of the *Archipelago* and argued that it was pointless to object that he had right-wing leanings or endorsed a religious ideology, as it was impossible to cast doubts upon the damning historical accuracy of what he was saying.[24]

Yet despite Glucksmann's admiration for Solzhenitsyn, something of the old *gauchiste* rhetoric survives in his polemic. When he speaks, in a single breathless denunciation, of the totalitarianism of the Hôpital Général, Nazism, 'the Chilean order' and Moscow,[25] the charge is so generalised that one easily hears echoes of his earlier denunciations of the fascism of Pompidou's France. The notion of the pleb also survives. In 1972, Glucksmann could claim: 'Today, the pleb is in the revolutionary camp: the Maoists are preserving for the people what the left has surrendered to fascism: the pleb, popular unity and victory.'[26] In 1977, the 'rabble' made up of common-law criminals, hippies, marginalised workers, immigrants and homosexuals is in some way analogous to Soviet dissidence. All are potential inhabitants of the concentration camp of the future, and the Soviet *contestataires* may help the West to understand itself better.[27]

The *gauchisme* of the GP had always contained an element of imaginary identification with the pleb, but the very terminology also implies a degree of disdain. Deleuze detected something very similar in the new philosophers' attitude towards the dissidents they claimed to be championing. 'What disgusts me is very simple: the new philosophers are creating a martyrology . . . feeding on corpses, blaming the inhabitants of the Gulag for not having "understood" earlier . . . If I belonged to an association, I would lay complaints against the new philosophers, who show rather too much scorn for the inhabitants of the Gulag.'[28] In his contribution to *Le Nouvel Observateur*'s 'Objectif 78' debate, Jacques Rancière spoke with similar disdain: 'In this mimed passion . . . in which intellectuals who occupy the place of the master, identify with all the persecuted (Socrates, Christ, the Jews, the victims of the Gulag), I see only the advertising display marking philosophy's entry into the speech style imposed by the state-commodity apparatus of domination.'[29]

If Solzhenitsyn was a new Dante, Foucault was, in Glucksmann's view, his prophet. *La Cuisinière* makes great use of *Histoire de la folie*: 'Confinement in Russia has caught up with and overtaken the "great confinement which inaugurated the bourgeois order in Western Europe" and the twentieth century is repeating the great confinement of the seventeenth'.[30] A book which had originally been conceived as a history of psychiatry and which had been turned into a treatise on anti-psychiatry was now becoming a denunciation of all totalitarianisms and of Soviet totalitarianism in particular.

Foucault himself endorsed this reinterpretation of his work. Discussing a film about the Soviet camps, he remarks: 'The Soviet Union punishes in accordance with the method of the "bourgeois order"', by which I mean an order established two centuries ago . . . The timeless, ubiquitous spectacle by which powers have constantly been manufacturing fear for two hundred years.'[31] He also reinterprets his own experience of the Eastern bloc in the light of his new concerns, telling an interviewer in 1978 that he had finished *Histoire de la folie* in Poland and 'Could not help but think, as was writing it, about what I could see around me'.[32] Nothing in the text of *Histoire de la folie*, or in any of the interviews given at the time, suggests that this was in fact the case; Foucault is clearly reinterpreting and reinscribing both his book and his experience within the context of the mid-1970s.

Yet while Foucault could and did argue that the 'confinement of the classical age' was part of the genealogy of the Gulag, he was wary of attempts to equate the two and of claims that 'we all have our own gulag'. As he argued in a written answer to questions put to him by Jacques Rancière, the danger was that such arguments threatened to let the PCF off the hook by allowing it to play on two propositions (namely that the problems of the USSR are the same as those of all other countries, and that the fact that the PCF criticised the Gulag demonstrated its non-subservience to the USSR) in order to avoid the real question by 'dissolving it into the muddy waters of political confinements in general'.[33]

Lévy had been known to Foucault since 1975. One of the new philosopher's less successful ventures had been the launch, with Michel Butel, of the daily *L'Imprévu*, which must have some claim to having set a journalistic record as it ran for only eleven issues (27 January to 7 February) before folding. It seems that Lévy's family was wealthy enough to absorb the considerable financial losses involved. Foucault gave it his backing by granting interviews that appeared in the first two issues.[34] What is more important is the way in which Foucault is invoked in Lévy's best-known book, *La Barbarie à visage humain*. In its opening pages, Lévy strikes a Foucauldian note by describing it as 'an archaeology of the present'.[35] The book does not in fact represent an 'archaeology' and is mainly a polemic against Marxism ('red fascism'), scientism and progressivism in general. The former supporter of revolution and radical change now finds himself asking whether revolution is desirable rather than possible.[36]

Like Glucksmann, Lévy concludes – or starts out from the conclusion – that there can be 'no socialism without camps' and that 'a Soviet camp is Marxist, as Marxist as Auschwitz was Nazi'.[37] Like Glucksmann, he finds that *Histoire de la folie*'s description of the great confinement is applicable to the Soviet Union and calls for 'a Foucaldian analysis' of that society.[38] The opening pages of Foucault's *Histoire* also provide Lévy with the iconography for his attack on 'Saint Gilles and Saint Félix, sailors on the modern ship of fools', who must have been somewhat surprised to learn that they were '*Marxist philosophers* whose rhetoric functions in accordance with the materialist model'.[39] It is, however, the theory of power elaborated in *Surveiller et punir* that is most important. For Lévy, the totalitarian state means 'scientists in power'; total power is synonymous with total knowledge, and the shadow of Bentham's panopticon looms large over all modern societies. The threat of totalitarianism is even greater when a society imposes the duty of 'telling all'; this is the danger of sexology and related practices.[40] In such formulations, Foucault becomes part of the new philosophy's vulgate.

Foucault and Lévy certainly shared doubts about the 'desirability of revolution', but the latter's attempts to coopt Foucault trap him in some odd contradictions. Outlining the theory of pleasures which he opposed to the philosophy of desire, in an interview devoted to *La Volonté de savoir*, Foucault told Lévy to read 'the book by Hocquenhem and Schérer'[41] Lévy does not take him up on this point, no doubt because it would have been a source of embarrassment: he himself had denounced the text in question as 'barbarian' and as representing 'another mode of decadence'.[42] Foucault could be an uncomfortable ally.

Foucault's most significant gesture of support for the new philosophers was the three-page review of Glucksmann's *Les Maîtres penseurs* published in *Le Nouvel Observateur* in May 1977. The book repeats and expands many of the points made in *La Cuisinière*, but extends criticism to what Glucksmann calls 'the Revolution-State' and argues that all philosophers display a will to domination which invitably leads them to collude with tyrants. As Foucault puts it, Glucksmann's basic question is: 'By what trick was German philosophy able to turn Revolution into the promise of a true, a good State, and the State into the serene and complete form of Revolution?'[43] The review provides Foucault with an opportunity for a final settling of accounts with Marxism:

> The whole of a certain left has attempted to explain the Gulag . . . in terms of the theory of history, or at least the history of theory. Yes, yes, there were massacres; but that was a terrible error. Just reread Marx or Lenin, compare them with Stalin and you will see where the latter went wrong. It is obvious that all those deaths could only result from a misreading. It was predictable: Stalinism-error was one of the principal agents behind the return to Marxism-truth, to Marxism-text which we saw in the 1960s. If you want to be against Stalin, don't listen to the victims; they will only recount their tortures. Reread the theoreticians; they will tell you the truth about the true.[44]

The target of such remarks is obviously Althusser, but they are also broad enough to take in Trotskyist theories of deviation or degeneration. Foucault had already made the same point two months earlier in a conversation with Claude Mauriac. The two met in the Mercure Galant, a restaurant near the Bibliothèque Nationale, where Foucault had spent the day. Conversation turned to the political situation in France, and to broader questions. Foucault described his generation as 'cowardly' because it had tacitly accepted the existence of the Gulag Archipelago as necessary; it was now obvious that the camps were not an accident, but an integral part of Marxism. Mauriac agreed and then attempted to argue that it might be possible to find something other than Marx, or to preserve something of Marx. That could, he thought, be Foucault's role. Foucault simply replied that it was 'too late'.[45] Nor

did China offer any alternative hope; on reading an account of the
Cultural Revolution, Foucault found a 'terribly worrying' similarity
between the ritual of public self-criticism and the extortion of
confessions in the camps: 'It is as though methods internal to the camps
had blossomed in the open, I was about to say like a hundred thousand
flowers, in the China of the "Cultural Revolution".'[46]

Foucault's political evolution was intersecting with that of the new
philosophers. His own 'leftist' period was over, his disillusionment with
Marxism was complete and he was moving into a political arena
dominated by dissidence and human rights. The political constellation
in which he moved was also changing. It was widely claimed that his
work, and particularly the theory of power elaborated in *Surveiller et
punir*, had prepared the ground for the new philosophers. Clavel wrote:
'Whether he likes it or not, Foucault has vanquished Marx and the
Enlightenment' and argued that all the new philosophers were
'walking down a road originally signposted by Foucault. And those on
the other side are incapable of even the least counter-offensive, for there
is no more Marxist thought, no more "human sciences" thought.'[47]
Foucault was close to Clavel at this time, and his comments could
always be seen as further evidence of his characteristic verbal inflation.
But when Deleuze began his counterattack on the new philosophy by
claiming that one explanation for its nullity was its use of 'big concepts
like *the* law, Power, the master . . .', the shaft directed against *Surveiller et
punir* and *La Volonté de savoir* was not easily deflected. Foucault's and
Deleuze's very different attitudes to the new philosophers led to an
increasing estrangement.

On the other hand, Foucault was not enthusiastic about being too
closely associated with the new philosophers and their publicity
machine. Autumn 1977 saw the appearance of an unusual issue of
L'Arc, a quarterly, each number of which was normally devoted to a
theme or a single author and his work. Issue 70 was to have been
devoted to Foucault, and had been advertised as such. Work on the
issue was well advanced when the *nouveaux philosophes* came on the
scene. Disturbed by their 'ideological marketing' and reluctant to be
involved in it, Foucault protested that he did not wish to see his name
on the cover, and that issue of *L'Arc* appeared as *La Crise dans la tête*.[48]

In the summer of 1977, it also seemed possible that a break with
Claude Mauriac was in the offing. Debates over the Soviet Union are
rarely exclusively Russian in their implications, and Mauriac noted
that this particular debate was going on only a year before France was
due to go to the polls. He also argued strongly that it was vital not to kill

hope, meaning that the Union of the Left had to be preserved. The Union was the Socialist-Communist electoral pact signed in 1972; it was now in crisis, largely because of disagreement between the two parties over the issue of nationalisations. Mauriac wrote in *Le Monde*: 'Michel Foucault has established a date at which hope shifted, at which the question was no longer how one could preserve, within Marxism, certain traditional values, but how it was still possible, knowing what we know, to remain a Marxist. He chose 1956, the year in which Soviet tanks imposed "socialist order" on Hungary.'[49] The reference is to Foucault's participation, along with Clavel, Glucksmann, Sollers, Jambet and Lardreau, in TF-1's *La Part de vérité* on 4 July. In the course of the programme, recorded at the home of Clavel in Vézelay, Foucault remarked: 'Since 1956, philosophers have no longer been able to think history by means of pre-established categories. They therefore have to resensitise themselves to events. Philosophers must become journalists.'[50]

Mauriac was not claiming that the Soviet camps were becoming any more tolerable, but he was concerned about the 'insidious, pernicious logic' that inferred necessary links between the Gulag and Marxism, between Marxism and communism, between communism and the Common Programme, between the Common Programme and the Gulag. His article at least implied that Foucault accepted or even promoted that logic. A fortnight later, he received a phone call from Foucault, 'apparently so approving, but I now [September 1977] wonder if it wasn't an elegant way of saying goodbye for ever'.[51] His fears were unjustified, but the article undoubtedly strained the friendship considerably.

Foucault was not a supporter of the Common Programme of the Left, mainly because of the Communist Party presence, and he was not sanguine about its electoral prospects. He refused, however, to be drawn into Giscard's camp and took a general stance of disenchantment. His disenchantment was, inevitably, based upon his theory of power:

> Socialisms do not need a new freedom charter or a new declaration of rights: easy, therefore useless. If they want to deserve being loved, and not to repel, if they want to be desired, they have to answer the question of power and of its exercise. They have to discover a way of exercising power that does not instil fear. That would be something new.[52]

Foucault was referring to *Liberté, libertés* which was the product of the reflections of a Socialist Party study group chaired by Robert Badinter.[53] It was basically a charter of rights and liberties, but when he discussed it in an address to a summer school organised by the Syndicat de la Magistrature, Foucault claimed that it represented a 'mutation in the techniques of power' which would extend the function of judges and courts by bringing ever-greater areas of civil society within their remit. It did not, that is, hold out the promise of a new mode of government.[54]

A similar argument underpinned one of Foucault's publishing projects of this period. While he was researching *Surveiller et punir*, Foucault had attended a CNRS colloquium at ENS on 'Delinquency and Social Exclusion' in March 1973.[55] One of the speakers was Michelle Perrot who, two years earlier, had defended an influential doctoral thesis on strikes in nineteenth-century France.[56] Her 1973 paper was on delinquency and the nineteenth-century penitentiary system, and she was delighted when Foucault requested a copy of it. Foucault duly cites it in *Surveiller et punir*, but wrongly gives the author's forename as 'Michèle'.[57]

The friendly relationship between Foucault and Perrot was fostered by Jean-Pierre Barou, who initially introduced himself to the historian because he was an admirer of her *Les Ouvriers en grève* and hoped to publish something by her. That ambition was finally realised in 1984, when, as an editor at Seuil, he was able to publish the abridged version of her thesis as *Jeunesse de la grève*. Although he had trained at an engineering school in Strasbourg, Barou had embarked on a literary career and had produced a small magazine entitled *Atoll* in the late 1960s, its first issue being devoted to Paul Nizan.[58] After the May events, he became involved in the emerging Maoist movement and then became a journalist on *J'Accuse* and *La Cause du peuple*. It was in that capacity that he was present on the famous occasion when Sartre was smuggled into Renault's fortresslike plant on the Ile Séguin in the back of a van. It was also through his work on the Maoist press that Barou met Foucault; he quite regularly called at Foucault's flat to collect copy or GIP press releases (not all of them signed), which Foucault often handed over – or even wrote at great speed – still in his dressing gown.[59]

In the course of a conversation with Perrot, Barou suggested that, given their common interests, she and Foucault should work together on something. Perrot blanched at the suggestion. She had met Foucault, but was rather frightened at the idea of approaching him directly. Eventually, she and Barou hit upon the idea of publishing Bentham's essay on the panopticon. It seemed to both that it was anomalous that a text which was being widely referred to as a result of *Surveiller et punir* was not actually available. *The Panopticon* exists in two different versions: the full text included in the fourth volume of Bentham's *Works* and a brief version commissioned by the French National Assembly in 1791. The latter was in the mid-1970s something of a bibliographical rarity, but Perrot, a collector, owned a copy purchased from a dealer in antiquarian books. The project gradually matured: the two would republish Bentham's French text and ask Foucault to write a preface, or at least to give them an interview which could be used as a preface. Barou was at the time a commissioning editor with the small publishing house owned and run by Pierre Belfond, and publication was therefore not a problem. Foucault was delighted to be approached by Barou and immediately agreed to an interview. That he was at once agreeable to being published by a small house with virtually no back list and little advertising capability may have been an early instance of what was to become a real disenchantment with commercial publishing, and even with life as a Gallimard author.

On a very hot morning in July 1976, Barou and a somewhat nervous Perrot went to Foucault's apartment. To their surprise, he opened the door dressed in a Japanese kimono and remained in that garb throughout the morning. Foucault was in a relaxed, cheerful mood and the interview was frequently interrupted by laughter. Eventually, the interview was completed and the three retired to the terrace for glasses of fruit juice. All three reread and revised a transcript of the tape, which appeared as the preface to Bentham's essay.[60]

The discussion was informal and wide-ranging. Much of it was naturally taken up with a reprise of the treatment of panopticism in *Surveiller et punir* but Perrot, in particular, opened it up to take in Taylorism and nineteenth-century industrialisation. Many of Foucault's ironic comments about the French left and power were expunged from the printed version, but some of his surviving remarks have a contemporary rather than a historical relevance. Thus, he argues that it is not enough to pose the question of power solely in terms of legislation or constitutions: 'Power is much more complicated, denser and more diffuse than a body of laws or a state apparatus.'[61] The final exchange with Perrot has an almost allegorical tone. She suggests that it might be pointless for the prisoners to take control of the central tower which is the locus of power. Foucault replies that such an action would be meaningful, 'provided that that is not the ultimate meaning of the operation. If the prisoners operated the panoptic apparatus and sat in the tower, do you really think that things would be much better than they were with the guards?' Foucault was using the panopticon metaphor to suggest that, in the event of a left electoral victory, nothing would really change in the absence of a profound meditation on the nature of power itself.[62]

By the autumn of 1977, Foucault was preoccupied not so much with Solzhenitsyn as with a rather different sort of dissident. In the summer, the West German lawyer Klaus Croissant slipped across the French border and surfaced at a press conference. Croissant had been one of the principal defence lawyers at the 1975 trial of members of the *Rote Armee Fraktion*, better known to the media as the 'Baader–Meinhof gang' (and to the French media as *'la bande à Baader'*), and now announced that he was seeking the political asylum guaranteed by the 1946 Constitution to anyone subjected to persecution for 'actions in favour of freedom'. The original charges against the lawyer were brought under a 1975 law which excluded from the defence anyone who supported a criminal organisation. Croissant was said to have attempted, ' "by means of numerous public demonstrations, press statements and political campaigns inside and outside the Federal Republic", to have tried "to arouse international interest in the members of the criminal association and their ostensible political aims" '.[63] In the eyes of many, his real crime had been to draw public attention to the conditions in the fortress-prison of Stannheim, which eventually drove Andreas Baader, Gudrun Ennslin and Jan-Karl Raspe to commit suicide in dubious circumstances in October 1977. It was sometimes said that they had been 'condemned to suicide'. By the time the Croissant affair reached its climax in Paris, the situation had been further inflamed by the murder of Hans-Martin Schleyer, the head of the West German employers' association, on 19 October, the day after the mass suicide.

Croissant had already been jailed twice; his passport had been confiscated and he was obliged to report to the police on a weekly basis. Given that he could no longer defend his clients in Germany, he had, he told the French press, chosen exile and hoped to continue his work in France.[64] As Croissant lodged his appeal for asylum, the West German authorities began extradition proceedings in the courts. At the end of September, Croissant was arrested in a house in the fourteenth *arrondissement* belonging to Hélène Châtelain, an actress and filmmaker who had worked with the GIP when it made its film, and an acquaintance of Foucault's. She and a second woman were arrested and charged with harbouring a fugitive from justice.

A Committee for the Immediate Liberation of Klaus Croissant was formed, and was responsible for a novel political gesture: one thousand croissants, each carefully wrapped in foil, were dispatched to lawyers, politicians and others, together with a note asking why a lawyer could not travel freely across the Common Market when a croissant could do so.[65]

Support for Croissant began to be organised, and a group of 'personalities' called for his immediate release on the grounds that 'handing over Klaus Croissant to the federal German government would mean abandoning a well-established tradition . . . in extradition affairs, contravening the constitutional principles of political asylum and giving way to the pressure brought to bear by the German government'. The fifty or so signatories included de Beauvoir, Clavel, Debray, Deleuze, Kiejman, Sartre and Françoise Sagan, but not Michel Foucault. He was, however, active in a variety of other ways.

His first salvo took the form of an article in *Le Nouvel Observateur* in which he argued that what was at stake in the Croissant affair was a right:

> The rights of the governed [*des gouvernés*] include a right which, slowly and in tortuous fashion, is beginning to be recognised and which is essential: the right to be defended in the courts. Now that right is not restricted to the possibility of having a lawyer to talk about you, in more or less contradictory terms, with the prosecutor, as though you were absent or as though you were . . . an inert object who was simply being asked either to confess or to remain silent. One of the rights of the governed is to have lawyers who are not, as they are in Eastern-bloc countries, people who defend you but make it quite clear to you that they would condemn you if their good fortune and your misfortune made them your judges. This is the right to have a lawyer who speaks for you, with you, who allows you to make yourself heard and to preserve your life, your identity and the strength of your refusal. . . . This is the right they wanted to deny the Baader group in Germany by persecuting their lawyers.[66]

The final extradition request and Croissant's appeal were to be heard on 16 November. Three days before the case was due to begin, Foucault and André Glucksmann had drafted a statement approving the position taken by the Syndicat des Avocats de la France at its Strasbourg congress, which had protested against the possible extradition because of the strong possibility that Croissant would face a long term of imprisonment for political reasons.[67] Foucault remarked in a telephone conversation with Claude Mauriac: 'The point is not to say that West Germany is fascist or that Croissant is a model for liberal lawyers, but to oppose the extradition.'[68] The signatories included a number of individuals close to Foucault: Barthes, Boulez, Clavel, Domenach, Costa-Gavras, Montand, Mauriac and Simone Signoret.

In the micro-world of political petitioning, a subtle battle was being fought out. Foucault had refused to lend his name to a petition being circulated by Félix Guattari. It too opposed the extradition of Croissant, but it referred to West Germany as 'fascist', and that was unacceptable to Foucault.[69] In other words, Foucault was prepared to fight for Croissant's right to asylum, but he would not lend his name to any statement which lent support to a thesis associated with the Red Army Fraction itself. Given the close association between Guattari and Deleuze, the ground had been prepared for a painful break between Foucault and a good friend. His refusal to countenance support for terrorism brought him bitter reproaches from some quarters. And, although there was no open exchange between the two, the position adopted by Genet was quite antithetical to Foucault's. Making a distinction between the brutality of 'the system' and the natural violence of 'resistance', Genet argued that everyone should be grateful to Baader, Meinhof and the RAF for having demonstrated that only violence could put an end to the brutality of men.[70] Support for such views was not rare in France, but Genet must have alienated many who held them by claiming in the same article that the USSR was, despite its failings, a friend to all oppressed peoples.

On 15 November, a planned demonstration taking the traditional route from the place de la République to the place de la Nation was banned by the Prefect of Police. A 'spontaneous' march therefore set out from Montparnasse to Saint-Germain, where violent scuffles broke out in the narrow side streets. Foucault was not present, but on the following evening he was outside the Santé prison as Croissant, having lost his case, was brought out to be returned to German custody. Foucault, Defert and a small group of people tried to form a symbolic human chain and were suddenly charged by some forty police in full riot gear. Foucault was struck and injured. Claude Mauriac received the news in a phone call while he, like most of the population, was watching France beat Bulgaria in the World Cup. The next day, he called Foucault, who told him:

Yes, I was manhandled. For the fun of it. I mean, there were only twenty or so of us, and there was no reason for them to charge so brutally . . . the cops are particularly fond of me . . . They obviously enjoyed beating me . . . A fairly heavy blow to the base of the spine. My lungs? I have difficulty breathing. Can't sit down, much less lie down.

Mauriac immediately diagnosed a cracked rib, but Foucault was, as usual, reluctant to see a doctor and did so only after considerable persuasion from Defert. The rib proved to be broken. Despite his injuries, Foucault read over the phone a call for a demonstration on 18 November.[71]

On the morning of the demonstration, Foucault's account of his experiences at the hands of the police appeared in *Le Matin*: 'I think that this brutal reaction is part of what might be called the "pleasure bonus" in a policeman's job. Taking it out on a *gauchiste* . . . is part of their wages. Besides, without that bonus, the police would be less reliable.' More generally, he argued that the government's obsession with law and order meant that security considerations were being placed above the law: 'We are currently moving towards a sort of world market in political justice which is designed to cut the number of sanctuaries constituted by asylum, which guarantee political dissidence in general.'[72]

The evening's demonstration had been called by an ad hoc group including Foucault, Jacques Debû-Bridel (president of France Terre d'Asile), Marguerite Duras, Sartre, Vercors and Mauriac. Despite his injuries, Foucault was in attendance but did not march the full distance and took the metro for part of the way. It rapidly became apparent that two demonstrations were taking place simultaneously. As the marchers chanted slogans denouncing Croissant's extradition, groups of self-styled 'autonomists' armed with iron bars began to attack a German-owned bank and even German-built cars. Foucault and Mauriac watched the spreading violence with great sadness, and eventually left the scene, only to be involved in another, if minor, confrontation. As they waited for a train, a man bleeding from a head wound was pursued into the station by a posse of CRS. Foucault and Mauriac attempted to intervene, and it seemed likely that Foucault was about to suffer another beating when total strangers began to protest: 'Leave him alone! It's Foucault.' To the surprise of all present, the police withdrew.[73]

Although Croissant had been deported and was now being held in Stannheim, Foucault's involvement in the affair was not over. In an open letter to 'certain leaders of the left', he argued that those who had expressed their indignation over the Croissant extradition – and who might well have done so earlier – should now take up the cause of Hélène Châtelain and Marie-Josèphe Sina, who faced charges for 'harbouring a fugitive'. Again, Foucault raised the issue of the right of the *gouvernés* to challenge the state:

> You aspire to governing us . . . It is important that we know how you will react to an affair like this: two women are being charged because they are accused of 'harbouring' the legal defender of 'terrorists', when all they did, even if the facts are proven, is to make one of the oldest gestures of appeasement bequeathed us by time; isn't the vindictiveness with which they are being charged an indication of a will to inflame the fear, and the fear of fear, that is one of the preconditions for the working of a security state? Do you agree that it is appropriate to press charges in the name of society, of our society?[74]

No leader of the left replied in public, but Foucault's passing reference to a 'Minister for Justice who had justified an extradition before the court had pronounced its opinion' did draw a response from Alain Peyrefitte, with whom Foucault had already clashed over the prison issue. Courteously addressing '*Mon cher camarade, maître et ami*' in an open letter, Peyrefitte, who had known Foucault as a student at ENS, challenged his account of events, and protested that he had refused to comment on a matter which was *sub judice*. Foucault's reply was brutally direct: Peyrefitte may not have mentioned Croissant by name, but he had addressed a meeting and had spoken in general terms of the need to combat Euroterrorism. What else was he talking about, if not the Croissant affair? 'Basically, you justified in advance an extradition order that was about to be granted. Rather than asking for it openly, you tried to make it acceptable by extending to France a climate which we must reject.'[75] The 'debate' went no further.

As the Croissant affair ran its course, Foucault and Defert went to Berlin in December, and paid a visit to the Eastern sector of the divided city. The border crossing brought an unpleasant encounter with the police, as their papers and notes were photocopied by officious bureaucrats who asked them to explain the references and book titles contained in a notebook. East Berlin did not make a good impression on them. Nor did West Berlin. As the two left their hotel, they were suddenly surrounded by police armed with machine guns and were searched with their hands above their heads in the street. Their mistake had been to allow themselves to be overheard discussing a book on Meinhof at breakfast. As Foucault told *Der Spiegel* when he was interviewed about this incident, the probable cause for their harassment was simply that, in the eyes of the police, they were, as intellectuals, an 'unclean species'.[76] Defert and Foucault were now in the tragicomic position of being criticised in France for not supporting Baader-Meinhof, and of almost being arrested in Germany for supposedly supporting them.

In January, Foucault returned to West Berlin to attend the huge gathering organised under the broad umbrella of TUNIX. TUNIX, which derived its name from a slang expression meaning 'Do nothing', was a loose coalition rather than a party or even a front, and brought together the disenchanted youth whose only real politics was a refusal to cooperate in any way with the authorities. Ecologists, feminists, anarchists, squatters and autonomists met in a cheerful confusion, with music and theatre groups all contributing to a circus-like atmosphere. Foucault revelled in the ambience and engaged in informal discussions and arguments with these members of the counterculture.

In a very real sense, this was his German public and he was its ideologue, just as he had become, thanks to his theory of the 'microphysics of power', something of a guru to Italy's autonomists, including those who, thanks to a liberal regime, were able to read Foucault in prison.[77] Academic philosophers in Germany had been slow to react to Foucault and, whereas in the United States his work had been disseminated through the universities, here it was the alternative press and small publishing houses like Merve, founded and run by his friends Peter Gente and Heidi Paris, that had done most to popularise him.[78] For this milieu, Foucault was an exciting, even dangerous thinker; the Nietzschean strand in his work added the frisson of breaking a taboo.[79] More academic philosophers found this disturbing. Interviewed in *Le Monde* some years later, Manfred Frank, who had been one of the first German academics to discuss Foucault seriously and who had considerable sympathy for his early work, spoke of his impression that Foucault was drifting into anti-rationalism and opined that it was precisely that which had coloured his reception in Germany, 'a rather uncritical reception, an alibi for giving a new lease of life to a political attitude which, in Germany, derives from a rather compromised tradition'.[80]

Nothing specific emerged from the TUNIX gathering, but Foucault enjoyed the experience. He also enjoyed exploring Berlin with his companion Catherine von Bülow, and particularly relished its seedier side, typified by the sleazy restaurants they discovered and by the clubs and bars into which he disappeared in the evening, leaving her to her own devices.[81] Nothing is on record of Foucault's nocturnal expeditions, but Berlin boasted a wide range of clubs catering for every taste, and it can be assumed that he was not abstemious.

The German expedition also had its more serious side. Foucault and von Bülow returned via Hanover, where they took part in a demonstration called in solidarity with Peter Bruckner, who had been dismissed from his post at the university after his involvement in the publication of a text which appeared to justify the murder of Federal Attorney-General Buback, the state's main terrorist hunter, who was shot dead in an ambush in April 1977. The text in question was actually published in a Göttingen student newspaper by a group using the pseudonym 'Mescaleros'; Bruckner did not particularly approve of its content or of the group's unconcealed joy at Buback's death, but insisted that its authors had the right to publish it. When legal action was taken against the newspaper, he and a group of other teachers republished it. As a result, and because of an earlier association with Ulrike Meinhof, he had become an 'enemy of the state' and fell victim to a *Berufsverbot*. Bruckner's denunciations of certain RAF actions, on the other hand, had led to his being denounced as a traitor by the said 'enemies of the state' and he fled his intolerable situation by going into exile in Denmark.[82]

If the Foucault who had marched through the cold streets of Hanover in solidarity with Bruckner provided a classic image of the professor militant, February found him in a rather different, and less dangerous, role. Together with Barthes and Deleuze, he was invited by Pierre Boulez to take part in 'Le Temps musical', a five-evening event organised by the Institut de Recherche et Coordination Acoustique/Musique at the recently opened Centre Georges Pompidou. Foucault and Boulez had been casually acquainted since the early 1950s, but were not close friends. They had, however, come to know one another better when, to the composer's surprise, Foucault put his name forward for election to the Collège de France in 1976 in an attempt to rejuvenate the institution.

'Le Temps musical' combined performances of works by Ligeti, Messiaen, Stockhausen, Carter and Boulez himself with workshops and a debate involving the three guests. To his astonishment, Boulez found himself facilitating a discussion in front of an audience of over two thousand on the last evening. The number of people present was not conducive to a real debate; Barthes read 'a Taoist story' about a butcher whose intellectual concentration on the cow he was butchering meant that, ultimately, he saw before him simply 'the principle of dissection', whereas Foucault effectively refused to participate and contented himself with answering questions. Only Deleuze entered into the public debate with any enthusiasm. The preparatory sessions had, on the other hand, been held in private and were much more successful.

To the extent that his contributions can be reconstructed from Boulez's published account, Foucault concentrated on a brief analysis of the musical culture of the Parisian intelligentsia, noting with some surprise that few of his colleagues or students took any serious interest in contemporary music and commenting on the anomaly between their philosophical and musical tastes: people who were passionately interested in Heidegger and Nietzsche followed the fortunes of mediocre rock groups rather than the experiments of IRCAM. His explanation was that, in the musical domain, such intellectuals were victims of a ready-packaged culture. Their condemnation of contemporary music as 'elitist' led them to listen to a more banal but more socially rooted music.[83] As he remarked in a later dialogue initiated by Boulez in an attempt to revive the IRCAM debate: 'Not only is rock music an integral part of the lives of many people (much more so than jazz used to be), but it is a cultural inductor; liking rock, liking one kind of rock rather than another is also a way of life, a way of reacting; it is a whole set of tastes and attitudes.' On the other hand, the apparently remote or elitist tendencies within music were in fact closer to the mainstream of modern intellectual culture: the investigation of 'form' which had characterised the work of Cézanne and the Cubists could also be found in Schoenberg, and the Russian formalists and the linguists of the Prague school.[84] Foucault himself had long been interested in serial music, though he was also an avid Mahler enthusiast who had recently been converted to Wagner by the Boulez–Chéreau production of *The Ring*. At the opposite extreme, he also enjoyed a David Bowie concert to which he was taken by Defert.[85] Foucault's comments on the sociology of rock music mask the fact that he seems not to have known a great deal about it: in conversation with Thierry Voeltzel, he proved incapable of distinguishing between Bowie and Mick Jagger.[86]

Foucault's second trip to Japan, in April 1978, was a rather more organised affair than his first visit in 1970. This time, he was not a guest of the Japanese and travelled under the auspices of the French Ministry of Culture. The other difference was that he was now accompanied by

Defert. The two were finally realising a project they had been thinking about since at least 1963.

They spent three weeks in the country and the schedule was a busy one. On 21 April Foucault took part in a debate following a showing of Allio's film version of *Moi, Pierre Rivière* at the Athenée Française, a cultural centre in Tokyo.[87] The screening allowed Foucault to outline elements of a theory of the role of the intellectual; by allowing Rivière to speak, he had, as an intellectual, given a voice to a subject who was alien, in terms of both his origins and his nature, to the structure of power. Speaking at the Institut Franco-Japonais, he also outlined the view that social developments were beginning to hint at the emergence of a non-disciplinary society.[88] In the course of a third public lecture on 27 April, he spoke in more general terms of power, expressing the hope that philosophy could become a counter-power, provided that the philosopher abandoned his prophetic role in order to reflect upon specific political struggles rather than universals. Tentatively, he also began to suggest that analytic philosophy could, if applied to the appropriate discursive areas, provide an analytic of power.[89]

Foucault was already working on the question of 'discipline' in Christianity, and the visit to Japan provided an opportunity to investigate the contrasting self-disciplinary techniques associated with Zen Buddhism. In preparation for the trip, he had read and studied some basic books on Zen, including those by Alan Watts and D. T. Suzuki. A few days spent in the 1,400-year-old Kóryú-ji Temple in Kyoto allowed him to move from theory to practice and to attempt meditation exercises, though not without a certain difficulty. Foucault's Zen apprenticeship later provided the basis for some rather banal remarks on the differences between Christianity and Buddhism. The former is a confessional religion in which the light of faith is required for the exploration of the soul, and in which only the purification of the soul can provide access to the truth, whereas 'in Buddhism, it is the same type of enlightenment which leads you to discover what you are and what is the truth. In this simultaneous enlightenment of yourself and the truth, you discover that your self was only an illusion.'[90]

Public lectures and Zen initiation did not take up all of the three weeks. Foucault and Defert also travelled south to Kyushu, in part because the latter was interested in early Jesuit missions to Japan and wanted to see their original ports of entry into the country. Foucault was involved in informal discussions with members of organisations corresponding to France's Syndicat de la Magistrature, with representatives of the Social Democratic Party, and with some of those involved in the campaign against the construction of Narita airport outside Tokyo, a campaign which involved an extraordinary alliance between peasant farmers and radical students and gave rise to pitched battles with the police that could have come from a film by Kurosawa. Despite the crowded schedule, there was also time to see at least something of the gay scene in Tokyo and Kyoto, which Foucault described in an interview given about a month after his return to Europe. He had visited some of the thousands of tiny clubs:

> They are tiny, and can't hold more than five or six. People sit on stools, talk, get drunk. There is little possibility of meeting anyone, and arrival of a newcomer is an event. It is a sort of communal life, organised in parallel with the Japanese imperative to get married when you reach adulthood. But when the evening comes, you go to your neighbourhood club, to the club in your block; a sort of small, faithful and slightly mobile community meets.[91]

The return flight to Paris involved a brief stopover in Moscow, where Foucault gave vent to his anti-Soviet feelings by refusing to buy the caviare he normally enjoyed so much; he simply would not spend money in the USSR, a country he never visited.[92]

On his return, Foucault was immediately plunged into a busy round of academic activity, beginning with a major discussion of *Surveiller et punir*. The book had received considerable acclaim, and it had of course also attracted the attention of professional historians. More specifically, the book attracted the attention of the Société d'Histoire de la Révolution de 1848 and its president, Maurice Agulhon, a specialist in nineteenth-century history and the author of a recent study of 1848 published in the 'Archives' series.[93] He had known Foucault since their days in the PCF in the 1950s. Perrot was a member of the Société and read a paper of 'Revolution and Prisons in 1848' to its annual general meeting. The Société then proposed the publication of a volume of studies devoted to the nineteenth-century penal system.[94] That volume should, it was suggested, contain a critical study of Foucault's latest work. Jacques Léonard, a specialist in medical history and in the nineteenth century, was delegated to write the review.

Léonard's title, 'The Historian and the Philosopher', suggests something of the distance between Foucault and academic historians and provides a useful indication of how he was perceived in their milieu. Although the review was not unfavourable, and praised

Foucault for the 'classicism' of his style and for his avoidance of the
patois parisien of the Left Bank. Léonard makes three primary criticisms.
His first reproach concerns the 'dazzling rapidity' of the analysis:
Foucault rushes through three centuries 'like a barbarian horseman'.
The Revolutionary period is largely passed over in silence and there is
no discussion of either the September massacres or the revolutionary
courts of the Terror.[95] Although Léonard does not make the point, the
omission is all the more surprising in that Foucault had discussed those
courts in his debate with Pierre Victor over the question of 'people's
justice' in 1972. Léonard also found it surprising that Foucault does not
discuss at any length the Restoration period, that he says nothing about
the *bagnes* (the penal barracks located in naval ports like Toulon and
Brest, where convicts were sentenced to forced labour[96]) and that he
presents so little statistical information about nineteenth-century
criminality. Rather more significantly, he raises the issue of the
apparent anonymity of the apparatuses described by Foucault, and
asks sardonically if the author is describing 'machinery' or 'machina-
tions'. He also casts doubts on Foucault's abilities as an archivist,
noting that French historians had a poor opinion of research carried out
in the Bibliothèque Nationale's printed-books room and not in the dust
of some provincial presbytery. Although expressed with some humour,
the comment is both telling and cutting, as is the remark about
statistics; the implication is that Foucault was an amateur historian.[97]

Léonard's review was sent to Foucault for comment, but the latter's
response was not published until *L'impossible Prison* appeared in 1980. It
centres on three methodological points: the procedural difference
between the analysis of a problem and the study of a period; the use of
the reality principle in history; and the distinction between the thesis
and the object of an analysis. The first and third points are almost self-
explanatory and relate to Foucault's perception of what he was about in
Surveiller et punir. The second refers to his insistence on the need to
demystify 'the overall instance of the real as a totality to be reconsti-
tuted'. In other words, his work is not concerned with an overall picture
of the nineteenth-century prison system, but with 'a chapter in the
history of "punitive reason" '.[98] He ends by expressing the hope, which
makes a playful reference to Part III of *Surveiller et punir* ('Discipline'),
that an exploration of relations between power and knowledge will
permit 'not an "interdisciplinary encounter" between "historians" and
"philosophers", but collective work with people who are trying to "de-
disciplinarise" themselves'.[99]

Although he was critical of Léonard's criticisms and basically argued that the historian had missed the point of his book, Foucault was delighted to be taken so seriously by a professional and rang Perrot to say that he would like to take part in a debate, with Léonard's review and his own comments as the topic for discussion. Perrot agreed to organise a round-table debate under the auspices of the Société d'Histoire de la Révolution de 1848. The joust took place on 20 May 1978. The historians involved were Maurice Agulhon, Nicole Castan, Catherine Duprat, Arlette Farge, Carlo Ginzburg, Remi Gossez, Jacques Léonard, Perrot and Jacques Revel. Foucault appeared in the company of François Ewald, Alexandre Fontana and Pasquale Pascino, all of whom were then members of his seminar group at the Collège de France. The proceedings, which lasted for some two hours, were taped in their entirety with a view to publication but the transcript proved to be very unwieldy and a compromise had to be found. It was not an entirely happy one. Ewald and Perrot condensed the debates, and all the comments by individuals became anonymous interventions by a 'collective historian'. Of all the participants, only Foucault has a voice of his own. This was not to everyone's satisfaction and Agulhon, who strongly objected to his collectivisation, insisted on making a signed contribution of his own. A copy of his text was sent to Foucault, who flew into a rage and telephoned Perrot, demanding that Agulhon's piece be withdrawn. Perrot did not wish to be put in the difficult position of trying to mediate between two men who had known each other since their student days and protested that they should sort matters out without her help. The published volume therefore finally appeared with an introduction by Agulhon and two 'afterwords', one by Foucault and the other by Agulhon.

The debate, as edited and condensed by Ewald and Perrot, centres on four main questions which are answered by Foucault at some length: Why study prisons?; 'Eventalisation' ['Événementialiser']; The Problem of rationalities; and the alleged 'anaesthetising effect' of the book. Foucault begins with a typical refusal to be defined in disciplinary terms – 'My books are neither philosophical treatises nor historical studies; at most, philosophical fragments on historical building sites' – and then argues that in concentrating on prisons he is attempting to pick up the theme of a genealogy of morals by tracing transformations in what might be termed 'moral technologies'. Although he does not speak directly of his own political activities or of the GIP, he insists that his subject is of direct political relevance, given recent events within the prison system.[100]

Turning to what he calls 'eventalisation', Foucault argues that his concentration on the 'event' is a way of challenging 'self-evident' truths on which knowledge and practices are based: 'Its theoretical-political function [is] to show that it was not as obvious as all that that the mad should be recognised as being mentally ill; it was not self-evident that the only thing to be done with a delinquent was to lock him up.'[101] Here, Foucault is deliberately courting controversy; *histoire évémentielle* (sometimes translated as 'event-bound history') has been a pejorative term ever since it was used by Braudel in the preface to his *La Méditerranée et le monde méditerranéen à l'époque de Philippe II* in 1949.[102] This is, however, little more than a flirtation with *Annales* terminology, though it is no doubt designed to annoy, as Foucault goes on to define his 'eventalisation' as an attempt to see how forms of rationalisation are inscribed in specific practices. He takes it as axiomatic that there is no higher rationality which allows other forms to be dismissed as 'irrational': 'My problem is that of knowing how men govern themselves and others . . . through the production of truth . . . Eventalising particular sets of practices so as to reveal them to be different regimes of jurisdiction and veridiction. That, to put it in extremely barbaric terms, is what I would like to do.'[103]

The debate finally turns to the allegedly 'anaesthetising effect' of *Surveiller et punir* when Foucault is asked about the transmission of his analyses: 'If, for example, one works with prison educators, one notes that the arrival of your book had an absolutely sterilising or, rather, anaesthetising effect on them in the sense that your logic had an implacability they could not get out of.'[104] Foucault is not entirely happy with the choice of terminology, but concurs that one of his aims is to ensure that certain 'obvious truths' and clichés about madness or criminality become more and more difficult to use, to ensure that, say, social workers in the prison service no longer know what to do or say, that words and practices which seemed self-evidently true become problematic.[105]

In their twin Afterwords, Agulhon and Foucault meet in 'single combat', as a reviewer put it.[106] Agulhon's arguments are political and ethical rather than historiographical in any strict sense. While he is critical of the optimism and self-satisfaction of the traditional socialist belief in 'progress', he is even more suspicious of the argument that nineteenth-century liberalism and philanthrophy, or even the Enlightenment itself, are a prefiguration of totalitarianism, and accused Foucault of having contributed to that argument. The subtext implies Agulhon's disapproval, as a supporter of the Socialist Party, of the *nouveaux philosophes* and of Foucault's association with them. In particular, he objects to the contrast drawn by Foucault between the old custom of leading away columns of prisoners in chains and the innovation of the police carriage, with its individual cells.[107] Foucault makes much of the almost carnivalesque scenes and popular violence that often surrounded the departure of *la chaîne* for the ports and which vanished with the appearance of the *fourgon cellulaire*, and at times seems to suggest that the old system was 'preferable' to individual confinement in a horse-drawn wagon.

For Agulhon, the disappearance of the old system is obviously a step towards the humanisation of the penal system. He ends by asking a rhetorical question: 'Is it horrible to recognise that there are degrees of horror? Does recognising that . . . there can be a humanisation of its modes of existence mean defending prisons?'[108]

Foucault first replies to Agulhon's second point, arguing: 'Revealing the system that supported the practice of *la chaîne* is no more a way of denying that it was abominable than saying that confinement is something other than a "humane" penalty is an excuse for not understanding the mechanisms in which it is inscribed.' He then denies attacking rationalism, claiming that he is interested in revealing the forms of rationality implemented in certain institutional practices. Finally, he makes a suggestion to Agulhon and his collaborators: 'Why not begin a major historical enquiry into the way the *Aufklärung* has been perceived, thought, lived, imagined, exorcised, anathemised and reactivated in the Europe of the nineteenth and twentieth centuries? That might be an interesting piece of "historico-philosophical" work. Relations between historians and philosophers could be "put to the test".'[109]

The suggestion was not taken up. As Agulhon remarks in his introduction to *L'impossible Prison*, the debate was a first stage in an improved mutual understanding between Foucault and historians,[110] but it was a first stage which went no further. To Foucault's lasting chagrin, he was never invited to lecture at the Ecole des Hautes Etudes.[111]

Had Agulhon attended Foucault's lecture to the Société Française de Philosophie on 27 May or the lectures he gave at the Collège de France in February, he would have been surprised to find that, far from disparaging the Enlightenment, Foucault was beginning to incorporate some of its values into his own work, notably by elaborating a theory of governmentality that would largely replace the earlier theory of power/knowledge. For Foucault, the Enlightenment meant a critical attitude and not a historical epoch. As he himself accepted, his theory that the *gouvernés* had an innate right to challenge governments, or to place limitations on their powers, came close to a theory of natural right.[112]

By the end of the year Foucault's academic interests and even his interest in domestic politics were eclipsed by something very new. On 28 September 1978, the Milan daily *Corriere della sera* announced on its front page that it had a distinguished new collaborator and promised its readers 'a series of reports . . . which will represent something new in European journalism and which will be entitled "Michel Foucault Investigates" '. Almost two months later, Foucault explained what he hoped to do. He introduced the first of the planned series – a report on Carter's America by Alain Finkielkraut – and went on:

> This will be followed by a series of other investigations, which we see as 'intellectual reportage' ['*reportages di idee*']. Some say that the great ideologies are dying, others that they overwhelm us with their monotony. On the other hand, the contemporary world is teeming with ideas which are born, are discussed, which disappear and reappear, and which stir up many people and many things. This is not only true of intellectual circles or of the universities of Western Europe; it is happening on a world scale, among people and minorities that, until now, history has not accustomed to speaking or making themselves heard.
>
> There are more ideas on earth than intellectuals themselves imagine. And these ideas are more active, more powerful and more stubborn than the politicians think. We have to be present at the birth of ideas, and at the explosion of their force, not in the books that formulate them, but in the events in which they manifest their strength, in the struggles led by ideas, for or against ideas.
>
> Ideas do not rule the world. But it is precisely because the world does have ideas (and because it continuously produces lots of them) that the world is not passively ruled by its rulers or by those who want to teach them what to think once and for all.
>
> That is the meaning that we want to give to these reports, in which an analysis of what is being thought will be linked to an analysis of what is happening. Intellectuals will work together with journalists at the point where ideas and events meet.[113]

Foucault speaks of having established a permanent team of collaborators based in Paris. The team in fact consisted of Thierry Voeltzel,

André Glucksmann and Alain Finkielkraut, then twenty-nine and enjoying the success of his first book, co-written with Pascal Bruckner; it was a denuciation of 'the genital reduction that the male body imprints on sexual life'.[114] Foucault's team included not one professional journalist.

Foucault had long been interested in journalism, and was a frequent 'occasional contributor' to *Le Nouvel Observateur*. His involvement with the GIP, with the Djellali Committee and with the small group that investigated the Jaubert case had, he believed, given him at least some competence in 'investigation' and 'news gathering'. He had written for the Maoist press in the early 1970s, and published occasional pieces in *Le Monde*. He had been one of the founders of *Libération* in 1973, but did not become a regular contributor. When he was approached by Alberto Cavallari, the head of the *Corriere*'s Paris desk, with a proposal for a series of articles, he readily agreed.[115] Foucault never explained his motives, but it is quite possible that he was contemplating a change of direction. From the newspaper's point of view, the advantage of the arrangement was the prestige attaching to Foucault's name; his work was available in Italian translation and was widely read. The fact that the copyright for the articles was held jointly by the newspaper and Rizzoli, a publishing house, indicates that at least the possibility of subsequent republication in book form was being considered.

In the event, the announced series did not materialise, and only Finkielkraut's piece was published. What did appear was a series of articles by Foucault on Iran. They were to prove very controversial in France, did Foucault's reputation little good, and taught him that journalism has its dangers for someone with his degree of public exposure. As he subsequently admitted:

> I cannot write the history of the future, and I am a somewhat clumsy explorer of the past. But I would like to pick up 'What is happening' because these days nothing is decided in advance [in Iran] and because the die is still rolling. Perhaps that is a journalist's job, but it is quite true that I am only a neophyte.[116]

The neophyte journalist was not an expert on Iran, though he had for some time taken an interest in the human-rights situation in that country, mainly because of his continued acquaintance with Thierry Mignon, a lawyer and a former comrade from the GIP days who now worked with a committee for the defence of Iranian political prisoners: Foucault had, for instance, signed a petition in *Le Monde* protesting against the execution of nineteen 'anti-fascist militants'.[117] Claude

Mauriac was now heavily involved in human-rights activities, and had recently been campaigning for the release of a group of Iranians wrongly imprisoned on a murder charge. He obviously discussed the campaign with Foucault, who was convinced that the French police was acting in collusion with SAVAK – the Shah's secret police, which was notorious for its covert activities on the campuses of European universities.[118] Foucault came up with the idea that the affair could be used to promote a confrontation between Giscard and a group of intellectuals. Foucault proposed that Giscard should be invited to lunch [déjeuner] in order to discuss the situation in Iran, but he immediately modified it: Giscard should be invited to a 'fast' [jeûne]. The proposal was also in part designed to embarrass those who had accepted Giscard's invitation to lunch in December 1976, and one guest in particular: 'Sollers has decided what is right and what is wrong for long enough. It's his turn to be judged.' Catherine von Bülow was to be left to make the arrangments, with Foucault joking that she might land them in Tehran if she was not careful. To which Mauriac laughingly replied that, if she did, they would never get home again.[119] The 'fast' plan went no further, but Foucault did go to Tehran, and did come home again.

Accompanied by Voeltzel (and not Defert), Foucault made two brief visits to Iran in September and October 1978. Before his departure, he did some preparatory research by talking to contacts made through Mignon, mixing with Iranian exiles, including some of Defert's students at Vincennes and moving in the shadowy milieu in which it was never quite certain just who was a genuine member of the opposition and who was a SAVAK agent.[120] It was a milieu characterised by fear: 'fear that it might become known that they were mixing with people on the left, fear that SAVAK agents might find out that they were reading such and such a book'.[121] Armed with at least some knowledge of the situation, he landed in Teheran days after Black Friday, on which the army had opened fire on a crowd of demonstrators, killing an untold number.

The first visit yielded two articles, written in French after Foucault's return to Paris rather than being phoned in, one for the *Corriere* and one for the *Nouvel Observateur*, which described him as 'our special correspondent'.[122] His contacts included sociologists, members of the opposition, met clandestinely on the outskirts of Teheran, and some members of the military, but on the whole he preferred to discuss the situation with casual acquaintances met in the street: ' "What do you want?" During the whole of my stay in Iran, I never once heard the word "revolution". But four times out of five, I got the answer "an Islamic government".[123] He quickly became convinced that a military coup followed by a dictatorship was not a likely development because of divisions within the military and because of the growing pressure for an Islamic state. The calls coming from the mosques, and distributed throughout the country on cassette, reminded him of the Florence of Savonarola, of the Anabaptists and of the Presbyterians of Cromwell's day. On the other hand, the mullahs were not a revolutionary force in the classic sense; something new and dangerously exciting was emerging in Iran: Shiite Islam was 'a religion which has, throughout the ages, constantly given an irreducible strength to everything within the people that can oppose state power'.[124]

Foucault's contacts were not restricted to anonymous spokesmen and students. He was also granted an interview with Ayatollah Madari in the holy city of Qom. The meeting, also attended by Mehdi Bazargan, who was later to become prime minister, took place under tight security, with guards carrying machine pistols at the door. Foucault was struck by Bazargan's claim that, although an Islamic government would restrict the rights of civil sovereignty, it would also be bound by religious duties which it could not escape; if it attempted to renege on them, the people would use Islam against it. He also appears to have been impressed by Madari's statement that Iran did not expect the return of the Mahdi, but was fighting day by day for a better government.[125]

The first visit was brief, but Foucault was back in Iran within the month, visiting Teheran again and travelling briefly to the oil town of Abadan, 1,000 kilometres to the south. This time, his visit produced four reports for the *Corriere*.[126] Before they could all be published, controversy broke out in Paris. On 6 November, *Le Nouvel Observateur* published a letter from an Iranian reader who identified herself simply as 'Atoussa H.' She violently objected to Foucault's article of 16 October and attacked him for suggesting that 'Muslim spirituality' was in some way preferable to the collapsing dictatorship of the Shah, and for offering the Iranian people a bleak choice between SAVAK and 'religious fanaticism'. More specifically, she pointed to the lowly position imposed upon women by Islam, and to the ominous spectacle of women being insulted for not wearing the veil. In her view, Islam would be used as a screen for feudal or pseudo-revolutionary oppression: if Islamic law was the cure, it might well be worse than the disease.[127] A week later, Foucault replied that, in view of the call for an Islamic government, it was his elementary duty to attempt to discover what that call meant. He further argued that 'Atoussa H.'s' letter contained two intolerable things. On the one hand, every possibility offered by Islam was being rejected in the name of the 'age-old reproach of fanaticism'; on the other, the writer seemed to suspect that any interest taken in Islam by a westerner was a sign of his scorn for it. 'The problem of Islam as a political force is an essential problem for our age and for the years to come. The precondition for approaching it with even a modicum of understanding is that we must not begin by bringing hatred into it.'[128]

Undeterred by criticism, Foucault continued to publish his reports in the *Corriere*. What impressed him most about the situation in Iran was its total unfamiliarity: this was neither China, Cuba nor Vietnam. Nor was it May 1968. What is happening in Iran . . . is a groundswell, with no vanguard, no party.'[129] He was convinced that he was seeing the emergence of a unified collective will: 'Perhaps the greatest ever insurrection against global systems, the most insane and the most modern form of revolt.'[130] It was the profoundly religious element that gave the Iranian revolution its unique force; religion had become 'a real force . . . the force that can make a whole people rise up, not only against a sovereign and his police, but against a whole regime, a whole way of life, a whole world'.[131] So impressed was he by the spectacle of this collective will that he sadly underestimated the power of Ayatollah Khomeini and the probable future of the developments he was witnessing, and argued that there would be no Khomeini party and no Khomeini regime, since the Ayatollah was the focal point for more anonymous collective forces.[132] As he had already put it in his *Nouvel Observateur* article, events in Iran recalled something the West had forgotten since the Renaissance and the great crises of Christianity, namely the possibility of 'a political spirituality'.[133]

Such statements were not acceptable to all Foucault's readers. He was aware that he would be laughed at in Paris, but was convinced that he was right. Even the loyal Mauriac had doubts about 'spirituality' where politics were concerned, but finally accepted that 'politics without spirituality' was equally dangerous.[134]

A particularly savage attack came from Claudie and Jacques Broyelle in the pages of *Le Matin*. They criticised Foucault for having become an apologist for 'a spirituality which punishes and disciplines', for an illegal regime. The attack also comprised some *ad hominem* remarks; Foucault was of course no more responsible for the blood that was flowing in Iran than western communists were responsible for the Gulag; on the other hand, all the 'models in the Foucault range bore the same anti-democratic, anti-legalist and anti-judiciary trademark'. The two also referred back to his 'debate with Maoists' about 'people's justice', implying a continuum between that and his vision of a collective will in Iran.[135]

Foucault did not deign to reply, saying that he had always refused to take part in polemics, and that he objected to being asked to 'admit my mistakes. The expression and the practice it refers to remind me of something, of many things. I have fought against them. I will not become involved, even in print, in a game whose form and effects seem to me to be detestable.'[136] He did, however, indicate his willingness to engage in a debate, and Le Matin mentioned that it hoped to publish an article by Foucault after the referendum called for the end of the month in Iran. No such article ever appeared.

There were two codas to the Iran affair. The first was an open letter to Mehdi Bazargan, now prime minister in the Khomeini government, which Foucault had believed would never take power. It was written at a time when officials and supporters of their ancien régime were being executed after summary trials. In it Foucault recalled their earlier discussions in Qom of the spiritual dimension of the revolution. The Iranian government was now in a position to honour its obligations: 'It is good that the governed should rise up to recall that they have not simply given rights to those who govern them, but that they intend to impose duties upon them. No government can escape those fundamental duties. And from that point of view, the trials which are now taking place in Iran are inevitably worrying.'[137]

Not surprisingly, no reply was forthcoming from Teheran. Foucault's last word came in an article published by Le Monde in May. He did not make any apology for the wave of executions taking place in Iran, but posed his own dilemma in terms of the duties of the intellectual. Replying to the imaginary strategist who could justify any death in terms of overriding necessity and who could sacrifice any general principle in the name of the needs of a particular situation, he argued that his own theoretical ethics was 'anti-strategic':

Be respectful when any singularity rises up, and intransigent when power infringes universals. A simple choice, but a difficult task, as one has to be at once slightly above history, watching for what is breaking or upsetting history, and slightly behind politics, watching unconditionally over anything that might limit politics. After all, that is my work. I am neither the first, the last, nor the only one to do it. But I chose it.[138]

In the early 1970s, Foucault had signed petitions denouncing American involvement in Vietnam and, along with countless others, had marched on the demonstrations against the war. By the end of the decade, Vietnam came to mean something other than a symbol of the struggle against oppression. The first hint of its changed meaning for Foucault and many others came during the reception at the Théâtre Récamier in June 1977. A small Vietnamese woman named Phung Anh spoke from the platform: 'I fought against the Thieu regime and there were thousands of French people with me. Today, thousands of Vietnamese are in prison and no one in France is protesting. What has changed? Who are you fighting for?'[139]

On the evening of 8 November 1978, television screens across the world showed the first pictures of the Hai Hong, a battered freighter crowded with 2,564 refugees from Vietnam being prevented from docking in Malaysia. The expression 'boat people' was about to enter both the English and French languages. For many, the film *Exodus* immediately sprang to mind: the emotive spectacle of a shipload of refugees being harassed by a navy was reminiscent of the ships carrying would-be Jewish settlers being fired upon by the British navy in 1947.[140]

At midnight Bernard Kouchner received a phone call from Jacques and Claudie Broyelle: something had to be done. The couple were former Maoists. Kouchner was a doctor whose experiences in Biafra in 1968 had led him to be instrumental in founding the international relief organisation Médecins Sans Frontières.[141] His political background was very different to that of the Broyelles, since he had been an active PCF militant in the early 1960s before becoming immersed in medical and Third World issues. Kouchner thought it only natural to approach Foucault for support, and still speaks with great affection of a man he regarded as 'a combatant in civil society', as a founder of associations like the GIP, associations which rejected the 'right' of governments to reduce individuals to 'the residue of politics'. As a result of his association with Kouchner, Foucault became a regular participant in the meetings of the so-called Académie Tarnier, a discussion group which met in the lecture theatre of the Hôpital Tarnier. Foucault was a constant presence, always sitting in the second row, sometimes with Simone Signoret at his side and usually with his head in his hands as he listened to papers on everything from Chad or Lebanon to the problems of the social-security system.[142]

An initial statement and an appeal for funds to charter a relief ship appeared in *Le Monde* on 9 November. The appeal eventually gathered hundreds of signatures from people as diverse as Brigitte Bardot and Eugène Ionesco. Foucault was one of the first to sign, but persuasion was required; he was not immediately convinced that the boat would ever set sail and argued that he would only support practical acts of solidarity.[143] He was, however, to prove an effective member of the Un Bateau pour Vietnam Committee. The committee's title 'A Boat for Vietnam' was taken from a leaflet distributed in 1966 and calling for medical relief for North Vietnam. It was Alain Geismar who unearthed it and gave it to Kouchner. Like many of the active members, Geismar was a former Maoist; the only self-professed Marxist to sign the appeal was Nicos Poulantzas. A number of the activists came from the old 'Vietnam base committees' which had flourished in the 1960s. Other supporters came from very different political backgrounds and one of the campaign's most surprising features was its success in bringing them together on a single platform. Foucault was not a leading figure in its day-to-day activities, but lent his name and influence in a variety of ways and greatly facilitated its work.

On 20 November, Yves Montand launched the campaign in an interview on the television news: 'Yes, we helped Vietnam to become independent; we fought against the American bombs which were killing Vietnamese people, and we were right. Now, Vietnamese people are being drowned, and we must help them too.'[144] The campaign was difficult, surrounded by political controversy and, for Kouchner himself, bitter and bruising. He was accused by former colleagues in Médecins Sans Frontières of courting media attention, of self-promotion and of appealing for *un bateau pour Saint-Germain* – a belittling charge equivalent, in British terms, of saying that he was involved in 'Hampstead politics'.[145] The organisation eventually split, and Kouchner founded the alternative Médecins du Monde in 1981.

In party-political terms, the work was difficult. No Trotskyist organisation would become involved, and sections of the Socialist Party also kept their distance. The Communist Party prevaricated, claiming that a human-rights issue was being exploited to anti-Communist ends and muddying the waters by raising the immigration issue: it was argued that Communist municipalities already had substantial immigrant populations and could accept no more refugees or migrants.

The most famous episode connected with the 'Boat for Vietnam' campaign involved Foucault in only a minor capacity. In June 1979, the Lutétia, an expensive hotel on the corner of the boulevard Raspail and the rue de Sèvres, was the setting for an unexpected encounter between Sartre and Raymond Aron. The two had been friends at the

Ecole Normale in the 1920s, were witnesses at the wedding of Paul Nizan, and Aron had been on the original editorial board of Sartre's *Les Temps Modernes*. Political differences had driven them apart and had resulted in decades of intermittent but bitter polemic. On 20 June, a nervous André Glucksmann led Sartre into the room and seated him next to Aron. Photographs of their handshake and reports of Aron's greeting '*Bonjour, mon petit camarade*' flashed around the world and threatened, in retrospect, to overshadow the reason for their meeting, as does the account given by Aron himself in his memoirs.[146] Despite press speculation, Sartre did not see the meeting as a reconciliation with Aron,[147] and was concerned solely with the issue of Vietnam.

Foucault arrived late and missed the beginning of the meeting,[148] but added his voice to those of Aron, Sartre, Simone Signoret, Alain Geismar, Bernard Stasi (vice-president of the National Assembly) and François Ponchaud, the chairman of the organisation representing those who survived their deportation from France to Auschwitz. All called for increased aid and for increased refugee quotas. Foucault was not the main speaker, but performed the essential task of organising a press conference afterwards.

On 26 June, he organised a second press conference, this time at the Collège de France, for a delegation from the committee consisting of Claudie Broyelle, Sartre, Glucksmann and Stasi. The delegation had been received by President Valéry Giscard d'Estaing, who proved to be sadly ill-informed about the situation but who eventually agreed that any refugees picked up by the boat that had now been acquired – the *Ile de Lumière* – would be accepted by France. The delegates left the Elysée in gloomy mood, unconvinced that anything would actually happen. Subsequent difficulties over visas justified their pessimism.[149] The difficulties were overcome, and the *Ile de Lumière* did set sail on its mercy mission, which Kouchner chronicles in detail in his book of the same name.

16

THE DANCE OF DEATH BEGINS

FOR more than twenty-five years, Foucault had, whenever resident in Paris, worked almost daily in the Bibliothèque Nationale. He finally abandoned that practice in the summer of 1979. His frustration with increasing delays in the book-delivery service had, according to Defert, been compounded by bitter personal quarrels with the library's director. At a dinner party given by Roger Stéphane (critic and author of classic studies of Malraux, T. E. Lawrence and Ernst von Salomon[1]), Foucault was introduced to Michel Albaric, the librarian of the Bibliothèque du Saulchoir, which is attached to the home of the Dominican community in the rue de la Glacière. Hearing of Foucault's problems at the Bibliothèque Nationale, Albaric told him that he would be more than welcome at the Saulchoir.

Foucault found there just what he was looking for. The Saulchoir is a small library, with a pleasant reading room built around a sunken garden. Whereas the Bibliothèque Nationale can, like many large libraries, be surprisingly noisy, the Saulchoir is peacefully quiet and tends to be frequented by nuns, monks, priests and students rather than by the cosmopolitan hordes who crowd into the great library in the rue de Richelieu. The atmosphere suited Foucault, who developed a firm friendship with Albaric. Both the library and its librarian appealed to the ascetic side of the man who once joked to Claude Mauriac that he was 'made for the monastery. If I were not a total atheist, I would be a monk . . . a good monk.'[2]

The Saulchoir's main collections are devoted to philosophy and the religious sciences; standard classical texts and works by the Church Fathers are available on open shelves. It was here that Foucault worked for the last years of his life, always sitting near the window at the same table, distracted from his work only by the occasional passage of attractive young men. The Saulchoir is a private foundation, and not a rich one. Over the coming years, Foucault would make discreet donations of unspecified amounts of money to its funds.[3]

The Saulchoir was ideal because the planned *Histoire de la sexualité* had now taken a new and rather different direction. One of the phenomena noted in *La Volonté de savoir* had been the contrast with the modern experience of 'sexuality' and the Christian experience of 'the flesh'. Both seemed, however, to be dominated by the figure of 'the man of desire'. Foucault therefore began to undertake a genealogy of desire and the desiring subject. At this point, he was faced with a choice: 'either keep the original plan, adding a rapid historical examination of this theme of desire; or organise the whole study around the slow formation, in antiquity, of a hermeneutics of the subject'. He opted for the latter course and began to assemble materials for 'a history of truth'.[4]

Foucault was now plunged deeply into classical Greek philosophy and the history of the Christian tradition. As he freely admitted, he was no classicist,[5] and he now had painfully to revive the knowledge of classical languages that he had acquired at school. That was a slow task, and he obviously also used translations and bilingual editions. Foucault states that he was helped with his research by Paul Veyne, one who 'knows what looking for the true means to a real historian; but he is also familiar with the labyrinth you enter when you want to write the history of games of true and false; he is one of those, and they are rare today, who are prepared to face the threat to all thought inherent in the question of the history of truth'.[6] For his part, Veyne speaks merely of general conversations at this time, and denies giving Foucault any specific help or advice.[7]

Foucault's lectures at the Collège de France were taking roughly the same direction as the *Histoire de la sexualité*. As in his 1978 lecture to the Société Française de Philosophie, in 1979–80, Foucault took as his title 'Du Gouvernement des vivants', and concentrated on 'the notion of government . . . in the broad sense of techniques and procedures designed to direct the conduct of men. The government of children, the government of souls or consciences, the government of a house, a state or the self.'[8] As a result, the old figure of power-knowledge began to be displaced by the theme of 'governmentality'.[9] The government of men demanded of men acts of obedience and submission, but also 'acts of truth', and Foucault was therefore led to ask: 'How did there take shape a form of government of men in which one is required not only to obey, but to manifest what one is by stating it [*en l'énonçant*]?' The answer lay, he thought, in the confessional and penitential practices of early Christianity and in the differences between those practices and the examination of conscience practised in the philosophical schools of antiquity. The seminar, in contrast, was devoted to aspects of nineteenth-century liberal thought.

The following year's lectures were devoted to 'Subjectivity and Truth', or to an investigation into the history of modes of self-knowledge. Rather than looking at philosophical theories of the soul, the passions or the body, Foucault spoke of investigating

'technologies of the self', that is, the procedures . . . which were proposed or prescribed for individuals in order to fix, maintain or transform their identity in accordance with a certain number of goals . . . How does one 'govern oneself' by performing actions in which one is oneself the object of those actions, the domain in which they are applied, the instrument to which they have recourse and the subject which acts?[10]

Plato's *Alcibiades* could be taken as a starting point because 'in this text, the question of the "care of the self" [*epimeleia heautou*] seems to be the general framework within which the imperative to know oneself takes on its meaning'.[11]

The Collège lectures were being used by Foucault to outline what would become the themes of his last two books. They also provided the subject matter for virtually all the guest lectures and seminars he would give in the last years of his life. A concern with liberation from the *dispositif* of sexuality was now giving way to a concern for an 'aesthetics of existence', to use the title of one of the very last interviews given by Foucault.[12] When read in sequence, the lectures and interviews from this period prove to be very repetitious, as the same themes are addressed over and over again from slightly different persepectives.

The return to the Greeks contained a certain irony. In the mid-1970s, when he was working on *Surveiller et punir*, Foucault had argued that the tendency, which he saw as originating with Heidegger and as exemplified in France by Derrida, to see Plato as the 'decadence after which everything began to crystallise', was 'disheartening'. He avoided talking about Greece because he did not want to 'fall into some Hellenistic archaism'. It was much more fun to philosophise about madness, policing and poverty.[13] The return to Greece and Rome proved to be rather less fun. When Daniel Defert told him how much he admired *L'Usage des plaisirs*, Foucault replied: 'But you know it was not the book I had most pleasure in writing.'[14]

The motive behind the final volumes of the *Histoire de la sexualité* was not, then, hedonism. Yet Foucault's motive was, he wrote, 'very simple'. It was curiosity, or 'the only kind of curiosity that it is worth pursuing with a little obstinacy; not that which allows us to assimilate what it is fitting to know, but that which allows one to lose one's fondness for oneself [*se déprendre de soi-même*]'.[15] Foucault's motive was very much in keeping with the Stoic and Christian traditions he was exploring. As he remarked in an interview given in California in 1983, 'Christian culture has developed the idea that, if you want to take care of yourself in the right way, you have to sacrifice yourself'.[16] It was also consonant with Foucault's conviction, derived at least in part from Nietzsche's comments on 'the great and rare art' of giving style to one's character,[17] that selfhood, rather like gay culture, was a question of aesthetic creation rather than of the expressive liberation of some personal essence. 'Losing one's fondness for oneself' can further be interpreted as a variant on the deindividualisation, and even the desexualisation, Foucault sought through the calculated use of pleasures, or on the dissolution of individuality common to Foucault, Deleuze and Klossowski. Although his terminology and philosophical frame of reference had changed somewhat, he was still 'writing in order to have no face' or 'writing in order to become other than what one is'.

Foucault's philosophical and even pedagogical concerns were changing in some senses, his sporadic political activities revealed that older concerns were still important to him. In the spring of 1980, he was, for instance, involved in the establishment of an Association Défense Libre. Its aims were to denounce the limitations placed upon defence lawyers, abuses of the accusatory system and violations of the rights of those facing prosecution. An initial meeting was held near Toulon in May, but Foucault appears not to have been present. He was involved in drawing up the preparatory documents for it, together with the lawyer Casamayor, Claude Mauriac, Jacques Vergès, Christian Revon and others. The introductory statement, which is reminiscent of the terminology once used by the GIP, was in part drafted by Foucault:

> Let us avoid the hackneyed problem of reformism and anti-reformism. It is not up to us to take responsibility for institutions which need to be reformed. It is up to us to defend ourselves so well that the institutions will be forced to reform themselves. . . .
> In the expression 'defend oneself', the reflexive pronoun is crucial. The point is to inscribe the life, the existence, the subjectivity and the very reality of the individual within the practice of the law.[18]

One of the cases which had inspired the founders of the association was the Ranucci affair, which had led Foucault to refuse Giscard d'Estaing's invitation to lunch. Foucault's involvement with Défense Libre did not go much beyond its foundation, but his presence is an indication that he had not forgotten the GIP experience. One contribution to the small orange-covered pamphlet published in May 1980 by the Dominican François Deltombe provides a surprising index of just how far his influence, and that of *Surveiller et punir* in particular, had spread. The fact that it was recommended reading for students of criminology in the universities is not surprising; that *Surveiller et punir* had also caught the attention of 'the very Catholic Justice and Peace commission, an organ of the French Conference of Bishops' was perhaps less predictable.[19]

Some of those involved with the Défense Libre project had been known to Foucault for a long time. Christian Revon, a Dominican and sometime psychiatric nurse turned lawyer, had known him since the GIP days. So too had Antoine Lazarus, once employed in the prison medical sevice at Fleury-Mérogis, and now running the Paris branch of the Groupe Multiprofessionnel des Prisons. In November 1979, Lazarus and François Colcombet (a former chairman of the Syndicat de la Magistrature) had been involved in a retrospective debate about the GIP with one 'Louis Appert'. 'Louis Appert', described as 'a member of the GIP', was Foucault. No one can give any convincing explanation for his adoption of a pseudonym, but it is intriguing that the name he chose should be so similar to his mother's maiden name of Malapert.

The debate goes some way towards providing the beginnings of the history of the GIP which Foucault could have written had he chosen to do so. Asked for his opinion as to the GIP's 'balance sheet', 'Appert' was uncertain what to say. The experience of working in the group had been positive, if only in that it represented a new way of combining theory and practice. In political groups, the two were combined thanks to 'a doctrine which binds, a practice which constrains'. In the GIP, on the other hand, 'knowledges, analyses, the practices of sociologists, a bit of historical knowledge, a little philosophy, a few anarchist ideas, the books we had read . . . all that came into play; it circulated, formed a sort of placenta around us'. However, he was far from convinced that anything had been actually achieved, and thought that most of the problems remained intact.[20] The transcript which appeared in *Esprit* was not a complete record of the discussion. On the original tape, Daniel Defert can be heard muttering in the background, to the amusement of all present, about penguins. His excursion into ornithology was not gratuitous; a right-wing politician had suggested in all seriousness that the real solution to the crime problem was to deport convicts to an Antarctic island.[21]

The concern with abuses of power that led Foucault to work with

Défense Libre was also apparent in his active participation in the work of the Defence Committee established to secure the release of Roger Knobelspiess. In 1972, Knobelspiess had been imprisoned for the theft of 800 francs; the only evidence against him was a denunciation. Despite his protestations of innocence, he was sentenced to fifteen years. Repeated hunger strikes and self-mutilations followed, but he was never granted leave to appeal against his conviction. Granted a forty-eight-hour pass in 1976, Knobelspiess disappeared, and was accused, on being recaptured, of having carried out several armed robberies. Now deemed to be a dangerous recidivist, he was confined in one of the newly opened *quartiers de haute sécurité*. These were secure units established after the mutinies at Clairvaux and elsewhere, and housed small numbers of supposedly dangerous prisoners in harsh conditions. Solitary confinement and video surveillance were part of the regime, and there was little association with other prisoners.[22] For the Comité d'Action des Prisonniers, which folded in 1980, the very existence of the high-security wings had represented a form of torture; in Foucault's view, they were an abuse of the law in that they were prisons within prisons and breached the principle that deprivation of liberty was in itself a final punishment.[23] No court could sentence a man to a QHS; the internal prison administration could and did. The establishment of the QHS system had frightening implications for the future. Given that there was a distinct possibility that the Socialist government elected in the spring of 1981 would abolish the death penalty, the QHS represented a potential threat; it was not impossible that death sentences would be replaced by sentences which condemned offenders to a QHS for an indefinite period.[24]

The Knobelspiess Defence Committee consisted of Foucault, Genet, Glucksmann, Mauriac, Montand, Signoret and Paul Thibaud, the editor of *Esprit*. In prison, Knobelspiess wrote his first book, part autobiography, part denunciation of the prisons in which he had, at the age of thirty-two, spent almost half his life. The book was published thanks to the efforts of the Defence Committee and was prefaced by Foucault: 'This is an unpolished document. It has not been written, and it has not been published, as one more account of prison life . . . Real and profound transformations are born of radical critiques, assertive refusals and voices which do not break. Knobelspiess's book is part of this battle.'[25] Perhaps more so than any of Foucault's 'theoretical' texts on the same subject,[26] his preface to Knobelspiess illustrates what he sees as the logic of the prison and of its construction of the dangerous individual:

Look at the case of Roger Knobelspiess: he was found guilty of a crime he strongly denies having committed. How could he accept prison without admitting that he was guilty? But you can see the mechanism: because he resists, he is put in a QHS. The reason why he is in a QHS is that he is dangerous. 'Dangerous' in prison, and therefore even more dangerous if he were at liberty. He is therefore guilty of having committed the crime of which he was accused. That he denies it is irrelevant: he could have done it. The QHS supplies proof; prison *shows* what the investigation may have demonstrated inadequately.[27]

In November 1981, Knobelspiess's case came to trial and, partly because of the campaign organised by the Defence Committee, with Mauriac playing the major role, he was pardoned by François Mitterrand.[28] Knobelspiess himself admitted the armed robberies of which he was accused. The presiding judge, on the other hand, seemed to be telling the jury that the crimes were the direct result of a wretchedly poor childhood and of an unsafe conviction in 1972.[29] Now something of a star, Knobelspiess was photographed at the side of Prime Minister Pierre Mauroy, appeared on television, became a sought-after dinner guest and wrote a second book, this time prefaced by Mauriac. In June 1983, Knobelspiess was arrested in Honfleur, and again charged with armed robbery and with having shot at two police officers. Further charges followed. Knobelspiess was again jailed, and was finally released on parole in August 1990, adamant that he wanted above all to be an ordinary citizen.[30]

When Knobelspiess was found guilty of armed robbery in 1983, Foucault expressed surprise that so many people had been surprised. Those who argued that the admission of guilt meant that Knobelspiess had also been guilty in 1972 were, he argued, being irrational. What was worse:

You are a danger to yourselves and a danger to us, if, that is . . . you do not wish to find yourself in the hand of a legal system that has been put to sleep by arbitrariness. You are also a historical danger. For, like a society, a justice which always has to question itself can exist only if it works on itself and its institutions.[31]

The Knobelspiess case obviously caused Foucault some embarrassment, and made him the object of not a little mockery. There was talk in the press of the disastrous effects of '*les foucades de Foucault*' ('Foucault's whims'), and references to the 'Prix Knobel' ('Knobel prize-winner') intellectuals who had defended him.[32] Despite the mocking criticisms addressed to him from certain quarters, Foucault had not been displaying naive liberalism in defending Knobelspiess. His decision to become involved, or to remain uninvolved, in such cases were based upon a political shrewdness which could disconcert some of his natural allies. When, in 1974, Pierre Goldman finally came to trial, accused of a double murder committed in the course of a robbery in 1969, most of the *gauchiste* world was convinced of his innocence. Once one of the PCF's best street-fighting men, Goldman was a romantic figure, deeply involved in *gauchisme* and linked to Latin American guerrilla movements. He was sentenced to life imprisonment, but was freed after a second trial in 1976. Although Goldman became a hero to certain sections of the left, Foucault, who said nothing about the case in public, was convinced that he was guilty and had no hand in publicising the Goldman cause.[33]

A brief exchange about Goldman with Mauriac and Signoret reveals something of Foucault's underlying beliefs about personal ethics. When Signoret, who had been one of Goldman's committed supporters, complained that he had failed to keep an appointment with her, Mauriac commented that no one had the right to expect gratitude from him. Foucault's face contorted, and for the first time Mauriac was subjected to the anger that had been directed at Catherine von Bülow when she foolishly suggested that Simone de Beauvoir should accompany '*les Montand boys*' to Madrid. Oblivious to Mauriac's stammered explanations, Foucault burst out: 'I won't stand for it. I'll never stand for it. The older I get, the more I believe in friendship and the duties it implies. That *gauchiste* offhandedness that consists in saying "I don't owe anyone anything. Especially not those who fought for me" . . . I won't stand for it.'[34] The outburst was short-lived, but it shook Mauriac.

Foucault's problems were not confined to difficulties with libraries. In both personal and professional terms, he was, despite his fame, surprisingly isolated as the 1970s gave way to the 1980s. After their disagreements over the Croissant affair, he had broken with Deleuze and Guattari. His articles on Iran had cost him other friends, and had done his reputation little good, and the resultant controversy had put a sudden end to his collaboration with the *Corriere della sera*.[35] His final contribution to the newspaper was a brief tribute to Lacan, 'the liberator of psychoanalysis', when he died in 1981.[36] The myth still persists that Foucault was an apologist for Khomeini and that he never criticised himself for having apparently saluted a 'nascent obscurantism as a new dawn'.[37] The positions adopted by Foucault in the autumn of 1978 were in fact little different from the views expressed in *Libération* and even *Le Nouvel Observateur*.[38] His visibility inevitably ensured that, while the errors of judgement made by professional journalists have been forgotten, Foucault's have not.

Foucault took no part in the *Etats généraux de la philosophie*, which brought together a huge gathering of philosophy teachers and students for a debate on the situation in French philosophy at the Sorbonne in June 1979,[39] possibly because its main organiser was Derrida, with whom there would be no reconciliation until 1981, when Derrida was arrested on trumped-up drug charges in Czechoslovakia; Foucault was one of the first to defend him. Foucault had been hurt by Baudrillard's attacks in his *Oublier Foucault*, and perceived, not entirely inaccurately, Aron and Kempf's study of nineteenth-century sexuality as a further attack on his *Volonté de savoir*. He resented its authors' challenge to what they called the 'currently accredited thesis' that 'the state apparatus . . . alienates its edifying mission to independent micro-executives – crèche, school, asylum, hospital'.[40] The book, worth reading for its title alone ('The Penis and the Demoralisation of the West'), was certainly seen as 'anti-Foucault' by reviewers.[41]

The appearance of a new journal in May 1980 led to a bitter quarrel with an old friend and colleague. *Le Débat*'s director was Pierre Nora, who had been Foucault's main editor at Gallimard since 1966. Its title – 'The Debate' – was chosen precisely because there was, in Nora's view, no debate in France. The first issue promised an open debate: the new journal had no system to impose and no message to deliver. It did not, however, seem to be open to Foucault, who was not invited to collaborate on it and who was not, according to many of his friends, consulted about the project. The first issue carried an article by Nora on the role – or absence thereof – of the intellectual. He ended by calling for an intellectual democracy which would put an end to the situation in which 'the *critical* function' helped to mask the political irresponsibility of intellectuals.[42] Foucault appears to have taken such comments as a personal attack on his political activities. He was also no doubt annoyed by other insinuations. Although he may well have agreed that the intellectual function had been degraded, Nora's pointed remark that Brigitte Bardot could one day be elected to the Collège de France because Simone Signoret to all intents and purposes had been,[43] might have been calculated to annoy: Foucault was extremely fond of Signoret and very close to her at this time. The result of Nora's article was a violent quarrel with Foucault, who threatened to leave Gallimard and publish his *Histoire de la Sexualité* elsewhere.[44] It was now common knowledge that his relations with Nora were execrable. According to Paul Veyne, there was an element of professional rivalry and jealousy in all this. Foucault had never been the editor of a major series or collection of books, and was envious of Nora's role.[45] It is further rumoured that he was trying to oust Nora from his position as the general editor of the Bibilothèque des Sciences Humaines.

Deteriorating relations with Nora were not the only reason for Foucault's annoyance with *Le Débat*. In a shallow but witty discussion of Paul Veyne, the journal's editor Marcel Gauchet picked up the historian's reference in an essay appended to his *Comment on écrit l'histoire* to Foucault's having 'negated' the natural object. For Veyne it was that negation that gave Foucault's work its stature. Gauchet commented: 'Philosophy, an eminently depredatory activity, can be practised only at the expense of the environment. For the philosopher to grow, the forest must shrink.'[46] Foucault was far from humourless, but comments like this added to his irritation with Nora's new journal. On the other hand, he himself ensured that relations with *Le Débat* would not be easy. Gauchet was the co-author, with Gladys Swain, of a history of Esquirol and the Salpetrière which went against the findings of *Histoire de la folie* by contending that it was a retrospective illusion to claim that the division between reason and unreason had been preceded by an age of tolerance.[47] To add insult to injury, the book appeared in the same series as *Les Mots et les choses*. Foucault agreed to review the book for *Le Monde* and other newspapers, but procrastinated, thus ensuring both that his own review did not appear and that no one else could review it either. Not suprisingly, this did nothing to improve relations with *Le Débat*. According to Nora, Foucault was 'afraid' of Gauchet, was disturbed by his association with his editor and saw the publication of *La Pratique de l'esprit humain* as a betrayal of his trust.[48]

Foucault was by now definitely thinking of leaving Gallimard. His decision to publish the panopticon text with a very small publisher may have been the first sign of a deeper dissatisfaction. The rumour that Foucault was planning to change his publisher spread quickly and aroused great excitement. Precisely what Foucault was planning was not entirely clear, but it is obvious that his unease was acute. To some friends, he talked of moving to Vrin, the academic philosophy specialists who had published his translation of Kant in 1964. Vrin is a classically academic house operating from premises that are literally in the shadow of the Sorbonne; it is extremely well respected in professional circles, but not given to advertising its titles on any great scale. At one point, Foucault was even discussing the possibility of direct publishing in the form of typescript. He spoke, at an unspecified date, to von Bülow of his wish to establish a 'community of scholars' which would be able to publish scholarly texts, small editions of lectures from the Collège de France and even doctoral theses. There was also a plan, discussed by an all-male gathering while von Bülow made the coffee, for a 'philosophical institute' whose members would include Foucault, Lardreau, Jambet and Glucksmann.[49] Mauriac also refers to a proposed 'Foucault foundation' which never came into being because there were too many manuscripts by Foucault to be examined – and some to be destroyed – before anything could be done.[50] Nora claims that, even at the height of their quarrel, Foucault was trying to convince him that he should leave Gallimard to set up a cooperative venture which could be financed by Foucault's royalties. A much more serious option was a move to Seuil.[51] The obstacle to any such move was of course that Foucault was tied by contract to Gallimard; the decision to turn to Gallimard for finance for the film version of *Moi, Pierre Rivière* was now a millstone. In 1983, Foucault was still claiming that *Le Souci de soi* would be published by Seuil,[52] but his last works inevitably appeared in Gallimard's 'Bibliothèque des histoires'.

It was in this context that Foucault told *Le Monde*, only half-jokingly, that for a year, all books should be published anonymously so that the critics would have to discuss them without reference to an author who was already situated or could be given a place within the intellectual firmament.[53] In the event, that suggestion, which reflects Foucault's recurrent fascination with the idea of personal and sexual anonymity, was never put into effect.

What did eventually emerge from Foucault's general dissatisfaction with the situation in publishing was a new collection at Seuil, jointly edited by Foucault, the linguist and psychoanalyst Jean-Claude Milner, Paul Veyne and François Wahl: *Des Travaux*. The collection was designed to publish research which, for economic and other reasons, could not find an outlet elsewhere: long-term research projects, brief accounts of research in progress and translations. The first title appeared in 1983: Paul Veyne's *Les Grecs ont-ils cru à leurs mythes?* The title of the collection was explained as follows: 'Work [*travail*] that is likely to introduce a significant difference into the field of knowledge, at the cost of a certain difficulty for both author and reader, and with the possible reward of a certain pleasure, or in other words access to another figure of the truth.' The word *travaux* (the plural of *travail*) had a particular significance for Foucault. He loathed the idea of being the author of an *oeuvre*, but when he said of a piece of work '*Ça, c'est un travail*', it was high praise indeed.[54] The publicity for the launch of the new collection included the announcement of a new book by Foucault: *Le Gouvernement de soi et des autres*. It never appeared.

Dissatisfaction with the publishing industry and with French intellectual life in general was to be a recurrent theme in the last interviews Foucault gave. On 25 April 1984, only a month before his death, Foucault again spoke of his 'anonymous publication' project in an interview with Alessandro Fontana. One way to put an end to the situation in which the actual reading of books was supplanted by the exchange of information and disinformation fostered by the media might be the adoption of a law prohibiting the use of an author's name on more than two occasions and encouraging the use of anonymity and pseudonyms. In most cases, the author's name was an irrelevance. With the exception of a few 'great authors', the name did not matter: 'For someone like me, and I am not a great author, but simply someone who manufactures books, one would like [the books] to be read for their own sake, with the imperfections and qualities they may or may not prove to have.'[55]

Similar concerns were expressed in a contemporaneous interview with Didier Eribon. One of the reasons that there could be no real debate in France was that the bookshop windows were piled up with hastily written books which, 'with lies and pronunciation mistakes, say anything and everything about the history of the world ever since its foundation, or which rewrite more recent histories with slogans and clichés'.[56] Journals and reviews, far from being the site of a real debate, had become either sectarian mouthpieces or supports for a bland eclecticism. There was a general tendency towards entropy in intellectual life, and it was affecting the reception of Foucault's works:

This passage of the philosophical question into the realm of the slogan, this transformation of the Marxist question, which becomes 'Marxism is dead', is not the responsibility of any one person in particular, but we can see the slide whereby philosophical thought, or a philosophical issue, becomes a consumer item . . . It took fifteen years to convert my book about madness into a slogan: all mad people were confined in the eighteenth century. But it did not even take fifteen months – it only took three weeks – to convert my book on will to knowledge into the slogan 'Sexuality has never been repressed'.[57]

Foucault was not alone in his pessimism about the state of French publishing. In 1980, Pierre Bourdieu was also complaining in an interview about the importation into the intellectual sphere of the marketing techniques that allowed a Golden Delicious to be passed off as an apple.[58]

To add to his general malaise at the start of the new decade, Foucault was now beginning to lose friends. Maurice Clavel died suddenly in April 1979. Despite his embarrassment and occasional annoyance at being hailed by him as the 'new Kant', Foucault had been very fond of Clavel. On Sunday, Clavel had been talking to Foucault on the phone about a whole host of topics: Freud, Christian penitence and the obligation to tell the truth . . . On Monday, Foucault was telephoned by *Le Matin* and asked to comment on his death. He had nothing to say: this day was not sufficient to the pain thereof.[59] Four days later, he wrote movingly in *Le Nouvel Observateur* of 'Clavel: impatient, jumping at the slightest noise, crying in the penumbra, calling down the storm . . . The great cycle which finds past and future in one another was not his problem. He was only interested in the atemporal that fractures the present.'[60] On 25 April, the basilica in Vézelay was filled with a strange company of Gaullists, *gauchistes*, royalists and philosophers old and new. Jean Daniel spoke: 'More and more of us understand that we have lost the last of the great Judaeo-Christian troublemakers.'[61]

In retrospect, the demise of the troublemaker must have looked like the beginning of a dance of death that would go on until the end of the year. Death's next partner was Barthes, who had, with some assistance from Foucault, been elected to the Collège de France at the end of 1976. On 25 February 1980, Roland Barthes and a number of other intellectuals had lunch with François Mitterrand, the first secretary of the Socialist Party. Presidential elections were due to take place in 1981 and the lunch, organised by Jack Lang, who was to become Mitterrand's minister of culture, was no doubt in part a way of sounding out the degree of support the Socialists could expect in 1981 and followed the precedent set by Giscard d'Estaing's famous lunches. Barthes chose to return on foot from the Marais to the Latin Quarter and, as he crossed the rue des Ecoles, he was struck by a delivery van. The accident, which occurred near the Collège de France, left him unconscious and bleeding, and he was rushed to the Salpêtrière by the emergency services. As he was carrying no papers, it was not until hours after his admission that his identity could be revealed.

The accident did not appear serious, and a bruised and battered

Barthes was soon receiving visitors, including Foucault, to whom he would mutter: 'How stupid [*quelle bêtise*]!' A month later, Barthes was dead at the age of sixty-four. His doctors announced that the accident had not been the direct cause of his death, but that it had exacerbated the respiratory problems of a man who had spent large portions of his youth in a TB sanatorium. Most of his friends believed that Barthes had simply lost any will to live and had never really recovered from the death of his adored mother in 1977. Some claimed that, immediately before stepping off the pavement, he had been looking in the direction of the van, and must have seen it coming towards him. In conversation with the translator of his *Raymond Roussel*, Foucault contested that widespread view, claiming that the rumours that Barthes wanted to die 'were completely false' and that his discussions with Barthes's doctors had confirmed his view of the matter. Mysteriously, he also claimed to have been with Barthes at the time of the accident, but no other account confirms this. A week before the accident, Foucault had watched Barthes teaching: 'I thought, "He's in his element, he's acquired the distinguished bearing of a man who is mature, serene, completely developed." I remember thinking, He'll live to be ninety years old; he is one of those men whose most important work will be written between the ages of sixty and ninety.'[62]

On Friday 28 March, a handful of friends and students gathered in the courtyard behind the Salpêtrière hospital as Barthes was brought down in an open coffin for the ritual *levée du corps*. When the mourners had paid their last respects, the coffin was then sealed and loaded into the hearse for the long journey to the southwest for private burial in Urt.[63]

For Foucault, the death of Barthes was a 'scandal' because he had died at the height of his creative powers.[64] The circumstances were also an uncannily graphic reminder of the accident which had left him hospitalised for a week in 1978. In a eulogy read to the assembled members of the Collège de France, he paid tribute to his late friend. Foucault described Barthes as a great writer and a wonderful teacher, as a man who paid for his fame with the pain of solitude, and then concluded:

Destiny would have it that the stupid violence of things – the only reality he was capable of hating – should put an end to all that, on the very steps of the house into which I asked you to invite him. The bitterness would be unbearable, were it not that I knew he was happy to be here, were it not that I felt entitled to pass on, from him to you, through the grief, the sign, the slightly smiling sign of friendship.[65]

The dance now continued. On 15 April 1980, Sartre died in the Hôpital Broussais. Four days later, his body was taken to the Père Lachaise cemetery for cremation. This was the occasion for what has sometimes been called the last demonstration of May 1968. An immense procession, estimated at between 20,000 and 30,000 people, followed his coffin through the streets in a hysterical atmosphere. At the very rear of the procession walked Foucault, Defert, Claude Mauriac, Robert Gallimard and Catherine von Bülow.[66]

Foucault had had to be persuaded to attend. When Defert asked him if he would be going to the funeral, he replied: 'Why should I? I don't owe him anything,' before capitulating in the face of the argument that Sartre had, in political and international terms, been the prototypical French intellectual of the post-war period. In the event, he found the experience moving.[67] As they moved slowly through the streets, Foucault spoke to von Bülow of his youth and of the 'intellectual terrorism' then exercised by Sartre and those around him.[68] When Mauriac remarked that very few of those present could ever have read Sartre in any real sense, Foucault agreed. He went on to observe that in other countries, intellectuals like Sartre did not have the role they had in France. His conclusion was startling and revealed that his knowledge of the English-speaking world was not as sophisticated as might have been expected: the American press and the British Parliament made the interventions and the position of French intellectuals pointless.[69]

Foucault's resentment of Sartre went back to 1967 and the appearance in *Les Temps Modernes* of very negative reviews of his *Les Mots et les choses*, and had been exacerbated by media attempts to construct a Foucault–Sartre opposition. Foucault and Sartre had nothing in common in philosophical terms and, even though they occasionally shared a platform, their political differences were considerable. Even so, Foucault did sometimes speak with some affection of Sartre as an individual.[70] The press coverage of Sartre's death did not improve Foucault's opinion of Sartre's entourage. In the account of Sartre's *gauchiste* involvement he published in *Le Monde*, Christian Zimmer spoke of his participation in anti-racist demonstrations in the Goutte d'Or and of his interventions in connection with the prison mutinies of 1972.[71] There was no mention of the fact that the demonstrations in the Goutte d'Or had been called by Foucault and

Mauriac, or of the existence of the GIP. It was as though Sartre had been the only committed intellectual, and Foucault understandably expressed a certain resentment at this.

Defert inherited something of Foucault's hostility towards *Les Temps Modernes* and identified completely with Foucault's reluctance to have anything to do with the journal. When he was approached by its editor Claude Lanzmann for a contribution to the two-volume 'Témoins de Sartre' issue published in 1990, he reacted badly. Lanzmann had asked him for a piece on 'Sartre and Foucault'; Defert replied that he could only write on 'Foucault and Sartre' and began by mentioning the 1967 reviews.[72] He finally contributed a short and not always completely objective account of relations between the two.

Foucault's discontent with France was almost directly proportional to his enthusiasm for America, and particularly for California. His increasingly solid reputation as one of Europe's pre-eminent intellectuals gave him a ready audience. Increasingly, he was tempted by the idea of taking up permanent residence in California, or at least of regularly spending part of the year there. He found intellectual life freer and more open there than in France. California offered ample opportunity for the further exploration of the use of pleasures. Even American cuisine appealed to him, and rather than eat sophisticated French dishes, he would, he said, take 'a good club sandwich with a Coke. That's my pleasure. It's true. With ice cream. That's true.'[73]

Derrida's reputation in the United States was also being consolidated at this time, but it was almost as though he and Foucault had established a geographical division of labour. Deconstructionism colonised Yale and the Ivy League universities, whereas Foucault found his audience, in which professional philosophers were usually underrepresented, in New York and on the West Coast. The establishment of these distinct spheres of influence meant that there were no direct encounters or confrontations between the two.

In October 1979, Foucault was invited to Stanford University in Palo Alto, California, to give the Tanner Lectures on Human Values.[74] Foucault's English was now sophisticated enough for him to deliver the lectures in that language. In seminars, he tended occasionally to lapse into French, particularly when tired. As he explained to a discussion group at Stanford when he was forced to fall back on the services of a hastily recruited interpreter, exhaustion rendered his English childishly poor.[75] Like any user of a second language, he was proud of his ability to employ colloquialisms and had an especial fondness for the phrase 'the Monday-morning quarterback', which he used to characterise the historian's beneficial hindsight.

It was while he was in California that Foucault first met Paul Rabinow and Hubert L. Dreyfus, both from Berkeley and respectively an anthropologist and a philosopher of the Heideggerean persuasion. Rabinow had recently attended a seminar given by Dreyfus and John Searle, and had objected to the characterisation of Foucault as a 'typical structuralist'.[76] Subsequent discussions led to a project for a joint article, and over the summer of 1979 the proposed article gradually grew into a book. The joint authors were involved in lengthy discussions with Foucault himself, and were to become good friends of his. Their book is a thorough, if at times very dense, survey of Foucault's work which, given the date of its composition, puts a surprising emphasis on *Les Mots et les choses* and *L'Archéologie du savoir*, and particularly on the theory of 'serious speech acts' that is allegedly to be found in the latter.

In late October of the following year, Foucault returned to Berkeley to give the Howinson Lectures on 'Truth and Subjectivity'.[77] The lectures were highly publicised and drew large audiences. Foucault was 'puzzled and made uncomfortable by the fanfare and notoriety',[78] but, as usual, enjoyed California. In November, he was in New York to give the James Lecture at the Institute for the Humanities. The lecture was part of a duet with the sociologist and novelist Richard Sennet, now a close friend.[79]

Foucault's reputation now gave him virtual cult status in certain quarters, and he was increasingly close to Leo Bersani and John Searle. But he also had his critics in the US. The *Village Voice* could speak with ironic mockery of his 'flashy use of graphic historical detail', and *Time* could cite Yale's Peter Gay's dismissal of him on the ground that 'he doesn't do any research, he just goes on instinct'.[80] Richard Rorty, for instance, was sceptical about Foucault's politics and dismissed his 'so-called anarchism' as 'self-indulgent radical chic' – a judgement which suggests little concrete knowledge and a lot of credit in hearsay.[81] In his 1981 James Lecture, Jürgen Habermas attacked Foucault as a 'Young Conservative' on the grounds that he juxtaposed in manichaean fashion 'instrumental reason' and principles 'only accessible through evocation, such as power'.[82] Although he was by no means unsympathetic to the book, the anthropologist Clifford Geertz from Princeton's Institute for Advanced Study began a review of *Discipline and Punish* in terms which capture something of the doubts that many had about Foucault's work as a whole. Foucault had become, he wrote:

a kind of impossible object: a nonhistorical historian, an anti-humanistic human scientist, and a counter-structuralist structuralist. If we add to this his tense, impacted prose style, which manages to seem imperious and doubt-ridden at the same time, and a method which supports sweeping summary with eccentric detail, the resemblance of his work to an Escher drawing – stairs rising to platforms lower than themselves, doors leading outside that bring you back inside – is complete.[83]

Foucault, of course, prided himself on his elusiveness and would no doubt have been amused at being described as an impossible object. Other criticisms must have been less welcome. In an article that continues to provoke controversy, H. C. Erik Midelfort argued not only that Foucault had greatly exaggerated the pan-European dimensions of *Histoire de la folie*'s 'great confinement', but that the *Narrenschiff* was a purely literary phenomenon, and that there was little or no proof that any such vessel had ever really drifted along the canals and rivers of northern Europe.[84]

The image of the mad being deported by sea had by now found its way into standard textbooks on the history of abnormal psychology; the authority cited for the existence of the ship of fools was invariably Foucault. Two American researchers, Winifred and Brendan Maher, began to investigate the claims for its empirical reality, and found that its existence was purely allegorical.[85] The Mahers then wrote to Foucault, asking for information about his sources. On 10 December 1980, he replied in a letter that abounds in Gallicisms:

> It is not easy for me to reply to the question that you have asked, as is also the case with others of the same kind that have been addressed to me. The documentation which I have utilised for *Histoire de la folie* comes in large part from the library at Upsala (sic) and it is very difficult to find these references in Paris. In the meantime I will try to retrieve those that you mention and will eventually send you the necessary citations.[86]

Correspondence between Foucault's two critics and librarians in Uppsala, in the meantime, had established that the only sources Foucault could have used were Brandt's *Das Narrenschiff* and a sixteenth-century anthology which reproduces Brandt's imagery. The authors concluded that the ship of fools did not exist, and that Foucault had succumbed to a 'structuralist' need to bring social behaviour into line with 'theoretical patterns of symbolism'.

Foucault did not respond to these criticisms. He did, however, reply to the comments made by Lawrence Stone in a long article on 'Madness' in the *New York Review of Books*. For Stone, the central challenge of Foucault's approach to madness was 'to the humanitarian values and achievements of the eighteenth-century Enlightenment'.[87] He conceded the influence of Foucault's work, but seriously challenged its empirical underpinnings: 'Foucault . . . provides us with a dark vision of modern society which accords with only some of the historical facts. Abstract and metaphoric in expression, unconcerned with historical detail of time or place or with rigorous documentation . . .'[88] Furthermore, Stone cast doubt on the very existence of the 'great confinement', and on the alleged emergence of a 'new principle that madness is shameful, and that the best treatment is forcible isolation from society under management by professionally trained doctors'. He then used the most extraordinary of arguments: 'So far from being isolated were the twenty-odd manacled madmen gibbering and rattling their chains in their filthy cage in Bedlam, one of the great tourist attractions of London from the early sixteenth century to the early nineteenth.'[89]

On this occasion, Foucault, who often claimed that he did not 'like to get involved in polemics',[90] did reply to his critic, and was not slow to exploit the weakness of Stone's comments on Bedlam: 'Do you really believe that locking people up and making an exhibition of them proves that they are not submitted to segregration? Just tell me if, fettered and howling in a yard or writhing behind bars, subject to the jibes of gawking onlookers, you would not feel slightly isolated?'[91] Most of the exchange did not take place at this level, but Foucault identified and refuted what he described as 'nine major errors'. He did not, however, take up the general issue of his allegedly anti-Enlightenment stance, nor did he produce any further empirical arguments or source materials to substantiate the claims of *Histoire de la folie*. His primary defence was to argue that Stone had not actually read his book, and to prove the point by supplying detailed references.

The last word was left to Stone, who basically repeated his original charges, to which he now added the most bizarre of all. He cited with obvious approval an article by a doctor of medicine published in *Hospital Practice* which argued that 'the recent discharge of thousands of helpless psychiatric patients onto the pitiless streets of New York' was a 'remote byproduct of Foucault's negative evaluation of the philanthropic dream of Pinel, coupled with the fashionable claims by the English revisionist psychiatrist R. D. Laing that schizophrenia is not a disease'. Foucault, it seemed, was the progenitor of the 'bag lady'.[92] It is reported that someone at the University of California asked Foucault why he chose to reply to Stone when he had ignored so many critics. Foucault replied: 'Because it was so easy.'[93]

While Foucault was in New York, the calm of ENS was brutally disturbed on the morning of 16 November 1980. Pierre Etienne, the school's doctor, was awakened by a furious hammering on his door. When he opened it, he found a frantic Althusser, who told him that he thought he had killed his wife. When he entered the Althussers' apartment, Etienne found Hélène sprawled on the bed. She was dead and her body was already cold, but there were no signs of a struggle. Etienne and the school authorities decided that Althusser should be taken to Sainte-Anne immediately, called an ambulance, and only then rang the police. An autopsy confirmed that Hélène had been strangled.[94] Attempts on the part of the police and an examining magistrate to interview Althusser merely demonstrated that the philosopher understood nothing of what was being said to him, and Althusser was committed to the care of his doctors. It was eventually decided that he had been temporarily insane at the time of the murder, and he was never brought to trial; according to the law of 1838 no crime or misdemeanour can be committed by anyone who is judged insane. The law also provides for indefinite commital to a psychiatric institution.

The remainder of Althusser's life was spent in Sainte-Anne, which he already knew well, and then in a series of private clinics (with occasional excursions into the outside world), where he tried to begin writing again. Althusser had already written a fragmentary auto-biography in 1976 (*Les Faits*), and now produced the much longer *L'Avenir dure longtemps* (1985). In his own view, the latter was a 'critical "confession" ', an equivalent to the memoir produced by Pierre Rivière.[95] With a desperate humour he also referred to it as his 'traumabiography'.[96] Deprived of any legal or civil existence by the law of 1838, Althusser was, in his own words, 'a man who had disappeared [*un disparu*]. Neither living nor dead, not yet buried, but *sans oeuvre* – the magnificent word Foucault uses to designate madness – dis-appeared.'[97] Althusser's disappearance lasted until his second death on 22 October 1990 in an old people's home, two years after his release from psychiatric care.

None of Althusser's close associates made any comment on the murder at the time. Derrida, for instance, merely said 'Too heavy' and refused to comment further.[98] Foucault too remained silent, but he kept in contact with his old teacher over the next ten years and visited him on at least three recorded occasions. As Althusser gradually recovered, he was able to discuss current events and developments in the intellectual world. The usual intermediary between the two was Father Stanislas Breton, a left-wing Catholic and a close friend of Althusser's since the mid-1960s. Foucault supplied Breton with a 'very special' telephone number where he could be contacted at any time. Both Althusser and Breton report one exchange with Foucault. Foucault was describing his research into the 'values' of Christianity and made the point that, while the Church had always set great value by love, it had always distrusted friendship. In his view, there was an obvious link between the revulsion from friendship and its ambivalent repulsion from homosexuality, or in other words its ill-repressed predilection for homosexuality. Breton replied by describing his life. At fifteen, he became a novice and had always lived a friendless life; friendship carried with it the threat of homosexual attachments and sin. Love was a means of salvation from the temptations of friendship. The priest then borrowed a phrase from Foucault and said; 'You know, man is a very recent invention in monasteries.'[99]

17

THE GREAT, STUBBORN LIGHT OF
POLISH FREEDOM

TO the jubilation of the crowds packed into the place de la Bastille on 10 May 1981, the huge video screens announced that Mitterrand had defeated Giscard d'Estaing in the presidential election. Just over a month later, the Socialist Party won an absolute majority in the National Assembly.

A month before Mitterrand's victory, Foucault had been ranked as France's 'third most influential intellectual' (his influence was outweighed by that of Lévi-Strauss and Raymond Aron).[1] He had not, however, used his alleged influence to rally support for Mitterrand or any other politician. In his view, people were old enough and big enough to choose for themselves who to vote for; the messianic role of the intellectual who advised others to vote for the politician he supported was one which did not suit him.[2]

Foucault had not been particularly optimistic about the possibility of a Socialist victory and had argued in 1980 that very little had changed or was likely to change: Mitterrand was in his usual position in the polls, and the PCF still commanded 20 per cent of votes.[3] The Union of the Left was not greatly to his taste, largely because of the pivotal role it was likely to give to the PCF in the event of a Socialist government being elected. He was wrong about voting patterns; one of the most striking features of the May election was the downturn in the PCF's vote. Although he had not urged anyone to vote for any particular party, Foucault was pleased with the decision of 10 May; people had used their ability to choose very effectively. He was optimistic about the immediate future and the 'left logic' which had put an end to the thirteen-year period in which France had been ruled by the right. In particular, he was impressed by the new government's likely attitude towards the issues of nuclear power, immigration and prisons. At a more general level, there was a real possibility of a new relationship between government and *gouvernés*, the governed.[4] Asked if he was now willing to work with the government, Foucault replied: 'Working with a government implies neither being subjugated to it nor total acceptance.

One can work and be restive. I even think that the two go together.'[5]
'Working with' was a variant on the 'working-alongside' principle that
had governed Foucault's attitude towards the Maoists a decade earlier,
and implied the right to maintain a critical attitude.

In many ways, Foucault's guarded optimism was justified. In
August, an estimated 300,000 illegal immigrants were invited to
'regularise' their situation. The new minister for justice, Robert
Badinter, who greatly admired *Surveiller et punir*, moved rapidly to
abolish the death penalty, to close the high-security wings in the
prisons (a move which Foucault urged in print in July[6]) and to abolish
the state-security court. The *loi anti-casseurs* of 1970, under which so
many *gauchistes* had been held, was repealed. In August, the Mirguet
amendment of 1960 was repealed, and the police were ordered to stop
keeping files on 'known homosexuals'. Any hope that Foucault may
have had of working 'with the government' in any official capacity was,
however, to be frustrated. He was offered a post as 'cultural counsellor'
in New York, but rejected the offer as unsuitable, given his age and
status in France. The one post which he did covet was that of director of
the Bibliothèque Nationale, but that went to one of Mitterrand's close
associates.

There was, then, no official role for Foucault, but he continued to be
politically active. In July, an international congress on the problem of
piracy opened at the UN in Geneva, where the corridors were decked
with giant photographs of the boat people staggering ashore from their
crippled vessels in Malaysia. Foucault addressed the conference
without any advance publicity. His brief intervention was drafted on a
scrap of paper and then read without any revision or hesitation.[7]
Foucault emphasised that he and his friends from Médecins du Monde
were present in their capacity as private individuals:

Then who mandated us? No one. And it is precisely that which
gives us the right to speak. It seems to me that we have to bear in
mind three principles . . .
　　1. There is such a thing as an international citizenship which
has its rights, which has its duties and which implies a commitment to rise up against any abuse of power, whoever its author,
whoever the victims. After all, we are all governed [*nous sommes tous
des gouvernés*] and, by that token, our fates are bound up together.
　　2. Because they claim to look after the happiness of societies,
governments arrogate to themselves the right to draw up profit-
and-loss accounts for the human misery which their decisions

provoke, or which their negligence causes. One of the duties of international citizenship is to reveal human misery to the eyes and ears of government, as it is not true that they are not responsible for it. Human misery must never be the silent residue of politics. It founds an absolute right to rise up and to address those who hold power.

3. We must reject the division of labour we are so often offered: it is up to individuals to become indignant and to talk; it is up to governments to think and to act . . . Amnesty International, Terre des Hommes and Médecins du Monde are the initiatives which have created this new right: the right of private individuals to intervene effectively in the order of international policies and strategies. The will of individuals must be inscribed in a reality over which governments wish to have a monopoly, a monopoly which we must wrest away from them, gradually and day by day.[8]

Foucault's words were to have an afterlife. In January 1987, Bernard Kouchner and Médecins du Monde organised an international conference in Paris under the joint patronage of the Polish politician Lech Walesa and the South African cleric Desmond Tutu. The conference insisted on the right and indeed the duty to interfere in the affairs of other countries in the name of human rights. The published proceedings are prefaced by Foucault's Geneva intervention, which can with some justification be regarded as the foundation for Kouchner's notion of a 'duty to interfere'.[9] As a direct result of the Paris conference, Kouchner was made secretary of state for humanitarian action by François Mitterrand in 1988.

The rest of the summer of 1981 passed quietly, but at the end of October Foucault participated in a grandiosely titled conference at the University of Southern California: 'Knowledge, Power, History. Interdisciplinary Approaches to the Works of Michel Foucault.'[10] The media interest in his presence was enormous, and even resulted in an article in *Time*, not normally noted for its concern for the philosophical.[11]

The conference was a lively affair. The University's Davidson Conference Centre overflowed with academics and students, journalists and a team hoping to make a video of the proceedings. Inevitably a forum for the display of academic and personal rivalries, for conspicuous displays of knowledge, it also became one for curious protests, like that from the unnamed woman who referred to the platform microphone as 'a voice-deforming penis'. Foucault himself spoke on 31 October, the closing day, and, given the size of his audience, settled for a fairly straightforward talk that retraced his intellectual trajectory. He ended by referring to his current work on 'pastoral power'; in other words, the model of power which originated in the religious practice of both tending a flock and establishing a link between the individual believer and Christ. Finally, Foucault asked: 'What are we and what could we be? What forms of new subjectivity can we create that will not originate in subjection?'[12]

Within a fortnight, Foucault was caught up in events that signified a very real 'subjection' and a concrete denial of the rights of the *gouvernés*. On 13 December 1981, General Woiciech Jaruzelski, who had been appointed prime minister of Poland in February, declared a 'state of war' and imposed martial law, thus suddenly putting an end to the hopes raised by the previous year's 'Polish August'.[13] Early next morning, Foucault was telephoned by Pierre Bourdieu. The two men were not close, even though they had known each other for almost thirty years, and Bourdieu was not normally one to take an active political stance. It seemed to him that Foucault was the obvious person to turn to in an attempt to protest against developments in Poland.

The result of the phone call was a text – drafted in Foucault's apartment by Bourdieu and Foucault – entitled 'Les Rendez-vous manqués', which was published, with some assistance from Didier Eribon, a young journalist Foucault had come to know in the mid-1970s, in *Libération* on 15 December and again on 17 December; extracts were also published in *Le Monde* on 18 December. The main signatories, in addition to the authors, included the theatre director Patrice Chéreau, Costa-Gavras, André Glucksmann, Bernard Kouchner, Claude Mauriac, Yves Montand, Jorge Semprun, Simone Signoret and Pierre Vidal-Naquet. The text was an angry response to Jaruzelski's 'seizure of power', and a reaction to the positions taken by the French government. It was to involve Foucault and his fellow signatories in a bitter wrangle with government spokesmen.

Speaking on *Europe 1* on 13 December, Foreign Minister Claude Cheysson had expressed surprise at developments in Poland, but had added that it was a purely internal matter for the Polish government; the French government would, 'obviously', do nothing. He voiced the hope that the crisis would be solved by the Poles themselves, adding that he saw no sign of possible 'outside intervention'.[14] Cheysson was to regret his unfortunate choice of words, which betrayed a serious failure to anticipate the wave of spontaneous sympathy with Poland that was soon to be seen in France. The minister did at least have the virtue of being consistent. Asked by *Le Monde* during the election campaign if he was optimistic or pessimistic about the future of Poland, he had refused to answer the question, saying that that was a matter for the Poles. He wished Poland good luck, but insisted that he had nothing to say about its internal affairs.[15]

On the morning of 15 December, the text of 'Les Rendez-vous manqués' was read out on *Europe 1* by Montand; it was then discussed by Foucault. Immediately after the broadcast, a motorcycle courier arrived from the Elysée, and left with a cassette recording of the comments made by Foucault and Montand. The text read as follows:

> The French government must not, like Moscow and Washington, allow it to be believed that the establishment of a military dictatorship in Poland is an internal matter which will allow the Poles to decide their destiny for themselves. That is an immoral and mendacious assertion. Poland has just woken up to find itself under martial law, with thousands of people interned, the trade unions outlawed, tanks in the streets and the promise of the death penalty for any disobedience.
>
> This is certainly a situation that the people of Poland did not want. It is a lie to describe the Polish army and the party with which it is so closely linked as instruments of national sovereignty.
>
> The Polish Communist Party, which controls the army, has always been the instrument of Poland's subjection to the Soviet Union. After all, the Chilean army is a national army too.
>
> By asserting in the face of all truth and all morality that the situation in Poland is a matter for Poles alone, are not the French Socialist leaders giving more importance to their alliances at home than to the assistance that is due to any nation in danger? Is a good understanding with the French Communist Party more important to them than the crushing of a labour movement under the boots of the military? In 1936, a socialist government was faced with a military putsch in Spain; in 1956, a socialist government was faced with repression in Hungary. In 1981, the socialist government is faced with the Warsaw coup. We do not want its attitude today to be that of its predecessors. We remind the government that it promised that the obligations of international morality would prevail over *Realpolitik*.[16]

The allusion to Spain was also a reference to the Blum government's controversial policy of non-intervention in the Spanish Civil War.

Foucault was well aware that France could not literally intervene in Polish affairs by sending in paratroopers or tanks; but he was convinced that for 'ethical reasons', it should make clear its 'non-acceptance' of what was happening. The *gouvernés* of France, in the meantime, should demonstrate their 'non-acceptance of the government's seeming passivity'.[17] In the event, the Mitterrand government was not particularly passive, and did protest about the Polish coup. France provided large amounts of relief aid during the martial-law period. Immediately after the December events, Pierre Mauroy made a point of cancelling his first official visit abroad as prime minister: a trip to Warsaw.[18] Cheysson's words had, however, sown the seeds for a controversy which quite destroyed the optimism Foucault had felt in May.

The first response came from Lionel Jospin, the first secretary of the Socialist Party, who used France-Inter's *Face au public* as a platform to denounce the Foucault–Bourdieu text as 'intellectually crazy' and, turning to more *ad hominem* arguments, to remind Montand that he had toured the Soviet Union after the 1956 invasion of Hungary. Whatever Montand's political past, there was no doubt of where his current sympathies lay: as he ended his performance at the Olympia on 15 December, a banner bearing the Solidarity logo was lowered from the flies. In a tart reply to Jospin's criticisms, the singer remarked that it was precisely because he had gone to Moscow in 1956 that he was in a position to denounce talk of 'counter-revolution', of 'calling on fraternal parties for help' and of 'non-interference in internal matters'.[19]

The Foucault–Bourdieu text was also denounced by Jack Lang, the minister for culture, a week later. He spoke of 'clowns', of 'dishonesty', of a 'typically structuralist fecklessness', and accused Glucksmann, Foucault and Montand of 'bawling without thinking'.[20] Immediate political issues aside, Lang's comments had a curiously anachronistic feel; he must have been the only man in France to have believed in the relevance of 'structuralism' in the winter of 1981. *Le Monde*'s editor, Jacques Fauvet, also joined in the chorus, claiming in a leader article that 'certain *intellectuels de gauche*' obviously had difficulty in accepting the Socialist victory of 10 May and criticising them for failing to mention the Soviet invasion of Czechoslovakia. In his view, their failure to do so could easily be explained: the left had not been in power in 1968.[21] Fauvet's reaction outraged Foucault, who refused ever again to read *Le Monde*. Friends who were careless enough to ask casually if he had seen such and such an article in that newspaper were rewarded with explosions of rage.[22]

Although *Le Monde* was critical of Cheysson's ill-advised words, it was broadly supportive of the government's stance and had refused to publish an earlier letter of protest drafted by Cornelius Castoriadis on 14 December. Castoriadis and his fellow signatories, who included Jean-Marie Domenach and Pierre Vidal-Naquet, made the point that the establishment of a Nazi dictatorship in pre-war Germany had also been an 'internal German affair', but it did not attract the hostile comments addressed to the Foucault–Bourdieu document. The text was eventually published in *Libération* on 21 December.

Petitions and open letters about Poland now began to proliferate. On 23 December, an 'Appeal from left-wing writers and scientists' appeared in *Le Monde*. Although the appeal begins by noting that 'The freedom of all is now at stake in Poland', the key sentence reads: 'We recognise ourselves in the words that declare an obvious truth in our name: "The Polish people must find in France's position an additional reason to believe in their ability to overcome the dangers which assail them." ' The quotation was from Mitterrand, and the text implied something of a reconcilation between government and intelligentsia. Significantly, Foucault was not one of the signatories to a statement published as an advertisement paid for by the government.

He did, however, sign the appeal from the CFDT trade union which was published the next day:

> Faithful to the spirit of Solidarnosc, in which trade unionists and intellectuals worked and struggled to free themselves from the hold of totalitarianism, [the signatories] declare that it is not enough to denounce the coup in Poland. Above all, we must immediately associate ourselves with the combat of the Polish people by combining intellectual criticism and social struggle, as Solidarity has done. No, this development was not inevitable. No, it is not the lesser of two evils. No, Solidarity has not gone too far. No, this is not an internal Polish affair.
>
> Invocations of the principle of non-interference must not lead to non-assistance. It is clear that the coup occurred as a result of pressure from the Soviet Union.
>
> We will not resign ourselves to it. Let us stop thinking about the situation in Poland purely in terms of geostrategic constraints, of state-to-state or bloc-to-bloc relations, which leads to human rights, the rights of peoples, the action of public opinion and international solidarity being seen as negligible quantities. We cannot accept a definitive partition of Euope which refuses Poland

and other countries under Soviet domination a democratic future.[23]

Of the fifty signatories, many were close associates or friends of Foucault: Allio, Bourdieu, Chéreau, Domenach, Ewald, Farge, Finkielkraut, Geismar, Glucksmann, Halbwachs, Jacob, Julliard, Mauriac, Montand, Nora, Semprun, Signoret, Stéphane, Veyne and Vidal-Naquet.

Partly in an attempt to rally support for the government position and to cement the cracking government–intelligentsia alliance, a gala evening in solidarity with Poland was organised at the Opéra on the evening of 22 December. Eleven members of the government were present, together with 2,000 invited guests, to hear Miguel Angel Estrella play Chopin and the chorus of the Opéra sing the 'Slaves' Chorus' from *Nabucco*. One uninvited guest was also present. On the morning of the gala, Foucault had spoken to a CFDT meeting on Poland. In the evening, he met Mauriac, Signoret, Semprun, Costa-Gavras and others in a café near the Opéra. Of those present, only Foucault had not received an official invitation to the gala. An invitation had indeed been taken by messenger to the rue de Vaugirard, but it was for Daniel Defert. 'Sarcastic, sardonic and jubilant',[24] Foucault was convinced that he had been deliberately ignored, whereas Mauriac was convinced that the Mauroy government held him personally responsible for the critical stance being taken in some quarters towards French policy over Poland.

Whether the omission of Foucault's name from the guest list was a matter of policy or merely an oversight is open to debate, but he had no difficulty in gaining admission to the Opéra. This may have been a source of disappointment to him; it is clear from Mauriac's account that he expected to be refused admittance and was looking forward to the scandal that would break when he telephoned *Libération*. In the event, there was no need to make the call and Foucault joined the assembled guests, but left for home before Joan Baez, not one of his favourite artistes, took the stage.[25]

A report in *Le Monde* illustrates some of the problems facing the intelligentsia over participating in any manifestation of solidarity with Poland. Fauvet had already been caustic about the Foucault–Bourdieu document. A reporter now commented sardonically on the migration from the Coupole and the Balzar (*brasseries* in Montparnasse and the Latin Quarter respectively) to the 'fief of the music-loving bourgeoisie' to celebrate the first 'post-May' gathering of the intelligentsia 'to the tune of freedom in Poland'.[26] Foucault's own solution was a much more practical commitment.

On 15 December, the CFDT announced that it had been contacted by 'a number of intellectuals' who were anxious to establish in France the 'worker–intellectual links' that had always been so important to the growth of Solidarity. An initial meeting was organised at the CFDT's offices for the following evening. The intellectuals present included Bourdieu, arguing the need for a permanent link between the union and its academic supporters, and Foucault, emphasising the need to establish an information centre or press agency. On 22 December, a much larger meeting was addressed by Foucault, Bourdieu and Edmond Maire, the CFDT's secretary general. Foucault again stressed the need for information if Solidarity was not to be silenced and proposed that a team of lawyers should be sent to Poland to supplement the work of Médecins du Monde, which was now organising convoys of medical supplies under the banner of the ad hoc 'Varsovivre' campaign.[27] It was in the course of this meeting that the badge campaign was launched; within hours, many Parisians began to buy and wear white badges with the Solidarity logo printed on them in red.

Foucault wore his for months. His solidarity with Poland was expressed by a devotion to fairly mundane tasks as well as by public declarations. He became associated with the Comité Solidarnosc en France, established by exiles, and spent hours on repetitive bureaucratic tasks. As a member of the Comité's finance committee, he would present detailed reports stuffed full of statistics, to the surprise of a senior member of the Comité who found that he could always count on Foucault, but could not stop himself thinking that he must have had more important things to do.[28]

Foucault and Bourdieu's decision to contact the CFDT brought them into contact with a trade-union world of which they knew almost nothing. The decision to establish links with that union in particular was significant. The CFDT has its origins in the Confédération Française des Travailleurs Chrétiens, a Christian union founded in 1919 which for a long time ended its meetings with a ritual 'Our Lady of Labour, pray for us'. In 1964, it broke its confessional links and took the name Confédération Française du Travail. Contacts with left-Catholic groups like Esprit were, however, maintained. In the eyes of many, the constitution of the CFDT marked the emergence of 'a second left', socialist but non-communist and committed to a self-management strategy.[29] The CFDT already had links with Solidarity: when Walesa visited Paris in October 1981, he had meetings with Maire, who stated:

'The bonds which unite us go well beyond ordinary friendship, even beyond a similarity of interests; they point to a destiny common to us all.'[30]

Foucault's interest in Poland and Solidarity obviously paralleled his support for Soviet dissidence. His experiences in Warsaw in 1958 had left him with an abiding affection for the country's people and dislike for its rulers. In 1977, he had signed petitions denouncing the imprisonment of members of KOR (Committee for Defence of Workers).[31] In January 1980, he publicly associated himself with the Oxford-based 'Free Learning in Poland' campaign and signed a collective open letter to the *New York Review of Books*:

> For many years, the struggle has been going on in Poland to keep alive an independent intellectual life, free from censorship and official restrictions. An extremely important aspect of this struggle is the 'Society for Academic Courses' (better known under the nickname of the 'Flying University'). This society arranges – in private flats – open lectures, seminars and discussions in fields which in official academic teaching are inevitably distorted by all sorts of suppressions, taboos and lies – especially in the social and human sciences.

'Free Learning in Poland' was set up to defend the Flying University and to promote exchanges between scholars in Poland and other countries. The letter's signatories included Alfred Ayer, Frank Kermode, Gunnar Myrdal, Joan Robinson, Edward Thompson, Jean Starobinski and Jean-Pierre Vernant.[32]

The Polish coup provided an obvious point around which the interests of the CFDT and of intellectuals like Foucault could converge. The convergence of interest was not confined to the Polish question. As an internal CFDT document put it, when Foucault and his associates approached Maire they were also taking up a stance critical of the French government. The CFDT was well aware of the danger of being seen as hostile to a socialist government, but argued that Foucault and others were expressing a real demand. They did not wish to be fellow travellers, nor did they wish simply to sign petitions. 'They wish, within the limits of their own competence, to find joint forms of work to promote thinking about the period our country has been experiencing since 10 May 1981.'[33] While it seemed impossible for Foucault to work with the government, work with an independent trade union might be a possibility, and he explored various projects in conversation with Edmond Maire, but none came to fruition.[34]

In the longer term, Foucault took part in the CFDT-led debates on the social-security system that resulted in the publication of a collective volume of studies.[35] Foucault's interlocutor was Robert Bruno, who developed a healthy respect for him:

> His was the perspective of the philosopher and *honnête homme* of the seventeenth century, transposed to the twentieth century – that is, an *honnête homme* with everything society has gained since the Enlightenment. I found in him the same persistence and dedication to understand the events of his time, and to apprehend them not in a partial or prejudiced fashion, but rather in their totality and their interactions.[36]

Foucault's involvement with Poland and Solidarity took a concrete form in the autumn of 1982, but before that he had a brief encounter with President Mitterrand. In September, he was invited, with a group that included Jean Daniel, Pierre Vidal-Naquet, Simone de Beauvoir (treated with icy politeness by Foucault) and Alain Finkielkraut, to a formal luncheon in the Elysée. There are no official records of what is said on such occasions, but it is known that the general theme proposed for discussion concerned Israel and the Middle East. As the discussion became more general, Mitterrand treated his guests to a homily on economics and economic policy. Foucault remained silent, but as he and the others left, he began to grumble to Vidal-Naquet about the 'obvious' economic incompetence of the president of the Republic.[37] This was the only occasion on which Foucault met a president.

A few days after the gathering at the Elysée, a blue minibus left Paris in the company of a large truck for the 3,000 kilometre trip to Warsaw. This was the last of sixteen convoys organised by Médecins du Monde and Varsovivre with financial support from both the French government and the European Community since December 1981. The minibus was carrying five passengers: Michel Foucault, Simone Signoret, Bernard Kouchner, Jacques Lebas and Jean-Pierre Maubert, the last three representing Médecins du Monde. The truck was carrying foodstuffs, medicines and – more or less clandestinely – books and some printing equipment. Books from France were particularly welcome in Warsaw; when André Glucksmann arrived with an earlier convoy, his reception committee was less than enthusiastic to find that his car was loaded with cheese and chocolate, and disappointed to learn that he had not even brought copies of his own books with him.[38]

Foucault's motives for joining the convoy were twofold. His involvement with France's Comité Solidarnosc had convinced him of the need for continued contact with Poland and of the necessity of talking to the Poles in order to be able to talk to the French about Poland.[39] The trip also no doubt provided a welcome break from work and from the long days spent in the Bibliothèque du Saulchoir, where he was researching the next two volumes of *Histoire de la sexualité*. For Signoret, who had met Walesa in August, it was a concrete way of expressing solidarity with the Polish people; even lowering a Solidarnosc banner from the flies of the Olympia was a somewhat abstract gesture.

The journey was to be a cheerful one. Signoret and Foucault, who adored one another, became characters from the *Tintin* cartoon books: she adopted the role of Mme Castafiore and he became *le professeur Tournesol* (Professor Calculus in the English version). Taking it in turns to drive, the five spent their time joking, exchanging life histories and singing. The general hilarity, in part the product of nervousness, eventually reached such a level that Foucault actually wet himself. As he had not thought fit to bring a change of trousers, his mishap necessitated a diversion to an airport to restore him to respectability. The repertoire of songs included Piaf and Montand. To the surprise of Kouchner and Lebas, Foucault – whose proclaimed taste in music ran to Boulez and Wagner rather than to the French *chanson* tradition – knew the words to all Montand's songs. His inability to sing in tune was a less pleasant surprise. The third surprise was Foucault's revelation that he had lived in Poland over twenty-five years earlier. Although he had known Kouchner for years, he had never mentioned the fact.

The journey to Warsaw was not without its tensions and it was expected that there would be long delays at the East German border. Foucault must have been reminded of his unpleasant encounter with border guards in East Berlin in 1978. Signoret, who had dressed down for the occasion and did not look like an international star, was the first to go through customs. As she removed her dark glasses and presented her passport, in her real name of 'Kaminker', the border guard gasped with astonishment and said: 'You are Simone Signoret.' He immediately waved them through customs, telling his superior officer that the actress and her companions were not to be held up. It transpired that her status in Eastern Europe approached the legendary and that she was still remembered for her 1956 tour with Montand. The convoy reached Warsaw without further incident.

In Warsaw, the group stayed in the Victoria Hotel, an establishment frequented by 'bogus prostitutes and real spies' and located a short distance from the Bristol, now abandoned and boarded up, where Foucault had completed *Histoire de la folie* by candlelight.[40] The visitors had a round of meetings with students, intellectuals and dissidents (including a future mayor of Cracow) and saw the flowers and crosses of Solidarity outside the churches. The queues outside the shops were even longer than the queues Signoret rememberd in wartime France. Her first impression had been one of horror: horror at the paranoid feeling of being under constant surveillance, horror at the moral decay apparent in the omnipresent prostitutes and the police spies masquerading as black-market currency dealers. Foucault was struck by the fragile equilibrium between the possibility of hope and the weight of an omnipresent dictatorship, an equilibrium known as 'socialism'. He had never seen such a gulf between the government and people of a country.[41]

The group were received by the minister for health, who thanked them for the medical aid they had brought, but an enquiry about the health of Lech Walesa was greeted with a frosty silence. Foucault did little to relax the situation by refusing to shake the ministerial hand. Throughout, the minister, accompanied by a political commissar, looked distinctly nervous. Aware of the danger of 'recuperation' and of appearing to be lending support to the Jaruzelski government, the party declined an invitation to a reception at which a cup was due to be presented to Kouchner on behalf of Médecins du Monde.

From Warsaw, they went to Cracow, which was also familiar territory to Foucault. More familiar then even he thought. Faced with a choice between an old hotel and an anonymously modern establishment, the group chose the former. The next morning, Lebas, Maubert and Kouchner found Foucault and Signoret laughing together. By coincidence, Foucault had been given the very room he had occupied in 1958, when an inspector from the French Ministry of Education had found him in bed with a 'charming young man'.

The schedule also included a short visit to Auschwitz, which is not far from Cracow. One by one, they walked though the red brick buildings and stood alone in silence – for 'such a long little instant', as Kouchner puts it – outside the crematorium ovens before moving on the square where the roll call had been taken. It was a fine day and the birds were singing. The square was astonishingly small, thought Kouchner; he had imagined that it would be large enough to contain the six million victims of genocide. Foucault never spoke of this experience.[42]

Foucault was now spending a lot of time abroad on the international lecture circuit. In May 1982, he had given a series of lectures at the

University of Louvain on the general topic of 'Mal faire, dire vrai' ('Do Evil, Speak Truthfully'), which dealt with 'the legal function of confession'. While Foucault was in Louvain, a videotape was made of his conversation with the School of Criminology's André Bertin.[43] In the summer, he taught on a seminar course at the University of Toronto.

His lectures were on the increasingly familiar themes of taboos on speaking and obligations to speak, on the cultivation or care of the self and on Christian and philosophical traditions of asceticism.[44] The opportunity to visit Canada was a welcome one. Foucault had always enjoyed the country, and especially Quebec. Before his first visit in 1971, he had been apprehensive and had expected to find a repressive, priest-ridden society. To his surprise, he found a lively and open society with a flourishing gay community.[45]

The transatlantic trip also provided the opportunity for a rapid visit to New York, where, turning away from the academic world, Foucault gave some of his more explicit interviews on gay culture and sexuality. The discursive presentation was, no doubt, combined with more physical explorations of the use of pleasures. In Toronto itself, pleasure was increasingly subject to a new regime. A number of S&M clubs and bath-houses had been recently closed by the local authorities. Despite their self-proclaimed tolerance, the authorities felt obliged to support the 'majority' view that the 'excesses' in which the gay community was indulging were no longer acceptable. In an interview published in *Gai Pied*, Foucault argued for intransigence: there could be no compromise between tolerance and intolerance. Police intervention in any aspect of sexual practice was totally unacceptable.[46]

Foucault's eulogy of the experimental laboratories of the bath-houses was made at a difficult moment. There was already talk of a mysterious 'gay cancer' and there had been deaths. In conversation with friends, Foucault, like the majority of his fellow experimenters, dismissed the notion of a 'gay cancer' with laughing incredulity. But fear was increasingly present. 'In San Francisco, the epidemic spread first through the leather scene. Gay men began suspiciously eyeing bar-room ionisers that helped eliminate tobacco smoke. Maybe those gadgets were emitting something else, something deadly.'[47]

In September, Foucault had been to Poland; in October, he was at the University of Vermont where he participated in a faculty seminar on 'Technologies of the Self'.[48] Foucault was on campus for three weeks and gave both seminar presentations and a public lecture. The lecture on 'The Political Technology of Individuals' was an abbreviated version of the 1980 Tanner Lectures; the seminar's content is very similar to that of the third volume of *Histoire de la sexualité*.[49] The Vermont faculty members were joined by distinguished scholars from other universities: Frank Lentricchia from Duke, Christopher Lasch from Rochester and Allan Megill from Iowa. Despite the heavyweight intellectual presence, the seminar took place in a relaxed atmosphere, but even so Foucault surprised his hosts with his unexpected shyness, which meant that he had to be pressed to take the platform for public presentations.

As usual, Foucault shunned 'intellectual cocktail parties', but was interested in everything else, from 'the local night life' to the concerns of children of faculty members. According to the organisers, he was 'happiest in the company of students'.[50] The interview given to the freelance journalist Rux Martin on 25 October certainly reveals a very relaxed Foucault, who at last stated that he had worked in French prisons and psychiatric hospitals, who spoke of reading for pleasure 'the books which produce in me the most emotion: Faulkner, Thomas Mann, Malcolm Lowry's *Under the Volcano*' and who admitted that, if he were younger, he might well emigrate to the United States.[51]

Foucault may well have been relaxed, but he could also be unintentionally hurtful. Jana Sawicki had just spent four years writing a doctoral dissertation on Foucault's critique of humanism and attempting to 'appropriate' it for feminism. The day after she submitted it for examination, she had the opportunity to attend part of Foucault's Vermont seminar. 'I told him that I had just finished writing a dissertation on his critique of humanism. Not surprisingly, he responded with some embarrassment and much seriousness. He suggested that I do not spend energy talking about him and, instead, do what he was doing, namely, write genealogies.' Foucault's reluctance to be seen as a philosophical monument is quite understandable, but so too is Sawicki's annoyance at his apparent dismissal of her four years' work. It did not, however, prevent her from going on to outline what she calls 'the contours of a viable Foucauldian feminism'.[52]

While Foucault was in Vermont, the Coral scandal broke in France. The Coral, in the mountains of the Gard *département*, was a *lieu de vie*, an 'alternative' centre for the treatment of severely disturbed children, strongly influenced by the anti-psychiatry movement and by various 'counterculture' ideologies. In October, the centre's director, Claude Sigala, and one of its teachers, Jean-Noël Bardy, were arrested and brought before an examining magistrate. They were under suspicion of having had sexual relations with their charges, and the centre became the focus for a major paedophile scandal.

The charges against Sigala and Bardy were brought as a result of information supplied by one Jean-Claude Krief, a young man with a history of psychiatric problems and a suspected police informer. Krief claimed that the Coral was at the centre of an extensive paedophile ring whose activities included an involvement in the production of child pornography in Amsterdam. He further claimed that by using the pretext of bringing him a book from Sigala, he had gained admittance to René Schérer's home, where he had discovered proof that Schérer was part of the ring. Schérer, who had visited the Coral for discussions, was held on charges of *excitation des mineurs à la débauche*. The scandal began to spread, and took on a distinctly political dimension: the list of those involved in the ring was now said to include a government minister. This was serious; while French political life tolerates a range of sexual behaviour unimaginable in Britain, paedophilia was beyond the pale. The list also included the name of Michel Foucault.

The ramifications of the Coral scandal have never been fully clarified. Krief withdrew many of his allegations (but subsequently retracted his retraction), and his list was shown to be false. Whether he was a mythomaniac acting on his own or was being used by one or another faction within the police is still unclear. For the defenders of the Coral, it seemed self-evident that, as a petition to the president of the Republic put it, France was witnessing 'a campaign of insinuation and intimidation directed at concentric circles: all alternative *lieux de vie*, homosexuals, and the Left'.[53] The official response from the government was a studied silence, and the defence campaign was organised mainly by the Comité d'Urgence Anti-Répression Homosexuelle, which held protest meeting, and demonstrations, and by Félix Guattari and Schérer, who was eventually freed without charges being brought. Guy Hocquenhem, in the meantime, made public the list of names supposedly involved in the Coral affair. Foucault was furious when he heard of this and his friendship with Hocquenhem was strained almost to breaking point.

Something of Hocquenhem's view of the matter can be glimpsed from his novel *Les petits Garçons*, a barely fictionalised account of the affair, in which Foucault fleetingly appears as 'Professor Couffauld, an authority on historical science and almost a Nobel Prize winner'.[54] *Les petits Garçons* includes an 'intermezzo' entitled 'Letter to a friend' which is a bitter attack on those who had failed to defend 'Stratos' (Schérer) because, previous positions notwithstanding, they had suddenly realised that they had never been against *all* of the police, *all* the legal system and *all* repression.[55] The addressee of the letter is a man whose work denounces the 'obsession with knowing characteristic of confessors, policemen, magistrates and psychoanalysts over the centuries', but who is now being told by the demands of public life that he should 'forget the telephone number of a man you clasped to your breast yesterday'.[56] Hocquenhem openly identifies Stratos with Alfred Dreyfus, the victim of prejudice and miscarriage of justice and asks: 'If Dreyfus came back, do you think anyone would recognise him?'[57] The parallel had already been drawn by Schérer himself in a letter published in *Le Monde* on 22 October 1982: the case did recall the Dreyfus affair, with the 'intellectual paedophile' playing the role of the Jew, but unfortunately no Zola had yet emerged. Hocquenhem was clearly implying that Foucault was no Zola.

On his return to France, Foucault did in fact take up the defence of Schérer and the others involved in the Coral affair, and was reconciled with Hocquenhem. Together with Châtelet, Deleuze, Derrida, Faye, Guattari, Hocquenhem and Lyotard, he signed a declaration protesting at the way the whole issue had been handled by the courts and by the press, and announcing their intention of producing a 'White Book' which would investigate the affair anew.[58] The 'White Book' never materialised. Charges were dropped, and the scandal gradually faded out of the public view, muddied and obscure to the last.[59]

Most of the lectures of 1982 relate in various ways to the *Histoire de la sexualité* project and to the 1981–82 lectures at the Collège de France on 'The Hermeneutics of the Subject'.[60] The year ended, however, with the final completion of a very old project first mentioned in *Histoire de la folie*. In his discussion of 'the correctional world', Foucault refers in passing to the *lettre de cachet* of the seventeenth and eighteenth centuries and remarks: 'Debauchery, prodigality, unacceptable relationships and shameful marriages are among the most common motives for confinement.' He adds: 'This repressive power, which is not quite justice and not exactly religion, this power which was directly linked to royal authority, does not really represent the arbitrariness of despotism, but the now rigorous character of demands from the family. The absolute monarch put confinement at the disposal of the bourgeois family.'[61]

The *lettre de cachet*, which allowed for the indefinite confinement of individuals on the order of the king or his *lieutenant de police*, is often viewed as the classic expression of absolutism and was one of the *bêtes noires* of the *philosophes* of the Enlightenment, and the Bastille has always been a symbol of oppression. De Sade, for instance, was held in the Bastille under this system. It was not in fact the case that *lettres de cachet* were used mainly against aristocratic libertines. They were often obtained by quite humble families and were, as Deleuze remarks, 'the ancestor of what we call "a voluntary committal" in psychiatry'.[62] As read by Foucault, the letters become social documents and an aid to the construction of a rather different theory of power.

The point made in *Histoire de la folie* about repressive power is illustrated by reference to Funck-Brentano's *Les Lettres de cachet* of 1903 and by an example taken from a manuscript in the Bibliothèque de l'Arsenal. The archives in question are known as the *Archives de la Bastille* and consist of police reports originally held in the Bastille, dispersed during the Revolution and then brought together again. The example given concerns one Noël Robert Huet, whose debauched conduct led his relatives to request his imprisonment because of the dishonour it was bringing upon them. Although Foucault does not elaborate on the point here, this appears to be the first hint of the later theory that power is not necessarily something which is imposed from on high by a sovereign authority, that it can also be something which proceeds from below.

The discovery of the Bastille archives quickly suggested a project for a book, and in 1964 Foucault signed a contract for a volume on *les embastillés*, which was supposed to appear in the 'Archives' series recently established by Pierre Nora at Julliard.[63] Early volumes in the series list as 'forthcoming' the title *'Les Fous: Michel Foucault raconte, du XVIIe au XIXe siècles, de la Bastille à Sainte-Anne, le voyage au bout de la nuit'*. It was never written.

In 1980, the young historian Arlette Farge received a packet of photocopies through the post. To her astonishment, the packet was from Foucault and contained transcripts of material from the Bastille archives. The two had met, but Farge was not a member of Foucault's close circle of friends and had, at this point, never attended his lectures at the Collège de France. Originally trained as a lawyer, Farge had turned to history, and had been present at the round-table discussion between Foucault and a group of historians that took place in May 1978. The two had also met briefly after a radio broadcast devoted to Farge's *Vivre dans la rue à Paris au XVIIIe siècle*, which appeared in the 'Archives' series in the spring of 1979 and exploits archive material and the work of authors like Jean-Sébastien Mercier to provide a detailed and vivid account of Parisian street life in the eighteenth century. They also knew one another's work. Farge was an admirer of *Surveiller et punir*, in which Foucault twice refers to her *Le Vol d'aliments à Paris au XVIIIe siècle*.[64] In the preface to her *Vivre dans la rue*, Farge notes that Foucault's acute analyses of the apparatuses of power was a stimulus to investigate archival sources from a new perspective. Finally, both Farge and Foucault knew Philippe Ariès, for whom they had both a great intellectual respect and a very real affection.

The letter accompanying the packet asked Farge for her opinion as to the advisability of publishing the archive material, which consisted of requests for the confinement of various individuals. Foucault was, he explained, fascinated by the beauty of the texts and wondered if they might not be published without any commentary. He had been particularly struck by the contrast between the exordium, usually written by an *écrivain public* in an ornate and conventional style, and the texts of the letters themselves, which were usually couched in an informal and often ungrammatical popular French.

Farge agreed about the beauty of the texts, but demurred at the suggestion that they did not require comment. After much hesitation, and with not a little apprehension, she wrote to Foucault saying that, in her view, the texts would help to restore a certain popular memory, but that they required an introduction and some explanation. She still recalls that it took a 'very long time' to write that short letter, but it had the desired effect. Foucault telephoned to say that he was convinced by her arguments and asked if they could work together on the project. Almost unable to believe her ears, Farge accepted the proposal after a moment of hesitation.

Le Désordre des familles is divided into two sections, devoted respectively to marital strife and relations between parents and children, and completed by an essay entitled 'Quand on s'adresse au roi' ('When One Writes to the King'). Each section is preceded by an introduction; in other respects, the texts are allowed to speak for themselves. The first task was obviously the selection of material from the documents collected by Foucault over a period of years. Because of the fragility of the material, photocopying had not been possible and the letters, written on either parchment or rag paper, and not always in a good state of preservation, had been copied out in longhand by Foucault. In the Bibliothèque Nationale, Foucault read; in the Arsenal, he had become involved in the 'banal and strange exercise' of copying, a 'painstaking and obsessional occupation'.[65] Eighteenth-century script is not always easy to decipher, and both spelling and punctuation can be erratic.

Even if it had been possible to photocopy the documents he wanted,

Foucault would probably not have done so. He frequently used the Bibliothèque Nationale's copying machines, but his attitude towards them was ambivalent. He told Claude Mauriac. 'It's so tempting . . . So easy . . . But it takes away the need to really read . . . And above all, it destroys the charm of the text, which becomes almost lifeless when you no longer have the printed page before your eyes and in your hands.'[66] There were no photocopiers to tempt him in the Arsenal and Foucault laboriously transcribed his material. His transcripts were then typed up by a secretary who, given the near-illegibility of Foucault's handwriting, must have been blessed with extraordinary patience. The secretary was a single parent, and was not in good health; a percentage of Foucault's royalties was quietly assigned to her.

This was a joint project, and there was no definite division of labour, though Farge explains that the introduction to the section on marital relations is 'predominantly' her work, whereas the longer piece on relations between parents and children is 'largely' Foucault's; she derives considerable amusement from seeing her words attributed to him. He was, she adds, reluctant to be too closely involved in any discussion of relations between husbands and wives, and was apprehensive about the feminist wrath that might descend upon him if he pronounced too emphatically on that aspect of sexual politics.

For at least some of the time, Farge worked while on holiday on Belle-Ile-en-Mer, the spectacularly beautiful island off the coast of Brittany; Foucault preferred to remain in Paris, and could not understand how anyone could work in such surroundings. He was convinced that he would have been distracted by watching the sea. Most of the discussions between the collaborators took place in Foucault's flat. Farge has no memory of any major disagreements, but speaks affectionately of dialogues in which 'the philosopher's intelligence – mobile, malicious and sometimes hilarious – made me loquacious'.[67] Nor did she sense any of the misogyny of which Foucault is sometimes accused, finding him very kind and even courteous. This was clearly the democracy of the Pierre Rivière seminar on a small scale. Not all the discussions between the collaborators centred on the work in hand, and Farge was particularly impressed by the stance taken by Foucault after the Socialist victory of May, and by his refusal to become a fellow traveller. She also recalls that, with her agreement, Foucault cancelled a planned television appearance on *Apostrophes* to promote *Le Désordre des familles*; instead, he appeared on Christine Ockrent's current-affairs programme to discuss Poland. An added attraction was that Ockrent – French television's 'Queen Christina' – was one of his favourite media personalities.

Some of the material used in the earlier 'La Vie des hommes infâmes' also appears in *Le Désordre*. Not all the documents transcribed by Foucault were used for the latter volume, and some of them found their way into Farge's contribution to *Histoire de la vie privée*. She had been asked to work on that volume by the ailing Ariès, who died in February 1984. With Foucault's permission, she used some of the material he had found in the Arsenal. For Foucault and Farge, this was a way of paying tribute to Ariès. The death of Foucault later the same year meant that Farge's work also became her tribute to him.

Le Désordre des familles was not a particular success, and attracted little critical attention.[68] Arlette Farge's explanation for its relative failure is that the book contained 'too many texts and not enough Foucault'. It was only after Foucault's death that she began to be approached with questions about its origins.[69]

18

AN UNFINISHED LIFE

FOUCAULT returned to Berkeley in April 1983 as the Regent's professor. This visit was the occasion for his true American apotheosis: a public lecture on 'The Culture of the Self' which drew an audience of over two thousand. Although he had a busy schedule, Foucault made himself available to students for informal discussions and took part in discussions and talks in a variety of academic departments, talking to the French department in April and to Rabinow's seminar on 26 April and 3 May. Among other plans, he discussed the possibility of returning in the autumn to teach a full course, and he was also investigating ways of arriving at some long-term arrangement, such as a permanent visiting professorship, which would allow him to return on a regular basis.[1] His enthusiasm about working in the United States was, as always, bound up with his increasing frustration with France, now so intense as to prompt him to talk of resigning his chair at the Collège de France.[2]

The lecture on 'The Culture of the Self' was not published but, as its title indicates, its content was very close to that of *Le Souci de soi*, which was published a year later. Foucault's return to California led to renewed contact with Dreyfus and Rabinow, with whom he engaged in a series of long conversations in English recorded between 15 and 21 April 1983.[3] The conversations were somewhat rambling, but were distilled into 'On the Genealogy of Ethics: An Overview of Work in Progress'. It provides useful documentary evidence on Foucault's progress with *Histoire de la sexualité*, and Foucault found the discussions a useful aid to his 'work on theoretical and methodological reformulation'.[4]

At this stage, the plans for the ongoing *Histoire de la sexualité* were still fluid, even confused. The first volume was to be *L'Usage des plaisirs*, followed by *Les Aveux de la chair*, which 'deals with Christian technologies of the self'. *Le Souci de soi* was now described by Foucault as being 'separate from the sex series'. He also stated that he had 'more than a draft of a book about sexual ethics in the sixteenth century, in which the problem of the techniques of the self, self-examination, the cure of souls, is very important, both in the Protestant and Catholic churches'.[5]

What emerges from the Berkeley conversations is both a rather confused project for future publications and a more general ethical project for an aesthetics of the self. Foucault's now considerable knowledge of the classics did not lead him to see antiquity as a golden age. It did not offer an alternative ethics of pleasure because it was linked to a virile society, to 'dissymmetry, exclusion of the other, an obsession with penetration, and a kind of threat of being dispossessed of your own energy, and so on. All that is quite disgusting!'[6] There was, however, something of a parallel between Greek ethics and contemporary problems. It was impossible for modern liberation movements to elaborate an ethics other than one 'founded on so-called scientific knowledge of what the self is, what desire is, what the unconscious is, and so on'.[7] The anti-liberationist strand that had already found expression in La Volonté de savoir also meant that Foucault had little time for the 'Californian cult of the self', in which 'one is supposed to discover one's true self, to separate it from that which might obscure or alienate it, to decipher its truth from that which is supposed to be able to tell you what your true self is'.[8] The Sartrean theory of authenticity appeared to him to be a return to the idea of a true self. Prompted by his interviewers, Foucault agreed that his own view was much closer to Nietzsche's contention that

One thing is needful – to 'give style' to one's character – a great and rare art. It is practised by those who survey all the strengths and weaknesses of their nature and then fit them into an artistic plan until every one of them appears as art and reason and even weakness delights the eye . . . through long practice and daily work at it.'[9]

The relationship to the self should, that is, be one of creative activity and not one designed to reveal a 'true' self.

The almost utopian charms – intellectual, climatic and erotic – of California contrasted with the dreariness of Paris, where Foucault was becoming caught up in a controversy not of his making and not to his liking. Foucault had not been alone in being somewhat reticent about the Socialist victory of 1981 and a general argument had developed about the phenomenon dubbed 'the silence of the intellectuals'. In the summer of 1983, Max Gallo, acting as a government spokesman, published an article in Le Monde expressing the fear that, in the cultural and intellectual domain, a right-wing resurgence was taking place. He noted that 'as an emblematic group', France's intellectuals had not played a particularly active part in May–June 1981: 'We know the itineraries of the veterans of 1968: from a return to God, to journalism and to a successful insertion in economic life; in many cases, one notes a rejection of politics and a refusal to consider power an issue.' He ended by calling for a new debate and for the renewed participation of the intelligentsia: 'In a democratic country, they [the intellectuals] are the channel through which a collective awareness finds expression. It may not be an exaggeration to say that the success of the left, and over and beyond that the destiny of France, will to a large extent depend upon the movement of ideas which will freely move minds.'[10]

Midsummer is a season when little happens in France, and when still less happens in the pages of *Le Monde*, which may explain why the ensuing controversy drew so much attention. There was a widespread realisation that, whereas in 1936 the intellectuals had rallied to the side of the Popular Front government, in 1981 they had remained largely indifferent. The historical comparison was not terribly accurate. As Jean Daniel was not slow to point out, what had united government and intellectuals in 1936 was above all the perceived threat of fascism,[11] something that was not a very real issue in the summer of 1983. The comparison with 1936 was also potentially embarrassing to the government, given the perceived parallel between Blum's nonintervention in Spain and Cheysson's comments on Poland.

Le Monde's Philippe Boggio undertook a short survey, asking a number of influential figures for their opinion about the silence of the intellectuals. Few had anything of interest to say, and their answers expressed boredom rather than any great insights. Some were more provocative. Lévy, in typically apocalyptic mood, speculated that the entire history of a certain form of commitment, which had begun with the Dreyfus affair, was finally coming to an end. Deleuze remarked that the intelligentsia seemed to be afraid of only one thing: communism. Foucault, like Simone de Beauvoir, simply refused to answer Boggio's queries.[12]

The name of Foucault was often mentioned in this debate. Boggio commented: 'The philosopher remains detached, silent about his fate.'[13] The debate was in some senses an absurd one. Foucault, for one, had certainly not been silent in 1981; on the contrary, he had been very vocal in his condemnation of Cheysson's inept remarks about Poland. As he told friends, when he tried to speak in December 1981, he was told to keep quiet; when he remained silent, people expressed surprise.[14] Jean-Claude Milner, one of Foucault's fellow editors on the

Des Travaux collection, now speculated that, given that he had always kept out of public debates when he was about to publish a new book, Foucault's silence might indicate that he was on the point of saying something.[15] Milner was both right and wrong.

Foucault was indeed planning to say something. He was planning to produce a book of interviews with Didier Eribon on the mistakes which had brought all left-wing governments in France to grief. What the Socialists lacked, he claimed, was 'the art of government' and in order to demonstrate his claim, he had begun to study the works of Léon Blum and the history of the Popular Front period. A provisional title had been found: *La Tête des socialistes*.[16] The book was never written, but it seems probable that its themes would have been similar to those of the address to the Syndicat de la Magistrature in 1977. It is unlikely that Foucault had any positive advice to offer the Socialist Party, but his analysis of 'parties and the party-function' would surely have been interesting to read.

Some of the probable content of the planned book emerges from one of the last interviews given by Foucault. Interviewed by François Ewald, he argued that the entire 'silence of the intellectuals' controversy had been based upon a lie, and had been engineered to avoid at all cost potential disagreements with the PCF. The intellectuals had been told to keep quiet, or at least given to understand that the government would not listen to anything they said:

> The problem is not, as it has been said, that the intellectuals ceased to be Marxists at the moment when the communists came to power; it stems from the fact that your worries about your alliance prevented you from doing in due course the work of thought with the intellectuals that would have made you capable of governing. Of governing other than with the dated slogans and poorly modernised techniques of others.[17]

Foucault had a poor opinion of Mitterrand, and was quite prepared to argue that the president of the National Assembly's talk of 'a new cultural model of solidarity and sacrifice' was the discourse of a latter-day Pétain.[18] His attitude to the Socialist Party itself was at best ambiguous. The 'new left' thinking of the past fifteen years, which had always appeared to be 'allergic to any party organisation, incapable of finding its real expression in anything but *groupuscules* and individualities', had to some extent been absorbed by the Socialists, and in particular by the tendency represented by Michel Rocard. Rocard's light was now 'hidden under a bushel' and 'the rather wooden pronouncements of many Socialist Party leaders at present are a betrayal of the earlier hopes expressed by a large part of this left thought. They also betray the recent history of the Socialist Party and they silence, in a fairly authoritarian manner, certain currents which exist within the party itself.'[19]

The book with Eribon was not the only project elaborated in the summer of 1983 to be abandoned. A second was the proposed discussion with Robert Badinter on 'the social function of punishment' that was to have been taped for publication in Le Débat at the suggestion of Pierre Nora. Badinter, a former professor of law and now minister for justice, was one of the few members of the government for whom Foucault had a genuine admiration; Badinter had long admired Foucault for 'the hard brilliance of his writing'.[20] The two men had first met in 1977, when, together with the psychoanalyst Jean Laplanche, they took part in a discussion on the death penalty at the suggestion of Jean Daniel.[21] Since then they had met occasionally, but became closer when Badinter became minister. Foucault was Badinter's occasional dinner guest in the Chancellerie, but accepted the invitation only if the meal was frugal enough for his tastes. The decor appealed to him, and he liked the faded silk hangings on the walls. In the somewhat decayed charms of this Republican splendour, he saw 'the festive old attractions and the mark of time past'.[22] Foucault found their joint discussions about legal and penal problems fascinating, and a new project gradually emerged. This was to be a seminar at Hautes Etudes on justice and the legal system; in part a genealogical exploration of the notion of justice, in part a return to the issues raised in *Surveiller et punir*, this time in more practical and less discursive terms. Foucault's death put an end to the project in its original form, but Badinter did lead a similar seminar with Michelle Perrot.[23]

Another proposed seminar that came to nothing was to have involved Jürgen Habermas, who met Foucault for the first time in 1983. In March, 'Foucault suggested that we meet with some American colleagues for a private conference in 1984 to discuss Kant's 200-year-old essay, "Answering the Question: What is Enlightenment?" '[24] The participants were to have been Dreyfus, Rabinow, Richard Rorty and Charles Taylor. Rabinow was unaware that Foucault had already explored this text in his 1978 lecture to the Société Française de Philosophie, and that he had returned to it in the first lecture he gave to the Collège de France in 1983.[25]

In the autumn, Foucault was again teaching in Berkeley, this time as a joint visiting professor of French and philosophy. His absence from Europe meant that he was unable to accept an invitation from the secretary of the Academy of International Law to give 'the philosopher's point of view' at a congress in The Hague on 'The Future of International Law in a Multicultural World'; his replacement was François Ewald.[26] In Berkeley, Foucault gave a series of six lectures on the topic of *parrhesia* or 'truth-telling' in ancient Greece; these survive in the shape of the bulky typescript notes made by Joseph Pearson of Northwestern University.[27] Although they probably seemed very novel to his American audience, Foucault's lectures were mining a seam he had first begun to excavate in the early 1970s, and they overlapped to a degree with *Le Souci de soi*. Foucault explored the meaning and evolution of the term *parrhesia* with specific reference to the tragedies of Euripides, the crisis of democratic institutions, and the general theme of the 'care of the self'.

At the invitation of Hans Sluga, the chairman of the philosophy department, Foucault also agreed to give a talk to a small, informal gathering. Sluga agreed not to publicise the event, but was unable to prevent rumours spreading across the campus. As Foucault entered the lecture room, deep in conversation with Sluga about the seminar planned for the next year, he suddenly realised that he faced not an informal gathering of philosophers, but a very disparate audience of at least 150. He turned pale, and whispered that he did not want all these people there, but eventually went ahead, in French, with another lecture on Kant's *Was ist Aufklärung?*[28] The lecture is to a large degree a reprise of the earlier discussions of the topic, but a slightly new note is struck by the reference to one of the key figures in any discussion of modernity: Baudelaire's *flâneur*.[29] The implication is that Foucault was being drawn into the all-pervasive debate about modernity, modernism and post-modernism, a term which he viewed with some suspicion.

A research project was also being set up for the future. Foucault was now looking forward to working on a contemporary topic: 'a history and a political critique of the present public policies in western societies . . . practices of government and targets of government'. After discussing a number of alternatives, he proposed as the research topics the period of the First World War and its aftermath because 'it witnessed the birth and spread of practices of government and exercises of power that are still with us today'.[30] A similar return to the concrete, if not the contemporary, is reported by Jacques Almira, who was told by Foucault that he was planning to read or reread the whole of Zola for the documentary value of his novels. At the opposite extreme, Dominique Seglard, who regularly attended Foucault's lectures, recalls him saying that he intended to explore the theme of 'truth-telling' in Byzantine culture, undeterred by the prospect of having to acquire at least the rudiments of medieval Greek.[31]

As usual, Foucault enjoyed informal contact with his students, both on and off campus. One undergraduate, writing in a little magazine, records an astonishing exchange with Foucault that autumn. After attempting to get Foucault to answer a rather confused question about the 'identity of the artist', Philip Horvitz was surprised to be invited to go for coffee. The context was bizarre. As they sat in a café waiting for their coffee, a sex talk show came over the radio: 'Martha, do you think your difficulty in achieving orgasm is a result of Jim's insensitivity?' 'I'm not sure, doctor. I wouldn't have called if I knew the answer to that one.' Foucault and Horvitz then began to talk of AIDS, and

of looking to authorities for lessons: doctors, the church. He is incensed that a group (gays) who have risked so much, are looking to standard authorities for guidance in a time of crisis. It is absurd. Unbelievable. 'How can I be scared of AIDS when I could die in a car? If sex with a boy gives me pleasure . . .' He returns to the theoretical: the world, the play is dangerous. That's what you've got. You have no choice. . . . He says, 'Good luck. And don't be scared!' I reply, 'You! You too. Don't you be scared.' He shrugs off the sentiment in French fashion. 'Oh,' he laughs, 'Don't cry for me if I die.' And with that turns, and vanishes.[32]

In February 1984, Philippe Ariès died at the age of sixty-nine. Foucault paid tribute to him in a piece in the *Nouvel Observateur* and in a dialogue with Arlette Farge published in *Le Matin*. In the latter, Foucault described for the first time how *Histoire de la folie* had been published twenty-three years earlier by the supposed 'banana merchant'.[33] In his *Nouvel Observateur* piece, Foucault described Ariès as 'a man whom it would have been difficult not to love', not least because of his endearing habit of attending mass wearing earplugs. Ariès was not a historian of mentalities, even though he did use that expression. He was, rather, a historian of practices. Here, Foucault was projecting his own concerns with the elaboration of an aesthetics of existence on to the man he described as having written a history of

both the practices which take the form of humble and stubborn habits, and those that can create a sumptuous art; and he tried to

detect the attitudes, the ways of being or doing that could lie at the
root of both. Attentive to both the mute gesture which is
perpetuated throughout the millennia and the individual art work
that sleeps in a museum, he founded the principle of a 'stylistics of
existence' – I mean a study of the forms through which man
manifests himself, invents himself, forgets himself or denies
himself in his fatality as a living and mortal being.

Ariès had given academic historians the unexpected gift of a 'new gaze',
with 'the mingled lordly generosity, irony and detachment one could
hear in his laughter'. Foucault had always admired the way in which
Ariès had come to terms with the problems posed him by his own
politics. How could a monarchist who believed in the continuity of the
nation come to terms with the discontinuities that marked a society's
sensibilities and attitudes? How could any importance be attached to
political structures, when one saw history as being the product of
obscure gestures of ill-defined groups? Foucault was, he wrote, tired of
the former Marxists who had noisily changed their principles and
values, but thought as carelessly as they had always done. He had
much more sympathy for someone who could, like Ariès, remain
faithful to his own values, but still rethink his personal choices and try
to change himself because of his 'concern for the truth'.[34]

When Mauriac telephoned on 10 March, Foucault was correcting
the proofs of *Le Souci de soi*, but he agreed to see Mauriac and a
delegation which included the Abbé de Broglie, an old acquaintance
from the Goutte d'Or. A month earlier, fifty-seven people had been
evicted from a house in the Goutte d'Or's rue Polonceau, and the
building was already partly demolished. It was officially claimed that
they were illegal squatters; Mauriac and his friends were convinced
that they were the victims of the notorious *marchands de sommeil*, who
rented out beds to immigrants by the hour. The evicted were now being
housed in the Salle Saint-Bruno, and a letter of protest was to be sent to
the mayor of Paris and other political figures, asking that they be
rehoused. Foucault drafted the text at Mauriac's request, and it was
eventually signed by Foucault, Deleuze, Châtelet and Mauriac. Any
response was to be addressed to 'Michel Foucault, Salle Saint-Bruno'.

Inevitably, talk of the Goutte d'Or revived nostalgic memories of
earlier activities in that area and a brief discussion of the efficacy of
different forms of action. Mauriac mentioned that a well-publicised
arrest could be effective, and went on: 'I've seen you in a cage . . . And
I've been in a cage myself.' Foucault replied that he had been arrested

on several occasions, but, to Mauriac's astonishment, had no memory of the incident when they were both arrested during the Diab demonstration of 1972. As Foucault drafted the letter, Mauriac looked out at the 'immense view and all the short red chimneys of Paris, only one of them smoking'. It was to be his last visit to the apartment, but not his last encounter with its owner.[35] That was to take place two months later.

On 14 May, Claude Mauriac met Foucault as he left Gallimard's premises in the rue Sébastien Bottin. Foucault was laughing and holding the first copies of *L'Usage des plaisirs*. Despite Mauriac's protestations, he insisted on signing a copy for him: '*Pour Claude Mauriac en signe d'une rencontre et comme témoignage d'amitié. MF.*' (For Claude Mauriac . . . and as a token of friendship'; the dedication contains an allusion to the seventh volume of Mauriac's journals: *Signes, rencontres et rendez-vous*.) He concurred with Mauriac's view that seeing a new book in print and holding the first copies was a marvellous moment and a great joy, and then hurried off. It was their last meeting.[36]

The book Mauriac was given outside Gallimard contained a small loose sheet known as a *prière d'insérer*. This uniquely French phenomenon is a description of a book written by its author in the third person. By their very nature, such documents tend all too often to be lost, but they provide valuable indications of authorial intent. That inserted into *L'Usage des plaisirs* reads:

> The initial project for this series of studies, as expounded in *La Volonté de savoir* (1976), was not to reconstitute the history of sexual behaviour and practices, nor to analyse the ideas (scientific, religious or philosophical) by means of which those behaviours were represented; it was to understand how, in modern western societies, there came to be constituted something like an 'experience' of 'sexuality', a familiar notion, yet one which is scarcely apparent before the beginning of the nineteenth century.
>
> To speak of sexuality as a historical experience implied undertaking the genealogy of the desiring subject and returning, not only to the beginnings of the Christian tradition, but to ancient philosophy.
>
> When he went back from the modern era, beyond Christianity, to antiquity, Michel Foucault encountered a question which is at once very simple and very general: why is sexual behaviour, and the activities and pleasures that derive from it, the object of a moral preoccupation? Why this ethical concern which, depending

on the moment, appears more or less important than the moral attention paid to other domains of individual or collective life, such as alimentary behaviour or the fulfilment of civic duties? This problematisation of existence, as applied to Graeco-Latin culture, seemed in its turn to be bound up with a set of practices which might be called 'arts of existence' or 'techniques of the self', and which was so important that a whole study could be devoted to it.

Hence, finally, the general recentring of this vast study on the genealogy of the man of desire, from classical antiquity to the first centuries of Christianity.

What had originally been a six-volume series now consisted of four volumes: *La Volonté de savoir*, *L'Usage des plaisirs*, *Le Souci de soi* and *Les Aveux de la chair*, the last-named described as 'forthcoming'. A version of part of the second volume was already in circulation, as was an early version of the first chapter of *Le Souci de soi*;[37] it seems improbable that the fourth will ever be published. An essay published in 1982, and then described as being part of Volume 3, predates the reorganisation of the series, and is presumably part of the unpublished fourth volume.[38] It is a discussion of the struggle against fornication and for chastity, as described by Cassian (360[?]–c. 435). Even as the first two volumes were about to go into production, Foucault was still uncertain about the order of publication. Finally rejecting the option of publishing a single book of some 750 pages, he thought of publishing *Les Aveux de la chair* first; this was the book he had begun to write first and it was now almost complete. Eventually, he accepted the advice of Nora and others and settled for the simultaneous publication of the two volumes in the chronological order of their content.[39]

It was not only the form of the project that had altered. In *La Volonté de savoir*, Foucault had made a tentative distinction between an *ars erotica* and a *scientia sexualis*, and had referred to the existence of the former in Greece and Rome, as well as in the Orient. Yet, as he told Dreyfus and Rabinow in May 1983, he later realised that he was wrong: 'The Greeks and Romans did not have any *ars erotica* to be compared with the Chinese *ars erotica* (or at least it was not something very important in their cultures). They had a *techne tou bio* ["art of life"] in which the economy of pleasure played a very large role.'[40] The fabled *ars erotica* is now held to exist in China but is never really explored in any detail,[41] and functions as an avatar of Foucault's long-standing concern with the 'limits of western reason'.

The second and third volumes of *Histoire de la sexualité* are by far the most plainly written of Foucault's books. They do not open with dramatic diptychs, and have none of the stylistic flourishes of the earlier works. The writing is plain, almost flat. The use of reference material is also very different. Foucault makes extensive use of a wide range of secondary literature, a suprising proportion of it in English. Both books include bibliographies, a feature absent from Foucault's work since *Naissance de la clinique*, though they are not fully comprehensive. Foucault can often be criticised for the inadequacy of his references, but not in these volumes. On the contrary, the books abound in page references to the works consulted in the Bibliothèque du Saulchoir. Strangely, this does not always give the impression of consummate scholarship, but rather the impression that Foucault is still exploring the domain he is attempting to master. At times, one has the impression of reading a working draft which should later have been completed and stylistically embellished. He summarises and expounds texts, and devotes a lot of space to the explanation and definition of the concepts he has uncovered. In *L'Usage des plaisirs*, for instance, over two pages are devoted to an exposition and explanation of the term *enkrateia*, which designates 'the form of relationship with oneself' implied by the ethics of pleasures.[42]

Foucault was quite conscious that he was not a classicist, and his concern to define terms seems to reflect that self-awareness. It also says something about his audience; a classicist writing for classicists does not write like this. Foucault was writing for the audience he had built up over the last twenty years, and few of them were Latinists or Hellenists. The degree of repetition is also greater than in any other text and indicates, perhaps, a slight uncertainty which is being overcome by insistence. Thus, the reader is told that, for the Greeks, sexual acts were not in themselves bad and 'were not in principle the object of any disqualification' and, only a few pages later, that 'the sexual act was certainly not seen by the Greeks as something bad; for them, it was not the object of an ethical disqualification'.[43]

Foucault's working hypothesis was that 'there is a whole field of rich and complex historicity in the way in which the individual is called upon to recognise himself as a moral subject of sexual behaviour'.[44] His aim was to look at how that 'subjectification' was defined and transformed 'from classical Greek thought to the constitution of the doctrine and Christian pastoral of the flesh'. Volume 2 of the *Histoire de la sexualité* therefore looks, not at sexuality in the modern sense, but at the field covered by the nominalised adjective *ta aphrodisia* or by the

Latin *venerea*, meaning roughly 'things' or 'pleasures' of love, 'sexual relations' or 'carnal acts'.

As in *La Volonté de savoir*, Foucault is not really concerned with sexual practices as such, but rather with the moral reflection of *ta aphrodisia* that established 'the style of what the Greeks called *chresis aphrodision*, the "use of pleasures" '. In general, the term referred to sexual activity, but it also covered 'the way in which an individual conducts his sexual activity, the way he conducts himself in this order of things, the regime he allows himself, the conditions in which he carries out sexual acts, the role he gives them in his life'.[45] What is at stake is a whole technology of the self, the relationship of the individual to his life and his pleasures. Foucault traces the emergence of this technology through a reading of a wide range of classical texts on the domestic economy of the household (which defined, among other things, permissible and nonpermissible sexual relations inside and outside marriage), dietetics (essential to the regulation of the body and sexual life), and the dialectic of freedom and self-mastery which is so basic to Stoic thought. That dialectic leads Foucault to write: 'The Greeks' moral reflection on sexual behaviour does not attempt to justify prohibitions, but to stylise a freedom: that exercised . . . by the free man.'[46]

Inevitably, the question of Greek homosexuality looms large throughout the text. Foucault was in fact uncertain about the application of the word 'homosexuality' to ancient Greece, as it refers to a rather different experience. The modern convention defines homosexuality in terms of the singularity of a desire that is not directed towards the opposite sex; for the Greeks, the same desire was directed to a desirable object – boy or girl – but was expected to give rise to a specific type of behaviour when two individuals of the same sex were involved.[47] He did not view Greece as some golden age; for the Greeks, 'homosexuality' was 'a theme of anxiety' and fraught with moral difficulties.[48]

The classic instance was, of course, the love felt for a boy by an older man who was an active participant in the life of the *polis*. Although accepted as normal, such relationships were problematical:

> On the one hand, the young man is recognised to be an object of pleasure – and even the sole legitimate and honourable object among the man's masculine partners . . . But on the other hand, the boy, because his youth must lead him to become a man, cannot agree to recognise himself as an object in this relationship, which is always conceived in the form of domination: he cannot

and must not identify with that role . . . In short, experiencing voluptousness and being the subject of pleasure with a boy was no problem for the Greeks; on the other hand, being the object of pleasure and recognising oneself as such constituted a major difficulty for the boy. The relationship he must establish with himself in order to become a free man, his own master and capable of dominating others, cannot coincide with a form of relationship in which he is the object of pleasure for another.[49]

The boy must therefore negotiate his surrender, refusing to submit to the passive role, and setting conditions (money, social advancement, lasting friendship . . .). Sexual love thus becomes a form of transition to something else: 'The love of boys can be morally honourable only if it comprises (thanks to the reasonable kindnesses of the lover, thanks to the reserved compliance of the loved one) elements which provide the foundations for the transformation of that love into a definitive and socially precious bond, that of *philia*.'[50]

The Greek emphasis on self-mastery and on the temperate, if not ascetic, use of pleasures meant that sexuality was not determined primarily by taboos or prohibitions: 'In Greek thought, sexual behaviour was constituted as a domain of moral practice in the form of *aphrodisia*, of acts of pleasure deriving from an agonistic field of forces which were difficult to master.'[51]

Le Souci de soi is in part an account of the passing of the figure of homosexual love and of its replacement by that of conjugal hetero-sexuality in the first two centuries of our era. As in the companion volume, Foucault traces his history of sexuality through a wide variety of texts, some well known, others remarkable mainly for their obscurity, and thus exposes himself to the criticisms of George Steiner: 'What we find in this book [*L'Usage des plaisirs*] is a curiously old-fashioned, academic discourse on certain seminal or neglected texts and motifs in Greek and Latin *verbalisations* of sexuality.'[52]

Le Souci de soi opens, somewhat unexpectedly, with a lengthy account of Artemidoris's *Oneirocritica*, one of the most famous dream-interpretation books of antiquity. Foucault is not particularly concerned with dream interpretation as such, but regards the book as illustrating a 'sexual scenography' centred on penetration. Insofar as the *Oneirocritica* was a guide to future behaviour, sexual dreams of penetration were important; dreams of penetrating a son, a daughter or a slave were warning signs of future behaviour which was to be avoided.[53] The interpretation of dreams was in that sense part of a technique of existence.

The two centuries discussed in the third volume of *Histoire de la sexualité* saw the development of a new concern with a form of individualism and of a related 'culture of the self'. A culture of the self already existed in Plato, but now takes on a rather different form; it becomes 'an attitude, a way of behaving, and it permeated ways of living; it developed into procedures, practices and recipes which were reflected upon, developed, perfected and taught; it thus constituted a social practice giving rise to interindividual relations, exchanges and communications and sometimes even institutions'.[54] The custom of making a daily examination of one's behaviour and actions was part of it; so too was the art of medicine, 'a voluntary and rational structure of behaviour'.[55] As a practice governing prophylaxis and diet (the avoidance of certain foods), personal knowledge of medicine provided 'a permanent armature' for the daily life of the individual who had attained a degree of rational self-mastery.[56]

Sexuality, or *ta aphrodisia*, was governed by the same arts or techniques of the self; sexuality was something to be managed, to be indulged in at appropriate times, in appropriate ways and with appropriate partners. Sexuality was both a source of pleasure and a potential source of danger because of the power of uncontrolled passions and desires. 'For a reasonable regime, the task is therefore to elide pleasure as the sought-after goal: to indulge in *aphrodisia* independently of the attraction of pleasure and as though it did not exist.' The sexual austerity of such a regime provided many of the themes that would later appear in early Christianity: 'a haunting fear of the individual misfortunes and collective ills that can result from disorderly sexual behaviour; the necessity for a rigorous mastery of desires . . . and for an annulment of pleasure as the goal of sexual relations'.[57]

On 2 June 1984, just over two weeks after he had given Mauriac the signed copy of *L'Usage des plaisirs*, Foucault collapsed at home and was hospitalised in the private Clinique Saint-Michel before being admitted to the Salpêtrière on 9 June. On Thursday 7 June, Defert had phoned Mauriac in tears to tell him that Foucault was very ill. Mauriac himself was not well, but went to the Salpêtrière three days later. He could not see Foucault, who had been taken for a scan, and could only scrawl a message on a book: '*Je vous embrasse, à bientôt*' ('See you soon, love . . .').[58] Although he was ill, Foucault was still convinced that he would be out of hospital within a fortnight; Defert thought it would take him two months or so to recover.

Over the next two weeks, Foucault did recover to some extent. He continued to make plans: a holiday in Andalusia with Defert; a trip to Elba with Hervé Guibert. He went ahead with plans to purchase and restore a former priest's house in Verrue, a few kilometres from Vendeuvre, 'not too far away and not too close'.[59] He complained when he had to go for treatment and was prevented from watching the Paris Open tennis game on television; he had particularly wanted to see the McEnroe–Lendl match.[60] He gave interviews and read the first reviews of his books. He received visitors and letters. One of the letters was from Deleuze, and Foucault was delighted that they had at last been reconciled.[61]

By 24 June, his condition had worsened and he was running a very high fever.[62] The next day, it was all over: Michel Foucault was dead. He was fifty-seven.

On Friday 29 June, several hundred people crowded into the courtyard outside the mortuary of the La Pitié-Salpêtrière hospital. The crowd was hushed as a voice, cracked with grief, began to read:

What is the point of striving after knowledge [savoir] if it ensures only the acquisition of knowledges [connaissances] and not, in a certain way and to the greatest extent possible, the disorientation of he who knows? ... What is philosophy today – I mean philosophical activity – if not the critical work of thought upon thought, if it does not, rather than legitimising what one already knows, consist of an attempt to know how and to what extent it is possible to think differently?

The voice was that of Gilles Deleuze; the text, a passage from the introduction to L'Usage des plaisirs.[63]

Lost in the crowd, Danièle Rancière, who had known Foucault for some twenty years, had the impression that she was seeing the very different strata that had gone to make up a complicated and active life. Her impression was not unreasonable. It had been announced that the funeral was to be strictly private, and the solemn removal of the body from the mortuary provided the only public opportunity for farewells. Old friends mingled with comrades from Foucault's militant days of the 1970s. The presence of Abbé de Broglie was a reminder of Foucault's support for the immigrants of the Goutte d'Or, while that of Hélène Cixous recalled both an affectionate friendship, the violence that had surrounded the work of the GIP, and the turmoil of the first years of the University of Vincennes. Jean-François Miquel, the biochemist who had met Foucault in Sweden in the mid-1950s, watched sadly as Georges Dumézil attempted to console his daughter – Foucault's godchild. The crowd included Robert Badinter and representatives of very different worlds. Yves Montand supported Simone Signoret, who was on the point of collapse. From the world of philosophy came Jacques Derrida and Michel Serres, and from that of publishing Pierre Nora, Claude Gallimard and Minuit's Jérôme Lindon. Paul Veyne, Pierre Boulez, the historion Jacques Le Goff, and Ariane Mnouchkine were also present, together with André Miquel, the director of the Bibliothèque National, where Foucault had spent so much of his working life. Surrounded by unknown faces and lost 'in the white shadows of a world drained of colour', Claude Mauriac mourned at the back of the crowd with his daugher Nathalie, who had dined with Foucault on 30 May and had been shocked to find him almost unable to breathe and to see his hands tremble as he took something out of the oven.[64] Jean Daniel and Serge Livrozet stood alongside Bernard-Henri Lévy, Bernard Kouchner and Alain Jaubert. Red roses were placed on the coffin.[65] The many floral tributes included a wreath bearing the Solidarity logo sent by a group of Polish exiles. There was also one significant absence: it had been intimated to Jack Lang, Mitterrand's minister for culture, that, given his all too public clashes with Foucault over the issue of Poland in 1982, his presence would not be appreciated.[66]

The assembled mourners filed past the open coffin, which was then sealed and lifted into the hearse which began the 300-kilometre journey to Vendeuvre-du-Poitou, where Foucault was buried in a graveyard within sight of Le Piroir. The ceremony was something of a compromise. Foucault's mother, who was to survive her elder son by two years, had wanted a full religious service, but Daniel Defert had demurred. The family had already approached a well-known priest, but he proved to be unavailable, and Defert suggested Michel Albaric, of the Bibliothèque du Saulchoir. Albaric, who had become very close to Foucault, agreed to bury his friend but was acutely aware of the possibility that a religious ceremony might look like a 'recuperation' of Foucault, whom he regarded, interestingly enough, as an agnostic rather than an atheist. He therefore suggested a ceremony of absolution rather than a full requiem mass, and orchestrated a combination of prayers, silence and meditation. Finally, he dropped roses into the open grave with the words 'May God keep you, Michel'. The simple ceremony was moving, short and included the reading of an extract from a poem by René Char:

Un couple de renards bouleversait la neige,
Piétinant l'orée du terrier nuptial;
Au soir le dur amour révèle à leurs parages
la soif cuisante en miettes de sang.

The lines ('A pair of foxes churned up the snow / Trampling the approach to the nuptial earth / In the evening, their harsh love revealed around them / Their burning thirst in gobbets of blood') are from 'Demi-jour en Creuse', dedicated to Foucault, dated four days before his death but not actually written for him. The manuscript had been given by Char to Paul Veyne, who lives near him in the south of France. Veyne still has a copy of the lines pinned to the wall of his office.[67] Char did not know that, at ENS, Foucault had been '*Le Fuchs*'. The poet is cited in Foucault's earliest writings and the back covers of the final two volumes of *Histoire de la sexualité* bear the inscription: ' "*L'histoire des hommes est la longue succession des synonymes d'un même vocable. Y contredire est un devoir.*" René Char.' ('The history of men is the long sequence of synonyms for a single term. Contradicting it is a duty.')

Foucault died on the afternoon of 25 June. A press release issued by Professor Paul Castaigne, the head of neurology at the Salpêtrière, and by Dr Bruno Sauron read as follows:

Monsieur Michel Foucault entered the ward for illnesses of the nervous system at the Salpêtrière Hospital in Paris on 9 June 1984 for further tests made necessary by neurological symptoms complicating septicemia. These explorations revealed the existence of several centres of suppuration in the brain. Antibiotic treatment initially had a beneficial effect; last week, a remission allowed Monsieur Michel Foucault to read the first reactions to the publication of his last books. A sudden deterioration in his condition removed all hope of effective treatment, and the death occurred on 25 June at 13.15.

Foucault's death was a shock to many and attracted wide media coverage. It also brought an official tribute from Alain Savary, the minister for education:

The death of Michel Foucault has robbed us of the greatest philosopher of his generation. He was one of the creators of the structuralist movement which completely renewed all of the human sciences. Yet his importance to the intellectual life of our country is perhaps due above all to the originality of his philosophical practice and to the way in which he opened up new fields to knowledge and to historical reflection: madness, the penal regime, medicine and, more recently, sexuality. The philosopher was also a tireless defender of freedom who on several occasions publicly demonstrated his rejection of constraint and repression. He will remain one of the basic references for all those who wish to understand the modernity of the late twentieth century.[68]

The press coverage alone gives an indication of the respect and affection with which Foucault was regarded. On 27 June, *Le Monde* announced his death on its front page and devoted three pages to tributes from friends and colleagues like Pierre Bourdieu and from the regular contributors Roger-Pol Droit and Bernard Poirot-Delpech. The previous day's *Libération* had appeared with its entire front page taken up with Michèle Bancilhon's wonderful photograph of Foucault speaking at the Collège de France. Lit from below and with a flask of water beside him, the Foucault who reminded Mauriac and Wiaz of an alchemist is reading a lecture, his right hand raised with the fingers slightly splayed in a characteristic gesture.[69] The headline, in white on black, read simply: 'Michel Foucault is dead'. Six pages were devoted to his life and work. The weekend issue, dated 30 June – 1 July and somewhat crassly described as a 'Foucault Special', carried a further ten pages. On 26 June, *Le Matin de Paris* also devoted its front page to Foucault's death, and three inside pages to tributes and reminiscences.

In the midst of all the media coverage, rumours were circulating. Many newspapers (*L'Humanité, Le Point, Figaro Magazine, Les Nouvelles, Le Figaro*) reported Foucault's demise without specifying any cause of death, while others, like *La Croix*, spoke of a brain tumour. In England, *The Times* simply said that Foucault died 'suddenly', and the *Guardian* spoke of 'a rare brain infection'. The *New York Times* mentioned 'a neurological disorder' but claimed that 'the cause of his death was not immediately disclosed'. An unsigned piece in *Libération*, no doubt well-intentioned but unfortunate, added to the confusion:

> As soon as he died, rumours began to circulate. It is being said that Foucault died of AIDS. As though an exceptional intellectual seemed, because he was also homosexual – a very discreet one, it is true – an ideal target for the fashionable disease. Quite apart from the fact that neither the medical files nor the transfer to the neurological ward of professors Castaigne and Sauron provides grounds for saying that Michel Foucault was suffering from a type

of cancer which represents scarcely two per cent of patients suffering from this 'modern' illness, one is amazed at the virulence of the rumour. As though Foucault had to die shamefully.[70]

It is quite disquieting to read such comments in *Libération*, whose personal columns have always carried lonely-hearts advertisements which make any notion of 'shame' or 'discretion' seem meaningless and which Foucault described as 'an erotic stage on which anyone can inscribe themselves and wander around, even if they are not looking for anything, even if they expect nothing'.[71] It might be added that, particularly in later years, Foucault was not particularly 'discreet' about his sexuality. *Libération*'s embarrassment is, however, an index of the difficulty of speaking openly of AIDS – an expression then rarely seen in the press – in the summer of 1984.

In America, the gay press proved to be cagey about the cause of Foucault's death. In a footnote to a 1982 interview published shortly after his death, the *Advocate* remarked that 'Foucault had been suffering from an illness of the nervous system',[72] while the *New York Native* criticised the *New York Times* for not giving AIDS as the cause of death . . . and then reported that he had died of 'an infection that attacked his central nervous system'.[73] Other obituarists were less guarded and actually disapproving. Criticising Foucault's apparent lack of political commitment in later years, Edward Said remarked: 'It was noticeable that he was more committed to exploring, if not indulging, his appetite for travel, for different kinds of pleasure (symbolised by his frequent sojourns in California), for less and less frequent political positions.'[74] That trips to California were, for many gay European men, as politically important as visits to Israel were for European and American Jews passes unnoticed.[75] So too are the talks reportedly given by Foucault in San Francisco's gay bath-houses in the late 1970s.[76]

Rumours breed rumours, and the author of an otherwise moving account of the AIDS epidemic can write that Foucault 'hid' the AIDS diagnosis 'from everyone, including his devoted lover'.[77] Foucault certainly suspected that he might have contracted AIDS, probably in California in 1982, but no positive diagnosis was ever made. Days before his death, his doctors were still saying: 'If it's AIDS . . .'[78] There appears to have been a general reluctance on the part of Parisian doctors to come to terms with their diagnoses and to impart them to their patients; it was not unknown for gay men to learn of their diagnoses by stealing medical notes which had been left conveniently available by a doctor who was unwilling or unable to speak openly. According to his friend and translator Alan Sheridan, Foucault told him: 'The doctors . . . did not know what was wrong with him. Among other possibilities, he talked about AIDS, only to dismiss it.'[79] Paul Veyne was convinced that Foucault knew what was wrong, and Pierre Nora insists that he had told those around him that he knew.[80]

In retrospect, one can only wonder at the rumours, now that references in obituaries to 'rare brain infections' and 'neurological disorders' are as obviously transparent metaphors for AIDS-related conditions as 'a long illness bravely borne' is for cancer. The symptoms displayed by Foucault in the eighteen months or so before his death now seem to be particularly clear: flulike symptoms, headaches, severe loss of weight, recurrent bouts of fever and a persistent dry cough. When he saw Foucault in February 1984, Alan Sheridan was shocked by his appearance: 'He now looked a good ten years older than he was.' Carl Gardner, then a television researcher for Britain's Channel Four, had the same reaction. He had first met Foucault in the summer of 1983, when he had tried unsuccessfully to persuade him to appear on *Voices*, a late-night discussion programme. Foucault was reluctant to take part in the programme, adding that he was on the point of going to California. The following spring, Gardner, who was now hoping to make a series of films about sexuality, prisons and medicine with comments from Foucault, found a noticeably older and more tired man who told him that he did not think he would be going to California again.[81] In retrospect, the words have a terrible irony. So too do the comments made again and again to Paul Rabinow and Herbert Dreyfus in Berkeley in the spring of 1983. Asked what he planned to do next, Foucault replied: 'I am going to take care of myself.'[82] The reference is of course to the title of the third volume of *Histoire de la Sexualité*, but the words now carry a tragic weight.

His illness did not stop Foucault from working. Until he was hospitalised, he was still working at the Saulchoir every day, sitting in his usual place by the window at the table that faces the entrance. Claude Mauriac reports a conversation with Daniel Defert at the beginning of July in which the latter said that Foucault had 'known' since December, when he had 'a serious warning'. At that point, he did not know if he had a fortnight or six months to live, but he did know that he was dying. Convinced that no treatment would be effective, he decided not to consult a doctor and went on working.[83] Only weeks before his death, he was in apparently good health and lifting weights regularly.[84] The final illness was mercifully short.

During his lifetime, Foucault was sometimes criticised for not being more openly gay, and he did occasionally avoid the issue in public debates. When, in March 1975, he was interviewed at length on Jacques Chancel's *Radioscopie*, Foucault was asked if he had children. The question was obviously loaded but Foucault somewhat clumsily avoided it by saying: 'No, I'm not married.'[85] In death, he was to be criticised for not 'coming out' about his illness.

The first French intellectual to 'come out' about AIDS was Jean-Paul Aron. Aron had known Foucault since 1950 and published his account of his own illness in 1987. The article itself is brave and moving, but contains some distasteful remarks. Discussing his *Les Modernes*, which is highly critical of Foucault's alleged privileging of discourse over lived experience, Aron comments: 'He was . . . homosexual. He was ashamed of it, but he lived it, sometimes in demented fashion. His silence in the face of his illness upset me because it was a shameful silence, not the silence of an intellectual. It went quite against everything he had always defended. It seemed ridiculous to me.' Aron does have the grace to admit that the real motive for his criticisms of Foucault in *Les Modernes* was simply envy, but seemed unrepentant about his other remarks.[86] As one activist remarks of the *New York Native*'s comments, such statements are 'morally indefensible'.[87] Given that no support networks existed to allow individuals with AIDS to speak out as anything other than victims, they are also anachronistic.

Aron's comments aroused Defert's anger. After the death of his partner, Defert founded AIDES (a major, and now nationwide, counselling and advisory organisation for people with AIDS) after discussions with London-based organisations such as the Terrence Higgins Trust. Commenting on Aron's remarks, he said: 'Jean-Paul Aron seems to be saying: "I am speaking because Foucault did not dare to speak" . . . I shared Foucault's life and moral choices for twenty-three years. If we had, as Aron says, been ashamed of being homosexual, I would never have created AIDES.'[88]

The issue of *Le Monde* which carried the news of Foucault's death also carried the last short text he wrote. It was an appeal for the liberation of two young Frenchmen who had been imprisoned in Poland and was published in the name of the Bureau d'Information et de Liaison pour la Pologne. The text was drafted by Foucault with his usual speed and fluency, but his handwriting was now shaky and he was forced to complete the draft on a typewriter.[89]

Foucault may have been uncertain of seeing California again, but in his last weeks he was debating the idea of leaving Paris once more. The

planned journey would have taken him to the South China Sea on a
boat chartered by Médicins du Monde to attempt to rescue Vietnamese
boat people. As he lay on his deathbed, he was assured by Bernard
Kouchner that he would command the *Jean Charcot*. When the boat
encountered the first refugees, they were greeted in the name of Michel
Foucault.[90]

Six years after his death, Foucault was at the centre of a scandal
occasioned by the publication of Hervé Guibert's novel *A l'Ami qui ne
m'a pas sauvé la vie*. Guibert had become part of Foucault's circle in 1977,
when he published *La Mort propagande*, an early piece of erotica. He was
a talented photographer, wrote on photography for *Le Monde* and had
startlingly good and deceptively angelic looks. Together with Mathieu
Lindon, a journalist and the son of the publisher Jérôme Lindon, he
soon became one of Foucault's intimates. Reviving a habit that dated
from his association with Barthes, Foucault dined with the two young
men three times a week. Some claim that Guibert was Foucault's last
lover, others that he was the object of an intensely platonic affection.

In 1988, Guibert had published a short story entitled 'Les Secrets
d'un homme', in which a surgeon performs a trepan on a philosopher.
On the surface of the brain he found 'unmasked discourses'; at a deeper
level, 'tunnels full of savings, stores, secrets, childhood secrets and
unpublished theories'. Then came the great discovery: 'The childhood
memories had buried themselves away deeper than everything, so as
not to come up against the imbecility of interpretations, the shady
weaving of a great and falsely transparent veil that could cover up his
work.' Among them were 'three terrible dioramas'. In the first, a
surgeon took a small boy into a ward in a Poitiers hospital to watch a
man having a leg amputated, 'in order to make a man of him'; in the
second, a small boy shook with delicious fear as he passed the courtyard
where the *séquestrée de Poitiers* had once languished in captivity. The
third showed the beginning of a story. A *lycéen* who had always been top
of his class lost his pre-eminence when Poitiers was invaded by children
from a Paris *lycée*. He cursed them, and the Jewish children who had
fled Paris disappeared into the death camps.

The unnamed philosopher was struggling to complete a book and,
despite the three abscesses on his brain, went to the library every day to
check his notes. He was, however, tempted to destroy all his work and
ordered a friend to burn his manuscripts. When he died only two
manuscripts were found on his desk. The coffin that left Paris for the
provinces was surmounted with a pyramid of roses and a card signed

with three forenames. Throughout the long journey, it remained motionless.[91]

In 1990, Guibert explained the origins of his short story. While Foucault was dying, Guibert had kept a diary and had noted down conversations with his friend. When Foucault died, Guibert said nothing and refused on several occasions to speak of their friendship. He then wrote 'Les Secrets d'un homme'. *A l'Ami qui ne m'a pas sauvé la vie* derived from the same diary notes, but was written because Guibert suddenly realised that 'by recounting his agony and his death, I was in the process of recounting my own destiny. As though in advance. As though I already knew, unconsciously, that I had AIDS'. He added: 'My best friend, who is ill, like me, tells: "You are a specialist in treachery". He sees everything I've written through that prism. Treachery may be the principal motive behind what I have done . . .'[92] Hervé Guibert died on 27 December 1991 at the age of thirty-six. He committed suicide by taking an overdose of an anti-AIDS drug.

A l'Ami qui ne m'a pas sauvé la vie is part autobiographical novel, part *roman à clef*. The philosopher 'Muzil' is readily recognisable as Foucault, his friend 'Stéphane' as Daniel Defert, and 'Marine' as the actress Isabelle Adjani; her fictional name is derived from the title of a song she recorded with Serge Gainsbourg. The portraits are cruel and certainly reveal Guibert's talent for treachery. Thus, 'Stéphane' confides to the narrator 'Hervé' that he feels guilty because Muzil's death had given him access to 'such a pretty house full of beautiful boys', the house in question being the villa on Elba Foucault had planned to visit with Guibert. Stéphane's solution to his guilt is to go to London to contact a self-help AIDS organisation and to establish something similar in France.[93]

After Muzil's death, Stéphane finds in a cupboard a bag full of whips, handcuffs, leather hoods and other sado-masochistic paraphernalia: 'Muzil adored violent orgies in saunas.' Hervé had on occasion seen him leaving his flat dressed in black leather, decked with chains and with metal rings in his epaulettes, and going off to look for victims in a bar in the twelfth *arrondissement*. Fear of being recognised kept him away from saunas in Paris, but when he taught his annual seminar in California, he took full advantage of the bath-houses and back rooms. In 1983, Muzil returned with a hacking cough, but was still talking about the pleasures of San Francisco's bath-houses:

That day, I said to him: 'There mustn't be a soul left in those places, because of AIDS.' 'That's what you think. On the contrary, there have never been more people in the bath-houses, and it's become extraordinary. That hovering threat has created new complicities, a new tenderness, new solidarities. Before, no one exchanged a word; now people talk to each other. Everybody knows exactly why he is there.'[94]

The veracity of Guibert's portrayal of Foucault-Muzil can neither be proven nor unproven. It is obviously coloured by the author's own fantasies and is not intended to be documentary. In general, it is an accurate picture, and many points of detail can be confirmed from other sources. Muzil, like Foucault, watched the Paris Open in hospital. He was preparing a book on 'the socialists and culture'. As a very small boy, he had wanted to be a goldfish, even though he detested cold water. Other details of the novel and the earlier short story cannot be confirmed – the amputation story; difficulties between Stéphane and Muzil's family over the absence of any proper will; Stéphane's discovery in the apartment of uncashed cheques to the value of millions of francs; the claim that the philosopher's death was 'stolen from him' by the falsification of a death certificate at the insistence of his sister.

Foucault liked to say that all his works were 'fictions', which did not necessarily mean that they were untrue. Asked by Claude Mauriac, for instance, if he had ever thought of writing a work of fiction, he replied: 'No, never. I've never even thought of novelistic fiction. On the other hand, in my books I do like to make fictional use of the materials I assemble or put together, and I deliberately make fictional constructions with authentic elements.'[95] In 1967, Foucault also told Raymond Bellour that Les Mots et les choses was 'a "fiction", pure and simple; it's a novel, but I didn't make it up . . .'[96] This notion of fiction derives from a passage in Daybreak: 'Facta! Yes, facta ficta! A historian has to do, not with what actually happened, but only with events supposed to have happened . . . All historians speak of things which have never existed except in imagination.'[97] A l'Ami qui ne m'a pas sauvé la vie belongs to this Nietzschean genre, and would have appealed to Foucault's 'concern for the truth'. He would no doubt have preferred the novel to a biography.

NOTES

Introduction

1. Michael Holroyd, *Bernard Shaw. Vol 1. 1856–1898. The Search for Love*, Harmondsworth: Penguin, 1990, p. 4.
2. Friedrich Nietzsche, *Untimely Meditations*, tr. R. J. Hollingdale, Cambridge University Press, 1983, p. 97.
3. The most useful of the general studies of Foucault are Alan Sheridan, *Michel Foucault: The Will to Truth*, London: Tavistock, 1980; Angèle Kremer Marietti, *Michel Foucault: Archéologie et Généalogie*, Paris: Livre de poche, 1985; Gary Gutting, *Michel Foucault's Archaeology of Scientific Reason*, Cambridge University Press, 1989; James W. Bernauer, *Michel Foucault's Force of Flight*, Atlantic Highlands, New Jersey: Humanities International Press, 1990.
4. Jürgen Habermas, 'Taking Aim at the Heart of the Present', in David Couzens Hoy, ed., *Foucault: A Critical Reader*, Oxford: Blackwell, 1986, p. 107.
5. Hubert L. Dreyfus and Paul Rabinow, *Michel Foucault: Beyond Structuralism and Hermeneutics*, Hemel Hempstead: Harvester, 1982.
6. Claudio Pogliano, 'Foucault, con interpreti', *Belfagor*, vol. 40, 1985, p. 147. For a transcript of the debate itself see 'Human Nature versus Power' in Fons Elders, ed., *Reflexive Water: The Basic Concerns of Mankind*, London: Souvenir Press, 1974, pp. 139–97.
7. 'L'Intellectuel et les pouvoirs' (propos recueillis le 14 mai 1981 et résumés par Christian Panier et Pierre Watté), *La Revue nouvelle*, vol. LXXX, no. 10, October 1984, p. 339.
8. Rux Martin, 'Truth, Power, Self: An Interview with Michel Foucault. October 25, 1982', in Luther H. Martin, Huck Gutman and Patrick H. Hutton, eds., *Technologies of the Self: A Seminar with Michel Foucault*, London: Tavistock, 1988, p. 11.
9. Charles Ruas, 'An Interview with Michel Foucault', in *Death and the Labyrinth: The World of Michel Foucault*, tr. Charles Ruas, London: Athlone Press, 1986, p. 184
10. 'The Minimalist Self', in Lawrence D. Kritzman, ed., *Politics, Philosophy, Culture. Interviews and Other Writings 1977–1984*, New York and London: Routledge, 1988, p. 16. The interview by Stephen Riggins, conducted in English on 22 June 1982, originally appeared in the Canadian journal *Ethos*, vol. 1, no. 2, Autumn 1983, pp. 4–9.
11. *L'Archéologie du savoir*, Paris: Gallimard, 1969, p. 28.
12. *La Pensée du dehors*, Montpellier: Fata Morgana, 1986, p. 37.
13. Michel de Certeau, 'The Laugh of Michel Foucault', *Heterologies. Discourse on the Other*, Manchester University Press, 1986, pp. 193–94.

14. 'Mal faire, dire vrai', unpublished lecture, Université Catholique de Louvain, May 1981. Typescript, Bibliothèque du Saulchoir, D202.
15. 'Che cos'è lei, Professor Foucault?', *La Fiera Letteraria*, 28 September 1967, p. 11 (interview with Paolo Caruso); 'Conversazione senza complessi con il filosofo che analizza le strutture del potere' (interview with Jerry Bauer), *Playmen* 12, 1978, p. 30.
16. 'Truth, Power, Self', p. 9.
17. Interview with Douglas Johnson.
18. Interview with Daniel Defert.
19. Jonathan Rée, personal communication.
20. Laurent Dispot, 'Une Soirée chez Michel Foucault', *Masques* 25–26, May 1985, pp. 163–67; interview with Laurent Dispot.
21. Interview with André Green.
22. Interview with Jean Laplanche.
23. 'Le Gai Savoir', interview with Jean Le Bitoux, *Mec Magazine* 5, June 1988, p. 36. The interview, dated 10 July 1978, was originally published in Dutch as 'Vijftien vragen von homosexele zijde san Michel Foucault' in M. Duyves and T. Maasen, eds., *Interviewen mit Michel Foucault*, Utrecht: De Woelsat, 1992, pp. 12–23.
24. Pierre Klossowski, 'Digression à partir d'un portrait apocryphe', *L'Arc* 49, *Deleuze*, new edn., 1990, p. 11.
25. 'Le Philosophe masqué', Christian Delacampagne, *Le Monde dimanche*, 6 April 1980, p. 1.
26. 'Deuxième Entretien: Sur les Façons d'écrire l'histoire' in Raymond Bellour, *Le Livre des autres*, Paris: L'Herne 1971, p. 203; originally published in *Les Lettres françaises*, 15 June 1967.
27. 'Sur "Histoire de Paul" par Michel Foucault et René Feret (Entretien)', *Cahiers du cinéma* 262–63, January 1976, p. 65.
28. Maurice Blanchot, *Michel Foucault tel que je l'imagine*, Montpellier: Fata Morgana, 1986, pp. 9–10.
29. Alan Sheridan, 'Diary', *London Review of Books*, 19 July–1 August 1984, p. 21.
30. Interview with Daniel Defert.
31. Reproduced in *Michel Foucault: Une Histoire de la vérité*, Paris: Syros, 1985, pp. 112–13.
32. *Les Mots et les choses*, Paris: Gallimard 1966, p. 7.
33. Jorge Luis Borges, *Obras Completas*, Buenos Aires: Emecé, 1974, p. 708.
34. 'Polemics, politics and problematizations: an interview', tr. Catherine Porter (an edited version of interviews with Paul Rabinow, Charles Taylor, Martin Jay, Richard Rorty and Leo Lowenthal, Berkeley, April 1983), in Paul Rabinow, ed., *The Foucault Reader*, Harmondsworth: Penguin 1986, pp. 383–84.
35. 'The Minimalist Self', p. 7.
36. Jean-Pierre Barou. 'Il aurait pu aussi bien m'arriver tout autre chose', *Libération*, 26 June 1984, p. 4.
37. Ibid.
38. Cited, Claude Mauriac, *Le Temps accompli*, Paris: Grasset, 1991, p. 43. For Guibert's fictionalised account, see his *A l'Ami qui ne m'a pas sauvé la vie*, Paris: Gallimard, 1990.
39. Mauriac, p. 43.
40. See Pierre Nora, 'Il avait un besoin formidable d'être aimé', *L'Evénement du jeudi*, 18–24 September 1986, pp. 82, 83.

41. *L'Archéologie du Savoir*, p. 35.
42. 'Maurice Florence' (i.e. Michel Foucault and François Ewald), 'Foucault, Michel, 1926–)', in Jean Huisman, ed., *Dictionnaire des philosophes*, Paris: PUF, 1981, Tôme I, p. 942; interview with François Ewald.
43. 'Un Problème qui m'intéresse depuis longtemps, c'est celui du système pénal', cited, Jélila Hafsia, *Visages et rencontres*, Tunis, 1981.
44. François Ewald and Pierre Macherey, 'Actualité de Michel Foucault', *L'Ane* 40, October–December 1989, pp. 4–5.
45. 'Sur la sellette', entretien avec Jean-Louis Ezine, *Les Nouvelles littéraires*, 17 March 1975, p. 3.
46. *Power/Knowledge. Selected Interviews and Other Writings 1972–1977*, edited by Colin Gordon, Brighton: Harvester, 1980; interview with Colin Gordon.
47. Duccio Trombadori, *Colloqui con Foucault*, Salerno: 10/17, 1981, tr. R. James Goldstein and James Casaito as *Remarks on Marx*, New York: Semiotext(e), 1991.
48. Mauriac, *Le Temps accompli*, p. 32.
49. Bernauer, *Foucault's Force of Flight*; Michael Clark, *Michel Foucault: An Annotated Bibliography*, New York: Garland, 1983. Lagrange's bibliography will be included in the forthcoming Gallimard edition. A copy is available in the Biblothèque du Saulchoir.
50. Thierry Voeltzel, *Vingt Ans et après*, Préface de Claude Mauriac, Paris: Grasset, 1978; interview with Claude Mauriac.
51. 'Faire vivre et laisser mourir. La Naissance du racisme', *Les Temps Modernes* 535, February 1991, pp. 37–61.
52. 'Sur la Justice populaire: débat avec les Maos', *Les Temps Modernes* 310bis, 1972, pp. 335–66.
53. Interview with Dominique Seglard.
54. Published under the generic title *De la Gouvernementalité. Leçons d'introduction aux cours des années 1978 et 1979*, Paris: Seuil/Productions de La Licorne, KS531, KS532.
55. Michel Foucault, *Résumé des cours 1970–1982*, Paris: Julliard, 1989.
56. Didier Eribon, *Michel Foucault*, Paris: Flammarion, 1989.

Chapter 1

1. In addition to the sources specifically mentioned in notes, this account is drawn from the oral testimonies of Denys Foucault, Francine Fruchaud, Henri Fruchaud, Sylvie-Claire d'Arvisenet, Anne Thalamy and Daniel Defert.
2. Paulin Malapert, *De Spinoza politica*, Paris 1907; *Les Eléments du caractère et leurs lois de combinaison*, Paris: Alcan, 1906; *Leçons de philosophie*, Paris: Hatier, 1918; *Psychologie*, Paris: Hatier, 1913.
3. Jean Plattard, ed., François Rabelais, *Oeuvres complètes*, Paris: Association Guillaume Budé, 1929 (five vols.); Michel de Montaigne, *Oeuvres complètes*, Paris: Association Guillaume Budé, 1931–32 (four vols.).
4. Eribon, *Michel Foucault*, p. 21.
5. Sheridan, 'Diary'; Voeltzel, *Vingt Ans et après*, p. 156.
6. Ibid., p. 182.
7. 'The Minimalist Self', p. 4.

484   THE LIVES OF MICHEL FOUCAULT

8. Ibid., pp. 6–7.

9. Interview with Jacqueline Verdeaux.

10. 'Structuralism and Post-Structuralism: An Interview with Michel Foucault', *Telos* 55, Spring 1983, p. 208, tr. Jeremy Harding; this interview with Gerard Raulet was originally published as 'Um welchen Preis sagt die Vernuft die Warheit?', *Spuren* 1–2, May–June 1983.

11. 'Hospicios, sexualidade, prisões' (interview with Claudio Bojunga), *Versus* (Rio de Janeiro), 1 October 1975.

12. 'Le Philosophe masqué', *Le Monde*, 6 April 1980.

13. Pierre Bourdieu and Jean-Claude Passeron, *Les Héritiers: les étudiants et la culture*, Paris: Minuit, 1964.

14. Mona Ozouf, *L'Ecole, l'église et la république*, Paris: Armand Colin, 1964.

15. *Radioscopie de Michel Foucault, propos recueillis par Jacques Chancel*, Radio-France, 3 October 1975. Cassette recordings of this interview may be consulted in the Bibliothèque du Saulchoir (C42) and in the Bibliothèque d'Information Publique, Centre Georges Pompidou.

16. Emmanuel Le Roy Ladurie, *Montpellier-Paris. PC-PSU, 1945–1963*, Paris: Gallimard, 1982, pp. 25–26.

17. Eribon, *Michel Foucault*, p. 25.

18. Etienne Burin des Roziers, 'Une Rencontre à Varsovie', *Le Débat* 41, September–November 1986, p. 134.

19. Eribon, *Michel Foucault*, p. 27.

20. Voeltzel, *Vingt Ans et après*, p. 55.

21. The term *khâgne* derives from *cagneux*, meaning 'knock-kneed', and apparently its educational usage stems from the science student's scorn for his counterpart in the humanities – an individual who is by definition ill-proportioned, graceless and clumsy.

22. Eribon, *Michel Foucault*, pp. 28–29.

23. Voeltzel, *Vingt Ans et après*, pp. 127–28.

24. Hervé Guibert, 'Les Secrets d'un homme' in *Mauve le vierge*, Paris: Gallimard, 1988, p. 106.

25. André Gide, *La Séquestrée de Poitiers*, in *Ne jugez pas*, Paris: Gallimard, 1930.

26. 'Deuxième Entretien: sur les façons d'écrire l'histoire', in Raymond Bellour, *Le Livre des autres*, Paris: L'Herne, 1971, pp. 201–202 (originally published in *Les Lettres françaises*, 15 June 1967).

27. Eribon, *Michel Foucault*, p. 29.

28. Interview with Jeannette Colombel.

29. Interview with Michel Albaric.

30. 'De l'amitié comme mode de vie', *Gai Pied* 25, April 1981, p. 4.

31. 'The Minimalist Self', p. 13.

32. Eribon, *Michel Foucault*, p. 30.

33. Interview with Jean Piel.

34. Le Roy Ladurie, *Paris-Montpellier*, p. 28.

35. 'Jean Hyppolite (1907–1968)', *Revue de métaphysique et de morale*, vol. 74, no 2., April–June 1969, p. 131.

36. Eribon, *Michel Foucault*, p. 40.

37. Ibid.

38. Jean-Paul Aron, *Les Modernes*, Paris: Folio, 1984, p. 9.

39. Jacques Piquemal, 'G. Canguilhem, professeur de Terminale (1937–1938). Un Essai de témoignage', *Revue de métaphysique et de morale*, 90-année, no. 1, January–March 1985, p. 78.
40. Interview with Dominique Seglard.
41. Louis Althusser, *L'Avenir dure longtemps, suivi de Les Faits: Autobiographies*, Paris: Stock/IMEC, 1992, p. 324.
42. Interview with Georges Canguilhem.
43. Interview with Jeannette Colombel.
44. Foucault describes his cycling in Paris thus: 'I've found a way not to dream when I go out: I cycle. It's the only way I get around now. A wonderful game in Paris. There again, there are people who travel by bike and see wonderful things. It seems that the Pont Royal is marvellous at seven on a September evening when there is a bit of mist. I never see that; I'm dicing with the hold-ups, dicing with the cars. The balance of power again.' 'A Quoi rêvent les philosophes' (interview with Emmanuel Lossowsky), *L'Imprévu*, 28 January 1975, p. 13.

Chapter 2

1. Jean-François Sirinelli, 'La Khâgne', in Pierre Nora, ed., *Les Lieux de mémoire. II La Nation*, Paris: Gallimard, 1986, vol. 3, p. 607.
2. Eribon, *Michel Foucault*, p. 42; Sirinelli, 'La Khâgne', p. 607.
3. Personal communication.
4. Régis Debray, *Teachers, Writers, Celebrities: The Intellectuals of Modern France*, tr. David Macey, London: Verso, 1981, p. 49.
5. Jean Hyppolite, 'La "Phénoménologie" de Hegel et la pensée française contemporaine', *Figures de la pensée philosophique*, Paris: PUF, 1971, p. 232.
6. Althusser, *L'Avenir dure longtemps*, p. 155.
7. Yann Moulier Boutang, *Louis Althusser: Une Biographie. Tome I. La Formation du mythe (1918–1956)*, Paris: Grasset, 1992, p. 362.
8. Elisabeth Roudinesco, *Jacques Lacan & Co.*, tr. Jeffrey Mehlman, London: Free Association Books, 1990, p. 376.
9. Boutang, *Louis Althusser*, p. 363.
10. Ibid., p. 461.
11. Ibid., p. 237.
12. Louis Althusser, 'Is It Simple to be a Marxist in Philosophy?', tr. Graham Locke in *Philosophy and the Spontaneous Philosophy of the Scientists and Other Essays*, edited with an Introduction by Gregory Elliott, London: Verso, 1990; *Montesquieu. La Politique et l'histoire*, Paris: PUF, 1959, tr. 'Montesquieu: Politics and History', in *Politics and History*, London: New Left Books, 1972
13. Douglas Johnson, 'Althusser's Fate', *London Review of Books*, 16 April–6 May 1981, p. 13.
14. Régis Debray, 'In Settlement of All Accounts', in *Prison Writings*, tr. Rosemary Sheed, London: Allen Lane, 1973, p. 197.
15. Interview with Douglas Johnson.
16. Althusser, *L'Avenir dure longtemps*, p. 124.
17. Ibid., p. 321.

18. Louis Althusser, *For Marx*, tr. Ben Brewster, London: Allen Lane, 1969, pp. 32, 256.

19. Boutang, *Louis Althusser*, pp. 449–59.

20. Personal communication.

21. Jean-François Sirinelli, 'Les Normaliens de la rue d'Ulm après 1945: une génération communiste?', *Revue d'histoire du monde moderne*, vol. 32, October–December 1986, pp. 569–88.

22. Interview with Jean Laplanche.

23. Maurice Agulhon, cited, *Libération*, 30 June–1 July 1984, p. 16.

24. Interviews with Didier Anzieu and Jacqueline Verdeaux.

25. Interview with Denys Foucault.

26. Interview with Jeanette Colombel.

27. Jean Delay, *La Jeunesse d'André Gide*, Paris: Gallimard, two vols., 1956, 1957; interview with Daniel Defert.

28. Interview with Jacqueline Verdeaux.

29. Maurice Pinguet, 'Les Années d'Apprentissage', p. 126.

30. 'Hospicios, sexualidade, prisões' (interview with Claudio Bojunga), *Versus*, 1 October 1975.

31. Interview with Francine and Henri Fruchaud.

32. Pinguet, 'Les Années d'apprentissage', p. 122.

33. Claude Mauriac, *Et comme l'Espérance est violente*, Paris: Livre de poche, 1986, p. 482; Bibliothèque du Saulchoir, C40.

34. Interview with Paul Veyne.

35. Janine Mossuz–Lavau, *Les Lois de l'amour. Les Politiques de la sexualité en France (1950–1990)*, Paris: Payot, 1991, p. 239.

36. Alexandre Koyré, 'Rapport sur l'état des études hégéliennes en France', *Etudes d'histoire de la pensée philosophique*, Paris: Armand Colin, 1961, pp. 205–30.

37. Maurice Merleau–Ponty, *Sens et non-sens*, Paris: Nagel, 1948, p. 125.

38. Georges Canguilhem, 'Hegel en France', *Revue d'histoire et de philosophie religieuses*, 4, 1948–49, p. 282.

39. Jean Hyppolite, 'La "Phénoménologie" de Hegel et la pensée française contemporaine', *Figures de la pensée philosophique* p. 235.

40. Vincent Descombes, *Modern French Philosophy*, tr. L. Scott–Fox and J. M. Harding, Cambridge University Press, 1980, p. 10.

41. It can, however, be argued that Bergson remained a powerful influence on Deleuze; see his *Le Bergsonisme*, Paris: PUF, 1966.

42. Alexandre Kojève, *Introduction à la lecture de Hegel. Leçons sur 'La Phénoménologie de l'Esprit' professées à l'Ecole des Hautes Etudes réunies et publiées par Raymond Queneau*, Paris: Gallimard, 1947. On the French reception of Hegel, see Judith P. Butler, *Subjects of Desire. Hegelian Reflections in Twentieth-Century France*, New York: Columbia University Press, 1987. The special issue of *Magazine littéraire* (293, November 1991) devoted to *Hegel et 'La Phénoménologie de l'esprit'*, also contains a wealth of information. I discuss Kojève's relevance for an understanding of Lacan in my *Lacan in Contexts*, London: Verso, 1988.

43. 'Jean Hyppolite', p. 131.

44. Jean Hyppolite, *Genèse et structure de la 'Phénoménologie de l'esprit'*, Paris: PUF, 1948. Hyppolite's account of his work can be found in his 1957 lecture on 'La "Phénoménologie" de Hegel et la pensée française contemporaine'.

45. Althusser's thesis will be included in the three volumes of his unpublished work announced for publication by IMEC. Extracts have been published under the title 'Esprit d'Iéna contre la Prusse' in the 'Hegel' issue of *Magazine littéraire*.

46. 'Le Retour de la morale', interview with Gilles Barbedette and André Scala, *Les Nouvelles*, 28 June–5 July 1984, p. 40.

47. Althusser, *L'Avenir dure longtemps*, p. 323.

48. Mauriac, *Et comme l'Espérance est violente*, p. 530.

49. 'Structuralism and Post-Structuralism', p. 198.

50. Interview with Paul Veyne.

51. 'La Vie: l'expérience et la science', *Revue de métaphysique et de morale*, 90- année, no. 1, January–March 1986, p. 4; originally published in Carolyn Fawcett's translation as the preface to Canguilhem, *On the Normal and the Pathological*, Boston: Riedel, 1978.

52. Pierre Bourdieu, 'Aspirant Philosophe. Un Point de vue sur le champ universitaire des années 50', in *Les Enjeux philosophiques des années 50*, Paris: Centre Georges Pompidou, 1989, pp. 19–20.

53. Cited, Mauriac, *Et comme l'Espérance est violente*, p. 600.

54. 'Le Retour de la morale', p. 40.

55. Jean Beaufret, 'M. Heidegger et le problème de l'existence', *Fontaine* 63, November 1947.

56. Edouard Gaede, 'Nietzsche et la littérature', in *Nietzsche (Cahiers de Royaumont)*, Paris: Minuit, 1967, pp. 141–52.

57. See for example *Colloqui con Foucault*, p. 27.

58. Maurice Pinguet, 'Les Années d'apprentissage', pp. 129–130.

59. 'Structuralism and Post-Structuralism', p. 198.

60. *Colloqui con Foucault*, p. 31.

61. Ibid., p. 39. On Bachelard, see Mary Tiles, *Bachelard: Science and Objectivity*, Cambridge University Press, 1984.

62. On the teaching of psychology, and on its relationship with psychoanalysis in this period, see Didier Anzieu, 'La Psychanalyse au service de la psychologie', *Nouvelle Revue de psychanalyse* 20, Autumn 1979, pp. 59–76.

63. Daniel Lagache, *L'Unité de la psychologie*, Paris: PUF, 1949.

64. Interview with Didier Anzieu.

65. The best introduction to Anzieu's work is his *A Skin for Thought. Interviews with Gilbert Tarrab*, tr. Daphne Nash Briggs, London and New York: Karnac Books, 1990.

66. Eribon, *Michel Foucault*, pp. 61–62.

67. *Colloqui con Foucault*, p. 33.

68. Ibid., pp. 28–29.

69. Cited, Otto Friedrich, 'France's Philosopher of Power', *Time*, 6 November 1981.

70. Interview with Francine Fruchaud.

71. Interview with Paul Veyne.

72. Pinguet, 'Les Années d'apprentissage', p. 127.

73. Eribon, *Michel Foucault*, p. 73.

74. Emmanuel Le Roy Ladurie, *Paris-Montpellier*, p. 46.

75. Georges Cogniot, 'Les Communistes et le sionisme', *La Nouvelle Critique* 44, March

1953, cited, Maxime Rodinson, *Cult, Ghetto, and State*, tr. Jon Rothschild, London: Al Saqi Books, 1983, p. 44, n. 19.

76. *Colloqui con Foucault*, pp. 31–32.
77. Ibid., p. 72.
78. Annie Besse, 'A Propos du sionisme et de l'anti-sémitisme', *Cahiers de communisme*, February 1953, cited, Rodinson, p. 43. Besse was at this time a PCF organiser. She subsequently moved far to the right and became an apologist for Zionism. Writing under the name Annie Kriegel, she became a cold warrior of no mean stature, but also one of the best academic historians of the PCF. See in particular her *Aux Origines du communisme français*, two vols., Paris: Mouton, 1964.
79. Pinguet, 'Les Années d'apprentissage', p. 127.
80. Cited, Friedrich, 'France's Philosopher of Power'.
81. Emmanuel Le Roy Ladurie, *Paris-Montpellier*, pp. 165–66.
82. Cited, Mossuz-Lavau, *Les Lois de l'amour*, p. 251.
83. Interview with Paul Veyne.
84. 'Postscript to *Death and the Labyrinth*, p. 174.
85. Aron, *Les Modernes*, Folio, 1984, pp. 75–76.
86. Mauriac, *Et comme l'Espérance est violente*, pp. 341–42.
87. Claude Mauriac, *Mauriac et fils*, Paris: Grasset, 1986, p. 291. The 'further montage' was published as *Une Certaine Rage*, Paris: Laffont, 1977.
88. Eribon, *Michel Foucault*, pp. 74–75.
89. Interview with Didier Eribon.
90. Rodinson, *Cult, Ghetto, and State*, p. 54.
91. Mauriac, *Et comme L'Espérance est violente*, pp. 557–76; *Mauriac et fils*, p. 291.
92. *Colloqui con Foucault*, p. 32.
93. For a good acount of the Lysenko affair, see Dominique Lecourt, *Lysenko. Histoire réelle d'une science prolétarienne*, Paris: Maspero, 1976; tr. *Proletarian Science? The Case of Lysenko*, London: New Left Books, 1977.
94. Pinguet, 'Les Années d'apprentissage', p. 127.
95. 'Vérité et pouvoir', interview with Alessandro Fontana, *L'Arc* 70; *La Crise dans la tête*, 1937, p. 16.
96. Eribon, *Michel Foucault*, pp. 54–55.
97. Boutang, *Louis Althusser*, p. 469.
98. Ibid.
99. Interview with Jean Laplanche.
100. Pinguet, 'Les Années d'apprentissage', p. 123.
101. On Aron, see Jean-Pierre Joecker and Alain Sanzio, 'Rencontre avec Jean-Paul Aron', *Masques* 21, Spring 1984, pp. 7–17.
102. Eribon, *Michel Foucault*, p. 56.
103. Interview with Georges Canguilhem.
104. Sironelli, 'La Khâne', p. 608.
105. Interview with Denys Foucault.

Chapter 3

1. 'La Recherche scientifique et la psychologie', in Jean-Edouard Morène, ed., *Des Chercheurs français s'interrogent*, Paris: PUF, 1957, pp. 178, 184.
2. Yvon Belaval, *L'Esthétique sans paradoxe de Diderot*, Paris: Gallimard, 1950.
3. Cited, Eribon, *Michel Foucault*, p. 83.
4. Jean-Paul Aron, *Le Mangeur au XIXe siècle*, Paris: Robert Laffont, 1973; tr. Nina Rootes, *The Art of Eating in France. Manners and Menus in the Nineteenth Century*, London: Peter Owen, 1975.
5. 'La Bibliothèque fantastique' in Gérard Genette and Tzvetan Todorov, eds., *Le Travail de Flaubert*, Paris: Seuil, 'Points', 1984; originally published as the afterword to Flaubert, *Die Versuchung des heiligen Antonius*, tr. Anneliese Botond, Frankfurt: Insel, 1964. First French publication as 'Un Fantastique de bibliothèque', *Cahiers Renaud-Barrault* 59, March 1967.
6. Aron, *Les Modernes*, pp. 72–73; 'Quelques souvenirs de Pierre Boulez, propos recueillis par Alain Jaubert', *Critique* 471–72, August–September 1986, p. 745.
7. 'Che cos'è lei Professore Foucault?', p. 14.
8. The most complete source of information on Barraqué is *Entretemps. Numéro spécial: Jean Barraqué*, 1987. This includes the valuable 'Essai de chrono-biographie' by Rose-Marie Janzen. See also G. W. Hopkins, 'Jean Barraqué', *Musical Times*, November 1966, pp. 952–55.
9. Michel Fano, 'Le Temps de l'amitié', *Entretemps*, p. 59; 'Autour de la musique', *Le Débat* 41, pp. 137–39.
10. 'The Minimalist Self', p. 13.
11. Jean Barraqué, 'Propos impromptu' (extracts), *Entretemps*, p. 133.
12. André Hodeir, 'Barraqué: Le Pari de la discontinuité', *Entretemps*, p. 39.
13. Friedrich Nietzsche, *Thus Spoke Zarathustra*, tr. R. J. Hollingdale, Harmondsworth: Penguin, 1961, p. 265–66. For the full French version used by Barraqué, see the score, *Séquence*, Florence: Hinrichsen Edition Ltd, 1963.
14. *The Death of Virgil*, tr. Jean Starr Untermeyer: New York: Pantheon, 1945.
15. Michel Habart, 'Hermann Broch et les rançons de la création poétique', *Critique* 83, April 1954, pp. 310–22.
16. Articles now in Maurice Blanchot, *Le Livre à venir*, Paris: Folio, 1986, pp. 160–72.
17. 'Pierre Boulez ou l'écran traversé', *Le Nouvel Observateur*, 2 October 1982, p. 51.
18. Jean Barraqué, *Debussy*, Paris: Seuil, 1962.
19. Fano, 'Le Temps de l'amitié', p. 61.
20. Maurice Pinguet, *La Mort volontaire au Japon*, Paris: Gallimard, 1984.
21. Pinguet, 'Les Années d'apprentissage', p. 125.
22. Interview with Serge Fauchereau.
23. Interview with Paul Veyne.
24. Pinguet, 'Les Années d'apprentissage', p. 130.
25. Nietzsche, *Untimely Meditations*, p. 104.
26. Friedrich Nietzsche, *The Gay Science*, tr. Walter Kaufmann, New York: Vintage Books, 1974, p. 81.
27. Pinguet, 'Les Années d'apprentissage', p. 124.
28. 'The Minimalist Self', p. 6.
29. 'Truth, Power, Self', p. 11.
30. *Maladie mentale et personnalité*, Paris: PUF, 1954, p. 108.

31. 'Michel Foucault. Conversazione senza complessi con il filosofo che analizza le "strutture del potere"', pp. 22–23.

32. 'The Minimalist Self', p. 6.

33. For an account of the centre's workings, see Dr Badonnel, 'Le Centre national d'orientation de Fresnes', *Esprit*, April 1955, pp. 585–92.

34. 'La Recherche scientifique et la psychologie', pp. 173–74. Maurice Pradines taught at the University of Strasbourg before becoming a member of the Institut. In the bibliographical note to his 'La Psychologie de 1850 à 1950', in A. Weber and D. Huisman, eds., *Histoire de la philosophie contemporaine*, Paris: Fischbacher, 1957, p. 607, Foucault credits him with having introduced, 'for the first time in the history of ideas, an authentically genetic method' in psychology.

35. Ruth Bochner and Florence Halpern, *The Clinical Application of the Rorschach Test*, New York: Grune and Stratton, 1942; tr. Jacqueline Verdeaux, *L'Interprétation clinique du test de Rorschach*;, Paris: PUF, 1947; Jacob Wyrsch, *Die Person des Schizophrenen*, Bern: Haupt, 1949; tr. Jacqueline Verdeaux, *La Personne du schizophréne, Paris: PUF, 1954*.

36. An English version of the text ('Dream and Existence') can be found in *Being in the World. Selected Papers of Ludwig Binswanger*, Translated and with a Critical Introduction to his Existential Psychoanalysis by Jacob Needleman, London: Souvenir Press, 1975, pp. 222–48. The text first appeared in *Neue Schweizer Rundschau*, 1930.

37. 'La Recherche scientifique et la psychologie', p. 199.

38. *Colloqui con Foucault*, p. 41.

39. Interview with Georges and Jacqueline Verdeaux.

40. 'La Folie n'existe que dans une société', *Le Monde*, 22 July 1961.

41. In addition to the introduction to Binswanger and 'La recherche scientifique en psychologie', Foucault's pre-1961 publications were *Maladie mentale et personnalité*, Paris: PUF, 1954; 'La Psychologie de 1850 à 1950', in A. Weber and D. Huisman, eds., *Histoire de la philosophie contemporaine. Tôme 2. Tableau de la philosophie contemporaine*, Paris: Fischbacher, 1957; translation, with Daniel Rocher, of Viktor von Weizsaecher, *Le Cycle de la structure (Der Gestaltkreis)*, Paris: Desclée de Brouwer, 1958.

42. Interview with Georges and Jacqueline Verdeaux.

43. 'Sur "Histoire de Paul" par Michel Foucault et René Feret (entretien)', *Cahiers du cinéma* 262–63, January 1976, p. 65.

44. Denis Huisman, 'Note sur l'article de Michel Foucault', *Revue internationale de philosophie*, vol. 44, no. 73, 2/1990, pp. 177–78.

45. 'La Psychologie', pp. 36, 37.

46. Ibid., p. 51.

47. Ibid.

48. Georges Canguilhem, 'L'Objet de l'histoire des sciences', *Etudes d'histoire et de philosophie des sciences*, Paris: Librarie philosophique J. Vrin, 1989, p. 13.

49. Reprinted in Georges Canguilhem, *Le Normal et le pathologique*, Paris: PUF, collection 'Quadrige', 1984. There is little available on Canguilhem in English. See Colin Gordon, 'The Normal and the Biological: A Note on Georges Canguilhem', *I&C* 7, Autumn 1980, *Technologies of the Human Sciences*. The same issue contains Howard Davies's translation of Canguilhem's 'What Is Psychology?' and Graham Burchell's translation of Foucault's 'Georges

Canguilhem, Philosopher of Error' (the preface to the English-language version of *The Normal and the Pathological*). See also Mike Shortland, 'Introduction to Georges Canguilhem', *Radical Philosophy* 29, Autumn 1981; Dominique Lecourt, 'Georges Canguilhem's Epistemological History' in *Marxism and Epistemology*, London: New Left Books, 1975, and Gutting, *Michel Foucault's Archaeology of Scientific Reason*, pp. 32–54.

50. 'La Psychologie', p. 37.
51. The best studies of the differences between the two editions are Pierre Macherey, 'Aux sources de l'*Histoire de la folie*', *Critique* 471–472, August–September 1986, pp. 753–75, and Ch. 2 of Bernauer's *Michel Foucault's Force of Flight*.
52. *Mental Illness and Psychology*, tr. Alan Sheridan, London; Harper and Row, 1976; reprinted with an introduction by Hubert Dreyfus, Berkeley and London: University of California Press, 1987. The translation is to be used with caution; 'Part II' is translated from the second edition.
53. *Maladie mentale*, p. 9.
54. Ibid., p. 2.
55. Ibid., p. 34.
56. Ibid., p. 53.
57. Ibid., p. 89.
58. Ibid., p. 102.
59. For an account of Pavlovianism and of its utilisation by the PCF, see Roudinesco, *Jacques Lacan & Co.*, pp. 30–43, 177–81. See also the relevant sections of David Joravsky, *Russian Psychology. A Critical History*, Oxford: Blackwell, 1989.
60. *Colloqui con Foucault*, p. 45.
61. Macherey, 'Aux sources de l'*Histoire de la folie*, p. 755.
62. Georges Politzer, *Critique des fondements de la psychologie*, Paris: Rieder, 1928. For an account of Politzer's work, see Roudinesco, *Jacques Lacan & Co.*, pp. 60–67.
63. 'La Psychologie', p. 44.
64. Jean Lacroix, 'La Signification de la folie', *Le Monde*, 8 December 1961, p. 8.
65. Roland Caillois, *Critique* 93, February 1955, pp. 189–90.
66. tr. Forrest Williams, 'Dream, Imagination and Existence', *Review of Existential Psychology and Psychiatry*, vol. XIX, no. 1, 1984–85, pp. 29–78. For recent discussions in English, see Gutting, pp. 29–78, Bernauer, pp. 25–35, and John Forrester, *The Seductions of Psychoanalysis*, Cambridge University Press, 1990, pp. 289ff.
67. Introduction to Binswanger, pp. 9–10.
68. Binswanger, 'Dream and Existence', p. 222.
69. Ibid., p. 223.
70. Ibid., p. 227.
71. Introduction, p. 9.
72. Ibid., pp. 11, 12.
73. Ibid., p. 15.
74. Ibid., p. 16.
75. The evolution of this relationship is traced in Jacques Lagrange, 'Versions de la psychanalyse dans le texte de Foucault', *Psychanalyse à l'université*, vol. 12, no. 45, 1987, pp. 99–120, and vol. 12, no. 46, pp. 259–80.
76. Introduction, pp. 18, 13.
77. Ibid., pp. 26–27.

78. Interview with Jacqueline Verdeaux. On Lacan's visit to Heidegger, see Roudinesco, *Jacques Lacan & Co.*, p. 298.

79. 'Merleau-Ponty à la Sorbonne. Résumé des cours établi par des étudiants et approuvé par lui-même', *Bulletin de la psychologie*, vol. XVII, nos. 3–6, 1964.

80. Daniel Defert, 'Lettre à Claude Lanzmann', *Les Temps Modernes* 531–33, October–December 1990, p. 1204. The texts by Sartre referred to are *L'Imaginaire. Psychologie phénoménologique de l'imagination*, Paris: Gallimard, 1940, and *Esquisse pour une théorie des émotions*, Paris: Herman, 1938.

81. The reference is to Gaston Bachelard, *L'Air et les songes. Essai sur l'imagination du mouvement*, Paris: Librairie José Corti, 1943.

82. 'Gaston Bachelard, le philosophe et son ombre: piéger sa propre culture', *Le Figaro*, 30 September 1972, p. 16.

83. Introduction, pp. 120, 125.

Chapter 4

1. Georges Dumézil, 'Un Homme heureux', *Le Nouvel Observateur*, 29 June 1984, p. x; *Entretiens avec Didier Eribon*, Paris: Folio, 1987, p. 214.

2. See his *Sémantique structurelle*, Paris: Larousse. 1966 and *Du Sens*, Paris: Seuil, 1970.

3. Louis-Jean Calvet, *Roland Barthes*, Paris: Flammarion, 1990, p. 154.

4. 'The Minimalist Self', pp. 4, 5.

5. 'Postscript' to *Death and the Labyrinth*, p. 174.

6. Ibid., p. 5.

7. 'La Philosophie structuraliste permet de diagnostiquer ce qu'est aujourd'hui' (propos recueillis par Gérard Fellous), *La Presse de Tunis*, 12 April 1967, p. 3.

8. *Colloqui con Foucault*, p. 42.

9. Interview with Denys Foucault.

10. Interview with Jean-François Miquel.

11. Eribon, *Michel Foucault*, p. 99.

12. 'Foucault à Uppsala, propos recueillis par Jean Piel', *Critique* 471–72, August–September 1986, p. 751. Piel's primary informant was Jean-François Miquel.

13. Interviews with Denys Foucault and Francine Fruchaud.

14. Mauriac, *Le Temps accompli*, p. 45.

15. *Histoire de la folie*, Paris: Gallimard, collection 'Tel', 1976, pp. 265–67.

16. Hyppolite's lecture on 'Histoire et existence' (December 1955) can be found in his *Figures de la pensée philosophique*, pp. 973–86. The same lecture was given at the French Institutes in Stockholm, Oslo and Copenhagen.

17. 'Foucault à Uppsala', p. 751.

18. Cited, Eribon, *Michel Foucault*, p. 105.

19. Dumézil, *Entretiens avec Didier Eribon*, pp. 214–15.

20. Georges Dumézil, *Le Festin de l'immortalité. Etude de mythologie comparée indo-européenne*, Paris: Annales du Musée Guimet, 1924. Dumézil's best-known work is probably the three-volume *Mythe et Epopée: L'Idéologie des trois fonctions dans les épopées des peuples indo-européens. Types épiques indo-européens: un héros, un sorcier, un roi* and *Histoires romaines*, Paris: Gallimard, 1968, 1971 and 1973. The *Entretiens* with Eribon provide a useful introduction to his work. For an extensive study, see C. Scott Littleton, *The New Comparative Mythology. An Anthropological Assessment of the*

Theories of Georges Dumézil, Berkeley: University of California Press, 1968.

21. See in particular Georges Duby, *Les Trois Ordres ou l'imaginaire du féodalisme*, Paris: Gallimard, 1978.

22. *Histoire de la folie*, Paris: Plon, 1961, p. x.

23. 'La Folie n'existe que dans une société', *Le Monde*, 22 July 1961, p. 9.

24. Yngve Lindung, 'En intervju med Michel Foucault', *Bonniers Litterära Magasin*, March 1968, p. 203.

25. Cited, Didier Eribon, *Michel Foucault*, second, revised edn. Paris: Flammarion, collection 'Champs', 1991, pp. 356–57. The uncertainty of the date arises from Foucault's habit of dating letters by day and month, but not year.

26. Letter of 10 August 1957 to Stirn Lindroth, cited Eribon, pp. 107–108. Interview with Jean-François Miquel.

27. Eribon, *Michel Foucault*, pp. 89, 90.

28. Ibid., p. 104; Calvet, *Roland Barthes*, p. 154.

29. Postscript to *Death and the Labyrinth*, pp. 171, 172.

30. Ibid., p. 185.

31. Jean Ferry, *Une Etude sur Raymond Roussel*, Paris: Arcanes, 1953.

32. Interview with Jean-François Miguel.

33. *Le Monde*, 14 December 1957.

34. *Colloqui con Foucault*, pp. 42, 60.

35. Eribon, p. 111.

36. Resolution adopted by the Fourteenth Congress of the PCF (June 1959), cited, M. Adereth, *The French Communist Party: A Critical History (1920–1984)*, Manchester University Press, 1984, p. 171; interview with Daniel Defert.

37. Cited, Eribon, *Michel Foucault*, p. 106.

38. *Colloqui con Foucault*, p. 71.

39. Neal Ascherson, *The Polish August*, Harmondsworth: Pelican, 1981, p. 76.

40. Ibid., p. 81.

41. 'L'Expérience morale et sociale des Polonais ne peut plus être effacée', *Les Nouvelles littéraires*, 14–20 October 1982, p. 8.

42. *Colloqui con Foucault*, p. 72.

43. Cited, Mauriac, *Et comme l'Espérance est violente*, p. 574.

44. Interview with Zygmunt Bauman.

45. Etienne Burin des Roziers, 'Une Rencontre à Varsovie', *Le Débat* 41, September–October 1986, pp. 133–34.

46. Interview with Zygmunt Bauman.

47. Interviews with Daniel Defert, Bernard Kouchner and Jacques Lebas.

48. Interviews with Jacques Lebas and Daniel Defert.

49. 'The Minimalist Self', p. 5.

50. Sheridan, 'Diary'.

51. Claude Mauriac, *Le Rire des pères dans les yeux des enfant*, Paris: Livre de poche, 1989, p. 197; 'Postscript' to *Death and the Labyrinth*, p. 172.

52. Interview with Daniel Defert.

53. Pierre Gascar, 'La Nuit de Sankt-Pauli', in *Portraits et souvenirs*, Paris: Gallimard, 1991.

54. Ibid., p. 64.

55. Foucault's translation was based on the second edition of 1780.

56. 'Thèse complementaire', p. 4. Copies of the typescript are available for

consultation in the Bibliothèque de la Sorbonne and the Bibliothèque du Saulchoir.

57. Ibid., p. 112.
58. Ibid., pp. 126–27.
59. *Les Mots et les choses*, Paris: Gallimard, 1966, pp. 396–97.
60. Cited, Boutang, *Louis Althusser*, p. 283.
61. Jean Lacouture, *Malraux: Une Vie dans le siècle*, Paris; Seuil, collection 'Points', 1976, pp. 337–38.
62. André Malraux, *La Tentation de l'Occident*, Paris: Livre de poche, 1972, p. 158.
63. See in particular Alexandre Kojève, *Introduction à la lecture de Hegel*, Paris: Gallimard, collection 'Tel', 1979, pp. 529–76.

Chapter 5

1. Jean-Paul Sartre, *Critique de la raison dialectique*, Paris: Gallimard, 1960, p. 17.
2. Mossuz-Lavau, *Les Lois de l'amour*, pp. 239–40.
3. Interview with Daniel Defert.
4. Interview with Daniel Defert.
5. 'Titres et travaux de Michel Foucault', Paris nd (1969).
6. 'Préface' *Histoire de la folie* (1961 edn.), p. ix.
7. References, other than to the preface, are to the 1976 'Tel' edition. Given its incomplete nature, it seems futile to use the English translation.
8. Blaise Pascal, *Pensées*, tr. A. J. Krailsheimer, Harmondsworth: Penguin, 1966, fragment 414 (Brunschwicg edition; 412 in Lafuma).
9. 'Préface', pp. i–ii.
10. Ibid., p. ii.
11. Ibid., p. iii.
12. Ibid., p. vi.
13. 'Deuxième Entretien: sur la façons d'écrire l'histoire', pp. 201–02.
14. *Histoire de la folie*, p. 366.
15. Ibid., p. 145.
16. Ibid., p. ix.
17. René Char, 'Partage formel' in *Fureur et mystère*, Paris: Gallimard, Poésies, 1967, p. 71. The earlier (acknowledged) quotation is on p. x: 'I will take away from things the illusion they produce to protect themselves from us, and will leave them the share they grant us' ('Suzerain', ibid., p. 193).
18. 'La Folie n'existe que dans une société'.
19. *Histoire de la folie*, p. 13.
20. Ibid., p. 27.
21. Ibid., p. 75. Foucault is citing Voltaire here. The definition is not as self-evident as he suggests, the original meaning of 'police' being simply the government or organisation of the *polis*.
22. Foucault does not devote much attention to the development of the factory; his analysis is to a large extent completed by the early chapters of Bernard Doray, *From Taylorism to Fordism. A Rational Madness*, tr. David Macey, London: Free Association Books, 1988.
23. *Histoire de la folie*, p. 58.

24. Ibid., p. 85.
25. Ibid., p. 106.
26. Ibid., p. 129.
27. Ibid., p. 181 ff.
28. Ibid., p. 364.
29. Foucault's choice of terminology is intriguing; *La Grande Peur de 1789* is the title of Georges Lefebvre's study of the panic that spread across France in 1789. It had recently been given a new relevance by the use Sartre makes of it in *Critique de la raison dialectique.*
30. *Histoire de la folie*, pp. 378–79.
31. Ibid., pp. 502–503.
32. Ibid., pp. 522–23.
33. Ibid., p. 115.
34. Ibid., p. 555.
35. Antonin Artaud, 'Le Pèse-nerfs' in *L'Ombilic des limbes, suivi de Le Pèse-nerfs et autres textes*, Paris: Gallimard, Collection 'Poèsies', 1968, p. 107.
36. 'La Folie, l'absence d'oeuvre', *La Table ronde* 196, May 1964, p. 11. This essay was reprinted as an appendix to the 1972 Gallimard edition of *Histoire de la folie*; it does not appear in the 'Tel' edition.
37. Ibid., p. 15.
38. Ibid., p. 19.
39. 'L'Obligation d'écrire', *Arts* 980, 11–17 November 1964, p. 3.
40. 'Van Gogh ou le suicidé de la société', in *Oeuvres complètes d'Antonin Artaud*, Paris: Gallimard, 1974, vol. 13, p. 17. For an introduction in English to Artaud, see Ronald Hayman, *Artaud and After*, Oxford University Press, 1977.
41. Georges Canguilhem, 'Sur *L'Histoire de la folie* en tant qu'événement', *Le Debat* 41, September–November 1986, p. 38.
42. 'Préface', p. x.
43. Interview with Georges Canguilhem.
44. Now in Georges Canguilhem, *Etudes d'histoire et de philosophie des sciences*, Paris: Vrin, 1989 (5th edn). The significance of the earlier reprint in *Cahiers pour l'analyse* 2, 1968, will be discussed below.
45. See especially his 'L'Objet de l'histoire des sciences' (1966) in *Etudes*, pp. 9–23.
46. Canguilhem, 'Qu'est-ce que la psychologie?', pp. 364–65, p. 381.
47. A copy of the original typescript may be consulted in the Bibliothèque du Saulchoir. The full text is given as 'Annexe 2' in Eribon, *Michel Foucault* (second, revised edition), pp. 358–61.
48. Canguilhem, 'Sur *L'Histoire de la folie* en tant qu'événement', *Le Débat*, 41, September–October 1986, p. 38.
49. Simon During, *Foucault and Literature: Towards A Genealogy of Writing*, London: Routledge, 1992, p. 32.
50. Brice Parain, *Recherches sur la nature et les fonctions du langage*, Paris: Gallimard, 1942; *Essais sur le logos platonicien*, Paris: Gallimard, 1942.
51. Annie Cohen-Solal, *Sartre 1905-1980*, Paris: Folio, 1985, pp. 222–24.
52. Dumézil, *Entretiens avec Didier Eribon*, p. 96; Pierre Assouline, *Gaston Gallimard*, Paris: Seuil, collection 'Points', 1985, pp. 126, 321.
53. For a brief profile, see 'Le Dernier Encyclopédiste: Roger Caillois, propos recueillis par Hector Biancotti', *Le Nouvel Observateur*, 4 November 1974, pp. 72–

73. On the Collège, see Denis Hollier, *Le Collège de sociologie*, Paris: Gallimard, collection 'Idées', 1979.

54. Blanchot, *Michel Foucault tel que je l'imagine*, p. 11.

55. Eribon, *Michel Foucault*, p. 130.

56. Ibid.

57. Michel Foucault and Arlette Farge, 'Le Style de l'histoire', *Libération*, 21 February 1984, p. 20.

58. Michel Winnock, preface to Philippe Ariès, *Un Historien du dimache*, Paris: Seuil, 1980, p. 9. See also the interview with André Burguière published as 'La Singulière Histoire de Philippe Ariès', *Le Nouvel Observateur*, 20 February 1978. *L'Enfant* is translated as *Centuries of Childhood*, London: Jonathan Cape, 1962.

59. Interviews with Philippe Meyer.

60. 'Philippe Ariès: Le Souci de la vérité', *Le Nouvel Observateur*, 17 February 1984, pp. 56–57.

61. Interview with Arlette Farge.

62. Ariès, *Un Historien*, p. 145.

63. Cited, Eribon, *Michel Foucault*, p. 155.

64. Gilles Deleuze, *Nietzsche et la philosophie*, Paris: PUF 1962. Deleuze's previous publications had been *David Hume, sa vie, son oeuvre*, with André Cresson, Paris: PUF, 1952: *Empirisme et subjectivité*, Paris: PUF, 1953, and *Instincts et institutions* (an edited anthology), Paris: Hachette, 1953.

65. Interview with Daniel Defert.

66. Gregory Elliott, *Althusser: The Detour of Theory*, London: Verso, 1987, p. 27.

67. See, for example, his *De l'Anathème au dialogue*, Paris: Editions sociales, 1965.

68. Eribon, *Michel Foucault*, p. 163.

69. Interview with Jean Duvignaud.

70. Interview with Pierre Vidal-Naquet.

71. Interview with Daniel Defert.

72. Aron, *Les Modernes*, pp. 216–17.

73. 'La Folie n'existe que dans une société'.

74. Eribon, *Michel Foucault*, pp. 136–37.

75. Interview with Pierre Macherey.

76. Aron, *Les Modernes*, p. 216.

77. Cited, Eribon, *Michel Foucault*, pp. 138–39.

78. See Maurice Blanchot, 'La Raison de Sade' in *Lautréamont et Sade*, Paris: Minuit, 1949.

79. See *Histoire de la folie*, pp. 32–33. The point is made by Roy Boyne, *Foucault and Derrida: The Other Side of Reason*, London, Unwin Hyman, 1990, p. 21.

80. 'Carceri e manicomi nel consegno del potere' (interview with Marco d'Erasmo), *Avanti*, 3 March 1974; cited, Mauriac, *Et comme l'Espérance est violente*, p. 403.

81. *Colloqui con Foucault*, pp. 43, 44.

82. Interview with Jean-Louis Ezine, *Les Nouvelles littéraires*, 17 March 1975, p. 3.

83. 'Vérité et pouvoir', Entretien avc M. Fontana, *L'Arc* 70, 1977, pp. 16–17.

84. Robert Castel, 'Les Aventures de la pratique', *Le Débat* 41, September–November 1986, p. 43.

85. 'La Folie n'existe que dans une société'.

86. Gaston Bachelard, letter of 1 August 1961 to Foucault, reproduced in *Michel Foucault: Une Histoire de la vérité*, p. 119.

87. Henry Amer, 'Michel Foucault: *Histoire de la folie à l'âge classique*', *Nouvelle Revue Française*, September 1961, pp. 530–31.
88. Maurice Blanchot, 'L'Oubli, la déraison', *Nouvelle Revue Française*, October 1961, pp. 679, 683, 686.
89. Roland Barthes, 'De Part et d'autre' in *Essais critiques*, pp. 168, 172.
90. Jean Lacroix, 'La Signification de la folie', *Le Monde*, 8 December 1961, p. 8. An expanded version appears in Lacroix's *Panorama de la philosophie française contemporaine*, Paris: PUF, 1966, pp. 208–16.
91. Octave Mannoni, *Les Temps modernes*, December 1961, pp. 802–05.
92. Robert Mandrou, 'Trois clefs pour comprendre la folie à l'âge classique', *Annales ESC*, 17 Années, no 4, July–August 1962, p. 761.
93. Ibid., p. 771.
94. Michel Serres, 'Géométrie de la folie', *Mercure de France*, August 1962, pp. 682, 686, 691.
95. Ibid., September 1962.
96. Eribon, *Michel Foucault*, p. 147.
97. Allan Megill, 'The reception of Foucault by historians', *Journal of the History of Ideas*, vol. 48, 1987, p. 126.
98. 'Le Mallarmé de J. -P. Richard, *Annales ESC*, vol. 19, no. 5, September–October 1964, pp. 996–1004.
99. John K. Simon, *Modern Language Notes*, vol. 78, 1963, pp. 85–88; Jacques Ehrmann, *French Review*, vol. 36, no. 1, October 1962, pp. 99–102.
100. *Madness and Civilization: A History of Insanity in the Age of Reason*, tr. Richard Howard, New York: Random House, 1965; London: Tavistock, 1967.
101. Richard Howard, 'The Story of Unreason', *Times Literary Supplement*, 6 October 1961, pp. 653–54.
102. Robert Castel, 'The two readings of *Histoire de la folie* in France', *History of the Human Sciences*, vol. 3, no. 1, February 1990, pp. 27–30; cf. the same author's 'Les Aventures de la pratique'.

Chapter 6

1. Klossowski's translation of Hölderlin's *Poèmes de la folie*, in collaboration with Pierre-Jean Jouve, first appeared in 1930 and was reprinted by Gallimard in 1963. His important translation of *Die fröhliche Wissenschaft* dates from 1954, and his version of Wittgenstein's *Tractatus* from 1961.
2. Leo Spitzer, 'Art du langage et linguistique' in *Etudes de style*, Paris: Gallimard, 1962, pp. 45–78. Original: '*Linguistics and Literary History*, Princeton University Press, 1948, pp. 1–39. Foucault had earlier collaborated with Daniel Rocher on a translation of Viktor von Weizsaecker, *Le Cycle de la structure (Der Gestaltkreis)*, Paris: Desclée de Brouwer, 1958.
3. Foucault's paper was published as 'Les Déviations religieuses et le savoir médical' in the conference proceedings: Jacques le Goff, ed., *Hérésies et sociétés dans l'Europe pré-industrielle 11–18 siècles*, Paris: Mouton, 1968, pp. 12–29.
4. Interview with Jean Piel.
5. Interview with Serge Fauchereau. See his 'Cummings', *Critique* 218, December 1964.

6. Eribon, *Michel Foucault*, p. 160. There is no record of the content of this lecture.
7. The Belgian lecture was on 'Langage et littérature' and deals with the same themes as the literary articles of this period. The typescript may be consulted in the Bibliothèque du Saulchoir, where it is catalogued at D1.
8. 'L'Eau et la folie', *Médecine et hygiène* (Geneva) 613, 23 October 1963, pp. 901–06; 'Wächter über die Nacht der Menschen', in Hanns Ludwig Spegg, ed., *Unterwegs mit Rolf Italiaander: Begegnungen, Betrachtungen, Bibliographie*, Hamburg: Freie Akademie der Kunst, 1963, pp. 46–49.
9. Preface to *Rousseau juge de Jean-Jacques: Dialogues*, Paris: Armand Colin, 1962, reviewed by M. Ciotti, *Studi Francesi*, vol. 8, 1964, p. 352.
10. Un Grand 'Roman de terreur', *France-Observateur*, 12 December 1963, p. 14, reprinted in Jean-Edern Hallier, *Chaque Matin qui se lève est une leçon de courage*, Paris: Editions libres, 1978, pp. 40–42. For Hallier's dubious account of his acquaintance with Foucault and for his very unpleasant account of the man he calls 'the disciplinarian Gandhi of the Latin Quarter', see his 'Cette Tête remarquable ne comprenait pas l'avenir', *Figaro Magazine*, 30 June–6 July 1984, pp. 76–77.
11. One of the most interesting exceptions to the rule of omission was the first chapter of John Rajchman, *Michel Foucault: The Freedom of Philosophy*, New York: Columbia University Press, 1985. The welcome appearance of During's *Foucault and Literature* does a lot to remedy the neglect of the literary Foucault.
12. *Nouvelle Revue Française*, December 1961, pp. 1123–24.
13. 'Le "Non" du père', *Critique* 178, March 1962, p. 201. The text under review is Jean Laplanche, *Hölderlin et la question du père*, Paris: PUF, 1961.
14. Ibid., 197.
15. Ibid., p. 204.
16. 'Un si cruel Savoir', *Critique* 182, July 1962, pp. 597–611 (on Crébillon and Reveroni); 'Distance, aspect, origine', *Critique* 198, November 1963, pp. 932–45 (on Sollers, *L'Intermédiare*, Pleynet, *Paysages en deux*, Baudry, *Les Images* and issues 1–14 of *Tel Quel*); 'Guetter le jour qui vient', *Nouvelle Revue Française* 130, October 1963, pp. 709–16 (on Laporte); 'Le Mallarmé de J.-P. Richard'.
17. 'La Bibliothèque fantastique', p. 107.
18. 'Le Langage à l'infini', *Tel Quel* 15, Autumn 1963, p. 48.
19. Ibid., p. 52. Borges's 'Library of Babel' is included in *Fictions*, tr. Anthony Kerrigan, London: Weidenfeld and Nicolson, 1962.
20. 'La Bibliothèque fantastique', p. 107.
21. 'Un si cruel Savoir', p. 597.
22. Alfred Jarry, *The Supermale*, tr. Barbara Wright, London: Cape Editions, 1968, p. 7.
23. 'Un si cruel Savoir', pp. 603–04.
24. Brisset's main works are *La Grammaire logique* (1878) and *La Science de dieu* (1900). For Brisset, see Jean-Jacques Lecercle, *Philosophy through the Looking-Glass*, London: Hutchinson, 1985, and *The Violence of Language*, London: Routledge, 1990.
25. André Breton, *Anthologie de l'humour noir*, Paris: Livre de poche, 1970, pp. 36–237.
26. 'Le Cycle des grenouilles', *Nouvelle Revue Française*, June 1962, pp. 1158, 1159.
27. Preface to Jean-Pierre Brisset, *La Grammaire logique*, Paris: Editions Tchou, 1970, reprinted in book form as *Sept Propos sur le septième ange*, Montpellier: Fata

Morgana, 1986. Other available texts by Brisset are *Les Origines humaines* (a revised version of *La Science de Dieu*), Paris: Baudouin, 1980, and *Le Mystère de dieu est accompli, Analytica*, vol. 31, 1983.

28. *Sept propos*, pp. 23–24.
29. See, however, the contributions of Raymond Bellour and Denis Hollier to the 1988 conference on Foucault, published as *Michel Foucault philosophe*, Paris: Seuil, 1989; see also Pierre Macherey, *A Quoi pense la littérature?*, Paris: PUF, 1990, pp. 177–92, and During, *Foucault and Literature*, pp. 74–80.
30. Postscript to *Death and the Labyrinth*, p. 185.
31. Rayner Heppenstall, *Raymond Roussel*, London: Calder and Boyars, 1966, p. 16.
32. Ferry, *Une Etude sur Raymond Roussel*; Michel Leiris, 'Conception et réalité chez Raymond Roussel', *Critique* 89, October 1954, see also his earlier 'Documents sur Raymond Roussel', *NRF* 259, April 1935.
33. Postscript, *Death and the Labyrinth*, p. 181.
34. Eribon, *Michel Foucault*, p. 173.
35. *Histoire de la folie*, p. 371.
36. Postscript, *Death and the Labyrinth*, p. 173.
37. 'Dire et voir chez Raymond Roussel', *Lettre ouverte* 4, Summer 1962, pp. 38–51.
38. Interview with Jean Piel.
39. 'La Métamorphose et le labyrinthe', *Nouvelle Revue Française* 124, April 1963, pp. 638–61; 'Pourquoi réédite-t-on l'oeuvre de Raymond Roussel? Un Précurseur de notre littérature moderne', *Le Monde*, 22 August 1964, p. 9.
40. Heppenstall, *Raymond Roussel*, p. 18.
41. Postscript, *Death and the Labyrinth*, pp. 184–85.
42. Ibid., p. 185.
43. Gilles Deleuze, *Foucault*, Paris: Minuit, 1986, p. 106n.
44. Michel Leiris, *La Règle du jeu I: Biffures*, Paris: Gallimard, 1948; *La Règle du jeu II: Fourbis*, Paris: Gallimard, 1955. The sequence is completed by two later volumes: *Fibrilles* (1966) and *Frêle Bruit* (1976).
45. *Raymond Roussel*, pp. 28–29.
46. Ibid., p. 22.
47. 'Pourquoi réédite-t-on l'oeuvre de Raymond Roussel?'
48. *Raymond Roussel*, p. 51.
49. Ibid., pp. 82–83.
50. Ibid., p. 23.
51. Ibid., pp. 102–03. The motif of minotaur and labyrinth also features in the discussion of Reveroni in 'Un si cruel Savoir'.
52. 'L'Arrière-fable', *L'Arc* 29, 1966, pp. 5–12.
53. 'Pourquoi réédite-t-on l'oeuvre de Raymond Roussel?'
54. *Raymond Roussel*, p. 61.
55. Ibid., p. 205.
56. Postscript, *Death and the Labyrinth*, p. 185.
57. Alan Sheridan, *Michel Foucault: The Will to Truth*, London: Tavistock, 1980, p. 37; J. G. Merquior, *Michel Foucault*, London: Fontana, 1985, p. 31.
58. Interview with Georges Canguilhem.
59. 'Entretien: Michel Foucault, *Les Mots et les choses*', in Raymond Bellour, *Le Livre des autres*, Paris: L'Herne, 1971, p. 139 (originally published in *Les Lettres françaises*, 31 March 1966).

60. *Naissance de la clinique*, Paris: PUF, 1963, p. v.
61. Ibid., p. vii.
62. Ibid., p. xiv.
63. Ibid., p. ix.
64. *Histoire de la folie*, p. ii.
65. *Raymond Roussel*, p. 207.
66. *Naissance de la clinique*, p. 197
67. Ibid., p. 182.
68. Jean Cavaillès, *Sur la Logique et la théorie de la science*, Paris: Librairie philosophique J. Vrin, 1987 (4th edn), p. 78, pp. 25–26. On the relevance of Cavaillès to Foucault, see Gutting, *Michel Foucault's Archaeology of Scientific Reason*, pp. 9–11.
69. *Naissance de la clinique*, p. 197.
70. Ibid., p. xi.
71. Ibid., p. 127.
72. Ibid., p. xv.
73. Bernauer, *Michel Foucault's Force of Flight*, p. 188.
74. *Naissance de la clinique*, p. 2.
75. Cited, ibid., p. 2.
76. Ibid., p. 3.
77. Ibid., p. 8.
78. Ibid., p. 14.
79. Ibid., p. 58.
80. Ibid., p. 29.
81. Ibid., p. 31.
82. Ibid., p. 92.
83. Ibid., p. 95.
84. Ibid., p. 149.
85. Ibid., p. 170.
86. 'Un si cruel Savoir', p. 602.
87. Ibid., p. 610.
88. *Naissance de la clinique*, p. 175.
89. Ibid., p. 147.
90. The other contributors were Alfred Metraux, Raymond Queneau, André Masson, Jean Bruno, Jean Piel, Jean Wahl and Philippe Sollers. For more recent studies of Bataille, see the material collected in Allan Stoekl, ed., *On Bataille, Yale French Studies* 78, 1990. For Bataille himself in English, see Allan Stoekl, ed., *Visions of Excess: Selected Writings 1927–1939*, University of Minneapolis Press, 1985.
91. 'Préface à la transgression, *Critique* 195–96, August–September 1963, pp. 751–69.
92. Now in Georges Bataille, *Oeuvres complètes*, vol. I, Paris: Gallimard, 1970.
93. 'Présentation', Georges Bataille, *Oeuvres complètes*, vol. I, p. 5.
94. 'Préface à la transgression', p. 751.
95. Ibid., p. 753.
96. Ibid., p. 754.
97. Ibid., p. 756.
98. Ibid., p. 761.
99. Ibid., p. 763.
100. Roland Barthes, 'La Métaphore de l'oeil', p. 771.

101. 'Préface', pp. 765–66.
102. *Naissance de la clinique*, p. 173.
103. Ibid., p. 176.
104. Ibid., pp. 201–02.
105. Alain Robbe-Grillet, 'Enigmes et transparence chez Raymond Roussel', *Critique* 199, December 1963, pp. 1027–33.
106. Yves Bertherat, *Esprit*, vol. 33, no. 1, January 1965, pp. 284–85, 286.
107. See, for example, Raphaël Sorin, 'Le Pendule de Foucault, ou le critique dans le labyrinthe', *Bizarre* 34–35, 1964, pp. 75–76; J. Bellemin-Noël, *Studi Francesi*, vol. 8, 1964, pp. 395–96; M. Lecomte, 'Signes kafkéens chez Roussel et Jules Verne, signes verniens chez Roussel', *Synthèses*, vol. 18, no. 207, 1963, pp. 95–98.
108. Philippe Sollers, 'Logicus Solus', *Tel Quel* 14, Summer 1963, pp. 46–50 and p. 50n.
109. F. N. L. Poynter, review of *Naissance de la clinique*, *History of Science* 3, 1964, pp. 140, 143.
110. François Dagognet, 'Archéologie ou histoire de la médecine', *Critique* 216, May 1965, pp. 436–47.
111. Bernard Kouchner, 'Un vrai Samuraï', in *Michel Foucault: Une Histoire de la vérité*, p. 85; interview with Bernard Kouchner.
112. Jacques Derrida, 'Cogito et histoire de la folie', in *L'Ecriture et la différence*, Paris: Seuil, 1967, p. 51.
113. Ibid., p. 52.
114. *Histoire de la folie*, pp. 56–59.
115. 'Cogito et histoire de la folie', p. 52.
116. For a full discussion of the respective readings of Descartes undertaken by Foucault and Derrida, see Boyne, *Foucault and Derrida*.
117. 'Cogito et histoire de la folie', p. 57.
118. Ibid., p. 85.
119. Ibid., pp. 69, 88.
120. Ibid., p. 95.
121. Interview with Daniel Defert.
122. Calvet, *Roland Barthes*, pp. 172–73.
123. 'Conversation', in Gérard Courant, ed., *Werner Schroeter*, Paris: Cinémathèque/Institut Goethe, 1982, p. 43.
124. 'Préface', *Histoire de la folie*, p. iv.
125. Cited, Eribon, *Michel Foucault*, p. 168.
126. Interview with Daniel Defert.
127. 'Déclaration', *Tel Quel* 1, 1960, p. 3.
128. Julia Kristeva, *La Révolution du langage poétique*, Paris: Seuil, 1974.
129. Philippe Sollers, '*Tel Quel* aujourd'hui', *France nouvelle*, 31 May 1967, cited Stephen Heath, *The Nouveau Roman*, London: Elek, 1972, p. 221.
130. Cited, ibid., p. 219.
131. 'Débat sur le roman', *Tel Quel* 17, Spring 1964, p. 12. Foucault's self-description (*un homme naïf avec mes gros sabots de philosophe*) is not easy to translate; '*je le vois venir avec ses gros sabots*' is roughly equivalent to 'I can see what he's after', but Foucault is also playing on the clumsiness implied by *sabots* – clogs.
132. Ibid., pp. 12–13.
133. Ibid., p. 14.
134. Ibid., p. 38.

135. Ibid., p. 45.
136. 'Débat sur la poésie', *Tel Quel* 17, Spring 1964, pp. 72, 73.

Chapter 7

1. 'Nietzsche, Freud, Marx', in *Cahiers de Royaumont: Nietzsche*, Paris: Minuit, 1967, p. 186.
2. Friedrich Nietzsche, *Daybreak*, tr. R. J. Hollingdale, Cambridge University Press, 1982, no. 446, no. 2. The first fragment is cited by Foucault.
3. 'Nietzsche, Freud, Marx,' p. 186–87.
4. Friedrich Nietzsche, *Beyond Good and Evil*, tr. R. J. Hollingdale, Harmondsworth; Penguin, 1990, no. 39.
5. 'Nietzsche, Freud, Marx', p. 189.
6. Ibid., p. 196.
7. Gilles Deleuze, 'Fendre les choses, fendre les mots', in *Pourparleurs*, Paris: Minuit, 1990, p. 115; originally published in *Libération*, 2–3 September 1986.
8. 'Nietzsche, Freud, Marx', p. 191.
9. Gilles Deleuze, 'Sur la Volonté de puissance et l'éternel retour', pp. 276–77.
10. Gilles Deleuze and Michel Foucault, 'Introduction générale', in Friedrich Nietzsche, *Oeuvres philosophiques. Vol 5: Le Gai Savoir*, Paris; Gallimard, 1967, pp. i–iv.
11. Claude Jannoud, 'Michel Foucault et Gilles Deleuze veulent rendre à Nietzsche son vrai visage', *Le Figaro littéraire*, 15 September 1966, p. 7. See also the interview with Jacqueline Piatier, 'La Publication des *Oeuvres complètes* de Nietzsche: La Volonté de puissance, texte capital, mais incertain, va disparaître, nous déclare Michel Foucault', *Le Monde*, 24 May 1967, 'supplément', p. vii.
12. 'Claude Jannoud, 'Michel Foucault et Gilles Deleuze . . .'.
13. Pierre Klossowski, 'Oubli et anamnèse dans l'expérience vécue de l'éternel retour du Même', *Nietzsche*, pp. 227–44.
14. Alain Arnaud, *Pierre Klossowski*, Paris: Seuil, 1990, p. 188. This is perhaps the best introduction to Klossowski; it is also one of the rare sources for reliable biographical information about him. See also the catalogue to the retrospective exhibition *Pierre Klossowski*, Paris: Editions La Différence/Centre National des Arts Plastiques, 1990.
15. The trilogy, published in one volume by Gallimard in 1965, comprises *Roberte, ce soir* (1954), *La Révocation de l'édit de Nantes* (1959) and *Le Souffleur, ou le Théâtre de société* (1960).'
16. See, for example, Anne-Marie Dardigna, *Les Châteaux d'Eros, ou l'infortune du sexe des femmes*, Paris: Maspero, 1980.
17. Cited, Arnaud, p. 26.
18. Cited, ibid., pp. 48–49, 52.
19. 'La Prose d'Actéon', *Nouvelle Revue Française* 135, March 1964, p. 447; Pierre Klossowski, 'Sur Quelques Themes fondamentaux de la "Gaya Scienza" de Nietzsche' (1958), in his *Un Si Funeste Désir*, Paris: Gallimard, 1963, p. 22.
20. Nietzsche, *The Gay Science*, p. 273.
21. *Les Lois de l'hospitalité*, pp. 146–47.
22. Gilles Deleuze, *Logique du sens*, Paris: 10/18, 1973, p. 382.

23. Interviews with Denise and Pierre Klossowski.
24. Arnaud, p. 19.
25. 'Les Mots qui saignent', *L'Express*, 29 August 1964, p. 21.
26. 'La Prose d'Actéon,' p. 451.
27. *La Pensée du dehors*, p. 19.
28. Arnaud, p. 139.
29. *Le Grand Renfermement II*, Zurich, Galerie Lelong, reproduced in *Pierre Klossowski*, p. 153. There is also a related 'Ship of Fools', ex. cat. Interview with Pierre Klossowski.
30. Alain Badiou, *Almagestes*, Paris: Seuil, 1964.
31. 'Philosophie et psychologie', *Dossiers pédagogiques de la radio-télévision scolaire*, 15–27 February, 1965, p. 20.
32. 'Philosophie et vérité', *Dossiers pédagogiques de la radio-télévision scolaire*, 27 March 1965, pp. 1–11.
33. Communication from Chaim Katz and Roberto Machado.
34. 'Lettre à Roger Caillois' (25 May 1966), reproduced, *Cahiers pour un temps. Hommage à R. Caillois*, Paris: Centre Georges Pompidou, 1981, p. 228.
35. 'La Prose du monde', *Diogène* 53, January–March 1966, pp. 20–41; 'The Prose of the World', tr. Victor Velen, *Diogenes* 53, Spring 1966, pp. 17–37.
36. During, *Foucault and Literature*, p. 239, citing Susan Sontag's *Against Interpretation*.
37. 'Du Pouvoir', interview with Pierre Boncenne (1978), *L'Express*, 13 July 1984, p. 58.
38. Sheridan, *The Will to Truth*, p. 47; Eribon, *Michel Foucault*, p. 183.
39. 'Foucault comme de petits pains', *Le Nouvel Observateur*, 10 August 1966, p. 58.
40. 'Les Succès du mois', *L'Express*, 8–14 August 1966, p. 32.
41. *Le Nouvel Observateur*, 26 May 1966, p. 33.
42. 'Sade mon prochain' (unsigned), *Le Nouvel Observateur*, 18 May 1966, p. 31. A revised version of Klossowski's lecture was published in *Tel Quel* 28, and then reprinted as 'Le Philosophe-scélérat' in the revised edition of his *Sade mon prochain*, Paris: Seuil, 1967. Translated by Alphonso Lingis as 'The Philosopher Villain' in *Sade My Neighbour*, Evanston, Illinois: Northwestern University Press, 1991.
43. Eribon, *Michel Foucault*, p. 182.
44. Marietti, *Michel Foucault*, p. 52.
45. *The Order of Things*, p. viii.
46. 'Entrevista com Michel Foucault par Sergio Paolo Rouanet e José Guilhermo Merquior', *O Homen e o discorso: A Arqueologia de Michel Foucault*, Rio de Janeiro: Tempo Brasiliero, 1971, pp. 17–42.
47. Dreyfus and Rabinow, *Michel Foucault*, p. vii.
48. *Maladie mentale et personnalité*, p. 26.
49. 'Thèse supplémentaire pour le Doctorat ès lettres', p. 4.
50. Bellour, 'Entretien avec Michel Foucault', p. 139.
51. *L'Archéologie du savoir*, p. 173.
52. 'Réponse au Cercle d'épistémologie', *Cahiers pour l'analyse* 8, Summer 1968, p. 19.
53. 'Monstrosities in Criticism', *Diacritics* 1, Fall 1971, p. 60.
54. Bernauer, *Michel Foucault's Force of Flight*, pp. 45, 202. With remarkable erudition, Bernauer traces the reference to Kant's *Welches sind die wirklichen Fortschrifte, die die Metaphysik seit Leibnitzens und Wolfs Zeiten in Deutschland gemacht hat?* in vol. 20 of the 1942 edition of the *Gesammelte Schriften*.

55. *The Order of Things*, pp. xi–xii. This foreword has not been published in French.
56. *Les Mots et les choses*, p. 177.
57. Ibid., p. 179.
58. Ibid., p. 214.
59. Ibid., p. 7.
60. *Les Mots et les choses*, p. 19.
61. Ibid., p. 31.
62. Eribon, *Michel Foucault*, p. 182.
63. *Les Mots et les choses*, p. 33.
64. Ibid., p. 42.
65. Ibid., p. 50.
66. Ibid., p. 55.
67. Ibid.
68. Ibid., p. 13.
69. Brice Parain, 'Michel Foucault: *L'Archéologie du savoir*', *Nouvelle Revue Française*, November 1969, pp. 726, 727.
70. *Les Mots et les choses*, p. 60.
71. Ibid., p. 61.
72. Ibid., p. 89.
73. See in particular Gutting's study, pp. 139–216.
74. *Les Mots et les choses*, pp. 94–95.
75. Ibid., p. 100.
76. Preface to Antoine Arnaud and Pierre Nicolle, *Grammaire générale et raisonnée*, Paris: Paulet, 1969, pp. iii–xxvii. An early version of the preface was published in *Langages* 7, September 1967, pp. 7–15.
77. *Les Mots et les choses*, p. 106.
78. Ibid., p. 107.
79. Ibid., p. 133.
80. Ibid., pp. 142, 157.
81. Ibid., p. 215.
82. Ibid., p. 177.
83. Ibid., p. 268.
84. Ibid., p. 274.
85. Ibid., p. 281.
86. Ibid., p. 59.
87. Ibid., p. 313.
88. Ibid., p. 220–21.
89. *Les Mots et les choses*, p. 398.
90. 'La Folie, l'absence d'oeuvre', p. 13.
91. The same interpretation is given by Judith P. Butler, *Figures of Desire*, p. 175.
92. See also the minor interview with Marie-Geneviève Foy, 'Qu'est-ce qu'un philosophe?', *Connaissance des arts* 22, Autumn 1966.
93. Chapsal, 'Entretien avec Michel Foucault', p. 137.
94. Ibid., p. 141.
95. *La Quinzaine littéraire*, 1–15 July 1967, p. 19.
96. *Naissance de la clinique*, p. xiii (1963), p. xiii (1972); for notes on the revisions, see Appendix 2 in Bernauer's *Michel Foucault's Force of Flight*.
97. Louis Althusser, 'Philosophy and the Spontaneous Philosophy of the Scientists',

tr. Warren Montag in the volume of the same title.

98. 'Entretien', *La Quinzaine littéraire*, 16 May 1966, pp. 14–15.

99. 'L'Homme est-il mort?' *Arts et loisirs* 38, 15 June 1966, p. 8.

100. De Certeau, 'The Black Sun of Language: Foucault' in *Heterologies*, p. 171.

101. 'C'était un nageur entre deux mots', *Arts et loisirs* 54, 5–11 October 1966, pp. 8–9.

102. Simone de Beauvoir, *Les Belles Images*, Paris: Folio, 1976, p. 94.

103. 'Simone de Beauvoir présente *Les Belles Images*', interview with Jacqueline Piatier, *Le Monde*, 23 December 1966, p. 1.

104. Letter of 4 June 1966 to Magritte, in André Blavier, ed., René Magritte, *Ecrits complets*, Paris: Flammarion, 1972, p. 521.

105. The essay appeared in *Cahiers du chemin* 2, January 1968, pp. 79–105; *Ceci n'est pas une pipe*, Montpellier: Fata Morgana, 1973, 1986. Magritte's two letters are reproduced, pp. 83–90.

106. Jean Lacroix, 'Fin de l'humanisme?', *Le Monde*, 9 June 1966.

107. François Châtelet, 'L'Homme, ce Narcisse incertain', *La Quinzaine littéraire*, 1 April 1966, p. 19.

108. Gilles Deleuze, 'L'Homme, une existence douteuse', *Le Nouvel Observateur*, 1 June 1966.

109. Madeleine Chapsal, 'La plus grande Révolution depuis l'existentialisme', *L'Express*, 23–29 May 1966, p. 121.

110. Robert Kanters, *Le Figaro littéraire*, 23 June 1966, p. 5.

111. François Mauriac, 'Bloc-notes', *Le Figaro*, 15 September 1966.

112. Jacques Brosse, 'L'Etude du language v-a-t-elle libérer un homme nouveau?', *Arts et loisirs*, 35, 25–31 May 1966.

113. Jean-Marie Domenach, 'Une Nouvelle Passion', *Esprit* 7–8, July–August 1966, pp. 77–78.

114. *L'Archéologie du savoir*, p. 19n.

115. 'Jean-Paul Sartre répond', *L'Arc* 30 October 1966, pp. 87–88.

116. Sylvie Le Bon, 'Un Positiviste désespéré'. *Les Temps Modernes* 248, January 1967, pp. 1299–319.

117. Ibid., p. 1299.

118. Ibid., pp. 1303, 1304.

119. Ibid., p. 1313.

120. Michel Amiot, 'Le Relativisme culturaliste de Michel Foucault', *Les Temps Modernes* 248, January 1967, pp. 1295, 1296. The Spengler association was also made by Maurice Corvez, 'Le Structuralisme de Michel Foucault', *Revue thomiste*, vol 68, 1968, p. 11.

121. Cited, Eribon, *Michel Foucault*, p. 190.

122. Jeannette Colombel, 'Les Mots de Foucault et les choses', *La Nouvelle Critique*, May 1967, p. 8.

123. Ibid., p. 13.

124. *Les Mots et le choses*, p. 274.

125. Olivier Revault d'Allonnes, 'Michel Foucault: Les Mots contre les choses', in *Structuralisme et marxisme*, Paris: 10/18, 1970, pp. 26, 34; originally published in *Raison présente* 2, 1967.

126. Ibid., p. 37.

127. Pierre Burgelin, 'L'Archéologie du savoir', *Esprit*, May 1967, pp. 859, 860.

128. Jean-Marie Domenach, 'Le système et la personne', ibid., pp. 776, 777.

129. Jean-Paul Sartre, 'M. François Mauriac et la liberté' (1939) in *Situations I*, Paris: Gallimard, 1947, p. 57.
130. Georges Canguilhem, 'Mort de l'homme ou épuisement du cogito?', *Critique* 242, July 1967, p. 599.
131. Ibid., p. 608.
132. Ibid., p. 617.
133. Interview with Daniel Defert.
134. *Colloqui con Foucault*, p. 51.
135. Ibid., p. 50.
136. Anne Coffin Hanson, *Manet and the Modern Tradition*, New Haven and London: Yale University Press, 1979, p. 119.
137. Chapsal, 'Entretien avec Michel Foucault', p. 15.
138. Eribon, *Michel Foucault*, p. 160.
139. For its content and importance, see Sadie Plant, *The Most Radical Gesture: The Situationist International in a Postmodern Age*, London: Routledge, 1992, pp. 94–96.
140. 'La Pensée du dehors', *Critique* 229, June 1966, pp. 523–46. In 1986, the article was reprinted in book form by Fata Morgana, Montpellier; references are to that edition.
141. 'La Pensée du dehors', pp. 12–13.
142. Ibid., p. 17.
143. Ibid., p. 19.
144. Ibid., p. 41.
145. 'Vérité et pouvoir', *L'Arc* 70, 1977; *La Crise dans la tête*, p. 23.

Chapter 8

1. Interview with Georges Canguilhem.
2. Communication from Chaim Katz and Roberto Machado.
3. Eribon, *Michel Foucault*, p. 169.
4. Ibid., p. 199.
5. Interview with Daniel Defert.
6. Jean Daniel, *La Blessure*, Paris: Grasset, 1992, p. 183.
7. Gérard Fellous, 'Michel Foucault: "La Philosophie 'structuraliste' permet de diagnostiquer ce qu'est aujourd'hui",' *La Presse de Tunis*, 12 April 1967, p. 3.
8. Cited, Mauriac, *Mauriac et fils*, p. 235.
9. Interview with Denise and Pierre Klossowski.
10. 'Des Espaces autres', *Architecture-Mouvement-Continuité*, 5, October 1984.
11. Baltimore, Johns Hopkins University Press, 1957.
12. Ariès's essay appeared in vol. CIX, 1966; reprinted in his *Essais sur l'histoire de la mort en Occident du Moyen Age à nos jours*, Paris: Seuil, 1975. The most attractive introduction to this aspect of Ariès's work is the richly illustrated *Images of Man and Death*, tr. Janet Lloyd, Cambridge, Massachusetts: Harvard University Press, 1985.
13. Wilfrid Knapp, *Tunisia*, London: Thames and Hudson, 1970, p. 181.
14. Daniel, *La Blessure*, pp. 164–65.
15. Interview with Jean Duvignaud; it is also claimed by Monique Bel, *Maurice Clavel*,

Paris: Bayard Editions, 1992, p. 221, that it was through Clavel that Foucault and Daniel first met.

16. Daniel, *La Blessure*, p. 182. The most readily accessible of Berque's books in English is his *Arab Rebirth: Pain and Ecstasy*, tr. Quintin Hoare, London: Al Saqi books, 1983.

17. Daniel, *La Blessure*, p. 19.

18. Jean Daniel, 'Le Flux des souvenirs', *Michel Foucault: Une Histoire de la vérité*, p. 58.

19. Jean Daniel, 'La Passion de Michel Foucault', *Le Nouvel Observateur*, 24 June 1984.

20. Interview with Jean Duvignaud.

21. Interview with Daniel Defert.

22. Interview with Catherine von Bülow.

23. Cited, Daniel, *La Blessure*, p. 184.

24. M. B. (Marc Beigbeder), 'En suivant le cours de Foucault', *Esprit*, June 1967, pp. 1066–67.

25. Jalila Hafsia, *Visages et rencontres*, Tunis, 1981, p. 51.

26. 'La Bibliothèque fantastique', p. 107.

27. Published in the French embassy's *Mission culturelle Française Information*, 10 April–10 May 1978; extracts republished in *La Presse de Tunis*, 10 April 1987, on the occasion of a three-day conference on the work of Foucault.

28. *L'Archéologie du savoir*, pp. 127–28.

29. Interview with Daniel Defert.

30. 'Linguistique et sciences sociales', *Revue tunisienne des sciences sociales* 19, December 1969, p. 251.

31. Samir Amin, *The Maghreb in the Modern World*, tr. Michael Perl, Harmondsworth: Penguin, 1970, pp. 198–210.

32. Lapassade's main interest at this time was in the traditional forms of psychodrama typified by the trance states induced by the *macumba* and *candomblé* of Latin America and the *stambuli* of North Africa. See his *Essai sur la transe*, Paris: Editions Universitaires, 1976.

33. Georges Lapassade, *Joyeux Tropiques*, Paris: Stock, 1978, pp. 51–52.

34. Georges Lapassade, *Le Bordel andalou*, Paris: L'Herne, 1971.

35. Lapassade, *Joyeux tropiques*, pp. 55–56.

36. François Châtelet, 'Foucault précise sa méthode', *La Quinzaine litteraire* 58, 1 October 1968, p. 28.

37. Bel, *Maurice Clavel*, pp. 117–19.

38. Ibid., pp. 220, 221.

39. Mauriac, *Et comme l'Espérance est violente*, p. 564.

40. Cited, Bel, *Maurice Clavel*, pp. 222–23.

41. 'Foucault répond à Sartre', *La Quinzaine littéraire* 46, 1–15 March 1969, p. 21.

42. Une Mise au point de Michel Foucault', *La Quinzaine littéraire*, 47, 15–31 March 1968, p. 21.

43. Interview with Didier Eribon.

44. 'Correspondance. A Propos des "Entretiens sur Foucault"', *La Pensée* 139, May–June 1968. For the Montpellier debates, see 'Entretiens sur Foucault', *La Pensée* 137, February 1968.

45. See *Esprit*, May 1967.

46. Interview with Jean-Marie Domenach, then its editor.

47. 'Réponse à une question', *Esprit* 371, May 1968, pp. 850–74.

48. Ibid., p. 851.
49. Ibid., p. 858.
50. Ibid., p. 871.
51. By far the best study to date is Gregory Elliott, *Althusser: The Detour of Theory*, London: Verso, 1987.
52. For a cogent account of controversies over humanism and theoretical anti-humanism, see Kate Soper, *Humanism and Anti-Humanism*, London: Hutchinson, 1986.
53. Althusser, 'A Letter to the Translator', *For Marx*, p. 256. The letter was never published in France in Althusser's lifetime.
54. The others were Roger Establet, Pierre Macherey and Jacques Rancière.
55. Interview with Etienne Balibar.
56. Eminently readable, if at times superficial, accounts of this period can be found in Hervé Hamon and Patrick Rotman, *Génération. Vol I. Les Années de rêve*, Paris: Seuil, 1987.
57. The editorial board consisted of Jacques-Alain Miller, Alain Grosrichard, Jean-Claude Milner, Alain Badiou and François Regnault. Most were also members of Lacan's Ecole Freudienne de Paris.
58. Althusser, *L'Avenir dure longtemps*, pp. 326, 344–45. For the purloined concept itself, see Jacques-Alain Miller, 'Action de la structure', *Cahiers pour l'analyse* 9, Summer 1968, pp. 93–105.
59. Roudinesco, *Jacques Lacan & Co.*, p. 398.
60. 'A Michel Foucault', *Cahiers pour l'analyse* 9, Summer 1968, p. 5.
61. 'Réponse au Cercle d'épistémologie', ibid., pp. 9–40.
62. 'Nouvelles Questions', ibid., pp. 42, 44.
63. *Les Mots et les choses*, p. 13n.
64. 'Réponse à une question', p. 854n.
65. 'La Naissance d'un monde' (interview with Jean-Michel Palmier), *Le Monde*, 3 May 1969, p. viii.
66. 'Truth, Power, Self', p. 11.
67. Frank Kermode, 'Crisis Critic', *New York Review of Books*, 17 May 1973, p. 37.
68. *L'Archéologie du savoir*, p. 27.
69. Ibid., p. 64 and n.
70. 'Nietzsche, Freud, Marx', pp. 198–99.
71. *L'Archéologie du savoir*, p. 74. and n.
72. Ibid., p. 9.
73. Ibid., p. 12.
74. Ibid., p. 38.
75. Ibid., p. 84.
76. Ibid., p. 64.
77. Ibid., p. 115.
78. Ibid., p. 107. See J. I. Austin, *How to Do Things with Words*, Oxford University Press, 1962, and John Searle, *Speech Acts*, Cambridge University Press, 1972. Neither book was available in French translation when Foucault was working on *L'Archéologie*. In a later correspondence with Searle, Foucault accepted that his statements were indeed speech acts, adding: 'I wanted to underline the fact that I saw them under a different angle than yours'; letter of 15 May 1979 to Searle, cited, Dreyfus and Rabinow, *Michel Foucault*, p. 46n.

79. *L'Archéologie du savoir*, p. 126.
80. Ibid., pp. 215–55.
81. Ibid., p. 250.
82. Voeltzel, *Vingt ans et après*, p. 72.
83. Cited, Eribon, *Michel Foucault*, p. 205.
84. *Colloqui con Foucault*, p. 73.
85. Ibid., p. 72.
86. Knapp, *Tunisia*, p. 184.
87. *Colloqui con Foucault*, p. 71.
88. Interview with Daniel Defert.
89. 'Folie et civilisation', cassette recording, Bibliothèque du Saulchoir, C32.
90. Régis Debray, *Contribution aux discoure et cérémonies du dixième anniversaire*, Paris: Maspero, 1978; Pierre Goldman, *Souvenirs obscurs d'un Juif polonais né en France*, Paris: Seuil, 1977, pp. 70–73.
91. *Colloqui con Foucault*, p. 74.
92. The literature on May is enormous. For relevant accounts in English, see Patrick Seale and Maureen McConville, *French Revolution 1968*, Harmondsworth: Penguin in association with William Heinemann Ltd, 1968 and Charles Posner, ed., *Reflections on the Revolution in France: 1968*, Harmondsworth: Penguin, 1970. The latter contains a useful chronology of events.
93. Daniel, *La Blessure*, pp. 184–85.
94. Cited, Eribon, *Michel Foucault*, p. 204.
95. Burin des Roziers, 'Une Rencontre à Varsovie', pp. 134–35.
96. Interview with Didier Anzieu.

Chapter 9

1. Pinguet, 'Les Années d'apprentissage', p. 126.
2. 'Qu'est-ce qu'un auteur?' *Bulletin de la Société française de philosophie*, 63, July–September 1969, pp. 73–104.
3. A. Geismar, S. July, E. Morance, *Vers la Guerre civile*, Paris: Editions premières, 1969.
4. Interview with Hélène Cixous.
5. Robert Castel, 'The two readings of *Histoire de la folie* in France', p. 28.
6. *Surveiller et punir*, Paris: 1975, p. 229.
7. 'Présentation', *Garde-fous arrêtez de vous serrer les coudes*, revised edn, Paris: Maspero, 1975, p. 5.
8. For a general account, see Robert Boyers and Robert Orril, eds., *Laing and Anti-Psychiatry*, Harmondsworth: Penguin, 1972.
9. For the controversy that has developed around readings based on this translation, see Colin Gordon, '*Histoire de la folie*: an unknown book by Michel Foucault', *History of the Human Sciences*, vol. 3, no. 1 February 1990, pp. 3–26, and the various 'responses' published in the same issue and in vol. 3, no. 3, October 1990.
10. David Cooper, 'Introduction', *Madness and Civilization*, p. vii.
11. Ibid., p. viii.
12. *New Statesman*, 16 June 1967, p. 844. Cooper's article was a review of Lacan's *Ecrits*, Thomas Scheff, *Being Mentally Ill*, K. Soddy and R. H. Ahrenfeld, *Mental*

Health and Contemporary Thought and Abraham Levinson, *The Mentally-Retarded Child.*

13. R. D. Laing, 'The invention of madness', *New Statesman*, 16 June 1967, p. 843.
14. Edmund Leach, 'Imprisoned by madmen', *Listener*, 8 June 1967, pp. 752–53; Hugh Freeman, 'Anti-psychiatry through history', 4 May 1967, pp. 665–66.
15. W. Ll. Parry-Jones, *British Journal of Social and Clinical Psychology* 8, 1969, p. 191.
16. 'Carceri e manicomi nel consegno del potere'.
17. David Cooper, ed., *The Dialectics of Liberation*, Harmondsworth: Penguin, 1968.
18. Proceedings published as 'Enfance aliénée', *Recherches*, September 1967, and 'Enfance aliénée II', *Recherches*, December 1968.
19. R. D. Laing and David Cooper, *Reason and Violence*, London: Laing's *The Divided Self*, London; Tavistock, 1959, is subtitled 'An Existential Study in Sanity and Madness' and its first chapter discusses 'The Existential-Phenomenological Foundations for a Science of Persons'.
20. On the origins and history of Evolution Psychiatrique, see Elisabeth Roudinesco, *La Bataille de cent ans. Histoire de la psychanalyse en France*, vol. I, Paris: Ramsay, 1982, pp. 413–31.
21. 'Du Pouvoir' (interview with Pierre Boncenne, 1978), *L'Express*, 13 July 1984; *Colloqui con Foucault*, p. 44.
22. 'La Conception idéologique de l'*Histoire de la folie* de Michel Foucault', *Evolution psychiatrique*, Tôme 36, fasc. 2, April–June 1971, pp. 225, 226.
23. Henri Ey, 'Commentaires critiques sur l'*Histoire de la folie* de Michel Foucault', ibid., pp. 257, 256.
24. Henri Sztulman, 'Folie ou maladie mentale', ibid., pp. 268, 277.
25. Georges Daumézon, 'Lecture historique de l'*Histoire de la folie*', ibid., pp. 228, 239.
26. Ibid., p. 282.
27. 'Intervention de E. Minkowski', ibid., pp. 218, 283.
28. 'La Situation de Cuvier dans l'histoire de la biologie', *Revue de l'histoire des sciences et de leurs applications*, vol. XXIII, no. 1, January–March 1970, pp. 63–92, followed by a transcript of the ensuing discussion.
29. 'Ariane s'est pendue', *Le Nouvel Observateur*, 31 March 1969, pp. 36–37.
30. 'Maxime Defert', *Les Lettres françaises*, 8–14 January 1969, p. 28.
31. 'La Naissance d'un monde', interview with Jean-Michel Palmier, *Le Monde*, 3 May 1969, p. viii. See also the interview with Jean-Jacques Brochier, 'Michel Foucault explique son dernier livre', *Magazine Littéraire* 28, April–May 1969, pp. 23–25.
32. François Châtelet, 'L'Archéologue du savoir', *La Quinzaine littéraire*, 1–15 March 1969, pp. 3–4.
33. Jean Duvignaud, 'Ce qui parle en nous, pour nous, mais sans nous', *Le Nouvel Observateur*, 21 April 1969, pp. 42–43.
34. Gilles Deleuze, 'Un Nouvel Archiviste', *Critique* 274, March 1970, pp. 195–209, reprinted in volume form, Montpellier: Fata Morgana, 1972. Expanded and republished under the same title for republication as the first chapter of *Foucault*, Paris: Minuit, 1986, and cited after that edition.
35. Ibid., p. 28, 22.
36. Ibid., p. 30.
37. A revised version of the article appeared as 'Sur L'Archéologie du savoir (à propos de Michel Foucault)' in Lecourt's *Pour Une Critique de l'épistémologie*, Paris:

Maspero, 1972, pp. 98–133. Interview with Dominique Lecourt.
38. Ibid., pp. 133, 113.
39. Georges Canguilhem, *Idéologie et rationnalité dans l'histoire des sciences de la vie* (second edn), Paris: Vrin, 1988, pp. 9–10.
40. 'Carceri et manicomi nel consegno del potere', p. 6.
41. Althusser, *For Marx*, pp. 87–128.
42. V. I. Lenin, *What is to be done? Selected Works*, Moscow: Progress Publishers, 1963, vol. 1, p. 150.
43. Michèle Manceaux, *Les 'Maos' en France*, Paris: Gallimard, 1972, p. 49.
44. Ibid., p. 20.
45. Ibid., p. 23.
46. Simone Weil, *La Condition ouvrière*, Paris: Gallimard, 1951.
47. Robert Linhart, *L'Etabli*, Paris: Minuit, 1978; interview with Daniel Defert.
48. Interview with Daniel Defert.
49. Emmanuel Terray, 'Nous n'irons pas voter', *Le Monde*, 12 January 1969, p. 10.
50. Hélène Cixous, *L'Exil de James Joyce ou l'art du remplacement*, Paris: Grasset, 1968. Cixous's first work of fiction was *Le Prénom de dieu*, a collection of short stories published in 1967.
51. Eribon, *Michel Foucault*, pp. 216–17.
52. Roudinesco, *Jacques Lacan & Co.*, pp. 550–51. See J. Laplanche and J. B. Pontalis, *The Language of Psycho-analysis*, tr. Donald Nicholson-Smith, London: The Hogarth Press and The Institute of Psycho-analysis, 1973.
53. Roudinesco, *Jacques Lacan & Co*, pp. 552–53.
54. Interview with Robert Castel.
55. Jacques Lacan, *Le Séminaire. Livre XVII. L'Envers de la psychanalyse*, Paris: Seuil, 1991, p. 240.
56. 'Une Petite Histoire', *Le Nouvel Observateur*, 17 March 1969, p. 43.
57. 'Précision', *Le Nouvel Observateur*, 31 May 1969.
58. Eribon, *Michel Foucault*, p. 216.
59. Interviews with Daniel Defert and Etienne Balibar.
60. Cited, Sherry Turkle, *Psychoanalytic Politics: Jacques Lacan and Freud's French Revolution*, London: Burnet Books in association with André Deutsch, 1979, p. 175.
61. Friedrich Nietzsche, *Twilight of the Idols*, tr. R. J. Hollingdale, Harmondsworth: Penguin, 1968, p. 110.
62. See Jean-Paul Sartre, 'La Jeunesse piégée', in *Situations VIII*, Paris; Gallimard, 1972, pp. 239–61.
63. *Le Monde*, 12 February 1969.
64. Ibid.
65. Hamon and Rotman, *Génération II*, pp. 57–58.
66. Ibid., p. 58.
67. Cited, Roudinesco, *Jacques Lacan & Co*, p. 558. The book in question is Michèle Manceaux and Madeleine Chapsal, *Les Professeurs, pour quoi faire?*, Paris: Seuil, 1970. See *L'Express*, 16–22 March 1970.
68. Interview with Bernard Doray.
69. Interview with Jacques Rancière.
70. Interview with Etienne Balibar.
71. Interview with Jeannette Colombel.

72. Letter of 3 July 1969 to Klossowski, in *Cahiers pour un temps: Pierre Klossowski*, Paris: Centre Georges Pompidou, 1985. See Pierre Klossowski, *Nietzsche et le cercle vicieux*, Paris: Mercure de France, 1969.

73. 'Le Piège de Vincennes', propos recueillis par Patrick Loriot, *Le Nouvel Observateur*, 9 February 1970.

74. 'Jean Hyppolite (1907–1968)', *Revue de métaphysique et de morale*, vol. 74, no. 2, April–July 1969, pp. 131–36.

75. Ibid., pp. 131–32.

76. Jean Hyppolite, 'Projet d'enseignement d'histoire de la pensée philosophique' (October 1962), *Figures de la pensée philosophique*, p. 998.

77. 'Nietzsche, La Généalogie, l'histoire', in *Hommage à Jean Hyppolite*, Paris: PUF, 1971, pp. 145–72.

78. Ibid., pp. 145–46.

79. Ibid., pp. 168, 167.

80. Ibid., p. 170.

81. Ibid., p. 169.

82. Bernauer, *Michel Foucault's Force of Flight*, p. 98.

83. *L'Ordre du discours*, pp. 77, 76.

84. Eribon, *Michel Foucault*, pp. 226-27.

85. Ibid., pp. 209-10.

86. 'Titres et travaux'; a photocopy of the original can be consulted in the Bibliothèque du Saulchoir, where it is catalogued at D314. The text is reproduced in the second revised edition of Eribon's biography.

87. *Titres et travaux*, p. 2.

88. Ibid. pp. 3-4.

89. Ibid. pp. 4-9.

90. Cited, Eribon, *Michel Foucault*, p. 231.

91. Ibid. pp. 231-32.

Chapter 10

1. Interview with Daniel Defert.

2. 'Folie, littérature et société', *Bugei* 12, 1970.

3. *Paideia*, September 1971. The reply was reprinted as an appendix to the 1972 edition of *Histoire de la folie*, pp. 583–603.

4. 'Mon corps . . .', p. 602.

5. Postscript, *Death and the Labyrinth*, p. 171.

6. Reproduced in *Michel Foucault. Une Histoire de la vérité*, p. 58.

7. Interview with Daniel Defert.

8. 'Le 28 Juillet 1983, Michel m'écrit un vrai texte dans une lettre', *L'Autre Journal* 10, December 1985, p. 5.

9. Rouanet and Merquior, 'Entravista com Michel Foucault'. In his *Foucault*, London: Fontana, 1985, p. 137, Merquior indicates that this interview took place in 1970, but does not give any precise date.

10. Jean Lacouture, 'Au Collège de France. Le cours inaugural de M. Michel Foucault', *Le Monde*, 4 December 1970, p. 8.

NOTES 513

11. Christophe Charle, 'Le Collège de France' in Pierre Nora, ed., *Les Lieux de mémoire II. La Nation*, vol. 3, Paris; Gallimard, 1986, p. 422.
12. Personal communication.
13. Interview with Danièle Rancière.
14. Paul Valéry, letter to Mme Roth-Mascagni, cited, Charle, 'Le Collège de France', ibid., p. 419.
15. Ibid., pp. 417–20.
16. Foucault, *L'Ordre du discours*, Paris: Gallimard, 1971, p. 8; Samuel Beckett, *L'Innommable*, Paris: Minuit, 1953, pp. 261–62.
17. *L'Ordre du discours*, pp. 73–74.
18. Ibid., pp. 74–75.
19. Ibid., pp. 81–82.
20. Ibid., p. 71.
21. 'Croître et multiplier', *Le Monde*, 15–16 November 1970, p. 13. Jacob's history of heredity is translated by Betty E. Spillmann as *The Logic of Living Systems: A History of Heredity*, London: Allen Lane, 1973.
22. *L'Ordre du discours*, pp. 30, 28.
23. Ibid., pp. 54–55.
24. Ibid., p. 55.
25. Ibid., p. 65.
26. Foucault described Lacan's seminar to a journalist thus: 'It is practically impossible to make sense of this esoteric language. In order to grasp all Lacan's allusions, you would need to have read everything. No one understands. But everyone feels concerned, and that is what is so wonderful. At one moment or another, each of his listeners has the feeling of having understood, and of being the only one to have done so. Every week, Lacan therefore accomplishes the feat of conducting, in front of a lecture theatre, a sort of abstract analysis which acts on every one of his listeners.' Cited, Gérard Petitjean, 'Les Grands Prêtres de l'Université française', *Le Nouvel Observateur*, 7 April 1975, p. 54.
27. Bernauer, *Michel Foucault's Force of Flight*, p. 3.
28. Mauriac, *Et comme l'Espérance est violente*, p. 498.
29. Interview with Anne Thalamy.
30. Petitjean, 'Les Grands Prêtres de l'université française', p. 55.
31. '*Radioscopie de Michel Foucault*. Propos recueillis par Jacques Chancel', 3 October 1975. Cassette recordings of this interview are held by the Bibliothèque du Saulchoir and by the Bibliothèque Public d'Information, Centre Georges Pompidou.
32. Interview with Arlette Farge.
33. *Foucault's Force of Flight*, p. 3.
34. Gérard Lefort, 'Au Collège de France: un judoka de l'intellect', *Libération*, 26 June 1984, p. 6.
35. Mauriac, *Et comme l'Espérance est violente*, p. 502.
36. *Résumé des cours*, p. 14.
37. J. P. Peter and Jeanne Favret, 'L'Animal, le fou, le mort' in *Moi, Pierre Rivière, ayant égorgé ma mère, ma soeur et mon frère. Un Cas de parricide au XIX siècle présenté par Michel Foucault*, Paris: Gallimard/Julliard, 1973, p. 249 and n.
38. 'About the Concept of the Dangerous Individual in Nineteenth-Century Legal Psychiatry', *International Journal of Law and Psychiatry* 1, 1978, pp. 1–18.

39. Ibid., p. 20.

40. Interview with Jean-Pierre Peter; Jean-Pierre Peter, 'Entendre Pierre Rivière', *Le Débat* 66, September–October 1991, p. 128.

41. *Résumé des cours*, p. 24.

42. 'Les Meurtres qu'on raconte', *Moi, Pierre Rivière*, p. 266.

43. Ibid., p. 275.

44. 'Présentation', ibid., p. 14.

45. The contributions, other than those already mentioned, are Patricia Moulin, 'Les Circonstances attenuantes', Blandine Barret-Kriegel, 'Régicide-parricide', Philippe Riot, 'Les Vies parallèles de P. Rivière', Robert Castel, 'Les Médicin et les juges', Alexandre Fontana, 'Les Intermittances de la raison'. A chronology was established by Georgette Legée, and a 'topography' of Riviere's wanderings by Gilbert Burlet-Torvic.

46. Pascal Kane, 'Entretien avec Michel Foucault', *Cahiers du cinéma* 271, November 1976, p. 52.

47. Peter, 'Entendre Pierre Rivière', p. 128.

48. Georges Lefranc, ed., *Juin 36*, Paris: Julliard, 1966; Annie Kriegel, ed., *Le Congrès de Tours*, Paris Julliard, 1964.

49. Emmanuel Le Roy Ladurie, 'Bocage au sang', *Le Monde*, 18 October 1973, pp. 19, 25. For more positive reviews, see Max Gallo, 'Histoire d'une folie', *L'Express*, 15–21 October 1973, pp. 59–60 ('total success Foucault's fascinating book'), and Marc Ferro, 'Au Croisement de l'histoire et du crime', *La Quinzaine littéraire*, 1–15 December 1973, pp. 25–26.

50. Jeanne Favret-Saada, *Les Mots, les morts, les sorts*, Paris: Gallimard, 1977.

51. Interview with Jean-Pierre Peter.

52. 'Theatrum philosophicum', *Critique* 282, November 1970, pp. 885–908.

53. 'Ariane s'est pendue', *Le Nouvel Observateur*, 31 March 1969, p. 61.

54. Good accounts of both books are given in Ronald Bogue, *Deleuze and Guattari*, London: Routledge, 1989.

55. Gilles Deleuze and Félix Guattari, *L'Anti-Oedipe*, Paris: Minuit, 1972.

56. 'Theatricum philosophicum', pp. 895–96.

57. Ibid., p. 901.

58. Ibid., p. 903.

59. Ibid., p. 904.

60. Ibid., pp. 907–08.

61. Pierre Klossowski, *La Monnaie vivante*, Paris: Eric Losfield, 1970.

62. Reproduced, *Pierre Klossowski*, p. 89.

63. Deleuze and Guattari, *L'Anti-Odipe*, Jean-François Lyotard, *Economie libidinale*, Paris: Minuit, 1972.

64. Letter to Pierre Klossowski (winter 1970–71), *Cahiers pour un temps: Pierre Klossowski*, Paris: Centre Georges Pompidou, 1985, pp. 89–90.

65. Jean-François Josselin, 'Le Continent noir', *Le Nouvel Observateur*, 7 September 1970, pp. 40–41. For Guyotat in general, see his interview with Gilles Barbedette, 'Pierre Guyotat par qui le scandale arrive', *Le Monde dimanche*, 21 March 1982, pp. I, IX.

66. 'Il y aura scandale, mais . . .', *Le Nouvel Observateur*, 7 September 1970, p. 40.

Chapter 11

1. *Garde à vue* refers to the common police practice of holding people without charge for a period of up to twenty-four hours. In theory, a suspect can only be detained on the specific orders of a senior officer and his or her alleged offence must be one punishable by imprisonment. The usual pretext for taking people into custody is the alleged need to check their identity.

2. The term is much broader than the English 'magistrate', and applies to all categories of judges and legal officials employed by the *magistrature*, which is directly controlled by the Ministry for Justice.

3. 'Création d'un Groupe d'Information sur les Prisons', *Esprit*, March 1971, p. 531. The whole statement was originally published in *La Cause du peuple* 35, 17 February 1971; the first paragraph was printed in *Le Monde* on 10 February.

4. Claude Angeli, 'Les Nouveaux Clandestins', *Le Nouvel Observateur*, 1 June 1970, p. 18.

5. Cf. its founding statement, partly drafted by Sartre: 'Secours Rouge will be a democratic, legally constituted and independent association; its main objective will be to ensure the political and legal defence of victims of oppression and to provide them and their families with material and moral aid . . . It is not possible to defend justice and freedom without organising popular solidarity. Secours Rouge has emerged from the people and will serve the people in its struggle.' Cited, Simone de Beauvoir, *La Cérémonie des adieux*, Paris: Gallimard, 1981, pp. 17–18.

6. *Le Monde*, 22 January 1971.

7. *Le Nouvel Observateur*, 17 January 1972.

8. *Le Monde*, 21 January 1971.

9. *Le Monde*, 9 February 1971.

10. VLR, founded in March 1969, was the most libertarian of the self-professed Maoist groups, and soon developed a distinctly 'underground' culture: its newpaper was more prone to featuring cartoons by Robert Crumb and Wolinksi than portraits of Chairman Mao.

11. *Le Monde*, 30 January 1971.

12. Simone Signoret, *La Nostalgie n'est plus ce qu'elle était*, Paris: Points, 1978, pp. 348–49.

13. See Jean-Paul Sartre, 'Premier procès populaire à Lens', *Situations VIII*, Paris: Gallimard, 1970, pp. 319–34.

14. Cited, Keith Gandal, 'Michel Foucault: Intellectual Work and Politics', *Telos* 67, Spring 1986, pp. 125–26.

15. Collection of Danièle Rancière; the original, in Foucault's handwriting and written on both sides of a small sheet of paper, is in the same collection.

16. Interview with Sylvie-Claire d'Arvisenet.

17. Michel Foucault, 'Je perçois l'intolérable', interview with Geneviève Armedler, *Journal de Genève: Samedi littéraire*, Cahier 135, 24 July 1971, p. 13.

18. Mauriac, *Et comme l'Espérance est violente*, pp. 410–11.

19. Cited, Samuelson, *Il était une fois 'Libération'*, p. 99.

20. Interviews with Jean-Marie Domenach and Pierre Vidal-Naquet. For Vidal-Naquet's stance on Algeria, see his *La Torture dans la République*, Paris: Maspero, 1972, and the essays collected in *Face à la raison d'état. Un historien dans la guerre*

d'Algérie, Paris: La Découverte, 1990. French censorship ensured that *La Torture* first appeared in English as *Torture: Cancer of Democracy*, Harmondsworth: Penguin, 1963. On French opposition to the war in Algeria, see Hervé Hamon and Patrick Rotman, *Les Porteurs de valises*, Paris: Albin Michel, 1979.

21. Interview with Bernard Kouchner; see his 'Prisons: les petits matons blêmes', *Actuel* 9, June 1971, pp. 41–43.

22. Hamon and Rotman, *Génération. II.*, p. 380.

23. Interview with Danièle Rancière.

24. 'Michel Foucault on Attica: An Interview', *Telos*, 19, Spring 1974, p. 161.

25. Mauriac, *Et comme l'Espérance est violente*, p. 482.

26. Interview with Philippe Meyer.

27. Interviews with Danièle Rancière and Hélène Cixous.

28. Hélène Cixous, *Dedans*, Paris: Grasset, 1969.

29. Interviews with Jean-Marie Domenach and Philippe Meyer.

30. 'Réponse de Michel Foucault', *Le Nouvel Observateur*, 11 December 1972, p. 63.

31. Patrick Sery, 'De quoi meurt un prisonnier', *Le Nouvel Observateur*, 30 October 1972, p. 52.

32. Interview with Jean-Marie Domenach and Edmond Maire.

33. Collection of Danièle Rancière.

34. Michel Foucault and Pierre Vidal–Naquet, 'Enquête sur les prisons, propos recueillis par Claude Angeli', *Politique-hebdo*, 18 March 1971, p.

35. Cited, ibid. A *maison centrale* holds convicted prisoners sentenced to more than one year's detention, as opposed to a *maison d'arrêt*, which holds remand and short-term prisoners. At this time, the distinction appears to have been technical rather than real.

36. Interview with Serge Livrozet.

37. Interview with Pierre Vidal–Naquet.

38. 'Foucault and the Prison', an interview with Gilles Deleuze conducted by Paul Rabinow and Keith Gandal, *History of the Present* 2, Spring 1986, p. 2.

39. Three other pamphlets were published in a series entitled 'Intolérable': *Enquête dans une prison-modèle: Fleury-Mérogis* (June 1971), *L'Assassinat de George Jackson* and *Suicides de prison* (1972). The last two pamphlets were published by Gallimard.

40. Groupe d'Information sur les Prisons, *Enquête dans vingt prisons*, Paris: Editions Champ Libre, 1971, pp. 3–4.

41. 'Les Intellectuels et le pouvoir', p. 5.

42. See, for instance, 'Vérité et pouvoir', p. 23.

43. François Paul–Boncour, 'Le Fer rouge', *Le Nouvel Observateur*, 19 June 1972, pp. 44–45. For a full description of the system and its history, see Christian Elek, *Le Casier judiciaire*, Paris: PUF, 1988.

44. Serge Livrozet's *De la Prison à la révolte* gives a first-hand account of the process.

45. 'Entretien', *C'est Demain la veille*, Paris: Seuil, 1974, p. 34; a slightly revised version of the interview published as 'Par-delà le bien et le mal', *Actuel* 14, November 1971.

46. 'Les Détenus parlent', *Esprit*, June 1971, pp. 1182–3.

47. Michel Foucault, 'La Prison partout', *Combat*, 5 May 1971, p. 1.

48. Ibid. Cf. *Le Monde*, 7 May 1971.

49. Foucault in fact gives two slightly different versions of this story. The above account is taken from the article in *Combat*. In a statement reproduced in *Le Monde*

on 23–24 May, he added that he was struck because he inadvertently picked up a police cape and not his overcoat as he left the *commissariat*.

50. Georges Kiejman, 'Un Combattant de rue', *Le Monde*, 27 June 1984; interview with Georges Kiejman, 23 November 1989. Precisely why this type of duplicator was known as a *vietnamienne* is something of a mystery. Presumably the name derives from a perceived analogy between guerrilla warfare in Vietman and illegal or semilegal activities in France.

51. Letter in the collection of Georges Kiejman; interview with Georges Kiejman.

52. Michel Foucault, cited, Madeleine Garrigou-Lagrange, 'Le Prisonnier est aussi un homme', *Témoignage chrétien*, 16 December 1971, p. 12.

53. Daniel Defert and Jacques Donzelot, 'La Charnière des prisons', *Magazine littéraire* 112–13, May 1976, p. 34.

54. Mauriac, *Et comme l'Espérance est violente*, p. 321.

55. Ibid., pp. 318–19.

56. Cited, *Le Nouvel Observateur*, 6 December 1971.

57. Cited, ibid.

58. 'I. A.', 'Prisons: réflexion faite', *L'Express*, 13–19 December 1971, p. 25.

59. 'L'Angoisse des "matons" ', *Le Nouvel Observateur*, 17 January 1972, p. 25.

60. *Le Monde*, 8 December 1971.

61. Jacqueline Remy, 'Noël au pain sec', *Le Nouvel Observateur*, 6 December 1971.

62. *Le Monde*, 8 December 1971.

63. Jean-Marie Domenach, 'Le Sang et la honte', *Le Monde*, 25 December 1971.

64. *Le Monde*, 16 December 1971.

65. Katia D. Kaupp, 'Le "Malentendu" de Toul', *Le Nouvel Observateur*, 20 December 1971.

66. Cited, ibid.

67. Interview with Antoine Lazarus.

68. Danièle Molho, 'Toul: l'école du désespoir', *L'Express*, 20–26 December 1971, pp. 12–15.

69. 'Le Discours de Toul', *Le Nouvel Observateur*, 27 December 1971, p. 15.

70. Mauriac, *Et comme l'Espérance est violente*, pp. 337–38.

71. Gilles Deleuze, 'Ce que les prisonniers attendent de nous . . .', *Le Nouvel Observateur*, 31 January 1972, p. 24.

72. *Le Monde*, 7 January 1972.

73. Cited, *Témoignage chrétien*, 23 December 1971.

74. Cited, *Le Monde*, 7 January 1972.

75. Mauriac, *Et comme l'Espérance est violente*, p. 354.

76. Jean-Marie Domenach, 'Le Détenu hors la loi', *Esprit*, February 1972, p. 167.

77. David Rousset, *L'Univers concentrationnaire*, Paris: Editions du pavois, 1946.

78. *Combat*, 18 January 1972.

79. *Le Monde*, 18 January 1972.

80. Ibid.

81. Mauriac, *Et comme l'Espérance est violente*, pp. 345–62.

82. 'Déclaration à la presse et aux pouvoirs publics émanant des prisonniers de la Maison Centrale de Melun', *Politique-Hebdo*, 20 January 1972, pp. 10–11.

83. *Le Monde*, 23–24 January 1972.

84. *Le Monde*, 11 January 1972.

85. 'Alice Dumas, former prostitute, has been saved from *le milieu* by her marriage to

an honest housepainter. Alice is a salesgirl in a chemist's shop. Her boss, René, loves her, but she rejects his advances. One day, her husband is poisoned and dies. Her mother-in-law, who hates Alice, accuses her of murder ... Sent to Hagenau women's prison, where the discipline is particularly strict, Alice is torn between despair and revolt.' *La Semaine Radio-Télévision*, 29 January–4 February 1972, p. 75.

86. Mauriac, *Et comme l'Espérance est violente*, pp. 367–8.
87. 'Les Dossiers (incomplets) de l'écran', *Le Nouvel Observateur*, 7 February 1972.
88. Cited, Mauriac, *Et comme l'Espérance est violente*, p. 374.
89. See the English-language summary by Stephen Davidson, *Acts (Proceedings of the Fourth Annual Conference on XVIIth Century French Literature)*, Graduate School of the University of Minnesota, vol. 1, pp. 22–23.
90. Interview with Hélène Cixous.
91. 'Michel Foucault on Attica', p. 158.
92. Deleuze, cited, Mauriac, *Et comme l'Espérance est violente*, p. 381.
93. 'Michel Foucault on Attica: An Interview', *Telos* 19, Spring 1974, p. 155.
94. Interview with Hélène Cixous.
95. Cited, Mauriac, *Et comme l'Espérance est violente*.
96. The entire transcript, with a prefatory note by Philippe Meyer, was published as 'La Justice telle qu'on la rend', *Esprit*, October 1971, pp. 524–55.
97. Mauriac, *Et comme l'Espérance est violente*, p. 416.
98. Interviews with Daniel Defert and Philippe Meyer.
99. Interview with Daniel Defert.
100. *Le Monde*, 28 October 1972, 31 October 1972.
101. GiP, *Suicides de prison*, Paris: Gallimard, 1973, p. 51.
102. Patrick Serry, 'De Quoi meurt un prisonnier?'
103. Mauriac, *Et comme l'Espérance est violente*, pp. 430–35; cf. *Le Monde*, 22 November 1972.
104. *Le Monde*, 1 July 1972. For a full, and harrowing, account of the trial by Bontems's lawyer, see Robert Badinter, *L'Exécution*, Paris: Grasset, 1973.
105. Mauriac, *Et comme l'Espérance est violente*, p. 415.
106. Michel Foucault, 'Les Deux Morts de Pompidou', *Le Nouvel Observateur*, 4 December 1972, pp. 56–57.
107. *Suicides de prison*, p. 9.
108. Ibid., p. 40.
109. Livrozet, *De la Prison à la révolte*, p. 220; interview with Serge Livrozet.
110. Mauriac, *Et comme l'Espérance est violente*, pp. 374, 397.
111. On the British and American experiences, see Mike Fitzgerald, *Prisoners in Revolt*, Harmondsworth: Penguin, 1977.
112. *Le Monde*, 22 May 1973.

Chapter 12

1. For his participation in a Vietnam demonstration in January 1973, see Mauriac, *Et comme l'Espérance est violente*, pp. 477–82, and for a description of his presence in March 1973 on a demonstration protesting against the threatened deportation of immigrant workers, see ibid., p. 500.

2. Ibid., p. 490ff.
3. Interview with Robert Castel.
4. Michel Foucault et les membres du GIS, 'Médecine et lutte des classes', *La Nef* 49, October–December 1972, pp. 67–73.
5. See Serge Karenty, 'La Médecine en question', *Magazine littéraire* 112–13, May 1976, pp. 38–41.
6. Jean-François Sirinelli, *Intellectuels et passions françaises. Manifestes et pétitions au XX siècle*, Paris: Fayard, 1990, pp. 21–23.
7. Christophe Charle, *Naissance des intellectuels 1880–1900*, Paris: Minuit, 1990, p. 8.
8. 'Mais à quoi servent les pétitions? Enquête de Pierre Assouline', *Les Nouvelles littéraires*, 1–8 February 1979, p. 4.
9. Interview with Daniel Defert.
10. 'Mais à quoi servent les pétitions?'
11. 'La Société disciplinaire en crise, développement de la diversité et l'indépendence en crise', *Asahi Janaru*, 12 May 1978.
12. 'Un Nouveau Journal?', *Zone des tempêtes* 2, May–June 1973, p. 3.
13. *Le Monde*, 1 June 1971.
14. *Le Monde*, 2 June 1971; Hamon and Rotman, *Génération: 2. Les Années de poudre*, pp. 344–48.
15. 'Michèle Manceaux "interpelée" ', *Le Nouvel Observateur*, 17 May 1971, p. 31.
16. Mariella Righini, 'Les Nouveaux passe-murailles', *Le Nouvel Observateur*, 22 February 1971, pp. 44–45.
17. *Le Monde*, 3 June 1971.
18. Langlois's *Dossiers noirs*, Paris: Seuil, 1971, is an examination of abuses of police power. In February 1972, Foucault testified in court to the probity and honesty Langlois had displayed in his search for the truth. See *Le Monde*, 6–7 February 1972. This was Foucault's only appearance in the witness box.
19. 'Déclaration de Michel Foucault à la conférence de presse d'Alain Jaubert', *La Cause du peuple – J'accuse*, 3 June 1971.
20. Mauriac, *Et comme l'Espérance est violente*, pp. 300–301.
21. René Backmann, 'Quatre Questions sur l'affaire Jaubert', *Le Nouvel Observateur*, 14 June 1971, p. 27.
22. Mauriac, *Et comme l'Espérance est violente*, p. 307.
23. *Rapports de la Commission d'information sur l'affaire Jaubert*, pp. 1–3.
24. 'Questions à Marcellin', *Le Nouvel Observateur*, 5 July 1971, p. 15.
25. *Le Monde*, 12 April 1973.
26. Sartre, 'Premier Procès populaire à Lens', p. 331.
27. See René Backmann, 'Le Procès des tribunaux populaires', *Le Nouvel Observateur*, 5 July 1971, p. 18.
28. Hamon and Rotman, *Génération: 2*, pp. 435–57.
29. 'Sur la Justice populaire. Débat avec les Maos', *Les Temps Modernes* 310bis, 1972 p. 338.
30. Ibid., pp. 357–58.
31. Ibid., p. 334.
32. Ibid., p. 360.
33. Mauriac, *Et Comme L'Espérance est violente*, p. 412.
34. 'Sur la Justice populaire', pp. 364–65.
35. Louis Althusser, 'Ideology and Ideological State Apparatuses (Notes Towards an

Investigation)', in *Lenin and Philosophy and Other Essays*, tr. Ben Brewster, London: New Left Books, 1971, pp. 121–76.

36. 'Sur la Justice populaire', p. 348.

37. The Bruay affair attracted massive press coverage. The most useful overall account is provided by Philippe Gavi, 'Bruay-en-Artois: Seul un bourgeois aurait pu faire ça?', *Les Temps Modernes* 312–313, July–August 1972, pp. 155–260. Gavi was a member of Vive la Révolution, and his article is also a good example of what emerged when the theses of *Histoire de la folie* were crossed with a certain *gauchisme*. Discussing the possibility that the crime was the work of a madman, he remarks (p. 186): 'It is true that it is the bourgeoisie that sets the norms according to which someone is mad or not mad. The bourgeoisie has forced into marginality everything that does not correspond to a productive function. It has normalised society so as to exercise its power more effectively.'

38. Interview with François Ewald.

39. Cited, Gavi, 'Bruay-en-Artois', p. 197.

40. *Coron* refers collectively to the miners' brick houses of the region often built in the shape of a hollow rectangle. Originally a Picard dialect term, the word gained national currency – or at least entered French dictionaries – thanks to Zola's *Germinal*.

41. Hayman, *Writing Against*, p. 416.

42. Mauriac, *Et comme l'Espérance est violente*, pp. 412–13.

43. Cited, ibid., 402–403.

44. Interview with François Ewald.

45. Beauvoir, *La Cérémonie des adieux*, p. 25.

46. See his *Parole d'ouvrier*, Paris: Grasset, 1978. Théret also contributed an article on '1930–1939: Les Mineurs contre le fascisme' to the *Nouveau Fascisme, nouvelle démocratie* issue of *Les Temps Modernes*.

47. An undated cassette recording in the Bibliothèque du Saulchoir (catalogued at C40) confirms the comments reported by Mauriac.

48. Mauriac, *Une Certaine Rage*, p. 73.

49. Hamon and Rotman, *Génération: 2*, pp. 432–33.

50. Cited, Gavi, 'Bruay-en-Artois . . .', p. 206.

51. Cited, Hamon and Rotman, *Génération: 2*, p. 435.

52. Cited, Hamon and Rotman, *Génération: 2*, p. 463.

53. René Backmann, 'La Bal des nervis', *Le Nouvel Observateur*, 24 July 1972, pp. 15–16.

54. On her experiences, see Catherine von Bülow and Fazia Ben Ali, *La Goutte d'Or, ou le mal des racines*, Paris: Stock, 1979; interview with Catherine von Bülow.

55. Mauriac, *Et comme l'Espérance est violente*, p. 315.

56. Ibid., p. 310.

57. Danièle Molho, 'M. Pigot achète un fusil', *L'Express*, 15–21 November 1971, p. 19. Katia D. Kaupp, 'L'Assassinat de Jillali', *Le Nouvel Observateur*, 15 November 1971, pp. 42–3.

58. 'Un Tribunal en France', *Le Nouvel Observateur*, 22 November 1971, p. 28.

59. Béatrix Andrade, 'Un Weekend à la Goutte d'Or', *L'Express*, 6–12 December 1971, p. 42.

60. Mauriac, *Et comme l'Espérance est violente*, p. 312.

61. Beauvoir, *La Cérémonie des adieux*, p. 37.

62. Mauriac, *Et comme l'Espérance est violente*, pp. 309, 318.
63. Ibid., p. 340.
64. Ibid., p. 411.
65. Ibid., p. 329.
66. Ibid., p. 349.
67. Interview with Daniel Defert. For Genet's Palestinian involvement, see the posthumously published (and rather disappointing) *Un Captif amoureux*, Paris: Gallimard, 1986.
68. *Le Monde*, 24 June 1977.
69. René Backmann, 'Fallait-il trois balles pour stopper un homme armé d'une chaise?', *Le Nouvel Observateur*, 11 December 1972, p. 58. Cf. Emmanuel Gabey, 'Après l'assassinat de Mohammed Diab', *Témoignage chrétien*, 21 December 1972, p. 10.
70. Jean-Paul Sartre, 'Le Nouveau racisme', *Le Nouvel Observateur*, 18 December 1972, p. 39.
71. Mauriac, *Et comme l'Espérance est violente*, p. 464.
72. Michel Foucault and Pierre Vidal-Naquet, 'Enquête sur les prisons', *Politique Hebdo*, 18 March 1971. For a graphic, and barely fictionalised, account of the events of October 1961, see François Maspero, *Le Figuier*, Paris: Seuil, 1988.
73. *Le Monde*, 19 December 1972; *Le Monde*, 21 December 1972; Jacques Derogy, 'Ratissage sélectif sur les grands boulevards', *L'Express*, 25–31 December 1972, p. 21; Claude Mauriac, *Les Espaces imaginaires*, Paris: Livre de poche, 1985, pp. 277–99; Mauriac *Et comme l'Espérance est violente*, pp. 462–63.
74. *Le Monde*, 15 April 1976; 11 June 1976; Mauriac, *Mauriac et fils*, pp. 329–31.
75. Cited, Samuelson, *Il était une fois 'Libération'*, p. 109. APL's manifesto first appeared in *L'Idiot international* 19–20, Summer 1971.
76. Althusser, *L'Avenir dure longtemps*, pp. 224–45.
77. Press release of 25 May 1973, cited, Samuelson, p. 128.
78. *On a raison de se révolter*, Paris: Gallimard 1974.
79. Mauriac's account of the meeting is given in his *Et comme l'Espérance est violente*, p. 447ff.
80. Ibid., pp. 449–50.
81. The silk workers of Lyon, whose rebellion of 1831 is one of the key dates in the history of French anarchism. It is said that this was the first time the black flag of anarchy was flown.
82. Mauriac, *Et comme l'Espérance est violente*, p. 454.
83. The full text of the manifesto is reproduced in Samuelson, pp. 140–45.
84. Ibid., p. 167. For Guattari's notion of the molecular, see his *Molecular Revolution: Psychiatry and Politics*, tr. Rosemary Sheed, Harmondsworth: Penguin, 1984.
85. 'L'Intellectuel sert à rassembler les idées . . . mais "son savoir est partiel par rapport au savoir ouvrier" ', *Libération*, 26 May 1973.
86. 'Sur la seconde révolution chinoise. Entretien 1. Michel Foucault et K. S. Karol', 31 January 1974, p. 10; 'Entretien 2', 1 February 1974, p. 10; 'Aller à Madrid', 24 September 1975, pp. 1, 7; 'Attention: danger', 22 March 1978.
87. Maurice Clavel, *Ce Que je crois*, Paris: Grasset, 1975, p. 98.
88. Interview with Philippe Gavi.
89. See the chronology in FHAR, *Rapport contre la normalité*, Paris: Editions Champ Libre, 1971, pp. 16–18.

90. Hamon and Rotman, *Génération: II*, p. 225.
91. Cited, ibid., p. 336.
92. Interviews with Laurent Dispot and René Schérer.
93. Guy Hocquenhem, *Le Désir homosexuel*, Paris: Editions universitaires, 1972, translated as *Homosexual Desire*, London: Alison and Busby, 1978. For discussions in English, see Philip Derbyshire, 'Odds and Sods', *Gay Left* 7, Winter 1978–79, pp. 18–19, and John de Weit, 'The Charming Passivity of Guy Hocquenhem', *Gay Left* 9, 1979, pp. 16–19. More generally, see *Cahier de l'imaginaire* 7, 1992: *Présence de Guy Hocquenhem*.
94. Bruno Frappat, 'Les Homosexuels par eux-mêmes', *Le Monde*, 19–20 August 1973, p. 14.
95. *Le Monde*, 7–28 May 1973; *Le Nouvel Observateur*, 9 April 1973; interviews with Laurent Dispot, Félix Guattari and George Kiejman.
96. The full text is reproduced in *Le Monde*, 11–12 February 1973. An expanded version was published under the same title by Maspero in March 1973.
97. 'La Condamnation du Dr Carpentier par le Conseil de l'Ordre; Texte de l'intervention de Michel Foucault à la conférence de presse de Jean Carpentier, le 29 juin 1972', *Psychiatrie aujourd'hui* 10, September 1972, p. 15.
98. 'Sexe, parole et répression', *Le Monde*, 20 October 1972, p. 14.
99. Mauriac, *Et comme l'Espérance est violente*, p. 532.
100. Ibid., p. 533.
101. Michel Foucault, Alain Landau, Jean-Yves Petit, 'Convoqués à la P.J.', *Le Nouvel Observateur*, 28 October 1973, p. 53.

Chapter 13

1. See, for instance, 'Entretien avec Michel Foucault: à propos de l'enfermement pénitentiare', *Pro Justitia*, vol. 1, no 3–4, 1974; 'Gefängnisse und Gefängnisrevolten', *Dokumente: Zeitschrift für übernationale Zusammenarbeit*, 29 June 1973, pp. 133–37.
2. 'Table ronde', *Esprit* 413, April–May 1972, pp. 678–703.
3. 'La Force de fuir', *Derrière le miroir* 202, March 1973, p. 1.
4. Ibid., p. 6.
5. Ibid., p. 6.
6. *Résumé des cours*, p. 44.
7. Interview with Anne Thalamy.
8. Interview with Félix Guattari.
9. Interview with Marie-Thérèse Vernier.
10. *Recherches* 13, December 1973. A second and revised edition was published in the 10/18 series in 1976. The introduction by François Fouquet and Lion Murard gives a good idea of how the collective worked.
11. *Recherches* 13, pp. 27–31, 183–186.
12. *Généalogie des équipements de normalisation*, Fontenay sous-Bois: CERFI, 1976. A slightly different edition appeared as *Les Machines à guérir*, Brussels: Pierre Mardaga, 1979. It includes Michel Foucault, 'La Politique de la santé au XVIIIè siècle'; Blandine Barret-Kriegel, 'L'Hôpital comme équipment'; Anne Thalamy, 'La Médicalisation de l'hôpital'; François Béguin, 'La Machine à guérir'; Bruno Fortier, 'Le Camp et la forteresse inversée'.

13. Georges Canguilhem, 'Les Machines à guérir', *Le Monde*, 6 April 1977, p. 16.
14. Published in a Portuguese translation by Roberto Machado as 'A Verdade e as formas juridicas', *Cademos do PUC*, 1974, pp. 5–102.
15. Ibid., p. 29.
16. 'O Mondo é om grande hospicio' (interview with Ricardo Gomes Leire), *Jornal de Belo Horizonte*, May 1973.
17. Interviews with Célio Garcia and Daniel Defert. Communication from Chaim Katz and Roberto Machado.
18. Foucault does not mention any specific title by Duvert, but was probably thinking of *Récidive*, Paris: Minuit, 1967, or *Paysage de fantaisie* Paris: Minuit, 1973.
19. Olga Bernal, *Alain Robbe-Grillet: le roman de l'absence*, Paris: Gallimard, 1964.
20. 'La Fête de l'écriture. Un Entretien avec Michel Foucault et Jacques Almira, propos recueillis par Jean Le Marchand', *Le Quotidien de Paris*, 25 April 1975, p. 13; Jacques Almira, 'La Reconnaissance d'un écrivain', *Le Débat* 41, September–December 1986, pp. 159–63; Mauriac, *Mauriac et fils*, pp. 225–26; interview with Jacques Almira.
21. 'Sade sergent du sexe', propos recueillis par Gérard Dupont', *Cinématographe* 16, December 1975–January 1976, pp. 3–5; Claude Mauriac, *Une Certaine Rage*, p. 34.
22. *Surveiller et punir*, Paris: Gallimard, 1975, pp. 9–13.
23. Ibid., p. 13.
24. Ibid., pp. 27, 28.
25. Ernst Kantorowicz, *The King's Two Bodies: A Study in Medieval Political Theology*, New Jersey: Princeton University Press, 1957.
26. *Surveiller et punir*, p. 82.
27. Ibid., pp. 96–103.
28. Ibid., p. 129.
29. Labour organisation is not a major theme of *Surveiller et punir*, but is explored in detail in Bernard Doray, *From Taylorism to Fordism: A Rational Madness*, tr. David Macey, London: Free Association Books, 1988. Doray admits to having been heavily influenced by Foucault, and to having been criticised for that fact by friends in the PCF.
30. *Surveiller et punir*, p. 179.
31. Ibid., p. 217.
32. Ibid., pp. 201–02.
33. Ibid., p. 252.
34. Ibid., p. 21.
35. Ibid., pp. 274–75.
36. Ibid., p. 276.
37. Ibid., p. 35.
38. *Le Nouvel Observateur*, 17 February 1975.
39. 'Des Supplices aux cellules', *Le Monde*, 21 February 1975, p. 16; Christian Jambet, 'L'Unité de la pensée: une interrogation sur les pouvoirs', ibid., p. 17.
40. 'Entretien sur la prison: le livre et sa méthode', *Magazine littéraire* 101, June 1975, pp. 27–35, Bernard-Henri Lévy, 'Le Système Foucault', ibid., pp. 7–10; 'Foucault et les historiens', ibid., pp. 10–12.
41. 'Sur la sellette' (with Jean-Louis Enzine), *Les Nouvelles Littéraires*, 17 March 1975, p. 3; Ferdinando Scianna, 'Il Carcere visto da un filosofo francese', *L'Europeo*, 3 April 1975, pp. 63–65.

42. Jean-Paul Enthoven, 'Crimes et châtiments', *Le Nouvel Observateur*, 3 March 1975, p. 58, 59; see also Adolfo Fernandez-Zoïla, 'La Machine à fabriquer des délinquants', *La Quinzaine littéraire*, 16–31 March 1975, pp. 3–4; Max Gallo, 'La Prison selon Michel Foucault', *L'Express*, 24 February–2 March 1975, pp. 65–66; Robert Kanters, 'Crimes et châtiments', *Le Figaro littéraire*, 22 February 1975, p. 17.

43. Arlette Farge, interviewed by Keith Gandal in 1985, cited, Gandal, 'Michel Foucault: Intellectual Work and Politics', p. 133n.

44. Gilles Deleuze, 'Ecrivain non: un nouveau cartographe', *Critique* 343, December 1975, pp. 1207–27 (revised as 'Un Nouveau Cartographe' in his *Foucault*, and cited here in that edition); François Ewald, 'Anatomie et corps politiques', ibid., pp. 1228–65; Philippe Meyer, 'La Correction paternelle, ou l'état, domicile de la famille', ibid., pp. 1266–76.

45. *Surveiller et punir*, p. 304, n. See Philippe Meyer, *L'Enfant et la raison d'état*, Paris: Seuil, 1977; interview with Philippe Meyer.

46. Ewald, p. 1256, cited, 'Nietzsche, la généalogie, l'histoire', p. 161.

47. Ewald, p. 1228; Nietzsche, *The Birth of Tragedy* and *The Genealogy of Morals*, tr. Francis Golffing, New York: Doubleday, 1956, pp. 154–55.

48. Ewald, p. 1265.

49. André Glucksmann, *La Cuisinière et le mangeur d'hommes*, Paris: Seuil, 1975.

50. Ewald, p. 1232.

51. *Surveiller et punir*, p. 305.

52. *Foucault*, pp. 31, 51. In the interview published in *Les Nouvelles littéraires*, 17 March 1975, Foucault described himself as a 'cartographer'.

53. *Foucault*, pp. 32, 33. Deleuze refers specifically to *Surveiller et punir*, pp. 32–33.

54. François Roustang, 'La visibilité est un piège', *Les Temps Modernes* 356, March 1976, pp. 1567–79; interview with François Roustang.

55. Personal communication.

56. 'La Peinture photogénique' in *Fromanger: Le Désir est partout*, Paris: Galerie Jeanne Bucher, 1975. Unpaginated.

57. *Résumé des cours*, p. 79.

58. Typescripts in the Bibliothèque du Saulchoir. Copies are also held in the 'History of the Present' collection in Berkeley. 'Discourse and repression' was transcribed by John Leavitt.

59. Mauriac, *Mauriac et fils*, p. 222.

60. Mauriac, *Le Temps accompli*, p. 44.

61. Roger-Pol Droit, 'Foucault, passe-frontières de la philosophie', *Le Monde*, 6 September 1986, p. 12.

62. Mauriac, *Et comme l'Espérance est violente*, p. 473.

63. The screenplay was published in *Cinéma* 183, 1977; see also the dossier in *Cahiers du cinéma* 271, November 1976.

64. Ibid., p. 631.

65. *Mauriac et fils*, p. 217.

66. Interview with Daniel Defert.

67. On FRAP, see *1 Congreso del Partido communista de Espana (Marxista-Leninista): Informe de Comité Central*, Madrid: Ediciones Vanguardia Obrera, n.d., pp. 95–97.

68. Mauriac, *Et comme l'Espérance est violente*, p. 582; interview with Catherine von Bülow. Mauriac's comprehensive account of these events is given in his *L'Espérance*, pp. 600–40.

69. Cited, Mauriac *Et comme l'Espérance est violente*, pp. 590–91.
70. Claude Mauriac, *Malraux ou le mal du héros*, Paris: Grasset, 1946.
71. Mauriac, *Et comme l'Espérance est violente*, pp. 259–60.
72. Ibid., p. 600.
73. Interview with Daniel Defert.
74. Personal communication.
75. Jean Daniel, 'Quinze jours en images', *Le Nouvel Observateur*, 29 September 1975, p. 28.
76. Catherine von Bülow, 'Contredire est un devoir', *Le Débat* 41, pp. 172–73.
77. Michel Foucault, 'Aller à Madrid', *Libération*, 24 September 1975, pp. 1, 7.
78. 'Hospicios, sexualidade, prisões' (interview with Claudio Bojunga), *Versus* (São Paulo), 1 October 1975.
79. Interview with Catherine von Bülow.
80. Cited, Mauriac, *Et comme l'Espérance est violente*, p. 628.
81. Jean Lacouture, *Malraux, une Vie dans le siècle*, Paris: Seuil, Points, 1976, p. 426.
82. 'Faire vivre et laisser mourir', *Les Temps Modernes* 535, February 1991, p. 47.
83. Foucault in 'Ils ont dit de Malraux', *Le Nouvel Observateur*, 29 November 1976, p. 83.
84. 'Aller à Madrid', *Libération*, 24 September 1975.
85. Mauriac, *Une Certaine Rage*, pp. 27–28.
86. 'Loucura – uma questão de poder' (interview with Silvia Helena Vianna Rodriguez), *Jornal do Brasil*, 12 November 1975.
87. Voeltzel, *Vingt Ans et après*, p. 157.
88. Mauriac, *Mauriac et fils*, p. 227.
89. Mauriac, *Une Certaine Rage*, pp. 30–36.
90. See *Le Procès de Draguignan*, Monaco: Editions du rocher, 1975; Robert Pelletier and Serge Ravat, *Le Mouvement des soldats*, Paris: Maspero, 1976.
91. See *Libération*, 8 December 1975.
92. *Le Monde*, 12 February 1976, p. 9.
93. Mauriac, *Une Certaine Rage*, p. 61.
94. *Le Cicogne en rogne* was also the title of the newsletter produced by the base's *comité de soldats*.
95. Interview with Jacques Lebas and Jean-Pierre Mignard.

Chapter 14

1. Maurice Clavel and Philippe Sollers, *Délivrance*, Paris: Seuil, 1977, p. 104.
2. 'Préface', *Histoire de la folie*, pp. iv–v.
3. 'Préface à la transgression', p. 751.
4. 'A Bas la dictature du sexe' (interview with Madeleine Chapsal), *L'Express*, 24–30 January 1977, p. 56.
5. Lecture on 'Discourse and repression', Berkeley, 8 May 1975, typescript, Bibliothèque du Saulchoir D246.
6. Mauriac, *Et comme l'Espérance est violente*, p. 574.
7. 'Le Jeu de Michel Foucault', *Ornicar?* 10, July 1977, p. 76.
8. Tr. Robert Hurley, *The History of Sexuality. Volume I: An Introduction*, New York: Random House, 1978.

9. *La Volonté de savoir*, p. 79n.

10. See in particular his comments in the preface to the German translation, *Sexualität und Warheit. 1. Der Wille zum Wissen*, Frankfurt: Suhrkamp, 1977.

11. 'Le Jeu de Michel Foucault', p. 76.

12. Ibid., pp. 63, 65.

13. Dreyfus and Rabinow, *Michel Foucault*, p. 121.

14. *La Volonté de savoir*, p. 13.

15. Ibid., p. 18.

16. Ibid., pp. 25, 26.

17. Ibid., p. 60.

18. Ibid., pp. 58–60.

19. Ibid., pp. 30–31.

20. Steven Marcus, *The Other Victorians. A Study of Pornography and Sexuality in Mid-Nineteenth-Century England*, London: Weidenfeld & Nicolson, 1966. Foucault habitually gives the author's forename as 'Stephen' (sic).

21. *La Volonté de Savoir*, pp. 31–32.

22. *My Secret Life*, tr. Christine Charnaux et al., Paris: Editions les formes du secret, 1978.

23. 'Préface', ibid., pp. 5–6.

24. *La Volonté du savoir*, p. 121.

25. Ibid., p. 137.

26. Ibid., pp. 76–77.

27. Ibid., p. 194.

28. Résumé des cours', p. 109.

29. For representative reviews, see André Burgière, 'Michel Foucault: La Preuve par l'aveu', *Le Nouvel Observateur*, 31 January 1977, pp. 64–66; J. Postel, *Esprit* 4–5, April–May 1977, pp. 294–96; Jacques Lagrange, '*La Volonté de savoir* de Michel Foucault ou une généalogie du sexe', *Psychanalyse à l'université*, vol. 2, no 7, June 1977, pp. 541–53; Dominique Wolton, 'Qui veut savoir?', *Esprit* 7–8, July–August 1977, pp. 37–47.

30. Roger-Pol Droit, 'Le Pouvoir et le sexe', *Le Monde*, 16 February 1977, pp. 1, 18.

31. Douglas Kellner, *Jean Baudrillard: From Marxism to Postmodernism and Beyond*, Cambridge: Polity, 1989, pp. 132, 231. Kellner's informants are, respectively, John Rachjman and Mark Poster.

32. Interview with Philippe Meyer.

33. Interview, *Lire*, June 1987, p. 87.

34. Jean Baudrillard, *Oublier Foucault*, Paris: Editions Galilée, 1977, pp. 12–13.

35. Interview with Jean-Pierre Barou.

36. Baudrillard, *Oublier Foucault*, p. 55; *L'Usage des plaisirs*, p. 11.

37. Jean Baudrillard, *Cool Memories*, Paris: Galilée, 1987, p. 198.

38. Ibid., p. 197.

39. 'La Vie des hommes infâmes', *Cahiers du chemin* 29, January 1977, pp. 12–29.

40. 'La Vie des hommes infâmes', p. 13.

41. *Histoire de la folie*, p. 105.

42. Ibid., pp. 22–23.

43. Foucault, cover note to *Herculine Barbin, dite Alexina B.*, Paris: Gallimard, 1978.

44. *Résumé des cours*, pp. 73–80. Much of the lecture course was devoted to the nineenth-century crusade against masturbation, which was to have been dealt

with in Volume 3 of the *Histoire: La Croisade des enfants*.

45. *Actes du Colloque Internationale:* 1, 2 and 3 November 1973, p. 9.

46. For a moving and barely fictionalised account of the transition from Arcadie to FHAR, see Dominique Fernandez's novel *L'Etoile rose*, Paris: Grasset, 1978.

47. Guy Hocquenhem, 'La Révolution des homosexuels', *Le Nouvel Observateur*, 10 January 1972, p. 34.

48. Mossuz-Lavau, *Les Lois de l'amour*, p. 246.

49. Interview with Daniel Defert.

50. Cited, Mossuz-Lavau, *Les Lois de l'amour*, p. 248.

51. Paul Veyne, 'Témoignage hétérosexuel d'un historien sur l'homosexualité', *Actes du Congrès International: Le Regard des autres*, Paris: Arcadie, 1979, p. 19.

52. 'Le vrai Sexe', *Arcadie* 323, November 1980, pp. 617–25. Foucault's paper did not appear in the *Actes* of the congress, where it was replaced (p. 25) by a summary; an offprint of 'Le vrai Sexe' was subsequently distributed to purchasers of the *Actes*. The reference to pleasure having no passport disappears from the slightly different version of the text published as the introduction to *Herculine Barbin. Being the Recently Discovered Memoirs of a Nineteenth-Century French Hermaphrodite*, introduced by Michel Foucault, tr. Richard MacDougall, Brighton: Harvester Press, 1980.

53. P. 208.

54. 'A Bas la dictature du sexe', pp. 56–57.

55. 'Foucault: Non au sexe roi', p. 98.

56. Ibid., p. 100. The reference is to Guibert's *La Mort propagande*.

57. René Schérer and Guy Hocquenhem, *Co-Ire. Album Systématique de l'enfance*, *Recherches* 22 (2nd edition, April 1977).

58. 'Le Gai Savoir II', *Mec Magazine* 6/7, July–August 1988, p. 32.

59. 'Le Gai Savoir', p. 34.

60. Jean Le Bitoux, 'Grandeur et décadence de la presse homosexuelle', *Masques* 25/26, May 1985, p. 75.

61. Frank Arnal, '*Gai Pied hebdo*, à l'origine de l'emergence de la visibilité homosexuelle', ibid., p. 85.

62. 'Un Plaisir si simple', *Gai Pied* 1, April 1979, pp. 1, 10.

63. Mauriac, *Mauriac et fils*, p. 368.

64. 'De l'Amitié comme mode de vie', *Gai Pied* 25, April 1981, pp. 38–39 'Non aux compromis', *Gai Pied* 43, October 1982, p. 9.

65. 'De l'Amitié comme mode de vie', p. 38.

66. 'The Social Triumph of the Sexual Will', interview with Gilles Barbedette, translated by Brendan Lemon, *Christopher Street* 64, May 1982, p. 36.

67. Mauriac, *Le Temps accompli*, p. 25.

68. 'The Social Triumph of the Sexual Will', p. 38.

69. 'Histoire et homosexualité: Entretien avec Michel Foucault (with Joecker, M. Oued and A. Sanzio)', *Masques* 13–14, Spring 1982, pp. 14–24. *Masques* failed for financial reasons in 1986.

70. 'The Social Triumph of the Sexual Will', p. 40.

71. Randy Shilts, *And the Band Played On*, Harmondsworth: Penguin, 1988, p. 19.

72. Ibid., p. 89.

73. 'An Interview: Sex, Power and the Politics of Identity', *Advocate*, 7 August 1984, p. 28. Translated as 'Lorsque l'amant part en taxi', *Gai Pied Hebdo* 151, January

1985, pp. 54–57. (Interview conducted in June 1982.)

74. Ibid., p. 30.

75. 'Sexual Choice, Sexual Acts: Foucault and Homosexuality', p. 298.

76. Ibid.

77. 'Le Gai Savoir', p. 36.

78. And the Band Played On, p. 23.

79. 'Sexual Choice, Sexual Act', p. 298.

80. Edmund White, States of Desire: Travels in Gay America, London: Picador, 1986, p. 267.

81. Ibid., p. 269.

82. 'Sex, Power and the Politics of Identity', p. 27.

83. Interview with Daniel Defert.

84. Eribon, Michel Foucault, p. 337.

85. Mauriac, Le Rire de pères dans les yeux des enfants, p. 619.

86. 'The Minimalist Self', p. 12.

87. Sheridan, 'Diary'.

88. Mauriac, Mauriac et fils, p. 328.

89. Ibid., p. 227.

90. Interview with Claude Mauriac.

91. Postscript, Death and the Labyrinth, p. 183.

92. Mauriac, Mauriac et fils, pp. 363, 364.

93. Voeltzel, Vingt Ans et après, p. 116.

94. Ibid., p. 119. For similar comments, see 'Sex, Power and the Politics of Identity'.

95. Claude Mauriac, 'Préface', Vingt Ans et après, p. 8.

96. Mauriac, L'Oncle Marcel, pp. 245–48, 243.

97. Voeltzel, Vingt Ans et après, pp. 119–20.

98. Mauriac, Mauriac et fils, p. 328.

99. 'The Minimalist Self', p. 12.

100. Michel Foucault, David Cooper, Jean-Pierre Faye, Marie-Odile Faye and Marine Zecca, 'Enfermement, psychiatrie, prison', Change 32–33, October 1977, (dated 12 May 1977); Michel Foucault, Guy Hocquenhem and Jean Danet, 'La Loi de la pudeur', Recherches 37, April 1979 (broadcast in France Culture's Dialogues series on 4 April 1978.

101. 'Enfermement, psychiatrie, prison', p. 109.

102. De Weit, 'The Charming Passivity of Guy Hocquenhem', p. 18.

103. 'Enfermement, psychiatre, prison', pp. 99–101.

104. See the three-part article by Michèle Solat, 'Les Féministes et le viol', Le Monde, 18, 19 and 20 October 1977.

105. Monique Plaza, 'Our costs and their benefits', tr. Wendy Harrison, m/f 4, 1980, p. 32.

106. Winnifred Woodhull, 'Sexuality, power, and the question of rape' in Irene Diamond and Lee Quinby, eds., Feminism and Foucault, Boston; Northeastern University Press, 1988, p. 170.

107. 'Sexual Choice, Sexual Acts', p. 289.

108. Susan Brownmiller, Against Our Will, Harmondsworth: Penguin, 1976, p. 15. Ann Villelaur's translation (Le Viol) was published by Stock in 1976.

109. Meaghan Morris, 'The Pirate's Fiancée', in Diamond and Quinby, Feminism and Foucault, p. 26.

110. 'Enfermement, psychiatrie, prison', p. 104.
111. Interview with René Schérer.
112. See Guy Hocquenhem, 'Homosexuals, Children and Violence', tr. Simon Watney, *Gay Left*, Summer 1978, pp. 14–15 (the original text appeared in *Gaie Presse* 1, January 1978).
113. 'Enfermement, psychiatrie, prison', pp. 103, 104.
114. 'Le Gai Savoir', p. 32.
115. 'La Loi de la pudeur', p. 74.
116. Ibid., pp. 77–78.

Chapter 15

1. See Simone de Beauvoir's letter to the Helsinki Conference, *Le Monde*, 12 January 1977, p. 9.
2. Maurice Clavel, ' "Vous direz trois rosaires" ', *Le Nouvel Observateur*, 27 December 1976, p. 55.
3. 'Du Pouvoir', interview with Pierre Boncenne, *L'Express*, 13 July 1984. This interview was recorded in 1978 but remained unpublished until after Foucault's death.
4. Mauriac, *Mauriac et fils*, p. 249.
5. For a reconstruction of the Ranucci case and for a convincing argument that he was not guilty, see Gilles Perrault, *Le Pull-over rouge*, Paris: Ramsay, 1978. Foucault's comments on both the case and Perrault's book will be found in 'Du bon Usage du criminel', *Le Nouvel Observateur*, 11 September 1978, pp. 40–42.
6. *Le Monde*, 23 June 1977.
7. Bernard Guetta, 'Le Salut à Brejnev', *Le Nouvel Observateur*, 27 June 1977, p. 31.
8. Mauriac, *Signes, rencontres et rendez-vous*, p. 249.
9. Ibid., pp. 249–50.
10. *Le Monde*, 23 June 1977; Mauriac, *Signes, Rencontres et Rendez-vous*, p. 249.
11. Cited, *Le Monde*, 23 June 1977.
12. Guetta, 'Le Salut à Brejnev'.
13. Régis Debray, 'Lettre à la Ligue communiste', *L'Espérance au purgatoire*, Paris: Alain Moreau, 1980, p. 62.
14. Interviews with Jeannette Colombel and Daniel Defert.
15. The two did not meet, but there is some dispute about why not; Hayman, *Writing Against*, p. 387, claims that it was Solzhenitsyn who refused to talk to Sartre because he had suggested that the 'hangman' Sholokov should receive the Nobel Prize. In an extraordinary speech delivered in Rome in October 1965, Sartre had referred to a 'false avant-garde' which was, despite itself, 'traditionalist' and involved in 'a dialogue with the dead': it included Joyce, Céline, Breton, Robbe-Grillet . . . and Solzhenitsyn. See Michel Contat and Michel Rybalka, *Les Ecrits de Sartre*, Paris: Gallimard, 1970, pp. 420–21.
16. Mauriac, *Signes Rencontres et Rendez-vous*, p. 247.
17. 'Les Nouveaux Philosophes', *Les Nouvelles Littéraires*, 10 June 1976; 'Les Nouveaux Gourous', *Le Nouvel Observateur*, 12 July 1976, pp. 62–68. See also Claude Sales, 'Les "Nouveaux Philosophes": La Révolte contre Marx', *Le Point*, 4 July 1977, pp. 33–37. For general accounts of the 'movement', see Peter Dews, 'The *Nouvelle*

Philosophie and Foucault', *Economy and Society*, vol. 8, no. 2, May 1979, pp. 127–171, and the same author's 'The "New Philosophers" and the end of leftism', *Radical Philosophy* 24, Spring 1980, pp. 2–11. François Aubral and Xavier Delcourt, *Contre la Nouvelle Philosophie*, Paris: Gallimard, collection 'Idées', 1977, Marxist-inspired and polemical to the point of near-apoplexy, is too partisan to provide any objective account, but does contain a wealth of information. Representative texts by the new philosophers include Philippe Nemo, *L'Homme structural*, Paris: Grasset 1975; Jean-Marie Benoist, *La Révolution structurale*, Paris: Grasset, 1975; Jean-Paul Dollé, *Haine de la pensée*, Paris: Editions Hallier, 1976; Guy Lardreau and Christian Jambet, *L'Ange*, Paris: Grasset, 1976.

18. J. Pasqualini, *Prisonnier de Mao*, Paris: Gallimard, 1975; Claudie and Jacques Broyelle and Evelyne Tschirhart, *Deuxième Retour de Chine*, Paris: Seuil, 1977.

19. 'Etes-vous un "nouveau philosophe"?', *Le Nouvel Observateur*, 1 August 1977, p. 46.

20. Lévy, *La Barbarie à visage humain*, pp. 9, 10.

21. André Glucksmann, *La Cuisinère et le mangeur d'hommes*, Paris; Seuil, collection 'Points', 1977, pp. 37, 40.

22. Lévy, *La Barbarie à visage humain*, p. 180.

23. Jean Daniel, *L'Ere des ruptures*, Paris: Livre de poche, 1980, pp. 261, 264.

24. Voeltzel, *Vingt Ans et après*, p. 142.

25. André Glucksmann, *La Cuisinière*, p. 205.

26. Glucksmann, 'Fascismes: l'ancien et le nouveau', *Les Temps Modernes* 310bis, 1972, p. 301.

27. Glucksmann, *La Cuisinière*, p. 11.

28. 'Gilles Deleuze contre les "nouveaux philosophes" ', *Le Monde*, 19–20 June 1977, p. 16 (extracts from Deleuze, 'A Propos des nouveaux philosophes et d'une question plus générale,' supplement to *Minuit* 24, 1977).

29. *Le Nouvel Observateur*, 25 July 1977, p. 40.

30. Ibid., pp. 103–107.

31. 'Crimes et châtiments en URSS et ailleurs . . .', *Le Nouvel Observateur*, 26 January 1976, p. 34.

32. 'Du Pouvoir' (interview with Pierre Boncenne), *L'Express*, 13 July 1984.

33. 'Pouvoirs et stratégies', *Les Révoltes logiques* 4, Winter 1977, pp. 89, 90.

34. 'La Politique est la continuation de la guerre par d'autres moyens' (interview with Bernard-Henri Lévy), *L'Imprévu*, 27 January 1975); 'A Quoi rêvent les philosophes?', ibid., 28 January 1975.

35. Lévy, *La Barbarie à visage humain*, p. 10.

36. Ibid., pp. 10–11.

37. Ibid., pp. 184, 181–82.

38. Ibid., p. 231.

39. Ibid., pp. 20, 23–24.

40. Ibid., pp. 170, 173.

41. 'Foucault: Non au sexe roi', *Le Nouvel Observateur*, 12 March 1977, p. 100.

42. Lévy. *La Barbarie*, p. 138.

43. 'La Grande Colère des faits', *Le Nouvel Observateur*, 9 May 1977, p. 85.

44. Ibid., pp. 84–85.

45. Mauriac, *Une Certaine Rage*, pp. 85–86.

46. 'Crimes et châtiments en URSS et ailleurs', p. 37

47. Clavel in *Nouvelle Action française*, 25 November 1976, cited Aubral and Delcourt, p. 284.

48. Catherine Clément and Bernard Pingaud, 'Raison de plus', *L'Arc* 70, 1977, pp. 1–2.

49. Claude Mauriac, 'Il ne faut pas tuer l'espérance', *Le Monde*, 17 July 1977 p. 1; also in *Signes, rencontres et rendez-vous*, pp. 252–55.

50. Cited, *Le Nouvel Observateur*, 11 July 1977, p. 51. Cf. Bel, *Maurice Clavel*, pp. 338–40.

51. Mauriac, *Signes, rencontres et rendez-vous*, p. 257.

52. 'Crimes et châtiments...', p. 37.

53. *Liberté, libertés. Réflexions du Comité pour une charte de liberté animé par Robert Badinter*, Paris: Gallimard, 1976.

54. 'Michel Foucault à Goutelas: la redéfinition du "judiciable"', *Justice* 115, June 1987, pp. 36–39.

55. The paper subsequently appeared as 'Délinquance et système pénitentiaire en France au XIXᵉ siècle', *Annales ESC*, vol. 30, no. 1, January–February 1975, pp. 67–91.

56. Michelle Perrot, *Les Ouvriers en grève (France 1870–1900)*, Paris: Mouton and CNRS, 1974. An abridged version was published as *Jeunesse de la grève*, Paris: Seuil, 1984, and translated by Chris Turner as *Workers on Strike*, Leamington Spa: Berg, 1987. On Perrot, see 'Michelle Perrot. Une Histoire des femmes. Propos recueillis par François Ewald', *Magazine littéraire* 286, March 1991, pp. 98–102.

57. *Surveiller et punir*, p. 287.

58. *Atoll* 1, November 1967–January 1968.

59. Interview with Jean-Pierre Barou.

60. Jeremy Bentham, *Le Panoptique, précédé de 'L'Oeil du pouvoir', entretien de Michel Foucault. Postface de Michelle Perrot*, Paris: Pierre Belfond, 1977. The volume contains a facsimile reproduction of the French text, a translation of the first chapter of the English version, and is completed by a bibliography compiled by Perrot.

61. 'L'Oeil du pouvoir', p. 23.

62. Interviews with Michelle Perrot and Jean-Pierre Barou.

63. Sebastian Cobler, *Law, Order and Politics in West Germany*, tr. Francis McDonagh, Harmondsworth: Penguin, 1978, p. 114, citing the Stuttgart District Court warrant against Croissant.

64. *Le Monde*, 14 July 1977.

65. *Le Monde*, 2 October 1977.

66. 'Va-t-on extrader Klaus Croissant?', *Le Nouvel Observateur*, 14 November 1977.

67. *Le Monde*, 15 November 1977.

68. Claude Mauriac, *Signes, Rencontres et Rendez-vous*, p. 266.

69. Ibid., p. 263.

70. Jean Genet, 'Violence et brutalité', *Le Monde*, 2 September 1977, pp. 1, 2.

71. Mauriac, *Signes, rencontre et rendez-vous*, p. 268.

72. 'Désormais, la sécurité est au-dessus des lois' (interview with Jean-Paul Kauffmann), *Le Matin*, 18 November 1977, p. 15.

73. Mauriac, *Signes, rencontres et rendez-vous*, pp. 271–72.

74. 'Lettre à quelques leaders de la gauche', *Le Nouvel Observateur*, 28 November 1977, p. 59.

75. 'Alain Peyrefitte s'explique ... et Michel Foucault lui répond', *Le Nouvel Observateur*, 23 January 1978, p. 25.

76. 'Wir fühlten uns als schmutzige Spezies', *Der Spiegel*, 19 December 1977, pp. 77–78.
77. Interview with Toni Negri. The key anthology is A. Fontana and P. Pasquino, eds., *Il microfisica del potere*, Turin: Einaudi, 1977.
78. See, for example, the anthologies *Mikrophysik der Macht*, Berlin: Maeve, 1976, and *Dispositive der Macht: Uber Sexualität, Wissen und Wahrheit*, Berlin: Maeve, 1978.
79. On the German reception of Foucault, see Uta Liebmann Schaub, 'Foucault, Alternative Presses, and Alternative Ideology in West Germany: A Report', *German Studies Review*, vol. XII, no. 1, February 1989, pp. 139–53.
80. Manfred Frank, 'Pourquoi la philosophie française plaît aux Allemands' (interview with Philippe Forget), *Le Monde dimanche*, 24 October 1982, pp. xv, xvi.
81. Interview with Catherine von Bülow.
82. See Foucault's preface, dated 28 February 1979, to Pascal Bruckner and Alfred Krovoza, *Ennemi de l'état*, Claix: La Pensée sauvage, 1979, pp. 3–4.
83. 'Quelques Souvenirs de Pierre Boulez' (propos recueillis par Alain Jaubert), *Critique* 471–72, August–September 1986, pp. 745–46.
84. Michel Foucault and Pierre Boulez, 'La Musique contemporaine et le public', *CNAC Magazine* 15, May–June 1983, p. 10.
85. Interview with Daniel Defert.
86. Voeltzel, *Vingt Ans et après*, p. 131.
87. Transcript of the debate made by Romei Yashimoto, Bibliothèque du Saulchoir.
88. 'La Société disciplinaire en crise: développement de la diversité et l'indépendence en crise', *Asahi janaru*, 12 May 1978.
89. A cassette recording of this lecture can be consulted in the Bibliothèque du Saulchoir.
90. Michel Foucault and Richard Sennett, 'Sexuality and Solitude', *London Review of Books*, 21 May–3 June 1981, p. 5.
91. 'Le Gai savoir (II)'.
92. Interview with Daniel Defert.
93. Maurice Agulhon, *Les Quarante-huitards*, Paris: Gallimard, collection 'Archives', 1975. Agulhon is primarily a historian of forms of sociability; see his *La Vie sociale en Province intérieure au lendemain de la Révolution*, Paris: Clavreuil, 1971. Much of his subsequent work is concerned with the imagery and iconography of French republicanism, as in his *Marianne au combat*, Paris: Flammarion, 1979.
94. Michelle Perrot, '1848. Révolution et prisons', in *L'impossible Prison. Recherches sur le système pénitentiare au XIXᵉ siècle*, Paris: Seuil, 1980, pp. 277–312. As the Société did not have its own publication, Perrot's study, together with the other papers in this volume, was first published in *Annales historiques de la Révolution française* 2, 1977.
95. Jacques Léonard, 'L'Historien et le philosophe' in *l'impossible Prison*, pp. 17, 16.
96. See André Zysberg, 'Politiques du bagne, 1820–1850', and Jacques Valette, 'Le Bagne de Rochefort, 1815–1856', in *L'impossible Prison*.
97. Jacques Léonard, 'L'Historien et le philosophe', especially pp. 11, 12, 14.
98. 'La Poussière et le nuage', ibid., pp. 30, 33, 34.
99. Ibid., p. 39
100. 'Débat avec Michel Foucault', ibid., pp. 41, 42–43.
101. Ibid., p. 44.
102. Peter Burke, *The French Historical Revolution: The 'Annales' School 1929–89*, Cambridge: Polity, 1990, p. 113.

103. 'Débat avec Michel Foucault', p. 47.
104. Ibid., p. 51.
105. Ibid., pp. 52, 53.
106. Maurice Duverger, 'Le Pouvoir et la prison'. Michel Foucault contesté par des historiens', *Le Monde*, 4 July 1980, pp. 15, 21.
107. *Surveiller et punir*, pp. 261ff.
108. Maurice Agulhon, 'Postface', *L'impossible prison*, pp. 313, 316.
109. Foucault, ibid., pp. 316-18.
110. Maurice Agulhon, 'Présentation', ibid., p. 6.
111. Interview with Arlette Farge.
112. 'Qu'est-ce que la critique? (Critique et *Aufklärung*)', *Bulletin de la Société Française de Philosophie*, vol. 84, 1990, pp. 35-63.
113. 'I "reportages" di idee', *Corriera della sera*, 12 November 1978, p. 1. Finkielkraut's article was 'La Diversa Destra che viene dal Pacifico', ibid., pp. 1, 2.
114. Pascal Bruckner and Alain Finkielkraut, *Le Nouveau Désordre amoureux*, Paris: Seuil, 1977, reprinted in collection 'Points', 1979, p. 180.
115. Interview with Alain Finkielkraut.
116. 'La Rivolta dell' Iran corre sui nastri delli minicassette', *Corriere della sera*, 19 November 1978, p. 1.
117. *Le Monde*, 4 February 1976.
118. Mauriac, *Mauriac et fils*, pp. 250-51.
119. Cited, *Mauriac et fils*, p. 252.
120. Interview with Daniel Defert.
121. 'Entretien avec Michel Foucault' in Claire Brière and Pierre Blanchet, *Iran: La Révolution au nom de dieu*, Paris: Seuil, 1979, p. 236.
122. 'L'Esercito, quando la terra trema', *Corriere della sera*, 28 September 1978, pp. 1-2; 'Teheran: la fede contro lo Scià', ibid., 8 October 1978, p. 11; 'A Quoi rêvent les Iraniens?', *Le Nouvel Observateur*, 16 October 1978, pp. 48-49.
123. 'A Quoi rêvent les Iraniens?', p. 49.
124. 'Teheran: La fede contro lo Scià'.
125. 'Lettre ouverte à Mehdi Bazargan', *Le Nouvel Observateur*, 14 April 1979; 'Teheran: la fede contro lo Scià'.
126. 'Una Rivolta con le mani nude', *Corriere*, 5 November 1978, pp. 1-2; 'Sfida all opposizione', ibid., 7 November 1978, pp. 1-2; 'La Rivolta dell' Iran corre sui nastri delli minicassette', ibid., 19 November 1978, pp. 1-2; 'Il mitico capo della rivolta nell Iran', ibid., pp. 1-2.
127. 'Une Iranienne écrit', *Le Nouvel Observateur*, 6 November 1978, p. 27.
128. 'Réponse à une lectrice iranienne', ibid., 13 November, p. 24.
129. 'Una Rivolta con le mani nude'.
130. 'Il mitico capo fella rivolta nell' Iran'.
131. 'Una polveriera chiamata Islam', *Corriere della sera*, 13 February 1979, p. 1.
132. 'Il mitico capo . . .'.
133. 'A Quoi rêvent les Iraniens?'
134. Mauriac, *Mauriac et fils*, pp. 322-23.
135. Claudie and Jacques Broyelle, 'A Quoi rêvent les philosophes?', *Le Matin*, 24 March 1979, p. 13.
136. 'Michel Foucault et l'Iran', *Le Matin*, 26 March 1979, p. 15.
137. 'Lettre ouverte à Mehdi Bazargan'.

138. 'Inutile de se soulever?', *Le Monde*, 11 May 1979.
139. Cited, Bernard Kouchner, *L'Ile de lumière*, Paris: Presses Pocket, 1989, p. 42.
140. Ibid., p. 14.
141. For a profile of Kouchner, see Paul Rambali, 'Minister of Mercy', *Weekend Guardian*, 1–2 June 1991, pp. 14–15.
142. Bernard Kouchner, 'Un vrai Samouraï', *Michel Foucault, Une Histoire de la vérité*, pp. 86–87; interview with Bernard Kouchner.
143. Kouchner, *L'Ile de lumière*, p. 39.
144. Cited, ibid., p. 51.
145. Xavier Emmanuelli, 'Un Bateau pour Saint-Germain-des-Près', *Quotidien du médecin*, 4 December 1978.
146. Raymond Aron, *Mémoires*, Paris: Julliard, 1983, pp. 709–11.
147. Beauvoir, *La Cérémonie des adieux*, p. 146.
148. Mauriac, *Le Rire des enfants dans les yeux des pères*, p. 601.
149. Kouchner, *L'Ile de Lumière*, pp. 263–65.

Chapter 16

1. Roger Stéphane, *Portrait de l'aventurier*, Paris: Le Sagittaire, 1950.
2. Mauriac, *Mauriac et fils*, p. 226.
3. Interview with Michel Albaric.
4. *L'Usage des plaisirs*, Paris: Gallimard, 1984, p. 12.
5. Ibid., p. 13, n.
6. Ibid., p. 14.
7. Interview with Paul Veyne.
8. *Résumé des cours*, p. 123.
9. For a general overview of the theme of governmentality, see Colin Gordon: 'Governmental Rationality: An Introduction', *The Foucault Effect*, pp. 1–52.
10. Ibid., p. 134.
11. Ibid.
12. 'Une Esthétique de l'existence', *Le Monde*, 15–16 July 1984, p. xi. The interview, conducted by Alessandro Fontana on 25 April 1984, originally appeared in a rather different form as 'Parla Michel Foucault: Alle fonti del piacere', *Panorama*, 28 May 1984, pp. 186–93.
13. 'Carceri e manicomi nel consegno del potere', p. 6.
14. Claude Mauriac, *Le Temps accompli*, p. 32.
15. *L'Usage des plaisirs*, p. 14.
16. 'The Power and Politics of Michel Foucault', interview with Peter Maas and David Brock, *Inside*, 22 April 1983, cited, Bernauer, *Michel Foucault's Force of Flight*, p. 180.
17. Nietzsche, *The Gay Science*, p. 232.
18. Michel Foucault, Henry Juramy, Christian Revon, Jacues Verges, Jean Lapeyrie and Dominique Nocaudie, 'Se Défendre' in *Pour la Défense libre*: Paris, Centre de Recherche et de Formation Juridique, 1980 (supplément à la revue *Actes* no. 24–25), p. 5. Interview with Christian Revon.
19. François Deltombe, 'Un Justiciable devant les problèmes de défense', ibid., p. 21.
20. 'Luttes autour de la prison', *Esprit* 35, November 1979, pp. 106, 108.

21. Interview with Antoine Lazarus.

22. For a description, see Bernard Guetta, 'Une Journée en "Haute Sécurité" ', *Le Nouvel Observateur*, 3 April 1978, pp. 84ff.

23. 'Il faut tout repenser la loi et la prison', *Libération*, 6 July 1981, p. 2.

24. 'De la Nécessité de mettre un terme à toute peine', *Libération*, 18 September 1981, p. 5.

25. ' "Se Prétend innocent et n'accepte pas sa peine" ' (31 March 1980) in Roger Knobelspiess, *QHS: Quartier de haute sécurité*, Paris: Stock, 1980, p. 11.

26. See, for example, the lecture on 'The Dangerous Individual' delivered to a symposium in Toronto in October 1977, *Politics, Philosophy, Culture*, pp. 125-51.

27. 'Se prétend innocent et n'accepte pas sa peine' p. 14.

28. Mauriac, *Mauriac et fils*, p. 349.

29. Irène Allier, 'Knobelspiess: un procès en trompe l'oeil', *Le Nouvel Observateur*, 31 October 1981, p. 30.

30. Dominique Le Guilledoux, 'La Libération de Roger Knobelspiess', *Le Monde*, 16 August 1990, p. 6.

31. 'Vous êtes dangereux', *Libération*, 10 June 1983, p. 20.

32. See François Caviglioli, 'Le Plongeon de Knobelspiess', *Le Nouvel Observateur*, 10 June 1983, p. 24.

33. Mauriac, *Mauriac et fils*, p. 254; interview with Daniel Defert. On the Goldman affair, see Goldman, *Souvenirs obscurs d'un Juif polonais né en France*, and Régis Debray, *Les Rendez-vous manqués (Pour Pierre Goldman)*, Paris: Seuil, 1975. Goldman was murdered in very suspicious circumstances in 1979.

34. Mauriac, *Mauriac et fils*, p. 253.

35. See in particular Pierre Manent, 'Lire Michel Foucault', *Commentaire* 7, Autumn 1979, pp. 369-75.

36. 'Lacan, il "liberatore" ', *Corriere della sera*, 11 September 1981, p. 1.

37. Bernard Henri-Lévy, *Les Aventures de la liberté*, Paris: Grasset, 1991, pp. 364-65.

38. Jacques Bureau, '*Libération* devant la révolution inattendue', *Esprit* 1, January 1980, pp. 56-58; Nicole Gnesotto, '*Le Nouvel Observateur*: "L'Histoire déraillée" ', ibid., pp. 64-69.

39. *Les Etats généraux de la philosophie (16 et 17 juin 1979)*, Paris: Flammarion, 1979.

40. Jean-Paul Aron and Roger Kempf, *Le Pénis et la démoralisation de l'occident*, Paris: Grasset, 1978, p. 17 and n.

41. See for instance Emmanuel Le Roy Ladurie, 'L'Offensive anti-sexe du dix-neuvième siècle', *Le Monde*, 27 October 1978, p. 24.

42. Pierre Nora, 'Que peuvent les intellectuels?', *Le Débat* 1, May 1980, p. 17.

43. Ibid., p. 10.

44. Pierre Nora, 'Il avait un besoin formidable d'être aimé', *L'Evénément du jeudi*, 18-24 September 1986, p. 82.

45. Interview with Paul Veyne.

46. Marcel Gauchet, 'De l'Inexistentialisme', *Le Débat* 1, p. 24. The reference is to Paul Veyne, 'Foucault révolutionne l'histoire' in *Comment on écrit l'histoire*, Paris: Seuil, collection 'Points', 1978, p. 227.

47. Marcel Gauchet and Gladys Swain, *La Pratique de l'esprit humain: L'Institution asilaire et la révolution démocratique*, Paris: Gallimard, 1980, p. 498. See also 'Un Nouveau Regard sur l'histoire de la folie: Entretien avec Marcel Gauchet et Gladys Swain', *Esprit* 11, November 1983, pp. 77-86.

48. Pierre Nora, 'Il avait un besoin formidable d'être aimé'.
49. Catherine von Bülow, 'Contredire est un devoir', p. 176.
50. Mauriac, *Le Temps accompli*, p. 43.
51. This was explored in discussions with François Wahl, with Jean-Pierre Barou acting as an intermediary. Interviews with Paul Veyne, Jean-Pierre Barou.
52. Transcript of discussion with Hubert L. Dreyfus and Paul Rabinow, April 1983 (Bibliothèque du Saulchoir, D250 [5]).
53. 'Le Philosophe masqué', p. 1.
54. Interview with Michelle Perrot.
55. 'Une Esthétique de l'existence', p. xi.
56. 'Pour en finir avec les mensonges', *Le Nouvel Observateur*, 21 June 1985, p. 60.
57. 'Structuralism and Post-Structuralism: An Interview with Michel Foucault', p. 211.
58. Didier Eribon, 'Pierre Bourdieu: La Grande Illusion des intellectuels', *Le Monde dimanche*, 4 May 1980, p. 1.
59. 'Le Moment de la vérité', *Le Matin*, 25 April 1979, p. 20.
60. 'Vivre autrement le temps', *Le Nouvel Observateur*, 30 April 1979, p. 20.
61. Bel, *Maurice Clavel*, p. 354.
62. Postscript, *Death and the Labyrinth*, pp. 186–87.
63. Calvet, *Roland Barthes*, pp. 293–97, 300–01.
64. Mauriac, *Le Rire des pères dans les yeux des enfants*, pp. 618–19.
65. 'Roland Barthes (12 novembre 1915–26 mars 1980)', *Annuaire du Collège de France*, 1979–80, pp. 61–62.
66. Mauriac, *Le Rire des pères dans les yeux des enfants*, p. 616.
67. Defert, 'Lettre à Claude Lanzmann', p. 1201.
68. Bülow, 'Contredire est un devoir', p. 177.
69. Mauriac, *Le Rire des pères dans les yeux des enfants*, p. 617.
70. Interviews with Daniel Defert and Jeannette Colombel.
71. Christian Zimmer, 'Dans le combat gauchiste', *Le Monde*, 17 April 1980, p. 17. The special edition of *Libération* published on the occasion of Sartre's death makes precisely the same error of omission.
72. Defert, 'Lettre à Claude Lanzmann', p. 1201.
73. 'The Minimalist Self', p. 12.
74. '*Omnes et singulatim*: Towards a Criticism of Political Reason', *Politics, Philosophy, Culture*, pp. 57–85. A French version appeared as '*Omnes et singulatim*: Vers une critique de la raison politique', *Le Débat* 41, September–November 1986.
75. Cassette recording of discussion at Stanford, 11 October 1979, Bibliothèque du Saulchoir (C9).
76. Dreyfus and Rabinow, *Michel Foucault: Beyond Structuralism and Hermeneutics*, p. vii.
77. The lectures remain unpublished; transcripts may be consulted in the Bibliothèque du Saulchoir.
78. Keith Gandal and Stephen Kotkin, 'Foucault in Berkeley', *History of the Present*, February 1985, p. 6.
79. Michel Foucault and Richard Sennet, 'Sexuality and Solitude', *London Review of Books*, 21 May–3 June 1981, pp. 3–7.
80. Carlin Romano, 'Michel Foucault's New Clothes', *Village Voice*, 29 April–5 May 1981, p. 1; Otto Friedrich, 'France's philosopher of Power', *Time*, 16 November 1981, p. 58.

81. Richard Rorty, 'Foucault and epistemology' in David Couzens Hoy, ed., *Foucault: A Critical Reader*, Oxford: Blackwell, 1986, p. 47.
82. Jürgen Habermas, 'Modernity Versus Post-Modernity', *New German Critique* 22, Winter 1981, p. 13. See also chapters 9 and 10 of his *Philosophical Discourse of Modernity*, tr. Frederick G. Lawrence, Cambridge: Polity, 1987.
83. Clifford Geertz, 'Stir Crazy', *New York Review of Books*, 26 January 1978, p. 3.
84. H. C. E. Midelfort, 'Madness and Civilization in Early Modern Europe: A Reappraisal of Michel Foucault' in B. C. Malament, ed., *After the Reformation: Essays in Honor of J. H. Hester*, Philadelphia: University of Pennsylvania Press, 1980, pp. 247–65. For similar comments on Foucault's tendency to exaggerate the geographical scope of the 'great confinement', see Roy Porter, *Mind-Forg'd Manacles: A History of Madness in England from the Restoration to the Regency*, London: Athlone Press, 1987.
85. Winifred Barbara Maher and Brendan Maher, 'The Ship of Fools: *Stultifera Navis* or *Ignis Fatuus?*', *American Psychologist*, July 1982, pp. 756–61.
86. Cited, ibid., p. 759.
87. Lawrence Stone, 'Madness', *New York Review of Books*, 16 December 1982, p. 29.
88. Ibid., p. 30.
89. Ibid., p. 28.
90. 'Polemics, Politics and Problematizations', *The Foucault Reader*, p. 381.
91. 'An Exchange with Michel Foucault', *New York Review of Books*, 31 March 1984, p. 42.
92. Ibid., p. 43, citing G. Weissmann, 'Foucault and the Bag Lady', *Hospital Practice*, August 1982.
93. Andrew Scull, 'Michel Foucault's History of Madness', *History of the Human Sciences*, vol. 3, no. 1, February 1990, p. 64, n.
94. For initial accounts of these events, see K. S. Karol, 'La Tragédie de Louis Althusser', *Le Nouvel Observateur*, 24 November 1980, pp. 26–27; an abridged translation appeared as 'The Tragedy of the Althussers', *New Left Review* 124, November–December 1980, pp. 93–95. The definitive account is Yann Moulier Boutang, *Louis Althusser*. For Althusser's own horrific description of the murder of Hélène, see his *L'Avenir dure longtemps*, pp. 11–12.
95. Ibid., p. 24.
96. Boutang, *Louis Althusser*, p. 59.
97. Althusser, *L'Avenir dure longtemps*, p. 19.
98. Philippe Boggio, 'Trop lourd', *Le Monde*, 19 November 1980, p. 16.
99. Althusser, *L'Avenir dure longtemps*, pp. 264–66; cf. 'Entretien avec le Père Stanislas Breton', in Lévy, *Les Aventures de la liberté*, pp. 423–25.

Chapter 17

1. See the poll published in *Lire*, April 1981.
2. 'Entretien: L'Intellectuel et les pouvoirs' (interview with Christian Panier and Pierre Watté, 14 May 1981), *La Revue nouvelle*, vol. 50, no. 10, October 1984, p. 338.

3. See 'Le Nouvel Observateur e l'union della sinistra', Spirali, 15 January 1980, pp. 53–55.

4. The neologism is fairly acceptable in French; it is common for a mayor, for instance, to speak of the inhabitants of his town as mes administrés.

5. 'Est-il donc important de penser?' (interview with Didier Eribon), Libération, 30–31 May 1981, p. 21.

6. 'Il faut tout repenser: La Loi et la prison', Libération, 6 July 1981, p. 2.

7. Interview with Bernard Kouchner.

8. 'Face aux gouvernements, les droits de l'homme', Actes: Les Cahiers d'action juridique 54, Summer 1986, p. 22. This text was never published during Foucault's lifetime, and first appeared in Libération, 1 July 1984.

9. Mario Bettati and Bernard Kouchner, Le Devoir d'ingérence, Paris: Denoël, 1987.

10. William R. Hackman, 'The Foucault Conference', Telos 51, Spring 1982, pp. 191–96.

11. Friedrich, 'France's Philosopher of Power'.

12. Cited, Hackman, 'The Foucault Conference', p. 196.

13. For a summary of events, see Oliver MacDonald, 'The Polish Vortex: Solidarity and Socialism', New Left Review 139, May–June 1983, pp. 5–48. For the earlier period, see Neal Ascherson, The Polish August, Harmondsworth: Penguin, 1981.

14. Le Monde, 15 December 1981.

15. Les Elections législatives de juin 1981, 'Supplément aux Dossiers et documents du Monde', June 1981, p. 43.

16. Cited Mauriac, Mauriac et fils, p. 351–2.

17. 'Politics and Ethics: An Interview', The Foucault Reader, p. 377.

18. Pierre Mauroy, A Gauche, Paris: Marabout, 1986, p. 245.

19. Le Monde, 19 December 1981.

20. Le Matin, 21 December 1981.

21. Le Monde, 17 December 1981.

22. Interview with Jacques Lebas.

23. Le Monde, 24 December 1981.

24. Mauriac, Mauriac et fils, p. 358.

25. Ibid., p. 360.

26. Frédéric Edelmann, 'Un hommage des artistes et des intellectuels à l'Opéra de Paris', Le Monde, 24 December 1981.

27. Varsovivre is a pun on Varsovie (Warsaw) and vivre (to live).

28. Seweryn Blumsztajn, in Michel Foucault: Une Histoire de la vérité, p. 98. Interview with Edmond Maire.

29. See Hervé Hamon and Patrick Rotman, La Deuxième Gauche: Histoire intellectuelle et politique de la CFDT, Paris: Editions Ramsay, 1982.

30. Lech Walesa, A Path of Hope: An Autobiography, London: Pan, 1988, p. 170.

31. Le Monde, 26–27 June 1977, p. 4.

32. 'The Flying University', New York Review of Books, 24 January 1980, p. 49.

33. Cited, Marcin Frybes, 'Rencontre ou malentendu autour de Solidarnosc?', CFDT aujourd'hui 100, March 1991, p. 106, Cf. 'Intellectuals and Labor Unions, An Interview with Robert Bono, conducted by Paul Rabinow and Keith Gandal', History of the Present, Spring 1986, pp. 3, 9–10.

34. See 'La Pologne, et après? Edmond Maire: Entretien Michel Foucault, Le Débat

25, May 1983, pp. 3–35

35. 'Un Système fini face à une demande infinie', in *Sécurité sociale: l'enjeu*, Paris: Syros, 1983, pp. 39–63.

36. Bono, 'Intellectuals and Labor Unions', p. 3.

37. Interviews with Alain Finkielkraut and Pierre Vidal-Naquet.

38. Interview with Jacques Lebas.

39. Michel Foucault, Simone Signoret and Bernard Kouchner, 'En abandonnant les Polonais, nous renonçons à une part de nous-mêmes', *Le Nouvel Observateur*, 9 October 1982, p. 36.

40. Bernard Kouchner, 'Un vrai Samouraï', p. 88.

41. 'En Abandonnant les Polonais . . .'

42. Kouchner, 'Un vrai Samouraï', p. 88. Interviews with Bernard Kouchner, Jacques Lebas.

43. Transcripts of the lectures can be consulted at the Bibliothèque du Saulchoir (catalogued at D201; typescript, pp. 159). The tape of the discussion with Bertin was shown on French television in 1988; transcribed as 'Entretien avec Michel Foucault', *Comités d'éthique à travers le monde: Recherches en cours*, Paris: Tierce/INSERM, 1989, pp. 228–35.

44. Typescripts of three lectures, University of Toronto, 1982, Bibliothèque du Saulchoir, D243.

45. Interview with Philippe Meyer.

46. 'Non aux compromis', *Gai Pied* 43, October 1982, p. 9.

47. *And the Band Played On*, p. 149.

48. 'Technologies of the Self: A Seminar with Michel Foucault'.

49. 'Technologies of the Self', ibid., pp. 16–49; 'The Political Technology of Individuals', ibid., 145–62.

50. Introduction, ibid., p. 11.

51. 'Truth, Power, Self: An Interview with Michel Foucault', ibid., pp. 11, 12, 13.

52. Jana Sawicki, *Disciplining Foucault: Feminism, Power, and the Body*, London: Routledge, 1991, p. 15.

53. Cited, Christian Colombani, 'Les "Lieux de vie" et l'affaire du Coral. 1. Une campagne et une enquête', *Le Monde*, 28 November 1982, p. 9.

54. Guy Hocquenhem, *Les petits Garçons*, Paris: Albin Michel, 1983, p. 144.

55. Ibid., p. 168.

56. Ibid., pp. 174, 175.

57. Ibid., p. 176.

58. See the report in *Le Monde*, 22 January 1983; interview with Jean-Pierre Mignon.

59. Interviews with René Schérer, Christian Revon, Laurent Dispot.

60. *Résumé des cours*, pp. 145–66. Extracts from the lectures given between January and March 1982 have been published as 'Herméneutique du sujet', *Concordia* 12, 1988, pp. 44–68. The extracts are retranslated from the German version established by Helmut Becker and Lothar Wolfstetter and first published in *Freiheit und Selbstsorge*, Frankfurt: Materalis Verlag, 1985.

61. *Histoire de la folie*, p. 105.

62. Deleuze, *Foucault*, p. 35.

63. Pierre Nora, 'Il avait un besoin formidable d'être aimé'.

64. *Surveiller et punir*, p. 79; Arlette Farge, *Le Vol d'aliments . . .*, Paris: Plon, 1974.

65. Arlette Farge, *Le Goût de l'archive*, Paris: Seuil, 1989, p. 24. This short but

delightful essay is probably the best account of what working on the Bastille archives actually involved.

66. Mauriac, *Et comme l'Espérance est violente*, p. 595.

67. Arlette Farge, 'Travailler avec Michel Foucault', *Le Débat* 41, September–November 1986, p. 166.

68. See, however, Emmanuel Todd, 'Ce que révèlent les lettres de cachet', *Le Monde*, 5 November 1982; Michal Ignatieff, 'At the Feet of the Father', *Times Literary Supplement*, 22 April 1983.

69. Interview with Arlette Farge.

Chapter 18

1. Keith Gondal and Stephen Kotkin 'Foucault in Berkeley', *History of the Present*, February 1985, p. 6.

2. Interview with Paul Veyne.

3. Transcripts of these discussions can be seen in the Bibliothèque du Saulchoir, which also holds cassette recordings of them.

4. *L'Usage des plaisirs*, p. 14.

5. 'On the Genealogy of Ethics', *The Foucault Reader*, p. 342.

6. Ibid., p. 346.

7. Ibid., p. 334.

8. Ibid., p. 362.

9. Ibid., p. 315; Nietzsche, *The Gay Science*, p. 232.

10. Max Gallo, 'Les Intellectuels, la politique et la modernité', *Le Monde*, 26 July 1983, p. 7.

11. Jean Daniel, 'Le Prince et les scribes', *Le Nouvel Observateur*, 19 August 1983, pp. 18–19.

12. Philippe Boggio, 'Le Silence des intellectuels de gauche. 1. Victoire à contre-temps', *Le Monde*, 27 July 1983, pp. 1, 10.

13. Philippe Boggio, 'Le Silence des intellectuels de gauche. 2. Les Chemins de traverse,' *Le Monde*, 28 July 1983, p. 6.

14. Eribon, *Michel Foucault*, p. 325.

15. Cited, ibid.

16. Ibid., pp. 325–26; interview with Didier Eribon.

17. 'Le Souci de la vérité', *Magazine littéraire* 207, May 1984, p. 23.

18. 'Structuralism and Post-Structuralism', p. 208.

19. Ibid., p. 209.

20. Robert Badinter, 'Au Nom des mots', in *Michel Foucault: Une Histoire de la vérité*, p. 73.

21. 'L'Angoisse de juger', *Le Nouvel Observateur*, 30 May 1977, pp. 92–126.

22. 'Au nom des mots', p. 74.

23. Interview with Robert Badinter.

24. Habermas, 'Taking Aim at the Heart of the Present', pp. 103–104.

25. Extracts published as 'Un cours inédit', *Magazine littéraire* 207, May 1984, pp. 35–39.

26. François Ewald, 'Droit: systèmes et stratégies', *Le Débat* 41, September–November 1986, pp. 63–69.

27. 'Discourse and Truth: The Problematization of Parrhesia', 121-page typescript, Bibliothéque du Saulchoir, D213.
28. 'What is Enlightenment?', tr. Catherine Porter, *The Foucault Reader*, pp. 32–50; Hans Sluga, 'Foucault à Berkeley: l'auteur et le discours', *Critique* 471–72, August–September 1986, pp. 840–57.
29. 'What Is Enlightenment?', pp. 39–42.
30. Keith Gandal and Stephen Kotkin, 'Governing Work and Social Life in the USA and the USSR', *History of the Present*, February 1985, p. 4.
31. Interviews with Jacques Almira and Dominique Seglard.
32. Philip Horvitz, 'Don't Cry for me. Academia', *Jimmy and Lucy's House of 'K'* 2, August 1984, p. 80.
33. Arlette Farge and Michel Foucault, 'Le Style de l'histoire', *Le Matin*, 21 February 1984, p. 21.
34. 'Le Souci de la vérité', *Le Nouvel Observateur*, 17 February 1984, pp. 56–57.
35. Mauriac, *Mauriac et fils*, pp. 387–91. The full text of the letter is reproduced, pp. 389–90.
36. Ibid., p. 394.
37. 'Usages des plaisirs et techniques de soi', *Le Débat* 27, November 1983, pp. 46–72; 'Rêver de ses plaisirs: sur l'onirocritique d'Artémidore', *Recherches sur la philosophie et le langage* 3, 1983, pp. 53–78.
38. 'Le Combat de la chasteté', *Communications* 35, May 1982, pp. 15–25.
39. Nora, 'Il avait un si formidable besoin d'être aimé'.
40. 'On the Genealogy of Ethics', pp. 347–48.
41. Thus, Foucault refers briefly to the existence in ancient China of texts containing 'advice on erotic behaviour designed to heighten as much as possible the pleasure of the partners, or at least the man' (p. 159). Foucault's authority for his brief comments is van Gulick, whose study of China appeared in French as *La Vie sexuelle dans la Chine ancienne* in 1971.
42. *L'Usage des plaisirs*, pp. 74–76.
43. Ibid., pp. 133, 141.
44. Ibid., p. 39.
45. Ibid., p. 63.
46. Ibid., p. 111.
47. Ibid., p. 212–13.
48. Ibid., p. 207.
49. Ibid., p. 243.
50. Ibid., p. 247.
51. Ibid., p. 274.
52. George Steiner, 'Power Play', *New Yorker*, 17 March 1986, pp. 108–109.
53. *Le Souci de soi*, pp. 43, 41.
54. Ibid., p. 59.
55. Ibid., p. 122.
56. Ibid., p. 123.
57. Ibid., p. 164.
58. Mauriac, *Le Temps accompli*, p. 22.
59. Interviews with Daniel Defert, Francine Fruchaud and Denys Foucault.
60. Bülow, 'Contredire est un devoir', p. 178.
61. Mauriac, *Le Temps accompli*, p. 49.

62. Ibid., p. 32.
63. *L'Usage des plaisirs*, pp. 14–15. For unexplained reasons, *Le Monde* had announced on 28 June that Deleuze would be reading the last page of *L'Archéologie du savoir*.
64. Mauriac, *Le Temps accompli*, pp. 39, 21.
65. Eribon, *Michel Foucault*, p. 354.
66. Mauriac, *Le Temps accompli*, p. 41.
67. Interviews with Michel Albaric and Paul Veyne.
68. *Le Monde*, 28 June 1984.
69. Reproduced as the cover illustration to James Bernauer and David Rasmussen, eds., *The Final Foucault*, Cambridge, Massachusetts: MIT Press, 1988.
70. 'Hier à 13 heures . . .' *Libération*, 26 June 1984, p. 2.
71. Cited, Samuelson, *Il Etait une fois 'Libération'*, p. 19.
72. 'Michel Foucault, an Interview: Sex, Power and the Politics of Identity', p. 28.
73. Shilts, *And the Band Played On*, p. 472.
74. Edward Said, 'Michel Foucault', *Raritan*, vol. 4, no. 2, 1984, p. 9. See Ed Cohen, 'Foucauldian necrologies: "gay" "politics?" politically gay?', *Textual Practice*, vol. 2, no. 1, Spring 1988.
75. On San Francisco as a gay's 'Israel', see Larry Kramer, *Reports from the Holocaust. The Making of an AIDS Activist*, Harmondsworth: Penguin, 1990, p. 254.
76. Cohen, 'Foucauldian necrologies', p. 91.
77. Shilts, *And the Band Played On*, p. 472.
78. Interview with Daniel Defert.
79. Sheridan, 'Diary'.
80. Paul Veyne, 'Le Dernier Foucault et sa morale', *Critique* 471–472, August–September 1986, p. 940; Pierre Nora, 'Il avait un besoin formidable d'être aimé'.
81. Interview with Carl Gardner.
82. 'On the Genealogy of Ethics', *The Foucault Reader*, p. 342.
83. Mauriac, *Le Temps accompli*, pp. 32–33.
84. Mauriac, *L'Oncle Marcel*, p. 449.
85. *Radioscopie de Michel Foucault*.
86. Jean-Paul Aron, 'Mon SIDA', *Le Nouvel Observateur*, 30 October–5 November 1987, p. 43. For his earlier criticisms of Foucault, see his *Les Modernes*.
87. Simon Watney, *Policing Desire. Pornography, AIDS and the Media*, London: Comedia, 1987, p. 123.
88. 'Daniel Defert: "Plus on est honteux, plus on avoue"', propos recueillis par Gilles Pail', *Libération*, 31 October–1 November 1978, p. 2.
89. Interview with Claude Mauriac.
90. Bernard Kouchner, 'Un vrai Samouraï', p. 89; interview with Bernard Kouchner.
91. Hervé Guibert, 'Les Secrets d'un homme', *Mauve le Vierge*, Paris: Gallimard, 1988, pp. 103–11.
92. 'La Vie SIDA. Le Nouveau roman de Hervé Guibert' (interview with Antoine de Gaudemar), *Libération*, 1 March 1990, p. 20.
93. Hervé Guibert, *A l'Ami qui ne m'a pas sauvé la vie*, Paris: Gallimard, 1990, pp. 117–18.
94. Ibid., p. 30.
95. Mauriac, *Mauriac et fils*, p. 244.
96. 'Deuxième Entretien avec Michel Foucault', p. 49.
97. Nietzsche, *Daybreak*, 307.

BIBLIOGRAPHY

The Works of Michel Foucault

Unless otherwise stated, the place of publication is Paris. All items listed as 'unpublished' are held in the Bibliothèque du Saulchoir, Paris. Insofar as it is possible to do so, items are listed in the order of their composition rather than their publication.

1. *Maladie mentale et personnalité*, Presses Universitaires de France, 1954.
2. 'Introduction' to Ludwig Binswanger, *Le Rêve et l'existence*, tr. Jacqueline Verdeaux, Desclée de Brouwer 1954, pp. 9–128. Tr. Forest Williams, 'Dream, Imagination and Existence', *Review of Existential Psychiatry*, vol. XIX, no. 1, 1984–85, pp. 29–78.
3. 'La Recherche scientifique et la psychologie', in Jean-Edouard Morère, ed., *Des Chercheurs français s'interrogent*, Presses Universitaires de France, 1957, pp, 171–201.
4. 'La Psychologie de 1850 à 1950', in A. Weber and D. Huisman, eds., *Histoire de la philosophie européenne. Tôme 2. Tableau de la philosophie contemporaine*, Fischbacher, 1957, pp. 591–606.
   Republished, *Revue internationale de philosophie*, Vol. 44, no. 173, 2/1990, pp. 159–76.
5. Translation, with Daniel Rocher, of *Le Cycle de la structure (Der Gestaltkreis)*, Desclée de Brouwer, 1958.
6. *Thèse complémentaire* for *Doctorat ès lettres*, 1961: introduction to and translation of Immanuel Kant, *Anthropologie in pragmatischer Hinsicht* (two volumes).
   Second volume published as *Anthropologie du point de vue pragmatique*, Vrin, 1964.
7. *Folie et déraison. Histoire de la folie à l'âge classique*, Plon, 1961.
   Abridged version published as *Histoire de la folie*, 10/18, Union Générale de l'Edition, 1964. Reprinted in complete form as *Histoire de la folie à l'âge classique*, Gallimard, 1972 with a new preface and two appendices: 'La Folie, l'absence d'oeuvre' (*La Table ronde*, May 1964) and 'Mon Corps, ce papier, ce feu' (*Paideia*, September 1971). Reprinted in Gallimard's 'Tel' collection, 1978, without the appendices.
   Tr. Richard Howard, *Madness and Civilization. A History of Insanity in the Age of Reason*., New York: Pantheon, 1965, introduction by José Barchilon; London: Tavistock, 1967, Introduction by David Cooper. This is a translation of the 1964 abridged edition, with some additions from the original version. Chapter 4 subsequently translated by Anthony Pugh as 'Experiences of Madness', *History of the Human Sciences*, vol. 4, no. 1, February 1991, pp. 1–25.

8. 'La Folie n'existe que dans une société' (interview with Jean-Paul Weber), *Le Monde*, 22 July 1961, p. 9.

9. Review of Alexandre Koyré, *La Révolution astronomique: Copernic, Kepler, Borelli*, *La Nouvelle Revue Française* 108, December 1961, pp. 1123–24.

10. *Maladie mentale et psychologie*, Presses Universitaires de France, 1962, 1966. A heavily rewritten version of *Maladie mentale et personnalité*. Tr. Alan Sheridan, *Mental Illness and Psychology*, New York: Harper and Row, 1976. Republished, Berkeley: University of California Press, with a foreword by Hubert Dreyfus, 1987.

11. 'Introduction' to Jean-Jacques Rousseau, *Rousseau juge de Jean-Jacques: Dialogues*, Armand Colin, 1962, pp. vii–xxiv.

12. 'Le "Non" du père', *Critique* 178, March 1962, pp. 195–209. Review of Jean Laplanche, *Hölderlin et la question du père*. Tr. 'The Father's "No" ', in *Language, Counter-Memory, Practice: Selected Essays and Interviews*, Edited by Donald Bouchard. Translated by Donald Bouchard and Sherry Simon, Ithaca: Cornell University Press, 1977, pp. 68–86.

13. 'Les Déviations religieuses et le savoir médical', in Jacques Le Goff, ed., *Hérésies et sociétés dans l'Europe occidentale, 11-1-8 siècles*, Mouton, 1968, pp. 19–29.

14. 'Le Cycle des grenouilles', *La Nouvelle Revue française* 114, June 1962, pp. 1159–60. Introduction to texts by Jean-Pierre Brisset.

15. 'Un Si Cruel Savoir', *Critique* 182, July 1962, pp. 597–611. On Claude Crébillon, *Les Egarements du coeur et de l'esprit* and J.A. Reveroni de Saint-Cyr, *Pauliska ou la perversité moderne*.

16. 'Dire et voir chez Raymond Roussel', *Lettre ouverte* 4, Summer 1962, pp. 38–51. Reprinted in a modified version as the first chapter of *Raymond Roussel*.

17. Translation into French of Leo Spitzer, 'Linguistics and Literary History' as 'Art du langage et linguistique', in Spitzer, *Etudes de style*, Gallimard, 1962, pp. 45–78.

18. *Naissance de la clinique : Une Archéologie du regard médical*, Presses Universitaires de France, 1963. Revised edition published under the same title, 1972. Tr. Alan Sheridan Smith, *The Birth of the Clinic : An Archaeology of Medical Perception*, London: Tavistock, New York: Pantheon, 1973. The translation is, with some interpolations from the first edition, of the 1972 edition.

19. *Raymond Roussel*, Gallimard, 1963. Tr. Charles Ruas, *Death and the Labyrinth : The World of Raymond Roussel*, with an introduction by John Ashbery, New York: Doubleday, 1986; London: Athlone Press, 1987.

20. 'Wächter über die Nacht der Menschen' in Hans Ludwig Spegg. ed. *Unterwegs mit Rolf Italiaander: Begegnungen, Betrachtungern, Bibliographie*, Hamburg: Freie Akademie der Kunst, 1963, pp. 46–49. 'Préface à la transgression', *Critique* 195–96, August–September 1963, pp. 751–69. Tr. 'A Preface to Transgression' in *Language, Counter-Memory, Practice*, pp. 29–52.

21. 'Débat sur le roman', *Tel Quel* 17, Spring 1964, pp. 15–24 (transcript of a discussion held at Cérisy La Salle in September 1963).

22. 'Débat sur la Poésie', *Tel Quel* 17, Spring 1964, pp. 69–82 (transcript of a discussion in which Foucault participated, Cérisy La Salle, September 1963).

23. 'Le Langage à l'infini', *Tel Quel* 15, Autumn 1963, pp. 931–45. Tr. 'Language to Infinity', *Language, Counter-Memory, Practice*, pp. 53–67.

24. 'L'Eau et la folie', *Médecine et hygiène* 613, 23 October 1963, pp. 901–906.

25. 'Afterword to Gustave Flaubert, tr. Annaliese Botond, *Die Versuchung des Heiligen*

Antonius, Frankfurt: Insel, 1964, pp. 217–251. French version, 'Un "Fantastique" de bibliothèque', *Cahiers Renaud-Barrault* 59, March 1967, pp. 7–30. Reprinted under the title 'La Bibliothèque fantastique' as preface to Flaubert, *La Tentation de Saint Antoine*, Livre de poche, 1971, pp. 7–33; reprinted, Tzvetan Todorov et al., *Travail de Flaubert*, Seuil, 1983, pp. 103–22.

26. 'Guetter le jour qui vient' *La Nouvelle Revue Française* 130, October 1963, pp. 709–16. On Roger Laporte, *La Veille*.

27. 'Distance, origine, aspect', *Critique* 198, November 1963, pp. 931–45. on Philippe Sollers, *L'Intermédiaire*, M. Pleynet, *Paysages en deux*, J.L. Baudry, *Les Images* and *Tel Quel* nos. 1–14.

28. 'Un Grand Roman de la terreur', *France-Observateur*, 12 December 1963, p. 14. Reprinted, Jean-Edern Hallier, *Chaque Matin qui se lève est une leçon de courage*, Editions Libres, 1978, pp. 40–42. On Edern's *Aventures d'une jeune fille*.

29. 'Langage et littérature', typescript of lecture, Saint-Louis, Belgium, 1964.

30. 'La Prose d'Actéon', *La Nouvelle Revue Française* 135, March 1964, pp. 444–59. On Pierre Klossowski.

31. 'Le Langage de l'espace', *Critique*, 203, April 1964, pp. 378–82.

32. 'La Folie, l'absence d'une oeuvre', *La Table ronde* 196, May 1964, pp. 11–21. Reprinted as an appendix to the 1972 edition of *Histoire de la folie*.

33. 'Nietzsche, Freud, Marx', *Cahiers de Royaumont 6: Nietzsche*, Minuit, 1967, pp. 183–207 (The conference at which this paper was delivered took place in July 1964).
Tr. Jon Anderson and Gary Hentzi, 'Nietzsche, Freud, Marx', *Critical Texts*, vol. 11, no. 2, Winter 1986, pp. 1–5.

34. 'Pourquoi réédite-t-on l'oeuvre de Raymond Roussel? Un Précurseur de notre littérature moderne', *Le Monde* 22 August 1964, p. 9.

35. 'Les Mots qui saignent', *L'Express* 22 August 1964, pp. 21–22. On Pierre Klossowski's translation of Virgil's *Aeneid*.

36. 'Le Mallarmé de J.P. Richard', *Annales*, vol 19, no 5, September–October 1964, pp. 996–1004. On Richard's *L'Univers imaginaire de Mallarmé*.

37. 'L'Obligation d'écrire', *Arts*, 980, 11–17 November 1964, p. 3. On Gérard de Nerval.

38. 'Philosophie et psychologie', discussion with Alain Badiou, *Dossiers pédagogiques de la radio-télévision scolaire* 10, 15–27 February 1965, pp. 61–67.

39. 'Philosophie et vérité', discussion with Jean Hyppolite, Georges Canguilhem, Paul Ricoeur, D. Dreyfus and Alain Badiou, *Dossiers pédagogiques de la radio-télévision scolaire*, 27 March 1965, pp. 1–11.

40. 'La Prose du monde', *Diogène* 53, January–March 1966, pp. 20–41. An abbreviated version of Chapter 2 of *Les Mots et les choses*.
Tr. Victor Velen, 'The Prose of the World', *Diogenes* 53, Spring 1963, pp. 17–37.

41. 'Les Suivantes', *Mercure de France* 1221–22, July–August 1965, pp. 366–84. A version of the first chapter of *Les Mots et les choses*.

42. *Les Mots et les choses: une archéologie ds sciences humaines*, Gallimard, 1966.
Tr., no translator identified (Alan Sheridan), *The Order of Things: An Archaeology of the Human Sciences*, London: Tavistock, New York: Pantheon, 1971.

43. 'L'Arrière-fable', *L'Arc* 29, 1966, pp. 5–12. On Jules Verne.

44. 'Entretien: Michel Foucault, *Les Mots et les choses*', *Les Lettres françaises* 31 March 1966, pp. 3–4.

Interview with Raymond Bellour, reprinted in Bellour's *Le Livre des autres*, Editions de l'Herne, 1971, pp. 135–44.

Tr. John Johnston, 'The Order of Things', Sylvère Lotringer, ed., *Foucault Live*, New York: Semiotext(e), 1989, pp. 1–10.

45. 'A la Recherche du présent perdu', *L'Express* 775, 25 April – 1 May 1966, pp. 114–15. On Jean Thibaudeau, *Ouverture*.

46. 'Entretien', *La Quinzaine littéraire* 5, 16 May 1966, pp. 14–15. Interview with Madeleine Chapsal.

47. 'Lettre à Roger Caillois', 25 May 1966, reprinted in *Cahiers pour un temps. Homage à R. Caillois*, Centre Georges Pompidou, 1981, p. 228.

48. Letter of 4 June 1966 to René Magritte, in René Magritte, *Ecrits complets*, André Blavier, ed., Flammarion, 1972, p. 521.

49. 'L'Homme est-il mort? Un Entretien avec Michel Foucault', *Arts et loisirs* 38, 15–21 June 1966, pp. 8–9. Interview with Claude Bonnefoy.

50. 'La Pensée du dehors', *Critique* 229, June 1966, pp. 523–46. On Maurice Blanchot. Reprinted as *La Pensée du dehors*, Montpellier: Fata Morgana, 1986.

Tr. Brian Massumi, 'Maurice Blanchot: The Thought from Outside' in *Foucault/Blanchot*, New York: Zone Press, 1987, pp. 7–60.

51. 'Une Histoire restée muette', *La Quinzaine littéraire* 8, 1 July 1966. On Ernst Cassirer, *La Philosophie des lumières*.

52. 'Michel Foucault et Gilles Deleuze veulent rendre à Nietzsche son vrai visage', *Le Figaro littéraire*, 15 Septembre 1966, p. 7. Interview with Claude Jannoud.

53. 'Qu'est-ce qu'un philosophe?', *Connaissance des hommes* 22, Autumn 1966. Interview with Marie-Geneviève Foy.

54. 'C'était un nageur entre deux mots', *Arts-Loisirs* 54, 5–11 October 1966, pp. 8–9. Interview with Claude Bonnefoy on André Breton. 'Message ou bruit?', *Le Concours médical* 22 October 1966, pp. 685–86.

55. 'Un archéologue des idées: Michel Foucault', *Synthèses* 245, October 1966, pp. 45–49. Interview with Jean-Michel Minon.

56. 'Des Espaces autres', lecture given in Paris on 14 March 1967. *Architecture-Mouvement-Continuité* 5, October 1986, pp. 46–49.

Tr. Jay Miskowiec, 'Of Other Spaces', *Diacritics*, vol. 16, no 1, Spring 1986, pp. 22–27.

57. 'Le Structuralisme et l'analyse littéraire', lecture at the Club Tahar Hadad, Tunis, 4 February 1967, *Mission culturelle française information*, 10 April-10 May 1978.

Extracts reprinted *La Presse de Tunis*, 10 April 1987.

58. 'La Philosophie structuraliste permet de diagnostiquer ce qu'est aujourd'hui', *La Presse de Tunis* 12 April 1967, p. 3. Interview with Gérard Fellous.

59. 'Introduction générale', Friedrich Nietzsche, *Oeuvres philosophiques. Vol. V. Le Gai Savoir*, Translated by Pierre Klossowski, Gallimard, 1967, pp. i–iv. With Gilles Deleuze.

60. '*La Volonté de puissance*, texte capital mais incertain, va disparaître', *Le Monde* 24 May 1967, p. vii. Interview with Jacqueline Piatier.

61. 'Deuxième Entretien: sur les façons d'écrire l'histoire', *Les Lettres françaises*, 15 June 1967, pp. 6–9.

Interview with Raymond Bellour, reprinted in Bellour's *Le Livre des autres*, Editions de l'Herne, 1971, 189–207.

Tr. John Johnston, 'The Discourse of History', *Foucault Live*, pp. 11–34.
62. 'Che cos'è lei Professore Foucault?' *La Fiera letteraria* 39, 28 September 1967, pp. 11–15.
Interview with Paolo Caruso, reprinted in Caruso's *Conversazione con Lévi-Strauss, Foucault, Lacan*, Milan: Mursia, 1969, pp. 91–131.
63. 'Préface', Antoine Arnaud and Pierre Nicolle, *Grammaire générale et raisonée*, Paulet, 1967, pp. iii–xxvii.
Extract published as 'La Grammaire générale de Port-Royal', *Langages* 7, September 1967, pp. 7–15.
64. 'Les Mots et les images' *Le Nouvel Observateur* 154, 25 October 1967, pp. 49–50. On Irwin Panofsky's *Essais d'iconologie* and *Architecture gothique et pensée scolastique*.
65. 'Ceci n'est pas une pipe', *Cahiers du chemin*, 2, January 1968, pp. 79–105. On René Magritte.
Expanded version published as *Ceci n'est pas une pipe*, Montpellier: Fata Morgana, 1973. Tr. James Harkness, *This Is Not a Pipe*, Berkeley: University of California Press, 1982.
66. 'En Intervju med Michel Foucault', *Bonniers Litteraria Magazin*, March 1968, pp. 203–11. Interview with Yngve Lindung.
67. 'Foucault répond à Sartre', *La Quinzaine littéraire* 46, 1–15 March 1968, pp. 20–22. Transcript of radio interview with Jean-Pierre El Kabbach.
Tr. John Johnston, 'Foucault Responds to Sartre', *Foucault Live*, pp. 35–44.
68. 'Une Mise au point de Michel Foucault', *La Quinzaine littéraire* 47, 15–31 March 1968, p. 21.
69. 'Linguistique et sciences sociales', paper read to a conference held in Tunis in March 1968, *Revue tunisienne de sciences sociales* 19, December 1969, pp. 248–55.
70. 'Réponse à une question', *Esprit* 371, May 1968, pp. 850–74.
Tr. Anthony Nazzaro, 'History, Discourse, Discontinuity', *Salmagundi* 20, Summer-Fall 1972, pp. 225–48. Revised tr. Colin Gordon, 'Politics and the Study of Discourse', *Ideology and Consciousness* 3, Spring 1978, 7–26; reprinted with further revisions, Graham Burchell, Colin Gordon and Peter Miller, eds., *The Foucault Effect: Studies in Governmentality*, Hemel Hemsptead: Harvester, 1991, pp. 53–72.
71. 'Lettre à Jacques Proust', *La Pensée* 139, May–June 1968, pp. 114–19.
72. 'Réponse au Cercle d'épistémologie', *Cahiers pour l'analyse* 9, Summer 1968, pp. 9–40.
Tr. (abridged; no translator identified), 'On the Archaeology of the Sciences' *Theoretical Practice* 3–4, Autumn 1971, pp. 108–27.
73. *L'Archéologie du savoir*, Gallimard, 1969. Tr. Alan Sheridan, *The Archaeology of Knowledge*, London: Tavistock, New York: Pantheon 1972.
74. *Titres et travaux de Michel Foucault*, privately printed, undated (1969).
75. 'Médecins, juges et sorciers au XVII siècle, *Médecine de France* 200, 1969, pp. 121–28.
76. 'Maxime Defert', *Les Lettres françaises* 8–14 January 1969, p. 28.
77. 'Jean Hyppolite (1907–1968)', speech at the memorial gathering for Jean Hyppolite held at ENS on 19 January 1969, *Revue de métaphysique et de morale* vol. 74, no. 2, April–June 1969, pp. 131–36.
78. 'Qu'est-ce qu'un auteur?', lecture delivered to the Société Française de Philosophie on 22 February 1969, *Bulletin de la Société Française de Philosophie* 63, July–September 1969, pp. 73–104.

Tr. Josué V. Harari, 'What is an Author?' in Paul Rabinow, ed., *The Foucault Reader*, Harmondsworth: Penguin, 1986, pp. 101–20. Omits the discussion that followed the lecture.

79. 'Ariane s'est pendue', *Le Nouvel Observateur* 229, 31 March 1969, pp. 36–37. On Gilles Deleuze, *Différence et répétition*.

80. 'Précision', *Le Nouvel Observateur* 299, 31 March 1969, p. 39.

81. 'La Naissance du monde', *Le Monde*, 3 May 1969, p. viii. Interview with Jean-Michel Palmier.
    Tr. John Johnston, 'The Birth of a World', *Foucault Live*, pp. 57–62.

82. 'Michel Foucault explique son dernier livre', *Magazine littéraire* 28, April–May 1969, pp. 23–25. Interview with Jean-Jacques Brochier.
    Tr. John Johnston, 'The Archaeology of Knowledge', *Foucault Live*, pp. 45–52.

83. 'La Situation de Cuvier dans l'histoire de la biologie', paper read to the 'Journées Cuvier' conference held on 30–31 May 1969, *Thalès: Revue d'histoire des sciences et de leurs applications* vol. XXIII, no 1, January–March 1970, pp. 63–92.
    Tr. Felicity Edholm, 'Cuvier's Position in the History of Biology', *Critique of Anthropology* vol IV, no. 13–14, Summer 1979, pp. 125–30.

84. Letter to Pierre Klossowski, 3 July 1969, in *Cahiers pour un temps: Pierre Klossowski*, Centre Georges Pompidou, 1985, pp. 85–88.

85. 'Folie, littérature et société', *Bugei* 12, 1970.

86. *L'Ordre du discours*, Gallimard 1971. Inaugural lecture at the Collège de France, 2 December 1970.
    Tr. Rupert Swyers, 'Orders of Discourse', *Social Sciences Information*, April 1971. Republished as 'The Discourse on Language', appendix to the US Edition of *The Archaeology of Knowledge*, pp. 215–37.

87. Letter to Pierre Klossowski, Winter 1970–71, *Cahiers pour un temps: Pierre Klossowski*, pp. 89–90.

88. 'Présentation', Georges Bataille, *Oeuvres complètes. Vol 1. Premiers Ecrits 1922–1940*, Gallimard 1970, pp. 5–6.

89. 'Sept Propos sur le septième ange', preface to Jean-Pierre Brisset, *La Grammaire logique*, Tchou, 1970. Reprinted as *Sept Propos sur le septième ange*, Montpellier: Fata Morgana, 1986.

90. 'Le Piège de Vincennes', *Le Nouvel Observateur* 274, 9 February 1970, pp. 33–35. Interview with Patrick Loriot.

91. 'Il y aura scandale, mais . . .', *Le Nouvel Observateur* 304, 7 September 1970, p. 40. On Pierre Guyotat.
    Tr. Edouard Roditi, 'Open Letter to Pierre Guyotat', *Paris Exiles* 2, 1985, p. 25.

92. 'Croître et multiplier', *Le Monde* 15 November 1970, p. 13. On François Jacob, *La Logique du vivant*.

93. 'Theatrum philosophicum', *Critique* 282, November 1970, pp. 165–96. On Gilles Deleuze, *Différence et répétition* and *Logique du sens*.
    Tr. 'Theatrum philosophicum', *Language, Counter-Memory, Practice*, pp. 165–96.

94. 'Foreword' to the English-language edition of *The Order of Things*, pp. ix–xiv.

95. 'Entravista com Michel Foucault' in Sergio Paulo Rouanet, ed., *O Homen e o discorso: A Arqueologia de Michel Foucault*, Rio de Janeiro: Tempo Brasiliero, 1971, pp. 17–42. Interview with Sergio Paolo Rouanet and José Guilhermo Merquior.

96. 'Nietzsche, la geneálogie, l'histoire' in *Homage à Jean Hyppolite*, Presses Universitaires de France, 1971, pp. 145–72.

Tr. 'Nietzsche, Genealogy, History', *Language, Counter-Memory, Practice*, pp. 139–64.

97. 'A Conversation with Michel Foucault', *Partisan Review*, vol 38, no. 2, 1971, pp. 192–201. Interview with John K. Simon.

98. 'Mon corps, ce papier, ce feu', *Paideia*, September 1971. Reprinted as appendix to 1972 edition of *Histoire de la folie*.
Tr. Geoff Bennington, 'My Body, this Paper, this Fire', *Oxford Literary Review* vol IV, no 1, Autumn 1979, pp. 5–28.

99. 'Enquête sur les prisons: brisons les barres du silence', *Politique Hebdo* 24, 18 March 1971, pp. 4–6. Interview with Foucault and Pierre Vidal-Naquet, conducted by C. Angeli.

100. 'Création d'un Groupe d'Information sur les Prisons', *Esprit*, 401, March 1971, pp. 531–32. Cosigned by Jean-Marie Domenach and Pierre Vidal-Naquet.

101. 'Introduction', Groupe d'Information sur les Prisons, *Enquête dans vingt prisons*, Editions Champ libre, 1971, pp. 3–5.

102. 'Folie et civilisation', lecture at the Club Tahar Hadid, Tunis, 23 April 1971, extracts published *La Presse de Tunis*, 10 April 1987

103. 'La Prison partout', *Combat*, 5 May 1971, p. 1.

104. 'L'Article 15', *La Cause du peuple-J'Accuse. No. spécial. Flics: l'affaire Jaubert*, 3 June 1971, p. 6.

105. 'Déclaration à la conférence de presse d'Alain Jaubert', *La Cause du peuple-J'Accuse*, 3 June 1971.

106. *Rapports de la Commission d'information sur l'affaire Jaubert présentés à la presse*, 21 June 1971.

107. 'Questions à Marcellin', open letter signed by Foucault, Gilles Deleuze, Denis Langlos, Claude Mauriac and Deni Perrier-Daville', *Le Nouvel Observateur*, 5 July 1971, p. 15.

108. Je perçois l'intolérable', *Journal de Génève*, (Samedi littéraire, Cahier 135), 24 July 1971, p. 13.

109. 'Lettre', *La Pensée* 159, September–October 1971, pp. 141–44.

110. 'Lettre ouverte à Monsieur le Ministre de l'Intérieur', *La Cause du peuple-J'Accuse* 10. 15 October 1971, p. 12.

111. 'Human Nature: Justice versus Power', dialogue with Noam Chomsky, televised in November 1971 by Dutch Broadcasting Company, in Fons Elders, ed., *Reflexive Water. The Basic Concerns of Mankind*, London: Souvenir Press, 1974, pp. 134–97.

112. 'Par delà le bien et le mal', *Actuel* 14, November 1971, pp. 42–47. Interview with M.-A. Burnier and P. Graine. Republished with slight modifications as 'Entretien' in *C'Est Demain la veille*', Seuil 1973, pp. 19–43.
Tr. 'Revolutionary Action: "Until Now" ', *Language, Counter-Memory, Practice*, pp. 218–33.

113. 'Monstrosities in Criticism', tr. Robert J. Matthews, *Diacritics*, vol 1, no. 1, Fall 1971, p. 59.

114. 'Foucault Responds 2', *Diacritics*, vol. 1, no 2., Winter 1971, p. 59.

115. 'Des Intellectuels aux travailleurs arabes', *La Cause du peuple-J'Accuse*, 14, 13 December 1971.

116. 'Le Discours de Toul', *Le Nouvel Observateur* 372, 27 December 1971, p. 15.

117. 'Histoire des systèmes de pensée', Summary of 1971 lectures at the Collège de France. *Annuaire du Collège de France*, 1971.

Republished as 'La Volonté de savoir', *Résumé des cours, 1970–1982,*Julliard, 1989, pp. 9–16. Tr. 'History of Systems of Thought', *Language, Counter-Memory, Practice,* pp. 199–204.

118. *Naissance de la clinique. Une Archéologie du regard médical,* revised edn., Presses Universitaires de France, 1972.

119. 'Préface' to new edn. of *Histoire de la folie,* Gallimard, 1972, pp. 7–9.

120. 'Die grosse Einsperrung', *Tages Anzeiger Magazin* 12, 25 March 1972, pp. 15, 17, 20, 37. Interview with Niklaus Meienberg.

121. 'Michel Foucault on Attica: An Interview', with John K. Simon, April 1972. *Telos* 19, Spring 1974, pp. 154–61. Republished as 'Rituals of Exclusion', *Foucault Live,* pp. 63–72.

122. 'Cérémonie, théâtre et politique au XVII siècle', lecture at the University of Minnesota, 7 April 1972. Summarized in English by Stephen Davidson, *Acta. Proceedings of the Fourth Annual Conference on XVIIth Century French Literature,* Minneapolis: Graduate School of the University of Minnesota vol. 1, pp. 22–23

123. 'Sur la Justice populaire: Débat avec les maos', *Les Temps Modernes* 310 bis *(hors série),* May 1972, pp. 335–66. Dialogue with Philippe Gavi and Pierre Victor. Tr. John Mepham, 'On Popular Justice: A Discussion with Maoists', in Colin Gordon. ed., *Power/Knowledge: Selected Interviews and Other Writings, 1972–1977,* New York: Pantheon, 1980, pp. 1–36.

124. 'Les Intellectuels et le pouvoir', *L'Arc* 49, 1972, pp. 3–10. Discussion with Gilles Deleuze, 4 March 1972.
Reprinted, *Le Nouvel Observateur,* 8 May 1972, pp. 68–70.
Tr. 'Intellectuals and Power', *Language, Counter-Memory, Practice,* pp. 205–17.

125. 'Table Ronde', *Esprit* 413, April–May 1972, pp. 678–703. Collective discussion on social work.

126. 'Texte de l'intervention de Michel Foucault à la conférence de presse de Jean Carpentier le 29 juin,1972', *Psychiatrie aujourd'hui* 10, September 1972, pp. 15–16.

127. 'Gaston Bachelard, le philosophe et son ombre: piéger sa propre culture', *Le Figaro,* 30 September 1972, p. 16.

128. 'Un Dibattito Foucault-Petri', *Bimestre* 2–23, September–December 1972, pp. 1–4. Debate moderated by Michele Dzieduszycki.
Tr. Jared Becker and James Cascaito, 'An Historian of Culture', *Foucault Live,* pp. 73–88.

129. 'Médecine et luttes de classes: Michel Foucault et le Groupe d'Information Santé', *Le Nef,* October–December 1972, pp. 67–73.

130. 'Comité Vérité-Justice: 1,500 Grenoblois accusent', *Vérité: Rhône-Alpes* 3, December 1972.

131. 'Une Giclée de sang ou un incendie', *La Cause du peuple-J'Accuse* 33, 1 December 1972.

132. 'Les Deux Morts de Pompidou', *Le Nouvel Observateur* 421, 4 December 1972, pp. 56–57. Extracts reprinted as 'Deux Calculs', *Le Monde,* 6 December 1972, p. 20.
Tr., abridged, Paul Auster, 'The Guillotine Lives', *New York Times,* 8 April 1973, section 4, p. 15.

133. 'Réponse', *Le Nouvel Observateur* 422, p. 63. Reply to comments by Aimé Paistre.

134. 'Histoire des systèmes de pensée', *Annuaire du Collège de France* 72, 1972, pp. 283–86.
Reprinted as 'Théories et institutions pénales', *Résumé des cours,* pp. 17–25.

135. 'Préface' to Serge Livrozet, *De la Prison à la révolte*, Mercure de France, 1973, pp. 7–14.

136. 'Présentation', *Moi, Pierre Rivière, ayant égorgé ma mère, ma soeur et mon frère* . . . *Un Cas de parricide au XIX siècle présenté par Michel Foucault*, Gallimard/Julliard, 1973, pp. 9–15.
Abbreviated version, with excerpts from Rivière's memoir, published as 'Un Crime fait pour être raconté', *Le Nouvel Observateur* 464, 1 October 1973, pp. 80–112.
Tr. Frank Jellinek, 'Foreword', *I, Pierre Rivière, Having Slaughtered my Mother, my Sister and my Brother* . . ., New York; Pantheon, 1975, pp. vii–xiv.

137. 'Les Meurtres qu'on raconte', in *Moi, Pierre Rivière*, pp. 265–75.
Tr. 'Tales of Murder', *I, Pierre Rivière*, pp. 199–212.

138. 'Pour une Chronique de la mémoire ouvrière', *Libération* 22 February 1973, p. 6.

139. 'En Guise de conclusion', *Le Nouvel Observateur* 435, 13 March 1973, p. 92.

140. 'La Force de fuir', *Derrière le miroir* 202, March 1973, pp. 1–8. On Paul Rebeyrolle.

141. 'Power and Norm: Notes', notes from lecture at the Collège de France, 28 March 1973.
Tr. W. Suchting, *Power Truth, Strategy*, pp. 59–66.

142. 'L'Intellectuel sert à rassembler les idées . . . mais son savoir est partiel par rapport au savoir ouvrier', *Libération* 26 May 1973, pp. 2–3.
Conversation with a worker known only as 'José'.

143. 'O Mondo é om grande hospicio', interview with Ricardo Gomes Leire, *Jornal de Belo Horizonte*, May 1973.

144. 'A Verdade e as Formas juridicas', *Cuadernos da PUC*, 1974, pp. 4–102. Five lectures given in Rio de Janeiro, 21–25 May 1973. Followed, pp. 103–33, by 'Mesa ronda', a discussion involving Foucault.

145. 'Un Nouveau Journal?', *Zone des tempêtes* 2, May–June 1973, p. 3.

146. 'Entretien avec Michel Foucault: A propos de l'enfermement pénitentiaire' *Pro Justitia*, vol 1. no. 3–4, Winter 1973. Interview with A. Krywin and F. Ringelheim.

147. 'Gefängnisse und Gefängnisrevolten', *Dokumente: Zeitschrift für übernationale Zusammenarbeit* 29, June 1973, pp. 133–37. Interview with Bodo Morawe.

148. 'Convoqués à la P.J.', *Le Nouvel Observateur* 468, 29 October 1973, p. 53. With Alain Landau and Jean-Yves Petit.

149. 'Entretien Foucault-Deleuze-Guattari', *Recherches* 13, December 1973, pp. 27–31, 183–88.

150. 'Histoire des systèmes de pensée', *Annuaire du Collège de France* 73, 1973, pp. 255–67.
Reprinted as 'La Société punitive', *Résumé des cours*, pp. 29–51.

151. 'Sur la Seconde Révolution chinoise. Entretien 1. Michel Foucault et K.S. Karol', *Libération* 31 January 1974, p. 10.

152. 'Sur la Seconde Révolution chinoise. Entretien 2', *Libération* 1 February 1974, p. 10.

153. 'Le Rayons noirs de Byzantios', *Le Nouvel Observateur* 483, 11 February 1974, pp. 56–57.

154. 'Carceri e manicomi nel congegno del potere', interview with Marco d'Erasmo, *Avanti* 3 March 1974, p. 6.

155. Letter of 22 May 1974 to Claude Mauriac, reprinted Mauriac, *Et Comme l'Espérance est violente*, Livre de poche, 1986, p. 454.

156. 'Sexualité et politique', *Combat*, 27–28 April 1974, p. 16.

157. 'L'Association de Défense des Droits des Détenus demande au gouvernement la discussion en plein jour du système pénitentiaire', *Le Monde* 28–29 July 1974, p. 8.

158. 'Anti-Rétro. Entretien avec Michel Foucault', with Pascal Bonitzer and Serge Toubiana, *Cahiers du cinéma* 251–52, July–August 1974, pp. 5–15.
Tr. abridged, Martin Jordan, 'Film and Popular Memory', *Radical Philosophy* 11, Summer 1975, pp. 24–29, republished *Foucault Live*, pp. 89–106..

159. 'Crisis de un modelo en la medicina?', lecture, Rio de Janeiro, October 1974. *Revista Centroamericano de Ciencas de la Salud* 3, January–April 1976, pp. 197–210.

160. 'La Nacimento de la medicina social', lecture, Rio de Janeiro, October 1974. *Revista Centroamericana de Ciencas de la Salud* 6, January–April 1977, pp. 89–108.

161. 'Incorporacion del medicina en la technologia moderna', lecture, Rio de Janeiro, October 1974. *Revista Centroamericana de Ciencas de la Salud* 10, May–August 1978, pp. 93–104.
French version published as 'Histoire de la médicalisation: l'incorporation de l'hôpital dans la technologie moderne', *Hermès* 2, 1988, pp. 13–40.

162. 'Table ronde sur l'expertise psychiatrique', *Actes: Cahiers d'action juridique* 5–6, December 1974–January 1975, pp. 93–104.
Reprinted *Actes: Délinquances et ordre*, Maspero, 1978, pp. 213–28. Foucault's interventions reprinted as 'L'Expertise psychiatrique', *Actes: Cahiers d'action juridique* 54, Summer 1986, p. 68.

163. 'Histoire des systèmes de pensée', *Annuaire du Collège de France* 74, 1974, pp. 293–300. Reprinted as 'Le Pouvoir psychiatrique', *Résumé des cours*, pp. 55–69.
A longer version later appeared as 'La Casa della follia', tr. C. Tarroni, in Franco Basaglia and Franca Basaglia-Ongaro, eds. *Crimini di pace*, Turin; Einaudi, 1975, pp. 151–69. The original French text subsequently appeared in Basaglia and Basagli-Ongaro, eds., *Les Criminels de paix: Recherches sur les intellectuels et leurs techniques comme préposés à l'oppression*, tr. Bernard Fréminville, Presses Universitaires de France, 1980, pp. 145–60.

164. *Surveiller et punir: Naissance de la prison*, Gallimard 1975.
Tr. Alan Sheridan, *Discipline and Punish*, London: Tavistock, New York: Pantheon, 1977.

165. 'La Peinture photogénique', introduction to the exhibition catalogue *Fromanger: Le Désir est partout*, Galerie Jeanne Bucher, 1975. 10 pp., no pagination.

166. 'Préface', Bruce Jackson, *Leurs Prisons*, Plon, 1975, pp. i–vi.

167. 'Un Pompier vend la mèche', *Le Nouvel Observateur* 531, 13 January 1975, pp. 56–57. Review of Jean-Jacques Lubrina, *L'Enfer des pompiers*.

168. 'La Politique est la continuation de la guerre par d'autres moyens', conversation with Bernard-Henri Lévy, *L'Imprévu* 1, 27 January 1975, p. 16.

169. 'A Quoi rêvent les philosophes?', *L'Imprévu* 2, 28 January 1975, p. 13.

170. 'Des Supplices aux cellules', *Le Monde* 21 February 1975, p. 16. Interview with Roger-Pol Droit.
Tr. abridged, Leonard Mayhew, 'Michel Foucault on the Role of Prisons', *New York Times*, 5 August 1975, p. 31.

171. 'Sur la sellette', *Les Nouvelles littéraires*, 17 March 1975, p. 3, interview with Jean-Louis Ezine.
Tr. Renée Morel, 'An Interview with Michel Foucault', *History of the Present* 1, February 1985, pp. 2–3, 14.

172. 'Il Carcere visto da un filosofo francese', *L'Europeo* vol. 31, no 4, 3 April 1975, pp. 63–65. Interview with Ferdinando Scianna.

173. 'La Fête de l'écriture. Un Entretien avec Michel Foucault and Jacques Almira', with Jean Le Marchand, *Le Quotidien de Paris* 25 April 1975, p. 13.

174. 'La Mort du père', with Pierre Daix, Philippe Gavi, Jacques Rancière and Yannakakis, *Libération* 30 April 1975, pp. 10–11.

175. 'On Infantile Sexuality', undated typescript. A slightly different and incomplete version transcribed by John Leavitt, entitled 'Discourse and Repression' (pp. 23), is described as an unpublished lecture and is dated 'Berkeley, 8 May 1975'.

176. 'Entretien sur la prison', *Magazine littéraire* 101, June 1975, pp. 27–33. Interview with Jean-Jacques Brochier.
   Tr. Colin Gordon, 'Prison Talk', *Radical Philosophy* 16, Spring 1977, pp. 10–15, reprinted in *Power/Knowledge*, pp. 37–54.

177. 'Pouvoir et corps', *Quel corps?* 2, 1975.
   Reprinted in *Quel Corps*, Maspero, 1978, pp. 27–35.
   Tr. Colin Gordon, 'Body/Power', *Power/Knowledge*, pp. 55–62.

178. 'Foucault, Passe-frontières de la philosophie', *Le Monde* 6 September 1986, p. 12. Interview with Roger-Pol Droit conducted on 20 June 1975.
   Tr. John Johnston, 'On Literature', *Foucault Live*, pp. 113–20.

179. 'La Machine à penser est-elle détraquée?, *Le Monde diplomatique*, July 1975, pp. 18–21. Brief responses to Maurice T. Maschino's survey of attitudes towards the alleged 'crisis in thought.'

180. 'Aller à Madrid', *Libération*, 24 September 1975, pp. 1, 7. Interview with Pierre Benoit.

181. 'Hospicios, sexualidade, prisoēs', *Versus*, 1 October 1975. Interview with Claudio Bojunga. 'Loucora – uma questaô de poder', *Jornal do Brasil*, 12 November 1975. Interview with Silvia Helena Vianna Rodrigues.

182. *Radioscopie de Michel Foucault. Propos recueillis par Jacques Chancel*, 3 October 1975.

183. 'Réflexions sur Histoire de Paul. Faire les fous', *Le Monde*, 16 October 1975, p. 17. On a film by René Feret.

184. 'A Propos de Marguerite Duras', *Cahiers Renaud-Barrault* 89, October 1975, pp. 8–22. Conversation with Hélène Cixous.

185. 'Sade, sergent du sexe', *Cinématographe* 16, December 1975-January 1976, pp. 3–5. Interview with Gérard Dupont.

186. 'Histoire des systèmes de pensée', *Annuaire du Collège de France* 75, 1975, pp. 335–39.
   Republished as 'Les Anormaux', *Résumé des cours*, pp. 73–81.

187. *Histoire de la sexualité I: La Volonté de savoir*, Gallimard 1976.
   Tr. Robert Hurley, *The History of Sexuality I: an Introduction*, New York: Pantheon, 1978.

188. 'Il faut défendre la société', Unpublished transcript by Jacques Lagrange of lecture of 7 January 1976 at the Collège de France.

189. 'Il faut défendre la société', unpublished transcript by Jacques Lagrange of lecture of 14 January 1976 at the Collège de France.
   Italian versions of these lectures published as 'Corso del 7 gennaio 1976' and 'Corso del 14 gennaio 1976' in Alessandro Fontana and Pasquale Pasquino, eds. *Microfisica del potere*, Turin: Einaudi, 1977, pp. 163–77, 179–94.
   Tr. (from the Italian), Kate Soper, 'Two Lectures', *Power/Knowledge*, pp. 78–108.

190. 'Les Têtes de la politique', preface to a collection of cartoons by Wiaz, *En attendant le grand soir*, Denoël, 1976, pp. 7–12.

191. 'Une Mort inacceptable', preface to Bernard Cuau, *L'Affaire Mirval, ou comment le récit abolit le crime*, Presses d'aujourd'hui, 1976, pp. vii–xi.

192. 'La Politique de la santé au XVII siècle', introduction to *Généalogie des équipements de normalisation: les équipements sanitaires*, Fontenay-sur-Bois: CERFI, 1976, pp. 1–11.
    Reprinted as *Les Machines à guérir (aux origins de l'hôpital moderne)*, Brussels: Pierre Mardaga, 1979, pp. 7–18.
    Tr. Colin Gordon, 'The Politics of Health in the Eighteenth Century', *Power/ Knowledge*, pp. 166–82.

193. 'La Voix de son maître, préface à un synopsis de Gérard Mordillat', unpublished typescript.

194. 'La Crisis de la medicina o la crisis de la antimedicina', *Education medica y salud*, vol. 10, no 2, 1976, pp. 152–70. Lecture given at the Instituto de Medecina Social, Centro Biomedico, Universidad Estatal de Rio Janeiro, October 1974.

195. 'Sur *Histoire de Paul*', *Cahiers du cinéma* 262–63, January 1976, pp. 63–65. A discussion with René Féret.

196. 'Questions à Michel Foucault sur la géographie', *Hérodote* 1, January–March 1976, pp. 71–85.
    Tr. Colin Gordon, 'Questions on Geography', *Power/Knowledge*, pp. 63–77.

197. 'Crimes et châtiments en URSS et ailleurs . . .', *Le Nouvel Observateur* 585, 26 January 1976, pp. 34–37. Conversation with K.S. Karol.
    Tr., abridged, Mollie Horwitz, 'The Politics of Crime', *Partisan Review* 43, 1976, pp. 453–59; republished, *Foucault Live*, pp. 121–30.

198. 'Mesures alternatives à l'emprisonnement', lecture delivered at the University of Montréal, 15 March 1976. *Actes: Cahiers d'action juridique* 73, December 1990, pp. 7–15.

199. 'Michel Foucault: L'Illégalisme et l'art de punir', Interview, *La Presse* (Montreal) 3, April 1976, 'Section D. Livres', pp. 2, 23.

200. 'L'Extension sociale de la norme', *Politique hebdo* 212, March 1976, pp. 14–16. A discussion, with P. Werner, of Szasz's *Fabriquer la folie*.

201. 'Faire vivre et laisser mourir: la naissance du racisme', lecture delivered at the Collège de France, March 1976, *Les Temps modernes* 535, February 1991, pp. 37–61.

202. 'Sorcellerie et folie', *Le Monde* 23 April 1976, p. 18. Discussion, with Roland Jacquard, of Szasz's *Fabriquer la folie*.
    Tr. John Johnson, 'Sorcery and Madness', *Foucault Live*, pp. 107–12.

203. 'Dialogue on Power: Michel Foucault and a Group of Students', Los Angeles, May 1976, *Quid* (Simon Wade, ed.), 1976, pp. 4–22.

204. 'Intervista a Michel Foucault'. Conducted in June 1976, this interview was published as the introduction to *Microfisica del potere*.
    Excerpts appeared as 'La Fonction politique de l'intellectuel', *Politique hebdo* 247, 29 November 1976. Full French text published as 'Vérité et pouvoir', *L'Arc* 70, 1977, pp. 16–26.
    Tr., Colin Gordon, 'Truth and Power', *Power/Knowledge*, pp. 109–33.

205. 'L'Expertise médico-légale', transcript of discussion on Radio-France, 8 October 1976.

206. 'Des Questions de Michel Foucault à *Hérodote*, *Hérodote* 3, July–September 1976, pp. 9–10.

207. 'Bio-histoire et bio-politique', *Le Monde*, 17–18 October 1976, p. 5. On Jacques Ruffié, *De la Biologie à la culture*.

208. 'L'Occident et la vérité du sexe', *Le Monde*, 5 November 1976, p. 24.
   Tr. Lawrence Winters, 'The West and the Truth of Sex', *Sub-Stance* 20, 1978, pp. 5–8.

209. 'Entretien avec Michel Foucault', *Cahiers du cinéma* 271, November 1976, pp. 52–53. Interview with Pascal Kane on René Allio's adaptation of *Moi, Pierre Rivière*.

210. 'Pourquoi le crime de Pierre Rivière? Dialogue: Michel Foucault et François Châtelet', *Pariscope*, 10–16 November 1976, pp. 5–7.
   Tr. John Johnston, 'I, Pierre Rivière . . .', *Foucault Live*, pp. 131–36.

211. 'Entretien avec Guy Gauthier', *Revue du cinéma* 312, December 1976, pp. 37–42.

212. 'Malraux', *Le Nouvel Observateur* 629, 29 November 1976, p. 83.

213. 'Histoire des systèmes de pensée', *Annuaire du Collège de France* 76, 1976, pp. 361–66.
   Republished as ' "Il faut défendre la société" ', *Résumé des cours*, pp. 85–94.
   Tr., Ian McLeod, 'War in the Filigree of Peace. Course Summary', *Oxford Literary Review*, vol 4, no. 2, 1980, pp. 15–19.

214. 'Michel Foucault à Goutelas : La Redéfinition du "justiciable" ', address to the Syndicat de la Magistrature, Spring 1977. *Justice* 115, June 1987, pp. 36–39.

215. 'Le Poster de l'ennemi public No 1', *Le Matin*, 7 March 1977, p. 11.

216. 'Preface' to English translation of Gilles Deleuze and Félix Guattari, *Anti-Oedipus: Capitalism and Schizophrenia*, tr. Robert Hurley, Mark Seem and Helen Lane, New York: Viking 1977, pp. 7–8.

217. 'Vorwort zur deutschen Ausgabe', introduction to German edition of *La Volonté de savoir: Sexualität und Wahrheit: I: Der Wille zum Wissen*, tr. Ulrich Raulf, Frankfurt: Suhrkamp, 1977, pp. 7–8.

218. 'Avant-propos', *Politiques de l'habitat 1800–1850*, CORDA, 1977, pp. 3–4.

219. 'L'Oeil du pouvoir', foreword to Jeremy Bentham, *Le Panoptique*, Pierre Belfond, 1977, pp. 9–31. Conversation with Jean-Pierre Barou and Michelle Perrot.
   Tr., Colin Gordon, 'The Eye of Power', *Power/Knowledge*, pp. 146–65.

220. 'Le Supplice de la vérité', *Chemin de ronde* 1, 1977, pp. 162–63.

221. 'Die Folter, das ist die Vernunft', *Literaturmagazin* 8, 1977, pp. 60–68. Discussion with Kurt Boesers.

222. 'La Sécurité et l'état', *Tribune socialiste*, 24 November 1977.

223. 'Préface' to Mireille Debard and Jean-Luc Hennig. *Les Juges Kaki*, Editions Alain Moreau, 1977. Also published as 'Les Juges Kaki', *Le Monde* 1–2 December 1977, p. 15.

224. 'Michel Foucault : "Les Rapports du pouvoir passent à l'intérieur du corps" ', interview with Lucette Finas, *La Quinzaine littéraire* 247, 1–15 January 1977.
   Tr. Leo Marshall, 'The History of Sexuality', *Power/Knowledge*, pp. 183–93.

225. 'La Vie des hommes infâmes', *Cahiers du chemin* 29, 15 January 1977, pp. 19–29.
   Tr., Paul Foss and Meaghan Morris, 'The Life of Infamous Men' in Foss and Morris, eds., *Power, Truth, Strategy*, Sydney: Feral, 1979, pp. 76–91.

226. 'Michel Foucault : A bas la dictature du sexe', interview with Madeleine Chapsal, *L'Express*, 24 January 1977, pp. 56–57.

227. 'Pouvoirs et stratégies', *Les Révoltes logiques* 4, Winter 1977, pp. 89–97. Written answers to questions from Jacques Rancière.
   Tr., Colin Gordon, 'Powers and Strategies', *Power/Knowledge*, pp. 134–45.

228. 'Non au sexe roi', *Le Nouvel Observateur* 644, 12 March 1977, pp. 92–130. Interview with Bernard-Henri Lévy.
Tr. David Parent, 'Power and Sex: An Interview with Michel Foucault', *Telos* 32, Summer 1977, pp. 152–61. Also by Dudley M. Marchi as 'The End of the Monarchy of Sex', *Foucault Live*, pp. 137–56.

229. 'Les Matins gris de la tolérance', *Le Monde* 23 March 1977, p. 24. On Pasolini's *Comizi d'amore*.

230. 'L'Asile illimité', *Le Nouvel Observateur* 646, 28 March 1977, pp. 66–67. On Robert Castel, *L'Ordre psychiatrique*.

231. 'La Géométrie fantastique de Maxime Defert', *Les Nouvelles littéraires*, 28 April 1977, p. 13.

232. 'La Grande Colère des faits', *Le Nouvel Observateur* 652, 9 May 1977, pp. 84–86. Reprinted in Sylvie Boucasse and Denis Bourgeois, eds., *Faut-il brûler les nouveaux philosophes?*, Nouvelles Editions Oswald, 1978, pp. 63–70. On André Glucksmann, *Les Maîtres penseurs*.

233. 'L'Angoisse de juger', *Le Nouvel Observateur* 655, 30 May 1977, pp. 92–116. Debate with Jean Laplanche and Robert Badinter.
Tr. John Johnston, 'The Anxiety of Judging', *Foucault Live*, pp. 157–78.

234. Comments on science fiction, 3 June and 20 November 1977, in Igor and Grichka Bogdanoff, *L'Effet science-fiction: à la recherche d'une définition*, Robert Laffont, 1979, pp. 35, 117.

235. 'Le Jeu de Michel Foucault', *Ornicar?* 10, July 1977, pp. 62–93. Discussion with Alain Grosrichard, Gérard Wajeman, Jacques-Alain Miller. Guy le Gaufey, Catherine Millot, Dominique Colas, Jocelyne Livi and Judith Miller.
Tr. Colin Gordon, 'The Confession of the Flesh', *Power/Knowledge*, pp. 194–228.

236. 'Une Mobilisation culturelle', *Le Nouvel Observateur* 670, 12 September 1977, p. 49.

237. 'Enfermement, psychiatrie, prison', *Change: La Folie encerclée* 32–33, October 1977. Discussion with David Cooper, Jean-Pierre Faye, Marie-Odile Faye and Marine Zecca.
Tr. Alan Sheridan, 'Confinement, Psychiatry, Prison', in Lawrence D. Kritzman, ed., *Politics, Philosophy, Culture: Interviews and Other Writings, 1977–1984*, London: Routledge, 1988, pp. 178–210.

238. 'About the Concept of the Dangerous Individual in Nineteenth-Century Legal Psychiatry', delivered to a symposium on law and psychiatry held at York University, Toronto, October 24–16 1977, tr. Alain Baudot and Jane Couchman, *International Journal of Law and Psychiatry* 1, 1978, pp. 1–18.
Republished as 'The Dangerous Individual', *Politics, Philosophy, Culture*, pp. 125–51. French version published as 'L'Evolution de la notion d'"individu dangereux" dans la psychiatrie légale', *Revue Déviance et société* 5, 1981, pp. 403–22.

239. 'Va-t-on extradier Klaus Croissant?', *Le Nouvel Observateur* 678, 14 November 1977, pp. 62–63.

240. 'Désormais, la sécurité est au-dessus des lois', *Le Matin*, 18 November 1977, p. 59. Interview with Jean-Paul Kauffman.

241. 'Lettre à quelques leaders de la gauche', *Le Nouvel Observateur* 681, 28 November 1977, p. 59.

242. ' "Wir fühlten uns als schmutzige Spezies" ', *Der Spiegel*, 19 December 1977, pp. 77–78.

243. 'Sécurité, térritoire, population', cassette recording of lecture of 11 January 1978

at Collège de France. Released by Seuil and Productions de la licorne as part of *De la Gouvernementalité*, KS S531A, 1989.

244. 'Préface' to *My Secret Life*, tr. Christine Charnaux et al., Editions les formes du secret, 1978, pp. 5–7.

245. 'Introduction' to Georges Canguilhem, *On the Normal and the Pathological*, tr. Carolyn Fawcett, Boston: Reidel, 1978, pp. ix–xx.
Subsequently published in French as 'La Vie: l'expérience et la science', *Revue de métaphysique et de morale* 90, January–March 1985, pp. 3–14.

246. 'Note', *Herculine Barbin dite Alexina B., présenté par Michel Foucault*, Gallimard, 1978, pp. 131–32.

247. 'La Grille politique traditionelle', *Politique Hebdo* 303, 1978, p. 20.

248. 'M. Foucault. Conversazione senza complessi con il filosofo che analizza le "struture del potere" ', *Playmen* 12, 1978, pp. 21–30. Interview with Jerry Bauer.

249. 'Un Jour dans une classe s'est fait un film', *L'Educateur*, vol. 51, no. 12, 1978, pp. 21–25.

250. 'Eugène Sue que j'aime', *Les Nouvelles littéraires*, 12–19 January 1978, p. 3.

251. 'Une Erudition étourdissante', *Le Matin* 20 January 1978, p. 25. On Philippe Ariès, *L'Homme devant la mort*.

252. 'Alain Peyrefitte s'explique . . . et Michel Foucault répond', *Le Nouvel Observateur* 689, 23 January 1978, p. 25.

253. 'La Governamentalita', *Aut-aut* 167–68, September–December 1978, Italian transcript, by Pasquale Pasquino, of a lecture given at the Collège de France in February 1978.
Tr. Rosi Braidotti, 'Govermentality', *Ideology and Consciousness* 6, Autumn 1979, pp. 5–12. Revised version in Graham Burchell, Colin Gordon and Peter Miller, eds., *The Foucault Effect: Studies in Governmentality*, Hemel Hempstead, 1991, pp. 87–105.
French version, tr. Jean-Claude Oswald, 'La Gouvernementalité', *Actes: Cahiers d'action juridique* 54, Summer 1986, pp. 7–15.

254. 'Precisazioni sul potere. Riposta ad alcuni critici', *Aut-aut* 167–68, September–December 1978, pp. 12–29. A reply to written questions from Pasquale Pasquino.
Tr. James Cascaito, 'Clarification on the Question of Power', *Foucault live*, pp. 179–92.

255. 'Attention: danger', *Libération*, 22 March 1978, p. 9.

256. 'La Loi de la pudeur', radio discussion on France-Culture's *Dialogues* on 4 April 1978 with Guy Hocquenhem and Jean Danet, transcript published *Recherches* 37, April 1979, pp. 69–82.
Tr. Alan Sheridan, 'Sexual Morality and the Law', *Politics, Philosophy, Culture*, pp. 271–85.

257. 'Débat avec Michel Foucault au Centre Culturel de L'Athénée Français', Tokyo, 21 April 1978. Transcript by Romei Yashimoto of debate following a screening of *Moi, Pierre Rivière*.

258. 'The Strategy of world-understanding: how to get rid of marxism', dialogue with Ryumei Yashimoto on April 25 1978, *UMI* 53, July 1978, pp. 302–28. In Japanese.

259. 'La Société disciplinaire en crise: développement de la diversité et l'indépendence en crise: Michel Foucault parle du pouvoir à l'Institut franco-japonais de Kansai à Tokyo', *Asahi janaru*, vol 20, no 19, 12 May 1978.

558   THE LIVES OF MICHEL FOUCAULT

260. 'On Sex and Politics', *Asahi janaru* vol. 20, no. 19, 12 May 1978. Interview with Moriaki Watanabe and Chobei Nemoto.
261. 'La Poussière et le nuage', in Michelle Perrot, ed., *Impossible Prison: Recherches sur le système pénitentiare au XIX siècle*, Seuil, 1980, pp. 29–39.
262. Table ronde du 20 mai 1978', *L'Impossible Prison*, pp. 40–56.
   Tr. Colin Gordon, 'Questions of Method', *Ideology and Consciousness* 8, Spring 1981, pp. 3–14. Republished, *The Foucault Effect*, pp. 73–86.
263. 'Postface', *L'Impossible Prison*, pp. 316–18.
264. 'Qu'est-ce que la critique? [Critique und Aufklärung]', lecture to the Société Française de Philosophie, 27 May 1978, *Bulletin de la Société Française de Philosophie*, vol. LXXXIV, 1990, pp. 35–63.
265. 'Vijftien vragen can homosexuele zijde san Michel Foucault' in M. Duyves and T. Maasen, eds., *Interviews met Michel Foucault*, Utrecht; De Woelrat, 1982, pp. 13–23.
   Interview dated 10 July 1978.
   French version published as 'Le Gai Savoir', *Mec Magazine*, 5 June 1988, pp. 32–36 and 'Le Gai Savoir (2)', *Mec Magazine* 6–7, July–August 1988, pp. 30–33.
266. 'Du Pouvoir', interview with Pierre Boncenne, July 1978, *L'Express* 13 July 1984, pp. 56–62.
   Tr. Alan Sheridan, 'On Power', *Politics, Philosophy, Culture*, pp. 96–109.
267. 'Il misterioso ermafrodito', *La Stampa*. August 5, 1978, p. 5.
268. 'Du Bon Usage du criminel' *Le Nouvel Observateur* 722, 11 September 1978, pp. 40–42.
269. 'Taccuina persiano: l'esercito, quando la terra trema', *Corriere della sera*, 28 September 1978, pp. 1–2.
270. 'Teheran: la fede contra lo Scia', *Corriere della sera*, 8 October 1978, p. 11.
271. 'A Quoi rêvent les Iraniens?', *Le Nouvel Observateur* 727, 16–22 October 1978, pp. 48–49.
272. 'Le Citron et le lait', *Le Monde* 21 October 1978, p. 14. On Philippe Boucher, *Le Ghetto judiciaire*.
273. 'Ein gewaltiges Erstaunen', *Der Spiegel* 32, 30 October 1978, p. 264. On the 1978 'Paris-Berlin' exhibition.
   Tr. J.D. Leakey, 'Interview with Michel Foucault', *New German Critique* 16, Winter 1979, pp. 155–56.
274. 'Una Rivolta con le mani nude', *Corriere della sera* 7 November 1978, pp. 1–2.
275. 'Sfida alla opposizione', *Corriere della sera*, 12 November 1978, , pp. 1–2.
276. 'I reportage di idee', *Corriere della sera*, 12 November 1978, p. 1.
277. 'Réponse de Michel Foucault à une lectrice iranienne', *Le Nouvel Observateur*, 13 November 1978, p. 26.
278. 'La Rivolta dell'Iran corre sui nastri delli minicassette', *Corriere della sera*, 19 November 1978, pp. 1–2.
279. 'Polemiche furiose: Foucault e i communisti italiani, a cura di Pascale Pasquino', *L'Espresso* 46, 19 November 1978, pp. 152–56.
280. 'Il mitico capo della rivolta nell'Iran', *Corriere della sera*, 26 November 1978, pp. 1–2.
281. *Colloqui con Foucault*, Salerno; 10/17 Cooperative editrice, 1978. A series of interviews with Duccio Trombadori.
   Tr. R. James Goldstein and James Cascaito, *Remarks on Marx*, New York: Semiotext(e), 1991.

282. 'Lettera di Foucault all '*Unità*', *Unità*, 1 December 1978, p. 1.
283. Unsigned contributions to Thierry Voeltzel, *Vingt Ans et après*, Seuil, 1978.
    Transcripts of dialogues recorded from July 1976 onwards.
284. 'Histoire des systèmes de pensée, *Annuaire du Collège de France* 78, 1978, pp. 445–49.
    Republished as 'Sécurité, térritoire et population', *Résumé des cours*, pp. 99–106.
    Tr. with an introduction, James Bernauer, 'Foucault at the Collège de France I:
    A Course Summary', *Philosophy and Social Criticism* vol. 8, no. 2, Summer 1981, pp.
    1–44.
285. 'L'Esprit d'un monde sans esprit', conversation with Claire Brière and Pierre
    Blanchet, published as an afterword to their *Iran: la Révolution au nom de Dieu*, Seuil,
    1979, pp. 235–41.
    Tr. Alan Sheridan, 'The Spirit of a World Without Spirit', *Politics, Philosophy,
    Culture*, pp. 211–26.
286. 'Préface', Peter Bruckner and Alfred Krovoza, *Ennemi de l'état*, Claix: La Pensée
    sauvage, 1979, pp. 4–5.
287. 'Naissance de la biopolitique'. Cassette recording of lecture of 10 January 1979 at
    Collège de France. Released by Seuil and Productions de la Licorne, as part of *De
    la Gouvernementalité*. KS 532, 1989.
288. 'La Phobie d'état', excerpt from lecture of 31 January 1979 at the Collège de
    France, *Libération* 30 June- 1 July 1984, p. 21.
289. 'Mais à quoi servent les pétitions?', response to questions from Pierre Assouline,
    Les Nouvelles littéraires 1–8 February 1979, p. 4.
290. 'Manières de justice', *Le Nouvel Observateur* 743, 5 February 1979, pp. 20–21.
291. 'Una Polveriera chimata Islam', *Corriere della sera*, 13 February 1979, p. 1.
292. 'Michel Foucault et l'Iran', *Le Matin*, 26 March 1979, p. 15.
293. 'Un Plaisir si simple', *Le Gai Pied* 1, April 1979, pp. 1, 10.
    Tr. Mike Riegle and Gilles Barbedette, 'The Simplest of Pleasures', *Fag Rag* 29,
    p. 3.
294. 'Lettre ouverte à Mehdi Bazarghan' *Le Nouvel Observateur* 753, 14 April 1979, p. 46.
295. 'Pour une Morale de l'inconfort', *Le Nouvel Observateur* 754, 23 April 1979, pp. 82–
    83. Review of Jean Daniel's *L'Ere des ruptures*.
    Reprinted as preface to the 1980 Livre de poche edn. of *L'Ere de ruptures*, pp. 9–16.
296. 'Le Moment de la vérité', *Le Matin*, 25 April 1979, p. 20. On the death of Maurice
    Clavel.
297. 'Vivre autrement le temps', *Le Nouvel Observateur* 755, 30 April 1979, p. 88. On the
    death of Maurice Clavel.
298. 'Le Vrai Sexe', read to *Arcadie* Congress, May 1979, *Arcadie* 27, November 1980,
    pp. 617–25.
    A modified version appeared in English as the 'Introduction' to *Herculine Barbin;
    Being the Recently Discovered Memoirs of a Nineteenth-Century French Hermaphrodite*, tr.
    Richard McDougall, Brighton: Harvester Press, 1980, pp. vii–xvii. Dated
    'January 1980'.
299. 'Inutile de se soulever?', *Le Monde*, 11 May 1979, pp. 1, 2.
    Tr. with an introduction James Bernauer, 'Is It Useless to Revolt?' *Philosophy and
    Social Criticism* vol. 8, no. 1, Spring 1981, pp. 1–9.
300. 'La Stratégie du pourtour', *Le Nouvel Observateur* 759, 28 May 1979, p. 57.
301. 'Omnes et Singulatim: Towards a Criticism of Political Reason' lectures
    delivered at Stanford University on 10 and 16 October 1979, in Sterling

McMurrin, ed., *The Tanner Lectures on Human Values II*, Salt Lake City: University of Utah Press, 1981, pp. 225–54.

Reprinted as 'Politics and Reason', *Politics, Philosophy, Culture*, pp. 57–85.

Tr. P. E. Dauzat, 'Omnes et singulatim: vers une critique de la raison politique', *Le Débat* 41, September-October 1986, pp. 5–35.

302. 'Luttes autour des prisons', *Esprit* 35, November 1979, pp. 102–11. Discussion with Antoine Lazarus and François Colcombet; Foucault uses the pseudonym 'Louis Appert'.

303. 'Histoire des systèmes de pensée', *Annuaire du Collège de France* 79, 1979, pp. 367–72.

Republished as 'Naissance de la biopolitique', *Résumé des cours*, pp. 109–19.

Tr. with an introduction, James Bernauer, 'Foucault at the Collège de France II: A Course Summary', *Philosophy and Social Criticism*, vol. 8, no. 3, Fall 1981, pp. 349–59.

304. 'Du Gouvernement des vivants', incomplete transcripts of lectures at the Collège de France on 9, 16 January 1980, 13, 20 February 1980 and 5 March 1990.

305. 'The Flying University', *New York Review of Books*, 24 January 1980, p. 49, collective open letter.

306. 'Les Quatre Cavaliers de l'Apocalypse et les vermisseaux quotidiens', *Cahiers du cinéma* 6, February 1980 (*Numéro hors série*), pp. 95–96. Interview with Bernard Sobel on Syberberg's *Hitler, a film from Germany*.

307. 'Se Défendre', preface to *Pour La Défense libre*, brochure issued by the Centre de Recherche et de Formation Juridique, 1980, pp. 5–6. Collectively signed by Michel Foucault, Henry Juramy, Christian Revon, Jacques Vergès, Jean Lapeyrie and Dominique Nocaudie.

308. '*Le Nouvel Observateur* e L'Unione della sinistra', *Spirali* 15, January 1980, pp. 53–55. Extracts from a conversation between Michel Foucault and Jean Daniel about Daniel's *L'Ere des ruptures*, originally broadcast on France-Culture.

309. 'Toujours les prisons', *Esprit*, 37, January 1980, pp. 184–86. Exchange of letters with Paul Thibaud and Jean-Marie Domenach.

310. 'Préface' to Roger Knobelspiess, QHS: *Quartier de Haute Sécurité*, Stock, 1980, pp. 11–16, dated 31 March 1980.

311. 'Le Philosophe masqué', *Le Monde dimanche*, 6 April 1980, pp. i, xvii. Interview with Christian Delacampagne; Foucault is not identified.

Tr. John Johnston, 'The Masked Philosopher', *Foucault Live*, pp. 193–202.

312. 'Conversation with Michel Foucault', *The Threepenny Review* vol. 1, no. 1, Winter-Spring 1980, pp. 4–5. Interview with Millicent Dillon.

313. 'Sexuality and Solitude', James Lecture delivered on 20 November 1980 at the New York Institute for the Humanities, published, *London Review of Books*, 21 May-3 June 1981, pp. 3, 5–6. Republished David Rieff, ed., *Humanities in Review I*, New York; Cambridge University Press, 1982, pp. 3–21.

314. 'Truth and Subjectivity' Howison Lectures delivered at Berkeley, 20 and 21 October 1980. Unpublished typescripts.

315. 'Power, Moral Values and the Intellectual', interview with Michael D. Bess, San Francisco 1980, typescript.

316. 'Foucault', in D. Huisman, ed., *Dictionnaire des philosophes*, Presses Universitaires de France, 1981, vol. 1., pp. 942–44. Signed 'Maurice Florence', sc. Michel Foucault and François Ewald.

317. 'Roland Barthes', *Annuaire du Collège de France* 80, 1980, pp. 61–62.

318. 'A mon retour de vacances . . .' letter of 16 December 1980 to Paul Rabinow. Typescript.

319. 'Histoire des systèmes de pensée', *Annuaire du Collège de France*, 80, 1980, pp. 449–52.
Republished as 'Du Gouvernement des vivants', *Résumé des cours*, pp. 123–129.

320. 'De L'Amitié comme mode de vie', *Le Gai Pied* 25, April 1981, pp. 38–39.
Tr. John Johnston, 'Friendship as a Way of Life' *Foucault Live*, pp. 203–11.

321. 'Mal faire, dire vrai', lectures given at the Faculté de Droit, Université Catholique de Louvain, May 1981. typescript, pp. 159.

322. 'Entretien avec Michel Foucault réalisé par André Berten', Louvain, May 1981, *Comités d'éthique à travers le monde*. *Recherches en cours 1988*, Tierce-Médecine/ INSERM, 1989, pp. 228–35.

323. 'L'Intellectuel et les pouvoirs', *La Revue nouvelle* vol. LXX, no. 10, October 1984, pp. 338–45. Interview with Christian Panier and Pierre Watté, conducted 14 May 1981.

324. 'Est-il donc important de penser?', *Libération* 30–31 May 1981. Interview with Didier Eribon.
Tr. with an afterword, Thomas Keenan, 'Is it really important to think?', *Philosophy and Social Criticism*, vol. 9, no. 1, Spring 1982, pp. 29–40.

325. 'Face aux gouvernements, les droits de l'homme', *Libération* 30 June-1 July 1984, p. 22. A statement made in June 1981.
Reprinted, *Actes: Cahiers d'action juridique* 54, Summer 1986, p. 2.

326. 'Il faut tout repenser la loi et la prison', *Libération*, 6 July 1981, p. 2.

327. 'Lacan, il "liberatore" della psicanalisi', *Corriere della sera*, 11 September 1981, p. 1. Interview with Jacques Nobécourt.

328. 'De la nécessité de mettre un terme à toute peine', *Libération*, 18 September 1981, p. 5.

329. 'Les Rendez-vous manqués'. Statement drafted by Foucault and Pierre Bourdieu and broadcast on *Europe 1*, 15 December 1981. Published *Libération* 15 December 1981.

330. 'Les Réponses de Pierre Vidal-Naquet et de Michel Foucault', *Libération*, 18 December 1981, p. 12.

331. 'Conversation' in Gérard Courant, ed., *Werner Schroeter*, Cinémathèque/Institut Goethe. Conversation with Schroeter.

332. 'Notes sur ce que l'on lit et entend', *Le Nouvel Observateur 893*, 19 December 1981, p. 21.

333. 'Histoire des systèmes de pensée', *Annuaire du Collège de France* 81, 1981, pp. 385–89.
Republished as 'Subjectivité et vérité', *Résumé des cours*, pp. 133–142.

334. *Le Désordre des familles. Lettres de cachet des Archives de la Bastille. Présenté par Arlette Farge et Michel Foucault*, Gallimard/Julliard, 1982.

335. 'Herméneutique du sujet', *Concordia* 12, 1988, pp. 44–68. Extracts from lectures at the Collège de France, 1982. French text established on the basis of transcripts by Helmut Becker and Lothar Wolfstetter, first published in *Freiheit und Selbstsorge*, Frankfurt: Materialis Verlag, 1985.

336. Typescript of three lectures, University of Toronto, 1982.

337. 'Nineteenth Century Imaginations', tr. Alex Susteric, *Semiotext(e)*, vol. 4, no. 2, 1982, pp. 182–90.

338. 'The Subject and Power', Afterword to Hubert L. Dreyfus and Paul Rabinow, *Michel Foucault: Beyond Structuralism and Hermeneutics*, Hemel Hempstead: Harvester, 1982, pp. 208–226.
339. *Les Lundis de l'histoire*. *Le Désordre des familles*, radio discussion with Arlette Farge, Michelle Perrot and André Béjin, 10 January 1982.
340. 'Response to speech by Susan Sontag', *Soho News*, 2 March 1982, p. 13.
341. 'Space, Knowledge and Power', *Skyline*, March 1982. Interview conducted by Paul Rabinow, tr. Christian Hubert, republished *The Foucault Reader*, pp. 239–56.
342. 'Histoire et homosexualité', *Masques* 13, Spring 1982, pp. 14–24. Discussion with J.-P. Joecker, M. Ouerd and A. Sanzio.
343. 'Sexual Choice, Sexual Act: An Interview with Michel Foucault', *Salmagundi* 58–59, Fall 1982-Winter 1983, pp. 10–24. Interview with James O'Higgins, reprinted *Foucault Live*, pp. 211–32.
    Republished as 'Sexual Choice, Sexual Act: Foucault and Homosexuality', *Politics, Philosophy, Culture*, pp. 286–303.
    French version published as 'Lorsque l'amant part en taxi', *Gai Pied hebdo* 151, January 5, 1985, pp. 22–24, 54–57.
344. 'Le Combat de la chasteté', *Communications* 35, May 1982, pp. 15–25. Tr. Anthony Foster, 'The Battle for Chastity' in Philippe Ariès and André Béjin, eds., *Western Sexuality: Practice and Precept in Past and Present Times*, Oxford: Basil Blackwell, 1985, pp. 14–25. Republished, *Politics, Philosophy, Culture*, pp. 242–55.
345. 'The Social Triumph of the Sexual Will', *Christopher Street* 64, May 1982, pp. 36–41. Conversation with Gilles Barbedette, tr. Brendan Lemon.
346. 'Des Caresses d'homme considérées comme un art', *Libération*, 1 June 1982, p. 27. Review of K.J. Dover, *L'Homosexualité grecque*.
347. 'An Interview', *Ethos* vol. 1, no. 2, Autumn 1983, pp. 4–9. Interview with Stephen Riggins, 22 June 1982.
    Republished as 'The Minimalist Self', *Politics, Philosophy, Culture*, pp. 3–16.
348. 'Michel Foucault, An Interview: Sex, Power and the Politics of Identity', *The Advocate* 400, 7 August 1984, pp. 26–30, 58. Conducted by Bob Gallagher and Alexander Wilson in June 1982.
    Tr. Jacques Hess, 'Que fabriquent donc les hommes ensemble?' *Le Nouvel Observateur* 1098, 22 November 1985, pp. 54–55.
349. 'Le Terrorisme ici et là', *Libération* 3 September 1982, p. 12. Interview with Didier Eribon.
350. 'Pierre Boulez ou l'écran traversé', *Le Nouvel Observateur* 934, 2 October 1982, pp. 51–52.
351. 'En Abandonnant les polonais, nous renonçons à une part de nous-mêmes', *Le Nouvel Observateur* 935, 9 October 1982, p. 36. With Simone Signoret and Bernard Kouchner.
352. 'L'Expérience morale et sociale des Polonais ne peut plus être effacée', *Les Nouvelles littéraires* 14–20 October 1982, pp. 8–9. Interview with Gilles Anquetil.
353. 'Truth, Power Self: An Interview with Michel Foucault', conducted by Rux Martin on 25 October 1982, in Luther H. Martin, Huck Gutman and Patrick H. Hutton, eds. *Technologies of the Self*: A Seminar with Michel Foucault, London: Tavistock, 1988, pp. 9–15.
354. 'Technologies of the Self', in *Technologies of the Self*, pp. 16–49.
355. 'The Political Technology of Individuals', in *Technologies of the Self*, pp. 145–62.

356. 'La Pensée, l'émotion', in *Duane Michals: Photographies de 1958–1982*, Paris Audiovisuel, Musée d'Art Moderne de la Ville de Paris, 1982, pp. iii–vii.

357. 'L'Age d'or de la lettre de cachet', *L'Express* 3 December 1982, pp. 35–36. Interview with Foucault and Arlette Farge, conducted by Yves Hersant.

358. 'Histoire des systèmes de pensée'. *Annuaire du Collège de France* 82, 1982, pp. 395–406.

Republished as 'L'Herméneutique du sujet' *Résumé des cours*, pp. 145–66.

359. 'L'Ecriture de soi', *Le Corps écrit* 5, 1983, pp. 3–23.

360. 'Rêver de ses plaisirs: sur l'onirocritique d'Artémidore', *Recherches sur la philosophie et le langage* 3, 1983, pp. 53–78. An early version of the first chapter of *Le Souci de soi*.

361. 'Un Système fini face à une demande infinie' in *Sécurité sociale: l'enjeu*, Editions Syros, 1983, pp. 39–63. Interview with R. Bono.

Tr. Alan Sheridan, 'Social Security', *Politics, Philosophy, Culture*, pp. 159–77.

362. 'Un Cours inédit' *Magazine littéraire* 207, May 1984, pp. 35–39. Lecture delivered at the Collège de France, 5 January 1983.

Tr. Colin Gordon, 'Kant on Enlightenment and Revolution', *Economy and Society* vol. 15 no. 1, February 1986, pp. 88–96.

363. 'A Propos des faiseurs d'histoire', *Libération*, 21 January 1983, p. 22.

364. 'An Exchange with Michel Foucault', exchange of letters between Foucault and Lawrence Stone, *New York Review of Books*, 13 March 1983, pp. 42–44.

365. 'Um welchen Preis sagt die Vernunft die Wahrheit?' *Spuren* 1–2, 1983. Interview with Gérard Raulet.

Tr. Jeremy Harding, 'Structuralism and Post-Structuralism: An Interview with Michel Foucault', *Telos* 55, Spring 1983, 195–211.

Tr. Mia Foret and Marion Martius, 'How Much Does it Cost to Tell the Truth', *Foucult Live*, pp. 257–76.

366. 'Sartre', fragmentary typescript, described as 'Extracts from a lecture at Berkeley'.

367. 'The Power and Politics of Michel Foucault', interview with Peter Maas and David Brock, *Inside*, 22 April 1983, pp. 7, 20–22.

368. 'Politics and Ethics: An Overview'. edited interviews, conducted in April 1983, with Paul Rabinow, Charles Taylor, Martin Jay, Richard Rorty and Leo Lowenthal, tr. Catherine Porter, in *The Foucault Reader*, pp. 373–80.

369. 'On the Genealogy of Ethics: An Overview of Work in Progress', interview with Hubert L. Dreyfus and Paul Rabinow, Dreyfus and Rabinow, *Michel Foucault: Beyond Structuralism and Hermeneutics* 2nd edn, University of Chicago Press, 1983, pp. 229–52.

Republished, *The Foucault Reader*, pp. 340–72.

Tr. (abridged) Jacques B. Hess, 'Le sexe comme une morale', *Le Nouvel Observateur*, 1 June 1984, pp. 62–66.

370. 'Discussion with Hubert L. Dreyfus and Paul Rabinow', Berkeley, 15 April 1983, typescript.

371. 'Discussion with Hubert L. Dreyfus and Paul Rabinow', Berkeley, 19 April 1983, typescript.

372. 'Discussion with Hubert L. Dreyfus and Paul Rabinow', Berkeley, 21 April 1983, typescript.

373. 'La Pologne et après', *Le Débat* 25, May 1983, pp. 3–34. Discussion with Edmond Maire.

374. 'La Musique contemporaine et le public' *CNAC Magazine* 15, May-June 1983, pp. 10-12. Discussion with Pierre Boulez.

Tr. John Rahn, 'Contemporary Music and the public', *Perspectives in New Music* 24, Fall-Winter 1985, pp. 6-12; republished *Politics, Philosophy, Culture*, pp. 314-330.

375. 'Vous êtes dangereux, *Libération*, 10 June 1983, p. 20.

376. 'Lettre à Hervé Guibert', dated July 1983, in 'L'Autre Journal d'Hervé Guibert', *L'Autre journal* 5, December 1985, p. 5.

377. 'An Interview with Michel Foucault', interview with Charles Ruas, published as the Postscript to *Death in the Labyrinth, pp. 169-86.*

'Archéologie d'une passion', *Magazine littéraire* 221, July-August 1985, pp. 100-105.

378. 'Usage des plaisirs et techniques de soi', *Le Débat* 27, November 1983, pp. 46-72. A slightly modified version of the first chapter of *L'Usage des plaisirs*.

379. 'Remarques sur la paix', *Géopolitique* 4, Autumn 1983, p. 76.

380. 'Discourse and Truth: The Problematization of Parrhesia', notes taken by Joseph Pearson on six lectures given by Foucault at the University of California at Berkely, October and November 1983. Typescript.

381. 'Qu'appelle-t-on punir?', Revue de l'Université de Bruxelles, 1984, pp. 35-46. Interview with Foulek Ringelheim, December 1983, revised and corrected by Foucault on 16 February 1984.

Tr. John Johnston, 'What Calls for Punishment?', *Foucault Live*, pp. 275-92.

382. 'Histoire des systèmes de pensée' *Annuaire du Collège de France* 83 (1983), p. 441.

383. 'Première Préface à *L'Usage des plaisirs*', undated typescript, pp. 51.

Tr., abridged, William Smock 'Preface to *The History of Sexuality, Volume II*', *The Foucault Reader, pp. 33-39.*

384. *Histoire de la sexualité 2: L'Usage des plaisirs*, Gallimard, 1984.

Tr. Robert Hurley, *The Use of Pleasure*, New York: Pantheon, 1985, London: Allen Lane, 1988.

385. *Histoire de la sexualité 3: Le Souci de soi*, Gallimard, 1984.

Tr. Robert Hurley, *The Care of the Self*, New York: Pantheon 1985, London: Allen Lane, 1988.

386. 'Interview met Michel Foucault', *Krisis: Tijdschrift voor filosofie* 14, 1984, pp. 47-58.

387. Interview with J. François and J. de Wit. 'L'Ethique du souci de soi comme pratique de la liberté', *Concordia* 6, 1984, pp. 99-116. Interview with Raul Fornet-Betancourt, Helmut Becker and Alfredo Gomez-Mûller, dated 20 January 1984.

Tr. Joseph Gauthier, 'The Ethics of the Care of the Self as a Practice of Freedom', *Philosophy and Social Criticism*, vol. 12, no. 2-3, 1987, pp. 2-3, 112-31.

388. 'Philippe Ariès: le souci de la vérité', *Le Nouvel Observateur* 1006, 17 February 1984, pp. 56-57.

389. 'Le Style de l'histoire', *Le Matin*, 21 February 1984, pp. 20-21. Interview with Arlette Farge, conducted by François Dumont and Jean-Paul Iommi-Amunstegui.

390. 'A Last Interview with French Philosopher Michel Foucault', conducted by Jamin Raskin, March 1984, *City Paper*, vol. 8. no. 3, 27 July-2 August 1984, p. 18.

391. 'Interview de Michel Foucault', conducted by Catherine Baker, April 1984, *Actes: Cahiers de l'action juridique* 45-46, 1984, pp. 3-6.

392. 'Le Souci de la vérité, interview with François Ewald,' *Magazine littéraire* 207, May 1984, pp. 18–23.

Tr., abridged, Paul Patton, 'The Regard for Truth', *Art and Text* 16, Summer 1984, pp. 20–31.

Tr. John Johnston, 'The Concern for Truth', *Foucault Live*, pp. 293–308.

393. 'Parla Michel Foucault: Alle fonti del piacere', *Panorama* 945, 28 May 1984. Interview with Alessandro Fontana, conducted 25 April 1984.

Modified French version published as 'Une Esthétique de l'existence, *Le Monde aujourd'hui* 1516 July 1984, p. x.

Tr. John Johnston, 'An Aesthetics of Existence', *Foucault Live*, pp. 309–16.

Tr. of French version, Alan Sheridan, 'An Aesthetics of Existence', *Politics, Philosophy, Culture*, pp. 47–53.

394. 'Polemics, Politics and Problematizations', tr. Lydia Davies, based on discussions with Paul Rabinow and Tom Zummer, May 1984, *The Foucault Reader*, pp. 381–90.

395. 'Pour en finir avec les mensonges', *Le Nouvel Observateur* 1076, pp. 76–77. Interview with Didier Eribon, dated June 1984.

396. 'Le Retour de la morale', *Les Nouvelles*, 28 June–5 July 1984, pp. 36–41. Interview with Gilles Barbedette and André Scala, conducted on 29 May 1984.

Tr. Thomas Levin and Isabelle Lorenz, 'Final Interview', *Raritan* vol 5, no. 1, Summer 1985, pp. 1–13. Republished as 'The Return of Morality', *Politics, Philosophy, Culture*, pp. 242–54.

Tr. John Johnston, 'The Return of Morality' *Foucault Live*, pp. 317–32.

397. *Résumé des cours 1970–1982*, Julliard, 1989.

OTHER WORKS CONSULTED

Adereth, M., *The French Communist Party: A Critical History (1920–1984)*, Manchester University Press, 1984.

Agulhon, Maurice, *La Vie sociale en Provence intérieure au lendemain de la Révolution*, Clavreuil, 1971.

—*Les Quarante-huitards*, Gallimard, 1975.

—*Marianne au combat*, Flammarion, 1979.

—'Présentation', in Michelle Perrot, ed., *L'Impossible Prison. Recherches sur le système pénitentiaire au XIX siècle*, Seuil, 1980, pp. 5–6.

—'Postface', ibid., pp. 313–16.

Allier, Irène, 'Knobelspiess: un procès en trompe l'oeil', *Le Nouvel Observateur*, 31 October 1981, p. 83.

—*Terras Hotel*, Gallimard 1984.

—'La Reconnaissance d'un écrivain', *Le Débat* 41, September–November 1986, pp. 159–63.

Almira, Jacques, *Le Voyage à Naucratis*, Gallimard, 1975.

Althusser, Louis, *Montesquieu: La Politique et l'histoire*, Presses Universitaires de France, 1959.

—*For Marx*, tr. Ben Brewster, London: New Left Books, 1969.

—*Lenin and Philosophy, and Other Essays*, tr. Ben Brewster, London: New Left Books, 1971.

—*Philosophy and the Spontaneous Philosophy of the Scientists, and Other Essays*, Gregory Elliott, ed., London: Verso, 1990.

—'*L'Avenir dure longtemps*', suivi de '*Les Faits*': *Autobiographies*, Stock/IMEC, 1992.

—et al., *Lire Le Capital*, Maspero, 1965, two vols.

Amer, Henry, 'Michel Foucault: Histoire de la folie à l'âge classique', *Nouvelle Revue Française*, September 1961, pp. 530–31.

Amin, Samir, *The Maghreb in the Modern World*, tr. Michael Perl, Harmondsworth: Penguin, 1970.

Amiot, Michel, 'Le Relativisme culturaliste de Michel Foucault', *Les Temps Modernes* 248, January 1967, pp. 1272–98.

Andrade, Béatrix, 'Un Weekend à la Goutte d'Or', *L'Express*, 6–12 December 1971, p. 42.

Angeli, Claude, 'Les Nouveaux Clandestins', *Le Nouvel Observateur*, 1 June 1970, p. 18.

Anzieu, Didier, 'La Psychanalyse au service de la psychologie', *Nouvelle Revue de psychanalyse* 20, Autumn 1979, pp. 59–76.

—*A Skin for Thought. Interviews with Gilbert Tarrah*, tr. Daphne Nash Briggs, London: Karnac, 1990.

Ariès, Philippe, *L'Enfant et la vie familiale sous l'Ancien Régime*, Plon, 1960.

—*Essais sur l'histoire de la mort en Occident du moyen âge à nos jours*, Seuil, 1975.

—'La Singulière Histoire de Philippe Ariès', *Le Nouvel Observateur*, 20 February 1978, p. 80 ff.

—*Un Historien du dimanche*, Seuil, 1980.

—'Le Souci de la vérité', *Le Nouvel Observateur*, 17 February 1984, pp. 56–57.

—*Images of Man and Death*, tr. Janet Lloyd, Cambridge, Massachusetts: Harvard University Press, 1985.

Arnal, Frank, '*Gai Pied hebdo*, à l'origine de l'émergence de la visibilité homosexuelle', *Masques* 25–26, May 19—5, pp. 83–85.

Arnaud, Alain, *Pierre Klossowski*, Seuil, 1990.

Aron, Jean-Paul, *Le Mangeur au XIX siècle*, Robert Laffont, 1973.

—*Les Modernes*, Folio, 1984.

—'Mon SIDA', *Le Nouvel Observateur*, 30 October 1987, p. 102 ff.

—and Kempf, Roger, *Le Pénis et la démoralisation de l'Occident*, Grasset, 1978.

Aron, Raymond, *Mémoires*, Julliard, 1983.

Artaud, Antonin, '*L'Ombilic des limbes*', suivi de '*La Pèse-nerfs*' et autres textes, Gallimard, Collection 'Poésies', 1968.

—*Oeuvres complètes*, vol. 13, Gallimard, 1974.

Ascherson, Neal, *The Polish August*, Harmondsworth, Penguin, 1981.

Assouline, Pierre, *Gaston Gallimard*, Points, 1985.

Aubral, François and Delcourt, Xavier, *Contre la nouvelle philosophie*, Gallimard, collection 'Idées', 1977.

Austin, J.L., *How To Do Things with Words*, Oxford University Press, 1962.

Bachelard, Gaston, *L'Air et les songes. Essai sur l'imagination du mouvement*, Librairie José Corti, 1942.

Backmann, René, 'Quatre Questions sur l'affaire Jaubert', *Le Nouvel Observateur*, 14 June 1971, p. 27. 'Le Procès des tribunaux populaires', *Le Nouvel Observateur*, 5 July 1971, p. 18.

—'Le Bal des nervis', *Le Nouvel Observateur*, 24 July 1972, pp. 15–16.

—'Fallait-il trois balles pour stopper un homme orné d'un chaise?' *Le Nouvel Observateur* 11 December 1972, p 58

Baddonel, Dr., 'Le Centre National d'Orientation de Fresnes', *Esprit*, April 1955, pp. 585–92.

Badinter, Robert, *L'Exécution*, Grasset, 1973.

—'Au Nom des mots', in *Michel Foucault: Une Histoire de la vérité*, Syros, 1985, pp. 73–75.

Badiou, Alain, *Almagestes*, Seuil, 1964.

Barbedette, Gilles, 'Pierre Guyotat par qui le scandale arrive', *Le Monde dimanche*, 21 March 1982, pp. 1, 18.

Barou, Jean-Pierre, 'Il aurait pu aussi bien m'arriver tout autre chose", *Libération* 26 June 1984, p. 4.

Barraqué, Jean, *Debussy*, Seuil, 1962.

Barthes, Roland, *Le Degré zéro de l'écriture*, Seuil, 1953.

—*Michelet par lui-même*, Seuil, 1954.

—*Mythologies*, Seuil, 1957.

—'La Métaphore de l'oeil', *Critique* 195–96, August–September 1963, pp. 770–77.

—*Essais critiques*, Seuil, 1964.

Bataille, Georges, *Oeuvres complètes*, vol. 1, Gallimard 1970.

—*Visions of Excess: Selected Writings 1927–1939*, ed. Allan Stoekl, University of Minneapolis Press, 1985.

Baudrillard, Jean, *Oublier Foucault*, Galilée, 1977.

—*Cool Memories*, Galilée, 1987.

Beaufret, Jean, 'M. Heidegger et le problème de l'existence, *Fontaine* 63, November 1947.

Beauvoir, Simone de, 'Simone de Beauvoir présente *Les Belles Images*', *Le Monde*, 23 December 1966, p. 1.

—*Les Belles Images*, Folio, 1976.

—*La Cérémonie des adieux*, Gallimard, 1981.

Beckett, Samuel, *L'Innommable*, Minuit, 1953.

Beigbeder, Marc, 'En Suivant le cours de Foucault', *Esprit*, vol 35., no. 7, June 1967, pp. 1066–69.

Bel, Monique, *Maurice Clavel*, Bayard Editions, 1992.

Belaval, Yvon, *L'Esthétique sans paradoxe de Diderot*, Gallimard, 1950.

Benoist, Jean-Marie, *La Révolution structurale*, Grasset, 1975.

Bernal, Olga, *Robbe-Grillet, Le Roman de l'absence*, Gallimard, 1964.

Bernauer, James W., *Michel Foucault's Force of Flight: Towards an Ethics for Thought*, Atlantic Highlands, New Jersey: Humanities Press International, 1990.

—and Rasmussen, David, eds., *The Final Foucault*, Cambridge, Massachusets: MIT Press, 1988.

Bettati, Mario and Kouchner, Bernard, *Le Devoir d'ingérence*, Denoël, 1987.

Biancotti, Hector, 'Le Dernier Encyclopédiste: Roger Caillois', *Le Nouvel Observateur* 4 November 1974, pp. 72–73.

Binswanger, Ludwig, *Being in the World: Selcted Papers of Ludwig Binswanger. Translated and with a Critical Introduction to his Existential Psychoanalysis by Jacob Needleman*, London: Souvenir Press, 1975.

Blanchot, Maurice, *Le Très-Haut*, Gallimard, 1948.

—*L'Arrêt de mort*, Gallimard, 1948.

—*Lautréamont et Sade*, Minuit, 1949.

—'L'Oubli, la déraison', *Nouvelle Revue Française* 106, October 1961, pp. 676–86.

—*Michel Foucault tel que je l'imagine*, Montpellier: Fata Morgana, 1986.

—*Le Livre à venir*, Folio, 1986.

—*L'Espace littéraire*, Folio, 1988.

Boggio, Philippe, 'Le Silence des intellectuels de gauche. 1. Victoire à contretemps', *Le Monde*, 27 July 1983, pp. 1, 10.

—'Le Silence des intellectuels de gauche. 2. Les Chemins de traverse', *Le Monde* 28 July 1983, p. 6.

—'Trop lourd', *Le Monde*, 19 November 1990, p. 16.

Bogue, Ronald, *Deleuze and Guattari*, London: Routledge, 1989.

Bourdieu, Pierre, 'Non chiedetemi chi sono. Un profilo di Michel Foucault', *l'Indice* 1, October 1984, pp. 4–50.

—'Aspirant philosophe. Un Point de vue sur le champ universitaire des années 50', in *Les Enjeux philosophiques des années 50*, Centre George Pompidou, 1989, pp. 15–24.

—and Passeron, Jean-Claude, *Les Héritiers: Les Etudiants et la culture*, Minuit, 1964.

Borges, Jorge Luis, *Fictions*, tr. Anthony Kerrigan, London: Weidenfeld and Nicolson, 1962.

—*Obras Completas*, Buenos Aires: Emecé, 1974.

Boutang, Yann Moulier, *Louis Althusser: Une Biographie. Tôme 1. La Formation du mythe (1918–1956)*, Grasset, 1992.

Boyers, Robert and Orill, Robert, eds., *Laing and Anti-Psychiatry*, Harmondsworth: Penguin, 1972.

Boyne, Roy, *Foucault and Derrida: The Other Side of Reason*, London Unwin Hyman, 1990.

Breton, André, *Anthologie de l'humour noir*, Livre de poche, 1970.

Brisset, Jean-Pierre, *La Grammaire logique*, Angers, 1878.

—*La Science de dieu*, Angers, 1900.

Broch, Hermann, *The Death of Virgil*, tr. Jean Starr Untermeyer, New York: Pantheon, 1945.

Brosse, Jacques, 'L'Etude du langage va-t-elle libérer un homme nouveau?', *Arts et loisirs* 35, 24–31 May 1966, pp. 8–9

Broyelle, Claudie, Broyelle, Jacques and Tschirart, Evelyne, *Deuxième Retour de Chine*, Seuil, 1977.

Broyelle, Claudie and Broyelle, Jacques, 'A Quoi rêvent les philosophes?', *Le Matin* 24 March 1979, p. 13.

Brownmiller, Susan, *Against Our Will*, Harmondsworth: Penguin, 1976.

Bruckner, Pascal and Finkielkraut, Alain, *Le Nouveau Désordre amoureux*, Seuil, 1977.

Bülow, Catherine von, 'l'Art de dire vrai', *Magazine littéraire* 207, May 1984, p. 34.

—'Contredire est un devoir', *Le Débat* 41, September–November 1986, pp. 168–78.

—and Ali, Fazia ben, *La Goutte d'Or, ou le mal des racines*, Stock, 1974.

Bureau, Jacques, 'Libération devant la révolution inattendue', *Esprit* 1, January 1980, pp. 56–58.

Burgelin, Pierre, 'L'Archéologie deu savoir' *Esprit*, May 1967, pp. 843–860.

Burguière, André, 'La Preuve par l'aveu', *Le Nouvel Observateur*, 31 January 1977, pp. 64–66.

Burin des Roziers, Etienne, 'Une Rencontre à Varsovie', *Le Débat* 41, September–November 1986, pp. 132–36.

Burke, Peter, *The French Historical Revoltution. The 'Annales' School 1929–89*, Cambridge: Polity, 1990.

Butler, Judith P. *Subjects of Desire: Hegelian Reflections in Twentieth-Century France*, New York: Columbia University Press, 1987.

Calvet, Louis-Jean, *Roland Barthes*, Flammarion, 1990.

Canguilhem, Georges, 'Hegel en France', *Revue d'histoire et de philosophie religieuses* 4, 1948–49, pp. 282–97.

—'Mort de l'homme ou épuisement du cogito?', *Critique* 242, July 1967, pp. 599–618.

—'Les Machines à guérir', *Le Monde*, 6 April 1977, p. 16.

—*Le Normal et le pathologique*, Presses Universitaires de France, Collection Quadrige, 1984.

—'Sur l'*Histoire de la folie* en tant qu'événement', *Le Débat* 41, September–November 1986, pp. 37–40.

—*La Connaissance de la vie*, Vrin, 1989.

—*Idéologie et rationalité dans l'histoire des sciences de la vie*, Vrin, 1988.

—*Etudes d'Histoire et de philosophie des sciences*, Vrin, 1989.

Castel, Robert, 'Les Aventures de la pratique', *Le Débat* 41, September–November 1986, pp. 41–51.

—'The Two Readings of *Histoire de la folie* in France', *History of the Human Sciences*, vol. 3, no 1, February 1990, pp. 27–30.

Cavaillès, Jean, *Sur la Logique et la théorie de la science*, Vrin, 1987.

Caviglioli, François, 'Le Plongeon de Knobelspiess', *Le Nouvel Observateur* 10 June 1983, p. 24.

Cercle d'Epistémologie, 'A Michel Foucault', *Cahiers pour l'analyse* 9, Summer 1968, pp. 5–8.

—'Nouvelles Questions', ibid., pp. 41–44.

Certeau, Michel de, *Heterologies: Discourse on the Other*, tr. Brian Massumi, Manchester University Press, 1986.

Chapsal, Madeleine, 'La Plus Grande Révolution depuis l'existentialisme', *L'Express* 23–29 May 1966, pp. 19–121.

Char, René, *Fureur et mystère*, Gallimard, Collection 'Poésie', 1967.

Charle, Christophe, 'Le Collège de France' in Pierre Nora, ed., *Les Lieux de mémoire. II. La Nation*, Gallimard 1986, vol 3., pp. 389–424.

—*Naissance des intellectuels 1880–1900*, Minuit, 1990.

Châtelet, François, 'L'Homme, ce narcisse incertain', *La Quinzaine Littéraire*, 1 April 1966, pp. 19–20.

—'Foucault précise sa méthode', *La Quinzaine littéraire*, 1 October 1968, p. 28.

—'L'Archéologie du Savoir' *La Quinzaine littéraire*, 1 March 1969, pp. 3–4.

Cixous, Hélène, *Le Prénom de Dieu*, Grasset, 1967.

—*L'Exil de James Joyce ou l'art du remplacement*, Grasset, 1968.

—*Dedans*, Grasset, 1969.

—'Cela n'a pas de nom, ce qui se passait', *Le Débat* 41, September–November 1986, pp. 153–58.

Clark, Michael, *Michel Foucault: An Annotated Bibliography*, New York: Garland, 1983.

Clavel, Maurice, *Ce Que je crois*, Grasset, 1975.

—' "Vous direz trois rosaires" ', *Le Nouvel Observateur* 27 February 1976, p. 55.

—and Sollers, Philippe, *Délivrance*, Seuil, 1977.

Clément, Catherine and Pingaud, Bernard, 'Raison de plus', *L'Arc* 70, 1977, pp. 1–2.

Cobler, Sebastian, *Law, Order and Politics in West Germany*, tr. Francis McDonagh, Harmondsworth: Penguin, 1978.

Cohen, Ed, 'Foucauldian Necrologies: "Gay" Politics, Politically Gay?', *Textual Practice*, vol. 2, no. 1, Spring 1988, pp. 87–99.

Cohen-Solal, Annie, *Sartre 1905–1980*, Folio, 1985.

Colombel, Jeannette, 'Les Mots de Foucault et les choses', *La Nouvelle Critique*, May 1967, pp. 8–13.

—'Contrepoints poétiques', *Critique* 471–72, August–September 1986, pp. 775–87.

Contat, Michel and Rybalka, Michel, *Les Ecrits de Sartre*, Gallimard, 1970.

Cooper, David, 'Who's Mad Anyway', *New Statesman*, 16 June 1967, p. 844.

—ed. *The Dialectics of Liberation*, Harmondsworth: Penguin, 1968.

Corvez, Maurice, 'Le Structuralisme de Michel Foucault', *Revue thomiste* 68, 1968, pp. 101–24.

Dagognet, François, 'Archéologie ou histoire de la médecine', *Critique* 216, May 1965, pp. 436–47.

Daniel, Jean, 'Quinze Jours en image', *Le Nouvel Observateur* 29 September 1975, p. 28.

—*L'Ere des ruptures*, Livre de poche, 1980.

—'Le Prince et les scribes', *Le Nouvel Observateur*, 19 August 1983, pp. 18–19.

—'Le Flux des souvenirs' in *Michel Foucault un histoire de la vérité*, Syros, 1985, pp. 57–60.

—'La Passion de Michel Foucault', *Le Nouvel Observateur* 24 June 1984.

—*La Blessure*, Grasset, 1992.

Dardigna, Anne-Marie, *Les Châteaux d'Eros, ou l'infortune du sexe des femmes*, Maspero, 1980.

Debray, Régis, *Prison Writings*, tr. Rosemary Sheed, London: Allen Lane, 1973.

—*Les Rendez-vous manqués (pour Pierre Goldman)*, Seuil, 1975.

—*Contribution aux discours et cérémonies du dixième anniversaire*, Maspero, 1978.

—*L'Espérance au purgatoire*, Alain Moreau, 1980.

—*Teachers, Writers, Celebrities: The Intellectuals of Modern France*, tr. David Macey, London: Verso, 1981.

'Déclaration à la presse et aux pouvoirs publics émanant des prisonniers de la Maison Centrale de Melun', *Politique Hebdo*, 20 January 1972, pp. 10–11.

Defert, Daniel, 'Lettre à Claude Lanzmann', *Les Temps modernes*, 531–33, October–December 1990, pp. 1201–06.

—and Donzelot, Jacques, 'La Charnière des prisons', *Magazine littéraire* 112–13, May 1976, pp. 33–35.

Delay, Jean, *La Jeunesse d'André Gide*, Gallimard, 1956, 1957. Two vols.

Deleuze, Gilles, *David Hume, sa vie, son oeuvre*, Presses Universitaires de France, 1952.

—*Empirisme et subjectivité*, Presses Universitaires de France, 1953.

—*Instincts et institutions*, Hachette, 1953.

—*Nietzsche et la philosophie*, Presses Universitaires de France, 1962.

—*Le Bergsonisme*, Presses Universitaires de France, 1966.

—'L'Homme, une existence douteuse', *Le Nouvel Observateur* 1 June 1966, pp. 32–34.

—'Ce Que les prisonniers attendent de nous', *Le Nouvel Observateur*, 31 January 1972, p. 24.

—'Gilles Deleuze contre les nouveaux philosophes', *Le Monde*, 19–20 June 1977, p. 16.

—*Foucault*, Minuit, 1986.

—*Pourparleurs*, Minuit, 1990.

—and Guattari, Félix, *Anti-Oedipe*, Minuit, 1972.

Derbyshire, Philip, 'Odds and Sods', *Gay Left* 7, Winter 1978–79, pp. 18–19.

Derogy, Jacques, 'Ratissage Sélectif sur les grands boulevards,' *L'Express*, 25–31 December 1975 p. 21.

Derrida, Jacques, *L'Ecriture et la différence*, Seuil, 1967.

'Les Détenus parlent', *Esprit* Vol. 39, no. 6 June 1971, pp. 1282–93

Descombes, Vincent, *Modern French Philosophy*, tr. L. Scott-Fox and J.M, Harding, Cambridge University Press, 1980.

Dews, Peter, 'The *Nouvelle Philosphie* and Foucault', *Economy and Society*, vol. 8, no. 2, May 1979, pp. 127–71.

—'The "New Philosophers" and the End of Leftism', *Radical Philosophy* 24, Spring 1980, pp. 2–11.

—*Logics of Disintegration: Post-Structuralist Thought and the Claims of Critical Theory*, London: Verso, 1987.

Diamond, Irene and Quinby, eds., *Feminism and Foucault*, Boston: Northeastern University Press, 1988.

Dispot, Laurent, 'Une Soirée chez Michel Foucault, *Masques* 25–26, May 1985, pp. 163–67.

Dollé, Jean-Paul, *Haine de la pensée*, Editions Hallier, 1976.

Domenach, Jean-Marie, 'Le Système et la personne' *Esprit* 5, May 1967, pp. 771–80.

—'Une Nouvelle Passion', *Esprit*, 7–8, July–August 1966, pp. 77–78.

—'Le Sang et la honte', *Le Monde*, 25 December 1971, p. 1.

—'Les Détenus hors la loi' *Esprit* Vol. 40, No. 2 February 1972, pp. 163–70.

Doray, Bernard, *From Taylorism to Fordism: A Rational Madness*, tr. David Macey, London: Free Association Books, 1988.

Dreyfus, Hubert L. and Rabinow, Paul, *Michel Foucault: Beyond Structuralism and Hermeneutics*, Hemel Hempstead, Harvester, 1982.

Droit, Roger-Pol, '*Le Pouvoir et le sexe*', *Le Monde* 16 February 1977, pp. 1, 18.

—Foucault, passe-frontières de la philosophie, *Le Monde*, 6 September 1986, p. 12.

Duby, Georges, *Les Trois Ordres, ou l'imaginaire de la société*, Gallimard, 1978.

Dumézil, Georges, *Le Festin de l'immortalité: Etude de la mythologie comparée*, Annales du Musée Guimet, 1924.

—*Mythe et épopée. Vol. 1. L'Idéologie des trois fonctions dans les épopées des peuples indo-européens*, Gallimard, 1968.

—*Mythe et épopée. Vol 2. Types épiques indo-européens: un héros, un sorcier un roi*, Gallimard 1971.

—*Mythe et épopée. Vol 3. Histoires romaines*, Gallimard, 1973.

—'Un Homme heureux', *Le Nouvel Observateur*, 29 June 1984.

—*Entretiens avec Didier Eribon*, Folio, 1987.

During, Simon, *Foucault and Literature: Towards A Genealogy of Writing*, London: Routledge, 1992.

Duverger, Maurice, 'Le Pouvoir et le prison. Michel Foucault contesté par des historiens', *Le Monde* 4 July 1980, pp. 15, 21.

Duvert, Tony, *Récidive*, Minuit, 1967.

—*Paysage de fantaisie*, Minuit, 1973.

Duvignaud, Jean, 'Ce Qui parle en nous, pour nous, mais sans nous', *Le Nouvel Observateur* 21 April 1969, pp. 42–43.

Elek, Christian, *Le Casier judiciaire*, Presses Universitaires de France, 1988.

Elliott, Gregory, *Althusser: The Detour of Theory*, London: Verso, 1987.

Emmanuelli, Xavier, 'Un Bateau pour Saint-Germain-des-Près', *Quotidien du médecin*, 4 December 1978.

Enthoven, Jean-Paul, 'Crimes et châtiments', *Le Nouvel Observateur* 3 March 1975, pp. 58–59.

'Entretiens sur Foucault', *La Pensée* 137, February 1978, pp. 3–37.

Entretemps. Numéro spécial: Jean Barraqué, 1987.

Eribon, Didier, 'Pierre Bourdieu: la grande illusion des intellectuels', *Le Monde dimanche* 4 May 1980, p. 1.

—*Michel Foucault (1926–1984)*, Flammarion, 1989.

—*Michel Foucault (1926–1984)* revised edn., Flammarion, Collection 'Champs', 1991.

Etats-généraux de la philosophie (16–17 juin 1979), Flammarion, 1979.

Ewald, François, 'Anatomie et corps politiques', *Critique* 343, December 1975, pp. 1228–65.

—'Droit: systèmes et stratégies, *Le Débat* 41, September–November 1986, pp. 63–69.

—'Michelle Perrot. Une Histoire de femmes', *Magazine littéraire* 286, March 1991, pp. 98–102.

—and Farge, Arlette and Perrot, Michelle, 'Une Pratique de la vérité' *Michel Foucault: Une Histoire de la vérité*, Syros, 1985, pp. 9–18.

—and Macherey, Pierre, 'Actualité de Michel Foucault', *L'Ane* 40, October–December 1989.

Fano, Michel, 'Autour de la musique', *Le Débat* 41, September–November 1986, pp. 137–39.

Farge Arlette, *Le Vol d'aliments à Paris au XVIP siècle*, Plon, 1974.

—*Vivre dans la rue à Paris au XVIP siècle*, Gallimard/Julliard, collection 'Archives', 1979.

—'Travailler avec Michel Foucault', *Le Débat* 41, September–November 1986, pp. 164–67.

—'Face à l'histoire', *Magazine littéraire* 207, May 1984, pp. 40–42.

—*La Vie fragile: Violence, pouvoirs et solidarités à Paris au XVIIP siècle*, Hachette, 1986.

—*Le Goût de l'archive*, Seuil 1989.

Fauchereau, Serge, 'Cummings', *Critique* 218, December 1964.

Favret-Saada, Jeanne, *Les Mots, les morts, les sorts*, Gallimard, 1977.

Fernandez, Dominique, *L'Etoile rose*, Grasset, 1978.

Fernandez-Zoila, Adolfo, 'La Machine à fabriquer des délinquants', *La Quinzaine littéraire* 16–31 March 1975, pp. 3–4.

Ferro, Marc, 'Au Croisement de l'histoire et du crime', *La Quinzaine littéraire*, 1–15 December 1973, pp. 25–26.

Ferry, Jean, *Une Etude sur Raymond Roussel*, Arcanes, 1953.

FHAR, *Rapport contre la normalité*, Editions Champ libre, 1971.

Fitzgerald, Mike, *Prisoners in Revolt*, Harmondsworth, Penguin, 1977.

Forrester, John, 'Foucault and Psychoanalysis', in *Ideas from France: The Legacy of French Theory*, London: ICA, 1985, pp. 24–25.

—*The Seductions of Psychoanalysis: Freud, Lacan and Derrida*, Cambridge University Press, 1990.

'Foucault à Uppsala. Propos recueillis par Jean Piel', *Critique* 471–72, August–September 1986, pp. 748–52.

Frank, Manfred, 'Pourquoi la philosophie française plaît aux Allemands', *Le Monde dimanche*, 24 October 1982, pp. xv–xvi.

Frappat, Bruno, 'Les Homosexuels par eux-mêmes', *Le Monde*, 19–20 August 1973, p. 14.

Freeman, Hugh, 'Anti-Psychiatry through History', *New Society* 4 May 1967, pp. 665–66.

Friedrich, Otto, 'France's Philosopher of Power', *Time*, 6 November 1981, pp. 147–48.

Frybes, Marcin, 'Rencontre ou malentendu autour de Solidarnosc?', *CFDT aujourd'hui* 100, March 1991, pp. 103–10.

Gabey, Emmanuel, 'Après l'assassinat de Mohammed Diab', *Témoignage chrétien*, 21 December 1972, p. 10.

Gaede, Edouard, 'Nietzsche et la littérature', in *Nietzsche: Cahiers de Royaumont*, Minuit, 1967, pp. 141–52.

Gallo, Max, 'Histoire d'une folie', *L'Express*, 15–21 October 1973, pp. 59–60.

—'La Prison selon Michel Foucault', *L'Express*, 24 February–2 March 1975, pp. 65–66.

—'Les Intellectuels, la politique et la modernité', *Le Monde*, 26 July 1983, p. 7.

Gandal, Keith, 'Michel Foucault: Intellectual Work and Politics', *Telos* 67, Spring 1986, pp. 121–35.

—and Kotkin, Stephen, 'Foucault in Berkeley', *History of the Present*, February 1985, pp. 6, 15

—'Governing Work and Social Life in the USA and the USSR', ibid, pp. 4–5, 7–14.

Garaudy, Roger, *De l'Anathème au dialogue*, Editions sociales, 1965.

Garde-fous, arrêtez de vous serrer les coudes, Maspero, 1975.

Garrigou-Lagrange, Madeleine, 'Le Prisonnier est aussi un homme', *Témoignage chrétien*, 16 December 1971, p. 12.

Gascar, Pierre, *Portraits et souvenirs*, Gallimard, 1991.

Gauchet, Marcel, 'De l'Inexistentialisme', *Le Débat* 1, May 1980, pp. 100–103.

—and Swain, Gladys, *La Pratique de l'esprit humain; l'institution asilaire et la révolution démocratique*, Gallimard, 1980.

Gaudemar, Antoine de, 'La Vie SIDA: Le Nouveau Roman d'Hervé Guibert, *Libération* 1 March 1990, pp. 19–21

Gavi, Philippe, 'Bruay-en-Artois: seul un bourgeois aurait pu faire ça?', *Les Temps modernes* 132–313, July–August 1972, pp. 155–260.

Geertz, Clifford, 'Stir Crazy', *New York Review of Books*, 26 January 1978.

Geismar, Alin, July, Serge and Morance, E., *Vers la guerre civile*, Editions premières, 1969.

Genet, Jean, 'Violence et brutalité', *Le Monde*, 2 September 1977, pp. 1, 2.

—*Un Captif amoureux*, Gallimard, 1986.

Gide, André, *Ne Jugez Pas*, Gallimard, 1930.

GIP, *Enquête dans 20 prisons*, Editions Champ libre, 1971.

—*Enquête dans une prison-modèle: Fleury-Mérogis*, Editions Champ libre, 1971.

—*L'Assassinat de George Jackson*, Gallimard, 1972.

—*Suicides de prison*, Gallimard, 1972.

Glucksmann, André, 'Fascismes: l'ancien et le nouveau', *Les Temps modernes* 310bis, 1972, pp. 266–34.

—*La Cuisinière et le mangeur d'hommes*, Points, 1977.

—*Les Maîtres penseurs*, Grasset, 1977.

Gnesotto, Nicole, '*Le Nouvel Observateur*: l'histoire déraillée', *Esprit* 1, January 1980, pp. 64–69.

Goldman, Pierre, *Souvenirs obscurs d'un Juif polonais né en France*, Points, 1977.

Gordon, Colin, 'The Normal and the Pathological: A Note on Georges Canguilhem', *I&C* 7, Autumn 1980, pp. 33–36.

—'*Histoire de la folie*: An Unknown Book by Michel Foucault', *History of the Human Sciences*, vol. 3, no. 1, February 1990, pp. 3–26.

—'Governmental Rationality: An Introduction' in Graham Burchell, Colin Gordon and Peter Miller. eds., *The Foucault Effect: Studies in Governmentality*, Hemel Hempstead: Harvester, 1991, pp. 1–52.

Greimas, A.J. *Sémantique structural*, Larousse, 1966.

—*Du Sens*, Seuil, 1970.

Guetta, Bernard, 'Le Salut à Brejnev', *Le Nouvel Observateur*, 27 June 1977, p. 31.

—'Une Journée en Haute Sécurité', *Le Nouvel Observateur*, 3 April 1978, pp. 84 ff.

Guattari, Félix, *Molecular Revolution: Psychiatry and Politics*, tr. Rosemary Sheed, Harmondsworth: Penguin, 1984.

Guibert, Hervé, *Mauve le vierge*, Gallimard, 1986.

—*A l'Ami qui ne m'a pas sauvé la vie*, Gallimard, 1990.

Gutting, Gary, *Michel Foucault's Archaeology of Scientific Reason*, Cambridge University Press, 1989.

Guyotat, Pierre, *Tombeau pour cinq cent mille soldats*, Gallimard, 1967.

—*Eden, Eden, Eden*, Gallimard, 1970.

Habart, Michel, 'Hermann Broch et les rançons de la création poétique', *Critique* 83, April 1954, pp. 310–22.

Habermas, Jürgen, 'Modernity versus Post-Modernity', *New German Critique* 22, Winter 1981, pp. 3–14.

—*The Philosophical Discourse of Modernity*, tr. Frederick G. Lawrence, Cambridge: Polity, 1987.

Hackmann, William R., 'The Foucault Conference', *Telos* 51, Spring 1982, pp. 191–96.

Hafsia, Jelila, *Visages et rencontres*, Tunis, 1981.

Hallier, Jean-Edern, 'Cette tête remarquable ne comprenait pas l'avenir', *Figaro Magazine*, 30 June–6 July 1984, pp. 76–77.

—*Chaque Matin qui se lève est une aventure*, Editions libres, 1978.

Hamon, Hervé and Rotman, Patrick, *Les Porteurs de valise*, Albin Michel, 1979.

—*La Deuxième Gauche: Histoire intellectuelle et politique de la CFDT*, Ramsay, 1982.

—*Génération I: Les Années de rêve*, Seuil, 1987.

—*Génération II: Les Années de poudre*, Seuil, 1988.

Hanson, Anne Coffin, *Manet and the Modern Tradition*, New Haven and London: Yale University Press, 1979.

Hayman, Ronald, *Artaud and After*, Oxford University Press, 1977.

—*Writing Against: A Biography of Sartre*, London: Weidenfeld & Nicolson, 1986.

Heath, Stephen, *The Nouveau Roman*, London: Elek, 1972.

Heppenstall, Rayner, *Raymond Roussel*, London: Calder and Boyers, 1966.

Hocquenhem, Guy, *Le Désir homosexuel*, Editions universitaires, 1972.

—'La Révolution des homosexuels', *Le Nouvel Observateur*, 10 January 1972, pp. 32–35.

—'Homosexuals, Children and Violence' tr. Simon Watney, *Gay Left*, Summer 1978, pp. 14–15.

—*Les Petits Garçons*, Albin Michel, 1983.

Hollier, Denis, *Le Collège de sociologie*, Gallimard, collection 'Idées', 1974.

Holroyd, Michael, *Bernard Shaw. Vol 1. 1856–1898: The Search for Love*, Harmondsworth: Penguin, 1990.

Hommage à Jean Hyppolite, Presses Universitaires de France, 1971.

Hopkins, J. W. 'Jean Barraqué', *Musical Times*, November 1966, pp. 952–55.

Horvitz, Philip, 'Don't Cry for Me, Academia', *Jimmy and Lucy's House of 'K'*, 2, August 1984, pp. 78–80.

Howard, Michael, 'The Story of Unreason', *Times Literary Supplement*, 6 October 1961, pp. 653–54.

Hoy, David Couzens, ed., *Foucault: A Critical Reader*, Oxford, Blackwell, 1986.

Huisman, Denis, 'Note sur l'article de Michel Foucault', *Revue Internationale de philosophie*, vol. 44, no 73, 2/1990, pp. 177–78.

Hyppolite, Jean, *Génèse et structure de 'La Phénomènologie de l'esprit'*, Presses Universitaires de France, 1948.

—*Figures de la pensée philosophique*, Presses Universitaires de France, 1971.

Ignatieff. Michael, 'At the Feet of the Father', *Times Literary Supplement*, 22 April 1983.

Jacob, François, *The Logic of Living Systems: A History of Heredity*, tr. Betty E. Spillmann, London: Allen Lane, 1973.

Jambet, Christian, 'L'Unité de la pensée: une interrogation sur les pouvoirs', *Le Monde*, 21 February 1975, p. 17.

Jarry, Alfred, *The Supermale*, tr. Barbara Wright, London: Cape Editions, 1968.

Joecker, Jean-Pierre and Sanzio, Alain, 'Rencontre avec Jean-Paul Aron', *Masques* 21, Spring 1984, pp. 7–17.

Johnson, Douglas, 'Althusser's Fate', *London Review of Books*, 16 April–6 May 1981, 13–15.

Joravsky, David, *Russian Psychology: A Critical History*, Oxford: Blackwell, 1989.

Josselin, Jean-François, 'Le Continent noir', *Le Nouvel Observateur*, 7 September 1970, pp. 40–41.

'Journées de l'Evolution Psychiatrique', *Evolution psychiatrique*, tôme 36, fasc. 2, April–June 1971, pp. 223–97.

'Justice telle qu'on la rend', *Esprit*, October 1971, pp. 524–55.

Kanters, Robert, 'Tu causes, tu causes, est-ce tout ce que tu sais faire?', *Figaro littéraire*, 23 June 1966, p. 5.

—'Crimes et châtiments', *Figaro littéraire* 22 February 1975, p. 17.

Kantorowicz, Ernst, *The King's Two Bodies: A Study in Medieval Political Theology*, New Jersey; Princeton University Press, 1957.

Karenty, Serge, 'La Médecine en question', *Magazine littéraire* 112–13, May 1976, pp. 38–41.

Karol, K.S., 'La Tragédie de Louis Althusser', *Le Nouvel Observateur*, 24 November 1980, pp. 26–27.

Kaupp, Katia D., 'L'Assassinat de Jillali', *Le Nouvel Observateur*, 15 December 1971, pp. 42–43

—'Le "Malentendu" de Toul', *Le Nouvel Observateur*, 20 December 1971, p. 27.

Kellner, Douglas, *Jean Baudrillard; From Marxism to Postmodernism and Beyond*, Cambridge: Polity, 1989.

Kermode, Frank, 'Crisis Critic', *New York Review of Books*, 17 May 1973, pp. 37–39.

Klossowski, Pierre, *La Vocation suspendue*, Gallimard, 1949.

—*Sade mon prochain*, Minuit, 1954, 1957.

—*Le Bain de Diane*, Jean-Jacques Pauvert, 1956.

—*Un Si Funeste Désir*, Gallimard, 1963.

—*Les Lois de l'hospitalité*, Gallimard, 1965.

—*Le Baphomet*, Mercure de France, 1965.

—*Nietzsche et le cercle vicieux*, Mercure de France, 1969.

—*La Monnaie vivante*, Eric Losfield, 1970.

—'Digression à partir d'un portrait apocryphe', *L'Arc* 49, 1990 (new edn.), pp. 11–22.

Knapp, Wilfrid, *Tunisia*, London: Thames and Hudson, 1970.

Knobelspiess, Roger, *QHS: Quartier de Haute Sécurité*, Stock, 1980.

Kojève, Alexandre, *Introduction à la lecture de Hegel*, Gallimard, 1947.

Kouchner, Bernard, 'Prisons: les petits matons blêmes', *Actuel* 9, June 1971, pp. 41–43.

—'Un Vrai samuraï', in *Michel Foucault: Une Histoire de la vérité*, Syros, 1985, pp. 85–89.

—*L'Ile de lumière*, Presses pocket, 1989.

Koyré, Alexandre, *From The Closed World to the Infinite Universe*, Baltimore: Johns Hopkins University Press, 1957

Etudes d'histoire de la pensée philosophique, Armand Colin, 1961.

Kramer, Larry, *Reports from the Holocaust. The Making of an AIDS Activist*, Harmondsworth: Penguin, 1990.

Kriegel, Annie, *Aux Origins du communisme français*, Paris: Mouton, 1964. Two vols.

Kristeva, Julia, *La Révolution du langage poétique*, Seuil, 1974.

Lacan, Jacques, *Le Séminaire. Livre XVII: L'Envers de la psychanalyse*, Seuil, 1991.

Lacouture, Jean, 'Au Collège de France: Le Cours inaugural de M. Michel Foucault', *Le Monde*, 4 December 1970, p. 8.

—*Malraux: Une Vie dans le siècle*, Points, 1976.

Lacroix, Jean, 'La Signification de la folie', *Le Monde*, 8 December 1961, p. 8.

—'Fin de l'humanisme?', *Le Monde*, 9 June 1966, p. 13.

—*Panorama de la philosophie française contemporaine*, Presses Universitaires de France.

Lagache, Daniel, *L'Unité de la psychologie*, Presses Universitaires de France, 1949.

Lagrange, Jacques, '*La Volonté de savoir* de Michel Foucault ou une généalogie du sexe', *Psychanalyse à l'université*, vol. 2, no. 7, June 1977, pp. 541–53.

—'Versions de la psychanalyse dans le texte de Foucault', *Psychanalyse à l'université*, vol. 12, no. 45, 1987, pp. 99–120, vol. 12., no. 46, 1987, pp. 259–80.

Laing, R. D., *The Divided Self*, London: Tavistock, 1959.

—'The Invention of Madness', *New Statesman*, 16 June 1963, p. 843.

—and Cooper, David, *Reason and Violence*, London: Tavistock, 1964.

Lapassade, Georges, *Le Bordel andalou*, L'Herne, 1971.

—*Essai sur la transe*, Editions universitaires, 1976.

—*Joyeux tropiques*, Stock, 1978.

Laplanche, J. and Pontalis, J.B., *The Language of Psychoanalysis*, tr. Donald Nicholson-Smith, London: Hogarth Press and Institute of Psychoanalysis, 1973.

Lardreau, Guy and Jambet, Christian, *L'Ange*, Grasset, 1976.

Leach, Edmund, 'Imprisoned by Madmen', *Listener* 8 June 1967, pp. 752–53.

Le Bitoux, Jean, 'Grandeur et décadence de la presse homosexuelle', *Masques* 25–26, May 1985, pp. 75–81.

Le Bon, Sylvie, 'Un Positiviste désesperé, *Les Temps modernes* 248, January 1967, pp. 1299–1319.

Lecercle, Jean-Jacques, *Philosophy Through the Looking Glass*, London: Hutchinson, 1985.

—*The Violence of Language*, London: Routledge, 1990.

Lecomte, M., 'Signes kafkéens chez Roussel et Jules Vernes, signes verniens chez Roussel', *Synthèses* vol. 18, no. 207, 1963, pp. 95–98.

Lecourt, Dominique, *Pour une Critique de l'épistémologie*, Maspero, 1972.

—*Lysenko: Histoire réelle d'une science prolétarienne*, Maspero, 1976.

Lefort, Gérard, 'Au Collège de France: un judoka de l'intellect', *Libération* 26 June 1984, p. 6.

Le Guilledoux, Dominique, 'La Libération de Roger Knobelspiess', *Le Monde*, 16 August 1990, p. 6.

Leiris, Michel, 'Documents sur Raymond Roussel', *Nouvelle Revue Française* 259, April 1935.

—'Conception et réalité chez Raymond Roussel', *Critique* 89, October 1954.

—*Biffures*, Gallimard, 1948.

—*Fourbis*, Gallimard, 1955.

—*Fibrilles*, Gallimard, 1966.

—*Frêle Bruit*, Gallimard, 1976.

Lenin V.I. 'What Is To Be Done?', *Selected Works*, Moscow: Progress Publishers, 1970, vol. 3, pp. 119–272.

Léonard, Jacques, 'L'Historien et le philosophe', in Michelle Perrot, ed., *L'Impossible Prison*, Seuil, 1980, pp. 9–28.

Le Roy Ladurie, Emmanuel, 'Bocage au sang', *Le Monde*, 18 October 1973, pp. 19, 25.

—'L'Offensive anti-sexe du dix-neuvième siècle', *Le Monde*, 27 October 1978, p. 24.

—*Paris-Montpellier, PC-PSU. 1945–1963*, Gallimard, 1982.

Lévy, Bernard-Henri, 'Le Système Foucault', *Magazine littéraire* 101, June 1975, pp. 7–9.

—*La Barbarie à visage humain*, Grasset, 1977.

—*Les Aventures de la liberté*, Grasset, 1991.

Liberté, libertés. Réflexions du Comité pour une charte de libertés animé par Robert Badinter, Gallimard, 1976.

Linhart, Robert, *L'Etabli*, Minuit, 1978.

Littleton, C. Scott, *The New Comparative Mythology. An Anthropological Assessment of the Theories of Georges Dumézil*, Berkeley: University of California Press, 1968.

Livrozet, Serge, *De La Prison à la révolte*, Mercure de France, 1973, 1986.

Lyotard, Jean-François, *Economie libidinale*, Minuit, 1972.

MacDonald, Oliver, 'The Polish Vortex: Solidarity and Socialism', *New Left Review* 139, May–June 1983, pp. 5–48.

Macey, David, *Lacan in Contexts*, London: Verso, 1988.

Macherey, Pierre, 'Aux Sources de l'*Histoire de la folie*: une rectification et ses limites', *Critique* 471–72, August–September 1986, pp. 753–74.

A Quoi pense la littérature?, Presses Universitaires de France, 1990.

Magazine littéraire 293, November 1991, special issue on 'Hegel and *The Phenomenology of Mind.*

Maher, Winifred Barbara and Maher, Brendan, 'The Ship of Fools: *Stultifera Navis* or *Ignis Fatuus?*', *American Psychologist*, July 1982, pp. 756–61.

Malapert, Paulin, *Les Eléments du caractère et leurs lois de combinaison*, Alcan, 1906.

—*De Spinoza politica*, Alcan 1907.

—*Psychologie*, Hatier, 1913.

—*Leçons de philosophie*, Hatier 1918.

Malraux, André, *La Tentation de l'Occident*, Livre de poche, 1976.

Manceaux, Michèle, *Les Maos en France*, Gallimard, 1972.

—and Chapsal, Madeleine, *Les Professeurs, pour quoi faire?*, Seuil, 1970.

Mandrou, Robert, 'Trois Clefs pour comprendre la folie à l'âge classique', *Annales ESC*, 17 année, no. 4, July–August 1962, pp. 761–71.

Manent, Pierre, 'Lire Michel Foucault', *Commentaire* 7, Autumn 1979, pp. 369–75.

Mannoni, Maude, *Le Psychiatre, son 'fou' et la psychanalyse*, Seuil, 1970.

Marcus, Steven, *The Other Victorians. A Study of Pornography and Sexuality in Mid-Nineteenth-Century England*, London: Weidenfeld and Nicolson, 1966.

Marietti, Angèle Kremer, *Michel Foucault: Archéologie et généalogie*, Livre de poche, 1985.

Maspero, François, *Le Figuier*, Seuil, 1988.

Mauriac, Claude, *Malraux ou le mal du héros*, Grasset, 1946.

—'Il ne faut pas tuer l'espérance', *Le Monde*, 17 July 1977, p. 1.

—*Le Temps immobile 2. Les Espaces imaginaires*, Livre de poche, 1985.

—*Le Temps immobile 3. Et comme l'espérance est violente*, Livre de poche, 1986.

—*Le Temps immobile 6. Le Rire des pères dans les yeux des enfants*, Livre de poche, 1989.

—*Le Temps immobile 7. Signes, rencontres et rendez-vous*, Grasset, 1983.

—*Le Temps immobile 9. Mauriac et fils*, Grasset, 1986.

—*Le Temps immobile 10. L'Oncle Marcel*, Grasset, 1988.

—*Une Certaine Rage*, Robert Laffont, 1977.

—*Le Temps accompli*, Grasset, 1991.

Mauriac, François, 'Bloc-notes', *Le Figaro*, 15 September 1966.

Mauroy, Pierre, *A Gauche*, Marabout, 1986.

Megill, Alan, 'The Reception of Foucault by Historians', *Journal of the History of Ideas*, vol. 48, 1987, pp. 117–41.

Merleau-Ponty, Maurice, *Sens et non-sens*, Nagel, 1948.

—'Merleau-Ponty à la Sorbonne. Résumé des cours établi par des étudiants et approuvé par lui-même', *Bulletin de psychologie*, vol. 17, nos. 3–6, 1964.

Merquior, J. G., *Foucault*, London: Fontana, 1985.

Meyer, Philippe, 'La Correction paternelle, ou l'état, domicile de la famille', *Critique* 343, December 1975, pp. 1266–76.

—*L'Enfant et la raison d'état*, Seuil, 1977.

—'Michel Foucault (1926–1984)', *Commentaire* vol. 13, no. 27, Autumn 1984, pp. 506–508.

Michel Foucault: Une Histoire de la vérité, Syros, 1985.

Midelfort, H. C. E., 'Madness and Civilization in Early Modern Europe: A Reappraisal of Michel Foucault', in B. C. Malament, ed., *After the Reformation: Essays in Honour of J. H. Hester*, Philadelphia: University of Pennsylvania Press, 1980, pp. 247–65.

Miller Jacques-Alain, 'Action de la structure', *Cahiers pour l'analyse* 9, Summer 1968, pp. 93–105.

Molho, Danièle, 'M. Pigot achète un fusil', *L'Express*, 15 November 1971, p. 19.

—'Toul: l'école du désespoir', *L'Express*, 27 December 1971, pp. 12–15.

Mossuz-Lavau, Janine, *Les Lois de l'amour. Les Politiques de la sexualité en France 1950–1990*, Payot, 1991.

Némo, Philippe, *L'Homme structural*, Grasset, 1975.

Nietzsche, Friedrich, *The Gay Science*, tr. Walter Kaufmann, New York: Vintage Books, 1974.

—*Untimely Meditations*, tr. R. J. Hollingdale, Cambridge University Press, 1983.

—*Twilight of the Idols*, tr. R. J. Hollingdale, Harmondsworth: Penguin, 1968.

—*The Birth of Tragedy* and *The Genealogy of Morals*, tr. Francis Golfing, New York: Doubleday, 1956.

—*Thus Spoke Zarathustra*, tr. R. J. Hollingdale, Harmondsworth: Penguin, 1961.

—*Daybreak*, tr. R.J. Hollingdale, Cambridge University Press, 1982.

—*Beyond Good and Evil*, tr. R.J. Hollingdale, Harmondsworth: Penguin, 1990.

Nora, Pierre, 'Que peuvent les intellectuels?', *Le Débat* 1, May 1980, pp. 3–19.

—'Il avait un besoin formidable d'être aimé', *L'Evénément du jeudi* 18–24 September 1986, pp. 82–83.

'Nouveau Regard sur l'histoire de la folie: entretien avec Marcel Gacuhet et Gladys Swain', *Esprit* 11, November 1983, pp. 77–86.

Ozouf, Mona, *L'Ecole, l'église et la république*, Armand Colin, 1964.

Pail, Gilles, 'Daniel Defert: "Plus on est honteux, plus on avoue"', *Libération* 31 October-1 November 1978, p. 27.

Parain, Brice, *Recherches sur la nature et les fonctions du langage*, Gallimard, 1942.

—*Essai sur le logos platonicien*, Gallimard, 1942.

—'Michel Foucault: l'Archéologie du savoir', *Nouvelle Revue Française*, November 1969, pp. 726–33.

Pascal, Blaise, *Pensées*, tr. A.J. Krailsheimer, Harmondsworth: Penguin, 1966.

Pasqualini, J., *Prisonnier de Mao*, Gallimard, 1975.

Paul-Boncour, François, 'Le Fer rouge', *Le Nouvel Observateur*, 19 June 1972, pp. 44–45.

Pelletier, Robert and Ravat, Serge, *Le Mouvement des soldats*, Maspero, 1976.

Pelorson, Marc, 'Michel Foucault et l'Espagne', *La Pensée* 152, July–August 1970, pp. 88–89.

Perrault, Gilles, *Le Pull-over rouge*, Ramsay, 1978.

Perrot, Michelle, *Les Ouvriers en grève*, Mouton/CNRS, 1974.

—'Délinquance et système pénitentiaire en France au XIXe siècle', *Annales ESC*, vol. 30, no. 1, January–February 1975, pp. 67–91.

—'L'Impossible Prison' in Perrot, *L'Impossible Prison: Recherches sur le système pénitentiaire au XIXe siècle*, Seuil 1980, pp. 59–63.

—'1848. Révolution et prisons', pp. 277–312.

—'La Leçon des ténèbres. Michel Foucault et la prison', *Actes: Cahiers d'action juridique* 54, Summer 1986, pp. 74–79.

Peter, Jean-Pierre, 'Entendre Pierre Rivière', *Le Débat* 66, September–October 1991, pp. 123–33.

Petitjean, Gérard, 'Les Grands Prêtres de l'université française', *Le Nouvel Observateur* 7 April 1975, pp. 52–57.

Pierre Klossowksi, Editions La Différence/Centre National des Arts Plastiques, 1990.

Piquemal, Jacques, 'G. Canguilhem, professeur de terminale (1937–1938). Un Essai de témoignage', *Revue de métaphysique et de morale* 90 èannée, no. 1, January–March 1985, pp. 63–83.

Plant, Sadie, *The Most Radical Gesture. The Situationist International in a Postmodern Age*, London: Routledge, 1992.

Plaza, Monique, 'Our Costs and their Benefits' tr. Wendy Harrison, *m/f* 4, 1980, pp. 28–40.

Pogliano, Claudio, 'Foucault, con interpreti', *Belfagor* vol. 40, 1985, pp. 147–78.

Politzer, Georges, *Critique des fondements de la psychologie*, Rieder, 1928.

Porter, Roy, *Mind-Forg'd Manacles: A History of Madness in England from the Restoration to the Regency*, London: Athlone Press, 1987.

Posner, Charles, ed., *Reflections on the Revolution in France: 1968*, Harmondsworth: Penguin, 1970.

Présence de Guy Hocquenhem. Cahiers de l'imaginaire 7, 1992.

Primero Congresso del Partido communista de España (marxista-leninista): Informe del Comité Central, Madrid: Ediciones Vanguardia Obrera, n.d.

Procès de Draguignon, Monaco: Edition du Rocher, 1975.

'Quelques souvenirs de Pierre Boulez. Propos recueillis par Alain Jaubert', *Critique* 471–72, August–September 1986, pp. 745–46.

Rabinow, Paul and Gandal, Keith, 'Foucault and the Prison: An Interview with Gilles Deleuze', *History of the Present* 2, Spring 1986, pp. 1–2, 20–21.

Rajchman, John, *Michel Foucault: The Freedom of Philosophy*, New York: Columbia University Press, 1955.

Rambali, Paul, 'Minister of Mercy', *Weekend Guardian*, 1–2 June 1991, pp. 14–15.

Recherches 13, December 1973, *Les Equipements du pouvoir*.

Remy, Jacqueline, 'Noël au pain sec', *Le Nouvel Observateur*, 6 December 1971, pp. 50–51.

Rencontre internationale. Michel Foucault philosophe, Seuil, 1989.

Revault d'Allonnes, Olivier, 'Michel Foucault: les mots contre les choses', in *Structuralisme et marxisme*, Union générale des editions, 10/18, 1970, pp. 13–38.

Revel, Jacques, 'Foucault et les historiens', *Magazine littéraire* 101, June 1975, pp. 10–12.

Righini, Mariella, 'Les Nouveaux Passe-murailles', *Le Nouvel Observateur*, 22 February 1971, pp. 44–45.

Robbe-Grillet, Alain, 'Enigmes et transpárence chez Raymond Roussel', *Critique* 199, December 1963, pp. 1027–33.

Romano, Carlin, 'Michel Foucault's New Clothes', *Village Voice*, 29 April–5 May 1981, pp. 1, 40–43.

Rodinson, Maxime, *Cult, Ghetto, and State*, tr. Jon Rothschild, London: Al Saqi Books, 1983.

Roudinesco, Elisabeth, *La Bataille de cent ans. Histoire de la psychanalyse en France. Volume 1: 1885–1939*, Ramsay, 1982.

—*Jacques Lacan & Co. A History of Psychoanalysis in France 1925–1985*, tr. Jeffrey Mehlman, London: Free Association Books, 1990.

Roussel, Raymond, *Impressions d'Afrique*, Pauvert, 1963.

—*Locus Solus*, Pauvert, 1963.

—*Comment j'ai écrit certains de mes livres*, Pauvert, 1963.

Rousset, David, *L'Univers concentrationnaire*, Editions du pavois, 1946.

Roustang, François, 'La Visibilité est un piège', *Les Temps Modernes* 356, March 1976, pp. 1567–79.

Saïd, Edward, 'Michel Foucault', *Raritan* vol. 4, no. 2, 1984, pp. 1.11.

Sales, Claude, 'Les "Nouveaux Philosophes": la révolte contre Marx', *Le Point*, 4 July 1977, pp. 33–37.

Samuelson, F.M. *Il Etait une fois 'Libération'*, Seuil, 1979.

Sartre, Jean-Paul, *Esquisse pour une théorie des émotions*, Hermann, 1938.

—*L'Imaginaire. Psychologie phénoménologique de l'imagination*, Gallimard, 1940.

—*L'Etre et le néant*, Gallimard, 1943.

—*Critique de la raison dialectique*, Gallimard, 1960.

—'Jean-Paul Sartre répond', *L'Arc* 30, October 1966, pp. 87–96.

—*Situations VIII*, Gallimard, 1972.

—'Le Nouveau Racisme', *Le Nouvel Observateur*, 18 December 1972, p. 39.

—Gavi, Philippe and Victor, Pierre, *On a raison de se révolter*, Gallimard, 1974.

Sawicki, Jana, *Disciplining Foucault: Feminism, Power and the Body*, London: Routledge, 1991.

Schaub, Uta Liebman, 'Foucault, Alternative Presses and Alternative Ideology in West Germany', *German Studies Review*, vol. 12, no. 1, February 1989, pp. 139–53.

Scianna, Ferdinando, 'Il Carcere visto da un filosofo francese', *L'Europeo*, 3 April 1975, pp. 63–65.

Scull, Andrew, 'Foucault's History of Madness', *History of the Human Sciences*, vol. 3, no. 1, February 1990, pp. 57–68.

Seale, Patrick and McConville, Maureen, *French Revolution 1968*, Harmondsworth: Penguin in association with William Heinemann, 1968.

Searle, John, *Speech Acts*, Cambridge University Press, 1972.

Schérer, René and Hocquenhem, Guy, *Co-Ire. Album systématique de l'enfance, Recherches 22*, 1977 (2nd. edn).

Serres, Michel, 'Géométrie de la folie', *Mercure de France*, August 1962, pp. 682–96, September 1962, pp. 62–81.

Sery, Patrick, 'De Quoi meurt un prisonnier?', *Le Nouvel Observateur*, 30 October 1972, pp. 50–52.

Sheridan, Alan, *Michel Foucault: The Will to Truth*, London: Tavistock, 1980.

—'Diary', *London Review of Books*, 19 July–1 August 1984, p. 21.

Shilts, Randy, *And the Band Played On*, Harmondsworth: Penguin, 1988.

Shortland, Mike, 'Introduction to Georges Canguilhem' *Radical Philosophy* 29, Autumn 1981.

Signoret, Simone, *La Nostalgie n'est plus ce qu'elle était*, Points, 1978.

Sirinelli, Jean-François, 'La Khâgne', in Pierre Nora, ed., *Les Lieux de mémoire. II. La Nation*, Gallimard 1986, vol. 3, pp. 589–624.

—'Les Normaliens de la rue d'Ulm après 1945: une génération communiste?', *Revue d'histoire du monde moderne*, vol. 32, October–December 1986, pp. 569–88.

—*Intellectuels et passions françaises. Manifestes et petitions au XX siècle*, Fayard, 1990.

Sluga, Hans, 'Foucault à Berkeley', *Critique* 471–72, August–September 1986, pp. 840–57.

Solat, Michèle, 'Les Féministes et le viol', *Le Monde*, 18, 19 and 20 October 1977.

Sollers, Philippe, 'Logicus Solus', *Tel Quel* 14, Summer 1963, pp. 46–80.

Soper, Kate, *Humanism and Anti-Humanism*, London: Hutchinson, 1986.

Sorin, Raphaël, 'Le Pendule de Foucault, ou le critique dans le labyrinthe', *Bizarre* 34–35, 1964, pp. 75–76.

Steiner, George, 'Power Play', *New Yorker*, 17 March 1986, pp. 108–109.

Stéphane, Roger, *Portrait de l'aventurier*, Le Sagittaire, 1950.

Stoekl, Allan, ed., *On Bataille: Yale French Studies*, 78, 1990.

Stone, Lawrence, 'Madness', *New York Review of Books*, 16 December 1982.

Terray, Emmanuel, 'Nous n'irons pas voter', *Le Monde*, 12 January 1969, p. 10.

Théret, André, *Parole d'ouvrier*, Grasset, 1978.

Tiles, Mary, *Bachelard: Science and Objectivity*, Cambridge University Press, 1984.

Todd, Emmanuel, 'Ce que révèlent les lettres de cachet', *Le Monde*, 5 November 1982.

Turkle, Sherry, *Psychoanalytic Politics: Jacques Lacan and Freud's French Revolution*, London: Barnet Books in Association with André Deutsch, 1979.

Veyne, Paul, *Comment on écrit l'histoire*, Points, 1978.

—'Témoignage hétérosexuel d'un historien sur l'homosexualité', *Actes du Congrès international: Le Regard des autres*, Arcadie, 1979.

—'Le Dernier Foucault et sa morale', *Critique* 471–72, August–September 1986, pp. 933–41.

Vidal-Naquet, Pierre, *La Torture dans la République*, Maspero, 1972.

—*Face à la raison d'état. Un Historien dans la guerre d'Algérie*, La Découverte, 1990.

Voeltzel, Thierry, *Vingt ans et après*, Grasset, 1978.

Walesa, Lech, *A Path of Hope: An Autobiography*, London: Pan, 1988.

Watney, Simon, *Policing Desire: Pornography, AIDS and the Media*, London: Comedia.

Weil, Simone, *La Condition ouvrière*, Gallimard, 1951.

Weit, John de, 'The Charming Passivity of Guy Hocquenhem', *Gay Left* 9, 1979, pp. 16–19.

White, Edmund, *States of Desire: Travels in Gay America*, London: Picador, 1986.

Wolton, Dominique, 'Qui veut savoir?', *Esprit* 7–8, July–August 1977, pp. 37–47.

Zimmer, Christian, 'Dans le combat gauchiste', *Le Monde*, 17 April 1980, p.17.

INDEX

Throughout this index, Michel Foucault is referred to as MF